THE

COMPLETE POETICAL WORKS

OF

ROBERT BURNS;

WITH

EXPLANATORY AND GLOSSARIAL NOTES,

AND

A LIFE OF THE AUTHOR.

BY JAMES CURRIE, M. D.

ADVERTISEMENT.

In the present day it would be a superfluous task to eulogize the poetry of Burns. No sooner had he given utterance to his exquisite strains, than they found an echo in the palace and the cottage. Men heard in them the voice of a master-poet—of one of those great minds who exercise an influence on the manners and sentiments of a people; and even before he died, his country did honor to his surpassing genius, and inscribed his name as the greatest of her minstrels, an award which has been continued with increasing reverence to the present day. And though other poets should arise to divide the national homage, still every succeeding age will continue to admire the truth and beauty of his sentiments and descriptions, upon the same principle that they will admire the simple manners and romantic scenery by which his inspiration was kindled, and which his patriotic heart loved to celebrate. To be dead to the poetry of Burns, is to be dead to Nature itself.

In reprinting the poetical works of one so distinguished in British literature, the Publishers considered it their duty to collate the various editions of his works, and to collect together the various poems which are the admitted productions of Burns, so as to render the present edition more complete than even the most expensive. The whole has been carefully revised.

and edited by one of our most talented living authors of Scottish Song; and to make the dialect and allusions fully accessible to English readers, glossarial definitions, and notes illustrative of the manners and customs which are described, have been added—not heaped together at the end, to fatigue the patience of the reader by a continual reference to the vocabulary, but subjoined to their respective pages, where they can be seen at a glance, in connection with the text. In addition to these, the Life of the Author, by the late Dr. Currie, of Liverpool, whose account, notwithstanding the numerous biographies of the poet which have been published, has never been surpassed, has been prefixed; and although it has been considerably abridged, still few particulars of any importance have been omitted. These advantages, combined with elegance and economy, will, it is hoped, secure a favorable reception for this edition of Burns's Poems, not only among his countrymen, but the public at large.

CONTENTS.

8 CONTENTS.

CONTENTS. 9

PAGE

10 CONTENTS.

MISCELLANEOUS PIECES LATELY COLLECTED.

ALPHABETICAL INDEX TO MISCELLANEOUS POEMS,

BY FIRST LINES.

14   CONTENTS.

16 CONTENTS.

ALPHABETICAL INDEX TO SONGS AND BALLADS

18   CONTENTS.

CONTENTS. 19

20   CONTENTS.

PAGE

The cooper o' Cuddie... 562
The country lassie.. 362
The Dean of Faculty... 406
The Deil's awa wi' the Exciseman.................................. 501
The deuk's dang owre my daddy..................................... 514
The Dumfries Volunteers 435
The Farewell to the brethren of St. James's Lodge, Tarbolton 403
The Farewell.. 569
The fête champêtre 570
The Five Carlins.. 514
The gallant weaver.. 486
The gloomy night is gathering fast 402
The Heron Ballads.................................. 596, 597, 600
The Highland laddie 564
The Highland lassie... 398
The Highland widow's lament 572
The jolly Beggars—a cantata....................................... 518
The joyful widower 532
The lass of Ballochmyle 411
The lass of Ecclefechan 561
The lass that made the bed to me 372
The lazy mist hangs from the brow of the hill 483
The lovely lass of Inverness 393
The ploughman.. 507, 530
The posie... 484
The ranting dog the daddie o't.................................... 440
The raving winds 393
The rigs of barley.. 353
The rose-bud 422
The ruin'd Maid's Lament.. 404
The soldier's return 387
The sons of old Killie 530
The tailor 539
The tither morn 549
The Union 436
The Vision 426
The weary pund o' tow... 550
The Whistle... 458
The winding Nith.. 437
The winter it is past 507
The young Highland rover 394
Their groves o' sweet myrtle...................................... 455
Theniel Menzie's bonnie Mary 417
There was a bonnie lass 509, 573
There was a lad was born at Kyle.................................. 503
There was a lass.. 535
There's a youth in this city...................................... 493
This is no my ain lassie.. 434
Tho' cruel fate should bid us part................................ 397
Thou hast left me ever, Jamie 350
Tibbie Dunbar... 509
To Anna 352
To Mary.. 399, 465
To Mary in heaven.... 401
To thee, loved Nith 566
'Twas na her bonnie blue een was my ruin 477

Up in the morning early 431

Wae is my heart 500

ALPHABETICAL INDEX TO SONGS,

BY FIRST LINES.

3

LIFE OF BURNS.

BY JAMES CURRIE, M. D.

ABRIDGED.

Robert Burns was born on the 29th day of January, 1759, in a small house about two miles from the town of Ayr, and within a few hundred yards of Alloway Church, which his poem of *Tam o' Shanter* has rendered immortal.* The name, which the poet and his brother modernized into Burns, was originally Burnes, or Burness. Their father, William Burnes, was the son of a farmer in Kincardineshire, and had received the education common in Scotland to persons in his condition of life; he could read and write, and had some knowledge of arithmetic. His family having fallen into reduced circumstances, he was compelled to leave his home in his nineteenth year, and turned his steps towards the south in quest of a livelihood. He undertook to act as a gardener, and shaped his course to Edinburgh, where he wrought hard when he could obtain employment, passing through a variety of difficulties. From Edinburgh William Burnes passed westward into the county of Ayr, where he engaged himself as a gardener to the laird of Fairly, with whom he lived two years; then changed his service for that of Crawford of Doonside. At length, being desirous of settling in life, he took a perpetual lease of seven acres of land from Dr. Campbell, physician in Ayr, with the view of commencing nurseryman and public gardener, and, having built a house upon it with his own hands, married in December, 1757, Agnes Brown. The first fruit of this marriage was Robert, the subject of these memoirs. Before William Burnes had made much progress in preparing his nursery, he was withdrawn from that undertaking by Mr. Ferguson, who purchased the estate of Doonholm, in the immediate neighborhood,

----

* This house is on the right-hand side of the road from Ayr to Mayhole, which forms a part of the road from Glasgow to Port-Patrick. It is now a country ale-house.

and engaged him as his gardener and overseer, and this was his
situation when our poet was born. When in the service of Mr.
Ferguson, he lived in his own house, his wife managing her family,
and her little dairy, which consisted of two, sometimes of three,
milch cows; and this state of unambitious content continued till
the year 1766. His son Robert was sent by him, in his sixth year,
to a school at Alloway Miln, about a mile distant, taught by a person
of the name of Campbell; but this teacher being in a few months
appointed master of the workhouse at Ayr, William Burnes, in con-
junction with some other heads of families, engaged John Murdoch
in his stead. The education of our poet, and of his brother Gilbert,
was in common; and whilst under Mr. Murdoch, they learned to
read English tolerably well, and to write a little. He also taught
them the elements of English grammar, in which Robert made
some proficiency—a circumstance which had considerable weight
in the unfolding of his genius and character; as he soon became
remarkable for the fluency and correctness of his expression, and
read the few books that came in his way with much pleasure and
improvement.

It appears that William Burnes approved himself greatly in the
service of Mr. Ferguson, by his intelligence, industry, and integ-
rity. In consequence of this, with a view of promoting his interest,
Mr. Ferguson leased to him the farm of Mount Oliphant, in the
parish of Ayr; consisting of upwards of seventy acres (about
ninety, English Imperial measure), the rent of which was to be
forty pounds annually for the first six years, and afterwards forty-
five pounds. Mr. Ferguson also lent him a hundred pounds to
assist in stocking the farm, to which he removed at Whitsuntide,
1766. But this, in place of being of advantage to William Burnes,
as it was intended by his former master, was the commencement
of much anxiety and distress to the whole family, which is forcibly
described by his son, Gilbert, in a letter to Mrs. Dunlop:

"Mount Oliphant, the farm my father possessed in the parish of
Ayr, is almost the very poorest soil I know of in a state of cultiva-
tion. A stronger proof of this I cannot give, than that, notwith-
standing the extraordinary rise in the value of lands in Scotland, it
was, after a considerable sum laid out in improving it by the pro-
prietor, let a few years ago five pounds per annum lower than the
rent paid for it by my father thirty years ago. My father, in con-
sequence of this, soon came into difficulties, which were increased
by the loss of several of his cattle by accidents and disease. To the
buffetings of misfortune, we could only oppose hard labor and the
most rigid economy. We lived very sparingly. For several years
butcher's meat was a stranger in the house, whi'e all the members

of the family exerted themselves to the utmost of their strength, and rather beyond it, in the labors of the farm. My brother, at the age of thirteen, assisted in thrashing the crop of corn, and at fifteen was the principal laborer on the farm, for we had no hired servant, male or female. The anguish of mind we felt at our tender years, under these straits and difficulties, was very great. To think of our father growing old (for he was now above fifty) broken down with the long-continued fatigues of his life, with a wife and five other children, and in a declining state of circumstances, these reflections produced in my brother's mind and mine sensations of the deepest distress. I doubt not but the hard labor and sorrow of this period of his life, was in a great measure the cause of that depression of spirits with which Robert was so often afflicted through his whole life afterwards. At this time he was almost constantly afflicted in the evenings with a dull headache, which, at a future period of his life, was exchanged for a palpitation of the heart, and a threatening of fainting and suffocation in his bed, in the night-time.

"By a stipulation in my father's lease, he had a right to throw it up, if he thought proper, at the end of every sixth year. He attempted to fix himself in a better farm at the end of the first six years, but failing in that attempt, he continued where he was for six years more. He then took the farm of Lochlea, of 130 acres, at the rent of twenty shillings an acre, in the parish of Tarbolton, of Mr. ——— ———, then a merchant in Ayr, and now (1797) a merchant at Liverpool. He removed to this farm at Whitsuntide, 1777, and possessed it only seven years. No writing had ever been made out of the conditions of the lease; a misunderstanding took place respecting them; the subjects in dispute were submitted to arbitration, and the decision involved my father's affairs in ruin. He lived to know of this decision, but not to see any execution in consequence of it. He died on the 13th of February, 1784."

Of this frugal, industrious, and good man, the following beautiful character has been given by Mr. Murdoch:—"He was a tender and affectionate father; he took pleasure in leading his children in the path of virtue; not in driving them, as some parents do, to the performance of duties to which they themselves are averse. He took care to find fault but very seldom; and therefore, when he did rebuke, he was listened to with a kind of reverential awe. A look of disapprobation was felt; a reproof was severely so; and a stripe with the *tawz*, even on the skirt of the coat, gave heartfelt pain, produced a loud lamentation, and brought forth a flood of tears.

"He had the art of gaining the esteem and good-will of those that were laborers ander him. I think I never saw him angry but twice : the one time it was with the foreman of the band, for not reaping the field as he was desired ; and the other time it was with an old man, for using smutty inuendoes and *double entendres.* Were every foul-mouthed old man to receive a seasonable check in this way, it would be to the advantage of the rising generation. As he was at no time overbearing to inferiors, he was equally incapable of that passive, pitiful, paltry spirit, that induces some people to *keep booing and booing* in the presence of a great man. He always treated superiors with a becoming respect ; but he never gave the smallest encouragement to aristocratical arrogance. But I must not pretend to give you a description of all the manly qualities, the rational and Christian virtues, of the venerable William Burnes. Time would fail me. I shall only add, that he carefully practised every known duty, and avoided every thing that was criminal ; or, in the apostle's words, ' Herein did he exercise himself, in living a life void of offence towards God and towards men.' Oh for a world of men of such dispositions ! We should then have no wars. I have often wished, for the good of mankind, that it were as customary to honor and perpetuate the memory of those who excel in moral rectitude, as it is to extol what are called heroic actions : then would the mausoleum of the friend of my youth overtop and surpass most of the monuments I see in Westminster Abbey !"

Under the humble roof of his parents, it appears indeed that our poet had great advantages ; but his opportunities of information at school were more limited as to time than they usually are among his countrymen, in his condition of life ; and the acquisitions which he made, and the poetical talent which he exerted, under the pressure of early and incessant toil, and of inferior, and perhaps scanty nutriment, testify at once the extraordinary force and activity of his mind. In his frame of body he rose nearly five feet ten inches, and assumed the proportions that indicate agility as well as strength. In the various labors of the farm he excelled all his competitors. Gilbert Burns declares that in mowing, the exercise that tries all the muscles most severely, Robert was the only man that, at the end of a summer's day, he was ever obliged to acknowledge as his master. But though our poet gave the powers of his body to the labors of the farm, he refused to bestow on them his thoughts or his cares. While the ploughshare under his guidance passed through the sward, or the grass fell under the sweep of his scythe, he was humming the songs of his country, musing on the deeds of ancient valor, or rapt in the illusions of Fancy, as her enchantments rose on his view. Happily the Sunday is yet a sabbath, on which man and beast rest from their labors. On this day, therefore, Burns could indulge in a freer intercourse with the charms of nature. It was his delight to wander alone on the banks of Ayr, whose stream is now immortal, and to listen to the song of the blackbird at the close of the summer's day. But still greater was his pleasure, as he himself informs us, in walking on the sheltered side of a wood, in a cloudy winter-day, and hearing the storm rave among the trees; and more elevated still his delight, to ascend some eminence during the agitations of nature, to stride along its summit while the lightning flashed around him, and, amidst the howlings of the tempest, to apostrophize the spirit of the storm. Such situations he declares most favorable to devotion—"Rapt in enthusiasm, I seem to ascend towards Him *who walks on the wings of the wind !*" If other proofs were wanting of the character of his genius, this might determine it. The heart of the poet is peculiarly awake to every impression of beauty and sublimity; but, with the higher order of poets, the beautiful is less attractive than the sublime.

The gayety of many of Burns's writings, and the lively and even cheerful coloring with which he has portrayed his own character, may lead some persons to suppose, that the melancholy which hung over him towards the end of his days was not an original part of his constitution. It is not to be doubted, indeed, that this melancholy acquired a darker hue in the progress of his life; but, independent of his own and of his brother's testimony, evidence is to be found among his papers that he was subject very early to those depressions of mind, which are perhaps not wholly separable from the sensibility of genius, but which in him rose to an uncommon degree. The following letter addressed to his father, will serve as a proof of this observation. It was written at the time when he was learning the business of a flax-dresser, and is dated

"HONORED SIR—   IRVINE, Dec. 27, 1781.

"I have purposely delayed writing, in the hope that I should have the pleasure of seeing you on New-year's day; but work comes so hard upon us, that I do not choose to be absent on that account, as well as for some other little reasons, which I shall tell you at meeting. My health is nearly the same as when you were here, only my sleep is a little sounder, and, on the whole, I am rather better than otherwise, though I mend by very slow degrees. The weakness of my nerves has so debilitated my mind, that I dare neither review past wants nor look forward into futurity; for the least anxiety or perturbation in my breast produces most unhappy effects on my whole frame. Sometimes, indeed, when for an hour or two my spirits are a little lightened, I *glimmer* a little into futurity; but my principal, and indeed my only pleasurable employment, is looking backwards and forwards in a moral and religious way. I am quite transported at the thought, that ere long, perhaps very soon, I shall bid an eternal adieu to all the pains, and uneasinesses, and disquietudes of this weary life; for I assure you I am heartily tired of it; and if I do not very much deceive myself, I could contentedly and gladly resign it.

> The soul, uneasy, and confined at home,
> Rests and expatiates in a life to come.

"It is for this reason I am more pleased with the 15th, 16th, and 17th verses of the 7th chapter of Revelations, than with any ten times as many verses in the whole Bible, and would not exchange the noble enthusiasm with which they inspire me for all that this world has to offer.* As for this world, I despair of ever making a figure in it. I am not formed for the bustle of the busy, nor the flutter of the gay. I shall never again be capable of entering into such scenes. Indeed, I am altogether unconcerned at the thoughts of this life. I foresee that poverty and obscurity probably await me, and I am in some measure prepared, and daily preparing, to meet them. I have but just time and paper to return you my grateful thanks for the lessons of virtue and piety you have given me, which were too much neglected at the time of giving them, but which, I hope, have been remembered ere it is yet too late. Present my dutiful respects to my mother, and my compliments to Mr. and Mrs. Muir; and, with wishing you a merry New-year's day, I shall conclude.

"I am, honored Sir,

"Your dutiful son,

"ROBERT BURNS.

"P. S. My meal is nearly out; but I am going to borrow, till I get more."

This letter, written several years before the publication of his poems, when his name was as obscure as his condition was humble, displays the philosophic melancholy which so generally forms the poetical temperament, and that buoyant and ambitious spirit which indicates a mind conscious of its strength. At Irvine, Burns at this time possessed a single room for his lodging, rented perhaps at the rate of a shilling a week. He passed his days in constant

---

* The verses of Scripture here alluded to, are as follow :

"15. Therefore are they before the throne of God, and serve him day and night in his temple ; and he that sitteth on the throne shall dwell among them.

"16. They shall hunger no more, neither thirst any more ; neither shall the sun light on them, nor any heat.

"17. For the Lamb that is in the midst of the throne shall feed them, and shall lead them unto living fountains of waters; and God shall wipe away all tears from their eyes."

labor as a flax-dresser, and his food consisted chiefly of oat-meal
sent to him from his father's family. The store of this humble,
though wholesome nutriment, it appears, was nearly exhausted,
and he was about to borrow till he should obtain a supply. Yet
even in this situation his active imagination had formed to itself
pictures of eminence and distinction. His despair of making a
figure in the world shows how ardently he wished for honorable
fame; and his contempt of life, founded on this despair, is the
genuine expression of a youthful and generous mind. In such a
state of reflection and of suffering, the imagination of Burns natu-
rally passed the dark boundaries of our earthly horizon, and rested
on those beautiful representations of a better world, where there is
neither thirst, nor hunger, nor sorrow, and where happiness shall
be in proportion to the capacity of happiness.

Such a disposition is far from being at variance with social enjoy-
ments. Those who have studied the affinities of mind know that
a melancholy of this description, after a while, seeks relief in the
endearments of society, and that it has no distant connection with
the flow of cheerfulness, or even the extravagance of mirth. It
was a few days after the writing of this letter that our poet, "in
giving a welcoming carousal to the new year, with his gay compan-
ions," suffered his flax to catch fire, and his shop to be consumed
to ashes.

The energy of Burns's mind was not exhausted by his daily la-
bors, the effusions of his muse, his social pleasures, or his solitary
meditations. Some time previous to his engagement as a flax-
dresser, having heard that a debating-club had been established in
Ayr, he resolved to try how such a meeting would succeed in the
village of Tarbolton. About the end of the year 1780, our poet,
his brother, and five other young peasants of the neighborhood,
formed themselves into a society of this sort, the declared objects
of which were to relax themselves after toil, to promote sociality
and friendship, and to improve the mind. The laws and regula-
tions were furnished by Burns. The members were to meet after
the labors of the day were over, once a week, in a small public-
house in the village; where each should offer his opinion on a giv-
en question or subject, supporting it by such arguments as he
thought proper. The debate was to be conducted with order and
decorum; and after it was finished, the members were to choose a
subject for discussion at the ensuing meeting. The sum expended
by each was not to exceed three-pence; and, with the humble po-
tation that this could procure, they were to toast their mistresses
and to cultivate friendship with each other.

After the family of our bard removed from Tarbolton to the

neighborhood of Mauchline, he and his brother were requested to
assist in forming a similar institution there. The regulations of the
club at Mauchline were nearly the same as those of the club at Tar-
bolton; but one laudable alteration was made. The fines for non-
attendance had at Tarbolton been spent in enlarging their scanty
potations: at Mauchline it was fixed, that the money so arising
should be set apart for the purchase of books; and the first work
procured in this manner was the Mirror, the separate numbers of
which were at that time recently collected and published in volumes.
After it followed a number of other works, chiefly of the same na-
ture, and among these the Lounger.

The society of Mauchline still subsists, and was in the list of
subscribers to the first edition of the works of its celebrated asso-
ciate.

Whether, in the humble societies of which he was a member,
Burns acquired much direct information, may perhaps be ques-
tioned. It cannot however be doubted, that by collision the facul-
ties of his mind would be excited, that by practice his habits of
enunciation would be established, and thus we have some explana-
tion of that early command of words and of expression which
enabled him to pour forth his thoughts in language not unworthy
of his genius, and which, of all his endowments, seemed, on his
appearance in Edinburgh, the most extraordinary. For associa-
tions of a literary nature, our poet acquired a considerable relish;
and happy had it been for him, after he emerged from the condition
of a peasant, if fortune had permitted him to enjoy them in the
degree of which he was capable, so as to have fortified his principles
of virtue by the purification of his taste, and given to the energies
of his mind habits of exertion that might have excluded other asso-
ciations, in which it must be acknowledged they were too often
wasted, as well as debased.

The whole course of the Ayr is fine; but the banks of that river,
as it bends to the eastward above Mauchline, are singularly beau-
tiful, and they were frequented, as may be imagined, by our poet
in his solitary walks. Here the muse often visited him. In one
of these wanderings, he met among the woods a celebrated Beauty
of the west of Scotland;* a lady, of whom it is said, that the charms
of her person corresponded with the character of her mind. This
incident gave rise, as might be expected, to a poem, of which an
account will be found in the following letter, in which he inclosed
it to the object of his inspiration:

* Miss Alexander, of Ballochmyle.

TO MISS ——.

"MADAM: MOSSGIEL, Nov. 18, 1778.

"Poets are such *outré* beings, so much the children of wayward fancy and capricious whim, that I believe the world generally allows them a larger latitude in the laws of propriety, than the sober sons of judgment and prudence. I mention this as an apology for the liberties that a nameless stranger has taken with you n the inclosed poem, which he begs leave to present you with. Whether it has poetical merit any way worthy of the theme, I am not the proper judge; but it is the best my abilities can produce; and, what to a good heart will perhaps be a superior grace, it is equally sincere as fervent.

"The scenery was nearly taken from real life, though I dare say, Madam, you do not recollect it, as I believe you scarcely noticed the poetic *reveur* as he wandered by you. I had roved out as chance directed, in the favorite haunts of my muse, on the banks of Ayr, to view nature in all the gayety of the vernal year. The evening sun was flaming over the distant western hills; not a breath stirred the crimson opening blossom, or the verdant spreading leaf. It was a golden moment for a poetic heart. I listened to the feathered warblers, pouring their harmony on every hand, with a congenial kindred regard, and frequently turned out of my path, lest I should disturb their little songs, or frighten them to another station. Surely, said I to myself, he must be a wretch indeed, who, regardless of your harmonious endeavor to please him, can eye your elusive flights to discover your secret recesses, and to rob you of all the property nature gives you, your dearest comforts, your helpless nestlings. Even the hoary hawthorn twig that shot across the way, what heart at such a time but must have been interested in its welfare, and wished it preserved from the rudely-browsing cattle, or the withering eastern blast? Such was the scene, and such the hour, when in a corner of my prospect I spied one of the fairest pieces of Nature's workmanship that ever crowned a poetic landscape, or met a poet's eye, those visionary bards excepted who hold commerce with aerial beings! Had Calumny and Villainy taken my walk, they had at that moment sworn eternal peace with such an object.

"What an hour of inspiration for a poet! It would have raised plain, dull, historic prose into metaphor and measure.

"The inclosed song was the work of my return home; and perhaps it but poorly answers what might have been expected from such a scene.   *   *   *   *   *   *   *

"I have the honor to be, Madam,
   "Your most obedient, and very humble servant,
                        "ROBERT BURNS."

4

'Twas even—the dewy fields were green,
　On every blade the pearls hang;*
The Zephyr wantoned round the bean,
　And bore its fragrant sweets alang:
In every glen the mavis sang,
　All nature listening seemed the while,
Except where green-wood echoes rang
　Amang the braes o' Ballochmyle!

With careless step I onward strayed,
　My heart rejoiced in nature's joy,
When, musing in a lonely glade,
　A maiden fair I chanced to spy;
Her look was like the morning's eye,
　Her air like nature's vernal smile,
Perfection whispered passing by,
　Behold the lass o' Ballochmyle!†

Fair is the morn in flowery May,
　And sweet is night in Autumn mild:
When roving through the garden gay,
　Or wandering in a lonely wild:
But woman, nature's darling child!
　There all her charms she does compile;
E'en there her other works are foiled
　By the bonny lass o' Ballochmyle.

O, had she been a country maid,
　And I the happy country swain,
Though sheltered in the lowest shed
　That ever rose in Scotland's plain,
Through weary winter's wind and rain,
　With joy, with rapture, I would toil;
And nightly to my bosom strain　.
　The bonny lass o' Ballochmyle.

Then pride might climb the slippery steep
　Where fame and honors lofty shine;
And thirst of gold might tempt the deep,
　Or downward sink the Indian mine;
Give me the cot below the pine,
　To tend the flocks or till the soil,
And every day have joys divine
　With the bonny lass o' Ballochmyle.

In the manuscript book in which our poet has recounted this incident, and into which the letter and poem were copied, he complains that the lady made no reply to his effusions, and this appears to have wounded his self-love. It is not, however, difficult to find an excuse for her silence. Her modesty might prevent her from perceiving that the muse of Tibullus breathed in this nameless poet, and that her beauty was awakening strains destined to im-

* *Hang*, Scotticism for *hung*.
† Variation.　The lily's hue and rose's dye
　　　　　Bespoke the lass o' Ballochmyle.

mortality on the banks of the Ayr. It may be conceived also, that
supposing the verses duly appreciated, delicacy might find it diffi-
cult to express its acknowledgments. The fervent imagination of
the rustic bard possessed more of tenderness than of respect. In-
stead of raising himself to the condition of the object of his admi
ration, he presumed to reduce her to his own, and to strain this
high-born beauty to his daring bosom.

The sensibility of our bard's temper, a: d the force of his imagi-
nation, exposed him in a particular manner to the impressions of
beauty; and these qualities, united to his impassioned eloquence,
gave him in turn a powerful influence over the female heart. The
banks of the Ayr formed the scene of youthful passions of a still
tenderer nature, the history of which it would be improper to re-
veal, were it even in our power, and the traces of which will soon
be discoverable only in those strains of nature and sensibility to
which they gave birth. The song entitled *Highland Mary* is known
to relate to one of these attachments. " It was written," says our
bard, "on one of the most interesting passages of my youthful
days." The object of this passion died early in life, and the im-
pression left on the mind of Burns seems to have been deep and
lasting. Several years afterwards, when he was removed to Niths-
dale, he gave vent to the sensibility of his recollections in the fol-
lowing impassioned lines addressed to " Mary in Heaven !"

Thou lingering star, with less'ning ray,
    That lov'st to greet the early morn,
Again thou usher'st in the day
    My Mary from my soul was torn.
O Mary, dear departed shade !
    Where is thy place of blissful rest ?
Seest thou thy lover lowly laid ?
    Hear'st thou the groans that rend his breast ?

That sacred hour can I forget ?
    Can I forget the hallowed grove,
Where by the winding Ayr we met,
    To live one day of parting love ?
Eternity will not efface
    Those records dear of transports past
Thy image at our last embrace !
    Ah ! little thought we 'twas our last !

Ayr gurgling kissed his pebbled shore,
    O'erhung with wild woods, thickening green ;
The fragrant birch and hawthorn hoar,
    Twined amorous round the raptured scene.
The flowers sprang wanton to be pressed,
    The birds sang love on every spray,
Till too, too soon, the glowing west
    Proclaimed the speed of winged day.

Still o'er these scenes my memory wakes,
And fondly broods with miser care !
Time but the impression deeper makes
As streams their channels deeper wear.
My Mary, dear departed shade !
Where is thy place of blissful rest ?
Seest thou thy lover lowly laid ?
Hear'st thou the groans that rend his breast ?

At this time Burns's prospects in life were so extremely gloomy, that he had decided upon going out to Jamaica, and had procured the situation of overseer on an estate belonging to Dr. Douglas ; not, however, without lamenting, that want of patronage should force him to think of a project so repugnant to his feelings, when his ambition aimed at no higher object than the station of an exciseman or gauger in his own country. But the situation in which he was now placed cannot be better illustrated than by introducing the letter which he wrote to Dr. Moore, giving an account of his life up to this period. As it was never intended to see the light, elegance, or perfect correctness of composition, will not be expected. These, however, will be compensated by the opportunity of seeing our poet, as he gives the incidents of his life, unfold the peculiarities of his character with all the careless vigor and open sincerity of his mind.

"SIR: MAUCHLINE, 2d August, 1787.

" For some months past I have been rambling over the country ; but I am now confined with some lingering complaints, originating, as I take it, in the stomach. To divert my spirits a little in this miserable fog of *ennui*, I have taken a whim to give you a history of myself. My name has made some little noise in this country ; you have done me the honor to interest yourself very warmly in my behalf ; and I think a faithful account of what character of a man I am, and how I came by that character, may perhaps amuse you in an idle moment. I will give you an honest narrative ; though I know it will be often at my own expense ;—for I assure you, sir, I have, like Solomon, whose character, except in the trifling affair of *wisdom*, I sometimes think I resemble—I have, I say, like him, ' turned my eyes to behold madness and folly,' and, like him, too frequently shaken hand with their intoxicating friendship. * * * After you have perused these pages, should you think them trifling and impertinent, I only beg leave to tell you, that the poor author wrote them under some twitching qualms of conscience, arising from a suspicion that he was doing what he ought not to do—a predicament he has more than once been in before.

"I have not the most distant pretensions to assume that character, which the pye-coated guardians of escutcheons call a Gentleman. When at Edinburgh last winter, I got acquainted in the Herald's Office; and looking through that granary of honors, I there found almost every name in the kingdom; but for me,

> My ancient but ignoble blood
> Has crept through scoundrels ever since the flood.

Gules, Purpure, Argent, &c., quite disowned me.

"My father was of the north of Scotland, the son of a farmer, and was thrown by early misfortunes on the world at large; where, after many years' wanderings and sojournings, he picked up a pretty large quantity of observation and experience, to which I am indebted for most of my pretensions to wisdom. I have met with few who understood *men, their manners, and their ways*, equal to him; but stubborn, ungainly integrity, and headlong, ungovernable irascibility, are disqualifying circumstances; consequently, I was born a very poor man's son. For the first six or seven years of my life, my father was gardener to a worthy gentleman of small estate in the neighborhood of Ayr. Had he continued in that station, I must have marched off to be one of the little underlings about a farm-house; but it was his dearest wish and prayer to have it in his power to keep his children under his own eye till they could discern between good and evil; so, with the assistance of his generous master, my father ventured on a small farm on his estate. At those years I was by no means a favorite with anybody. I was a good deal noted for a retentive memory, a stubborn sturdy something in my disposition, and an enthusiastic idiot piety. I say *idiot* piety, because I was then but a child. Though it cost the schoolmaster some thrashings, I made an excellent English scholar; and by the time I was ten or eleven years of age, I was a critic in substantives, verbs, and particles. In my infant and boyish days, too, I owed much to an old woman who resided in the family, remarkable for her ignorance, credulity, and superstition. She had, I suppose, the largest collection in the country of tales and songs concerning devils, ghosts, fairies, brownies, witches, warlocks, spunkies, kelpies, elf-candles, deadlights, wraiths, apparitions, cantraips, giants, enchanted towers, dragons, and other trumpery. This cultivated the latent seeds of poetry; but had so strong an effect on my imagination, that to this hour, in my nocturnal rambles, I sometimes keep a sharp look-out in suspicious places: and though nobody can be more skeptical than I am in such matters, yet it often takes an effort of philosophy to shake off these idle terrors. The earliest composition that I recollect taking pleasure in was *The Vision of Mirza*, and a hymn of Addison's, beginning:

'How are thy servants blessed, O Lord!' I particularly remember
one half-stanza, which was music to my boyish ear—

For though on dreadful whirls we hung
High on the broken wave.

I met with these pieces in Mason's English Collection, one of my
school-books. The two first books I ever read in private, and
which gave me more pleasure than any two books I ever read since,
were, *The Life of Hannibal,* and *The History of Sir William Wallace.*
Hannibal gave my young ideas such a turn, that I used to strut in
raptures up and down after the recruiting drum and bagpipe, and
wish myself tall enough to be a soldier; while the story of Wallace
poured a Scottish prejudice into my veins, which will boil along
there till the flood-gates of life shut in eternal rest.

"Polemical divinity about this time was putting the country half
mad; and I, ambitious of shining in conversation parties on Sun-
days, between sermons, at funerals, &c., used a few years after-
wards to puzzle Calvinism with so much heat and indiscretion, that
I raised a hue-and-cry of heresy against me, which has not ceased
to this hour.

"My vicinity to Ayr was of some advantage to me. My social
disposition, when not checked by some modifications of spirited
pride, was, like our catechism definition of infinitude, *without
bounds or limits.* I formed several connections with other yonkers
who possessed superior advantages, the *youngling* actors, who were
busy in the rehearsal of parts in which they were shortly to appear
on the stage of life, where, alas! I was destined to drudge behind
the scenes. It is not commonly at this green age that our young
gentry have a just sense of the immense distance between them and
their ragged play-fellows. It takes a few dashes into the world, to
give the young great man that proper, decent, unnoticing disregard
for the poor, insignificant, stupid devils, the mechanics and peas-
antry around him, who were perhaps born in the same village.
My young superiors never insulted the *clouterly* appearance of my
plough-boy carcase, the two extremes of which were often exposed
to all the inclemencies of all the seasons. They would give me
stray volumes of books: among them, even then, I could pick up
some observations; and one, whose heart I am sure not even the
Munny Begum scenes have tainted, helped me to a little French.
Parting with these my young friends and benefactors, as they oc-
casionally went off for the East or West Indies, was often to me a
sore affliction; but I was soon called to more serious evils. My
father's generous master died; the farm proved a ruinous bargain;
and, to clench the misfortune, we fell into the hands of a factor,
who sat for the picture I have drawn of one in my *Tale of Twa Dogs*

My father was advanced in life when he married ; I was the eldest
of seven children; and he, worn out by early hardships, was unfit
for labor. My father's spirit was soon irritated, but not easily
broken. There was a freedom in his lease in two years more; and,
to weather these two years, we retrenched our expenses. We lived
very poorly : I was a dexterous ploughman for my age ; and the next
eldest to me was a brother (Gilbert), who could drive the plough
very well, and help me to thrash the corn. A novel-writer might
perhaps have viewed these scenes with some satisfaction ; but so
did not I ; my indignation yet boils at the recollection of the s——l
factor's insolent threatening letters, which used to set us all in
tears.

"This kind of life—the cheerless gloom of a hermit, with the
unceasing moil of a galley-slave, brought me to my sixteenth year :
a little before which period I first committed the sin of rhyme.
You know our country custom of coupling a man and woman together
as partners in the labors of harvest. In my fifteenth autumn, my
partner was a bewitching creature, a year younger than myself.
My scarcity of English denies me the power of doing her justice in
that language, but you know the Scottish idiom—she was a *bonnie,
sweet, sonsie lass*. In short, she, altogether unwittingly to herself,
initiated me into that delicious passion, which, in spite of acid dis-
appointment, gin-horse prudence, and book-worm philosophy, I
hold to be the first of human joys, our dearest blessing here below !
How she caught the contagion, I cannot tell : you medical people
talk much of infection from breathing the same air, the touch, &c. ;
but I never expressly said I loved her. Indeed, I did not know
myself why I liked so much to loiter behind with her, when return-
ing in the evening from our labors; why the tones of her voice
made my heart-strings thrill like an Æolian harp ; and particularly
why my pulse beat such a furious rattan when I looked and finger-
ed over her little hand to pick out the cruel nettle-stings and this-
tles. Among her other love-inspiring qualities, she sung sweetly ;
and it was her favorite reel to which I attempted giving an em-
bodied vehicle in rhyme. I was not so presumptuous as to imagine
that I could make verses like printed ones, composed by men who
had Greek and Latin ; but my girl sung a song, which was said to
be composed by a small country laird's son, on one of his father's
maids, with whom he was in love! and I saw no reason why I
might not rhyme as well as he : for, excepting that he could smear
sheep, and cast peats, his father living in the moorlands, he had no
more school-craft than myself.

"Thus with me began love and poetry ; which at times have
been my only, and till within the last twelve months, have been my

highest enjoyment. My father struggled on till he reached the freedom in his lease, when he entered on a larger farm, about ten miles farther in the country. The nature of the bargain he made was such as to throw a little ready money into his hands at the commencement of his lease ; otherwise the affair would have been impracticable. For four years we lived comfortably here ; but a difference commencing between him and his landlord as to terms, after three years' tossing and whirling in the vortex of litigation, my father was just saved from the horrors of a jail by a consumption, which, after two years' promises, kindly stepped in, and carried him away, to 'where the wicked cease from troubling, and where the weary are at rest.'

"It is during the time that we lived on this farm that my little story is most eventful. I was, at the beginning of this period, perhaps the most ungainly, awkward boy in the parish—no *solitaire* was less acquainted with the ways of the world. What I knew of ancient story was gathered from Salmon's and Guthrie's geographical grammars ; and the ideas I had formed of modern manners, of literature and criticism, I got from the Spectator. These, with *Pope's Works*, some plays of *Shakspeare, Tull and Dickson on Agriculture, The Pantheon, Locke's Essay on the Human Understanding, Stackhouse's History of the Bible, Justice's British Gardener's Directory, Bayle's Lectures, Allan Ramsay's Works, Taylor's Scripture Doctrine of Original Sin, A Select Collection of English Songs*, and *Hervey's Meditations*, had formed the whole of my reading. The collection of songs was my *vade mecum*. I pored over them driving my cart, or walking to labor, song by song, verse by verse ; carefully noting the true, tender, or sublime, from affectation and fustian. I am convinced I owe to this practice much of my critic craft, such as it is.

"In my seventeenth year, to give my manners a brush, I went to a country dancing-school.—My father had an unaccountable antipathy against these meetings ; and my going was, what to this moment I repent, in opposition to his wishes. My father, as I said before, was subject to strong passions ; from that instance of disobedience in me, he took a sort of dislike to me, which I believe was one cause of the dissipation which marked my succeeding years. I say dissipation, comparatively with the strictness, and sobriety, and regularity of Presbyterian country life ; for though the Will-o'-Wisp meteors of thoughtless whim were almost the sole lights of my path, yet early ingrained piety and virtue kept me for several years afterwards within the line of innocence. The great misfortune of my life was to want an aim. I had felt early some stirrings of ambition, but they were the blind gropings of Homer's Cyclops round the walls of his cave. I saw my father's

situation entailed on me perpetual labor. The only two openings
by which I could enter the temple of Fortune, was the gate of nig-
gardly economy, or the path of little chicaning bargain-making.
The first is so contracted an aperture, I never could squeeze myself
into it;—the last I always hated—there was contamination in the
very entrance! Thus abandoned of aim or view in life, with a
strong appetite for sociability, as well from native hilarity, as from
a pride of observation and remark; a constitutional melancholy or
hypochondriasm, that made me fly solitude; add to these incen-
tives to social life, my reputation for bookish knowledge, a certain
wild logical talent, and a strength of thought, something like the
rudiments of good sense; and it will not seem surprising that I was
generally a welcome guest, where I visited, or any great wonder
that, always where two or three met together, there was I among
them.⟩ But far beyond all other impulses of my heart, was *un pen-
chant à l'adorable moitié du genre humain.* My heart was complete-
ly tinder, and was eternally lighted up by some goddess or other;
and as in every other warfare in this world, my fortune was vari-
ous—sometimes I was received with favor, and sometimes I was
mortified with a repulse. At the plough, scythe, or reap-hook, I
feared no competitor, and thus I set absolute want at defiance; and
as I never cared farther for my labors than while I was in actual
exercise, I spent the evenings in the way after my own heart. A
country lad seldom carries on a love-adventure without an assisting
confidant. I possessed a curiosity, zeal, and intrepid dexterity,
that recommended me as a proper second on these occasions; and
I dare say I felt as much pleasure in being in the secret of half the
loves of the parish of Tarbolton, as ever did statesman in knowing
the intrigues of half the courts of Europe.—The very goose-feather
in my hand seems to know instinctively the well-worn path of my
imagination, the favorite theme of my song; and is with difficulty
restrained from giving you a couple of paragraphs on the love-
adventures of my compeers, the humble inmates of the farm-house
and cottage; but the grave sons of science, ambition, or avarice,
baptize these things by the name of Follies. To the sons and daugh-
ters of labor and poverty, they are matters of the most serious na-
ture: to them the ardent hope, the stolen interview, the tender
farewell, are the greatest and most delicious parts of their enjoy-
ments.

"Another circumstance in my life which made some alteration
in my mind and manners, was that I spent my nineteenth summer
on a smuggling coast, a good distance from home, at a noted school,
to learn mensuration, surveying, dialling, &c., in which I made a
pretty good progress. But I made a greater progress in the knowl-
edge of mankind. The contraband trade was at that time very suc-

cessful, and it sometimes happened to me to fall in with those who carried it on. Scenes of swaggering riot and roaring dissipation were till this time new to me: but I was no enemy to social life. Here, though I learnt to fill my glass, and to mix without fear in a drunken squabble, yet I went on with a high hand with my geometry, till the sun entered Virgo, a month which is always a carnival in my bosom, when a charming *fillette*, who lived next door to the school, overset my trigonometry, and sent me off at a tangent from the sphere of my studies. I, however, struggled on with my *sines* and *co-sines* for a few days more; but stepping into the garden one charming noon to take the sun's altitude, there I met my angel,

> Like Proserpine, gathering flowers,
> Herself a fairer flower.——

"It was in vain to think of doing any more good at school. The remaining week I staid, I did nothing but craze the faculties of my soul about her, or steal out to meet her; and the two last nights of my stay in the country, had sleep been a mortal sin, the image of this modest and innocent girl had kept me guiltless.

"I returned home very considerably improved. My reading was enlarged with the very important addition of Thomson's and Shenstone's Works; I had seen human nature in a new phasis; and I engaged several of my schoolfellows to keep up a literary correspondence with me. This improved me in composition. I had met with a collection of letters by the wits of Queen Anne's reign, and I poured over them most devoutly; I kept copies of any of my own letters that pleased me; and a comparison between them and the composition of most of my correspondents flattered my vanity. I carried this whim so far, that though I had not three farthings' worth of business in the world, yet almost every post brought me as many letters as if I had been a broad plodding son of a day-book and ledger.

"My life flowed on much in the same course till my twenty-third year. *Vive l'amour, et vive la bagatelle*, were my sole principles of action. The addition of two more authors to my library gave me great pleasure; Sterne and M'Kenzie—*Tristram Shandy* and *The Man of Feeling*—were my bosom favorites. Poesy was still a darling walk for my mind; but it was only indulged in according to the humor of the hour. I had usually half a dozen or more pieces in hand; I took up one or the other, as it suited the momentary tone of the mind, and dismissed the work as it bordered on fatigue. My passions, when once lighted up, raged like so many devils till they got vent in rhyme; and then the conning over my verses, like a spell, soothed all into quiet! None of the rhymes of those days are in print, except *Winter, a Dirge*, the eldest of my printed pieces; *The Death of Poor Mailie, John Barleycorn*, and songs, first, second, and third. Song second was the ebullition of that passion which ended the forementioned school business.

"My twenty-third year was to me an important era. Partly through whim, and partly that I wished to set about doing something in life, I joined a flax-dresser in a neighboring town (Irvine) to learn his trade. This was an unlucky affair. My * * * * * * *; and, to finish the whole, as we were giving a welcoming carousal to the new year, the shop took fire, and burnt to ashes; and I was left, like a true poet, not worth a sixpence.

"I was obliged to give up this scheme; the clouds of misfortune were gathering thick round my father's head; and what was worst of all, he was visibly far gone in a consumption; and, to crown my distresses, a *belle fille* whom I adored, and who had pledged her soul to meet me in the field of matrimony, jilted me with peculiar circumstances of mortification. The finishing evil that brought up the rear of this infernal file was, my constitutional melancholy being increased to such a degree, that for three months I was in a state of mind scarcely to be envied by the hopeless wretches who have got their mittimus—*Depart from me, ye accursed!*

"From this adventure, I learned something of a town life; but the principle thing which gave my mind a turn was a friendship I formed with a young fellow, a very noble character, but a hapless son of misfortune. He was a son of a simple mechanic; but a great man in the neighborhood taking him under his patronage, gave him a genteel education, with a view of bettering his situation in life. The patron dying just as he was ready to launch out into the world, the poor fellow in despair went to sea; where, after a variety of good and ill fortune, a little before I was acquainted with him, he had been set ashore by an American privateer, on the wild coast of Connaught, stripped of every thing. I cannot quit this poor fellow's story without adding, that he is at this time master of a large West-Indiaman, belonging to the Thames.

"His mind was fraught with independence, magnanimity, and every manly virtue. I loved and admired him to a degree of enthusiasm, and of course strove to imitate him. In some measure I succeeded; I had pride before, but he taught it to flow in proper channels. His knowledge of the world was vastly superior to mine, and I was all attention to learn. He was the only man I ever saw who was a greater fool than myself, where woman was the presiding star; but he spoke of illicit love with the levity of a sailor, which hitherto I had regarded with horror. Here his friendship did me a mischief; and the consequence was, that soon after I resumed the plough, I wrote the *Poet's Welcome.** My reading only increased, while in this town, by two stray volumes of *Pamela*, and one of *Ferdinand Count Fathom*, which gave me some idea of novels. Rhyme, except some religious pieces that are in print, I had given up; but meeting with *Fergusson's Scottish Poems*, I strung anew my wildly-sounding lyre with emulating vigor. When my father died, his all went among the hell-hounds that growl in the kennel of justice; but we made a shift to collect a little money in the family among us, with which, to keep us together, my brother and I took a neighboring farm. My brother wanted my hair-brained imagination, as well as my social and amorous madness; but, in good sense, and every sober qualification, he was far my superior.

"I entered on this farm with a full resolution, 'Come, go to, I will be wise!' I read farming books; I calculated crops; I attended markets: and, in short, in spite of 'the devil, and the world, and the flesh,' I believe I should have been a wise man; but the first year, from unfortunately buying bad seed,—the second, from a late harvest,—we lost half our crops. This overset all my wisdom, and I returned, 'like the dog to his vomit, and the sow that was washed to her wallowing in the mire.'

"I now began to be known in the neighborhood as a maker of rhymes. The first of my poetic offspring that saw the light was a burlesque lamentation on a quarrel between two reverend Calvinists, both of them *dramatis personæ* in my *Holy Fair*. I had a notion myself, that the piece had some merit; but to prevent the worst, I gave a copy of it to a friend who was very fond of such things, and told him that I could not guess who was the author of it, but that I thought it pretty clever. With a certain description of the clergy, as well as laity, it met with a roar of applause. *Holy Willie's Prayer* next made its appearance, and alarmed the kirk-session so much, that they held several meetings to look over their spiritual artillery, if haply any of it might be pointed against profane rhymers. Unluckily for me, my wanderings led me on another side, within point-blank shot of their heaviest metal. This is the unfortunate story that gave rise to my printed poem *The Lament*. This was a most melancholy affair, which I cannot yet bear to reflect on, and had very nearly given me one or two of the principal qualifications for a place among those who have lost the chart, and mistaken the reckoning, of Rationality. I gave up my part of the farm to my brother,—in truth, it was only nominally mine,—and made what little preparation was in my power for Jamaica But,

* Rob the Rhymer's Welcome to his Bastard Child.

before leaving my native country forever, I resolved to publish my poems. I weighed my productions as impartially as was in my power; I thought they had merit; and it was a delicious idea that I should be called a clever fellow, even though it should never reach my ears—a poor negro-driver,—or perhaps a victim to that inhospitable clime, and gone to the world of spirits! I can truly say, that *pauvre inconnu* as I then was, I had pretty nearly as high an idea of myself and my works as I have at this moment, when the public has decided in their favor. It ever was my opinion, that the mistakes and blunders, both in a rational and religious point of view, of which we see thousands daily guilty, are owing to their ignorance of themselves.—To know myself has been all along my constant study. I weighed myself alone; I balanced myself with others; I watched every means of information, to see how much ground I occupied as a man and as a poet: I studied assiduously Nature's design in my formation—where the lights and shades in my character were intended. I was pretty confident my poems would meet with some applause; but, at the worst, the roar of the Atlantic would deafen the voice of censure, and the novelty of West Indian scenes make me forget neglect. I threw off six hundred copies, of which I had got subscriptions for about three hundred and fifty.—My vanity was highly gratified by the reception I met with from the public; and besides, I pocketed, all expenses deducted, nearly twenty pounds. This sum came very seasonably, as I was thinking of indenting myself, for want of money to procure my passage. As soon as I was master of nine guineas, the price of wafting me to the torrid zone, I took a steerage passage in the first ship that was to sail from the Clyde; for

Hungry ruin had me in the wind.

"I had been for some days skulking from covert to covert, under all the terrors of a jail; as some ill-advised people had uncoupled the merciless pack of the law at my heels. I had taken the last farewell of my friends; my chest was on the road to Greenock; I had composed the last song I should ever measure in Caledonia, The gloomy night was gathering fast,' when a letter from Dr. Blacklock, to a friend of mine, overthrew all my schemes, by opening new prospects to my poetic ambition. The Doctor belonged to a set of critics, for whose applause I had not dared to hope. His opinion that I would meet with encouragement in Edinburgh for a second edition fired me so much, that away I posted for that city, without a single acquaintance, or a single letter of introduction. The baneful star, that had so long shed its blasting influence in my zenith, for once made a revolution to the Nadir; and a kind Provi-

5

dence placed me under the patronage of one of the noblest of men, the Earl of Glencairn. *Oublie moi, Grand Dieu, si jamais je l'oublie!* "I need relate no farther. At Edinburgh I was in a new world; I mingled among many classes of men, but all of them new to me, and I was all attention to catch the characters and 'the manners living as they rise.' Whether I have profited, time will show."

The letter alluded to from Dr. Blacklock was addressed to the Rev. Mr. Laurie, Minister of Loudoun, a kind and steady friend, who felt so much interested in the poet, that he immediately forwarded it to him. The letter was received with so much surprise and delight, that, although the ship was unmooring and ready to sail, he at once decided to post to Edinburgh. This letter, so creditable to Dr. Blacklock, deserves to be preserved in any Life of our poet:

"I ought to have acknowledged your favor long ago, not only as a testimony of your kind remembrance, but as it gave me an opportunity of sharing one of the finest, and, perhaps, one of the most genuine entertainments, of which the human mind is susceptible. A number of avocations retarded my progress in reading the poems; at last, however, I have finished that pleasing perusal. Many instances have I seen of Nature's force and beneficence exerted under numerous and formidable disadvantages: but none equal to that with which you have been kind enough to present me. There is a pathos and delicacy in his serious poems, a vein of wit and humor in those of a more festive turn, which cannot be too much admired, nor too warmly approved; and I think I shall never open the book without feeling my astonishment renewed and increased. It was my wish to have expressed my approbation in verse; but whether from declining life, or a temporary depression of spirits, it is at present out of my power to accomplish that agreeable intention.

"Mr. Stewart, Professor of Morals in this University, formerly read me three of the poems, and I had desired him to get my name inserted among the subscribers; but whether this was done, or not, I never could learn. I have little intercourse with Dr. Blair, but will take care to have the poems communicated to him by the intervention of some mutual friend. It has been told me by a gentleman, to whom I showed the performances, and who sought a copy with diligence and ardor, that the whole impression is already exhausted. It were, therefore, much to be wished, for the sake of the young man, that a second edition, more numerous than the former, could immediately be printed: as it appears certain that its intrinsic merit, and the exertion of the author's friends, might give it a more universal circulation than any thing of the kind which has been published within my memory."

Burns set out for Edinburgh in the month of November, 1786, and arrived on the second day afterwards, having performed his journey on foot. He was furnished with a letter of introduction to Dr. Blacklock, from Mr. Laurie, to whom the Doctor had addressed the letter which has been represented as the immediate cause of his visiting the Scottish metropolis. He was acquainted with Mr. Stewart, Professor of Moral Philosophy in the University, and had been entertained by that gentleman at Catrine, his estate in Ayrshire. He had been introduced by Mr. Alexander Dalzel to the Earl of Glencairn, who had expressed his high approbation of his poetical talents. He had friends, therefore, who could introduce him into the circles of literature, as well as of fashion, and his own manners and appearance exceeding every expectation that could have been formed of them, he soon became an object of general curiosity and admiration.

The scene that opened on our bard in Edinburgh was altogether new, and in a variety of other respects highly interesting, especially to one of his disposition of mind. To use an expression of his own, he found himself "suddenly translated from the veriest shades of life" into the presence, and indeed into the society, of a number of persons, previously known to him by report as of the highest distinction in his country, and whose characters it was natural for him to examine with no common curiosity.

From the men of letters, in general, his reception was particularly flattering. The late Dr. Robertson, Dr. Blair, Dr. Gregory, Mr. Stewart, Mr. Mackenzie, and Mr. Fraser Tytler, may be mentioned in the list of those who perceived his uncommon talents, who acknowledged more especially his powers in conversation, and who interested themselves in the cultivation of his genius. In Edinburgh, literary and fashionable society are a good deal mixed. Our bard was an acceptable guest in the gayest and most elevated circles, and frequently received from female beauty and elegance those attentions above all others most grateful to him. At the table of Lord Monboddo he was a frequent guest; and while he enjoyed the society, and partook of the hospitalities of the venerable judge, he experienced the kindness and condescension of his lovely and accomplished daughter. The singular beauty of this young lady was illuminated by that happy expression of countenance which results from the union of cultivated taste and superior understanding, with the finest affections of the mind. The influence of such attractions was not unfelt by our poet. "There has not been any thing like Miss Burnet," said he in a letter to a friend, "in all the combinations of beauty, grace, and goodness, the Creator has formed, since Milton's Eve on the first day of her existence."

In his Address to Edinburgh, she is celebrated in a strain of still greater elevation:

> Fair Burnet strikes th' adoring eye,
> Heaven's beauties on my fancy shine;
> I see the *sire of love on high*,
> And own his work indeed divine !

This lovely woman died a few years afterwards in the flower of youth. Our bard expressed his sensibility on that occasion, in verses addressed to her memory.

Among the men of rank and fashion, Burns was particularly distinguished by James, Earl of Glencairn. On the motion of this nobleman, the *Caledonian Hunt* (an association of the principal of the nobility and gentry of Scotland) extended their patronage to our bard, and admitted him to their gay orgies. He repaid their notice by a dedication of the enlarged and improved edition of his poems, in which he has celebrated their patriotism and independence in very animated terms.

A taste for letters is not always conjoined with habits of temperance and regularity ; and Edinburgh, at the time of which we speak, contained perhaps an uncommon proportion of men of considerable talents, devoted to social excesses, in which their talents were wasted and debased.

Burns entered into several parties of this description, with the usual vehemence of his character. His generous affections, his ardent eloquence, his brilliant and daring imagination, fitted him to be the idol of such associations ; and accustoming himself to conversation of unlimited range, and to festive indulgences that scorned restraint, he gradually lost some portion of his relish for the more pure, but less poignant pleasures, to be found in the circles of taste, elegance, and literature. The sudden alteration in his habits of life operated on him physically as well as morally. The humble fare of an Ayrshire peasant he had exchanged for the luxuries of the Scottish metropolis, and the effects of this change on his ardent constitution could not be inconsiderable. But whatever influence might be produced on his conduct, his excellent understanding suffered no corresponding debasement. He estimated his friends and associates of every description at their proper value, and appreciated his own conduct with a precision that might give scope to much curious and melancholy reflection. He saw his danger, and at times formed resolutions to guard against it ; but he had embarked on the tide of dissipation, and was borne along its stream.

By the new edition of his poem, Burns acquired a sum of money that enabled him not only to partake of the pleasures of Edinburgh, but to gratify a desire he had long entertained, of visiting those

parts of his native country most attractive by their beauty or
their grandeur; a desire which the return of summer naturally re-
vived. The scenery of the banks of the Tweed, and of its tribu-
tary streams, strongly interested his fancy; and, accordingly, he
left Edinburgh on the 6th of May, 1787, on a tour through a country
so much celebrated in the rural songs of Scotland. He travelled
on horseback, and was accompanied, during some part of his jour-
ney, by Mr. Ainslie, writer to the signet, a gentleman who enjoyed
much of his friendship and of his confidence.

Having spent three weeks in exploring the interesting scenery of
the Tweed, the Jed, the Tiviot, and other border districts, Burns
crossed over into Northumberland. Mr. Kerr and Mr. Hood, two
gentlemen with whom he had become acquainted in the course of
his tour, accompanied him. He visited Alnwick Castle, the princely
seat of the Duke of Northumberland; the hermitage and old castle
of Warksworth; Morpeth, and Newcastle. In this town he spent
two days, and then proceeded to the southwest by Hexham and
Wardrue, to Carlisle. After spending a day at Carlisle with his
friend Mr. Mitchell, he returned into Scotland by way of Annan.

Of the various persons with whom he became acquainted in the
course of this journey, he has, in general, given some account, and
almost always a favorable one. From Annan, Burns proceeded to
Dumfries, and thence through Sanquhar, to Mossgiel, near Mauch-
line, in Ayrshire, where he arrived about the 8th of June, 1787,
after a long absence of six busy and eventful months. It will easily
be conceived with what pleasure and pride he was received by his
mother, his brothers, and sisters. He had left them poor, and com-
paratively friendless; he returned to them high in public estima-
tion, and easy in his circumstances. He returned to them unchanged
in his ardent affections, and ready to share with them, to the utter-
most farthing, the pittance that fortune had bestowed.

Having remained with them a few days, he proceeded again to
Edinburgh, and immediately set out on a journey to the High-
lands.

From this journey Burns returned to his friends in Ayrshire,
with whom he spent the month of July, renewing his friendships,
and extending his acquaintance throughout the county, where he
was now very generally known and admired. In August he again
visited Edinburgh, whence he undertook another journey, towards
the middle of this month, in company with Mr. M. Adair, now Dr.
Adair, of Harrowgate, of which this gentleman has favored us with
the following account:

"Burns and I left Edinburgh together in August, 1787. We rode
by Linlithgow and Carron, to Stirling. We visited the iron-works

at Carron, with which the poet was forcibly struck. The resem-
blance between that place, and its inhabitants, to the cave of the
Cyclops, which must have occurred to every classical visitor, pre-
sented itself to Burns. At Stirling, the prospects from the castle
strong'y interested him; in a former visit to which, his national
feelings had been powerfully excited by the ruinous and roofless
state of the hall in which the Scottish Parliaments had frequently
been held. His indignation had vented itself in some imprudent,
but not unpoetical lines, which had given much offence, and which
he took this opportunity of erasing, by breaking the pane of the win-
dow at the inn on which they were written.

"At Stirling, we met with a company of travellers from Edin-
burgh, among whom was a character, in many respects congenial
with that of Burns. This was Nicol, one of the teachers of the
High Grammar School at Edinburgh—the same wit and power
of conversation, the same fondness for convivial society, and
thoughtlessness of to-morrow, characterized both. Jacobitical
principles in politics were common to both of them; and these have
been suspected, since the revolution of France, to have given place
in each to opinions apparently opposite. I regret that I have pre-
served no *memorabilia* of their conversation, either on this, or on
other occasions, when I happened to meet them together. Many
songs were sung, which I mention for the sake of observing, that
when Burns was called on in his turn, he was accustomed, instead
of singing, to recite one or other of his own shorter poems, with a
tone and emphasis, which, though not correct or harmonious, were
impressive and pathetic. This he did on the present occasion.

"From Stirling we went next morning through the romantic and
fertile vale of Devon to Harviestone, in Clackmannanshire, then
inhabited by Mrs. Hamilton, with the younger part of whose family
Burns had been previously acquainted. He introduced me to the
family, and there was formed my first acquaintance with Mr.
Hamilton's eldest daughter, to whom I have been married for nine
years. Thus was I indebted to Burns for a connection from which
I have derived, and expect further to derive, much happiness.

"During a residence of about ten days at Harviestone, we made
excursions to visit various parts of the surrounding scenery, in
ferior to none in Scotland, in beauty, sublimity, and romantic inter-
est; particularly Castle Campbell, the ancient seat of the family o.
Argyll; and the famous cataract of the Devon, called the Cauldron
Lynn; and the Rumbling Bridge, a single broad arch, thrown by
the devil, if tradition is to be believed, across the river, at about the
height of a hundred feet above its bed. I am surprised that none
of these scenes should have called forth an exertion of Burns's

muse. But I doubt if he had much taste for the picturesque. I well remember, that the ladies at Harviestone, who accompanied us on this jaunt, expressed their disappointment at his not expressing in more glowing and fervid language his impressions of the Cauldron Linn scene, certainly highly sublime, and somewhat horrible.

"A visit to Mrs. Bruce, of Clackmannan, a lady above ninety, the lineal descendant of that race which gave the Scottish throne its brightest ornament, interested his feelings more powerfully. This venerable dame, with characteristical dignity, informed me, on my observing that I believed she was descended from the family of Robert Bruce, that Robert Bruce was sprung from her family. Though almost deprived of speech by a paralytic affection, she preserved her hospitality and urbanity. She was in possession of the hero's helmet and two-handed sword, with which she conferred on Burns and myself the honor of knighthood, remarking, that she had a better right of conferring that title than *some people.* * * * You will of course conclude that the old lady's political tenets were as Jacobitical as the poet's, a conformity which contributed not a little to the cordiality of our reception and entertainment. She gave as her first toast after dinner, ' Awa Uncos,' or, Away with the Strangers. Who these strangers were, you will readily understand. Mrs. A. corrects me by saying it should be ' Hooi, or Hoohi, Uncos,' a sound used by shepherds to direct their dogs to drive away the sheep.

"We returned to Edinburgh by Kinross (on the shore of Lochleven) and Queensferry. I am inclined to think Burns knew nothing of poor Michael Bruce, who was then alive at Kinross, or had died there a short while before. A meeting between the bards, or a visit to the deserted cottage and early grave of poor Bruce, would have been highly interesting.*

"At Dunfermline we visited the ruined abbey, and the abbey-church, now consecrated to Presbyterian worship. Here I mounted the *cutty stool,* or stool of repentance, assuming the character of a penitent for fornication; while Burns from the pulpit addressed to me a ludicrous reproof and exhortation, parodied from that which had been delivered to himself in Ayrshire, where he had, as he assured me, once been one of seven who mounted the *seat of shame* together.

"In the church-yard two broad flag-stones marked the grave of Robert Bruce, for whose memory Burns had more than common veneration. He knelt and kissed the stone with sacred fervor, and

* Bruce died some years before.

heartily (*suus ut mos erat*) execrated the worse than gothic neglect
of the first of Scottish heroes."[*]

The different journeys already mentioned did not satisfy the
curiosity of Burns. About the beginning of September he again
set out from Edinburgh, on a more extended tour to the Highlands,
in company with Mr. Nicol, with whom he had contracted a partic-
ular intimacy, which lasted during the remainder of his life. Mr.
Nicol was of Dumfriesshire, of a descent equally humble with our
poet. Like him he rose by the strength of his talents, and fell by
the strength of his passions. He died in the summer of 1797.
Having received the elements of a classical instruction at his parish
school, Mr. Nicol made a very rapid and singular proficiency; and
by early undertaking the office of an instructor himself, he acquired
the means of entering himself at the University of Edinburgh.
There he was first a student of theology, then a student of medi-
cine, and was afterwards employed in the assistance and instruc-
tion of graduates in medicine, in those parts of their exercises in
which the Latin language is employed. In this situation he was
the contemporary and rival of the celebrated Dr. Brown, whom he
resembled in the particulars of his history, as well as in the leading
features of his character. The office of assistant-teacher in the
High-school being vacant, it was as usual filled up by competition;
and in the face of some prejudices, and perhaps of some well-
founded objections, Mr. Nicol, by superior learning, carried it from
all the other candidates. This office he filled at the period of which
we speak.

Mr. Nicol and our poet travelled in a post-chaise, which they en-
gaged for the journey, and passing through the heart of the High-
lands, stretched northwards about ten miles beyond Inverness.
There they bent their course eastward, across the island, and re-
turned by the shore of the German Sea to Edinburgh. In the
course of this tour, they visited a number of remarkable scenes,
and the imagination of Burns was constantly excited by the wild
and sublime scenery through which he passed. Of the history of
one of these poems, *The humble petition of Bruar water*, and of the
bard's visit to Athole House, the following particulars are given by
Mr. Walker of Perth, then residing in the family of the Duke of Athol.

"On reaching Blair, he sent me notice of his arrival (as I had
been previously acquainted with him), and I hastened to meet him
at the inn. The Duke, to whom he had brought a letter of intro-
duction, was from home; but the Duchess being informed of his
arrival, gave him an invitation to sup and sleep at Athole House.

---

[*] Extract from a letter of Dr. Adair to the Editor.

"My curiosity was great to see how he would conduct himself in company so different from what he had been accustomed to.* His manner was unembarrassed, plain, and firm. He appeared to have complete reliance on his own native good sense for directing his behavior. He seemed at once to perceive and appreciate what was due to the company and to himself, and never to forget a proper respect for the separate species of dignity belonging to each. He did not arrogate conversation, but when led into it, he spoke with ease, propriety, and manliness. He tried to exert his abilities, because he knew it was ability alone gave him a title to be there. The Duke's fine young family attracted much of his admiration; he drank their healths as *honest men and bonnie lasses*, an idea which was much applauded by the company, and with which he has very felicitously closed his poem.

"Much attention was paid to Burns both before and after the Duke's return, of which he was perfectly sensible, without being vain; and at his departure I recommended to him, as the most appropriate return he could make, to write some descriptive verses on any of the scenes with which he had been so much delighted. After leaving Blair, he, by the Duke's advice, visited the *Falls of Bruar*, and in a few days I received a letter from Inverness, with the verses inclosed."

It appears that the impression made by our poet on the noble family of Athole was in a high degree favorable; it is certain he was charmed with the reception he received from them, and he often mentioned the two days he spent at Athole House as among the happiest of his life. He was warmly invited to prolong his stay, but sacrificed his inclinations to his engagement with Mr. Nicol; which is the more to be regretted, as he would otherwise have been introduced to Mr. Dundas (then daily expected on a visit to the Duke), a circumstance that might have had a favorable influence on Burns's future fortunes. At Athole House he met, for the first time, Mr. Graham of Fintry, to whom he was afterwards indebted for his office in the Excise.

The letters and poems which he addressed to Mr. Graham bear testimony of his sensibility,† and justify the supposition that he would not have been deficient in gratitude, had he been elevated to a situation better suited to his disposition and to his talents.

A few days after leaving Blair of Athole, our poet and his fellow-

* In the preceding winter, Burns had been in company of the highest rank in Edinburgh; but this description of his manners is perfectly applicable to his first appearance in such society.

† See the First and Second Epistles to Mr. Graham, soliciting an employment in the Excise.

traveller arrived at Fochabers. In the course of the preceding
winter Burns had been introduced to the Duchess of Gordon at
Edinburgh, and presuming on this acquaintance, he proceeded to
Gordon Castle, leaving Mr. Nicol at the inn in the village. At the
castle our poet was received with the utmost hospitality and kind-
ness, and the family being about to sit down to dinner, he was in-
vited to take his place at the table as a matter of course. This invi-
tation he accepted, and after drinking a few glasses of wine, he
rose up, and proposed to withdraw. On being pressed to stay, he
mentioned, for the first time, his engagement with his fellow-trav-
eller ; and his noble host offering to send a servant to conduct Mr
Nicol to the castle, Burns insisted on undertaking that office him-
self. He was, however, accompanied by a gentleman, a particular
acquaintance of the Duke, by whom the invitation was delivered
in all the forms of politeness. The invitation, however, came too
late ; the pride of Nicol was inflamed to the highest degree by the
neglect which he had already suffered. He had ordered the horses
to be put to the carriage, being determined to proceed on his jour-
ney alone ; and they found him parading the streets of Fochabers,
before the door of the inn, venting his anger on the postillion, for
the slowness with which he obeyed his commands. As no expla-
nation nor entreaty could change the purpose of his fellow-travel-
ler, our poet was reduced to the necessity of separating from him en-
tirely, or of instantly proceeding with him on their journey. He chose
the last of these alternatives ; and seating himself beside Nicol in
the post-chaise, with mortification and regret he turned his back
on Gordon Castle; where he had promised himself some happy
days. Sensible, however, of the great kindness of the noble family,
he made the best return in his power by the following poem.*

Streams that glide in orient plains,
Never bound by winter's chains ;
Glowing here on golden sands,
There commix'd with foulest stains
From tyranny's empurpled bands :
These, their richly-gleaming waves,
I leave to tyrants and their slaves—
Give me the stream that sweetly laves
The banks by Castle-Gordon.

Spicy forests, ever gay,
Shading from the burning ray
Hapless wretches sold to toil,
Or the ruthless native's way,
Bent on slaughter, blood, and spoil ;

* This information is extracted from a letter of Dr. Couper, of Fochabers, to the
Editor.

Woods that ever verdant wave,
I leave the tyrant and the slave—
Give me the groves that lofty brave
The storms, by Castle-Gordon.

Wildly here, without control,
Nature reigns and rules the whole ;
In that sober, pensive mood,
Dearest to the feeling soul,
She plants the forest, pours the flood ;
Life's poor day I'll musing rave,
And find at night a sheltering cave,
Where waters flow and wild woods wave,
By bonnie Castle-Gordon.*

Burns remained at Edinburgh during the greater part of the
winter, 1787-8, and again entered into the society and dissipation
of that metropolis. It appears, that on the 31st of December, he at-
tended a meeting to celebrate the birthday of the lineal descend-
ant of the Scottish race of kings, the late unfortunate Prince Charles
Edward. On this occasion our bard took upon himself the office
of poet-laureate, and produced an ode, which, though deficient in
the complicated rhythm and polished versification that such compo-
sitions require, might on a fair competition, where energy of feel-
ings and of expression were alone in question, have won the butt of
Malmsey from the real Laureate of that day.†

In relating the incidents of our poet's life in Edinburgh, we ought
to have mentioned the sentiments of respect and sympathy with
which he traced out the grave of his predecessor Fergusson, over
whose ashes, in the Canongate churchyard, he obtained leave to
erect an humble monument, which will be viewed by reflecting
minds with no common interest, and which will awake in the bo-
som of kindred genius, many a high emotion. Neither should we
pass over the continued friendship he experienced from the amia-
ble and accomplished Blacklock. To his encouraging advice it was
owing (as has already appeared) that Burns, instead of emigrating
to the West Indies, repaired to Edinburgh. He received him there
with all the ardor of affectionate admiration ; he eagerly introduced
him to the respectable circle of his friends ; he consulted his in-
terest ; he blazoned his fame ; he lavished upon him all the kindness
of a generous and feeling heart, into which nothing selfish or en-
vious ever found admittance. Among the friends to whom he in-
troduced Burns was Mr. Ramsay, of Ochtertyre, to whom our poet
paid a visit in the autumn of 1787, at his delightful retirement in
the neighborhood of Stirling, and on the banks of the Teith.

* These verses our poet composed to be sung to *Morag*, a Highland air of which he
was extremely fond.
† See page 191.

On settling with his publisher, Mr. Creech, in February, 1789, Burns found himself master of nearly five hundred pounds, after discharging all his expenses. Two hundred pounds he immediately advanced to his brother Gilbert, who had taken upon himself the support of their aged mother, and was struggling with many difficulties in the farm of Mossgiel. With the remainder of this sum, and some farther eventual profits from his poems, he determined on settling himself for life in the occupation of agriculture, and took from Mr. Miller, of Dalswinton, the farm of Ellisland, on the banks of the river Nith, six miles above Dumfries, on which he entered at Whitsunday, 1788. Hav'ng been previously recommended to the Board of Excise, his name had been put on the list of candidates for the humble office of a gauger, or exciseman ; and he immediately applied to acquiring the information necessary for filling that office, when the honorable Board might judge it proper to employ him. He expected to be called into service in the district in which his farm was situated, and vainly hoped to unite with success the labors of the farmer with the duties of the exciseman.

When Burns had in this manner arranged his plans for futurity, his generous heart turned to the object of his most ardent attachment, and listening to no considerations but those of honor and affection, he joined with her in a public declaration of marriage, thus legalizing their union, and rendering it permanent for life.

It was not convenient for Mrs. Burns to remove immediately from Ayrshire, and our poet therefore took up his residence alone at Ellisland, to prepare for the reception of his wife and children, who joined him towards the end of the year.

The situation in which Burns now found himself was calculated to awaken reflection. The different steps he had of late taken were in their nature highly important, and might be said to have, in some measure, fixed his destiny. He had become a husband and a father; he had engaged in the management of a considerable farm, a difficult and laborious undertaking ; in his success the happiness of his family was involved ; it was time, therefore, to abandon the gayety and dissipation of which he had been too much enamored : to ponder seriously on the past, and to form virtuous resolutions respecting the future.

He commenced by immediately rebuilding the dwelling-house on his farm, which, in the state he found it, was inadequate to the accommodation of his family. On this occasion, he himself resumed at times the occupation of a laborer, and found neither his strength nor his skill impaired. Pleased with surveying the grounds he was about to cultivate, and with the rearing of a building that should give shelter to his wife and children, and, as he fondly hoped, to his own gray hairs, sentiments of independence buoyed up his mind, pictures of domestic content and peace rose on his imagination; and a few days passed away, as he himself informs us, the most tranquil, if not the happiest, which he had ever experienced.

His fame naturally drew upon him the attention of his neighbors, and he soon formed a general acquaintance in the district in which he lived. The public voice had now pronounced on the subject of his talents; the reception he had met with in Edinburgh had given him the currency which fashion bestows; he had surmounted the prejudices arising from his humble birth, and he was received at the table of the gentlemen of Nithsdale with welcome, with kindness, and even with respect. Their social parties too often seduced him from his rustic labors, and it was not long, therefore, before Burns began to view his farm with dislike and despondence, if not with disgust.

Unfortunately he had for several years looked to an office in the Excise as a certain means of livelihood, should his other expectations fail. As has already been mentioned, he had been recommended to the Board of Excise, and had received the instructions necessary for such a situation. He now applied to be employed; and by the interest of Mr. Graham, of Fintry, was appointed to be exciseman, or, as it is vulgarly called, gauger, of the district in which he lived. His farm was, after this, in a great measure, abandoned to servants, while he betook himself to the duties of his new appointment.

He might indeed still be seen in the spring directing his plough, a labor in which he excelled; or with a white sheet containing his seed-corn, slung across his shoulders, striding with measured steps along his turned-up furrows, and scattering the grain in the earth. But his farm no longer occupied the principal part of his care or his thoughts. It was not at Ellisland that he was now in general to be found. Mounted on horseback, this high-minded poet was pursuing the defaulters of the revenue among the hills and vales of Nithsdale, his roving eye wandering over the charms of nature, and *muttering his wayward fancies* as he moved along.

Besides his duties in the Excise and his social pleasures, other circumstances interfered with the attention of Burns to his farm. He engaged in the formation of a society for purchasing and circulating books among the farmers of his neighborhood, of which he undertook the management; and he occupied himself occasionally in composing songs for the musical work of Mr. Johnson, then in the course of publication. These engagements, useful and honor able in themselves, contributed, no doubt, to the abstraction of his thoughts from the business of agriculture.

The consequences may be easily imagined. Notwithstanding the uniform prudence and good management of Mrs. Burns, and though his rent was moderate and reasonable, our poet found it convenient, if not necessary, to resign his farm to Mr. Miller, after having occupied it three years and a half. His office in the Excise had originally produced about fifty pounds per annum. Having acquitted himself to the satisfaction of the Board, he had been appointed to a new district, the emoluments of which rose to about seventy pounds per annum. Hoping to support himself and his family on his humble income till promotion should reach him, he disposed of his stock and of his crop on Ellisland by public auction, and removed to a small house which he had taken in Dumfries, about the end of the year 1791.

Hitherto Burns, though addicted to excess in social parties, had abstained from the habitual use of strong liquors, and his constitution had not suffered any permanent injury from the irregularities of his conduct. In Dumfries, temptations to "the sin that so easily beset him" continually presented themselves; and his irregularities grew by degrees into habits. These temptations unhappily occurred during his engagements in the business of his office, as well as during his hours of relaxation; and though he clearly foresaw the consequence of yielding to them, his appetites and sensations, which could not pervert the dictates of his judgment, finally triumphed over the powers of his will.

Still, however, he cultivated the society of persons of taste and respectability, and in their company could impose upon himself the restraints of temperance and decorum. Nor was his muse dormant. In the four years which he lived at Dumfries, he produced many of his beautiful lyrics, though it does not appear that he attempted any poem of considerable length.

Burns had entertained hopes of promotion in the Excise; but circumstances occurred which retarded their fulfilment, and which, in his own mind, destroyed all expectation of their being ever fulfilled. The extraordinary events which ushered in the revolution of France interested the feelings, and excited the hopes, of men in every corner of Europe. Prejudice and tyranny seemed about to disappear from among men, and the day-star of reason to rise upon a benighted world. In the dawn of this beautiful morning, the genius of French freedom appeared on our southern horizon with the countenance of an angel, but speedily assumed the features of a demon, and vanished in a shower of blood.

Though previously a Jacobite and a cavalier Burns had shared

in the original hopes entertained of this astonishing revolut.on by
ardent and benevolent minds. The novelty and the hazard of the
attempt meditated by the First, or Constituent Assembly, served
rather, it is probable, to recommend it to his daring temper; and
the unfettered scope proposed to be given to every kind of talents
was doubtless gratifying to the feelings of conscious but indignant
genius. Burns foresaw not the mighty ruin that was to be the
immediate consequence of an enterprise, which, on its commence-
ment, promised so much happiness to the human race. And even
after the career of guilt and of blood commenced, he could not im-
mediately, it may be presumed, withdraw his partial gaze from a
people who had so lately breathed the sentiments of universal peace
and benignity, or obliterate in his bosom the pictures of hope and
of happiness to which those sentiments had given birth. Under
these impressions, he did not always conduct himself with the cir-
cumspection and prudence which his dependent situation seemed
to demand. He engaged indeed in no popular associations, so
common at the time of which we speak; but in company he did
not conceal his opinions of public measures, or of the reforms re-
quired in the practice of our government: and sometimes, in his
social and unguarded moments, he uttered them with a wild and
unjustifiable vehemence. Information of this was given to the
Board of Excise, with the exaggerations so general in such cases.
A superior officer in that department was authorized to inquire
into his conduct. Burns defended himself in a letter addressed to
one of the Board, written with great independence of spirit, and
with more than his accustomed eloquence. The officer appointed
to inquire into his conduct gave a favorable report. His steady
friend, Mr. Graham, of Fintry, interposed his good offices in his
behalf; and the imprudent ganger was suffered to retain his situ-
ation, but given to understand that his promotion was deferred, and
must depend on his future behavior.

This circumstance made a deep impression on the mind of Burns.
Fame exaggerated his misconduct, and represented him as actually
dismissed from his office; and this report induced a gentleman of
much respectability to propose a subscription in his favor. The
offer was refused by our poet in a letter of great elevation of senti-
ment, in which he gives an account of the whole of this transaction,
and defends himself from the imputation of disloyal sentiments on
the one hand, and on the other from the charge of having made
submissions for the sake of his office, unworthy of his character.

In the midst of all his wanderings, Burns met nothing in his do-
mestic circle but gentleness and forgiveness, except in the gnawings
of his own remorse. He acknowledged his transgressions to the

wife of his bosom, promised amendment, and again received pardon for his offences. But as the strength of his body decayed, his resolution became feebler, and habit acquired predominating strength.

From October, 1795, to the January following, an accidental complaint confined him to the house. A few days after he began to go abroad, he dined at a tavern, and returned about three o'clock in a very cold morning, benumbed and intoxicated. This was followed by an attack of rheumatism, which confined him about a week. His appetite now began to fail; his hand shook, and his voice faltered on any exertion or emotion. His pulse became weaker and more rapid, and pain in the larger joints, and in the hands and feet, deprived him of the enjoyment of refreshing sleep. Too much dejected in his spirits, and too well aware of his real situation to entertain hopes of recovery, he was ever musing on the approaching desolation of his family, and his spirits sunk into a uniform gloom.

It was hoped by some of his friends, that if he could live through the months of spring, the succeeding season might restore him. But they were disappointed. The genial beams of the sun infused no vigor into his languid frame; the summer wind blew upon him, but produced no refreshment. About the latter end of June he was advised to go into the country, and, impatient of medical advice, as well as of every species of control, he determined for himself to try the effects of bathing in the sea. For this purpose he took up his residence at Brow, in Annandale, about ten miles east of Dumfries, on the shore of the Solway-Frith.

At first, Burns imagined bathing in the sea had been of benefit to him; the pains in his limbs were relieved; but this was immediately followed by a new attack of fever. When brought back to his own house in Dumfries, on the 18th July, he was no longer able to stand upright. At this time a tremor pervaded his frame: his tongue was parched, and his mind sunk into delirium, when not roused by conversation. On the second and third day the fever increased, and his strength diminished. On the fourth, the sufferings of this great but ill-fated genius were terminated, and a life was closed in which virtue and passion had been at perpetual variance.

The death of Burns made a strong and general impression on all who had interested themselves in his character, and especially on the inhabitants of the town and country in which he had spent the latter years of his life. The Gentlemen-Volunteers of Dumfries determined to bury their illustrious associate with military honors, and every preparation was made to render this last service solemn and impressive. The Fencible Infantry of Angus-shire, and the

regiment of cavalry of the Cinque Ports, at that time quartered in
Dumfries, offered their assistance on this occasion; the principal
inhabitants of the town and neighborhood determined to walk in
the funeral procession; and a vast concourse of persons assembled,
some of them from a considerable distance, to witness the obsequies
of the Scottish Bard. On the evening of the 25th of July, the re-
mains of Burns were removed from his house to the Town Hall, and
the funeral took place on the succeeding day. A party of the Vol-
unteers, selected to perform the military duty in the churchyard,
stationed themselves in the front of the procession with their arms
reversed; the main body of the corps surrounded and supported
the coffin, on which were placed the hat and sword of their friend
and fellow-soldier; the numerous body of attendants ranged them-
selves in the rear; while the Fencible regiments of infantry and
cavalry lined the streets from the Town Hall to the burial-ground
in the Southern churchyard, a distance of more than half a mile.
The whole procession moved forward to that sublime and affecting
strain of music, the *Dead March* in Saul: and three volleys fired
over his grave marked the return of Burns to his parent earth!
The spectacle was in a high degree grand and solemn, and accord-
ing with the general sentiments of sympathy and sorrow which the
occasion had called forth.

It was an affecting circumstance, that, on the morning of the day
of her husband's funeral, Mrs. Burns was undergoing the pains of
labor, and that during the solemn service we have just been de-
scribing, the posthumous son of our poet was born. This infant
boy, who received the name of Maxwell, was not destined to a long
life. He has already become an inhabitant of the same grave with
his celebrated father.

The sense of his poverty, and of the approaching distress of his
infant family, pressed heavily on Burns as he lay on the bed of
death. Yet he alluded to his indigence, at times, with something
approaching to his wonted gayety.—" What business," said he to
Dr. Maxwell, who attended him with the utmost zeal, "has a phy-
sician to waste his time on me? I am a poor pigeon not worth
plucking. Alas! I have not feather enough upon me to carry me
to my grave." And when his reason was lost in delirium, his ideas
ran in the same melancholy train: the horrors of a jail were con-
tinually present to his troubled imagination, and produced the
most affecting exclamations.

On the death of Burns, the inhabitants of Dumfries and its
neighborhood opened a subscription for the support of his wife
and family. The subscription was extended to other parts of Scot-
land, and of England also, particularly London and Liverpool. By

this means a sum was raised amounting to seven hundred pounds
and thus the widow and children were rescued from immediate
distress, and the most melancholy of the forebodings of Burns hap-
pily disappointed.

Burns, as has already been mentioned, was nearly five feet ten
inches in height, and a form that indicated agility as well as strength.
His well-raised forehead, shaded with black curling hair, indicated
extensive capacity. His eyes were large, dark, full of ardor and
intelligence. His face was well formed; and his countenance un-
commonly interesting and expressive. The tones of his voice hap-
pily corresponded with the expression of his features, and with the
feelings of his mind. When to these endowments are added a
rapid and distinct apprehension, a most powerful understanding,
and a happy command of language—of strength as well as bril-
liancy of expression—we shall be able to account for the extraordi-
nary attractions of his conversation—for the sorcery which, in his
social parties, he seemed to exert on all around him. In the com-
pany of women this sorcery was more especially apparent. Their
presence charmed the fiend of melancholy in his bosom, and awoke
his happiest feelings; it excited the powers of his fancy, as well as
the tenderness of his heart; and, by restraining the vehemence and
the exuberance of his language, at times gave to his manners the
impression of taste, and even of elegance, which in the company of
men they seldom possessed. This influence was doubtless recip-
rocal.

———

We conclude with the character of Burns as given by his country-
man, Mr. Allan Cunningham, which is alike creditable to his taste,
and does justice to the illustrious fame of the poet:—

As a poet, Burns stands in the first rank: his conceptions are
original; his thoughts new and weighty; his manner unborrowed;
and even his language is his own. He owes no honor to his sub-
jects, for they are all of an ordinary kind, such as humble life
around him presented: he sought neither in high station nor in
history for matter to his muse, and yet all his topics are simple,
natural, and to be found without research. The Scottish bards
who preceded him selected subjects which obtained notice from
their oddity, and treated them in a way singular and outré. The
verses of the first and fifth James, as well as those of Ramsay and
Fergusson, are chiefly a succession of odd and ludicrous pictures,
as true as truth itself, and no more. To their graphic force of de-

lineation Burns added sentiment and passion, and an elegant ten-
derness and simplicity. He took topics familiar to all; the Daisy
grew on the lands he ploughed; the Mouse built her nest on his
own stubble-field; the Haggis smoked on his own board; the Scotch
Drink which he sung was distilled on the banks of Doon; the
Dogs that conversed so wittily and wisely were his own collies;
Tam O'Shanter was a merry husbandman of his own acquaintance;
and even the "De'il himsel" was familiar to all, and had often
alarmed, by his eldritch croon and the marks of his cloven foot,
the pastoral people of Kyle. Burns was the first who taught the
world that in lowly subjects high poetry resided. Touched by
him, they were lifted at once into the regions of inspiration. His
spirit ascended into an humble topic, as the sap of spring ascends a
true to endow it with beauty and fragrance.

Burns is our chief national Poet; he owes nothing of the struc-
ture of his verse or of the materials of his poetry to other lands—he
is the offspring of the soil; he is as natural to Scotland as the heath
is to her hills, and all his brightness, like our nocturnal aurora, is
of the north. Nor has he taken up fleeting themes; his song is
not of the external manners and changeable affections of man—it
is of the human heart—of the mind's hopes and fears, and of the
soul's aspirations. Others give us the outward form and pressure
of society—the court-costume of human nature—the laced lapelle
and the epauleted shoulder. He gives us flesh and blood; all he
has he holds in common with mankind, yet all is national and
Scottish. We can see to whom other bards have looked up for in-
spiration—like fruit of the finest sort, they smack of the stock on
which they were grafted. Burns read Young, Thomson, Shen-
stone, and Shakspeare; yet there is nothing of Young, Thomson,
Shenstone, or Shakspeare about him; nor is there much of the old
ballad. His light is of nature, like sunshine, and not reflected.
When, in after-life, he tried imitation, his "Epistle to Grahame of
Fintray" showed satiric power and polish little inferior to Dryden.

He is not only the truest and best of Scottish Poets, but, in ease,
fire, and passion, he is second to none save Shakspeare. I know
of no one besides, whose verse flows forth so sparkling and spon-
taneous. On the lines of other bards, we see the marks of care
and study—now and then they are happy, but they are as often
elaborated out and brightened like a key by frequent handling.
Burns is seldom or never so—he wrote from the impulse of nature
—he wrote because his passions raged like so many demons till
they got vent in rhyme. Others sit and solicit the muse, like a
coy mistress, to be kind; she came to Burns "unsent for," like
the "bonnie lass" in the song, and showered her favors freely.

The strength was equal to the harmony; rugged westlin words were taken from the lips of the weaver and the ploughman, and adorned with melody and feeling; and familiar phrases were picked up from shepherds and mechanics, and rendered as musical as is Apollo's lute. "I can think of no verse since Shakspeare's," said Pitt to Henry Addington, "which comes so sweetly and at once from nature." "Out of the eater came forth meat:"—the premier praised whom he starved. Burns was not a poet by fits and starts; the mercury of his genius stood always at the inspired point; like the fairy's drinking cup, the fountain of his fancy was ever flowing and ever full. He had, it is true, set times and seasons when the fruits of his mind were more than usually abundant; but the songs of spring were equal to those of summer—those of summer were not surpassed by those of autumn; the quantity might be different, the flavor and richness were ever the same.

His variety is equal to his originality. His humor, his gayety, his tenderness, and his pathos, come all in a breath; they come freely, for they come of their own accord; nor are they huddled together at random, like doves and crows in a flock; the contrast is never offensive; the comic slides easily into the serious, the serious into the tender, and the tender into the pathetic. The witch's cup, out of which the wondering rustic drank seven kinds of wine at once, was typical of the muse of Burns. It is this which has made him welcome to all readers. "No poet," says Scott, "with the exception of Shakspeare, ever possessed the power of exciting the most varied and discordant emotions with such rapid transitions."

Notwithstanding the uncommon ease and natural elegance of his musings—the sweet and impassioned tone of his verse—critics have not been wanting who perceived in his works the humility of his origin. His poems, I remember well enough, were considered by many, at first, as the labors of some gentleman who assumed the rustic for the sake of indulging in satire; their knowledge was reckoned beyond the reach, and their flights above the power, of a simple ploughman. Something of this belief may be seen in Mrs. Scott of Wauchope's letter: and when it was known for a truth that the author was a ploughman, many lengthy discussions took place concerning the way in which the Poet had acquired his knowledge. Ayr race-course was pointed out as the likely scene of his studies of high life, where he found what was graceful and elegant. When Jeffrey wrote his depreciating criticism, he forgot that Burns had studied politeness in the very school where he himself was polished:

"I've been at drunken writers' feasts,"

claims a scholarship which the critic might have respected. If sharp epigrams, familiar gallantry, love of independence, and a leaning to the tumid be, as that critic assures us, true symptoms of vulgar birth, then Swift was a scavenger, Rochester a coalheaver Pope a carman, and Thomson a boor. He might as well see lowness of origin in the James Stuart who wrote "Christ's Kirk on the Green," as in the Robert Burns who wrote "Tam O'Shanter." The nature which Burns infused into all he wrote deals with internal emotions: feeling is no more vulgar in a ploughman than in a prince.

In all this I see the reluctance of an accomplished scholar to admit the merits of a rustic poet who not only claimed, but took, the best station on the Caledonian Parnassus. It could be no welcome sight to philosophers, historians, and critics, to see a peasant, fragrant from the furrow, elbowing his way through their polished ranks to the highest place of honor, exclaiming—

"What's a' your jargon o' your schools ?"

Some of them were no doubt astonished and incensed; nature was doing too much: they avenged themselves by advising him to leave his vulgar or romantic fancies and grow classical. His best songs they called random flights; his happiest poems the fruit of a vagrant impulse; they accounted him an accident—"a wild colt of a comet"—a sort of splendid error: and refused to look upon him as a true poet, raised by the kindly warmth of nature; for they thought nothing beautiful which was not produced or adorned by learning.

Burns is a thorough Scotchman: his nationality, like cream on milk, floats on the surface of all his works; it mingles in his humor as well as in his tenderness; yet it is seldom or never offensive to an English ear; there is nothing narrow-souled in it. He rejoices in Scotland's ancient glory and in her present strength: he bestows his affection on her heathery mountains, as well as on her romantic vales; he glories in the worth of her husbandmen, and in the loveliness of her maidens. The brackeny glens and thistly brae-sides of the North are more welcome to his sight than are the sunny dales of Italy, fragrant with ungathered grapes; its men, if not quite divinities, are more than mortal; and the women are clothed in beauty, and walk in a light of their own creating; a haggis is food fit for gods; brose is a better sort of ambrosia; "wi' twopenny we fear nae evil;" and whiskey not only makes us insensible of danger, but inspires noble verse and heroic deeds. There is something at once ludicrous and dignified in all this: to excite mingled emotions was the aim of the Poet. Besides a love of country, there is an intense love of freedom about him : not the savage joy in the boundless forest and the unlicensed range, but the calm determination and temperate delight of a reflecting mind. Burns is the bard of liberty—not that which sets fancy free and fetters the body; he resists oppression—he covets free thought and speech—he scorns slavish obedience to the mob as much as he detests tyranny in the rulers. He spoke out like a bold-inspired person ; he knew his word would have weight with the world, and sung his "Man's a man for a' that," as a watchword to future generations—as a spell against slavery.

The best poems of Burns are about rural and pastoral life, and relate the hopes, joys, and aspirations, of that portion of the people falsely called the humble, as if grandeur of soul were a thing "born in the purple," and not the free gift and bounty of heaven. The passions and feelings of man are disguised, not changed, in polished society ; flesh and blood are the same beneath hoddin' gray as beneath three-piled velvet. This was what Burns alluded to when he said he saw little in the splendid circles of Edinburgh which was new to him. His pictures of human life and of the world are of a mental as well as national kind. His "Twa Dogs" prove that happiness is not unequally diffused : "Scotch Drink" gives us fireside enjoyments; the "Earnest Cry and Prayer" shows the keen eye which humble people cast on their rulers; the "Address to the Deil" indulges in religious humanities, in which sympathy overcomes fear ; "The Auld Mare," and "The Address to Mailie," enjoin, by the most simple and touching examples, kindness and mercy to dumb creatures ; "The Holy Fair" desires to curb the licentiousness of those who seek amusement instead of holiness in religion ; "Man was made to Mourn" exhorts the strong and the wealthy to be mindful of the weak and the poor; "Halloween" shows us superstition in a domestic aspect ; "Tam O'Shanter" adorns popular belief with humorous terror, and helps us to laugh old dreads away ; "The Mouse," in its weakness, contrasts with man in his strength, and preaches to us the instability of happiness on earth ; while "The Mountain Daisy" pleads with such moral pathos the cause of the flowers of the field sent by God to adorn the earth for man's pleasure, that our feet have pressed less ungraciously on the "wee, modest, crimson-tipped flower," since his song was written.

Others of his poems have a still grander reach. "The Vision" reveals the Poet's plan of Providence, proves the worth of eloquence, bravery, honesty, and beauty, and that even the rustic bard himself is a useful and ornamental link in the great chain of being. "The Cotter's Saturday Night" connects us with the invisible world, and shows that domestic peace, faithful love, and patri-

otic feelings are of earthly things most akin to the joys of heaven,
while the divine "Elegy on Matthew Henderson" unites human
nature in a bond of sympathy with the stars of the sky, the fowls
of the air, the beasts of the field, the flowery vale, and the lonely
mountain. The hastiest of his effusions has a wise aim ; and the
eloquent Curran perceived this when he spoke of the "sublime
morality of Burns."

Had Burns, in his poems, preached only so many moral sermons,
his audience might have been a select, but it would have been a
limited, one. The sublimest truths, like the surest medicines, are
sometimes uneasy to swallow : for this the Poet provided an effec-
tual remedy : he associated his moral counsel with so much tender-
ness and pathos, and garnished it all about with such exquisite
humor, that the public, like the giant drinking the wine in Homer,
gaped, and cried, "More! this is divine!" If a reader has such
a limited soul as to love humor only, why Burns is his man—he
has more of it than any modern poet ; should he covet tenderness,
he cannot read far in Burns without finding it to his mind ; should
he desire pathos, the Scottish Peasant has it of the purest sort ; and
if he wish for them altogether let him try no other bard—for in
what other poet will he find them woven more naturally into the
web of song ? It is by thus suiting himself to so many minds and
tastes, that Burns has become such a favorite with the world ; if,
in a strange company, we should chance to stumble in quoting
him, an English voice, or an Irish one, corrects us ; much of the
business of life is mingled with his verse ; and the lover, whether
in joy or sorrow, will find that Burns has anticipated every throb
of his heart :—

> "Every pulse along his veins,
> And every roving fancy."

He was the first of our northern poets who brought deep passion
and high energy to the service of the muse, who added sublimity
to simplicity, and found loveliness and elegance dwelling among
the cottages of his native land. His simplicity is graceful as well
as strong ; he is never mean, never weak, never vulgar, and but
seldom coarse. All he says is above the mark of other men : his
language is familiar, yet dignified ; careless, yet concise ; and he
touches on the most ordinary—nay, perilous themes, with a skill
so rare and felicitous, that good fortune seems to unite with good
taste in helping him through the Slough of Despond, in which so
many meaner spirits have wallowed. No one has greater power in
adorning the humble, and dignifying the plain—no one else has so
happily picked the sweet fresh flowers of poesy from among the
thorns and brambles of the ordinary paths of existence.

"The excellence of Burns," says Thomas Carlyle, a true judge, "is, indeed, among the rarest, whether in poetry or prose; but at the same time it is plain and easily recognized—his sincerity—his indisputable air of truth. Here are no fabulous woes or joys; no hollow fantastic sentimentalities; no wire-drawn refinings either in thought or feeling: the passion that is traced before us has glowed in a living heart; the opinion he utters has risen in his own understanding, and been a light to his own steps. He does not write from hearsay, but from sight and experience: it is the scenes he has lived and labored amidst that he describes; those scenes, rude and humble as they are, have kindled beautiful emotions in his soul, noble thoughts, and definite resolves; and he speaks forth what is in him, not from any outward call of vanity or interest, but because his heart is too full to be silent. He speaks it, too, with such melody and modulation as he can—in homely rustic jingle—but it is his own, and genuine. This is the grand secret for finding readers, and retaining them: let him who would move and convince others, be first moved and convinced himself."

It must be mentioned, in abatement of this high praise, that Burns occasionally speaks with too little delicacy. He violates without necessity the true decorum of his subject, and indulges in hidden meanings and allusions, such as the most tolerant cannot applaud. Nor is this the worst: he is much too free in his treatment of matters holy. He ventures to take the Deity to task about his own passions, and the order of nature, in a way less reverent than he employs when winning his way to woman's love. He has, in truth, touches of profanity which make the pious shudder. In the warmth of conversation such expressions might escape from the lips; but they should not have been coolly sanctioned in the closet with the pen. These deformities are not, however, of frequent occurrence; and, what is some extenuation, they are generally united to a noble or natural sentiment. He is not profane or indecorous for the sake of being so: his faults, as well as his beauties, come from an overflowing fulness of mind.

His songs have all the beauties, and none of the faults, of his poems. As compositions to be sung, a finer and more scientific harmony, and a more nicely-modulated dance of words were required, and Burns had both in perfection. They flow as readily to the music as if both the air and verse had been created together, and blend and mingle like two uniting streams. The sentiments are from nature; and they never, in any instance, jar or jangle with the peculiar feeling of the music. While humming the air over during the moments of composition, the words came and took their proper places, each according to the meaning of the air: rugged

expressions could not well mingle with thoughts inspired by har
mony.

In his poems, Burns supposes himself in the society of men, and
indulges in reckless sentiments and unmeasured language: in his
songs he imagines himself in softer company: when woman's eye
is on him he is gentle, persuasive, and impassioned; he is never
boisterous; he seeks not to say fine things, yet he never misses
saying them; his compliments are uttered of free will, and all his
thoughts flow naturally from the subject. There is a natural grace
and fascination about his songs; all is earnest and from the heart:
he is none of your millinery bards who deal in jewelled locks, laced
garments, and shower pearls and gems by the bushel on youth
and beauty. He makes bright eyes, flushing cheeks, the music of
the tongue, and the pulses' maddening play, do all. Those charms
he knew came from heaven, and not out of the tirewoman's basket,
and would last when fashions changed. It is remarkable that the
most naturally elegant and truly impassioned songs in the lan-
guage were written by a ploughman-lad in honor of the rustic
lasses around him.

If we regard the songs of Burns as so many pastoral pictures, we
will find that he has an eye for the beauties of nature as accurate and
as tasteful as the happiest landscape painter. Indeed, he seldom
gives us a finished image of female loveliness without the accom-
paniment of blooming flowers, running streams, waving woods,
and the melody of birds: this is the framework which sets off the
portrait. He has recourse rarely to embellishments borrowed from
art; the lighted hall and the thrilling strings are less to him than
a walk with her he loves by some lonely rivulet's side, when the
dews are beginning to glisten on the lilies and weigh them down,
and the moon is moving not unconsciously above them. In all
this we may recognize a true poet—one who felt that woman's
loveliness triumphed over these fragrant accompaniments, and
who regarded her still as the "blood-royal of life," the brightest
part of creation.

Those who desire to feel, in their full force, the songs of Burns,
must not hope it from scientific singers in the theatres. The right
scene is the pastoral glen; the right tongue for utterance is that of
a shepherd lass; and the proper song is that which belongs to her
present feelings. The gowany glen, the nibbling sheep, the warb-
ling birds, and the running stream, give the inanimate, while the
singer herself personates the living beauty of the song. I have
listened to a country girl singing one of his songs, while she spread
her webs to bleach by a running stream—ignorant of her audi-
ence—with such feeling and effect as were quite overpowering.

7

This will keep the fame of Burns high among us; should the
printer's ink dry up, ten thousand melodious tongues will preserve
his songs to remote generations.

The variety, too, of his lyrics is equal to their truth and beauty.
He has written songs which echo the feelings of every age and con-
dition in life. He personates all the passions of man and all the
gradations of affection. He sings the lover hastening through
storm and tempest to see the object of his attachment—the swell-
ing stream, the haunted wood, and the suspicious parents, are all
alike disregarded. He paints him again on an eve of July, when
the air is calm, the grass fragrant, and no sound is abroad save
'he amorous cry of the partridge, enjoying the beauty of the eve-
ning as he steals by some unfrequented way to the trysting thorn,
whither his mistress is hastening; or he limns him on a cold and
snowy night, enjoying a brief parley with her whom he loves, from
a cautiously opened window, which shows her white arm and
bright eyes, and the shadow perhaps of a more fortunate lover,
which accounts for the marks of feet impressed in the snow
on the way to her dwelling. Nor is he always sighing and
vowing: some of his heroes answer scorn with scorn, are saucy
with the saucy, and proud with the proud, and comfort themselves
with sarcastic comments on woman and her fickleness and folly;
others drop all allegiance to that fantastic idol beauty, and while
mirth abounds, and "the wine-cup shines in light," find wondrous
solace. He laughs at the sex one moment, and adores them the
next—he ridicules and satirizes—he vows and entreats—he 'traduces
and he defies—all in a breath. Burns was intimate with the female
heart, and with the romantic mode of courtship practised in the
pastoral districts of Caledonia. He was early initiated into all the
mysteries of rustic love, and had tried his eloquence with such
success among the maidens of the land, that one of them said,
"Open your eyes and shut your ears with Rob Burns, and there's
nae fear o' your heart; but close your eyes and open your ears, and
you'll lose it."

Of all lyric poets he is the most prolific and various. Of one
hundred and sixty songs which he communicated to Johnson's
Museum, all, save a score or so, are either his composition, or
amended with such skill and genius as to be all but made his own.
For Thomson he wrote little short of a hundred. He took a pe-
culiar pleasure in ekeing out and amending the old and imperfect
songs of his country. He has exercised his fancy and taste to a
greater extent that way than antiquarians either like or seem will-
ing to acknowledge. Scott, who performed for the ballads of
Scotland what Burns did for many of her songs, perceived this:—

"The Scottish tunes and songs," he remarked, "preserved for
Burns that inexpressible charm which they have ever afforded to
his countrymen. He entered into the idea of collecting their frag-
ments with the zeal of an enthusiast; and few, whether serious or
humorous, passed through his hands without receiving some of
those magic touches, which, without greatly altering the song, re-
stored its original spirit, or gave it more than it previously pos-
sessed. So dexterously are those touches combined with the an-
cient structure, that the *rifacciamento*, in many instances, could
scarcely have been detected without the avowal of the Bard him-
self. Neither would it be easy to mark his share in the individual
ditties. Some he appears to have entirely rewritten; to others he
added supplementary stanzas; in some he retained only the lead-
ing lines and the chorus; and others he merely arranged and orna-
mented." No one has ever equalled him in these exquisite imita-
tions: he caught up the peculiar spirit of the old song at once;
he thought as his elder brother in rhyme thought, and communi-
cated an antique sentiment and tone to all the verses which he
added. Finer feeling, purer fancy, more exquisite touches of na-
ture, and more vigorous thoughts, were the result of this inter-
course. Burns found Scottish song like a fruit-tree in winter, not
dead, though unbudded; nor did he leave it till it was covered
with bloom and beauty. He sharpened the sarcasm, deepened the
passion, heightened the humor, and abated the indelicacy of his
country's lyrics.

"To Burns's ear," says Wilson—a high judge in all poetic ques-
tions—"the lowly lays of Scotland were familiar, and most dear
were they all to his heart. Often had he 'sung aloud old songs
that are the music of the heart;' and, some day, to be able himself
to breathe such strains was his dearest, his highest ambition. His
genius and his moral frame were thus imbued with the spirit of our
old traditionary ballad poetry; and, as soon as all his passions were
ripe, the voice of song was on all occasions of deep and tender in-
terest—the voice of his daily, his nightly speech. Those old songs
were his models; he felt as they felt, and looked up with the same
eyes on the same objects. So entirely was their language his lan-
guage, that all the beautiful lines, and half-lines, and single words
that, because of something in them most exquisitely true to nature,
had survived the rest of the compositions to which they had long
ago belonged, were sometimes adopted by him, almost uncon-
sciously it might seem, in his finest inspirations; and oftener still
sounded in his ear like a key-note, on which he pitched his own
plaintive tune of the heart till the voice and language of the old and
new days were but as one." He never failed to surpass what he

imitated; he added fruit to the tree and fragrance to the flower.
That his songs are a solace to Scottish hearts in far lands we know
from many sources; the poetic testimony of an inspired witness is
all we shall call for at present:—

> " Encamped by Indian rivers wild,
> The soldier, resting on his arms,
> In Burns's carol sweet recalls
> The scenes that blessed him when a child,
> And glows and gladdens at the charms
> Of Scotia's woods and waterfalls."

A want of chivalry has been instanced as a radical fault in the
lyrics of Burns. He certainly is not of the number who approach
beauty with much awe or reverence, and who raise loveliness into
an idol for man to fall down and worship. The polished courtesies
and romantic affectations of high society had not found their way
among the maidens of Kyle; the midnight tryste, and the stolen
interview—the rapture to meet—and the anguish to part—the secret
vow, and the scarce audible whisper, were dear to their bosoms;
and they were unacquainted with moving in parallel lines, and
breathing sighs into roses, in the affairs of the heart. To draw a
magic circle of affection round those he loved, which could not be
passed without lowering them from the station of angels, forms no
part of the lyrical system of Burns's poetic wooing: there is no affec-
tation in him; he speaks like one unconscious of the veneered and
varnished civilities of artificial life; he feels that true love is unac-
quainted with fashionable distinctions, and in all he has written
has thought but of the natural man and woman, and the unin-
fluenced emotions of the heart. Some have charged him with a
want of delicacy—an accusation easily answered: he is rapturous,
he is warmed, he is impassioned—his heart cannot contain its ec-
stasies; he glows with emotion as a crystal goblet with wine; but
in none of his best songs is there the least indelicacy. Love is with
him a leveller; passion and feeling are of themselves as little in-
fluenced by fashion and manners as the wind is in blowing, or the
sun is in shining; chivalry, and even notions of delicacy, are change-
able things; our daughters speak no longer with the free tongues
of their great-grandmothers, and young men no longer challenge
wild lions, or keep dangerous castles, in honor of their ladies' eyes.

The prose of Burns has much of the original merit of his poetry;
but it is seldom so pure, so natural, and so sustained. It abounds
with bright bits, fine outflashings, gentle emotions, and uncommon
warmth and ardor. It is very unequal; sometimes it is simple and
vigorous; now and then inflated and cumbrous; and he not seldom
labors to say weighty and decided things, in which a "double

double toil and trouble" sort of labor is visible. "But hundreds even of his most familiar letters"—I adopt the words of Wilson—"are perfectly artless, though still most eloquent compositions. Simple we may not call them, so rich are they in fancy, so overflowing in feeling, and dashed off in every other paragraph with the easy boldness of a great master, conscious of his strength even at times when, of all things in the world, he was least solicitous about display; while some there are so solemn, so sacred, so religious, that he who can read them with an unstirred heart can have no trust, no hope, in the immortality of the soul." Those who desire to feel him in his strength must taste him in his Scottish spirit. There he spoke the language of life: in English, he spoke that of education; he had to think in the former before he could express himself in the latter. In the language in which his mother sung and nursed him he excelled; a dialect reckoned barbarous by scholars, grew classic and elevated when uttered by the tongue of Robert Burns.

Of the family and fame of the Poet something should be said. Good and active friends bestirred themselves after his death: Currie munificently wrote his Life and edited his works; Robert, his eldest son, was placed in the Stamp-office by Lord Sidmouth; cadetships in India were generously obtained for William and James by Sir James Shaw, who otherwise largely befriended the family; and Lord Panmure nobly presented one hundred pounds annually to his widow, till the success of her sons in India enabled them to interpose, and take—not without remonstrance—that pious duty on themselves. The venerable Mrs. Burns lives* in the house where her eminent husband died: all around her has an air of comfort, and she has been enabled to save a small sum out of her annual income: her brother, a London merchant of much respectability, has long interested himself in her affairs; and her brother-in-law, Gilbert, died lately, after having established his family successfully in the world.

The citizens of my native Dumfries feel the honor which the Poet's ashes confer on them; Mill-hole-brae has been named Burns-street: the walks are reverenced where he loved to muse; and his grave may be traced by the well-trodden pathways which pass the unnoticed tombs of the learned, the pious, the brave, and the far-descended, and lead to that of the inspired Peasant. Honors have elsewhere been liberally paid to his name; a fair monument is raised to him on the Doon; a noble statue, from the hand of Flaxman, stands in Edinburgh; and Burns-clubs celebrate his

* Mrs. Burns died 1834.

birthday in the chief towns and cities of Britain. On the banks of
the Amazon, Mississippi, St. Lawrence, Indus, and the Ganges,
his name is annually invoked and his songs sung; Wordsworth,
Coleridge, and Campbell, have celebrated him in verse; statues
are made from his chief characters; pictures painted from his vivid
delineations; and even the rafters of Alloway-kirk have been
formed into ornaments for the necks of ladies, and quaighs for the
hands of men.   Such is the influence of genius!

The following beautiful tribute to the memory of Burns is by
Mr. Roscoe:

Rear high thy bleak majestic hills,
    Thy sheltered valleys proudly spread,
And, Scotia, pour thy thousand rills,
    And wave thy heaths with blossoms red:
But, ah! what poet now shall tread
    Thy airy heights, thy woodland reign,
Since he, the sweetest bard, is dead,
    That ever breathed the soothing strain!

As green thy towering pines may grow,
    As clear thy streams may speed along,
As bright thy summer suns may glow,
    As gayly charm thy feathery throng;
But now, unheeded is the song,
    And dull and lifeless all around,
For his wild harp lies all unstrung,
    And cold the hand that waked its sound.

What though thy vigorous offspring rise,
    In arts, in arms, thy sons excel;
Though beauty in thy daughters' eyes,
    And health in every feature dwell;
Yet who shall now their praises tell,
    In strains impassioned, fond, and free,
Since he no more the song shall swell
    To love, and liberty, and thee!

With step-dame eye and frown severe
    His hapless youth why didst thou view?
For all thy joys to him were dear,
    And all his vows to thee were due:
Nor greater bliss his bosom knew,
    In opening youth's delightful prime,
Than when thy favoring ear he drew
    To listen to his chanted rhyme.

Thy lonely wastes and frowning skies
    To him were all with rapture fraught·
He heard with joy the tempest rise
    That waked him to sublimer thought·

And oft thy winding dells he sought,
  Where wild-flowers poured their rath perfume,
And with sincere devotion brought
  To thee the summer's earliest bloom.

But ah! no fond maternal smile
  His unprotected youth enjoyed;
His limbs inured to early toil,
  His days with early hardships tried!
And more to mark the gloomy void,
  And bid him feel his misery,
Before his infant eyes would glide
  Day-dreams of immortality.

Yet, not by cold neglect depressed,
  With sinewy arm he turned the soil,
Sunk with the evening sun to rest,
  And met at morn his earliest smile.
Waked by his rustic pipe meanwhile,
  The powers of fancy came along,
And soothed his lengthened hours of toil
  With native wit and sprightly song.

— Ah! days of bliss too swiftly fled,
  When vigorous health from labor springs,
And bland Contentment soothes the bed,
  And Sleep his ready opiate brings;
And hovering round on airy wings
  Float the light forms of young Desire,
That of unutterable things
  The soft and shadowy hope inspire.

Now spells of mightier power prepare,
  Bid brighter phantoms round him dance
Let Flattery spread her viewless snare,
  And Fame attract his vagrant glance:
Let sprightly Pleasure too advance,
  Unveiled her eyes, unclasped her zone,
Till lost in love's delirious trance,
  He scorn the joys his youth has known.

Let Friendship pour her brightest blaze,
  Expanding all the bloom of soul;
And Mirth concentre all her rays,
  And point them from the sparkling bowl;
And let the careless moments roll
  In social pleasures unconfined,
And confidence that spurns control
  Unlock the inmost springs of mind!

And lead his steps those bowers among,
  Where elegance with splendor vies,
Or Science bids her favored throng
  To more refined sensations rise;
Beyond the peasant's humbler joys,
  And freed from each laborious strife,
There let him learn the bliss to prize
  That waits the sons of polished life.

Then, whilst his throbbing veins beat high
  With every impulse of delight,
Dash from his lips the cup of joy,
  And shroud the scene in shades of night ;
And let Despair with wizard light
  Disclose the yawning gulf below,
And pour incessant on his sight
  Her spectred ills and shapes of woe :

And show beneath a cheerless shed,
  With sorrowing heart and streaming eyes
In silent grief where droops her head,
  The partner of his early joys ;
And let his infants' tender cries
  His fond parental succor claim,
And bid him hear in agonies
  A husband's and a father's name.

'Tis done, the powerful charm succeeds ;
  His high reluctant spirit bends ;
In bitterness of soul he bleeds,
  Nor longer with his fate contends.
An idiot laugh the welkin rends,
  As Genius thus degraded lies ;
Till pitying Heaven the veil extends
  That shrouds the Poet's ardent eyes.

Rear high thy bleak majestic hills,
  Thy shelter'd valleys proudly spread,
And, Scotia, pour thy thousand rills,
  And wave thy heaths with blossoms red
But never more shall poet tread
  Thy airy heights, thy woodland reign,
Since he, the sweetest bard, is dead
  That ever breathed the soothing strain.

PREFACE TO THE FIRST EDITION.

THE following trifles are not the production of the poet, who, with all the advantages of learned art, and perhaps amid the elegances and idlenesses of upper life, looks down for a rural theme, with an eye to Theocritus or Virgil. To the Author of this, these and other celebrated names, their countrymen, are, at least in their original language, *a fountain shut up, and a book sealed.* Unacquainted with the necessary requisites for commencing poet by rule, he sings the sentiments and manners he felt and saw in himself and his rustic compeers around him, in his and their native language. Though a rhymer from his earliest years, at least from the earliest impulses of the softer passion, it was not till very lately that the applause, perhaps the partiality, of friendship, wakened his vanity so far as to make him think any thing of his worth showing; and none of the following works were composed with a view to the press. To amuse himself with the little creations of his own fancy, amid the toil and fatigues of a laborious life; to transcribe the various feelings, the loves, the griefs, the hopes, the fears, in his own breast; to find some kind of counterpoise to the struggles of a world, always an alien scene, a task uncouth to the poetical mind;—these were his motives for courting the Muses, and in these he found Poetry to be its own reward.

Now that he appears in the public character of an Author, he does it with fear and trembling. So dear is fame to the rhyming tribe, that even he, an obscure, nameless Bard, shrinks aghast at the thought of being branded as—an impertinent blockhead, obtruding his nonsense on the world; and, because he can make a shift to jingle a few doggerel Scottish rhymes

together, looking upon himself as a Poet of no small conse-
quence forsooth!

It is an observation of that celebrated poet, Shenstone, whose
divine Elegies do honor to our language, our nation, and our
species, that "*Humility* has depressed many a genius to a her-
mit, but never raised one to fame!" If any critic catches at
the word *genius*, the Author tells him, once for all, that he cer-
tainly looks upon himself as possessed of some poetic abilities,
otherwise his publishing in the manner he has done would be
a manœuvre below the worst character, which, he hopes, his
worst enemy will ever give him. But to the genius of a Ram-
say, or the glorious dawnings of the poor, unfortunate Fergus-
son, he with equal, unaffected sincerity, declares, that even in
his highest pulse of vanity, he has not the most distant preten-
sions. These two justly admired Scottish Poets he has often
had in his eye in the following pieces; but rather with a view
to kindle at their flame, than for servile imitation.

To his Subscribers, the Author returns his most sincere
thanks—not the mercenary bow over a counter—but the heart-
throbbing gratitude of the Bard, conscious how much he owes
to benevolence and friendship, for gratifying him, if he deserves
it, in that dearest wish of every poetic bosom—to be distin-
guished. He begs his readers, particularly the learned and the
polite, who may honor him with a perusal, that they will make
every allowance for education and circumstances of life; but
if, after a fair, candid, and impartial criticism, he shall stand
convicted of dullness and nonsense, let him be done by as he
would in that case do by others—let him be condemned, with-
out mercy, to contempt and oblivion.

DEDICATION TO THE SECOND EDITION.

TO THE NOBLEMEN AND GENTLEMEN OF THE CALEDONIAN HUNT.

MY LORDS AND GENTLEMEN—

A SCOTTISH Bard, proud of the name, and whose highest ambition is to sing in his Country's service—where shall he so properly look for patronage as to the illustrious names of his native Land—those who bear the honors and inherit the virtues of their Ancestors? The Poetic Genius of my Country found me, as the prophetic bard Elijah did Elisha—at the plough; and threw her inspiring mantle over me. She bade me sing the loves, the joys, the rural scenes and rural pleasures of my native soil in my native tongue. I tuned my wild, artless notes as she inspired. She whispered me to come to this ancient Metropolis of Caledonia, and lay my songs under your honored protection.

Though much indebted to your goodness, I do not approach you, my Lords and Gentlemen, in the usual style of Dedication, to thank you for past favors. That path is so hackneyed by prostituted learning, that honest rusticity is ashamed of it. Nor do I present this address with the venal soul of a servile Author, looking for a continuation of those favors. I was bred to the plough, and am independent. I come to claim the common Scottish name with you, my illustrious countrymen; and to tell the world that I glory in the title. I come to congratulate my Country that the blood of her ancient heroes still runs uncontaminated; and that from your courage, knowledge, and public spirit, she may expect protection, wealth, and liberty. In the last place, I come to proffer my warmest wishes to the great Fountain of honor, the Monarch of the universe, for your welfare and happiness.

When you go forth to waken the Echoes, in the ancient and favorite amusement of your forefathers, may Pleasure ever be of your party; and may social Joy await your return! When harassed in courts or camps with the jostlings of bad men and bad measures, may the honest consciousness of injured worth attend your return to your native Seats; and may domestic Happiness, with a smiling welcome, meet you at your gates! May Corruption shrink at your kindling, indignant glance! and may Tyranny in the Ruler, and Licentiousness in the People, equally find you an inexorable foe!

I have the honor to be,
With the sincerest gratitude, and highest respect,
My Lords and Gentlemen,
Your most devoted, humble Servant,
ROBERT BURNS.

Edinburgh, April 4, 1787.

POEMS,

CHIEFLY SCOTTISH.

THE TWA DOGS.

A TALE.

'Twas in that place o'[1] Scotland's isle,
That bears the name o' Auld King Coil,
Upon a bonnie day in June,
When wearing thro' the afternoon,
Twa dogs that were na thrang at hame,[2]
Forgather'd[3] ance upon a time.
　The first I'll name, they ca'd him *Cæsar*,
Was keepit for his honor's pleasure;
His hair, his size, his mouth, his lugs,[4]
Show'd he was nane o' Scotland's dogs,
But whalpit[5] some place far abroad,
Where sailors gang to fish for cod.
　His locked, letter'd, braw[6] brass collar,
Show'd him the gentleman and scholar;
But though he was o' high degree,
The fient'[7] a pride nae pride had he;
But wad hae[8] spent an hour caressin',
Ev'n wi' a tinkler-gipsy's messin':[9]
At kirk or market, mill or smiddie,[10]
Nae tawted[11] tyke,[12] tho' e'er sae duddie,[13]
But he wad stan't,[14] as glad to see him,
And stroan't[15] on stanes and hillocks[16] wi' him.
　The tither[17] was a ploughman's collie,[18]
A rhyming, ranting, roaring billie,[19]

---

[1] Of.—[2] Had nothing to do at home.—[3] Met.—[4] Ears.—[5] Whelped.—
[6] Large, handsome.—[7] Fiend, devil.—[8] Would have.—[9] A small dog.—
[10] Smithy, or smith's workshop.—[11] Having the hair matted together.—
[12] Dog.—[13] Ragged.—[14] Stand, or stop.—[15] To piss.—[16] Stones and little
hills.—[17] The other.—[18] A country cur.—[19] A young fellow.

8

Wha for his friend an' comrade had him,
And in his freaks had *Luath* ca'd him,
After some dog in Highland sang,[1]
Was made lang syne[2]—Lord knows how lang.
  He was a gash[3] and faithful tyke,
As ever lap[4] a sheugh[5] or dyke.
His honest, sonsie,[6] baws'nt[7] face,
Ay gat him friends in ilka[8] place.
His breast was white, his touzie[9] back
Weel clad wi' coat o' glossy black;
His gawcie[10] tail, wi' upward curl,
Hung o'er his hurdies[11] wi' a swirl.[12]
  Nae doubt but they were fain o' ither,[13]
An' unco pack and thick[14] thegither;
Wi' social nose whyles[15] snuff't and snowkit,[16]
Whyles[17] mice and moudieworts[18] they howkit;[19]
Whyles scour'd awa in lang excursion,
An' worried ither in diversion;
Until wi' daffin'[20] weary grown,
Upon a knowe[21] they sat them down,
And there began a lang digression
About the *Lords o' the Creation.*

CÆSAR.

  I've aften wonder'd, honest Luath,
What sort o' life poor dogs like you have;
An' when the gentry's life I saw,
What way poor bodies liv'd ava.[22]
  Our laird gets in his racked rents,
His coals, his kain,[23] and a' his stents:[24]
He rises when he likes himsel;
His flunkies[25] answer at the bell:
He ca's[26] his coach, he ca's his horse;
He draws a bonnie silken purse
As lang 's my tail, where, thro' the steeks,[27]
The yellow-letter'd Geordie keeks.[28]

---

[1] 'Cuchullin's dog in Ossian's Fingal. — [2] Long since. — [3] Sagacious.—
[4] Leaped.—[5] Trench, or sluice.—[6] Engaging.—[7] Having a white stripe down
the face.—[8] Every.—[9] Shaggy.—[10] Large.—[11] Loins.—[12] Curve.—[13] Fond
of each other. — [14] And very intimate. — [15] Sometimes. — [16] Scented.—
[17] Sometimes.—[18] Moles.—[19] Digged.—[20] Merriment, foolishness.—[21] A
small hillock.—[22] At all.—[23] Fowls, &c., paid as rent by a farmer.—[24] Trib-
ute, dues of any kind.—[25] Livery-servants,—[26] Calls.—[27] Stitches.—[28] Peeps.

Frae morn to e'en it's nought but toiling,
At baking, roasting, frying, boiling;
An' tho' the gentry first are stechin',[1]
Yet ev'n the ha' folk[2] fill their pechan[3]
Wi' sauce, ragouts, and sic like thrastrie,
That 's little short o' downright wastrie.
Our whipper-in, wee[4] blastit[5] wonner,[6]
Poor worthless elf, it eats a dinner,
Better than onie tenant man
His honor has in a' the lan':
An' what poor cot-folk pit[7] their painch[8] in,
I own it 's past my comprehension.

LUATH.

Trowth, Cæsar, whyles they 're fasht[9] eneugh,
A cotter howkin[10] in a sheugh,[11]
Wi' dirty stanes biggin[12] a dyke,
Baring a quarry, and sic like,
Himself, a wife, he thus sustains,
A smytrie[13] o' wee duddie weans,[14]
An' nought but his han' darg,[15] to keep
Them right and tight in thack an' rape.[16]
An' when they meet wi' sair disasters,
Like loss o' health or want o' masters,
Ye maist wad think a wee touch langer,
An' they maun[17] starve o' cauld and hunger.
But how it comes I never kenn'd yet,
They 're maistly wonderfu' contented;
And buirdly chiels,[18] and clever hizzies,[19]
Are bred in sic a way as this is.

CÆSAR.

But then to see how ye 're negleckit,
How huff'd, and cuff'd, and disrespeckit!
L—d, man, our gentry care but little
For delvers, ditchers, and sic cattle;
They gang as saucy by poor folk,
As I wad by a stinking brock.[20]

[1] Cramming.—[2] Hall-folk, servants.—[3] Stomach.—[4] Little.—[5] Blasted.—
[6] A contemptuous appellation.—[7] Put.—[8] Paunch.—[9] Troubled.—[10] Digging.
—[11] Trench.—[12] Building.—[13] A numerous collection of small individuals.
—[14] Ragged children.—[15] Day's work.—[16] Clothing, necessaries.—[17] Must.
—[18] Stout-made young men.—[19] Hussies, young women.—[20] A badger.

I've noticed, on our laird's court-day,
And monie a time my heart's been wae,
Poor tenant bodies, scant o' cash,
How they maun thole[1] a factor's snash :[2]
He'll stamp an' threaten, curse an' swear,
He'll apprehend them, poind[3] their gear;
While they maun stan', wi' aspect humble,
An' hear it a', an' fear an' tremble!
I see how folk live that hae riches;
But surely poor folk maun be wretches?

LUATH.

They're nae sae wretched's ane wad think;
Tho' constantly on poortith's[4] brink:
They're sae accustom'd wi' the sight,
The view o't gies them little fright.

Then chance an' fortune are sae guided,
They're ay in less or mair provided;
An' tho' fatigued wi' close employment,
A blink o' rest's a sweet enjoyment.

The dearest comfort o' their lives,
Their grushie[5] weans[6] an' faithfu' wives;
The prattling things are just their pride,
That sweetens a' their fireside.

An' whyles twalpennie-worth o' nappie[7]
Can make the bodies unco[8] happy;
They lay aside their private cares,
To mind the kirk and state affairs;
They'll talk o' patronage and priests,
Wi' kindling fury in their breasts,
Or tell what new taxation's comin',
An' ferlie[9] at the folk in Lon'on.

As bleak-faced Hallowmas returns,
They get the jovial, rantin' kirns,[10]
When *rural life* o' every station,
Unite in common recreation:
Love blinks, wit slaps, and social mirth,
Forgets there's care upo' the earth.

That merry day the year begins,
They bar the door on frosty winds;

Suffer, endure.—[2] Abuse.—[3] To seize for rent.—[4] Poverty.—[5] Of thriving growth.—[6] Children.—[7] Ale.—[8] Very.—[9] Wonder.—[10] The harvest supper

The nappie reeks wi' mantling ream,[1]
And sheds a heart-inspiring steam;
The luntin'[2] pipe, and sneeshin' mill,[3]
Are handed round wi' right guid will;
The cantie[4] auld folks cracking crouse,
The young anes ranting thro' the house—
My heart has been sae fain[6] to see them,
That I for joy hae barkit[7] wi' them.
 Still it 's owre[8] true that ye hae said,
Sic game is now owre aften play'd.
There 's monie a creditable stock
O' decent, honest, fawsont[9] folk,
Are riven out baith root and branch,
Some rascal's pridefu' greed[10] to quench,
Wha thinks to knit himsel the faster
In favor wi' some gentle master,
Wha, aiblins,[11] thrang a-parliamentin',
For Britain's guid[12] his saul indentin'[13]—

CÆSAR.

Haith,[14] lad, ye little ken about it;
For Britain's guid! guid faith I doubt it:
Say rather, gaun[15] as Premiers lead him,
An' saying *aye* or *no* 's they bid him:
At operas an' plays parading,
Mortgaging, gambling, masquerading;
Or maybe, in a frolic daft,[16]
To Hague or Calais takes a waft,
To make a tour, and tak a whirl,
To learn *bon ton*, an' see the worl'.
 There at Vienna or Versailles,
He rives[17] his father's auld entails;
Or by Madrid he takes the rout,
To thrum guitars, an' fecht[18] wi' nowt;[19]
Or down Italian vista startles,
Wh-re-hunting among groves o' myrtles:
Then bouses drumly[20] German water,
To mak himsel look fair and fatter,

[1] To foam, or froth.—[2] Smoking.—[3] Snuff-box.—[4] Cheerful—[5] Conversing; merrily.—[6] Glad, happy.—[7] Shouted, hallooed.—[8] Over.—[9] Respectable.—[10] Avarice, selfishness.—[11] Perhaps.—[12] Good.—[13] Making a bargain, or selling his vote for seven years.—[14] A petty oath.—[15] Going.—[16] Mad, foolish.—[17] Divides and squanders.—[18] Fight.—[19] Black cattle; in allusion to the Spanish bull-fights.—[20] Muddy.

An' clear the consequential sorrows,
Love-gifts of carnival signoras.
For Britain's guid! for her destruction!
Wi' dissipation, feud, an' faction.

LUATH.

Hech[1] man! dear sirs! is that the gate[2]
They waste sae monie a braw[3] estate!
Are we sae foughten[4] an' harass'd
For gear to gang that gate at last!
  O, would they stay aback frae courts,
An' please themselves wi' countra[5] sports,
It wad for ev'ry ane be better,
The laird, the tenant, an' the cotter![6]
For thae[7] frank, rantin', ramblin' billies,[8]
Fient haet[9] o' them 's ill-hearted fellows:
Except for breakin' o' their timmer,[10]
Or speakin' lightly o' their limmer,[11]
Or shootin' o' a hare or moor-cock,
Tho ne'er a bit they 're ill to poor folk.
  But will you tell me, master Cæsar,
Sure great folk's life 's a life o' pleasure?
Nae cauld or hunger e'er can steer them,
The very thought o't need na fear them.

CÆSAR.

L—d, man, were ye but whyles[12] whare I am,
The gentles ye wad ne'er envy 'em.
  It 's true they need na starve or sweat,
Thro' winter's cauld, or simmer's heat;
They 've nae sair wark to craze their banes,
An' fill auld age wi' gripes an' granes:
But human bodies are sic fools,
For a' their colleges and schools,
That when nae real ills perplex them,
They make enow themsels to vex them;
An' ay the less they hae to sturt[13] them,
In like proportion less will hurt them.
A country fellow at the pleugh,
His acre 's till'd, he 's right eneugh;
A country-girl at her wheel,

---

[1] Oh! strange.—[2] The way.—[3] Large.—[4] Troubled.—[5] Country.—[6] Cottager.—[7] These.—[8] Young men.—[9] A petty oath of negation.—[10] Timber.—[11] A strumpet, or kept mistress.—[12] Sometimes.—[13] To trouble or molest.

Her dizzen 's[1] done, she 's unco weel :[2]
But gentlemen, an' ladies warst,
Wi' ev'ndown want o' wark are curst;
They loiter, lounging, lank, an' lazy;
Tho' deil haet[3] ails them, yet uneasy;
Their days insipid, dull, an' tasteless;
Their nights unquiet, lang, an' restless:
An' e'en their sports, their balls, an' races,
Their galloping thro' public places;
There 's sic[4] parade, sic pomp an' art,
The joy can scarcely reach the heart.
The men cast out in party matches,
Then souther[5] a' in deep debauches;
Ae[6] night they 're mad wi' drink an' wh-ring,
Niest[7] day their life is past enduring.
The ladies arm-in-arm in clusters,
As great and gracious a' as sisters;
But hear their absent thoughts o' ither,
They 're a' run deils[8] an' jades thegither.
Whyles o'er the wee bit cup an' platie,[9]
They sip the scandal potion pretty:
Or lee-lang[10] nights, wi' crabbit leuks,
Pore owre the devil's pictur'd beuks ;[11]
Stake on a chance a farmer's stack-yard,
An' cheat like onie unhang'd blackguard.
    There 's some exception, man an' woman;
But this is gentry's life in common.
    By this, the sun was out o' sight,
An' darker gloaming[12] brought the night;
The bum-clock[13] humm'd wi' lazy drone;
The kye[14] stood routin' i' the loan;[15]
When up they gat, and shook their lugs,[16]
Rejoiced they were na *men* but *dogs ;*
An' each took aff his several way,
Resolved to meet some ither day.

---

[1] A dozen.—[2] Very happy.—[3] The deuce of any thing.—[4] Such.—[5] Solder, cement.—[6] One.—[7] Next.—[8] Right-down devils.—[9] Cup and saucer.—[10] Live-long.—[11] Playing cards.—[12] Twilight.—[13] A humming beetle that flies in the summer evenings.—[14] Cows.—[15] Lowing in the place of milking.—[16] Ears.

TAM O' SHANTER.

A TALE.

Of Brownyis and of Bogilis full is this Buke.—*Gawin Douglas.*

WHEN chapman billies' leave the street,
And drouthy neebors neebors meet,
As market-days are wearing late,
An' folk begin to tak the gate;[2]
While we sit bousing at the nappy,
An' getting fou and unco happy,
We think na on the lang Scots miles,
The mosses, waters, slaps,[3] and styles,
That lie between us and our hame,
Whare sits our sulky, sullen dame,
Gath'ring her brows like gath'ring storm,
Nursing her wrath to keep it warm.
   This truth fand[4] honest *Tam o' Shanter,*
As he, frae Ayr, ae[5] night did canter,
(Auld Ayr, wham ne'er a town surpasses,
For honest men and bonnie lasses.)
   O Tam! hadst thou but been sae wise,
As taen thy ain wife Kate's advice!
She tauld thee weel thou was a skellum,[6]
A bleth'ring, blust'ring, drunken blellum;[7]
That frae November till October,
Ae market-day thou was na sober,
That ilka[8] melder,[9] wi' the miller,
Thou sat as lang as thou had siller:
That every naig was ca'd a shoe on,
The smith and thee gat roaring fou[10] on:
That at the L——d's house, ev'n on Sunday,
Thou drank wi' Kirton Jean till Monday.
She prophesied, that, late or soon,
Thou would be found deep drown'd in Doon;
Or catch'd wi' warlocks[11] in the mirk,[12]
By Alloway's auld haunted kirk.

---

[1] Hawkers, or peddlers.—[2] To ge their way.—[3] Gates.—[4] Found.—[5] One.—
[6] A worthless fellow.—[7] A nonsensical, idle-talking fellow.—[8] Every.—[9] A
grist, or small quantity of corn taken to the mill to be ground.—[10] Drunk.—
[11] Wizards.—[12] Dark.

Ah, gentle dames! it gars me greet,[1]
To think how monie counsels sweet,
How monie lengthen'd sage advices,
Tho husband frae the wife despises!
 But to our tale: Ae[2] market night,
Tam had got planted unco right,
Fast by an ingle,[3] bleezing finely,
Wi' reaming swats,[4] that drank divinely;
And at his elbow souter[5] Johnny,
His ancient, trusty, drouthy crony;
Tam lo'ed him like a vera brither;
They had been fou for weeks thegither.
The night drave on wi' sangs and clatter;
And ay the ale was growing better:
The landlady and Tam grew gracious,
Wi' favors secret, sweet, and precious;
The souter tauld his queerest stories;
The landlord's laugh was ready chorus;
The storm without might rair[6] and rustle,
Tam did na mind the storm a whistle.
 Care, mad to see a man sae happy,
E'en drown'd himself amang the nappy;
As bees flee hame wi' lades[7] o' treasure,
The minutes wing'd their way wi' pleasure;
Kings may be blest, but Tam was glorious,
O'er a' the ills o' life victorious.
 But pleasures are like poppies spread,
You seize the flow'r, its bloom is shed;
Or like the snow-falls in the river,
A moment white—then melts forever;
Or like the borealis race,
That flit ere you can point their place;
Or like the rainbow's lovely form,
Evanishing amid the storm—
Nae man can tether time or tide;
The hour approaches Tam maun ride;
That hour o' night's black arch the key-stane,
That dreary hour he mounts his beast in;
And sic a night he takes the road in,
As ne'er poor sinner was abroad in.

---

[1] Makes me ween —[2] One.—[3] Fireplace.—[4] Frothing ale.—[5] A shoemaker.
—[6] Roar.—[7] Loads.

The wind blew as 'twad blawn its last;
The rattling showers rose on the blast;
The speedy gleams the darkness swallow'd;
Loud, deep, and lang, the thunder bellow'd: ·
That night a child might understand,
The Deil had business on his hand.

Weel mounted on his gray mare, Meg,
(A better never lifted leg,)
Tam skelpit[1] on thro' dub and mire,
Despising wind, and rain, and fire;
Whyles[2] holding fast his guid blue bonnet;
Whyles crooning[3] o'er some auld Scots sonnet;
Whyles glow'ring[4] round wi' prudent cares,
Lest bogles[5] catch him unawares;
Kirk-Alloway was drawing nigh,
Where ghaists and houlets[6] nightly cry.—

By this time he was cross the ford,
Whare in the snaw the chapman[7] smoor'd;[8]
And past the birks[9] and meikle stane,[10]
Whare drunken Charlie brak 's neck bane;
And thro' the whins,[11] and by the cairn,[12]
Whare hunters fand[13] the murder'd bairn;
And near the thorn, aboon[14] the well,
Whare Mungo's mither hang'd hersel.—
Before him Doon pours all his floods;
The doubling storm roars thro' the woods ·
The lightnings flash from pole to pole;
Near and more near the thunders roll;
When glimmering thro' the groaning trees,
Kirk-Alloway seem'd in a bleeze;
Thro' ilka[15] bore[16] the beams were glancing;
And loud resounded mirth and dancing.—

Inspiring bold John Barleycorn!
What dangers thou canst make us scorn!
Wi' tippenny,[17] we fear nae evil;
Wi' usquabae,[18] we 'll face the Devil!—
The swats sae ream'd[19] in Tammie's noddle,
Fair play, he cared na Deils a bodle.[20]

---

[1] Galloped.—[2] Sometimes.—[3] Humming a tune.—[4] Looking.—[5] Spirits, hobgoblins.—[6] Owls.—[7] A travelling peddler.—[8] Was smothered.—[9] Birch trees.—[10] A large stone.—[11] Furze.—[12] A heap of stones.—[13] Found.—[14] Above.—[15] Every.—[16] A hole in the wall.—[17] Ale.—[18] Whisky.—[19] The ale so foamed.—[20] A small copper coin.

But Maggie stood right sair astonish'd,
Till, by the heel and hand admonish'd,
She ventured forward on the light;
And, vow! Tam saw an unco' sight;
Warlocks[2] and witches in a dance;
Nae cotillon brent new[3] frae France,
But hornpipes, jigs, strathspeys, and reels,
Put life and mettle in their heels.
A winnock-bunker[4] in the east,
There sat auld Nick, in shape o' beast;
A towzie tyke,[5] black, grim, and large,
To gie them music was his charge;
He screw'd the pipes and gart[6] them skirl,[7]
Till roof an' rafters a' did dirl.[8]—
Coffins stood round like open presses,
That shaw'd the dead in their last dresses;
And by some devilish cantrip[9] slight,
Each in its cauld hand held a light,—
By which, heroic Tam was able
To note upon the haly[10] table,
A murderer's banes in gibbet airns;[11]
Twa span-lang, wee,[12] unchristen'd bairns;
A thief, new cutted fra a rape,[13]
Wi' his last gasp his gab[14] did gape;
Five tomahawks, wi' bluid red rusted;
Five scymitars, wi' murder crusted;
A garter, which a babe had strangled;
A knife a father's throat had mangled,
Whom his ain son o' life bereft,
The gray hairs yet stack to the heft;
Three lawyers' tongues turn'd inside out,
Wi' lies seam'd like a beggar's clout,
And priests' hearts, rotten, black as muck,
Lay stinking, vile, in every neuk:
Wi' mair o' horrible and awfu',
Which ev'n to name wad be unlawfu'.
As Tammie glower'd,[15] amazed and curious,
The mirth and fun grew fast and furious;
The piper loud and louder blew;

[1] Strange, frightful.—[2] Wizards.—[3] Quite new.—[4] Window-seat.—[5] A shaggy dog.—[6] Made, forced.—[7] To make a shrill noise.—[8] Tremble.—[9] A charm or spell—[10] Holy.—[11] Irons.—[12] Little.—[13] Rope.—[14] Mouth.—[15] Stared.

The dancers quick and quicker flew;
They reel'd, they set, they cross'd, they cleekit,[1]
Till ilka carlin swat and reekit,[2]
And coost her duddies[3] to the wark,
And linket[4] at it in her sark.[5]
Now Tam, O Tam! had they been queans,
A' plump and strapping in their teens;
Their sarks, instead o' creeshie flannen,[6]
Been snaw-white seventeen-hunder linen;[7]
Thir[8] breeks o' mine, my only pair,
That ance were plush, o' guid blue hair,
I wad hae gi'en them aff my hurdies,[9]
For ae blink o' the bonnie burdies![10]
But wither'd beldams, auld and droll,
Rigwoodie hags[11] wad spean a[12] foal,
Lowping[13] an' flinging on a crummock,[14]
I wonder did na turn thy stomach.
But Tam kenn'd what was what fu' brawlie,[15]
There was ae winsome[16] wench and walie,[17]
That night inlisted in the core,
(Lang after kenn'd[18] on Carrick shore!
For monie a beast to dead she shot,
And perish'd monie a bonnie boat,
And shook baith meikle corn and bear,[19]
And kept the country-side in fear,)
Her cutty-sark[20] o' Paisley harn,[21]
That while a lassie she had worn,
In longitude tho' sorely scanty,
It was her best, and she was vauntie.[22]
Ah! little kenn'd[23] thy reverend grannie,
That sark she coft[24] for her wee Nannie,
Wi' twa pund Scots[25] ('twas a' her riches),
Wad ever graced a dance o' witches!
But here my Muse her wing maun cower;
Sic flights are far beyond her power;
To sing how Nannie lap[26] and flang,

<hr>

[1] Caught.—[2] Till every old woman was in a reeking sweat.—[3] Cast off her rags.—[4] Tripped.—[5] Shirt.—[6] Greasy flannel.—[7] Linen of the finest quality.—[8] These.—[9] The loins, &c.—[10] Plural of burd, a damsel.—[11] Gallows hags.—[12] To wean.—[13] Leaping.—[14] A cow with crooked horns.—[15] Full well—[16] One hearty.—[17] Jolly.—[18] Seen or known.—[19] Much corn and barley.—[20] Short shirt.—[21] Paisley linen.—[22] Proud of it.—[23] Thought, or knew.—[24] Bought.—[25] Two pounds Scotch, 3s. 4d. sterling.—[26] Leaped.

(A souple jad she was and strang,)
And how Tam stood, like ane bewitch'd,
And thought his very een enrich'd ;
Ev'n Satan glower'd,[1] and fidged fu' fain,[2]
And hotch'd and blew wi' might and main :
Till first ae caper, syne[3] anither,
Tam tint[4] his reason a' thegither,
And roars out, *Weel done, Cutty-sark !*[5]
And in an instant a' was dark :
And scarcely had he Maggie rallied,
When out the hellish legion sallied.
  As bees biz out wi' angry fyke,[6]
When plundering herds assail their byke ;[7]
As open pussie's[8] mortal foes,
When, pop ! she starts before their nose ;
As eager runs the market-crowd,
When *Catch the thief !* resounds aloud ;
So Maggie runs, the witches follow,
Wi' monie an eldritch[9] skreech and hollow.
  Ah, Tam ! ah, Tam ! thou 'll get thy fairin' ![10]
In hell they 'll roast thee like a herrin' !
In vain thy Kate awaits thy comin' !
Kate soon will be a woefu' woman !
Now, do thy speedy utmost, Meg,
And win the key-stane[11] of the brig :
There at them thou thy tail may toss,
A running stream they dare na cross.
But ere the key-stane she could make,
The fient a tail she had to shake ;
For Nannie, far before the rest,
Hard upon noble Maggie prest,
And flew at Tam wi' furious ettle ;[12]
But little wist she Maggie's mettle—
Ae spring brought aff her master hale,

[1] Looked on with rapture.—[2] Manifested a fidgety kind of joy or pleasure.—
[3] Then.—[4] Lost.—[5] Short shirt.—[6] In a great fuss.—[7] A bee-hive.—[8] A hare,
—[9] Frightful, ghastly.—[10] Get the reward of thy temerity.
[11] It is a well-known fact, that witches, or any evil spirits, have no power
to follow a poor wight any farther than the middle of the next running
stream. It may be proper likewise to mention to the benighted traveller,
that when he falls in with *bogles,* whatever danger may be in his going for-
ward, there is much more hazard in turning back.
[12] Attempt.
9

But left behind her ain gray tail:
The carlin claught[1] her by the rump,
And left poor Maggie scarce a stump.
    Now, wha this tale o' truth shall read,
Ilk[2] man and mother's son take heed:
Whene'er to drink you are inclined,
Or cutty-sarks run in your mind,
Think, ye may buy the joys o'er dear,
Remember Tam o' Shanter's mare.[3]

[1] Laid hold of.—[2] Every.

[3] Died at Lochwinnoch, on the 9th inst. (August, 1823,) Thomas Reid, laborer. He was born on the 21st of October, 1745, in the clachan of Kyle, Ayrshire. The importance attached to this circumstance arises from his being the celebrated equestrian hero of Burns's Poem "Tam O'Shanter." He has at length surmounted the "mosses, rivers, slaps, and styles" of life. For a considerable time by-past he has been in the service of Major Hervey, of Castle-Semple, nine months of which he has been incapable of labor; and to the honor of Mr. Hervey be it named, he has, with a fostering and laudable generosity, soothed, as far as it was in his power, the many ills of age and disease. He, however, still retained the desire of being "fou' for weeks thegither."—*Glasgow Chronicle.* Another version of this story is the following: That Tam O'Shanter was no imaginary character. Shanter is a farm near the village of Kirkoswald, where Burns, when nineteen years old, studied mensuration, and "first became acquainted with scenes of swaggering riot." The then occupier of Shanter, by name "Douglas Grahame," was, by all accounts, equally what the *Tam* of the poet appears—a jolly, careless rustic, who took much more interest in the contraband traffic of the coast, then carried on, than in the rotation of crops. Burns knew the man well; and to his dying day, he, nothing loath, passed among his rural compeers by the name of "Tam O'Shanter."—*Lockhart's Life of Burns.*

    This admirable tale was written for Grose's "Antiquities of Scotland," where it first appeared, with a beautiful engraving of "Alloway's auld haunted Kirk."

DEATH AND DR. HORNBOOK.

A TRUE STORY.

[The following circumstance occasioned the composition of this poem:—
"The schoolmaster of Tarbolton parish, to eke up the scanty subsistence
allowed to that useful class of men, had set up a shop of grocery goods.
Having accidentally fallen in with some medical books, and become most
hobby-horsically attached to the study of medicine, he had added the sale of
a few medicines to his little trade. He had got a shop-bill printed, at the
bottom of which, overlooking his own incapacity, he had advertised, that
'Advice would be given in common disorders at the shop gratis.'"—*Lock-
hart's Life of Burns.*]

Some books are lies frae end to end,
And some great lies were never penn'd;
Ev'n ministers, they hae been kenn'd,
    In holy rapture,
A rousing whid,[1] at times, to vend,
    And nail 't wi' Scripture.

But this that I am gaun to tell,
Which lately on a night befel,
Is just as true 's the deil 's in hell,
    Or Dublin city:
That e'er he nearer comes oursel
    's a muckle pity.

The clachan yill[2] had made me canty,[3]
I was na fou,[4] but just had plenty;
I stacher'd[5] whyles, but yet took tent[6] ay
    To free the ditches;
An' hillocks, stanes, and bushes kenn'd ay
    Frae ghaists[7] and witches.

The rising moon began to glower[8]
The distant Cumnock hills out-owre;
To count her horns wi' a' my power,
    I set mysel;
But whether she had three or four,
    I cou'd na tell.

---

[1] A lie.—[2] Village ale.—[3] Merry.—[4] Drunk.—[5] Staggered.—[6] Took heed.
—[7] From ghosts.—[8] To shine faintly.

I was come round about the hill,
And todlin[1] down on Willie's mill,
Setting my staff wi' a' my skill,
　　To keep me sicker;[2]
Tho' leeward whyles, against my will,
　　I took a bicker.[3]

I there wi' *something* did forgather[4]
That put me in an eerie swither;[5]
An awfu' scythe out-owre ae shouther,
　　Clear, dangling hang;
A three-taed leister[6] on the ither
　　Lay, large an' lang.

Its stature seem'd lang Scotch ells twa,
The queerest shape that e'er I saw,
For fient a wame[7] it had ava![8]
　　And then, its shanks,
They were as thin, as sharp, an' sma'
　　As cheeks o' branks![9]

"Guid-e'en," quo' I; "Friend! hae ye been mawin
When ither folk are busy sawin'?"[10]
It seem'd to mak a kind o' stan',
　　But naething spak;
At length, says I, "Friend, whare ye gaun,
　　Will ye go back?"

It spak right howe[11]—"My name is Death,
But be na fley'd."[12]—Quoth I, "Guid faith!
Ye 're maybe come to stap my breath;
　　But tent me, billie;[13]
I red[14] ye weel, tak care o' scaith,[15]
　　See there 's a gully!"[16]

"Gudeman," quo' he, "put up your whittle,
I 'm no design'd to try its metal;
But if I did, I wad be kittle[17]
　　To be mislear'd;[18]

---

[1] Tottering.—[2] Steady.—[3] A short run.—[4] Meet.—[5] Frightful hesitation.
—[6] A three-pronged dart.—[7] Belly.—[8] At all.—[9] A kind of wooden curb for
norses.—[10] This rencounter happened in seed-time, 1785.—[11] With a hollow
tone of voice.—[12] Frightened.—[13] Heed me, good fellow.—[14] To counsel, or
advise.—[15] Injury.—[16] A large knife.—[17] Ticklish, difficult.—[18] Mischievous;
i. e. it would be no easy matter for you to hurt, or do me any mischief.

I wad na mind it, no that spittle
    Out-owre my beard."

" Weel, weel!" says I, " a bargain be 't;
Come, gie 's your hand, an' sae we 're gree't;[1]
We 'll ease our shanks an' tak a seat,
    Come, gie 's your news;
This while[2] ye hae been monie a gate,[3]
    At monie a house."

" Ay, ay!" quo' he, an' shook his head,
" It 's e'en a lang, lang time indeed,
Sin' I began to nick the thread,
    An' choke the breath:
Folk maun do something for their bread,
    An' sae maun Death.

" Sax thousand years are near hand fled
Sin' I was to the butching[4] bred,
An' monie a scheme in vain 's been laid,
    To stap or scaur[5] me;
Till ane Hornbook 's[6] taen up the trade,
    An' faith, he 'll waur[7] me.

" Ye ken Jock Hornbook i' the clachan,[8]
Deil mak his king's-hood[9] in a spleuchan![10]
He 's grown sae weel acquaint wi' Buchan[11]
    An' ither chaps,
The weans[12] haud out their fingers laughin',
    An' pouk my hips.

" See here 's a scythe, and there 's a dart,
They hae pierced monie a gallant heart;
But Doctor Hornbook, wi' his art
    And cursed skill,
Has made them baith no worth a f—t,
    Damn'd haet[13] they 'll kill!

---

[1] Agreed.—[2] An epidemical fever was then raging in that part of the coun-
try.—[3] Many a road.—[4] Butchering.—[5] Stop or scare.

[6] This gentleman, Dr. Hornbook, is professionally a brother of the sovereign
Order of the Ferula; but, by intuition and inspiration, is at once an apothe-
cary, surgeon, and physician.

[7] Worst, or defeat.—[8] Hamlet, or village.—[9] A part of the entrails.—[10] A
tobacco pouch.—[11] Buchan's Domestic Medicine.—[12] Children.

[13] An oath of negation; i. e. in Dr. Hornbook's opinion he has rendered
my weapons harmless; they'll kill nobody.

"'Twas but yestreen,[1] nae farther gane,
I threw a noble throw at ane;
Wi' less I 'm sure I 've hundreds slain;
      But Deil-ma-care,[2]
It just play'd dirl[3] on the bane,
      But did nae mair.

"Hornbook was by, wi' ready art,
And had sae fortified the part,
That when I looked to my dart,
      It was sae blunt,
Fient haet[4] o 't wad hae pierced the heart
      Of a kail-runt.[5]

"I drew my scythe in sic a fury,
I near had cowpit[6] wi' my hurry,
But yet the bauld apothecary
      Withstood the shock;
I might as well hae tried a quarry
      O' hard whin[7] rock.

"Ev'n them he canna get attended,[8]
Altho' their face he ne'er had kenn'd it,
Just —— in a kail-blade and send it,
      As soon 's he smells 't,
Baith their disease, and what will mend it,
      At once he tells 't.

"And then a' doctor's saws an' whittles,[9]
Of a' dimensions, shapes, an' mettles,
A' kinds o' boxes, mugs, an' bottles,
      He 's sure to hae;
Their Latin names as fast he rattles
      As A B C.

"Calces o' fossils, earth, and trees;
True sal-marinum o' the seas;
The farina of beans and pease,
      He has 't in plenty;

[1] Yesternight.—[2] No matter!—[3] A slight tremulous stroke.—[4] An oath of negation.—[5] The stem of Colewort.—[6] Tumbled.—[7] The hard stone found in the Scottish hills; granite.
[8] Those patients who cannot attend upon the doctor, or cannot be seen by him, must send their water in a vial, from the sight of which he pretends to know and cure their various diseases.
[9] Knives.

Aqua-fontis, what you please,
    He can content ye.

"Forbye[1] some new uncommon weapons,
Urinus spiritus of capons:
Or mite-horn shavings, filings, scrapings,
    Distill'd *per se;*
Sal-alkali o' midge-tail clippings,
    And monie mae."[2]

" Waes me for Johnny Ged's Hole[3] now,"
Quo' I, "if that the news be true!
His braw calf-ward,[4] where gowans grew[5]
    Sae white and bonnie,
Nae doubt they 'll rive it wi' the pleugh;
    They 'll ruin Johnny!"

The creature grain'd an eldritch laugh,[6]
And says, " Ye need na yoke the pleugh,
Kirk-yards will soon be till'd eneugh.
    Tak ye nae fear:
They 'll a' be trench'd wi' monie a sheugh,[7]
    In twa-three year.

" Whare I kill'd ane a fair straa death,[8]
By loss o' blood or want o' breath,
This night I 'm free to tak my aith,
    That Hornbook's skill
Has clad a score i' their last claith,[9]
    By drap an' pill.

" An honest wabster[10] to his trade,
Whase wife's twa nieves[11] were scarce weel bred,
Gat tippence-worth to mend her head,
    When it was sair;
The wife slade cannie[12] to her bed,
    But ne'er spak mair.

" A countra laird had taen the batts,[13]
Or some curmurring[14] in his guts;

His only son for Hornbook sets,
    An' pays him well :
The lad, for twa guid gimmer pets,[1]
    Was laird himsel.

"A bonnie lass, ye kenn'd her name,
Some ill-brewn drink had hoved her wame,[2]
She trusts hersel, to hide the shame,
    In Hornbook's care ;
Horn sent her aff to her lang hame,
    To hide it there.

"That 's just a swatch[3] o' Hornbook's way ;
Thus goes he on from day to day,
Thus does he poison, kill, an' slay,
    An 's weel paid for 't ;
Yet stops me o' my lawfu' prey,
    Wi' his d-mn'd dirt :[4]

"But, hark ! I 'll tell you of a plot,
Tho' dinna ye be speaking o 't ;
I 'll nail the self-conceited sot,
    As dead 's a herrin' ;
Niest[5] time we meet, I 'll wad a groat,
    He gets his fairin'!"

But just as he began to tell,
The auld kirk-hammer strak the bell
Some wee short hour ayont the *twal*,[6]
    Which raised us baith :
I took the way that pleased mysel,
    And sae did Death.[7]

---

[1] Ewe lambs.—[2] Swelled her belly.—[3] A sample.—[4] By sending his patients to the church-yard.—[5] Next.—[6] The hour of one.

[7] So irresistible was the tide of ridicule, on the publication of this poem, that John Wilson, alias Dr. Hornbook, was not only compelled to shut up shop as an apothecary, or druggist rather, but to abandon his school also, as his pupils one by one deserted him.

THE COTTER'S SATURDAY NIGHT.

INSCRIBED TO R. AIKEN, ESQ.

Let not ambition mock their useful toil,
Their homely joys and destiny obscure ;
Nor grandeur hear, with a disdainful smile,
The short and simple annals of the poor.—*Gray.*

MY loved, my honor'd, much respected friend!
    No mercenary bard his homage pays;
With honest pride I scorn each selfish end,
    My dearest meed, a friend's esteem and praise:
To you I sing in simple Scottish lays,
    The lowly train in life's sequester'd scene;
The native feelings strong, the guileless ways;
    What Aiken in a cottage would have been;
Ah! tho' his worth unknown, far happier there, I ween.

November chill blaws loud wi' angry sugh ;[1]
    The shortening winter-day is near a close;
The miry beasts retreating frae the pleugh;
    The blackening trains o' craws to their repose;
The toil-worn Cotter frae his labor goes,
    This night his weekly moil is at an end,
Collects his spades, his mattocks, and his hoes,
    Hoping the morn in ease and rest to spend,
And weary, o'er the moor, his course does hameward
            bend.

At length his lonely cot appears in view,
    Beneath the shelter of an aged tree;
Th' expectant wee-things,[2] todlin,[3] stacher[4] thro',
    To meet their dad wi' flichterin[5] noise and glee.
His wee bit ingle[6] blinkin' bonnilie,
    His clean hearth-stane, his thriftie wifie's smile,
The lisping infant prattling on his knee,
    Does a' his weary, carking cares beguile,
An' makes him quite forget his labor and his toil.

[1] The continued rushing noise of a strong wind.—[2] Little children.—
[3] Tottering.—[4] Stagger.—[5] Fluttering.—[6] Small fireplace.

belyve[1] the elder bairns come drappin' in,
  At service out, amang the farmers roun';
Some ca' the pleugh, some herd, some tentie[2] rin
  A cannie errand to a neebor town;
Their eldest hope, their Jenny, woman grown,
  In youthfu' bloom, love sparkling in her e'e,
Comes hame, perhaps, to show a braw new gown,
  Or deposite her sair-won penny-fee,
To help her parents dear, if they in hardship be.

Wi' joy unfeign'd brothers and sisters meet,
  An' each for other's weelfare kindly spiers:[3]
The social hours, swift-wing'd, unnoticed fleet;
  Each tells the uncos[4] that he sees or hears:
The parents, partial, eye their hopeful years;
  Anticipation forward points the view.
The mother, wi' her needle an' her shears,
  Gars[5] auld claes look amaist[6] as weel 's the new;
The father mixes a' wi' admonition due.

Their masters' and their mistresses' command,
  The younkers a' are warned to obey;
An' mind their labors wi' an eydent[7] hand,
  An' ne'er, tho' out o' sight, to jauk[8] or play;
An' oh! be sure to fear the Lord alway!
  An' mind your *duty*, duly, morn an' night!
Lest in temptation's path ye gang[9] astray,
  Implore his counsel and assisting might:
They never sought in vain that sought the Lord aright!

But hark! a rap comes gently to the door:
  Jenny, wha kens the meaning o' the same,
Tells how a neebor lad cam o'er the moor,
  To do some errands, and convoy her hame.
The wily mother sees the conscious flame
  Sparkle in Jenny's e'e, and flush her cheek;
Wi' heart-struck anxious care, inquires his name,
  While Jenny hafflins[10] is afraid to speak;
Weel pleased the mother hears, it 's nae wild, worthless
  rake.

---

[1] By and by.—[2] Carefully.—[3] To inquire.—[4] Strange sights, tales, or stories
—[5] Makes.—[6] Almost.—[7] Diligent.—[8] Dally, or trifle.—[9] Go.—[10] Partly.

Wi' kindly welcome Jenny brings him ben ;[1]
A strappan youth; he taks the mother's eye;
Blythe Jenny sees the visit's no ill ta'en;
The father cracks of horses, pleughs, and kye;
The youngster's artless heart o'erflows wi' joy,
But blate[2] and laithfu',[3] scarce can weel behave;
The mother, wi' a woman's wiles, can spy
What makes the youth sae bashfu' and sae grave;
Weel pleased to think her bairn[4]'s respected like the lave.[5]

O happy love! where love like this is found!
O heart-felt raptures! bliss beyond compare!
I 've paced much this weary mortal round,
And sage experience bids me this declare—
If Heaven a draught of heavenly pleasure spare
One cordial in this melancholy vale,
'Tis when a youthful, loving, modest pair,
In other's arms breathe out the tender tale,
Beneath the milk-white thorn that scents the evening gale.

Is there in human form that bears a heart—
A wretch! a villain! lost to love and truth!
That can, with studied, sly, ensnaring art,
Betray sweet Jenny's unsuspecting youth?
Curse on his perjured arts! dissembling smooth!
Are honor, virtue, conscience, all exiled?
Is there no pity, no relenting ruth,[6]
Points to the parents fondling o'er their child?
Then paints the ruin'd maid, and their distraction wild!

But now the supper crowns their simple board!
The halesome parritch,[7] chief o' Scotia's food:
The soup their only hawkie[8] does afford,
That 'yont[9] the hallan[10] snugly chows her cud:
The dame brings forth, in complimental mood,
To grace the lad, her weel-hain'd kebbuck[11] fell,[12]
An' aft he 's press'd, an' aft he ca's it good;
The frugal wifie, garrulous will tell,
How 'twas a towmond auld,[13] sin' lint was i' the bell.[14]

[1] In the country parlor.—[2] Bashful.—[3] Sheepish.—[4] Child.—[5] The rest, the others.—[6] Sorrow.—[7] Wholesome porridge.—[8] Cow.—[9] Beyond.—[10] A partition-wall in a cottage, or a seat of turf at the outside.—[11] Well-saved or well-kept cheese.—[12] Well-savored, of good relish.—[13] A twelvemonth old.—[14] Since flax was in the flower.

The cheerfu' supper done, wi' serious face,
    They, round the ingle,[1] form a circle wide;
The sire turns o'er, wi' patriarchal grace,
    The big Ha'-Bible,[2] ance his father's pride:
His bonnet rev'rently is laid aside,
    His lyart[3] haffets[4] wearin' thin and bare;
Those strains that once did sweet in Zion glide,
    He wales[5] a portion with judicious care;
And *"Let us worship God!"* he says with solemn air.

They chant their artless notes in simple guise;
    They tune their hearts, by far the noblest aim;
Perhaps Dundee's wild warbling measures rise,
    Or plaintive Martyrs, worthy o' the name:
Or noble Elgin[6] beets[7] the heavenward flame,
    The sweetest far o' Scotia's holy lays:
Compared with these, Italian trills are tame;
    The tickled ears no heartfelt raptures raise;
Nae unison hae they with our Creator's praise.

The priest-like father reads the sacred page,
    How Abraham was the friend of God on high;
Or, Moses bade eternal warfare wage
    With Amalek's ungracious progeny;
Or, how the royal bard did groaning lie
    Beneath the stroke of Heaven's avenging ire;
Or, Job's pathetic plaint, and wailing cry;
    Or, rapt Isaiah's wild seraphic fire;
Or other holy seers that tune the sacred lyre.

Perhaps the Christian volume is the theme,
    How guiltless blood for guilty man was shed;
How *He*, who bore in heaven the second name,
    Had not on earth whereon to lay his head;
How his first followers and servants sped;
    The precepts sage they wrote to many a land:
How *he*, who lone in Patmos banished,
    Saw in the sun a mighty angel stand,
And heard great Bab'lon's doom pronounced by Heaven's
    command.

---

[1] Fireplace.—[2] The large hall-Bible.—[3] Gray, or of a mixed color.—[4] Temples, side of the head.—[5] Chooses, selects.—[6] Dundee, Martyrs, Elgin, names of sacred melodies used in singing psalms.—[7] Adds fuel to or increases devotion.

Then kneeling down to heaven's eternal King,
The *saint*, the *father*, and the *husband* prays:
Hope "springs exulting on triumphant wing,"[1]
That *thus* they all shall meet in future days;
There, ever bask in uncreated rays,
No more to sigh, or shed the bitter tear,
Together hymning their Creator's praise,
In such society, yet still more dear,
While circling time moves round in an eternal sphere.

Compared with this, how poor religion's pride,
In all the pomp of method and of art,
When men display to congregations wide,
Devotions every grace except the *heart!*
The *Power*, incensed, the pageant will desert,
The pompous strain, the sacerdotal stôle;
But haply, in some cottage far apart,
May hear, well pleased, the language of the soul;
And in his *book of life* the inmates poor enrol.

Then homeward all take off their several way;
The youngling cottagers retire to rest:
The parent-pair their *secret homage* pay,
And proffer up to Heaven the warm request,
That He who stills the raven's clamorous nest,
And decks the lily fair in flowery pride,
Would, in the way his wisdom sees the best,
For them and for their little ones provide;
But chiefly in their hearts with *grace divine* preside.

From scenes like these old Scotia's grandeur springs,
That makes her loved at home, revered abroad.
Princes and lords are but the breath of kings,
"An honest man 's the noblest work of God:"[2]
And *certes*, in fair virtue's heavenly road,
The *cottage* leaves the *palace* far behind:
What is a lordling's pomp? a cumbrous load,
Disguising oft the wretch of human-kind,
Studied in arts of hell, in wickedness refined!

O Scotia! my dear, my native soil!
For whom my warmest wish to Heaven is sent!
Long may thy hardy sons of rustic toil,
Be blest with health, and peace, and sweet content!

[1] Pope's Windsor Forest.—[2] Pope's Essay on Man.
10

And, oh! may Heaven their simple lives prevent
   From luxury's contagion weak and vile!
Then, howe'er *crowns* and *coronets* be rent,
   A *virtuous populace* may rise the while,
And stand a wall of fire around their much-loved Isle.

O Thou! who pour'd the patriotic tide
   That stream'd thro' Wallace's undaunted heart;
Who dared to nobly stem tyrannic pride,
   Or nobly die, the second glorious part,
(The patriot's God peculiarly thou art,
   His friend, inspirer, guardian, and reward!)
O never, never, Scotia's realm desert:
   But still the *patriot* and the *patriot bard*,
In bright succession raise, her ornament and guard!

The "Cotter's Saturday Night is, perhaps, of all Burns's pieces, the one whose exclusion from the collection, were such things possible now-a-days, would be the most injurious, if not to the genius, at least to the character, of the man. Loftier flights he certainly has made, but in these he remained but a short while on the wing, and effort is too often perceptible; here the motion is easy, gentle, placidly undulating. There is more of the conscious security of power, than in any other of his serious pieces of considerable length; the whole has the appearance of coming in a full stream from the fountain of his heart—a stream that soothes the ear, and has no glare on the surface."—*Lockhart's Life of Burns.*

∴

[The following Poem will, by many readers, be well enough understood; but
for the sake of those who are unacquainted with the manners and traditions
of the country where the scene is cast, *Notes* are added, to give some ac-
count of the principal charms and spells of that night, so big with prophecy
to the peasantry in the west of Scotland. The passion of prying into fu-
turity makes a striking part of the history of human nature in its rude
state in all ages and nations; and it may be some entertainment to a phi-
losophic mind, if any such should honor the Author with a perusal, to see
the remains of it among the more unenlightened in our own.]

HALLOWEEN.[1]

Yes! let the rich deride, the proud disdain,
The simple pleasures of the lowly train;
To me more dear, congenial to my heart,
One native charm, than all the gloss of art.—*Goldsmith.*

UPON that night, when fairies light
On Cassilis Downans[2] dance,
Or owre the lays, in splendid blaze,
On sprightly coursers prance;
Or for Colean the rout is taen,
Beneath the moon's pale beams;
There up the Cove,[3] to stray an' rove
Amang the rocks an' streams,
To sport that night.

Amang the bonnie winding banks,
Where Doon rins, wimplin',[4] clear,
Where Bruce ance ruled the martial ranks
And shook the Carrick[5] spear,
Some merry, friendly, countra folks,
Together did convene,

Is thought to be a night when witches, devils, and other mischief-mak-
ing beings, are all abroad on their baneful, midnight errands; particularly
those aerial people, the fairies, are said on that night to hold a grand an-
niversary.

[2] Certain little, romantic, rocky, green hills, in the neighborhood of the
ancient seat of the earls of Cassilis.

[3] A noted cavern near Colean-house, called the Cove of Colean; which, as
well as Cassilis Downans, is famed in country story for being a favorite haunt
of fairies.

[4] Meandering.

[5] The famous family of that name, the ancestors of Robert, the great de-
liverer of his country, were earls of Carrick.

To *burn* their nits,[1] an' *pou*[2] their stocks,
  An' haud their *Halloween*
     Fu' blythe that night.

The lasses feat,[3] an' cleanly neat,
  Mair braw than when they 're fine;
Their faces blythe, fu' sweetly kythe,[4]
  Hearts leal,[5] an' warm, an' kin':[6]
The lads sae trig,[7] wi' wooer-babs,[8]
  Weel knotted on their garten,
Some unco blate,[9] and some wi' gabs,[10]
  Gar lasses' hearts gang startin'
     Whyles fast that night.

Then first and foremost, thro' the kail,
  Their *stocks*[11] maun a' be sought ance;
They steek their een,[12] an' graip, an' wale,[13]
  For muckle anes an' straught anes.[14]
Poor hav'rel[15] Will fell aff the drift,
  An' wander'd thro' the *bow-kail*,[16]
An' pou 't,[17] for want o' better shift,
  A *runt*[18] was like a sow-tail,
     Sae bow't[19] that night.

Then straught or crooked, yird[20] or nane,
  They roar an' cry a' throu'ther;[21]
The vera wee-things,[22] todlin', rin[23]
  Wi' stocks out-owre their shouther;

---

[1] Nuts.—[2] Pull, or pluck.—[3] Nice, trim.—[4] Discover, or show themselves.—
[5] Loyal, true, faithful.—[6] Kind.—[7] Spruce, neat.—[8] The garter knotted below
the knee with a couple of loops.—[9] Very bashful.—[10] To talk boldly.
[11] The first ceremony of Halloween is pulling each a *stock* or plant of kail.
They must go out, hand in hand, with eyes shut, and pull the first they meet
with. Its being big or little, straight or crooked, is prophetic of the size
and shape of the grand object of all their spells—the husband or wife. If
any *yird*, or earth, stick to the root, that is *tocher*, or fortune; and the taste
of the *custock*, that is, the heart of the stem, is indicative of the natural tem-
per and disposition. Lastly, the stems, or, to give them their ordinary appel-
lation, the *runts*, are placed somewhere above the head of the door; and the
Christian names of the people whom chance brings into the house, are, ac-
cording to the priority of placing the *runts*, the names in question.
[12] Shut their eyes.—[13] Grope and choose, or pick.—[14] For large and straight
ones.—[15] A half-witted, talkative person.—[16] Cabbages.—[17] Pulled.—[18] Stem
of cabbage, or colewort.—[19] Crooked.—[20] With earth, or dirt.—[21] Pell-mell,
confusedly.—[22] Young children.—[23] Tottering run.

An' gif[1] the *custock 's*[2] sweet or sour,
Wi' jocktelegs[3] they taste them;
Syne coziely,[4] aboon the door,
Wi' cannie care, they 've placed them
To lie that night.

The lasses staw[5] frae 'mang them a'
To pou their *stalks o' corn;*[6]
But Rab slips out, an' jinks[7] about,
Behint the muckle thorn;
He grippet Nelly hard an' fast;
Loud skirled[8] a' the lasses;
But her *tap-pickle*[9] maist was lost,
When kiuttlin[10] i' the fause-house[11]
Wi' him that night.

The auld guidwife's[12] weel hoordet[13] *nits*[14]
Are round an' round divided,
An' monie lads' an' lasses' fates
Are there that night decided;
Some kindle, couthie,[15] side by side,
An' burn thegither trimly;
Some start awa' wi' saucy pride,
An' jump out-owre the chimlie
Fu' high that night.

Jean slips in twa wi' tentie e'e;[16]
Wha 'twas she wadna[17] tell;

1 If.—2 The stalk of the kail, or colewort.—3 A kind of knife.—4 Snugly.
—5 Stole away.
6 They go to the barn-yard and pull each, at three several times, a stalk of oats. If the third stalk wants the *top-pickle*, that is, the grain at the top of the stalk, the party in question will come to the marriage-bed any thing but a maid.
7 To turn a corner.—8 Shrieked.—9 Supposed to have allusion to something of which ladies are said to be very careful.—10 Cuddling.
11 When the corn is in a doubtful state, by being too green, or wet, the stack-builder, by means of old timber, &c., makes a large apartment in his stack, with an opening in the side which is fairest exposed to the wind; this he calls the *fause-house.*
12 Mistress of the house.—13 Hoarded.
14 Burning the nuts is a famous charm. They name the lad and lass to each particular nut, as they lay them in the fire, and accordingly as they burn quietly together, or start from beside one another, the course and issue of the courtship will be.
15 Lovingly.—16 With watchful eye.—17 Would not.

But this is *Jock*, an' this is *me*,
 She says in to hersel;
He bleez'd owre her an' she owre him,
 As they wad ne'er mair part!
Till fuff!¹ he started up the lum,²
 An' Jean had e'en a sair heart
   To see 't that night.

Poor Willie wi' his *bow-kail-runt*,³
 Was *brunt*⁴ wi' primsie⁵ Mallie;
An' Mallie, nae doubt took the drunt,⁶
 To be compared to Willie;
Mall's nit lap⁷ out wi' pridefu' fling,
 An' her ain fit⁸ it brunt it;
While Willie lap an' swoor by *jing*,
 'Twas just the way he wanted
   To be that night.

Nell had the fause-house⁹ in her min'
 She pits¹⁰ hersel an' Rob in;
In loving bleeze they sweetly join,
 Till white in ase¹¹ they 're sobbin';
Nell's heart was dancin' at the view,
 She whisper'd Rob to look for 't;
Rob, stowlins,¹² pried¹³ her bonnie mou,¹⁴
 Fu' cozie¹⁵ in the neuk¹⁶ for 't,
   Unseen that night.

But Merran sat behint their backs,
 Her thoughts on Andrew Bell;
She lea'es them gashin'¹⁷ at their cracks,
 And slips out by hersel:
She thro' the yard the nearest taks,
 An' to the kiln she goes then,
An' darklins grapit¹⁸ for the bauks,¹⁹
 And in the *blue-clue*²⁰ throws then,
   Right fear't that night.

---

¹ With a puff, or bounce.—² The chimney.—³ Cabbage-stalk.—⁴ Burnt.—
⁵ Demure.—⁶ Pet, crabbed humor.—⁷ Leaped.—⁸ Foot.—⁹ False-house; see
a foregoing note.—¹⁰ Puts.—¹¹ Ashes.—¹² By stealth.—¹³ Tasted, or kissed.—
¹⁴ Mouth, or lips.—¹⁵ Snugly.—¹⁶ Nook.—¹⁷ Talking.—¹⁸ Groped in the
dark.—¹⁹ Cross-beams.
²⁰ Whoever would, with success, try this spell, must strictly observe these
directions: Steal out, all alone, to the *kiln*, and darkling, throw into the *pot*

An' ay she win't,[1] an' ay she swat,[2]
I wat she made nae jaukin';[3]
Till something held within the pat,[4]
Guid L—d! but she was quakin'!
But whether 'twas the Deil himsel,
Or whether 'twas a bauk-en',[5]
Or whether it was Andrew Bell,
She did na wait on talkin'
To spier[6] that night.

Wee Jenny to her graunie says,
"Will ye go wi' me, graunie?
I 'll *eat the apple[7] at the glass*,
I gat frae uncle Johnnie:"
She fuff't[8] her pipe wi' sic a lunt,
In wrath she was sae vap'rin',
She noticed na[10] an aizle[11] brunt
Her braw new worset[12] apron
Out thro' that night.

" Ye little skelpie limmer's[13] face!
How daur you try sic sportin',
As seek the foul Thief ony place,
For him to spae[14] your fortune?
Nae doubt but ye may get a *sight!*
Great cause ye hae to fear it;
For monie a ane has gotten a fright,
An' lived an' died deleeret[16]
On sic a night.

" Ae hairst afore[16] the Sherra-moor,[17]
I mind 't as weel 's yestreen,[18]

a clue of blue yarn; wind it in a new clue off the old one; and, towards the latter end, something will hold the thread; demand, *Wha hauds?* i. e. Who holds? An answer will be returned from the kiln pot, by naming the Christian and surname of your future spouse.

[1] Wound, did wind.—[2] Did sweat.—[3] Dallying, trifling.—[4] Pot.—[5] The end of a beam.—[6] To inquire.

[7] Take a candle, and go alone to a looking-glass; eat an apple before it, and some traditions say, you should comb your hair all the time; the face of your conjugal companion *to be* will be seen in the glass, as if peeping over your shoulder.

[8] Puffed out the smoke.—[9] A column of smoke.—[10] Not.—[11] A hot cinder.—[12] Worsted.—[13] A technical term in female scolding.—[14] To divine, or prophesy.—[15] Delirious.—[16] One harvest before.—[17] The battle of Sheriff Moor, in the year 1715.—[18] I remember it as well as if it had been but yesterday.

I was a gilpey[1] then, I 'm sure
I was na past fyfteen:
The simmer had been cauld an' wat,
An' stuff was unco green;
An' ay a rantin' kirn[2] we gat,
An' just on *Halloween*
    • It fell that night.

"Our stibble-rig[3] was Rab M'Graen,
A clever, sturdy fallow;
He 's sin[4] gat Eppie Sim wi' wean,
That lived in Achmacalla;
He gat *hemp-seed*,[5] I mind it weel,
An' he made unco light o 't;
But monie a day was *by himsel*,[6]
He was sae sairly frightet
    That very night."

Then up gat fechtin[7] Jamie Fleck,
An' he swoor by his conscience,
That he could *saw*[8] *hemp-seed* a peck;
For it was a' but nonsense:
The auld guidman raught[9] down the pock,[10]
An' out a handfu' gied him;
Syne[11] bade him slip frae 'mang the folk,
Some time when nae ane see'd him,
    An' try 't that night.

He marches thro' amang the stacks,
Tho' he was something sturtin;[12]
The *graip*[13] he for a *harrow* taks,
An' haurls at his curpin:[14]

[1] A half-grown girl.—[2] Harvest-supper.—[3] The reaper in harvest who takes the lead.—[4] Son.

[5] Steal out, unperceived, and sow a handful of hemp-seed; harrowing it with any thing you can conveniently draw after you. Repeat now and then. "Hempseed, I saw thee; hempseed, I saw thee; and him (or her) that is to be my true-love, come after me and pou thee." Look over your left shoulder and you will see the appearance of the person invoked, in the attitude of pulling hemp. Some traditions say, "Come after me, and shaw thee;" that is, show thyself: in which case, it simply appears. Others omit the harrowing, and say, "Come after me, and harrow thee."

[6] Out of his senses.—[7] Fighting.—[8] Sow.—[9] Reached.—[10] Bag, or sack.—
[11] Then.—[12] Frighted.—[13] A three-pronged dung-fork.—[14] Crupper.

An' every now an' then, he says,
"Hemp-seed I saw thee,
An' her that is to be my lass,
Come after me, and draw thee
As fast this night."

He whistled up Lord Lennox march,
To keep his courage cheery:
Altho' his hair began to arch,
He was sae fley'd[1] an' eerie;[2]
Till presently he hears a squeak,
An' then a grane[3] an' gruntle;[4]
He by his shouther gae a keek,[5]
An' tumbled wi' a wintle[6]
Out-owre that night.

He roar'd a horrid murder-shout,
In dreadfu' desperation!
An' young an' auld cam rinnin' out,
An' hear the sad narration:
He swoor 'twas hilchin[7] Jean M'Craw,
Or crouchie[8] Merran Humphie,
'Till stop! she trotted thro' them a';
An' wha was it but *grumphie*[9]
Asteer[10] that night!

Meg fain wad to the *barn* hae gaen
To *win*[11] *three wechts*[12] o' *naething*;[13]
But for to meet the Deil her lane,[14]
She pat but little faith in:
She gies the herd a pickle[15] nits,[16]
An' twa red checkit apples,

- Scared, frighted. — [2] Afraid of spirits.—[3] Groan. — [4] Grunting noise. —
[5] To peep. — [6] A stagger. — [7] Halting. — [8] Crooked-backed. — [9] A sow. —
[10] Abroad.—[11] To winnow as corn.—[12] An instrument for winnowing corn.
[13] This charm must likewise be performed unperceived, and alone. You
go to the *barn*, and open both doors, taking them off the hinges if possible;
for there is danger that the *being*, about to appear, may shut the doors, and
do you some mischief. Then take that instrument used in winnowing the
corn, which, in our country dialect we call a *wecht;* and go through all the
attitudes of letting down corn against the wind. Repeat it three times; and
the third time an apparition will pass through the barn, in at the windy door,
and out at the other, having both the figure in question, and the appearance
or retinue, marking the employment or station in life.
[14] Herself alone.—[15] A few.—[16] Nuts.

To watch, while for the barn she sets,[1]
In hopes to see Tam Kipples
That vera night.

She turns the key wi' cannie thraw,
And owre the threshold ventures;
But first on Sawnie gies a ca',
Syne[2] bauldly in she enters;
A *ratton*[3] rattled up the wa',
An' she cried, L—d preserve her!
An' ran thro' middon-hole[4] an' a',
An' pray'd wi' zeal an' fervor,
Fu' fast that night.

They hoy't[5] out Will, wi' sair advice:
They hecht[6] him some fine braw ane;[7]
It chanced the *stack* he *faddom'd[8] thrice,*
Was timmer-propt for thrawin':[10]
He taks a swirlie,[11] auld moss oak,
For some black, grousome carlin;[12]
An' loot a winze,[13] an' drew a stroke,
Till skin in blypes[14] came haurlin'[15]
Aff 's nieves[16] that night.

A wanton widow Leezie was,
As canty as a kittlen;[17]
But, och! that night, amang the shaws,
She got a fearfu' settlin'!
She thro' the whins,[18] an' by the cairn,[19]
An' owre the hill gaed scrievin',[20]
Whare *three lairds' lands meet at a burn,*[21]
To dip her left sark-sleeve in,
Was bent that night.

[1] Sets off.—[2] Then.—[3] A rat.—[4] A dung-hole.—[5] Urged.—[6] Promised to foretell something that is to be got or given.—[7] A fine handsome sweetheart.—[8] Fathomed.
[9] Take an opportunity of going, unnoticed, to a *bean-stack*, and fathom it three times round. The last fathom of the last time, you will catch in your arms the appearance of your future conjugal yoke-fellow.
[10] Twisting, or inclining to fall, therefore propt with timber.—[11] Knotty.—[12] Grim-looking, ugly old woman.—[13] Swore an oath.—[14] Shreds.—[15] Peeling.—[16] Off his knuckles.—[17] Frisky as a kitten.—[18] Furze, or gorse.—[19] A heap of stones.—[20] Swiftly.
[21] You go out, one or more, for this is a social spell, to a south-running spring or rivulet, where three lairds' lands meet, and dip your left shirt-sleeve.

Whyles[1] owre a linn[2] the burnie plays,
   As thro' the glen it wimpl't;[3]
Whyles round a rocky scaur it strays;
   Whyles in a wiel[4] it dimpl't;
Whyles glitter'd to the nightly rays,
   Wi' bickering, dancing dazzle;
Whyles cookit[5] underneath the braes,[6]
   Below the spreading hazel,
        Unseen that night.

Amang the brachens,[7] on the brae
   Between her an' the moon,
The Deil, or else an outler quey,[8]
   Gat up an' gae a croon:[9]
Poor Leezie's heart maist lap the hool;[10]
   Near lav'rock[11] height she jumpit,
But mist a fit,[12] an' in the *pool*
   Out-owre the lugs she plumpit,[13]
        Wi' a plunge that night.

In order, on the clean hearth-stane,
   The *luggies* three[14] are ranged,
And every time great care is ta'en
   To see them duly changed:
Auld uncle John, wha wedlock's joys
   Sin' *Mar's-year*[15] did desire,
Because he got the toomdish[16] thrice,
   He heaved them on the fire
        In wrath that night.

Go to bed in sight of a fire, and hang your wet sleeve before it to dry. Lie awake; and some time near midnight, an apparition, having the exact figure of the grand object in question, will come and turn the sleeve, as if to dry the other side of it.

[1] Sometimes.—[2] A waterfall.—[3] Waved. — [4] Whirlpool.—[5] Appeared and disappeared by fits.—[6] Declivity or precipice.—[7] Fern.—[8] A young cow running at large, not housed.—[9] To roar, or bellow.—[10] Leaped out of her skin.—[11] Lark.—[12] Missed a foot.—[13] Over head and ears.

[14] Take three dishes: put clean water in one, foul water in another, leave the third empty: blindfold a person, and lead him to the hearth where the dishes are ranged: he (or she) dips the left hand: if by chance in the clean water, the future husband or wife will come to the bar of matrimony a maid: if in the foul, a widow: if in the empty dish, it foretells with equal certainty no marriage at all. It is repeated three times; and every time the arrangement of the dishes is altered.

[15] The year 1715.—[16] Empty dish.

Wi' merry sangs, an' friendly cracks,[1]
    I wat they did na weary;
An' unco[2] tales, an' funny jokes,
    Their sports were cheap an' cheery,
'Till *butter'd so'ns*[3] wi' fragrant lunt,[4]
    Set a' their gabs[5] a-steerin';[6]
Syne[7] wi' a social glass o' strunt,[8]
    They parted aff careerin'
            Fu' blythe that night.

SCOTCH DRINK.

Gie him strong drink until he wink,
    That 's sinking in despair;
An' liquor guid to fire his bluid,
    That 's prest wi' grief an' care;
There let him bouse an' deep carouse,
    Wi' bumpers flowing o'er,
Till he forgets his *loves* or *debts*,
    An' minds his griefs no more.
            Solomon's Proverbs, xxxi. 6, 7.

LET other poets raise a fracas
'Bout vines, an' wines, an' drunken Bacchus,
An' crabbit names an' stories wrack us,
            An' grate our lug,
I sing the juice *Scots bear* can mak us,
            In glass or jug.

O thou, my Muse! guid auld *Scotch drink*,
Whether thro' wimplin' worms thou jink,
Or, richly brown, ream o'er the brink,
            In glorious faem,
Inspire me, till I lisp and wink,
            To sing thy name!

Let husky Wheat the haughs adorn;
An' Aits set up their awnie horn,
An' Peas an' Beans, at e'en or morn,
            Perfume the plain,
Leeze me on thee, *John Barleycorn*,
            Thou king o' grain!

To converse.—[2] Strange, marvellous.
    Sowens—oatmeal made into a kind of pudding. This is always the
Halloween supper.
    [4] Smoke of tobacco—[5] Mouths.—[6] Stirring.—[7] Then.—[8] Spirituous liquor.

On thee aft Scotland chows her cood,
In souple scones,[1] the wale[2] o' food!
Or tumblin' in the boiling flood,
    Wi' kail an' beef;
But when thou pours thy strong heart's blood,
    There thou shines chief.

Food fills the wame,[3] an' keeps us livin';
Tho' life's a gift no worth receivin',
When heavy dragg'd wi' pine an' grievin';[4]
    But, oil'd by thee,
The wheels o' life gae down hill, scrievin',[5]
    Wi' rattlin' glee.

Thou clears the head o' doited[6] Lear;[7]
Thou cheers the heart o' drooping Care;
Thou strings the nerves o' Labor sair,
    At 's weary toil;
Thou even brightens dark Despair
    Wi' gloomy smile.

Aft clad in massy siller weed,[8]
Wi' gentles thou erects thy head;
Yet humbly kind in time o' need,
    The poor man's wine,[9]
His wee drap parritch, or his bread,
    Thou kitchens[10] fine.

Thou art the life o' public haunts;
But[11] thee, what were our fairs and rants?
Even godly meetings o' the saunts,
    By thee inspired,
When gaping they besiege the tents,
    Are doubly fired.

That merry night we get the corn in,
O sweetly then thou reams[12] the horn in!

[1] Flexible bread; i. e. Bannocks made of barley meal, &c., which when baked are so flexible as to admit of being easily rolled together.
[2] The choice.—[3] The belly.—[4] Grieving.—[5] Swiftly.—[6] Stupefied, fatigued with study.—[7] Learning, knowledge.
[8] Silver dress; alluding to the silver cups and tankards used at the tables of the gentry.
[9] Ale is here intended, a small portion of which is frequently mixed with the porridge of the poorer sort of people.
[10] Gives a relish to.—[11] Without.—[12] Foams.

11

Or reeking on a New-year mornin'
  In cog or bicker,[1]
An' just a wee drap sp'ritual burn in,[2]
  An' gusty[3] sucker![4]

When Vulcan gies his bellows breath,
An' ploughmen gather wi' their graith,[5]
O rare! to see thee fizz[6] an' freath[7]
  I' th' lugget caup![8]
Then Burnewin[9] comes on like death
  At every chaup.[10]

Nae mercy then for airn[11] or steel;
The brawnie, bainie,[12] ploughman chiel,
Brings hard owrehip, wi' sturdy wheel,
  The strong fore-hammer,[13]
Till block an' studie[14] ring an' reel
  Wi' dinsome clamor.

When skirlin' weanies[15] see the light,
Thou maks the gossips clatter[16] bright,
How fumblin' cuifs[17] their dearies slight;
  Wae worth the name;
Nae howdie[18] gets a social night,
  Or plack frae them.

When neebors anger at a plea,
An' just as wud[19] as wud can be,
How easy can the *barley bree*[20]
  Cement the quarrel!
It 's aye the cheapest lawyer's fee,
  To taste the barrel.

Alake! that e'er my Muse has reason
To wyte[21] her countrymen wi' treason!
But monie daily weet their weason[22]
  Wi' liquors nice,
An' hardly, in a winter's season
  E'er spier[23] her price.

---

[1] A wooden cup or dish.—[2] A small quantity of spirits burnt in a spoon, and put into the ale.—[3] Tasteful.—[4] Sugar.—[5] Tackle, geer.—[6] To make a hissing noise.— [7] Froth.—[8] A cup with a handle. — [9] Burn-the-wind; the blacksmith.—[10] Stroke.—[11] Iron.—[12] Bony.—[13] The smith's large hammer. —[14] Anvil.—[15] Crying children. — [16] Tell idle stories. — [17] Ninnies.—[18] A midwife —[19] Mad.—[20] Juice.—[21] To blame.—[22] Weasand.—[23] To ask, to inquire.

Wae worth that *brandy*, burning trash!
Fell source o' monie a pain an' brash![1]
Twins[2] monie a poor, doylt,[3] drunken hash,[4]
    O' half his days;
An' sends, beside, auld Scotland's cash
    To her warst faes.

Ye Scots wha wish auld Scotland well,
Ye chief, to you my tale I tell,
Poor plackless[5] devils like mysel!
    It sets you ill,
Wi' bitter dearthfu' wines to mell,[6]
    Or foreign gill.

May gravels round his blether wrench,
An' gouts torment him inch by inch,
Wha twists his gruntle[7] wi' a glunch[8]
    O' sour disdain,
Out-owre a glass o' *whisky punch*
    Wi' honest men.

O *Whisky!* soul o' plays an' pranks!
Accept a Bardie's humble thanks!
When wanting thee, what tuneless cranks
    Are my poor verses!
Thou comes!—they rattle i' their ranks
    At ither's a—s!

Thee, *Ferintosh!*[9] O sadly lost!
Scotland, lament frae coast to coast!
Now colic grips, an' barkin' hoast,[10]
    May kill us a';
For loyal Forbes's charter'd boast[11]
    Is ta'en awa!

Thae curst horse-leeches o' th' excise,
Wha mak the *whisky stells* their prize!

[1] Sudden illness.—[2] Parts, deprives.—[3] Stupid.—[4] A fellow who knows neither how to act or dress with propriety.—[5] Pennyless.—[6] To meddle.—[7] The phiz.—[8] A frown; sour look.—[9] A very superior kind of whisky made in a district of the Highlands called by that name.—[10] Coughing.

[11] Lord Forbes, of Ferintosh, in the county of Cromarty, formerly held by charter a right for all his tenantry to distil whisky without paying any duty to the king.

Haud up thy hand, Deil! ance, twice, thrice!
   There, seize the blinkers![1]
An' bake them up in brunstane[2] pies
   For poor d—n'd drinkers.

Fortune! if thou 'll but gie me still
Hale breeks,[3] a scone,[4] an' *whisky gill*,
An' rowth[5] o' rhyme to rave at will,
   Tak a' the rest,
An' deal 't about as thy blind skill
   Directs thee best.

THE AUTHOR'S EARNEST CRY AND PRAYER[6]

TO THE SCOTCH REPRESENTATIVES IN THE HOUSE OF COMMONS

Dearest of distillation ! last and best—
—How art thou lost !——
Parody on Milton.

YE Irish Lords, ye Knights an' Squires,
Wha *represent* our brughs an' shires,
An' doucely manage our affairs
   In parliament,
To you a simple Poet's prayers
   Are humbly sent.

Alas! my roupet[7] Muse is hearse![8]
Your Honors' heart wi' grief twad pierce!
To see her sitting on her a—e
   Low i' the dust,
An' scriechin' out prosaic verse,
   An' like to brust!

Tell them wha hae the chief direction,
Scotland an' me 's in great affliction,
E'er sin' they laid that curst restriction
   On *Aquavitæ;*
An' rouse them up to strong conviction,
   An' move their pity.

[1] A term of contempt.—[2] Brimstone.—[3] Whole breeches.—[4] A cake; kind of bread.—[5] Plenty.
[6] This was written before the act anent the Scotch distilleries, of Session 1786; for which Scotland and the Author return their most grateful thanks.
[7] Hoarse, as with a cold.—[8] Hoarse.

Stand forth, an' tell yon Premier youth,
The honest, open, naked truth:
Tell him o' mine an' Scotland's drouth,
    His servants humble:
The muckle[1] Devil blaw ye south,
    If ye dissemble!

Does onie great man glunch[2] an' gloom?
Speak out, an' never fash your thumb![3]
Let posts an' pensions sink or soom[4]
    Wi' them wha grant 'em:
If honestly they canna come,
    Far better want 'em.

In gathering votes you were na slack;
Now stand as tightly by your tack;
Ne'er claw your lug,[5] an' fidge your back,
    An' hum an' haw;
But raise your arm, an' tell your crack
    Before them a'.

Paint Scotland greetin'[6] owre her thrissle,[7]
Her mutchkin stoup[8] as toom 's a whissle;[9]
An' d-mn'd Excisemen in a bussle,
    Seizin' a *stell*,[10]
Triumphant crushin' 't like a mussel
    Or lampit[11] shell.

Then on the tither hand present her,
A blackguard Smuggler right behint her,
An' cheek-for-chow a chuffie[12] Vintner,
    Colleaguing join,
Picking her pouch[13] as bare as winter
    Of a' kind coin.

Is there that bears the name o' Scot,
But feels his heart's bluid rising hot,
To see his poor auld mither's pot
    Thus dung in staves,[14]
An' plunder'd o' her hindmost groat
    By gallows knaves?

[1] Great.—[2] Frown.—[3] Don't be afraid, never trouble your head about it.
—[4] Swim. — [5] Ear.—[6] Weeping.—[7] Thistle, the national emblem.—[8] Pint mug.—[9] Empty.—[10] A still, used for making whisky.—[11] Lympet, a shell fish.—[12] Fat-faced.—[13] Pocket.—[14] Knocked to pieces.

Alas! I 'm but a nameless wight,
Trode i' the mire an' out o' sight!
But could I like Montgomeries fight,
       Or gab[1] like Boswell,
There 's some sark-necks[2] I wad draw tight,
       An' tie some hose well.

God bless your honors, can ye see 't,
The kind, auld, cantie carlin[3] greet,[4]
An' no[5] get warmly to your feet,
       An' gar[6] them hear it,
An' tell them wi' a patriot heat,
       Ye winna[7] bear it!

Some o' you nicely ken the laws,
To round the period, an' pause,
An' wi' rhetoric clause on clause
       To mak harangues;
Then echo thro' Saint Stephen's wa's
       Auld Scotland's wrangs.

Dempster,[8] a true-blue Scot I'se warran;
Thee, aith[9]-detesting, chaste Kilkerran;[10]
An' that glib-gabbet[11] Highland baron,
       The laird o' Graham;[12]
An' ane, a chap that 's d-mn'd auldfarran,[13]
       Dundas his name.

Erskine, a spunkie Norland billie;
True Campbells, Frederick, an' Ilay;
An' Livingstone, the bauld Sir Willie;
       An' monie ithers,
Whom auld Demosthenes or Tully
       Might own for brithers.

Thee, sodger Hugh,[14] my watchman stented,
If bardies e'er are represented;

---

[1] To speak boldly.—[2] Shirt-collars.—[3] Old lady.—[4] Weep.—[5] Not.—[6] Make.
—[7] Will not.
     [8] George Dempster, Esq., of Dunnichen, Forfarshire. He was many years M. P. for the Dundee district of boroughs, and always spoke and voted on the liberal side of politics.
     [9] An oath.—[10] Sir Adam Ferguson.—[11] That speaks smoothly and readily.
—[12] The Duke of Montrose.—[13] Sagacious, cunning.—[14] Earl of Eglintoun, then Colonel Montgomery, and representative for Ayrshire.

I ken if that your sword were wanted,
        Ye 'd lend your hand,
But when there 's aught to say anent it,
        Ye 're at a stand.

Arouse, my boys! exert your mettle,
To get auld Scotland back her *kettle ;*[1]
Or, faith! I 'll wad[2] my new pleugh-pettle,[3]
        Ye 'll see 't or lang,[4]
She 'll teach you wi' a reekin' whittle,[5]
        Anither sang.

This while she 's been in crankous[6] mood,
Her *lost Militia*[7] fired her bluid ;
(Deil na they never mair do guid,
        Play'd her that pliskie![8])
An' now she 's like to rin red-wud,[9]
        About her whisky.

An' L—d! if ance they pit her till 't,[10]
Her tartan petticoat she 'll kilt,[11]
An' dirk an' pistol at her belt,
        She 'll tak the streets,
An' rin her whittle to the hilt,
        I' the first she meets.

For G—d's sake, Sirs! then speak her fair,
An' straik her cannie[12] wi' the hair,
An' to the muckle House[13] repair,
        Wi' instant speed,
An' strive, wi' a' your wit an' lear,[14]
        To get remead.[15]

Yon ill-tongued tinkler, Charlie Fox,
May taunt you wi' his jeers an' mocks ;
But gie him 't het,[16] my hearty cocks !
        E'en cowe the caddie ;[17]
An' send him to his dicing box
        An' sporting lady.

---

[1] Her still.—[2] To bet or wager.—[3] Plough-staff.—[4] Ere lorg.—[5] A bloody
sword.—[6] Fretful.
[7] Burlesque allusion to the bill for a Scotch militia, which was, shortly be-
fore that time, negatived in Parliament.
[8] A trick.—[9] Run stark mad.—[10] Put her to it.—[11] To truss up the clothes.
—[12] Stroke her gently.—[13] The parliament house.—[14] Learning.—[15] Remedy.
—[16] Hot.—[17] Frighten the fellow, make him knock under.

Tell yon guid bluid[1] o' auld Boconnock's,
I 'll be his debt twa mashlum bonnocks,[2]
An' drink his health in auld Nanse Tinnock's,[3]
    Nine times a week,
If he some scheme, like tea an' winnocks,[4]
    Wad kindly seek.

Could he some *commutation* broach,
I 'll pledge my aith in guid braid Scotch,
He need na fear their foul reproach
    Nor erudition,
Yon mixtie-maxtie[5] queer hotch-potch,
    The *Coalition.*

Auld Scotland has a raucle[6] tongue ;
She 's just a devil wi' a rung ;[7]
An' if she promise auld or young
    To tak their part,
Though by the neck she should be strung,
    She 'll no desert.

An' now, ye chosen *Five-and-Forty*,[8]
May still your mither's heart support ye ;
Then, though a minister grow dorty,[9]
    An' kick your place,
Ye 'll snap your fingers, poor an' hearty,
    Before his face.

God bless your honors a' your days
Wi' sowps o' kail[10] an' brats o' claise,[11]
In spite o' a' the thievish kaes[12]
    That haunt Saint Jamie's !
Your humble poet sings an' prays
    While Rab his name is.

POSTSCRIPT.

Let half-starved slaves, in warmer skies,
See future wines, rich-clustering, rise—

---

[1] Good blood.—[2] Two bannocks or cakes made of mixed corn.
[3] A worthy old hostess of the Author's in Mauchline, where he sometimes studied politics over a glass of guid auld Scotch drink.
[4] Tea and windows ; an allusion to Mr. Pitt's commutation tax
[5] Confusedly mixed.—[6] Rash, fearless.—[7] A cudgel.—[8] The Scotch members of parliament—[9] Saucy.—[10] Sups of kail-broth.—[11] Rags of clothes.—[12] Jackdaws.

Their lot auld Scotland ne'er envies,
　　But blythe and frisky,
She eyes her free-born, martial boys
　　Tak aff their whisky.

What tho' their Phœbus kinder warms,
While fragrance blooms and beauty charms!
When wretches range, in famish'd swarms,
　　The scented groves,
Or hounded forth, dishonor arms
　　In hungry droves:

Their gun's a burden on their shouther;
They downa[1] bide the stink o' pouther;
Their bauldest thought's a hank'ring swither[2]
　　To stan' or rin,
Till skelp—a shot!—they 're aff a' throwther,[3]
　　To save their skin.

But bring a Scotsman frae his hill,
Clap in his cheek a Highland gill,[4]
Say, such is royal George's will,
　　An' there 's the foe,
He has nae thought but how to kill
　　Twa at a blow.

Nae cauld, faint-hearted doubtings tease him;
Death comes, wi' fearless eye he sees him;
Wi' bluidy hand a welcome gies him:
　　An' when he fa's,
His latest draught o' breathin' lea'es[5] him
　　In faint huzzas.

Sages their solemn een may steek,[6]
An' raise a philosophic reek,[7]
An' physically causes seek,
　　In clime an' season;
But tell me *whisky's* name in Greek,
　　I 'll tell the reason.

Scotland, my auld respected Mither!
Tho' whyles[8] ye moistify your leather,

- Cannot.—[2] Hesitation.—[3] All pell-mell, or in confusion.—[4] A gill of High-
land whisky.—[5] Leaves.—[6] Shut.—[7] Smoke.—[8] Sometimes.

4*

Till whare ye sit, on craps[1] o' heather,
    Ye tine your dam;[2]
(*Freedom* and *Whisky* gang thegither!)
    Tak aff your dram![3]

* * *

THE VISION.

DUAN FIRST.[4]

THE sun had closed the winter day,
The curlers' quat[5] their roaring play,
An' hunger'd maukin[6] ta'en her way
    To kail-yards green,
While faithless snaws ilk[7] step betray
    Whar she has been.

The thresher's weary *flingin-tree*[8]
The lee-lang[9] day had tired me;
And whan the day had closed his e'e,
    Far i' the west,
Ben i' the *spence*[10] right pensivelie,
    I gaed to rest.

There, lanely, by the ingle-cheek,[11]
I sat and eyed the spewing reek,[12]
That fill'd, wi' hoast-provoking smeek,[13]
    The auld clay biggin;[14]
An' heard the restless rattons squeak
    About the riggin'.

All in this mottie,[15] misty clime,
I backward mused on wasted time,

---

[1] Crops.—[2] Lose your urine.

[3] Burns was not so much the votary of Bacchus as this and "Scotch Drinks," the preceding poem, would lead the reader to suppose. When "Auld Nanse Tinnock," the Mauchline landlady, found her name celebrated in this poem, she said, "Robin Burns may be a clever enough lad, but he has little regard to truth; for I'm sure the chiel' was never in a' his life aboon three times i' my house."

[4] Duan, a term of Ossian's for the different divisions of a digressive poem. See his Cath-Loda.

[5] A game on the ice.—[6] Did quit.—[7] A hare.—[8] Each.—[9] A flail.—[10] Live-long.—[11] In the country parlor.—[12] Fireside.—[13] Smoke.—[14] Cough-provoking smoke.—[15] Building.—[16] Full of motes.

How I had spent my youthfu' prime,
　　　An' done nae-thing,
But stringin' blethers[1] up in rhyme,
　　　For fools to sing.

Had I to guid advice but harkit,[2]
I might, by this, hae led a market,
Or strutted in a bank and clarkit[3]
　　　My cash-account:
While here, half-mad, half-fed, half-sarkit,[4]
　　　Is a' th' amount.

I started, muttering, blockhead! coof![5]
And heaved on high my waukit loof,[6]
To swear by a' yon starry roof,
　　　Or some rash aith,[7]
That I, henceforth, would be *rhyme proof*
　　　Till my last breath—

When click! the string the snick[8] did draw;
And jee! the door gaed to the wa';
An' by my ingle lowe[9] I saw,
　　　Now bleezin[10] bright,
A tight, outlandish *Hizzie*,[11] braw,
　　　Come full in sight.

Ye need na doubt, I held my whisht;[12]
The infant aith, half-form'd, was crusht;
I glower'd as eerie 's I 'd been dush't[13]
　　　In some wild glen;
When sweet, like modest Worth, she blusht,
　　　And stepped ben.[14]

Green, slender, leaf-clad *holly-boughs*
Were twisted, gracefu', round her brows;
I took her for some *Scottish Muse*,
　　　By that same token;
An' come to stop those reckless vows,
　　　Would soon been broken.

[1] Foolish or romantic ideas.—[2] Hearkened.—[3] Wrote.—[4] Badly provided with shirts.—[5] Ninny.—[6] Thick or clumsy hand.—[7] Oath.—[8] The latch of a door.—[9] Flame of the fire.—[10] Blazing.—[11] A young girl.—[12] Was silent. [13] Stared frightfully, as if I had been suddenly pushed, or attacked by an ox. [14] Into the parlor.

A "hair-brain'd sentimental trace,"
Was strongly marked in her face;
A wildy-witty, rustic grace
    Shone full upon her;
Her eye, even turn'd on empty space,
    Beam'd keen with Honor.

Down flow'd her robe, a tartan sheen,[1]
Till half a leg was scrimply[2] seen;
And such a leg! my bonnie Jean
    Could only peer[3] it;
Sae straught,[4] sae taper, tight, and clean,
    Nane else came near it.

Her *mantle* large, of greenish hue,
My gazing wonder chiefly drew;
Deep *lights* and *shades*, bold-mingling, threw
    A lustre grand;
And seem'd, to my astonish'd view,
    A *well-known* land.

Here, rivers in the sea were lost;
There, mountains to the skies were tost;
Here, tumbling billows mark'd the coast,
    With surging foam;
There, distant shone Art's lofty boast,
    The lordly dome.

Here, Doon pour'd down his far-fetch'd floods;
There, well-fed Irwine stately thuds;[5]
Auld hermit Ayr staw[6] thro' his woods,
    On to the shore;
And many a lesser torrent scuds,
    With seeming roar.

Low, in a sandy valley spread,
An ancient *borough* rear'd her head;
Still, as in Scottish story read,
    She boasts a race,
To every nobler virtue bred,
    And polish'd grace.

---

[1] A bright, or shining tartan, or checkered woollen stuff, much worn in Scotland, particularly in the Highlands.
[2] Scantily.—[3] Equal.—[4] Straight.—[5] To make a loud continued noise.—[6] Stole.

By stately tower or palace fair,
Or ruins pendent in the air,
Bold stems of heroes, here and there,
    I could discern;
Some seem'd to muse, some seem'd to dare,
    With feature stern.

My heart did glowing transport feel,
To see a race[1] heroic wheel,
And brandish round the deep-dyed steel
    In sturdy blows;
While back-recoiling seem'd to reel
    Their Suthron foes.

His *Country's Saviour*,[2] mark him well;
Bold Richardton's[3] heroic swell;
The chief on Sark[4] who glorious fell,
    In high command;
And He whom ruthless fates expel
    His native land.

There, where a scepter'd Pictish shade[5]
Stalk'd round his ashes lowly laid,
I mark'd a martial race, portray'd
    In colors strong;
Bold, soldier-featured, undismay'd
    They strode along.

Thro' many a wild, romantic grove,[6]
Near many a hermit-fancied cove,
(Fit haunts for Friendship or for Love,)
    In musing mood,
An *aged Judge*, I saw him rove,
    Dispensing good

[1] The Wallaces.—[2] William Wallace.

[3] Adam Wallace, of Richardton, cousin to the immortal preserver of Scottish Independence.

[4] Wallace, laird of Craigie, who was second in command, under Douglas, earl of Ormond, at the famous battle on the banks of Sark, fought *anno* 1448. That glorious victory was principally owing to the judicious conduct and intrepid valor of the gallant laird of Craigie, who died of his wounds after the action.

[5] Coilus, King of the Picts, from whom the district of Kyle is said to take its name, lies buried, as tradition says, near the family seat of the Montgomeries of Coil's-field, where his burial-place is still shown.

[6] Barskimming, the seat of the late Lord Justice Clerk.

With deep-struck reverential awe[1]
The learned *Sire* and *Son* I saw,
To Nature's God and Nature's law
    They gave their lore:
This, all its source and end to draw;
    That, to adore.

Brydone's brave ward[2] I well could spy,
Beneath old Scotia's smiling eye;
Who call'd on Fame, low standing by,
    To hand him on
Where many a Patriot-name on high,
    And hero shone.

DUAN SECOND.

WITH musing deep, astonish'd stare,
I view'd the heavenly-seeming *Fair*,
A whispering throb did witness bear,
    Of kindred sweet,
When, with an elder sister's air,
    She did me greet:—

All hail! my own inspired Bard!
In me thy native Muse regard:
Nor longer mourn thy fate is hard,
    Thus poorly low!
I come to give thee such reward
    As we bestow.

Know, the great *Genius* of this land
Has many a light aerial band,
Who, all beneath his high command,
    Harmoniously,
As arts or arms they understand,
    Their labors ply.

They Scotia's race among them share;
Some fire the Soldier on to dare;
Some rouse the Patriot up to bare
    Corruption's heart;
Some teach the Bard, a darling care,
    The tuneful art.

[1] Catrine, the seat of the late Doctor, and present Professor Stewart.
[2] Colonel Fullarton.

'Mong swelling floods of reeking gore,
They ardent, kindling spirits pour;
Or 'mid the venal Senate's roar,
       They, sightless, stand,
To mend the honest Patriot-lore,
       And grace the hand.

And when the Bard, or hoary Sage,
Charm or instruct the future age,
They bind the wild poetic rage
       In energy,
Or point the inconclusive page
       Full on the eye.

Hence Fullarton, the brave and young;
Hence Dempster's zeal-inspired tongue;
Hence sweet harmonious Beattie sung
       His *Minstrel* lays;
Or tore, with noble ardor stung,
       The *Skeptic's*[1] bays.

To lower orders are assign'd,
The humbler ranks of human kind,
The rustic Bard, the laboring Hind,
       The Artisan;
All choose, as various they're inclined,
       The various man.

When yellow waves the heavy grain,
The threatening storm some strongly rein;
Some teach to meliorate the plain
       With tillage skill;
And some instruct the shepherd train
       Blithe o'er the hill.

Some hint the lover's harmless wile;
Some grace the maiden's artless smile;
Some soothe the laborer's weary toil
       For humble gains,
And make his cottage-scenes beguile
       His cares and pains.

Some, bounded to a district-space,
Explore at large man's infant race,

[1] David Hume.

To mark the embryotic trace,
       Of *rustic Bard;*
And careful note each opening grace,
       A guide and guard.

Of these am I—Coïla[1] my name;
And this district as mine I claim,
Where once the Campbells, chiefs of fame,
       Held ruling power;
I mark'd thy embryo tuneful flame,
       Thy natal hour.

With future hope, I oft would gaze,
Fond, on thy little early ways,
Thy rudely caroll'd, chiming phrase,
       In uncouth rhymes,
Fired at the simple, artless lays
       Of other times.

I saw thee seek the sounding shore,
Delighted with the dashing roar;
Or when the North his fleecy store
       Drove thro' the sky,
I saw grim Nature's visage hoar,
       Struck thy young eye.

Or when the deep green-mantled earth
Warm cherish'd every floweret's birth,
And joy and music pouring forth
       In every grove,
I saw thee eye the general mirth
       With boundless love.

When ripen'd fields and azure skies,
Call'd forth the reapers' rustling noise,
I saw thee leave their evening joys,
       And lonely stalk,
To vent thy bosom's swelling rise
       In pensive walk.

When youthful love, warm-blushing, strong,
Keen-shivering shot thy nerves along,

---

[1] Coïla, from Kyle, a district in Ayrshire, so called, saith tradition, from Coil, or Coilus, a Pictish monarch.

Those accents, grateful to thy tongue,
    Th' adored *name*,
I taught thee how to pour in song,
    To soothe thy flame.

I saw thy pulse's maddening play
Wild send thee pleasure's devious way
Misled by Fancy's meteor ray,
    By passion driven;
But yet the *light* that led astray
    Was *light* from Heaven.

I taught thy manners-painting strains,
The loves, the ways of simple swains,
Till now, o'er all my wide domains
    Thy fame extends:
And some, the pride of Coila's plains,
    Become thy friends.

Thou canst not learn, nor can I show,
To paint with Thomson's landscape glow;
Or wake the bosom-melting throe,
    With Shenstone's art;
Or pour, with Gray, the moving flow
    Warm on the heart.

Yet all beneath the unrivall'd rose,
The lowly daisy sweetly blows;
Tho' large the forest's monarch throws
    His army shade,
Yet green the juicy hawthorn grows,
    Adown the glade.

Then never murmur nor repine;
Strive in thy humble sphere to shine;
And trust me, not Potosi's' mine,
    Nor kings' regard,
Can give a bliss o'ermatching thine,
    A *rustic Bard.*

To give my counsels all in one,
Thy tuneful flame still careful fan;

[1] In South America, famed for its gold mines.

Preserve *the Dignity of Man,*
  With soul erect;
And trust the *Universal Plan*
  Will all protect.

And wear thou this!—she solemn said,
And bound the *Holly* round my head:
The polish'd leaves and berries red
  Did rustling play;
And, like a passing thought, she fled
  In light away.

A DREAM.

Thoughts, words, and deeds, the statute blames with reason,
But surely *Dreams* were ne'er indicted treason.

[On reading in the public papers, the Laureate's Ode, with the other parade of June 4, 1786, the Author was no sooner dropt asleep, than he imagined himself transported to the birth-day levee; and in his dreaming fancy made the following address.]

GUID-MORNIN' to your Majesty!
  May Heaven augment your blisses,
On every new *birth-day* ye see,
  A humble poet wishes!
My Bardship here, at your levee,
  On sic a day as this is,
Is sure an uncouth sight to see,
  Amang thae[1] birth-day dresses
      Sae fine this day.

I see ye 're complimented thrang,[2]
  By monie a lord and lady;
God save the king! 's a cuckoo sang,
  That 's unco[3] easy said ay;
The *Poets* too, a venal gang,
  Wi' rhymes weel-turn'd and ready,
Wad gar ye trow[4] ye ne'er do wrang,
  But ay unerring steady,
      On sic a day.

For me! before a monarch's face,
  Even *there* I winna[5] flatter;

[1] Among those.—[2] By a crowd.—[3] Very.—[4] Believe.—[5] Will not.

For neither pension, post, nor place,
    Am I your humble debtor;
So, nae reflection on *your grace*,
    Your kingship to bespatter;
There's monie waur[1] been o' the race,
    And aiblins ane[2] been better
                Than you this day.

'Tis very true, my sovereign King,
    My skill may weel be doubted;
But facts are chiels that winna ding,[3]
    An' downa[4] be disputed:
Your royal nest,[5] beneath your wing,
    Is e'en right reft an' clouted,[6]
And now the third part o' the string,
    And less, will gang about it.
                Than did ae day.[7]

Far be't frae me that I aspire
    To blame your legislation,
Or say, ye wisdom want, or fire,
    To rule this mighty nation!
But, faith! I muckle[8] doubt, my Sire,
    Ye've trusted ministration
To chaps, wha in a barn or byre[9]
    Wad better fill'd their station
                Than courts yon day.

And now ye've gien auld Britain peace,
    Her broken shins to plaster:
Your sair taxation does her fleece,
    Till she has scarce a tester:
For me, thank God, my life's a *lease*,
    Nae *bargain* wearing faster,
Or, faith! I fear, that wi' the geese,
    I shortly boost[10] to pasture
              I' the craft[11] some day.

I'm no mistrusting Willie Pitt,
    When taxes he enlarges,

[1] Worse.—[2] Perhaps one.—[3] Will not give way.—[4] Cannot.—[5] Your dominions.—[6] Torn and patched.—[7] Written in allusion to the recent loss of America.—[8] Must.—[9] A cow stable.—[10] Must needs.—[11] Croft, grass field.

(An' Will 's a true guid fallow's get,
 A name not envy spairges,[1])
That he intends to pay your debt,
 An' lessen a' your charges;
But, G—d sake! let nae *saving-fit*
 Abridge your bonnie barges[2]
    An' boats this day.

Adieu, my liege! may freedom geck[3]
 Beneath your high protection;
An' may ye rax[4] corruption's neck,
 An' gie her for dissection!
But since I 'm here, I 'll no neglect,
 In loyal, true affection,
To pay your Queen, with due respect,
 My fealty an' subjection
    This great birth-day.

Hail, *Majesty most excellent!*
 While nobles strive to please ye,
Will ye accept a compliment
 A simple Poet gies ye?
Thae bonnie bairn-time,[5] Heaven has lent,
 Still higher may they heeze[6] ye
In bliss, till fate some day is sent,
 Forever to release ye
    Frae care that day.

For you, young Potentate o' Wales,
 I tell your Highness fairly,
Down pleasure's stream, wi' swelling sails,
 I 'm tauld you 're driving rarely;
But some day ye may gnaw your nails,
 An' curse your folly sairly,
That e'er you brak Diana's pales,
 Or rattled dice wi' Charlie,
    By night or day.

Yet aft a ragged cowte[7] 's been known
 To mak a noble aiver;[8]
So, ye may doucely[9] fill a throne,
 For a' their clish-ma-claver;[10]

---

[1] Soils or disparages.—[2] Ships of the navy.—[3] Hold up her head.—[4] Stretch
—[5] Family of children.—[6] Elevate.—[7] Colt.—[8] Horse.—[9] Wisely.—[10] Idle conversation.

There, him at Agincourt[1] wha shone,
   Few better were or braver;
An' yet wi' funny queer Sir John,[2]
   He was an unco[3] shaver
      For monie a day.

For you, right reverend Osnaburg,
   Nane sets the *lawn-sleeve* sweeter,
Altho' a ribbon at your lug[4]
   Wad been a dress completer:
As ye disown yon paughty[5] dog
   That bears the keys of Peter,
Then swith![6] an' get a wife to hug,
   Or, trouth! ye 'll stain the mitre
      Some luckless day.

Young, royal Tarry Breeks,[7] I learn,
   Ye 've lately come athwart her;
A glorious *galley*,[8] stem an' stern,
   Weel rigg'd for Venus' barter;
But first hang out, that she 'll discern
   Your hymeneal charter,
Then heave aboard your grapple airn,[9]
   An' large upo' her quarter
      Come full that day.

Ye, lastly, bonnie blossoms a',
   Ye royal lasses dainty,
Heaven mak you guid as weel as braw,[10]
   An' gie you lads a plenty:
But sneer na British boys awa',
   For kings are unco scant[11] ay;
An' German gentles are but *sma'*,
   They 're better just than *want ay*
      On onie day.

God bless you a', consider now,
   Ye 're unco muckle dantet:[12]
But, ere the course o' life be thro',
   It may be bitter sautet:[13]

---

[1] ,King Henry V.— [2] Sir John Falstaff. *Vide* Shakspeare.— [3] Strange, whimsical.— [4] Ear.— [5] Proud, haughty.— [6] Get away.— [7] Breeches.— [8] Alluding to the newspaper accounts of a certain royal sailor's amour.— [9] Iron.— [10] Fine, handsome. — [11] Very few.— [12] Very much caressed. — [13] Salted, pickled.

An' I hae seen their coggie fou,[1]
That yet hae tarrow'd[2] at it:
But or the day was done, I trow,
The laggen[3] they hae clautet[4]
Fu' clean that day.

ADDRESS TO THE DEIL.

O Prince! O Chief of many throned Powers,
That led th' embattled Seraphim to war.—*Milton.*

O THOU! whatever title suit thee,
Auld Hornie, Satan, Nick, or Clootie,
Wha in yon cavern, grim an' sootie,
Closed under hatches,
Spairges[5] about the brunstane cootie,[6]
To scaud[7] poor wretches!

Hear me, auld Hangie, for a wee,[8]
And let poor damned bodies be;
I'm sure sma'[9] pleasure it can gie,[10]
E'en to a Deil,
To skelp[11] an' scaud poor dogs like me,
An' hear us squeel!

Great is thy power, an' great thy fame;
Far kenn'd[12] and noted is thy name;
An' tho' yon lowin' heugh[13]'s thy hame,
Thou travels far;
An' faith! thou 's neither lag nor lame,
Nor blate,[14] nor scaur.[15]

Whyles[16] ranging like a roaring lion
For prey, a' holes an' corners tryin';
Whyles on the strong-wing'd tempest flyin',
Tirling[17] the kirks:
Whyles in the human bosom pryin',
Unseen thou lurks.

[1] Cup or dish full.—[2] Murmured.—[3] The angle between the side and bottom of a wooden dish.—[4] Scraped.—[5] To dash, or throw about.—[6] Brimstone dish, or ladle.—[7] Scald.—[8] Little.—[9] Small.—[10] Give.—[11] Strike, or beat.—[12] Known.—[13] Flaming pit.—[14] Bashful.—[15] Apt to be scared.—[16] Sometimes.—[17] Uncovering.

I 've heard my reverend *grannie* say,
In lanely glens ye like to stray;
Or where auld, ruin'd castles, gray,
    Nod to the moon,
Ye fright the nightly wanderer's way
    Wi' eldritch croon.[1]

When twilight did my *graunie* summon,
To say her prayers, douce,[2] honest woman!
Aft yont[3] the dyke she 's heard you bummin',
    Wi' eerie[4] drone;
Or, rustlin', thro' the boortries[5] comin',
    Wi' heavy groan.

Ae[6] dreary, windy, winter night,
The stars shot down wi' sklentin[7] light;
Wi' you, mysel, I gat a fright,
    Ayont the lough;[8]
Ye, like a rash-bush,[9] stood in sight,
    Wi' waving sugh.[10]

The cudgel in my nieve[11] did shake,
Each bristled hair stood like a stake,
When wi' an eldritch stour,[12] quaick—quaick—
    Amang the springs,
Awa' ye squatter'd[13] like a drake,
    On whistling wings.

Let *warlocks*[14] grim, an' wither'd *hags*,
Tell how wi' you on ragweed[15] nags,
They skim the muirs an' dizzy crags,
    Wi' wicked speed;
And in kirk-yards renew their leagues
    Owre howkit[16] dead.

[1] Frightful hollow moan.—[2] Wise, good.—[3] Beyond.—[4] Frighted, or fright
ful.—[5] Elder-trees.—[6] One.—[7] Glimmering.—[8] A pool, or sheet of water.—
[9] A bush, or large tuft of rushes.—[10] Rushing noise of wind or water.—
[11] Hand, or fist.—[12] The raising a cloud of dust.—[13] Fluttered in water.—
[14] Wizards.—[15] Ragwort.
[16] Digged up, or disinterred. Those who are, or were, believers in the old
traditions relative to witchcraft, supposed that the incantations of these de
moniacs were frequently performed over dead bodies, which they dug
scratched, or conjured out of their graves in order to perform their devilish
orgies more effectually.

Thence countra wives wi' toil an' pain,
May plunge an' plunge the kirn[1] in vain;
For, oh! the yellow treasure 's ta'en
    By witching skill:
An' dawtit,[2] twal-pint[3] Hawkie 's[4] gaen[5]
    As yell 's[6] the Bill.[7]

Thence mystic knots mak great abuse,
On young guidmen,[8] fond, keen, an' crouse;[9]
When the best wark-lume[10] i' the house,
    By cantrip[11] wit,
Is instant made no worth a louse,
    Just at the bit.

When thowes[12] dissolve the snawy hoord,
An' float the jingling icy-boord,
Then *Water kelpies*[13] haunt the foord,
    By your direction,
An' 'nighted travellers are allured
    To their destruction.

An' aft your moss-traversing *Spunkies*,[14]
Decoy the wight that late an' drunk is,
The bleezin', curst, mischievous monkeys
    Delude his eyes,
Till in some miry slough he sunk is,
    Ne'er mair to rise.

When *Masons'* mystic *word* an' *grip*
In storms an' tempests raise you up,

---

[1] Churn. — [2] Fondled, caressed. — [3] Twelve-pint. — [4] Cow. — [5] Gone. — [6] Barren.

[7] Bull.—The literal English meaning of these last two lines is, that a favorite cow, that gave daily twelve Scotch pints of milk (equal to forty-eight English pints), is becoming as barren as a bull, in consequence of witchcraft.

[8] Men newly married.—[9] Courageous.

[10] A working tool. Fully to appreciate the meaning of the stanza beginning "Thence mystic knots," it is necessary for the English reader to know, that a tradition was entertained in Scotland of the power of witchcraft to prevent consummation on the bridal night, by rendering the "young guid man" powerless "just at the bit," or moment when, &c.

[11] A charm or spell.—[12] Thaws.

[13] A mischievous kind of spirits, said to haunt fords, or ferries, particularly n stormy nights.

[14] Will-o'-the-wisp, or Jack-a-lantern.

Some cock or cat your rage maun stop,
  Or, strange to tell!
The youngest brother ye wad whip
  Aff straught to h-ll!

Lang syne in Eden's bonnie yard,
When youthfu' lovers first were pair'd,
An' a' the soul of love they shared
  The raptured hour,
Sweet on the fragrant, flowery swaird,
  In shady bower:

Then you, ye auld, snick-drawing[1] dog!
Ye came to Paradise *incog.*
An' played on man a cursed brogue,
  (Black be your fa'!)
An' gied the infant warld a shog,[2]
  'Maist ruin'd a'.

D'ye mind that day, when in a bizz,[3]
Wi' reekit duds,[4] an' reestit gizz,[5]
Ye did present your smoutie[6] phiz,
  'Mang better folk,
An' sklented[7] on the *man of Uz*
  Your spitefu' joke?

An' how ye gat him i' your thrall,
An' brak him out o' house an' hall,
While scabs an' blotches did him gall,
  Wi' bitter claw,
An' lows'd[8] his ill-tongued wicked scawl,[9]
  Was warst ava?

But a' your doings to rehearse,
Your wily snares an' fechting[10] fierce,
Sin' that day Michael[11] did you pierce,
  Down to this time,
Wad ding[12] a' Lallan tongue, or Erse,
  In prose or rhyme.

An' now, auld *Cloots*, I ken ye're thinkin',
A certain Bardie's rantin', drinkin',

[1] Trick-contriving.—[2] A violent shock.—[3] Bustle.—[4] Smoky clothes.—[5] Withered, or scorched wig.—[6] Ugly, or smutty.—[7] Hit aslant, or obliquely.—[8] Loosed.—[9] A scold.—[10] Fighting.—[11] Vide Milton, book vi.—[12] Puzzle.

13

Some luckless hour will send him linkin',[1]
    To your black pit;
But, faith! he 'll turn a corner jinkin',[2]
    An' cheat you yet.

But fare you weel, auld *Nickie-ben!*
O wad ye tak a thought an' men'!
Ye aiblins[3] might—I dinna ken[4]—
    Still hae a *stake*—
I 'm wae to think upon yon den,
    Even for your sake![5]

ADDRESS TO EDINBURGH.

EDINA! Scotia's darling seat!
  All hail thy palaces and towers,
Where once beneath a monarch's feet
  Sat Legislation's sovereign powers!
From marking wildly-scatter'd flowers,
  As on the banks of Ayr I stray'd,
And singing, lone, the lingering hours,
  I shelter in thy honor'd shade.

Here Wealth still swells the golden tide,
  As busy Trade his labors plies;
There Architecture's noble pride
  Bids elegance and splendor rise;
Here Justice, from her native skies,
  High wields her balance and her rod;
There Learning, with his eagle eyes,
  Seeks Science in her coy abode.

Thy sons, Edina, social, kind,
  With open arms the stranger hail;
Their views enlarged, their liberal mind,
  Above the narrow, rural vale;
Attentive still to sorrow's wail,
  Or modest merit's silent claim;

[1] Tripping.—[2] Dodging.—[3] Perhaps.—[4] Do not know.

[5] Written in the winter of 1784-5. "The idea of an Address to the Deil was suggested to the poet, by running over in his mind the many ludicrous accounts and representations we have, from various quarters, of this august personage."—*Gilbert Burns.*

And never may their sources fail!
　　And never envy blot their name!

Thy daughters bright thy walks adorn!
　　Gay as the gilded summer sky,
Sweet as the dewy milk-white thorn,
　　Dear as the raptured thrill of joy!
Fair Burnet[1] strikes th' adoring eye,
　　Heaven's beauties on my fancy shine,
I see the Sire of love on high,
　　And own his work indeed divine!

There, watching high the least alarms,
　　Thy rough, rude fortress gleams afar;
Like some bold veteran, gray in arms,
　　And mark'd with many a seamy scar;
The ponderous wall and massy bar,
　　Grim-rising o'er the rugged rock;
Have oft withstood assailing war,
　　And oft repell'd the invader's shock.

With awe-struck thought, and pitying tears,
　　I view that noble, stately dome,
Where Scotia's kings of other years,
　　Famed heroes, had their royal home.
Alas! how changed the times to come;
　　Their royal name low in the dust!
Their hapless race wild-wandering roam!
　　Tho' rigid law cries out, 'twas just!

Wild beats my heart to trace your steps,
　　Whose ancestors, in days of yore,
Thro' hostile ranks and ruin'd gaps,
　　Old Scotia's bloody lion bore:
Even I who sing in rustic lore,
　　Haply my sires have left their shed,
And faced grim danger's loudest roar,
　　Bold-following where your fathers led!

Edina! Scotia's darling seat!
　　All hail thy palaces and towers,
Where once beneath a monarch's feet
　　Sat Legislation's sovereign powers!

[1] Miss Burnet of Monboddo.

From marking wildly-scatter'd flowers,
   As on the banks of Ayr I stray'd,
And singing, lone, the lingering hours,
   I shelter in thy honor'd shade.[1]

ADDRESS TO THE SHADE OF THOMSON,

ON CROWNING HIS BUST, AT EDNAM, ROXBURGHSHIRE, WITH BAYS

[Written by desire of the poet's friend, the Earl of Buchan.]

WHILE virgin Spring, by Eden's flood,
   Unfolds her tender mantle green,
Or pranks the sod in frolic mood,
   Or tunes Eolian strains between:

While Summer, with a matron grace,
   Retreats to Dryburgh's cooling shade,
Yet oft, delighted, stops to trace
   The progress of the spiky blade:

While Autumn, benefactor kind,
   By Tweed erects his aged head,
And sees, with self-approving mind,
   Each creature on his bounty fed:

While maniac Winter rages o'er
   The hills whence classic Yarrow flows,
·Rousing the turbid torrent's roar,
   Or sweeping wild, a waste of snows:

So long, sweet Poet of the Year,
   Shall bloom that wreath thou well hast won;
While SCOTIA, with exulting tear,
   Proclaims that THOMSON was her son.

THE POET'S WELCOME

TO HIS ILLEGITIMATE CHILD.[2]

THOU'S welcome, wean, mishanter fa' me,
If aught of thee or of thy mammy,

---

[1] This poem is chiefly remarkable for the grand stanzas on the castle and Holyrood with which it concludes.—*Lockhart.*

[2] This "Address" is omitted by Dr. Currie, and as its contents are rather of too indelicate a complexion to need elucidation, the commentator has withheld his pen.

Shall ever danton me or awe me,
>> My sweet wee lady,
Or if I blush when thou shalt ca' me
>> Tit-ta or daddy.

Wee image of my bonnie Betty,
I, fatherly, will kiss an' daut thee,
As dear an' near my heart I set thee,
>> Wi' as gude will,
As a' the priests had seen me get
>> That's out o' h–ll.

What tho' they ca' me fornicator,
An' tease my name in kintry-clatter:
The mair they tauk I'm kent the better,
>> E'en let them clash;
An auld wife's tongue's a feckless matter
>> To gie ane fash.

Sweet fruit o' monie a merry dint,
My funny toil is now a' tint,
Sin' thou came to the warl' asklent,
>> Which fools may scoff at;
In my last plack thy part's be in 't—
>> The better half o't.

An' if thou be what I wad hae thee,
An' tak the counsel I shall gie thee,
A lovin' father I'll be to thee,
>> If thou be spared;
Thro' a' thy childish years I'll e'e thee,
>> An' think 't weel war'd.

Gude grant that thou may ay inherit
Thy mither's person, grace, an' merit,
An' thy poor worthless daddy's spirit,
>> Without his failin's!
'Twill please me mair to hear an' see 't
>> Than stocket mailins.

TO A HAGGIS.[1]

Fair fa' your honest, sonsie[2] face,
Great chieftain o' the puddin'-race!
Aboon[3] them a' ye tak your place,
      Painch,[4] tripe, or thairm:[5]
Weel are ye wordy[6] of a *grace*
      As lang 's my arm.

The groaning trencher there ye fill,
Your hurdies like a distant hill,
Your pin wad help to mend a mill
      In time o' need,
While thro' your pores the dews distil
      Like amber bead.

His knife see rustic labor dight,[7]
An' cut you up wi' ready slight,
Trenching your gushing entrails bright
      Like onie ditch;
And then, O what a glorious sight,
      Warm-reeking rich!

Then horn for horn[8] they stretch an' strive:
Deil tak the hindmost! on they drive,
Till a' their weel-swall'd kytes[9] belyve[10]
      Are bent like drums,
Then auld guidman, maist like to rive,[11]
      Bethankit[12] hums.

Is there that o'er his French *ragout*,
Or *olio* that wad staw[13] a sow,
Or *fricassee* wad make her spew
      Wi' perfect sconner,[14]
Looks down wi' sneering, scornfu' view
      On sic a dinner?

Poor devil! see him owre his trash,
As feckless[15] as a wither'd rash,

---

[1] A kind of pudding boiled in the stomach of a cow, or sheep.—[2] Engaging, pleasing.—[3] Above.—[4] Paunch.—[5] A small gut.—[6] Worthy.—[7] Wipe clean.—[8] A spoon made of horn.—[9] Bellies.—[10] By and by.—[11] To split.—[12] Grace after meat.—[13] Surfeit.—[14] Loathing.—[15] Puny, weak.

His spindle-shank a guid whip-lash,
　　　　His nieve[1] a nit;[2]
Thro' bloody flood or field to dash,
　　　　O how unfit!

But mark the rustic, *haggis-fed*,
The trembling earth resounds his tread,
Clap in his walie[3] nieve a blade,
　　　　He 'll mak it whissle;
An' legs, an' arms, an' heads will sned,[4]
　　　　Like taps o' thrissle.[5]

Ye Powers wha mak mankind your care,
And dish them out their bill o' fare,
Auld Scotland wants nae skinking[6] ware
　　　　That jaups[7] in luggies[8];
But, if ye wish her gratefu' prayer,
　　　　Gie her a *Haggis!*

ADDRESS TO THE TOOTHACHE.

My curse upon thy venom'd stang,
That shoots my tortured gums alang;
And thro' my lugs[9] gies monie a twang,
　　　　Wi' gnawing vengeance;
Tearing my nerves wi' bitter pang,
　　　　Like racking engines.

When fevers burn, or ague freezes,
Rheumatics gnaw, or colic squeezes;
Our neighbor's sympathy may ease us,
　　　　Wi' pitying moan;
But thee—thou hell o' a' diseases,
　　　　Ay mocks our groan!

Adown my beard the slavers trickle!
I throw the wee stools o'er the mickle,[10]

---

[1] The fist.—[2] Nut.—[3] Large, ample.—[4] To lop off.—[5] Tops of thistles.—[6] Small portions.—[7] A jerk of waters, or a thin potion that will jerk or quash like water. — [8] A small wooden dish with a handle. — [9] Ears. — [10] The greater.

As round the fire the giglets[1] keckle[2]
     To see me loup ;[3]
While, raving mad, I wish a heckle[4]
     Were in their doup.[5]

O' a' the numerous human dools,[6]
Ill har'sts,[7] daft bargains,[8] *cutty-stools*,[9]
Or worthy friends raked i' the mools,[10]
     Sad sight to see!
The tricks o' knaves, or fash[11] o' fools,
     Thou bear'st the gree.[12]

Where'er that place be priests ca' hell,
Whence a' the tones o' misery yell,
And ranked plagues their numbers tell,
     In dreadfu' raw,[12]
Thou, Toothache, surely bear'st the bell
     Aboon[14] them a'!

O thou grim, mischief-making chiel',
That gars[16] the notes of *discord* squeel,
Till daft mankind aft dance a reel
     In gore a shoe-thick,—
Gie a' the faes o' Scotland's weal
     A towmond's[16] Toothache!

TO A POSTHUMOUS CHILD,

BORN IN PECULIAR CIRCUMSTANCES OF DISTRESS.

SWEET floweret, pledge o' meikle[17] love,
     And ward o' monie a prayer,
What heart o' stane wad thou na move,
     Sae helpless, sweet, and fair!

November hirples[18] o'er the lea,
     Chill, on thy lovely form;

---

* Fools.—[2] Laugh.—[3] Leap, jump.
[4] A board in which are driven a number of sharp iron pins, used for dressing hemp, flax, &c.
[5] Backside.—[6] Sorrows.—[7] Bad harvests.—[8] Foolish bargains.—[9] Stool of repentance.—[10] Laid in the grave.—[11] Trouble.—[12] The victory.—[13] Row.—[14] Above. — [15] Makes. — [16] A twelvemonth. — [17] Much. — [18] Creeps, or limps.

And gane, alas! the shelt'ring tree,
  Should shield thee frae the storm.

May He, who gives the rain to pour,
  And wings the blast to blaw,
Protect thee frae the driving shower,
  The bitter frost and snaw!

May He, the friend of woe and want,
  Who heals life's various stounds,[1]
Protect and guard the mother-plant,
  And heal her cruel wounds!

But late she flourish'd, rooted fast,
  Fair on the summer morn;
Now, feebly bends she in the blast,
  Unshelter'd and forlorn.

Blest be thy bloom, thou lovely gem,
  Unscathed[2] by ruffian hand!
And from thee many a parent stem
  Arise to deck our land!

TO A MOUNTAIN DAISY,

On turning one down with the plough, In April, 1786.

Wee,[3] modest, crimson-tippéd flower,
Thou 'st met me in an evil hour;
For I maun crush amang the stoure[4]
    Thy slender stem;
To spare thee now is past my power,
    Thou bonnie gem.

Alas! it 's no[5] thy neebor sweet!
The bonnie *Lark*, companion meet!
Bending thee 'mang the dewy weet![6]
    Wi' spreckled breast,
When upward-springing, blythe, to greet
    The purpling East.

Cauld blew the bitter-biting North
Upon thy early, humble birth,

---

[1] Acute pains.—[2] Unhurt.—[3] Small.—[4] Dust.—[5] Not.—[6] Wet, wetness.

Yet cheerfully thou glinted[1] forth
         Amid the storm,
Scarce rear'd above the parent earth
         Thy tender form.

The flaunting flowers our gardens yield,
High sheltering woods and wa's maun shield;
But thou, beneath the random bield[2]
         O' clod or stane,
Adorns the histie[3] *stibble-field*,
         Unseen, alane.

There, in thy scanty mantle clad,
Thy snawie bosom sunward spread,
Thou lifts thy unassuming head
         In humble guise;
But now the *share* up-tears thy bed,
         And low thou lies!

Such is the fate of artless Maid,
Sweet *flow'ret* of the rural shade!
By love's simplicity betray'd,
         And guileless trust,
Till she, like thee, all soil'd, is laid
         Low i' the dust.

Such is the fate of simple Bard,
On life's rough ocean luckless starr'd:
Unskilful he to note the card
         Of *prudent lore*,
Till billows rage, and gales blow hard,
         And whelm him o'er!

Such fate to *suffering worth* is given,
Who long with wants and woes has striven,
By human pride or cunning driven,
         To mis'ry's brink,
Till wrenched of ev'ry stay but *Heaven*,
         He, ruin'd, sink!

Even thou who mourn'st the Daisy's fate,
That fate is thine—no distant date;

---

[1] Peeped.—[2] Shelter.—[3] Dry, chapt, barren.

Stern Ruin's *plough-share* drives, elate,
   Full on thy bloom,
Till crush'd beneath the furrow's weight,
   Shall be thy doom![1]

TO A MOUSE,

On turning her up in her nest, with the plough, November, 1785

WEE, sleekit,[2] cow'rin',[3] tim'rous beastie,
Oh, what a panic 's in thy breastie!
Thou need na start awa' sae hasty,
   Wi' bick'rin' brattle![4]
I wad be laith[5] to rin an' chase thee,
   Wi' murd'ring *pattle.*[6]

I 'm truly sorry man's dominion
Has broken Nature's social union,
An' justifies that ill opinion
   Which makes thee startle
At me, thy poor earth-born companion,
   An' *fellow-mortal.*

I doubt na, whyles, but thou may thieve:
What then? poor beastie, thou maun live;
A *daimen icker*[7] in a *thrave*[8]
   'S a sma' request:
I 'll get a blessing wi' the lave,[9]
   And never miss 't.

Thy wee bit *housie*, too, in ruin!
Its silly wa's the wins[10] are strewin'!
An' naething, now, to big[11] a new ane,
   O' foggage[12] green!
An' bleak December's wins ensuin',
   Baith snell[13] and keen!

[1] When Burns first arrived in Edinburgh, the "Lounger," a weekly paper, edited by Henry Mackenzie, Esq., author of the "Man of Feeling," was in course of publication. In that periodical a whole number (the "Lounger for Saturday, December 9, 1786") was devoted to "An account of Robert Burns, the Ayrshire ploughman," in which were given the address "To a Mountain Daisy," and an extract from the "Vision," as specimens of his poetry.
[2] Sleek.—[3] Cowering.—[4] A short race.—[5] Loth.—[6] Plough-staff.—[7] An ear of corn now and then.—[8] A shock of corn.—[9] The rest.—[10] Winds.—[11] To build.—[12] Aftergrass.—[13] Bitter, biting.

Thou saw the fields laid bare an' waste,
And weary winter comin' fast,
An' cozie[1] here, beneath the blast,
    Thou thought to dwell,
Till, crash! the cruel *coulter* pass'd
    Out thro' thy cell.

That wee bit heap o' leaves an' stibble,
Has cost thee monie a weary nibble!
Now thou 's turn'd out, for a' thy trouble,
    But[2] house or hald,[3]
To thole[4] the winter's sleety dribble,
    An' cranreuch[5] cauld!

But, Mousie, thou art no thy lane,[6]
In proving *foresight* may be vain:
The best-laid schemes o' *mice* an' *men*,
    Gang aft a-gley,[7]
And lea'e us naught but grief and pain,
    For promised joy.

Still thou art blest, compared wi' *me!*
The *present* only toucheth thee:
But, och! I backward cast my e'e,
    On prospects drear!
An' forward, tho' I canna *see,*
    I *guess* an' *fear.*[8]

LINES

ON SCARING SOME WATER-FOWL IN LOCH-TURIT,

A wild scene among the hills of Ouchterfyre.

Why, ye tenants of the lake,
For me your watery haunt forsake?
Tell me, fellow-creatures, why
At my presence thus you fly?
Why disturb your social joys,

---

[1] Snugly.—[2] Without.—[3] Hold, home.—[4] To endure.—[5] The hoar frost.—
Not alone.—[7] Off the right time.

[8] "The verses to the Mouse, and Mountain Daisy, were composed on the occasions mentioned, and while the author was holding the plough."—*Gilbert Burns.*

Parent, filial, kindred ties,—
Common friend to you and me,
Nature's gifts to all are free:
Peaceful keep your dimpling wave,
Busy feed, or wanton lave;
Or beneath the shelt'ring rock,
Bide the surging billow's shock.
  Conscious, blushing for our race,
Soon, too soon, your fears I trace:
Man, your proud usurping foe,
Would be lord of all below;
Plumes himself in Freedom's pride,
Tyrant stern to all beside.
  The eagle from the cliffy brow,
Marking you his prey below,
In his breast no pity dwells,
Strong necessity compels:
But Man, to whom alone is given
A ray direct from pitying Heaven,
Glories in his heart humane—
And creatures for his pleasure slain.
  In these savage, liquid plains,
Only known to wandering swains,
Where the mossy rivulet strays,
Far from human haunts and ways;
All on Nature you depend,   •
And life's poor season peaceful spend.
  Or, if man's superior might,
·Dare invade your native right,
On the lofty ether borne,
Man with all his powers you scorn;
Swiftly seek on clanging wings,
Other lakes and other springs;
And the foe you cannot brave,
Scorn at least to be his slave.
14

SONNET.

WRITTEN JANUARY 25, 1793, THE BIRTH-DAY OF THE
AUTHOR,

On hearing a thrush in a morning walk.

SING on, sweet thrush, upon the leafless bough ;
 Sing on, sweet bird, I listen to thy strain;
 See aged Winter, 'mid his surly reign,
At thy blythe carol clears his furrow'd brow .

So in lone Poverty's dominion drear,
 Sits meek Content with light, unanxious heart,
 Welcomes the rapid moments, bids them part,
Nor asks if they bring aught to hope or fear.

I thank thee, Author of this opening day !
 Thou whose bright sun now gilds yon orient skies!
 Riches denied, thy boon was purer joys,
What wealth could never give nor take away !

Yet come, thou child of Poverty and Care ;
The mite high Heaven bestow'd, that mite with thee
  I 'll share.

VERSES

On seeing a wounded hare limp by me, which a fellow had just shot.

INHUMAN man ! curse on thy barbarous art,
 And blasted be thy murder-aiming eye:
 May never Pity soothe thee with a sigh,
Nor ever Pleasure glad thy cruel heart !

Go, live, poor wanderer of the wood and field,
 The bitter little that of life remains :
 No more the thickening brakes and verdant plains
To thee shall home, or food, or pastime yield.

Seek, mangled wretch, some place of wonted rest—
 No more of rest, but now thy dying bed !
 The sheltering rushes whistling o'er thy head,
The cold earth with thy bloody bosom press'd.

Oft as by winding Nith I, musing, wait
The sober eve, or hail the cheerful dawn,
I 'll miss thee sporting o'er the dewy lawn,
And curse the ruffian's aim, and mourn thy help-
less fate.

THE AULD FARMER'S

NEW-YEAR MORNING SALUTATION TO HIS AULD MARE MAGGIE,

On giving her the accustomed ripp of corn to hansel in the New-Year.

A GUID new year, I wish thee, Maggie!
Hae there 's a ripp[1] to thy auld baggie;[2]
Tho' thou 's howe-backit,[3] now, an' knaggie,[4]
        I 've seen the day
Thou could hae gaen like onie staggie[5]
        Out-owre the lay.

Tho' now thou 's dowie,[6] stiff, an' crazy,
An' thy auld hide 's as white 's a daisy,
I 've seen thee dappled, sleek, and glaizie,[7]
        A bonnie gray :
He should been tight that daur't to *raise*[8] thee,
        Ance in a day.

Thou ance was i' the foremost rank,
A *filly*, buirdly,[9] steeve,[10] an' swank,[11]
An' set weel down a shapely shank,
        As e'er tread yird ;[12]
An' could hae flown out-owre a stauk,[13]
        Like onie bird.

It 's now some nine-an'-twenty year,
Sin' thou was my guid-father's *meere ;*
He gied me thee, o' tocher[14] clear,
        An' fifty mark ;
Tho' it was sma', 'twas weel won gear,
        An' thou was stark.[15]

---

[1] A handful of unthreshed corn.—[2] Belly.—[3] Sunk in the back.—[4] Like knaggs, or points of rocks.—[5] Diminutive of stag.—[6] Worn with fatigue.—[7] Smooth like glass.—[8] To inflame, or madden.—[9] Stout made.—[10] Firm, compacted.—[11] Stately.—[12] Earth.—[13] A pool of standing water.—[14] A marriage portion.—[15] Stout.

When first I gaed to woo my Jenny,
Ye then was trottin' wi' your minnie:[1]
Tho' ye was trickie, slee, an' funnie,
          Ye ne'er was donsie;[2]
But hamely, tawie,[3] quiet, an' cannie,
          An' unco sonsie.[4]

That day ye danced wi' muckle pride,
When ye bure hame my bonnie *bride;*
An' sweet an' gracefu' she did ride,
          Wi' maiden air!
Kyle Stewart[5] I could bragged[6] wide,
          For sic a pair.

Tho' now ye dow[7] but hoyte[8] and hobble,
An' wintle like a saumont-cobble,[9]
That day ye was a jinker[10] noble,
          For heels an' win'!
An' ran them till they a' did wauble,[11]
          Far, far behin'.

When thou an' I were young an' skeigh,[12]
An' stable-meals at fairs were dreigh,[13]
How thou wad prance, an' snore, an' skreigh,[14]
          An' tak the road!
Town's bodies[15] ran and stood abeigh,[16]
          And ca't thee mad.

When thou was corn't,[17] an' I was mellow,
We took the road ay like a swallow:
At Brooses[18] thou had ne'er a fellow,
          For pith an' speed;
But ev'ry tail thou paid them hollow,
          Where'er thou gaed.

The sma', droop-rumpl't,[19] hunter-cattle,
Might aiblins[20] waur't[21] thee for a brattle;[22]

[1] Mother, dam.—[2] Unlucky.—[3] Peaceable to be handled.—[4] Good-looking.
—[5] A district in Aberdeenshire.—[6] Challenged.—[7] Can.—[8] Amble crazily.—
[9] Salmon fishing-boat.—[10] That turns quickly.—[11] To reel.—[12] Proud, high-
mettled.—[13] Tedious, long about it.—[14] To scream.—[15] Town people.—[16] At
a shy distance.—[17] Well fed with oats.
[18] A race at country weddings, who shall first reach the bridegroom's house
on returning from church.
[19] That droops at the crupper.—[20] Perhaps.—[21] Worsted.—[22] A short
race.

But sax Scotch miles, thou try't their mettle
  An' gar't them whaizle:[1]
Nae whip nor spur, but just a wattle[2]
  O' saugh[3] or hazle.

Thou was a noble *fittie-lan*',[4]
As e'er in tug or tow[5] was drawn!
Aft thee an' I, in aught[6] hours gaun,[7]
  On guid March weather,
Hae turn'd sax[8] rood beside our han'
  For days thegither.

Thou never braindg't,[9] an' fecht,[10] an' fliskit,[11]
But thy auld tail thou wad hae whiskit,
An' spread abreed thy weel-fill'd brisket,[12]
  Wi' pith and power,
Till spritty knowes[13] wad rair't and risket,[14]
  And slypet[15] owre.

When frosts lay lang an' snaws were deep,
An' threaten'd labor back to keep,
I gied thy cog[16] a wee bit heap
  Aboon the timmer;[17]
I kenn'd my Maggie wad na sleep
  For that, or simmer.[18]

In cart or car thou never reestit;[19]
The steyest brae[20] thou wad hae faced it;
Thou never lap,[21] and stent,[22] and breastit,[23]
  Then stood to blaw;
But just thy step a wee thing hastit,[24]
  Thou snoov't[25] awa.

My *pleugh* is now thy bairn-time a';[26]
Four gallant brutes as e'er did draw:

[1] Made them wheeze.—[2] A twig.—[3] Willow.—[4] The near-horse of the hindmost pair in the plough.—[5] Rope.—[6] Eight.—[7] Going.—[8] Six.—[9] Reeled forward.—[10] Fought.—[11] Fretted.—[12] The breast.—[13] Small hills full of tough-rooted plants or weeds.—[14] Make a noise like the tearing of roots.—[15] Fell. —[16] Wooden dish.—[17] Above the brim.—[18] Summer.—[19] Stood restive.— [20] Steepest hill. —[21] Leaped. —[22] Reared. —[23] Sprung up, or forward.— [24] Hastened. —[25] Went smoothly.—[26] All the team belonging to my plough are of thy brood.

Forbye sax mae I 've sell't awa',[1]
     That thou hast nurst:
They drew me thretteen pund an' twa"[2]
     The vera warst.

Monie a sair darg[3] we twa hae wrought,
An' wi' the weary warl' fought!
An' monie an anxious day I thought
     We wad be beat!
Yet here to crazy age we 're brought
     Wi' something yet.

An' think na', my auld trusty servan',
That now perhaps thou 's less deservin',
An' thy auld days may end in starvin'
     For my last *fou*,[4]
A heapet[5] *stimpart*,[6] I 'll reserve ane,
     Laid by for you.

We 've worn to crazy years thegither;
We 'll toyte[7] about wi' ane anither;
Wi' tentie[8] care I 'll flit thy tether,
     To some hain'd[9] rig,
Where ye may nobly rax[10] your leather,
     Wi' sma' fatigue.

THE DEATH AND DYING WORDS OF POOR MAILIE,

The Author's only pet yowe.

AN UNCO MOURNFU' TALE.

As Mailie, an' her lambs thegither,
Were ae day nibbling on the tether,
Upon her cloot[11] she coost[12] a hitch,
An' owre she warsled[13] in the ditch:
There, groaning, dying, she did lie,
When Hughoc[14] he came doytin'[15] by.

---

[1] Besides six more which I have sold.
[2] Thirteen pounds and two—perhaps fifteen pounds is here meant, as the poet praises the goodness of Maggie's stock,
[3] Day's labor.—[4] My last drinking bout.—[5] Heaped.—[6] The eighth part of a bushel.—[7] Totter.—[8] Cautious. — [9] Spared. — [10] Stretch.—[11] Hoof. — [12] Did cast.—[13] Wrestled, or fell struggling.—[14] A neebor herd callan.—[15] Stupidly

Wi' glowrin' een,[1] an lifted han's,
Poor Hughoc like a statue stan's;
He saw her days were near-hand ended,
But, waes my heart! he could na mend it;
He gapéd wide, but naething spak!
At length poor Mailie silence brak:
"O thou, whase lamentable face
Appears to mourn my wofu' case!
My *dying words* attentive hear,
And bear them to my Master dear.
"Tell him, if e'er again he keep
As muckle gear as buy a sheep,
Oh, bid him never tie them mair
Wi' wicked strings o' hemp or hair!
But ca' them out to park or hill,
An' let them wander at their will;
So may his flock increase, and grow
To scores o' lambs, and packs o' woo'!
"Tell him he was a Master kin',
An' ay was guid to me and mine;
An' now my dying charge I gie him,
My helpless lambs I trust them wi' him.
"Oh, bid him save their harmless lives,
Frae dogs, an' tods,[2] an' butchers' knives!
But gie them good cow-milk their fill,
Till they be fit to fend themsel':
An' tent them duly, e'en and morn,
Wi' teats o' hay an' rips o' corn.
"An' may they never learn the gaets[3]
Of ither vile wanrestfu'[4] *pets;*
To slink thro' slaps,[5] an' reave,[6] an' steal,
At stacks o' pease or stocks o' kail.
So may they, like their great forbears,[7]
For monie a year come thro' the shears:
So wives will gie them bits o' bread,
An' bairns greet[8] for them when they 're dead
"My poor *toop-lamb,*[9] my son an' heir,
Oh, bid him breed him up wi' care!
An' if he live to be a beast,
To pit some havins[10] in his breast!

[1] Staring eyes.—[2] Foxes. — [3] Manners. — [4] Restless.—[5] Gates.—[6] Rove.—
[7] Forefathers.—[8] Weep.—[9] Ram-lamb.—[10] Good-manners.

An' warn him, what I winna name,
To stay content wi' yowes[1] at hame;
An' no to rin an' wear his cloots[2]
Like ither menseless,[3] graceless brutes.
  "An' niest[4] my *yowie*, silly thing,
Gude[5] keep thee frae a tether string!
Oh, may thou ne'er forgather[6] up
Wi' onie blastit,[7] moorland toop;[8]
But ay keep mind to moop[9] an' mell[10]
Wi' sheep o' credit like thysel!
  "And now, my bairns, wi' my last breath,
I lea'e my blessin' wi' you baith;
An' when you think upo' your mither,
Mind to be kin' to ane anither.
  "Now, honest Hughoc, dinna fail
To tell my Master a' my tale;
An' bid him burn this cursèd tether,
An' for thy pains, thou 's get my blether."[11]
  This said, poor Mailie turn'd her head,
An' closed her een[12] amang the dead.

POOR MAILIE'S ELEGY.

LAMENT in rhyme, lament in prose,
Wi' saut[13] tears trickling down your nose;
Our Bardie's fate is at a close,
            Past a' remead;[14]
The last sad cap-stane[15] of his woes;
            Poor Mailie 's dead!

It 's no the loss o' warl's gear,
That could sae bitter draw the tear,
Or mak our Bardie, dowie,[16] wear
            The mourning weed:
He 's lost a friend and neebor dear,
            In Mailie dead.

Thro' a' the town she trotted by him;
A lang half mile she could descry him;

[1] Ewes.—[2] Hoofs.—[3] Ill-bred.—[4] Next.—[5] God.—[6] To meet.—[7] Blasted.—[8] Ram.—[9] To nibble as a sheep.—[10] Meddle.—[11] Bladder.—[12] Eyes—[13] Salt. [14] Remedy.—[15] Cope-stone, or top-stone.—[16] Worn with grief.

Wi' kindly bleat, when she did spy him,
    She ran wi' speed:
A friend mair faithfu' ne'er cam nigh him,
    Than Mailie dead.

I wat she was a sheep o' sense,
An' could behave herself wi' mense :[1]
I 'll say 't, she never brak a fence
    Thro' thievish greed;[2]
Our Bardie, lanely, keeps the spence[3]
    Sin' Mailie 's dead.

Or, if he wanders up the howe,[4]
Her living image in her *yowe*
Comes bleating to him, o'er the knowe,
    For bits o' bread ;
An' down the briny pearls rowe[5]
    For Mailie dead.

She was nae get o' moorland tips,[6]
Wi' tauted ket[7] an' hairy hips;
For her forbears[8] were brought in ships
    Frae 'yont the Tweed ;
A bonnier *fleesh*[9] ne'er cross'd the clips
    Than Mailie dead.

Wae worth the man wha first did shape
That vile wanchancie[10] thing—*a rape!*[11]
It maks guid fellows girn[12] an' gape,
    Wi' chokin' dread ;
An' Robin's bonnet wave wi' crape,
    For Mailie dead.

Oh, a' ye bards on bonnie Doon!
An' wha on Ayr your chanters tune!
Come, join the melancholious croon[13]
    O' Robin's reed!
His heart will never get aboon
    His Mailie dead!

[1] Decency.—[2] Greediness.—[3] The country parlor.—[4] A hollow, or dell.—[5] Roll.—[6] Ram.—[7] Matted fleece.—[8] Progenitors.—[9] Fleece.—[10] Unlucky.—[11] Rope.—[12] To twist the features in agony.—[13] A hollow moan.

THE HUMBLE PETITION OF BRUAR WATER.[1]

To the noble Duke of Athole.

My Lord, I know your noble ear
　Woe ne'er assails in vain;
Embolden'd thus, I beg you 'll hear
　Your humble slave complain,
How saucy Phœbus' scorching beams,
　In flaming summer-pride,
Dry-withering, waste my foamy streams,
　And drink my crystal tide.

The lightly-jumping glowrin'[2] trouts,
　That thro' my waters play,
If, in their random, wanton spouts,
　They near the margin stray;
If, hapless chance! they linger lang,
　I 'm scorching up so shallow,
They 're left the whit'ning stanes amang,
　In grasping death to wallow.

Last day I grat[3] wi' spite and teen,[4]
　As Poet *Burns* came by,
That, to a Bard, I should be seen
　Wi' half my channel dry:
A panegyric rhyme, I ween,
　E'en as I was he shor'd[5] me;
But had I in my glory been,
　He, kneeling, wad adored me.

Here, foaming down the shelvy rocks,
　In twisting strength I rin;
There, high my boiling torrent smokes,
　Wild-roaring o'er a linn;[6]
Enjoying large each spring and well,
　As Nature gave them me,
I am, altho' I say 't mysel,
　Worth gaun[7] a mile to see.

---

[1] Bruar Falls, in Athole, are exceedingly picturesque and beautiful; but the effect is much impaired by the want of trees and shrubs.
[2] Staring.—[3] Wept.—[4] Grief, sorrow.—[5] Offered.—[6] A precipice, or water-fall.—[7] Going.

Would then my noble master please
 To grant my highest wishes,
He 'll shade my banks wi' tow'ring trees,
 And bonnie spreading bushes;
Delighted doubly then, my Lord,
 You 'll wander on my banks,
And listen monie a grateful bird
 Return you tuneful thanks.

The sober lav'rock[1] warbling wild,
 Shall to the skies aspire;
The gowdspink,[2] music's gayest child,
 Shall sweetly join the choir:
The blackbird strong, the lintwhite[3] clear,
 The mavis[4] mild and mellow;
The robin pensive autumn cheer,
 In all her locks of yellow:

This, too, a covert shall insure,
 To shield them from the storm;
And coward maukin[5] sleep secure,
 Low in her grassy form:
Here shall the shepherd make his seat,
 To weave his crown of flowers;
Or find a shelt'ring, safe retreat,
 From prone descending showers.

And here, by sweet, endearing stealth,
 Shall meet the loving pair,
Despising worlds with all their wealth,
 As empty, idle care.
The flowers shall vie in all their charms,
 The hour of heaven to grace,
And birks[6] extend their fragrant arms,
 To screen the dear embrace.

Here haply too, at vernal dawn,
 Some musing Bard may stray,
And eye the smoking dewy lawn,
 And misty mountain, gray;
Or, by the reaper's nightly beam,
 Mild-check'ring thro' the trees,

[1] Lark.—[2] Goldfinch.—[3] Linnet.—[4] Thrush.—[5] The hare.—[6] Birch-trees.

Rave to my darkly dashing stream,
Hoarse-swelling on the breeze.

Let lofty firs and ashes cool
  My lowly banks o'erspread,
And view, deep-bending in the pool,
  Their shadows' wat'ry bed :
Let fragrant birks,[1] in woodbines drest,
  My craggy cliffs adorn ;
And for the little songster's nest,
  The close embow'ring thorn.

So may old Scotia's darling hope,
  Your little angel band,
Spring, like their fathers, up to prop
  Their honor'd native land !
So may, thro' Albion's farthest ken,
  To social-flowing glasses,
The grace be—" Athole's honest men,
  And Athole's bonnie lasses !"

THE BRIGS[2] OF AYR.

Inscribed to J. Ballantyne, Esq., Ayr.

THE simple Bard, rough at the rustic plough,
Learning his tuneful trade from ev'ry bough;
The chanting linnet, or the mellow thrush,
Hailing the setting sun, sweet, in the green thorn-bush ;
The soaring lark, the perching red-breast shrill,
Or deep-toned plovers, gray, wild whistling o'er the hill'
Shall he, nursed in the peasant's lowly shed,
To hardy Independence bravely bred,
By early Poverty to hardship steel'd,
And train'd to arms in stern Misfortune's field ;
Shall he be guilty of their hireling crimes,
The servile, mercenary Swiss of rhymes?
Or labor hard the panegyric close,
With all the venal soul of dedicating Prose?
No ! though his artless strains he rudely sings,
And throws his hand uncouthly o'er the strings,

---

[1] Birch-trees.—[2] Bridges.

He glows with all the spirit of the Bard—
Fame, honest fame, his great, his dear reward!
Still, if some patron's generous care he trace,
Skill'd, in the secret, to bestow with grace;
When Ballantyne[1] befriends his humble name,
And hands the rustic stranger up to fame,
With heart-felt throes his grateful bosom swells,
The god-like bliss, to give, alone excels.

* * * * * *

'Twas when the stacks get on their winter-hap,[1]
And thack and rape[2] secure the toil-won crap;
Potatoe-bings are snugged up frae skaith[4]
Of coming Winter's biting, frosty breath;
The bees, rejoicing o'er their summer toils,
Unnumber'd buds, an' flowers' delicious spoils,
Seal'd up with frugal care in massive waxen piles,
Are doom'd by man, that tyrant o'er the weak,
The death o' devils—smoor'd[5] wi' brimstone reck;[6]
The thundering guns are heard on ev'ry side,
The wounded coveys, reeling, scatter wide;
The feather'd field-mates, bound by Nature's tie,
Sires, mothers, children, in one carnage lie:
(What warm poetic heart, but inly bleeds,
And execrates man's savage, ruthless deeds!)
Nae mair the flower in field or meadow springs;
Nae mair the grove with airy concert rings,
Except perhaps the robin's whistling glee,
Proud o' the height o' some bit half-lang tree:
The hoary morns precede the sunny days,
Mild, calm, serene, wide spreads the noon-tide blaze,
While thick the gossamer waves wanton in the rays.
'Twas in that season, when a simple Bard,
Unknown and poor, simplicity's reward;
Ae night within the ancient burgh of Ayr,
By whim inspired, or haply press'd wi' care;
He left his bed, and took his wayward rout,
And down by Simpson's[7] wheel'd the left about:
(Whether impell'd by all-directing Fate,
To witness what I after shall narrate;

* John Ballantyne, Esq., Banker, Ayr, one of our poet's earliest patrons.—
[2] Covering. — [3] Thatch secured with ropes of straw, &c. — [4] Damage.—
[5] Smothered.—[6] Smoke.—[7] A noted tavern at the Auld Brig end.
15

Or whether, rapt in meditation high,
He wander'd out, he knew not where nor why:)
The drowsy Dungeon-clock had numbered two,
And Wallace Tower[1] had sworn the fact was true;
The tide-swoln Firth, with sullen-sounding roar,
Through the still night dash'd hoarse along the
    shore;
All else was hush'd as Nature's closed e'e;
The silent moon shone high o'er tower and tree:
The chilly frost, beneath the silver beam,
Crept, gently-crusting, o'er the glittering stream.
   When, lo! on either hand the list'ning Bard,
The clanging sugh[2] of whistling wings he heard;
Two dusky forms dart thro' the midnight air,
Swift as the Gos[3] drives on the wheeling hare;
Ane on th' *Auld Brig* his hairy shape uprears,
The ither flutters o'er the *rising piers;*
Our warlock[4] Rhymer instantly descried
The Spirits that owre the *Brigs of Ayr* preside.
(That bards are second-sighted is nae joke,
And ken the lingo o' the sp'ritual folk;
Fays, spunkies, kelpies, a', they can explain them,
And even the vera deils they brawly ken them.)
Auld Brig appear'd of ancient Pictish race,
The vera wrinkles Gothic in his face:
He seem'd as he wi' Time had warstled[5] lang,
Yet teughly doure,[6] he bade[7] an unco bang.[8]
New Brig was buskit[9] in a braw new coat,
That he, at Lon'on, frae ane Adams, got;
In 's hand five taper staves as smooth 's a bead,
Wi' virls[10] and whirlygigums[11] at the head.
The Goth was stalking round with anxious search
Spying the time-worn flaws in every arch;
It chanced his new-come neebor took his e'e,
And e'en a vex'd and angry heart had he!
Wi' thieveless[12] sneer to see his modish mien,
He, down the water, gies him this guid-e'en:[13]

<hr>

[1] Dungeon-clock and Wallace Tower, the two steeples.—[2] The continued rushing noise of wind.—[3] The gos-hawk, or falcon.—[4] Wizard.—[5] Wrestled. —[6] Toughly durable.—[7] Did bide, sustain, or endure.—[8] Sustained the repeated shocks of the floods and currents.—[9] Dressed.—[10] A ring which surrounds a column, &c.—[11] Useless ornaments.—[12] Cold, dry—spoken of a person's demeanor.—[13] Salutation, or good evening.

AULD BRIG.

I doubt na', frien', ye 'll think ye 're nae sheep-
    shank,[1]
Ance ye were streekit[2] o'er frae bank to bank!
But gin ye be a brig as auld as me,
Tho' faith that day, I doubt, ye 'll never see;
There 'll be, if that date come, I 'll wad a bodle,[3]
Some fewer whigmeleeries[4] in your noddle.

NEW BRIG.

Auld Vandal, ye but show your little mense,[5]
Just much about it wi' your scanty sense;
Will your poor, narrow foot-path of a street,
Where twa wheel-barrows tremble when they meet:
Your ruin'd, formless bulk o' stane an' lime,
Compare wi' bonnie brigs o' modern time?
There 's men o' taste would take the Duckat st:eam,[6]
Tho' they should cast the very sark[7] and swim,
Ere they would grate their feelings wi' the view
Of sic an ugly Gothic hulk as you.

AULD BRIG.

Conceited gowk![8] puff'd up wi' windy pride!
This monie a year I 've stood the flood an' tide;
And tho' wi' crazy eild[9] I 'm sair forfairn,[10]
I 'll be a brig when ye 're a shapeless cairn;[11]
As yet ye little ken about the matter,
But twa-three winters will inform ye better.
When heavy, dark, continued, a'-day rains,
Wi' deepening deluges o'erflow the plains;
When from the hills where springs the brawling
    Coil,
Or stately Lugar's mossy fountains boil,
Or where the Greenock winds his moorland course,
Or haunted Garpal[12] draws his feeble source,

---

[1] No mean personage.—[2] Stretched.—[3] Bet a bodle; i. e. a small coin.—
[4] Whims, fancies.—[5] Good-breeding.—[6] A noted ford just above Auld Brig.
—[7] Shirt.—[8] Cuckoo; applied as a term of contempt.—[9] Old age.—[10] Worn
out.—[11] A loose heap of stones.
[12] The banks of Garpal Water is one of the few places in the west of Scot-
land, where those fancy-scaring beings, known by the name of *Ghaists*, still
continue pertinaciously to inhabit.

Aroused by blustering winds an' spotting thowes,[1]
In monie a torrent down his snaw-broo rowes;[2]
While crashing ice, borne on the roaring speat,[3]
Sweeps dams, an' mills, an' brigs, a' to the gate;
And from Glenbuck,[4] down to the Ratton-key,[5]
Auld Ayr is just one lengthen'd, tumbling sea;
Then down ye 'll hurl—deil nor ye never rise;
And dash the gumlie jaups[6] up to the pouring skies:
A lesson sadly teaching, to your cost,
That architecture's noble art is lost.

NEW BRIG.

Fine architecture! trowth, I needs must say 't o 't,
The L—d be thankit that we 've tint the gate[7] o 't!
Gaunt, ghastly, ghaist-alluring edifices,
Hanging with threatening jut, like precipices;
O'er-arching, mouldy, gloom-inspiring coves,
Supporting roofs fantastic, stony groves;
Windows and doors in nameless sculpture drest,
With order, symmetry, or taste unblest;
Forms like some bedlam statuary's dream,
The crazed creations of misguided whim;
Forms might be worshipp'd on the bended knee,
And still the *second* dread *command* be free,
Their likeness is not found on earth, in air, or sea.
Mansions that would disgrace the building taste
Of any mason, reptile, bird, or beast;
Fit only for a doited[8] monkish race,
Or frosty maids, forsworn the dear embrace;
Or cuifs[9] of latter times, wha held the notion
That sullen gloom was sterling true devotion;
Fancies that our guid Burgh[10] denies protection,
And soon may they expire, unbless'd with resurrection

AULD BRIG.

O ye, my dear-remember'd ancient yealings,[11]
Were ye but here to share my wounded feelings!
Ye worthy Proveses, an' monie a Bailie,
Wha in the paths of righteousness did toil ay;

---

[1] Thaws.—[2] Snow-water rolls.—[3] A sweeping torrent after a thaw.—[4] The source of the river Ayr.—[5] A small landing-place above the large quay.—[6] The muddy jerks of agitated water.—[7] Lost the way of it.—[8] Stupefied.—[9] Blockheads.—[10] Borough.—[11] Coevals.

Ye dainty Deacons, and ye douce[1] Conveeners,
To whom our moderns are but causey-cleaners;
Ye godly Councils wha hae bless'd this town,
Ye godly Brethren of the sacred gown,
Wha meekly gae your hurdies[2] to the smiters;
And (what would now be strange) ye godly Writers:
A' ye douce folk I 've borne aboon the broo,
Were ye but here, what would you say or do?
How would your spirits groan in deep vexation,
To see such melancholy alteration;
And, agonizing, curse the time and place,
When ye begat the base, degenerate race?
Nae langer reverend men, their country's glory,
In plain braid[3] Scots hold forth a plain braid story!
Nae langer thrifty citizens an' douce,[4]
Meet owre a pint, or in the council-house;
But staumrel,[5] corky-headed, graceless gentry,
The herryment[6] and ruin of the country;
Men, three-parts made by tailors and by barbers,
Wha waste your weel-hain'd gear[7] on d—d new *brigs*
    and *harbors!*

NEW BRIG.

Now haud[8] you there! for faith ye 've said enough,
And muckle[9] mair than ye can make to through.[10]
As for your priesthood, I shall say but little,
Corbies[11] and *clergy* are a shot right kittle:[12]
But under favor o' your langer beard,
Abuse o' magistrates might weel be spared:
To liken them to your auld-warld squad,
I must needs say comparisons are odd.
In Ayr, wag-wits nae mair can hae[13] a handle
To mouth a " citizen," a term o' scandal;
Nae mair the council waddles down the street,
In all the pomp of ignorant conceit;
Men wha grew wise priggin'[14] owre hops an' raisins,
Or gather'd liberal views in bonds and seisins.
If haply Knowledge, on a random tramp,
Had shor'd[15] them with a glimmer of his lamp,

[1] Wise.—[2] The loins.—[3] Broad.—[4] Wise, prudent.—[5] Half-witted.—[6] Plunderers.—[7] Well-saved money.—[8] Hold.—[9] Much.—[10] Make out, or prove.—[1] A species of crows.—[12] Ticklish, difficult to come at.—[13] To have.—[14] Cheapening.—[15] Offered.

And would to Common-sense, for once betray'd them,
Plain, dull Stupidity stept kindly in to aid them.

  * * * * * *

 What farther clishmaclaver[1] might been said,
What bloody wars, if sprites had blood to shed,
No man can tell; but all before their sight,
A fairy train appear'd in order bright:
Adown the glitt'ring stream they featly danced,
Bright to the moon their various dresses glanced;
They footed o'er the wat'ry glass so neat,
The infant ice scarce bent beneath their feet;
While arts of minstrelsy among them rung,
And soul-ennobling bards heroic ditties sung.
O had M'Lauchlan,[2] thairm[3]-inspiring sage,
Been there to hear this heavenly band engage,
When through his dear *strathspeys* they bore with
   Highland rage;
Or when they struck old Scotia's melting airs,
The lover's raptured joys or bleeding cares;
How would his Highland lug[4] been nobler fired,
And e'en his matchless hand with finer touch inspired!
No guess could tell what instrument appear'd,
But all the soul of Music's self was heard;
Harmonious concert rung in every part,
While simple melody pour'd moving on the heart.
 The Genius of the stream in front appears,
A venerable chief advanced in years;
His hoary head with water-lilies crown'd,
His manly leg with garter-tangle[5] bound;
Next came the loveliest pair in all the ring,
Sweet Female Beauty hand in hand with Spring;
Then, crown'd with flowery hay, came Rural Joy,
And Summer, with his fervid-beaming eye;
All-cheering Plenty, with her flowing horn,
Led yellow Autumn, wreathed with nodding corn;
Then Winter's time-bleach'd locks did hoary show,
By Hospitality, with cloudless brow.
Next follow'd Courage with his martial stride,
From where the Feal[6] wild-woody coverts hide;
Benevolence, with mild, benignant air,

[1] Idle tale.—[2] A well-known performer of Scottish music on the violin.—
Fiddle-string.—[4] Ear.—[5] Sea-weed.—[6] Field, meadow.

A female form,[1] came from the towers of Stair;
Learning and Worth in equal measures trode
From simple Catrine,[2] their long-loved abode;
Last, white-robed Peace, crown'd with a hazel wreath,
To rustic Agriculture did bequeath
The broken iron instruments of Death;
At sight of whom our Sprites forgot their kindling
    wrath.

LINES

Written with a pencil, standing by the Fall of Fyers, near Loch-Ness.

Among the heathy hills and ragged woods
The roaring Fyers pours his mossy floods;
Till full he dashes on the rocky mounds,
Where, thro' a shapeless breach, his stream resounds.
As high in air the bursting torrents flow,
As deep recoiling surges foam below.
Prone down the rock the whitening sheet descends,
And viewless Echo's ear, astonish'd, rends.
Dim seen thro' rising mists and ceaseless showers,
The hoary cavern, wide-surrounding, lowers.
Still thro' the gap the struggling river toils,
An' still, below, the horrid cauldron boils—

     *   *   *   *   *   *

LINES

Written with a pencil, over the chimney-piece, in the parlor of an inn
at Kenmore, Taymouth.

Admiring Nature in her wildest grace,
These northern scenes with weary feet I trace;
O'er many a winding dale and painful steep,
The abodes of covey'd grouse and timid sheep,
My savage journey, curious, I pursue,
Till famed Breadalbane opens to my view.
The meeting cliffs each deep-sunk glen divides,
The woods, wild-scatter'd, clothe their ample sides;
Th' outstretching lake, embosom'd 'mong the hills,

---

1 Mrs. Stewart.—2 See note 1, p. 134.

The eye with wonder and amazement fills;
The Tay meand'ring sweet in infant pride,
The palace rising on his verdant side;
The lawns wood-fringed in Nature's native taste;
The hillocks dropt in Nature's careless haste;
The arches striding o'er the new-born stream;
The village glittering in the noon-tide beam—
   *   *   *   *   *
Poetic ardors in my bosom swell,
Lone, wandering by the hermit's mossy cell:
The sweeping theatre of hanging woods;
Th' incessant roar of headlong tumbling floods—
   *   *   *   *   *
Here Poesy might wake her heaven-taught lyre,
And look through Nature with creative fire;
Here, to the wrongs of Fate half reconciled,
Misfortune's lighten'd steps might wander wild;
And Disappointment, in these lonely bounds,
Find balm to sooth her bitter, rankling wounds.
Here heart-struck Grief might heavenward stretch
     her scan,
And injured Worth forget and pardon man.[1]
   *   *   *   *   *

INSCRIPTION FOR AN ALTAR TO INDEPENDENCE,

At Kerroughtry, the seat of Mr. Heron, author of a Life of the poet, History of Scotland, &c., &c.; written in the summer, 1795.

Thou of an independent mind,
With soul resolved, with soul resign'd;
Prepared power's proudest frown to brave,
Who wilt not be, nor have a slave;
Virtue alone who dost revere,
Thy own reproach alone dost fear,—
Approach this shrine, and worship here.

[1] These two Fragments were composed in the autumn of 1787, when the poet was on a tour to the Highlands with Mr. W. Nicol, of the High School, Edinburgh.

ON PASTORAL POETRY.

HAIL, Poesie! thou nymph reserved!
In chase o' thee what crowds hae swerved
Frae common sense, or sunk enerved
    'Mang heaps o' clavers;[1]
And och! o'er aft' thy joes[3] hae starved,
    'Mid a' thy favors!

Say, lassie, why thy train amang,
While loud the trump's heroic clang,
And sock or buskin, skelp[4] alang
    To death or marriage,
Scarce ane has tried the shepherd-sang,
    But wi' miscarriage?

In Homer's craft Jock Milton thrives;
Eschylus' pen Will Shakspeare drives;
Wee[5] Pope, the knurlin,[6] till' him 'rives
    Horatian fame;[8]
In thy sweet sang, Barbauld, survives
    Even Sappho's flame.

But thee, Theocritus! wha matches?
They're no herd's ballats, Maro's catches:
Squire Pope but busks[9] his skinklin[10] patches
    O' heathen tatters:
I pass by hunders,[11] nameless wretches,
    That ape their betters.

In this braw age o' wit and lear,[12]
Will nane the shepherd's whistle mair
Blaw sweetly in its native air
    And rural grace;
And wi' the far-famed Grecian, share
    A rival place?

Yes, there is ane—a Scottish callan![13]
There's ane—come forrit,[14] honest *Allan!*[15]

[1] Idle stories.—[2] Over often.—[3] Thy lovers.—[4] Trip.—[5] Little.—[6] Dwarf.—[7] To.—[8] 'Rives Horatian fame; i. e. divides, or shares fame with Horace.—[9] Dresses.—[10] A small portion.—[11] Hundreds.—[12] Learning.—[13] Boy.—[14] Forward.—[15] Allan Ramsay.

Thou need na jouk[1] beyond the hallan,[2]
    A chiel sae clever;
The teeth o' time may gnaw *Tamtallan*,[3]
    But thou 's forever!

Thou paints auld Nature to the nines,
In thy sweet *Caledonian* lines:
Nae gowden[5] stream thro' myrtles twines,
    Where Philomel,
While nightly breezes sweep the vines,
    Her griefs will tell!

In gowany glens[6] thy burnie' strays,
Where bonnie lasses bleach their claes;[8]
Or trots by hazelly shaws and braes,
    Wi' hawthorns gray,
Where blackbirds join the shepherd's lays
    At close o' day.

Thy rural loves are Nature's sel';[9]
Nae bombast spates[10] o' nousense swell;
Nae snap[11] conceits, but that sweet spell
    O' witchin' love,
That charm, that can the strongest quell,
    The sternest move.

ON THE LATE CAPTAIN GROSE'S PEREGRINATIONS THROUGH SCOTLAND,

COLLECTING THE ANTIQUITIES OF THAT KINGDOM.

HEAR, Land o' Cakes, and brither Scots,
Frae Maidenkirk to Johnie Groat's;
If there 's a hole in a' your coats,
    I rede you tent it:[12]
A chield 's amang you takin' notes,
    And, faith, he 'll prent it.

If in your bounds ye chance to light
Upon a fine, fat, fodgel[13] wight,

[1] To hang the head.—[2] A party-wall in a cottage.—[3] The name of a mountain. — [4] Exactly, to a nicety.—[5] Golden. — [6] Daisied dales.—[7] Rivulet.—[8] Clothes.—[9] Self.—[10] Torrents.—[11] Short.—[12] I advise you to be cautious.—[13] Pursy, bloated.

O' stature short, but genius bright,
    That 's he, mark weel—
And wow !¹ he has an unco slight²
    O' cauk and keel.³

By some auld houlet⁴-haunted biggin',⁵
Or kirk deserted by its riggen,
It 's ten to ane ye 'll find him snug in
    Some eldritch⁶ part,
Wi' deils they say, L—d safe 's ! colleaguin'
    At some black art.—

Ilk ghaist⁷ that haunts auld ha' or cham'er,⁸
Ye gipsey gang that deal in glamor,⁹
And you deep-read in hell's black grammar,
    Warlocks¹⁰ an' witches;
Ye 'll quake at his conjuring hammer,
    Ye midnight b—es !

It 's tauld he was a sodger¹¹ bred,
And ane wad rather fa'n than fled;
But now he 's quat¹² the spurtle blade,¹³
    And dog-skin wallet,
And taen the—*Antiquarian trade*,
    I think they call it.

He has a fouth¹⁴ o' auld nick-nackets:
Rusty airn caps¹⁵ and jingling jackets,¹⁶
Wad haud the Lothians three in tackets,¹⁷
    A towmont guid;¹⁸
An' parritch-pats,¹⁹ and auld saut-backets,
    Before the flood.

Of Eve's first fire he has a cinder;
And Tubal-Cain's fire-shool and fender;
That which distinguished the gender
    O' Balaam's ass;

¹ An exclamation of pleasure, or wonder.—² Great sleight, or dexterity.—
³ Chalk and red clay.—⁴ An owl.—⁵ Building. See his Antiquities of Scotland.—⁶ Frightful, ghastly.—⁷ Each ghost.—⁸ Old hall, or chamber.—⁹ Fortune-telling, pretending to a knowledge of future events by magic, &c.—
¹⁰ Wizards.—¹¹ Soldier.—¹² Did quit.—¹³ A sort of nickname for a sword.
—¹⁴ A plenty.—¹⁵ Iron helmets.—¹⁶ Coats of mail, &c. See his Treatise on Ancient Armor.—¹⁷ Small nails.—¹⁸ Would furnish tacks enough to supply the three counties of Lothian for a twelvemonth.—¹⁹ Porridge-pots.

A broom-stick o' the Witch of Endor,
    Weel shod wi' brass.

Forbye,[1] he 'll shape you aff, fu' gleg,[2]
The cut of Adam's philibeg;[3]
The knife that nicket Abel's craig,[4]
    He 'll prove you fully
It was a faulding jocteleg,[5]
    Or long-kail gullie.[6]

But wad ye see him in his glee,
(For meikle glee and fun has he,)
Then set him down, and twa or three
    Guid fellows wi' him;
And *port, O port!* shine thou a wee,
    And then ye 'll see him!

Now, by the powers o' verse and prose!
Thou art a dainty chield,[7] O Grose!
Whae'er o' thee shall ill suppose,
    They sair misca' thee;
I 'd take the rascal by the nose,
    Wad say, Shame fa' thee!

VERSES WRITTEN AT SELKIRK.[8]

Auld chuckie Reekie[9]'s sair distrest,
Down droops her ance weel burnisht crest,
Nae joy her bonnie buskit[10] nest
    Can yield ava,[11]
Her darling bird that she lo'es best,
    Willie 's awa!

O Willie was a witty wight,[12]
And had o' things an unco[13] slight;
Auld Reekie ay he keepit tight,
    And trig an' braw:[14]

[1] Besides.—[2] Quite readily.—[3] The short petticoat, part of the Highland dress.—[4] Throat.—[5] A folding or clasp knife.—[6] A large knife used for cutting kail.—[7] Fellow.

[8] To William Creech, Esq., Edin! urgh, author of "Fugitive Pieces," &c., and the Poet's worthy publisher.

[9] Edinburgh.—[10] Dressed.—[11] At all.—[12] A superior genius.—[13] Very great.—[14] Spruce and fine.

But now they 'll busk[1] her like a fright,
    Willie 's awa!

The stiffest o' them a' he bow'd,
The bauldest o' them a' he cow'd ;[2]
They durst nae mair than he allow'd,
    That was a law:
We 've lost a birkie[3] weel worth gowd,
    Willie 's awa!

Now gawkies, tawpies, gowks and fools,[4]
Frae colleges, and boarding-schools,
May sprout like simmer puddock-stools,[5]
    In glen or shaw ;[6]
He who could brush them down to mools,[7]
    Willie 's awa!

The brethren o' the Commerce-chaumer[8]
May mourn their loss wi' doolfu' clamor;
He was a dictionar and grammar
    Amang them a';
I fear they 'll now mak mony a stammer,
    Willie 's awa!

Nae mair we see his levee door
Philosophers and poets pour,[9]
And toothy critics by the core,
    In bloody raw!
The adjutant o' a' the score,
    Willie 's awa!

Now worthy Gregory's Latin face,
Tytler's and Greenfield's modest grace;
M'Kenzie, Stuart, such a brace
    As Rome ne'er saw;
They a' maun[10] meet some ither place,
    Willie 's awa!

Poor Burns—e'en Scotch drink canna quicken,
He cheeps[11] like some bewilder'd chicken,

: Dress.—[2] Frightened.—[3] Clever fellow.—[4] Foolish, thoughtless young persons.—[5] Mushrooms.—[6] A small wood in a hollow.—[7] Dust.
  [8] The Chamber of Commerce of Edinburgh, of which Mr. C. was secretary.
  [9] Many literary gentlemen were accustomed to meet at Mr. C.'s house at breakfast.
[10] Must.—[11] Chirps.

Scared frae its minnie[1] and the clecken[2]
      By hoodie-craw;[3]
Grief's gien[4] his heart an unco kickin',
      Willie's awa!

Now every sour-mou'd, girnin'[5] blellum,[6]
And Calvin's fock[7] are fit to fell him;
And self-conceited critic skellum[8]
      His quill may draw;
He wha could brawlie[9] ward their bellum,[10]
      Willie's awa!

Up wimpling,[11] stately Tweed I've sped,
And Eden scenes on crystal Jed,
And Ettrick banks now roaring red,
      While tempests blaw;
But every joy and pleasure's fled,
      Willie's awa!

May I be slander's common speech;
A text for infamy to preach;
And, lastly, streekit[12] out to bleach
      In winter snaw;
When I forget thee! Willie Creech,
      Tho' far awa!

May never wicked fortune touzle him!
May never wicked men bamboozle him!
Until a pow[13] as auld[14]'s Methusalem!
      He canty claw![15]
Then to the blessèd, new Jerusalem,
      Fleet wing awa!

LIBERTY.—A FRAGMENT.

Thee, Caledonia, thy wild heaths among—
Thee famed for martial deed and sacred song—
   To thee I turn with swimming eyes;
   Where is that soul of freedom fled?

Immingled with the mighty dead!
  Beneath that hallow'd turf where Wallace lies!
Hear it not, Wallace, in thy bed of death!
  Ye babbling winds, in silence sweep;
  Disturb not ye the hero's sleep,
Nor give the coward secret breath.—
  Is this the power in freedom's war
  That wont to bid the battle rage?
Behold that eye which shot immortal hate,
  Crushing the despot's proudest bearing,
That arm which, nerved with thundering fate,
  Braved usurpation's boldest daring!
One quenched in darkness like the sinking star,
And one the palsied arm of tottering, powerless age.

THE VOWELS.—A TALE.

'Twas where the birch and sounding thong are plied,
The noisy domicile of pedant pride;
Where Ignorance her darkening vapor throws,
And cruelty directs the thickening blows;
Upon a time, Sir Abece the great,
In all his pedagogic powers elate,
His awful chair of state resolves to mount,
And call the trembling vowels to account.
  First enter'd A, a grave, broad, solemn wight,
But, ah! deform'd, dishonest to the sight!
His twisted head look'd backward on his way,
And flagrant from the scourge, he grunted, *ai!*
  Reluctant, E stalk'd in; with piteous grace
The justling tears ran down his honest face!
That name, that well-worn name, and all his own.
Pale he surrenders at the tyrant's throne!
The pedant stifles keen the Roman sound
Not all his mongrel diphthongs can compound;
And next the title following close behind,
He to the nameless, ghastly wretch assign'd.
  The cobweb'd gothic dome resounded Y!
In sullen vengeance, I, disdain'd reply:
The pedant swung his felon cudgel round,
And knock'd the groaning vowel to the ground!

In rueful apprehension enter'd O,
The wailing minstrel of despairing woe;
Th' Inquisitor of Spain the most expert,
Might there have learnt new mysteries of his art:
So grim, deform'd, with horrors entering U,
His dearest friend and brother scarcely knew!
  As trembling U stood staring all aghast,
The pedant in his left hand clutch'd him fast,
In helpless infants' tears he dipp'd his right,
Baptized him *eu*, and kick'd him from his sight.

FRAGMENT,

Inscribed to the Right Hon. C. J. Fox.

How wisdom and folly meet, mix, and unite;
How virtue and vice blend their black and their white:
How genius, the illustrious father of fiction,
Confounds rule and law, reconciles contradiction—
I sing: If these mortals, the critics, should bustle,
I care not, not I, let the critics go whistle.
  But now for a patron, whose name and whose glory
At once may illustrate and honor my story.
  Thou first of our orators, first of our wits;
Yet whose parts and acquirements seem mere lucky hits;
With knowledge so vast, and with judgment so strong,
No man with the half of 'em e'er went far wrong;
With passions so potent, and fancies so bright,
No man with the half of 'em e'er went quite right;
A sorry, poor misbegot son of the Muses,
For using thy name offers fifty excuses.
  Good L—d, what is man! for as simple he looks,
Do but try to develop his hooks and his crooks;
With his depths and his shallows, his good and his evil,
All in all he 's a problem must puzzle the devil.
  On his one ruling passion Sir Pope hugely labors,
That, like th' old Hebrew walking-switch, eats up its
    neighbors:
Mankind are his show-box—a friend, would you know
    him?
Pull the string, ruling passion, the picture will show him.
What pity, in rearing so beauteous a system,

One trifling particular, truth, should have miss'd him;
For, spite of his fine, theoretic positions,
Mankind is a science defies definitions.
Some sort all our qualities each to its tribe,
And think human nature they truly describe;
Have you found this, or t'other? there's more in the
 wind,
As by one drunken fellow his comrades you'll find.
But such is the flaw, or the depth of the plan,
In the make of that wonderful creature call'd Man,
No two virtues, whatever relation they claim,
Nor even two different shades of the same,
Though, like as was ever twin brother to brother,
Possessing the one shall imply you've the other.

SKETCH.[1]

A LITTLE, upright, pert, tart, tripping wight,
And still his precious self his dear delight;
Who loves his own smart shadow in the streets,
Better than e'er the fairest she he meets:
A man of fashion too, he made his tour,
Learn'd *vive la bagatelle, et vive l'amour;*
So travell'd monkeys their grimace improve,
Polish they grin, nay, sigh for ladies' love.
Much specious lore but little understood;
Veneering oft outshines the solid wood;
His solid sense—by inches you must tell,
But mete his cunning by the old Scots ell;
His meddling vanity, a busy fiend,
Still making work his selfish craft must mend.

----

[1] This sketch seems to be one of a series, intended for a projected work, under the title of "The Poet's Progress." This character was sent as a specimen, accompanied by a letter, to Professor Dugald Stewart, in which it is thus noticed: "The fragment beginning 'A little, upright, pert, tart,' &c., I have not shown to any man living, till I now show it to you. It forms the postulata, the axioms, the definition of a character, which, if it appear at all, shall be placed in a variety of lights. This particular part I send you merely, as a sample of my hand at portrait sketching."

SCOTS PROLOGUE.

For Mr. Sutherland's Benefit Night, Dumfries.

WHAT needs this din about the town o' Lon'on,
How this new play an' that new sang is comin'?
Why is outlandish stuff sae mickle courted?
Does nonsense mend like whisky, when imported?
Is there nae poet, burning keen for fame,
Will try to gie us sangs and plays at hame?
For comedy abroad he need na toil,
A fool and knave are plants of every soil;
Nor need he hunt as far as Rome and Greece,
To gather matter for a serious piece;
There 's themes enough in Caledonian story,
Would show the tragic muse in a' her glory.—
    Is there no daring bard will rise, and tell
How glorious Wallace stood, how hapless fell?
Where are the muses fled that could produce
A drama worthy o' the name o' Bruce;
How here, even here, he first unsheath'd the sword
'Gainst mighty England and her guilty lord;
And after mony a bloody, deathless doing,
Wrench'd his dear country from the jaws of ruin?
O for a Shakspeare or an Otway scene,
To draw the lovely, hapless Scottish queen!
Vain all th' omnipotence of female charms
'Gainst headlong, ruthless, mad Rebellion's arms.
She fell, but fell with spirit truly Roman,
To glut the vengeance of a rival woman:
A woman, tho' the phrase may seem uncivil,
As able and as cruel as the devil!
One Douglas lives in Home's immortal page,
But Douglases were heroes every age:
And though your fathers, prodigal of life,
A Douglas follow'd to the martial strife,
Perhaps if bowls row right, and Right succeeds,
Ye yet may follow where a Douglas leads!
    As ye hae generous done, if a' the land,
Would take the muses' servants by the hand;
Not only hear, but patronize, befriend them,
And where ye justly can commend, commend them;

And aiblins[1] when they winna stand the test,
Wink hard and say, the folks hae done their best;
Would a' the land do this, then I 'll be caution[2]
Ye 'll soon hae poets o' the Scottish nation,
Will gar[3] Fame blaw until her trumpet crack,
An' warsle[4] Time an' lay him on his back!
　For us and for our stage should ony spier,[5]
"Whase aught thae chiels[6] maks a' this bustle here?"
My best leg foremost, I 'll set up my brow,
We have the honor to belong to you!
We 're your ain bairns, e'en guide us as ye like,
But like good mithers, shore[7] before you strike,—
An' gratefu' still I hope ye 'll ever find us,
For a' the patronage and meikle kindness
We 've got frae a' professions, sets and ranks:
God help us! we 're but poor—ye 'se get but thanks.

────

PROLOGUE,

Spoken at the Theatre, Dumfries, on New-Year-Day evening.

No song nor dance I bring from yon great city
That queens it o'er our taste—the more 's the pity:
Tho', by the by, abroad why will you roam?
Good sense and taste are natives here at home:
But not for panegyric I appear,
I come to wish you all a good new-year!
Old Father Time deputes me here before ye,
Not for to preach, but tell his simple story.
The sage grave ancient cough'd, and bade me say,
"You 're one year older this important day:"
If *wiser too*—he hinted some suggestion,
But 'twould be rude, you know, to ask the question;
And with a would-be-roguish leer and wink,
He bade me on you press this one word—"think!"
　Ye sprightly youths, quite flush with hope and
　　spirit,
Who think to storm the world by dint of merit,
To you the dotard has a deal to say,

[1] Perhaps.—[2] Security.—[3] Make.—[4] To struggle.—[5]Inquire.—[6] Fellows.—
To chide

In his sly, dry, sententious, proverb way!
He bids you mind, amid your thoughtless rattle,
That the first blow is ever half the battle;
That tho' some by the skirt may try to snatch him,
Yet by the forelock is the hold to catch him;
That whether doing, suffering, or forbearing,
You may do miracles by persevering.

 Last, tho' not least in love, ye youthful fair,
Angelic forms, high Heaven's peculiar care!
To you old Bald-pate smooths his wrinkled brow,
And humbly begs you 'll mind th' important—now!
To crown your happiness he asks your leave,
And offers, bliss to give and to receive.

 For our sincere, tho' haply weak endeavors,
With grateful pride we own your many favors;
And howsoe'er our tongues may ill reveal it,
Believe our glowing bosoms truly feel it.

PROLOGUE,

Spoken by Mr. Woods, on his Benefit Night, Monday, April 16, 1787

WHEN by a generous public's kind acclaim,
That dearest meed is granted—honest fame;
When here your favor is the actor's lot,
Nor even the man in private life forgot;
What breast so dead to heavenly virtue's glow,
But heaves impassion'd with the grateful throe?

 Poor is the task to please a barbarous throng,
It needs no Siddons' power in Southern's song:
But here an ancient nation, famed afar
For genius, learning high, as great in war—
Hail, Caledonia! name forever dear!
Before whose sons I 'm honor'd to appear!
Where every science, every nobler art—
That can inform the mind, or mend the heart,
Is known; as grateful nations oft have found,
Far as the rude barbarian marks the bound.
Philosophy, no idle, pedant dream,
Here holds her search, by heaven-taught Reason's
  beam;
Here History paints, with elegance and force,

The tide of Empire's fluctuating course;
Here Douglas forms wild Shakspeare into plan,
And Harley[1] rouses all the god in man.
When well-form'd taste, and sparkling wit unite,
With manly lore, or female beauty bright,
(Beauty, where faultless symmetry and grace
Can only charm us in the second place,)
Witness my heart, how oft with panting fear,
As on this night, I've met these judges here!
But still the hope Experience taught to live,
Equal to judge—you're candid to forgive.
No hundred-headed Riot here we meet,
With decency and law beneath his feet,
Nor Insolence assumes fair Freedom's name;
Like Caledonians, you applaud or blame.

O Thou, dread Power! whose empire-giving hand
Has oft been stretch'd to shield the honor'd land,
Strong may she glow with all her ancient fire;
May every son be worthy of his sire;
Firm may she rise with generous disdain
At Tyranny's, or direr Pleasure's chain;
Still self-dependent in her native shore,
Bold may she brave grim Danger's loudest roar,
Till Fate the curtain drop on worlds to be no more.

TRAGIC FRAGMENT.

[The following verses were written when our Poet was in his eighteenth or nineteenth year. It is an exclamation by a great character on meeting with a child of misery.]

ALL devil as I am, a damnéd wretch,
A harden'd, stubborn, unrepenting villain,
Still my heart melts at human wretchedness;
And with sincere tho' unavailing sighs,
I view the helpless children of distress.
With tears indignant I behold th' oppressor
Rejoicing in the honest man's destruction,
Whose unsubmitting heart was all his crime.
Even you, ye helpless crew, I pity you;

[1] The Man of Feeling, written by Mr. Mackenzie.

Ye, whom the seeming good think sin to pity:
Ye poor despised, abandon'd vagabonds,
Whom vice, as usual, has turn'd o'er to ruin.
—O, but for kind, tho' ill-requited friends,
I had been driven forth like you forlorn,
The most detested, worthless wretch among you.

———

REMORSE.—A FRAGMENT.

[These lines were found in a note-book of the Poet's, written in
early life.]

Of all the numerous ills that hurt our peace,
That press the soul, or wring the mind with anguish,
Beyond comparison, the worst are those
That to our folly or our guilt we owe.
In every other circumstance, the mind
Has this to say—" It was no deed of mine ;"
But when to all the evil of misfortune
This sting is added—"Blame thy foolish self,"
Or, worser far, the pangs of keen remorse ;
The torturing, gnawing consciousness of guilt—
Of guilt, perhaps, where we 've involved others ;
The young, the innocent, who fondly loved us,
Nay more, that very love their cause of ruin !
O burning hell ! in all thy store of torments,
There 's not a keener lash !
Lives there a man so firm, who, while his heart
Feels all the bitter horrors of his crime,
Can reason down its agonizing throbs ;
And after proper purpose of amendment,
Can firmly force his jarring thoughts to peace ?
O happy, happy, enviable man !
O glorious magnanimity of soul !

ODE

ON THE BIRTHDAY OF PRINCE CHARLES EDWARD.

[Burns having been present at a meeting held at Edinburgh, on the 31st Dec.,
1787, to celebrate the birth-day of the unfortunate Prince Charles Edward,
and being appointed poet-laureate for the occasion, he produced an ode, of
which an extract is here presented to the reader.]

*   *   *   *   *   *

*   *   *   *   *

False flatterer, Hope, away!
Nor think to lure us as in days of yore;
  We solemnize this sorrowing natal day,
To prove our loyal truth—we can no more;
  And, owning Heaven's mysterious sway,
    Submissive, low, adore.
    Ye honor'd, mighty dead!
Who nobly perish'd in the glorious cause,
Your king, your country, and her laws!
  From great Dundee, who smiling victory led,
    And fell a martyr in her arms,
    (What breast of northern ice but warms?)
To bold Balmerino's undying name,
Whose soul of fire lighted at Heaven's high flame,
Deserves the proudest wreath departed heroes claim.

Not unrevenged your fate shall be,
  It only lags the fatal hour;
Your blood shall with incessant cry
  Awake at last th' unsparing power.
As from the cliff, with thundering course,
  The snowy ruin smokes along
With doubling speed and gathering force,
Till deep it crashing whelms the cottage in the vale:
So vengeance   *   *   *   *

ADDRESS,

Spoken by Miss Fontenelle, on her Benefit Night, Dec. 4, 1795, at the Theatre,
Dumfries.

STILL anxious to secure your partial favor,
And not less anxious, sure, this night than ever,
A Prologue, Epilogue, or some such matter,
'Twould vamp my bill, said I, if nothing better:

So, sought a Poet, roosted near the skies;
Told him I came to feast my curious eyes;
Said, nothing like his works was ever printed:
And last my Prologue-business slily hinted.
"Ma'am, let me tell you," quoth my man of rhymes,
"I know your bent—these are no laughing times:
Can you—but Miss, I own I have my fears,—
Dissolve in pause—and sentimental tears,
With laden sighs, and solemn-rounded sentence,
Rouse from his sluggish slumbers fell Repentance;
Paint Vengeance as he takes his horrid stand,
Waving on high the desolating brand,
Calling the storms to bear him o'er a guilty land?"
     I could no more—askance the creature eyeing,
D've think, said I, this face was made for crying?
I'll laugh, that's poz—nay more, the world shall
          know it;
And so, your servant! gloomy Master Poet!
     Firm as my creed, sirs, 'tis my fixed belief,
That Misery's another word for Grief;
I also think—so may I be a bride!
That so much laughter, so much life enjoy'd.
     Thou man of crazy care and ceaseless sigh,
Still under bleak Misfortune's blasting eye;
Doom'd to that sorest task of man alive—
To make three guineas do the work of five:
Laugh in Misfortune's face—the beldam witch!
Say, you'll be merry, tho' you can't be rich.
     Thou other man of care, the wretch in love,
Who long with jiltish arts and airs hast strove;
Who, as the boughs all temptingly project,
Measur'st in desperate thought—a rope—thy neck—
Or, where the beetling cliff o'erhangs the deep,
Peerest to meditate the healing leap;
Wouldst thou be cured, thou silly, moping elf,
Laugh at her follies—laugh e'en at thyself;
Learn to despise those frowns now so terrific,
And love a kinder—that's your grand specific.
     To sum up all, be merry, I advise;
And as we're merry may we still be wise.

THE RIGHTS OF WOMAN:

An Occasional Address spoken by Miss Fontenelle on her Benefit Night.

WHILE Europe's eye is fix'd on mighty things,
The fate of empires and the fall of kings;
While quacks of state must each produce his plan,
And even children lisp *the Rights of Man ;*
Amid this mighty fuss just let me mention,
The Rights of Woman merit some attention.
　First, in the sexes' intermix'd connection,
One sacred Right of Woman is *protection*—
The tender flower that lifts it head elate,
Helpless must fall before the blasts of fate,
Sunk on the earth, defaced its lovely form,
Unless your shelter ward the impending storm.
　Our second Right—but needless here is caution,
To keep that right inviolate 's the fashion,
Each man of sense has it so full before him,
He 'd die before he 'd wrong it—'tis *decorum.*—
There was, indeed, in far less polish'd days,
A time when rough, rude man had naughty ways;
Would swagger, swear, get drunk, kick up a riot,
Nay, even thus invade a lady's quiet:
Now, thank our stars! these Gothic times are fled,
Now, well-bred men—and you are all well-bred—
Most justly think (and we are much the gainers)
Such conduct neither spirit, wit, nor manners.
　For Right the third, our last, our best, our dearest,—
That right to fluttering female hearts the nearest,
Which even the Rights of Kings in low prostration
Most humbly own—'tis dear, dear *admiration !*
In that blest sphere alone we live and move;
There taste that life of life—immortal love.—
Smiles, glances, sighs, tears, fits, flirtations, airs,
'Gainst such an host what flinty savage dares—
When awful Beauty joins with all her charms,
Who is so rash as rise in rebel arms?
　But truce with kings, and truce with constitutions,
With bloody armaments and revolutions;
Let Majesty your first attention summon,
Ah! ça ira ! the Majesty of Woman!

17

VERSES

Written under the portrait of Fergusson, the poet, in a copy of the Author's works presented to a young lady in Edinburgh, March 19, 1787.

CURSE on ungrateful man, that can be pleased,
And yet can starve the author of the pleasure!
O thou, my elder brother in misfortune,
By far my elder brother in the muses,
With tears I pity thy unhappy fate!
Why is the bard unpitied by the world,
Yet has so keen a relish of its pleasures?

THE HENPECKED HUSBAND.

CURSED be the man, the poorest wretch in life,
The crouching vassal to the tyrant wife!
Who has no will but by her high permission;
Who has not sixpence but in her possession;
Who must to her his dear friend's secret tell,
Who dreads a curtain lecture worse than hell.—
Were such the wife had fallen to my part,
I'd break her spirit, or I'd break her heart:
I'd charm her with the magic of a switch,
I'd kiss her maids and kick the perverse b—h.

LINES ON AN INTERVIEW WITH LORD DAER.

THIS wot ye all whom it concerns,
I, Rhymer Robin, alias Burns,
        October twenty-third,
A ne'er-to-be-forgotten day,
Sae far I sprachled[1] up the brae,[2]
        I dinner'd wi' a Lord.

I've been at drunken writers' feasts,
Nay, been bitch-fou 'mang godly priests,
        (Wi' reverence be it spoken;)

---

[1] Crawled, or clambered on the hands and knees.—[2] Hill.

I 've even join'd the honor'd jorum,
When mighty Squireships of the quorum
      Their hydra drouth[1] did sloken.[2]

But wi' a Lord—stand out my shin,
A Lord—a Peer—an Earl's son,
      Up higher yet, my bonnet ;
An' sic a Lord—lang Scotch ells twa,[3]
Our Peerage, he o'erlooks them a'
      As I look o'er my sonnet!

But oh for Hogarth's magic power!
To show Sir Bardie's willyart[4] glower,
      And how he stared and stammer'd,
When goavan[5] as if led wi' branks,[6]
An' stumpin' on his ploughman shanks,
      He in the parlor hammer'd.

To meet good Stuart little pain is,
Or Scotia's sacred Demosthenes,
      Thinks I, they are but men!
But Burns, my Lord—Guid God! I doited,[7]
My knees on ane anither knoited,[8]
      As faltering I gaed ben![9]

I sidling shelter'd in a nook,
An' at his Lordship steal 't a look
      Like some portentous omen ;
Except good sense and social glee,
An' (what surprised me) modesty,
      I markéd naught uncommon.

I watch'd the symptoms of the great,
The gentle pride, the lordly state,
      The arrogant assuming ;
The fient a pride, nae pride had he,
Nor sauce, nor state that I could see,
      Mair than an honest ploughman.

[1] Thirst.—[2] Slacken, or quench.—[3] i. e. he was six feet high.—[4] Bashful look.—[5] Going, or walking.—[6] A kind of wooden curb for horses.—[7] Was stupified.—[8] Knocked together.—[9] Went into the parlor.

Then from his Lordship I shall learn,
Henceforth to meet with unconcern
    One rank as weel 's another;
Nae honest, worthy man need care,
To meet with noble, youthful Daer,
    For he but meets a brother.

A PRAYER.

Left in a room of a reverend friend's house, where the Author slept.

O THOU, dread Power who reign'st above!
    I know thou wilt me hear;
When for this scene of peace and love,
    I make my prayer sincere.

The hoary sire—the mortal stroke,
    Long, long, be pleased to spare!
To bless his little filial flock,
    And show what good men are.

She, who her lovely offspring eyes
    With tender hopes and fears,
Oh bless her with a mother's joys,
    But spare a mother's tears!

Their hope, their stay, their darling youth,
    In manhood's dawning blush;

[1] Dr. Laurie, minister of Loudoun, from whom the poet received many essential favors, one of which, and none of the least, will be best explained in his own words:—"I had taken the last farewell of my few friends—my chest was on the road to Greenock, from whence I was to embark in a few days for America. I had composed the last song I should ever measure in Caledonia, 'The gloomy night is gathering fast,' when a letter from Dr. Blacklock, to a friend of mine (Dr. Laurie, who had sent to Dr. Blacklock a copy of our Poet's works), overthrew all my schemes, by opening new prospects to my poetic ambition. The doctor belonged to a set of critics for whose applause I had not dared to hope. His opinion that I would meet with encouragement in Edinburgh for a second edition, fired me so much, that away I posted for that city, without a single acquaintance, or a single letter of introduction. The baneful star that had so long shed its blasting influence in my zenith, for once made a revolution to the nadir; and a kind Providence placed me under the patronage of one of the noblest of men, the Earl of Glencairn."

Bless him, thou God of love and truth,
Up to a parent's wish!

The beauteous seraph sister-band,
With earnest tears I pray,
Thou know'st the snares on every hand,
Guide thou their steps alway!

When soon or late they reach that coast,
O'er life's rough ocean driven,
May they rejoice, no wanderer lost,
A family in heaven!

A PRAYER,

UNDER THE PRESSURE OF VIOLENT ANGUISH.

O thou, great Being! what thou art
Surpasses me to know;
Yet sure I am, that known to Thee
Are all thy works below.

Thy creature here before Thee stands,
All wretched and distrest;
Yet sure those ills that wring my soul
Obey thy high behest.

Sure Thou, Almighty, canst not act
From cruelty or wrath!
Oh, free my weary eyes from tears!
Or close them fast in death!

But if I must afflicted be,
To suit some wise design;
Then man my soul with firm resolves
To bear and not repine!

A PRAYER,

IN THE PROSPECT OF DEATH.

O thou, unknown, Almighty cause
Of all my hope and fear!
In whose dread presence, ere an hour
Perhaps I must appear!

If I have wander'd in those paths
    Of life I ought to shun;
As *something*, loudly, in my breast
    Remonstrates I have done:

Thou know'st that Thou hast forméd me
    With passions wild and strong;
And listening to their witching voice
    Has often led me wrong.

Where human weakness has come short,
    Or frailty stept aside,
Do Thou, All-Good! for such Thou art,
    In shades of darkness hide.

Where with intention I have err'd,
    No other plea I have,
But, Thou art good; and goodness still
    Delighteth to forgive.

STANZAS ON THE SAME OCCASION.

Why am I loth to leave this earthly scene?
    Have I so found it full of pleasing charms?
Some drops of joy with draughts of ill between;
    Some gleams of sunshine 'mid renewing storms.
Is it departing pangs my soul alarms;
    Or death's unlovely, dreary, dark abode?
For guilt, for guilt, my terrors are in arms;
    I tremble to approach an angry God,
And justly smart beneath his sin-avenging rod.

Fain would I say, Forgive my foul offence!
    Fain promise never more to disobey;
But should my Author health again dispense,
    Again I might desert fair virtue's way;
Again in folly's path might go astray;
    Again exalt the brute and sink the man;
Then how should I for heavenly mercy pray,
    Who act so counter heavenly mercy's plan?
Who sin so oft have mourn'd, yet to temptation ran?

O Thou, great Governor of all below!
  If I may dare a lifted eye to Thee,
Thy nod can make the tempest cease to blow,
  Or still the tumult of the raging sea;
With that controlling power assist even me,
  Those headlong furious passions to confine,
For all unfit I feel my powers to be,
  To rule their torrent in th' allowéd line;
Oh, aid me with thy help, Omnipotence Divine!

THE FIRST PSALM.

The man in life, wherever placed,
  Hath happiness in store,
Who walks not in the wicked's way,
  Nor learns their guilty lore!

Nor from the seat of scornful pride
  Casts forth his eyes abroad,
But with humility and awe
  Still walks before his God.

That man shall flourish like the trees
  Which by the streamlets grow;
The fruitful top is spread on high,
  And firm the root below.

But he whose blossom buds in guilt,
  Shall to the ground be cast,
And, like the rootless stubble, tost
  Before the sweeping blast.

For why? That God, the good adore,
  Hath given them peace and rest,
But hath decreed that wicked men
  Shall ne'er be truly blest.

THE FIRST SIX VERSES OF THE 90TH PSALM.

O Thou, the first, the greatest Friend
  Of all the human race!
Whose strong right hand has ever been
  Their stay and dwelling-place!

Before the mountains heaved their heads
    Beneath thy forming hand,
Before this ponderous globe itself
    Arose at thy command:

That Power which raised and still upholds
    This universal frame,
From countless, unbeginning time
    Was ever still the same.

Those mighty periods of years
    Which seem to us so vast,
Appear no more before thy sight
    Than yesterday that's past.

Thou giv'st the word: thy creature, man,
    Is to existence brought:
Again, thou sayest, " Ye sons of men,
    Return ye into naught!"

Thou layest them, with all their cares,
    In everlasting sleep:
As with a flood thou tak'st them off
    With overwhelming sweep.

They flourish like the morning flower,
    In beauty's pride array'd;
But long ere night cut down it lies
    All wither'd and decay'd.

A GRACE BEFORE DINNER.

O THOU, who kindly dost provide
    For every creature's want!
We bless thee, God of Nature wide,
    For all thy goodness lent:
And, if it please thee, heavenly Guide,
    May never worse be sent;
But whether granted or denied,
    Lord, bless us with content.—*Amen.*

VERSE

Written in Friar's-Carse Hermitage on Nith-side.

Thou whom chance may hither lead,
Be thou clad in russet weed,
Be thou deck'd in silken stole,
Grave these counsels on thy soul!—
Life is but a day at most,
Sprung from night, in darkness lost;
Hope not sunshine every hour,
Fear not clouds will always lower.
As youth and love with sprightly dance,
Beneath thy morning-star advance,
Pleasure, with her syren air,
May delude the thoughtless pair;
Let prudence bless enjoyment's cup,
Then raptured sip, and sip it up.
As thy day grows warm and high,
Life's meridian flaming nigh,
Dost thou spurn the humble vale?
Life's proud summits wouldst thou scale?
Check thy climbing step, elate.
Evils lurk in felon wait;
Dangers, eagle-pinion'd, bold
Soar around each cliffy hold;
While cheerful peace, with linnet song,
Chants the lowly dells among.[1]
As the shades of evening close,
Beckoning thee to long repose;
As life itself becomes disease,
Seek the chimney-neuk of ease;
There, ruminate with sober thought,
On all thou 'st seen, and heard, and wrought;
And teach the sportive younkers round,
Saws of experience, sage and sound.
Say, "Man's true, genuine estimate,
The grand criterion of his fate,
Is not, Art thou high or low?
Did thy fortune ebb or flow?
Did many talents gild thy span?

[1] See "Grongar Hill," a Poem by Dyer.

Or frugal nature grudge thee one?"
Tell them, and press it on their mind,
As thou thyself must shortly find,
The smile or frown of awful Heaven
To virtue or to vice is given.
Say, "To be just, and kind, and wise,
There solid self-enjoyment lies;
That foolish, selfish, faithless ways
Lead to the wretched, vile, and base."
　　Thus resign'd and quiet creep
To the bed of lasting sleep;
Sleep, whence thou shalt ne'er awake,
Night, where dawn shall never break,
Till future life—future no more,
To light, and joy, and good restore—
To light and joy unknown before!
　　Stranger, go! Heaven be thy guide!
Quoth the Beadsman of Nith-side.

WINTER.—A DIRGE.

The wintry west extends his blast,
　　And hail and rain does blaw;
Or the stormy north sends driving forth
　　The blinding sleet and snaw:
While tumbling brown, the burn comes down,
　　And roars frae bank to brae;
And bird and beast in covert rest
　　And pass the heartless day.

"The sweeping blast, the sky o'ercast,"[1]
　　The joyless winter-day,
Let others fear, to me more dear
　　Than all the pride of May:
The tempest's howl, it soothes my soul,
　　My griefs it seems to join;
The leafless trees my fancy please,
　　Their fate resembles mine!

Thou Power Supreme, whose mighty scheme
　　These woes of mine fulfil,

[1] Dr. Young.

Here, firm, I rest—they must be best,
    Because they are Thy will!
Then all I want (oh, do thou grant
    This one request of mine!)
Since to enjoy thou dost deny,
    Assist me to resign.

———

MAN WAS MADE TO MOURN.—A DIRGE.

WHEN chill November's surly blast
    Made fields and forests bare,
One evening, as I wander'd forth
    Along the banks of Ayr,
I spied a man, whose aged step
    Seem'd weary, worn with care;
His face was furrow'd o'er with years,
    And hoary was his hair.

"Young stranger, whither wand'rest thou?"
    Began the reverend sage;
"Does thirst of wealth thy step constrain,
    Or youthful pleasure's rage?
Or, haply, prest with cares and woes,
    Too soon thou hast began
To wander forth with me to mourn
    The miseries of man!

"The sun that overhangs yon moors,
    Outspreading far and wide,
Where hundreds labor to support
    A haughty lordling's pride!
I've seen yon weary winter-sun
    Twice forty times return;
And every time has added proofs
    That man was made to mourn.

"O man! while in thy early years
    How prodigal of time!
Misspending all thy precious hours,
    Thy glorious youthful prime!
Alternate follies take the sway;
    Licentious passions burn;

Which tenfold force gives Nature's law,
    That man was made to mourn.

"Look not alone on youthful prime,
    Or manhood's active might;
Man then is useful to his kind,
    Supported is his right;
But see him on the edge of life,
    With cares and sorrows worn,
Then age and want, oh! ill-match'd pair!
    Show man was made to mourn.

"A few seem favorites of Fate,
    In pleasure's lap carest;
Yet, think not all the rich and great
    Are likewise truly blest.
But, oh! what crowds in every land,
    Are wretched and forlorn!
Thro' weary life this lesson learn,
    That man was made to mourn.

"Many and sharp the numerous ills
    Inwoven with our frame!
More pointed still we make ourselves,
    Regret, remorse, and shame!
And man, whose heaven-erected face
    The smiles of love adorn,
Man's inhumanity to man
    Makes countless thousands mourn!

"See yonder poor, o'erlabor'd wight,
    So abject, mean, and vile,
Who begs a brother of the earth
    To give him leave to toil;[1]
And see his lordly *fellow-worm*
    The poor petition spurn,
Unmindful, though a weeping wife
    And helpless offspring mourn.

"If I'm design'd yon lordling's slave—
    By Nature's law design'd—

---

[1] The contrast between his own worldly circumstances and intellectual rank, was never perhaps more bitterly nor more loftily expressed by our Poet, than in these four lines, and the first half of the following stanza.

Why was an independent wish
 E'er planted in my mind?
If not, why am I subject to
 His cruelty or scorn?
Or why has man the will and power
 To make his fellow mourn?

" Yet let not this too much, my son,
 Disturb thy youthful breast:
This partial view of human kind
 Is surely not the *last!*
The poor, oppresséd, honest man
 Had never, sure, been born,
Had there not been some recompense
 To comfort those that mourn!

" O Death! the poor man's dearest friend!
 The kindest and the best!
Welcome the hour my agéd limbs
 Are laid with thee at rest!
The great, the wealthy, fear thy blow,
 From pomp and pleasure torn;
But, oh! a blest relief to those
 That weary-laden mourn!"'

DESPONDENCY.—AN ODE.

OPPRESS'D with grief, oppress'd with care,
A burden more than I can bear,
 I sit me down and sigh:
O Life! thou art a galling load,
Along a rough, a weary road,
 To wretches such as I!
Dim, backward, as I cast my view,
 What sickening scenes appear!
What sorrows *yet* may pierce me thro',
 Too justly I may fear!
  Still caring, despairing,
  Must be my bitter doom;

[1] In " Man was made to Mourn," Burns appears to have taken many hints from an ancient ballad, entitled "The Life and Age of Man."

18

My woes here shall close ne'er,
  But with the closing tomb!

Happy, ye sons of busy life,
Who, equal to the bustling strife,
  No other view regard!
Even when the wishéd *end*'s denied,
Yet while the busy *means* are plied,
  They bring their own reward:
Whilst I, a hope-abandon'd wight,
  Unfitted with an *aim*,
Meet every sad returning night,
  And joyless morn, the same.
    You, bustling, and justling,
      Forget each grief and pain;
    I listless, yet restless,
      Find every prospect vain.

How blest the Solitary's lot!
Who, all-forgetting, all-forgot,
  Within his humble cell,
The cavern wild, with tangling roots,
Sits o'er his newly-gather'd fruits,
  Beside his crystal well!
Or, haply, to his evening thought,
  By unfrequented stream,
The ways of men are distant brought,
  A faint collected dream:
    While praising, and raising
      His thoughts to Heaven on high,
    As wandering, meandering,
      He views the solemn sky.

Than I, no lonely hermit placed
Where never human footstep traced,
  Less fit to play the part;
The lucky moment to improve,
And *just* to stop and *just* to move,
  With self-respecting art:
But ah! those pleasures, loves, and joys,
  Which I too keenly taste,
The *Solitary* can despise,
  Can want, and yet be blest!
    He needs not, he heeds not,

Or human love or hate,
  Whilst I here must cry here,
    At perfidy ingrate!

Oh! enviable, early days,
When dancing thoughtless pleasure's maze,
  To care, to guilt unknown!
How ill exchanged for riper times,
To feel the follies, or the crimes,
  Of others, or my own!
Ye tiny elves that guiltless sport,
  Like linnets in the bush,
Ye little know the ills ye court,
  When manhood is your wish!
    The losses, the crosses,
      That *active man* engage!
    The fears all, the tears all,
      Of dim declining *age!*

TO RUIN.

ALL hail! inexorable lord!
At whose destruction-breathing word
  The mightiest empires fall!
Thy cruel, woe-delighted train,
The ministers of grief and pain,
  A sullen welcome, all!
With stern-resolved despairing eye,
  I see each aiméd dart;
For one has cut my *dearest tie,*
  And quivers in my heart.
    Then lowering and pouring,
      The *storm* no more I dread;
    Tho' thickening and blackening,
      Round my devoted head.

And thou, grim Power, by life abhorr'd,
While life a *pleasure* can afford,
  Oh! hear a wretch's prayer!
No more I shrink, appall'd, afraid,
I court, I beg thy friendly aid,
  To close this scene of care!

When shall my soul, in silent peace,
  Resign life's *joyless* day;
My weary heart its throbbing cease,
  Cold mouldering in the clay?
    No fear more, no tear more,
      To stain my lifeless face:
    Enclasped and grasped
      Within thy cold embrace!

A WINTER NIGHT.

Poor naked wretches, wheresoe'er you are,
That bide the pelting of this pitiless storm !
How shall your houseless heads, and unfed sides,
Your loop'd and window'd raggedness, defend you
From seasons such as these!—*Shakspeare.*

When biting Boreas, fell and doure,[1]
Sharp shivers thro' the leafless bower;
When Phœbus gies a short-lived glower[2]
      Far south the lift,[3]
Dim darkening thro' the flaky shower
      Or whirlin' drift:

Ae[4] night the storm the steeples rock'd,
Poor labor sweet in sleep was lock'd,
While burns,[5] in snawy wreaths up-chock'd,
      Wild-eddying swirl,[6]
Or thro' the mining outlet bock'd,[7]
      Down headlong hurl.

Listening the doors and winnocks[8] rattle,
I thought me on the ourie[9] cattle,
Or silly sheep, wha bide this brattle
      O' winter war,
And thro' the drift, deep-lairing[10] sprattle
      Beneath a scar.[11]

Ilk happing[12] bird, wee, helpless thing,
That, in the merry months o' spring,
Delighted me to hear thee sing,

Sullen.—[2] Glimmer.—[3] The sky.—[4] One.—[5] Rivulets.—[6] Curve.—
[7] Gushed.—[8] Windows,—[9] Shivering.—[10] Wading and sinking in snow, or
mud,—[11] A cliff, or precipice.—[12] Each hopping.

What comes o' thee?
Whare wilt thou cower thy chittering wing,
And close thy e'e?

E'en you cn murdering errands toil'd,
Lone, from your savage homes exiled,
The blood-stain'd roost, and sheep-cote spoil'd,
My heart forgets,
While pitiless the tempest wild
Sore on you beats.

Now Phœbe, in her midnight reign,
Dark, muffled, view'd the dreary plain;
Still crowding thoughts a pensive train,
Rose in my soul,
When on my ear this plaintive strain,
Slow, solemn, stole—

"Blow, blow, ye winds, with heavier gust!
And freeze, thou bitter-biting frost!
Descend, ye chilly, smothering snows!
Not all your rage, as now united, shows
More hard unkindness, unrelenting,
Vengeful malice, unrepenting,
Than heaven-illumined man on brother man bestows.

"See stern oppression's iron grip,
Or mad ambition's gory hand,
Sending, like bloodhounds from the slip,
Woe, want, and murder o'er a land!

"E'en in the peaceful rural vale,
Truth, weeping, tells the mournful tale,
How pamper'd Luxury, Flattery by her side,
The parasite empoisoning her ear,
With all the servile wretches in the rear,
Looks o'er proud property, extended wide;
And eyes the simple rustic hind,
Whose toil upholds the glittering show,
A creature of another kind,
Some coarser substance, unrefined,
Placed for her lordly use thus far, thus vile, below.

"Where, where is Love's fond, tender throe,
With lordly Honor's lofty brow,

The powers you proudly own?
Is there, beneath Love's noble name,
Can harbor, dark, the selfish aim,
    To bless himself alone!
Mark maiden-innocence a prey
    To love-pretending snares,
This boasted Honor turns away,
Shunning soft Pity's rising sway,
    Regardless of her tears, and unavailing prayers!
Perhaps, this hour, in misery's squalid nest,
She strains your infant to her joyless breast,
And with a mother's fears shrinks at the rocking blast!

"O ye! who, sunk in beds of down,
Feel not a want but what yourselves create,
Think for a moment on his wretched fate,
    Whom friends and fortune quite disown!
Ill-satisfied keen nature's clamorous call,
    Stretch'd on his straw, he lays himself to sleep,
While, through the ragged roof and chinky wall,
    Chill o'er his slumbers piles the drifty heap!

"Think on the dungeon's grim confine,
Where guilt and poor misfortune pine!
    Guilt, erring man, relenting, view;
    But shall thy legal rage pursue
    The wretch, already crushéd low
    By cruel Fortune's undeservéd blow?
Affliction's sons are brothers in distress,
A brother to relieve, how exquisite the bliss!"

I heard nae mair, for chanticleer
    Shook off the pouthery snaw,[1]
And hail'd the morning with a cheer,
    A cottage-rousing craw.

But deep this truth impress'd my mind—
    Through all his works abroad,
The heart, benevolent and kind,
    The most resembles God.

[1] Flaky snow.

THE LAMENT,

OCCASIONED BY THE UNFORTUNATE ISSUE OF A FRIEND'S AMOUR.

Alas ! how oft does Goodness wound itself,
And sweet Affection prove the spring of woe !—Home.

O THOU pale orb, that silent shines,
　While care-untroubled mortals sleep !
Thou seest a wretch that inly pines,
　And wanders here to wail and weep !
With woe I nightly vigils keep,
　Beneath thy wan unwarming beam ;
And mourn in lamentation deep,
　How life and love are all a dream.

I joyless view thy rays adorn
　The faintly-markéd distant hill :
I joyless view thy trembling horn,
　Reflected in the gurgling rill :
My fondly fluttering heart, be still !
　Thou busy power, Remembrance, cease !
Ah ! must the agonizing thrill
　Forever bar returning peace !

No idly-feign'd poetic pains,
　My sad love-lorn lamentings claim ;
No shepherd's pipe—Arcadian strains ;
　No fabled tortures, quaint and tame :
The plighted faith ; the mutual flame ;
　The oft attested Powers above ;
The promised father's tender name—
　These were the pledges of my love !

Encircled in her clasping arms,
　How have the raptured moments flown !
How have I wish'd for Fortune's charms
　For her dear sake, and hers alone !
And must I think it ! Is she gone,
　My secret heart's exulting boast ?
And does she heedless hear my groan ?
　And is she ever, ever lost ?

Oh ! can she bear so base a heart,
　So lost to honor, lost to truth,

As from the fondest lover part,
  The plighted husband of her youth!
Alas! life's path may be unsmooth!
  Her way may lie through rough distress!
Then, who her pangs and pains will soothe,
  Her sorrows share, and make them less?

Ye wingéd hours that o'er us past,
  Enraptured more, the more enjoy'd,
Your dear remembrance in my breast
  My fondly treasured thoughts employ'd.
That breast, how dreary now and void,
  For her too scanty once of room!
Even every ray of hope destroy'd,
  And not a wish to gild the gloom!

The morn that warns the approaching day,
  Awakes me up to toil and woe:
I see the hours in long array,
  That I must suffer, lingering, slow.
Full many a pang, and many a throe,
  Keen recollection's direful train,
Must wing my soul, ere Phœbus, low,
  Shall kiss the distant western main.

And when my nightly couch I try,
  Sore harass'd out with care and grief,
My toil-beat nerves, and tear-worn eye,
  Keep watchings with the nightly thief:
Or, if I slumber, Fancy, chief,
  Reigns haggard-wild, in sore affright:
Even day, all-bitter, brings relief
  From such a horror-breathing night!

O thou bright queen, who o'er the expanse
  Now highest reign'st, with boundless sway!
Oft has thy silent-marking glance
  Observed us, fondly-wandering, stray!
The time, unheeded, sped away,
  While love's luxurious pulse beat high,
Beneath thy silver-gleaming ray,
  To mark the mutual-kindling eye.

Oh! scenes in strong remembrance set!
  Scenes never, never, to return!

Scenes, if, in stupor, I forget,
  Again I feel, again I burn:
From every joy and pleasure torn,
  Life's weary vale I'll wander through:
And hopeless, comfortless, I'll mourn
  A faithless woman's broken vow.[1]

LAMENT.[2]

Written when the Author was about to leave his native country.

O'er the mist-shrouded cliffs of the lone mountain straying,
  Where the wild winds of winter incessantly rave,
What woes wring my heart while intently surveying
  The storm's gloomy path on the breast of the wave!

Ye foam-crested billows, allow me to wail,
  Ere ye toss me afar from my loved native shore;
Where the flower which bloom'd sweetest in Coila's green
    vale,
  The pride o' my bosom, my Mary's no more.

No more by the banks of the streamlet we'll wander,
  And smile at the moon's rimpled face in the wave;
No more shall my arms cling with fondness around her,
  For the dewdrops of morning fall cold on her grave.

Nor more shall the soft thrill of love warm my breast,
  I haste with the storm to a far distant shore;
Where unknown, unlamented, my ashes shall rest,
  And joy shall revisit my bosom no more.

LAMENT,

FOR JAMES, EARL OF GLENCAIRN.

The wind blew hollow frae the hills,
  By fits the sun's departing beam
Look'd on the fading yellow woods
  That waved o'er Lugar's winding stream:

---

[1] A detail of the circumstance on which this affecting Poem was composed
will be found in Lockhart's Life of the Poet, p. 85.
[2] First published in the Dumfries Weekly Journal, July 5th, 1815.

Beneath a craigy steep, a Bard,
  Laden with years and meikle[1] pain,
In loud lament bewail'd his lord,
  Whom death had all untimely taen.[2]

He lean'd him to an ancient aik,[3]
  Whose trunk was mouldering down with years;
His locks were bleachéd white wi' time,
  His hoary cheek was wet wi' tears!
And as he touch'd his trembling harp,
  And as he tuned his doleful sang,
The winds, lamenting thro' their caves,
  To echo bore the notes alang.

"Ye scatter'd birds that faintly sing,
  The relics of the vernal choir!
Ye woods that shed on a' the winds
  The honors of the agéd year!
A few short months, and glad and gay,
  Again ye 'll charm the ear and e'e;
But nocht[4] in all revolving time
  Can gladness bring again to me.

"I am a bending agéd tree,
  That long has stood the wind and rain,
But now has come a cruel blast,
  And my last hald[5] of earth is gane:
Nae leaf o' mine shall greet the spring,
  Nae simmer sun exalt my bloom;
But I maun lie before the storm,
  And ithers plant them in my room.

"I 've seen sae monie changefu' years,
  On earth I am a stranger grown;
I wander in the ways of men,
  Alike unknowing and unknown:
Unheard, unpitied, unrelieved,
  I bare alane my lade o' care,
For silent, low, on beds of dust,
  Lie a' that would my sorrows share.

"And last (the sum of a' my griefs!)
  My noble master lies in clay;

[1] Much.—[2] Taken.—[3] Oak.—[4] Naught.—[5] Hold.

The flower amang our barons bold,
  His country's pride, his country's stay:
In weary being now I pine,
  For a' the life of life is dead,
And hope has left my agéd ken,
  On forward wing forever fled.

" Awake thy last sad voice, my harp!
  The voice of woe and wild despair!
Awake! resound thy latest lay,
  Then sleep in silence evermair!
And thou, my last, best, only friend,
  That fillest an untimely tomb,
Accept this tribute from the Bard
  Thou brought from Fortune's mirkest[1] gloom.

" In poverty's low barren vale,
  Thick mists, obscure, involved me round;
Tho' oft I turn'd the wistful eye,
  Nae ray of fame was to be found:
Thou found'st me like the morning sun
  That melts the fogs in limpid air;
The friendless Bard and rustic song
  Became alike thy fostering care.

" Oh! why has worth so short a date?
  While villains ripen gray with time,
Must thou, the noble, generous, great,
  Fall in bold manhood's hardy prime?
Why did I live to see that day?
  A day to me so full of woe!
Oh! had I met the mortal shaft
  Which laid my benefactor low!

" The bridegroom may forget the bride
  Was made his wedded wife yestreen;
The monarch may forget the crown
  That on his head an hour has been;
The mother may forget the child
  That smiles sae sweetly on her knee;
But I 'll remember thee, Glencairn,
  And a' that thou hast done for me!"[2]

[1] Darkest.—[2] See note on page 196.

LINES

Sent to Sir John Whitefoord, of Whitefoord, Bart., with the
foregoing Poem.

Thou, who thy honor as thy God rever'st,
Who, save thy mind's reproach, naught earthly fear'st,
To thee this votive offering I impart,
The tearful tribute of a broken heart.
The *friend* thou valued'st, I the *patron* loved;
His worth, his honor, all the world approved.
We'll mourn till we too go as he has gone,
And tread the dreary path to that dark world unknown.

LAMENT OF MARY, QUEEN OF SCOTS.

ON THE APPROACH OF SPRING.

Now Nature hangs her mantle green
   On every blooming tree, .
And spreads her sheets o' daisies white
   Out o'er the grassy lea:
Now Phœbus cheers the crystal streams,
   And glads the azure skies;
But nocht can glad the weary wight
   That fast in durance lies.

Now lav'rocks wake the merry morn,
   Aloft on dewy wing;
The merle,[1] in his noontide bower,
   Makes woodland echoes ring;
The mavis[2] mild, wi' many a note,
   Sings drowsy day to rest:
In love and freedom they rejoice,
   Wi' care nor thrall opprest.

Now blooms the lily by the bank,
   The primrose down the brae;
The hawthorn's budding in the glen,
   And milk-white is the slae:
The meanest hind in fair Scotland
   May rove their sweets amang;

[1] The Blackbird.—[2] The Thrush.

But I, the Queen of a' Scotland,
  Maun[1] lie in prison strang.[2]

I was the Queen o' bonnie France,
  Where happy I hae been;
Fu'[3] lightly raise I in the morn,
  As blythe lay down at e'en:
And I'm the Sovereign of Scotland,
  And monie a traitor there:
Yet here I lie in foreign bands,
  And never-ending care.

But as for thee, thou false woman,
  My sister and my fae,
Grim Vengeance, yet, shall whet a sword
  That through thy soul shall gae:
The weeping blood in woman's breast
  Was never known to thee;
Nor th' balm that drops on wounds of woe
  Frae woman's pitying e'e.

My son! my son! may kinder stars
  Upon thy fortune shine;
And may those pleasures gild thy reign,
  That ne'er wad blink[4] on mine!
God keep thee frae thy mother's faes,
  Or turn their hearts to thee;
And where thou meet'st thy mother's friend,
  Remember him for me!

Oh! soon, to me, may summer suns
  Nae mair[5] light up the morn!
Nae mair, to me, the autumn winds
  Wave o'er the yellow corn!
And in the narrow house o' death
  Let winter round me rave;
And the next flowers that deck the spring,
  Bloom on my peaceful grave!

[1] Must.—[2] Strong.—[3] Full.—[4] Would shine.—[5] No more.
19

EPISTLES.

EPISTLE TO JAMES SMITH.[1]

Friendship! mysterious cement of the soul!
Sweet'ner of life, and solder of society!
I owe thee much.—Blair.

DEAR Smith, the sleest,[2] pawkie[3] thief,
That e'er attempted stealth or rief,[4]
Ye surely hae some warlock-breef[5]
　　　　Owre human hearts;
For ne'er a bosom yet was prief[6]
　　　　Against your arts.

For me, I swear by sun and moon,
And every star that blinks aboon,
Ye 've cost me twenty pair o' shoon
　　　　Just gaun to see you;
And every ither pair that 's done,
　　　　Mair taen[7] I 'm wi' you.

That auld capricious carlin[8] Nature,
To mak amends for scrimpit[9] stature,
She 's turn'd you aff, a human creature
　　　　On her first plan,
And in her freaks, on every feature,
　　　　She 's wrote "the man."

Just now I 've taen the fit o' rhyme,
My barmy[10] noddle 's working prime,
My fancy yerkit[11] up sublime
　　　　Wi' hasty summon:
Hae ye a leisure-moment's time
　　　　To hear what 's comin?

---

[1] Then a shopkeeper in Mauchline. He afterwards went to the West Indies, where he died.

[2] Pronounced *slee-est*, slyest.—[3] Cunning.—[4] Plunder.—[5] Wizard-spell.—[6] Proof.—[7] More delighted.—[8] A stout old woman.—[9] Scanty.—[10] Like barm, or yeast.—[11] Jerked, lashed.

Some rhyme, a neebor's name to lash;
Some rhyme (vain thought!) for needfu' cash;
Some rhyme to court the countra clash,[1]
   An' raise a din;
For me, an aim I never fash![2]
   I rhyme for fun.

The star that rules my luckless lot,
Has fated me the russet coat,
An' damn'd my fortune to the groat;[3]
   But, in requit,
Has bless'd me wi' a random shot
   O' countra wit.

This while my notion's taen a sklent,[4]
To try my fate in guid black prent;
But still the mair I'm that way bent,
   Something cries—"Hoolie![5]
I red[6] you, honest man, tak tent![7]
   Ye'll shaw your folly.

"There's ither poets, much your betters,
Far seen in Greek, deep men o' letters,
Hae thought they had insured their debtors
   A' future ages;
Now moths deform in shapeless tetters
   Their unknown pages."

Then fareweel hopes o' laurel-boughs,
To garland my poetic brows!
Henceforth I'll rove where busy ploughs
   Are whistling thrang,
And teach the lanely heights an' howes[8]
   My rustic sang.

I'll wander on wi' tentless[9] heed
How never-halting moments speed,
Till fate shall snap the brittle thread;
   Then, all unknown,
I'll lay me with th' inglorious dead,
   Forgot and gone!

---

[1] Country talk.—[2] To care for.—[3] Doomed me to poverty.—[4] Aslant.—Take time and consider.—[6] Counsel.—[7] Take heed.—[8] Hollows, or dales.—Thoughtless.

But why o' death begin a tale?
Just now we 're living, sound, and hale,
Then top and main-top crowd the sail,
          Heave care owre-side!
And large, before enjoyment's gale,
          Let 's tak the tide.

This life, sae far 's I understand,
Is a' enchanted, fairy land,
Where pleasure is the magic wand,
          That, wielded right,
Maks hours like minutes, hand in hand,
          Dance by fu' light.

The magic wand then let us wield;
For, ance[1] that five-an'-forty 's speel'd,[2]
See crazy, weary, joyless eild,[3]
          Wi' wrinkled face,
Come hostin',[4] hirplin',[5] owre the field,
          Wi' creepin' pace.

When ance life's day draws near the gloamin,[6]
Then fareweel vacant careless roamin';
An' fareweel cheerfu' tankards foamin',
          An' social noise;
An' fareweel, dear, deluding woman,
          The joy of joys!

O Life! how pleasant in thy morning,
Young Fancy's rays the hills adorning!
Cold-pausing Caution's lesson scorning,
          We frisk away,
Like school-boys at th' expected warning,
          To joy and play.

We wander there, we wander here,
We eye the rose upon the brier,
Unmindful that the thorn is near
          Amang the leaves;
And tho' the puny wound appear,
          Short while it grieves.

Once.—[2] To climb.—[3] Old age.—[4] Coughing.—[5] Hobbling.—[6] Twilight.

Some, lucky, find a flowery spot,
For which they never toil'd nor swat;[1]
They drink the sweet, and eat the fat,
        But[2] care or pain;
And, haply, eye the barren hut
        With high disdain.

With steady aim some fortune chase;
Keen Hope does every sinew brace;
Thro' fair, thro' foul, they urge the race,
        And seize the prey;
Then cannie,[3] in some cozie[4] place,
        They close the day.

And others, like your humble servan',
Poor wights! nae rules nor roads observin',
To right or left, eternal swervin',
        They zig-zag on;
Till curst with age, obscure an' starvin',
        They aften groan.

Alas! what bitter toil an' straining—
But truce with peevish, poor complaining!
Is Fortune's fickle *luna* waning?
        E'en let her gang!
Beneath what light she has remaining
        Let's sing our sang.

My pen I here fling to the door,
And kneel, " Ye Powers!" and warm implore.
" Though I should wander *terra* o'er,
        In all her climes,
Grant me but this, I ask no more,
        Ay rowth[5] o' rhymes.

" Gie dreeping roasts to countra lairds,
Till icicles hang frae their beards;
Gie fine braw claes[6] to fine life-guards,
        And maids of honor:
And yill[7] an' whisky gie to cairds,[8]
        Until they sconner.[9]

" A title, Dempster[10] merits it;
A garter gie to Willie Pitt;

---

[1] Did sweat.—[2] Without.—[3] Dexterously.—[4] Snug.—[5] Plenty.—[6] Clothes.
—[7] Ale.—[8] Tinkers.—[9] Loathe it.—[10] George Dempster, Esq., of Dunnichen.

Gie wealth to some be-ledger'd cit,
    In cent. per cent.;
But gie me real, sterling wit,
    And I'm content.

" While ye are pleased to keep me hale,
I'll sit down o'er my scanty meal,
Be 't water-brose[1] or muslin-kail,[2]
    Wi' cheerfu' face,
As lang 's the Muses dinna fail
    To say the grace."

An anxious e'e I never throws
Behint my lug, or by my nose;
I jouk[3] beneath misfortune's blows
    As weel 's I may;
Sworn foe to sorrow, care, and prose,
    I rhyme away.

O ye douce[4] folk that live by rule,
Grave, tideless-blooded, calm and cool,
Compared wi' you—O fool! fool! fool!
    How much unlike!
Your hearts are just a standing pool,
    Your lives, a dyke!

Nae hair-brain'd, sentimental traces
In your unletter'd, nameless faces!
In arioso trills and graces
    Ye never stray,
But, gravissimo, solemn basses
    Ye hum away.

Ye are sae grave, nae doubt ye 're wise;
Nae ferly[5] tho' you do despise
The harum-scarum, ram-stam[6] boys,
    The rattlin' squad:
I see you upward cast your eyes—
    Ye ken the road.—

Whilst I—but I shall haud me there—
Wi' you I'll scarce gang onie where—

[1] Made of meal and water only.—[2] Broth, composed of water, shelled barley, and greens.—[3] To stoop.—[4] Wise.—[5] With contempt.—[6] Thoughtless.

Then, Jamie, I shall say nae mair,
      But quit my sang,
Content wi' you to make a pair,
      Where'er I gang.

TO JOHN LAPRAIK,

AN OLD SCOTTISH BARD.

APRIL 1, 1785.

WHILE briers an' woodbines budding green,
An' paitricks[1] scraichin' loud at e'en,
An' morning pousie[2] whiddin'[3] seen,
      Inspire my Muse,
This freedom in an unknown frien'
      I pray excuse.

On Fasten-e'en[4] we had a rockin',[5]
To ca' the crack[6] and weave the stockin';
And there was muckle fun an' jockin',
      Ye need nae doubt;
At length we had a hearty yokin'
      At sang about.

There was ae sang,[7] amang the rest,
Aboon them a' it pleased me best,
That some kind husband had addrest
      To some sweet wife:

[1] Partridges.—[2] A hare.—[3] Running as a hare does.—[4] Fastens-even.

[5] This is a term derived from those primitive times, when the country women employed their leisure hours in spinning on the rock or distaff. This instrument being very portable, was well fitted to accompany its owner to a neighbor's house; hence the phrase of *going a rocking* or *with the rock*. The connection, however, which the phrase had with the implement was forgotten after the rock gave place to the spinning-wheel, and men talked of going a-rocking as well as women. It was at one of these rockings, or social parties, that Mr. Lapraik's song was sung. Burns being informed who was the author, wrote his first epistle to Lapraik; and his second in reply to his answer.

[6] To call upon some one in the company for a song or a story.

[7] The song here alluded to was written by Mr. Lapraik after sustaining a considerable pecuniary loss. In consequence of some connection as security for several persons concerned in the failure of the Ayr bank, he was obliged to sell his farm of Dalfram, near Muirkirk. One day, while his wife was fret-

It thirl'd the heart-strings thro' the breast,
  A' to the life.

I 've scarce heard aught describes sae weel,
What generous, manly bosoms feel;
Thought I, "Can this be Pope, or Steele,
  Or Beattie's wark?"
They tauld me 'twas an odd kind chiel[1]
  About Muirkirk.

It pat me fidgin'-fain[2] to hear 't,
And sae about him there I spier't;[3]
Then a' that kent him round declared
  He had ingine,[4]
That nane excell'd it, few cam near 't,
  It was sae fine.

ting over their misfortunes, he composed it with a view to moderate her grief
and fortify her resignation. It is as follows:

  When I upon thy bosom lean,
   And fondly clasp thee a' my ain,
  I glory in the sacred ties
   That made us ane, wha ance were twain:
  A mutual flame inspires us baith,
   The tender look, the melting kiss:
  Even years shall ne'er destroy our love,
   But only gie us change o' bliss.

  Hae I a wish? It 's a' for thee;
   I ken thy wish is me to please;
  Our moments pass sae smooth away,
   That numbers on us look and gaze;
  Weel pleased they see our happy days,
   Nor Envy's sel finds aught to blame;
  And ay when weary cares arise,
   Thy bosom still shall be my hame.

  I 'll lay me there, and take my rest,
   And if that aught disturb my dear,
  I 'll bid her laugh her cares away,
   And beg her not to drap a tear:
  Hae I a joy? it 's a' her ain;
   United still her heart and mine;
  They 're like the woodbine round the tree,
   That 's twined till death shall them disjoin.

[1] A droll, good fellow.—[2] Very anxious.—[3] Inquired.—[4] Possessed of wit
and genius.

That, set him to a pint of ale,
An' either douce,[1] or merry tale,
Or rhymes an' sangs he 'd made himsel,
    Or witty catches,
'Tween Inverness and Tiviotdale,
    He had few matches.

Then up I gat, an' swoor an aith,
Tho' I should pawn my pleugh and graith,[2]
Or die a cadger-pownie's[3] death,
    At some dyke-back,
A pint an' gill I 'd gie them baith
    To hear your crack.[4]

But, first an' foremost, I should tell,
Amaist as soon as I could spell
I to the crambo-jingle[5] fell,
    Tho' rude an' rough,
Yet crooning[6] to a body's sel,
    Does weel enough.

I am nae Poet, in a sense,
But just a Rhymer, like, by chance,
An' hae to learning nae pretence,
    Yet, what the matter?
Whene'er my Muse does on me glance,
    I jingle at her.

Your critic-folk may cock their nose,
And say, "How can you e'er propose,
You wha ken hardly verse frae prose,
    To mak a sang?"
But, by your leaves, my learned foes,
    Ye 're may be wrang.

What 's a' your jargon o' your schools,
Your Latin names for horns and stools;
If honest Nature made you fools,
    What sairs[7] your grammars?
Ye 'd better taen up spades and shools,
    Or knappin'-hammers.

[1] Serious.—[2] Furniture.—[3] A carrier's poney.—[4] Converse.—[5] Rhyming.
—[6] Humming.—[7] Serves, what service.

A set o' dull, conceited hashes,[1]
Confuse their brains in college classes!
They gang in stirks,[2] and come out asses,
      Plain truth to speak;
An' syne[3] they think to climb Parnassus
      By dint o' Greek!

Gie me ae spark o' Nature's fire,
That's a' the learning I desire;
Then tho' I drudge thro' dub,[4] and mire,
      At pleugh or cart,
My Muse, tho' hamely in attire,
      May touch the heart.

Oh for a spunk o' Allan's glee,
Or Fergusson's, the bauld and slee,[5]
Or bright Lapraik's, my friend to be,
      If I can hit it!
That would be lear[6] enough for me,
      If I could get it.

Now, Sir, if ye hae friends enow,
Tho' real friends, I b'lieve, are few,
Yet if your catalogue be fu',[7]
      I'se no insist,
But gif ye want a friend that's true,
      I'm on your list.

I winna blaw[8] about mysel;
As ill I like my fauts to tell;
But friends, and folk that wish me well,
      They sometimes roose[9] me,
Tho' I maun own, as monie still
      As sair[10] abuse me.

There's ae wee faut[11] they whiles lay to me,
I like the lasses—Gude forgie me!
For monie a plack[12] they wheedle frae me!
      At dance or fair;
Maybe some ither thing they gie me,
      They weel can spare.

[1] Stupid fellows, who know neither how to dress, or to behave with propriety.
[2] Large calves.—[3] Then.—[4] A pond.—[5] Sly.—[6] Learning.—[7] Full.—[8] Will not boast.—[9] Praise me.—[10] Sore.—[11] One small fault.—[12] An old Scotch coin, the third part of a Scotch penny.

But Mauchline race, or Mauchline fair;
I should be proud to meet you there;
We 'se gie a night's discharge to care,
   If we forgather,[1]
An' hae a swap o' rhymin'-ware
   Wi' ane anither.

The four-gill chap,[2] we 'se gar[3] him clatter
An' kirsen[4] him wi' reeking water;
Syne[5] we 'll sit down an' tak our whitter,[6]
   To cheer our heart;
An' faith wo 'se be acquainted better
   Before we part.

There 's naething like the honest nappy!
Whaur 'll ye e'er see men sae happy,
Or women sonsie, saft an' sappy,
    'Tween morn an' morn,
As them wha like to taste the drappie
   In glass or horn?

I 've seen me daez't[7] upon a time;
I scarce could wink or see a styme;
Just ae half muchkin does me prime,
   Aught less is little;
Then back I rattle on the rhyme
   As gleg 's a whittle!

Awa' ye selfish, warly[8] race,
Wha think that havins,[9] sense, an' grace,
Even love an' friendship should give place
   To catch the plack![10]
I dinna like to see your face
   Nor hear your crack.

But ye whom social pleasure charms,
Whose hearts the tide of kindness warms,
Who hold your being on the terms—
   "Each aid the others!"
Come to my bowl, come to my arms,
   My friends, my brothers!

---

[1] Meet.—[2] A pot or measure, in which whisky or other spirits was served out to customers at alehouses.

[3] Make.—[4] To christen.—[5] Then.—[6] A hearty draught of liquor.—[7] Stupid. —[8] Worldly.—[9] Good manners.—[10] To get money.

But to conclude my lang epistle,
As my auld pen 's worn to the grissle;
Twa lines frae you wad gar me fissle,[1]
        Who am most fervent,
While I can either sing or whissle,
        Your friend and servant.

————

TO THE SAME.

Aꜰʀɪʟ 21, 178ᶓ.

Wʜɪʟᴇ new-ca'd kye[2] rout at the stake,
An' pownies reek in pleugh or braik,[3]
This hour, on e'enin's edge, I take,
        To own I 'm debtor
To honest-hearted, auld Lapraik,
        For his kind letter.

Forjesket[4] sair, with weary legs,
Rattlin' the corn out-owre the rigs,
Or dealing thro' amang the naigs
        Their ten-hours[5] bite,
My awkwart Muse sair pleads and begs,
        I would na write.

The tapetless[6] ramfeezl'd[7] hizzie,
She 's saft at best, and something lazy,
Quo' she, " Ye ken we 've been sae busy,
        This month an' mair,
That trouth my head is grown right dizzie,
        An' something sair."

Her dowff[8] excuses pat me mad:
" Conscience," says I, " ye thowless jad!
I 'll write, an' that a hearty blaud,
        This vera night;
So dinna ye affront your trade,
        But rhyme it right.

" Shall bauld Lapraik, the king o' hearts,
Tho' mankind were a pack o' cartes,

———

[1] Bustle.—[2] Cows having newly calved.—[3] A kind of harrow.—[4] Jaded
with fatigue.—[5] A slight bate given to horses in the forenoon, while in the
yoke.—[6] Foolish.—[7] Fatigued.—[8] Pithless, wanting force.

Roose[1] you sae weel for your deserts,
   In terms sae friendly,
Yet ye'll neglect to shaw your parts,
   An' thank him kindly!"

Sae I gat paper in a blink,
An' down gaed stumpie in the ink;
Quoth I, "Before I sleep a wink,
   I vow I'll close it;
An' if you winna mak it clink,
   By Jove I'll prose it!"

Sae I've begun to scrawl, but whether
In rhyme or prose, or baith thegither,
Or some hotch-potch that's rightly neither,
   Let time mak proof;
But I shall scribble down some blether[2]
   Just clean aff-loof.[3]

My worthy friend, ne'er grudge an' carp,
Tho' Fortune use you hard and sharp;
Come, kittle up your moorland harp
   Wi' gleesome touch!
Ne'er mind how Fortune waft and warp;
   She's but a bitch.

She's gien me mony a jirt an' fleg,
Sin' I could striddle[4] owre a rig;[5]
But, by the Lord, tho' I should beg
   Wi' lyart pow,[6]
I'll laugh an' sing, an' shake my leg
   As lang's I dow![7]

Now comes the sax-an'-twentieth simmer
I've seen the bud upo' the timmer,[8]
Still persecuted by the limmer[9]
   Frae year to year;
But yet, despite the kittle kimmer,[10]
   I, Rob, am here.

Do ye envy the city *gent.*,
Behind a kist[11] to lie and sklent,[12]

[1] Praise, commend.—[2] Nonsense.—[3] Unpremeditated, off-hand.—[4] Straddle.—[5] Ridge.—[6] With gray hairs.—[7] Can.—[8] Tree.—[9] Kept mistress.—[10] Skittish girl.—[11] Shop counter.—[12] To look sideways, and cunning.

Or purse-proud, big wi' *cent. per cent.*
    And muckle wame,[1]
In some bit burgh[2] to represent
    A bailie's name?

Or, is 't the paughty, feudal thane,
Wi' ruffled sark[3] an' glancing cane,
Wha thinks himself nae sheep-shank bane,
    But lordly stalks,
While caps and bonnets aff are taen,
    As by he walks?

"O Thou, wha gies us each good gift!
Gie me o' wit an' sense a lift,
Then turn me, if thou please, adrift,
    Thro' Scotland wide;
Wi' cits nor lairds I wadna shift,
    In a' their pride!"

Were this the charter of our state—
"On pain of hell be rich and great;"
Damnation then would be our fate,
    Beyond remead;[4]
But, thanks to Heaven! that's no the gate[5]
    We learn our creed:—

For thus the royal mandate ran,
When first the human race began—
"The social, friendly, honest man,
    Whate'er he be,
'Tis he fulfils great Nature's plan,
    An' none but he."

O mandate glorious and divine!
The ragged followers of the Nine,
Poor, thoughtless devils! yet may shine
    In glorious light,
While sordid sons of Mammon's line
    Are dark as night.

Tho' here they scrape, an' squeeze, an' growl,
Their worthless nievefu'[7] of a soul
May in some future carcase howl,
    The forest's fright;

---

[1] Large belly. — [2] Small borough. — [3] Shirt. — [4] No mean personage. —
[5] Remedy. — [6] The way. — [7] Handful.

Or in some day-detesting owl,
　　　May shun the light.

Then may Lapraik and Burns arise,
To reach their native, kindred skies,
And sing their pleasures, hopes, an' joys,
　　　In some mild sphere,
Still closer knit in friendship's ties
　　　Each passing year!

TO THE SAME.

Sept. 13th, 1785

Guid speed an' furder to you, Johnie,
Guid health, hale han's, an' weather bonnie;
Now when ye 're nickan[1] down fu' cannie[2]
　　　The staff o' bread,
May ye ne'er want a stoop[3] o' brany
　　　To clear your head.

May Boreas never thresh your rigs,
Nor kick your rickles aff their legs,
Sendin' the stuff o'er muirs an' haggs[4]
　　　Like drivin' wrack;
But may the tapmast grain that wags
　　　Come to the sack.

I 'm bizzie[5] too, an' skelpin[6] at it,
But bitter, daudin showers hae wat it,
Sae my auld stumpie pen I gat it,
　　　Wi' muckle wark,
An' took my jocteleg[7] an' whatt[8] it,
　　　Like ony clerk.

It 's now twa month that I 'm your debtor,
For your braw, nameless, dateless letter,
Abusin' me for harsh ill nature
　　　On holy men,
While deil a hair yoursel ye 're better,
　　　But mair profane.

[1] Cutting.—[2] Dexterous.—[3] Jug or dish with a handle.—[4] Scars or gulfs in mosses.—[5] Busy.—[6] Driving or pressing forward.—[7] A kind of knife.—[8] To polish by cutting.

But let the kirk-folk ring their bells,
Let's sing about our noble sels;
We'll cry nae jads frae heathen hills
    To help, or roose us,
But browster wives and whiskie stills,
    They are the muses.

Your friendship, Sir, I winna quat[1] it,
An' if ye mak objections at it,
Then han' in nieve[2] some day we'll knot it,
    An' witness take,
An' when wi' usquabae we've wat it
    It winna break.

But if the beast and branks[3] be spared
Till kye[4] be gaun[5] without the herd,
An' a' the vittel in the yard,
    An' theckit[6] right,
I mean your ingle-side to guard
    Ae winter night.

Then muse-inspirin' aqua-vitœ
Shall make us baith sae blithe an' witty,
Till ye forget ye're auld an' gatty,[7]
    An' be as canty,[8]
As ye were nine years less than thretty,
    Sweet ane an' twenty!

But stooks[9] are cowpet[10] wi' the blast,
An' now the sun keeks[11] in the west,
Then I maun rin[12] amang the rest
    An' quat my chanter;
Sae I subscribe mysel in haste,
    Yours, Rab the Ranter.

Quit.—[2] Hand in hand.—[3] A kind of wooden curb.—[4] Cows.—[5] Going—[6] Thatched.—[7] Infirm.—[8] Merry.—[9] Shocks of corn.—[10] Upset.—[11] Peeps—[12] Must run.

EPISTLE TO DAVIE,[1]

A BROTHER POET.

JAN. ——.

While winds frae aff Ben-Lomond blaw,
And bar the doors wi' driving snaw,
  And hing[2] us owre the ingle,[3]
I set me down to pass the time,
And spin a verse or twa o' rhyme,
  In hamely westlin[4] jingle.
While frosty winds blaw in the drift,
  Ben to the chimla lug,[5]
I grudge a wee the great folks' gift,
  That live sae bien[6] and snug:
    I tent[7] less, and want less
      Their roomy fireside;
    But hanker and canker,
      To see their cursed pride.

It's hardly in a body's power
To keep, at times, frae being sour,
  To see how things are shared;
How best o' chiels[8] are whiles in want,
While coofs[9] on countless thousands rant,
  And ken na how to wair 't:[10]
But, Davie lad, ne'er fash[11] your head
  Tho' we hae little gear,
We 're fit to win our daily bread
  As lang 's we 're hale and fier;[12]
    "Mair spier[13] na, nor fear na',[14]
      Auld age ne'er mind a feg,[15]
    The last o 't, the warst o 't,
      Is only for to beg.

To lie in kilns and barns at e'en,
When banes are crazed and bluid is thin,
  Is, doubtless, great distress!
Yet then content could make us blest:

---

[1] David Sillar, author of a volume of Poems in the Scottish dialect.—
[2] Hang.—[3] Fireplace.—[4] West country.—[5] The fireside.—[6] In plenty.—[7] Heed.
—[8] Best of men.—[9] Blockheads.—[10] To spend it.—[11] Trouble.—[12] Sound.—
[13] More ask not.—[14] Ramsay.—[15] Fig.

Even then, sometimes, we'd snatch a taste
  Of truest happiness.
The honest heart that's free frae a'
  Intended fraud or guile,
However Fortune kick'd the ba',
  Has ay some cause to smile:
    And mind still, you'll find still,
      A comfort this nae sma';
    Nae mair then, we'll care then,
      Nae farther can we fa'.

What tho', like commoners of air,
We wander out, we know not where,
  But[1] either house or hall?
Yet Nature's charms, the hills and woods,
The sweeping vales and foaming floods,
  Are free alike to all.
In days when daisies deck the ground,
  And blackbirds whistle clear,
With honest joy our hearts will bound,
  To see the coming year:
    On braes when we please, then,
      We'll sit an' sowth[2] a tune;
    Syne[3] rhyme till 't,[4] we'll time till 't,
      And sing 't when we hae done.

It's no in titles nor in rank;
It's no in wealth like Lon'on bank,
  To purchase peace and rest:
It's no in makin' muckle mair;[5]
It's no in books; it's no in lear,
  To make us truly blest:
If happiness hae not her seat
  And centre in the breast,
We may be wise, or rich, or great,
  But never can be blest:
    Nae treasures, nor pleasures,
      Could make us happy lang;
    The heart ay's the part ay,
      That makes us right or wrang.

Think ye, that sic as you and I,
Wha drudge and drive thro' wet an' dry,

---

[1] Without.—[2] Hum, or whistle.—[3] Then.—[4] To it.—[5] Much more.

Wi' never-ceasing toil;
Think ye, are we less blest than they,
Wha scarcely tent us in their way,
  As hardly worth their while?
Alas! how aft in haughty mood,
  God's creatures they oppress!
Or else, neglecting a' that 's good,
  They riot in excess!
    Baith careless and fearless
      Of either heaven or hell!
    Esteeming and deeming
      It 's a' an idle tale!

Then let us cheerfu' acquiesce;
Nor make our scanty pleasures less,
  By pining at our state;
And even should misfortunes come,
I, here wha sit, hae met wi' some,
  An' 's thankfu' for them yet.
They gie the wit o' age to youth;
  They let us ken oursel;
They make us see the naked truth,
  The real good and ill.
    Tho' losses and crosses
      Be lessons right severe,
    There 's wit there, ye 'll get there,
      Ye 'll find nae other where.

But tent me, Davie, ace o' hearts!
(To say aught less wad wrang the cartes,
  And flattery I detest,)
This life has joys for you and I;
And joys that riches ne'er could buy;
  And joys the very best.
There 's a' the pleasures o' the heart,
  The lover an' the frien';
Ye hae your Meg, your dearest part,
  And I, my darling Jean!
    It warms me, it charms me,
      To mention but her name:
    It heats me, it beets[1] me,
      And sets me a' on flame!

[1] Adds fuel to fire.

O all ye powers who rule above!
O Thou, whose very self art love!
  Thou know'st my words sincere!
The life-blood streaming thro' my heart,
Or my more dear immortal part,
  Is not more fondly dear!
When heart-corroding care and grief
  Deprive my soul of rest,
Her dear idea brings relief
  And solace to my breast.
    Thou Being, all-seeing,
      Oh hear my fervent prayer;
    Still take her, and make her
      Thy most peculiar care!

All hail, ye tender feelings dear!
The smile of love, the friendly tear,
  The sympathetic glow;
Long since, this world's thorny ways
Had number'd out my weary days,
  Had it not been for you!
Fate still has blest me with a friend,
  In every care and ill;
And oft a more endearing band,
  A tie more tender still:
    It lightens, it brightens
      The tenebrific[1] scene,
    To meet with and greet with,
      My Davie or my Jean.

Oh, how that name inspires my style!
The words come skelpin[2] rank and file,
  Amaist before I ken!
The ready measure rins as fine,
As Phœbus and the famous Nine
  Were glow'rin[3] o'er my pen.
My spaviet[4] Pegasus will limp,
  Till ance he's fairly het;[5]
And then he'll hilch,[6] and stilt,[7] and jimp,[8]
  An' rin an unco fit:[9]

- Dark, gloomy.—[2] Tripping.—[3] Looking.—[4] Having the spavin.—[5] Heated.
—[6] Hobble.—[7] Limp, or halt.—[8] Jump.—[9] Go speedily.

But lest then, the beast then
  Should rue this hasty ride,
I 'll light now, and dight now,
  His sweaty, wizen'd[1] hide.

TO THE SAME.[2]

AULD NEEBOR—

I 'M three times doubly o'er your debtor,
For your auld-farrant,[3] frien'ly letter;
Tho' I maun say 't, I doubt ye flatter,
    Ye speak sae fair;
For my puir, silly, rhymin' clatter,
    Some less maun sair.[4]

Hale be your heart, hale be your fiddle;
Lang may your elbuck[5] jink[6] an' diddle,
To cheer you thro' the weary widdle
    O' war'ly cares,
Till bairns' bairns' kindly cuddle
    Your auld, gray hairs.

But, Davie lad, I 'm red[8] ye 're glaikit;[9]
I 'm tauld the Muse ye hae negleckit;
An' gif[10] it 's sae, ye sud[11] be licket[12]
    Until ye fyke;[13]
Sic hauns as you sud ne'er be faikit,[14]
    Be hain't[15] wha like.

For me, I 'm on Parnassus' brink,
Rivin' the words to gar them clink;
Whyles dais't[16] wi' love, whyles dais't wi' drink,
    Wi' jads[17] or masons;
An' whyles, but ay owre late, I think
    Braw sober lessons.

---

[1] Shrunk, hide-bound.
[2] This is prefixed to the poems of David Sillar, published at Kilmarnock, 1789.
[3] Sagacious.—[4] Must serve.—[5] Elbow.—[6] A sudden turning.—[7] Children's children.—[8] Informed.—[9] Inattentive, foolish.—[10] If.—[11] Should.—[12] Licked, beaten.—[13] Become agitated.—[14] Such hands as you should ne'er be unknown.—[15] Spared, or excused.—[16] Sometimes stupified.—[17] Women.

Of a' the thoughtless sons o' man,
Commen' me to the Bardie clan;
Except it be some idle plan
O' rhymin' clink,
The devil-haet,[1] that I sud ban,[2]
They ever think.

Nae thought, nae view, nae scheme o' livin',
Nae cares to gie us joy or grievin';
But just the pouchie[3] put the nieve[4] in,
An' while aught's there,
Then, hiltie, skiltie, we gae scrievin',[5]
An' fash nae mair.[6]

Leeze me[7] on rhyme! it's aye a treasure,
My chief, amaist my only pleasure,
At hame, a-fiel',[8] at wark or leisure,
The Muse, poor hizzie!
Though rough an' raploch[9] be her measure,
She's seldom lazy.

Haud[10] to the Muse, my dainty Davie;
The warl' may play you monie a shavie;
But for the Muse, she'll never leave ye,
Tho' e'er sae puir,
Na, even tho' limpin' wi' the spavie[11]
Frae door to door.

TO MR. WILLIAM TYTLER,

With a portrait of the Author.

EDINBURGH, 1787.

REVERED defender of beauteous Stuart,
Of Stuart, a name once respected,
A name, which to love was the mark of a true heart,
But now 'tis despised and neglected.

Tho' something like moisture conglobes in my eye,
Let no one misdeem me disloyal;

The devil forbid.—[2] Swear.—[3] Pouch, or purse.—[4] The hand.—[5] Dashing away.—[6] Care for nothing more.—[7] A phrase of endearment.—[8] In the field.—[9] Coarse.—[10] Hold.—[11] Spavin.

A poor friendless wanderer may well claim a sigh,
    Still more if that wanderer were royal.

My fathers that name have revered on a throne;
    My fathers have fallen to right it;
Those fathers would spurn their degenerate son,
    That name should he scoffingly slight it.

Still in prayers for King George I most heartily join,
    The Queen, and the rest of the gentry,
Be they wise, be they foolish, is nothing of mine;
    Their title 's avow'd by my country.

But why of this epocha make such a fuss,
    *   *   *   *   *
    *   *   *   *   *
    *   *   *   *   *

But loyalty, truce! we 're on dangerous ground,
    Who knows how the fashions may alter?
The doctrine to-day that is loyalty sound,
    To-morrow may bring us a halter.

I send you a trifle, a head of a Bard,
    A trifle scarce worthy your care;
But accept it, good Sir, as a mark of respect;
    Sincere as a saint's dying prayer.

Now life's chilly evening dim shades on your eye,
    And ushers the long dreary night;
But you, like the star that athwart gilds the sky,
    Your course to the latest is bright.

<hr />

TO WILLIAM SIMPSON, OCHILTREE.

MAY, 1785.

I GAT your letter, winsome Willie;
Wi' gratefu' heart I thank you brawlie;
Tho' I maun say 't, I wad be silly,
    And unco vain,
Should I believe, my coaxing billie,
    Your flatterin' strain.

But I 'se believe ye kindly meant it,
I sud[1] be laith[2] to think ye hinted
Ironic satire, sidelins[3] sklented
  On my poor Musie;
Tho' in sic phrasin'[4] terms ye 've penn'd it,
  I scarce excuse ye.

My senses wad be in a creel,[5]
Should I but dare a hope to speel,[6]
Wi' Allan or wi' Gilbertfield,
  The braes o' fame;
Or Fergusson, the writer-chiel;
  A deathless name!

(O Fergusson! thy glorious parts
Ill suited law's dry, musty arts!
My curse upon your whunstane[7] hearts,
  Ye E'nburgh[8] gentry!
The tithe o' what ye waste at cartes,[9]
  Wad stow'd his pantry!)

Yet when a tale comes i' my head,
Or lasses gie my heart a screed,[10]
As whyles they 're like to be my dead,[11]
  (O sad disease!)
I kittle up my rustic reed;
  It gies me ease.

Auld Coila[12] now may fidge fu' fain,[13]
She 's gotten Poets o' her ain,
Chiels wha their chanters[14] winna hain,[15]
  But tune their lays,
Till echoes a' resound again
  Her weel-sung praise.

Nae Poet thought her worth his while,
To set her name in measured style;
She lay like some unkenn'd-of-isle,
  Beside New Holland,
Or whare wild-meeting oceans boil
  Besouth Magellan.

Ramsay and famous Fergusson
Gied Forth and Tay a lift aboon;
Yarrow an' Tweed, to monie a tune,
      Owre Scotland rings,
While Irwin, Lugar, Ayr, an' Doon,
      Nae body sings.

Th' Ilissus, Tiber, Thames, an' Seine,
Glide sweet in monie a tunefu' line!
But, Willie, set your fit[1] to mine,
      An' cock your crest,
We 'll gar[2] our streams and burnies' shine
      Up wi' the best.

We 'll sing auld Coila's plains and fells,[4]
Her moors red brown wi' heather bells,
Her banks an' braes, her dens an' dells,
      Where glorious Wallace
Aft bure the gree,[5] as story tells,
      Frae Southron billies.[6]

At Wallace' name what Scottish blood
But boils up in a spring-tide flood!
Oft have our fearless fathers strode
      By Wallace' side,
Still pressing onward, red-wat shod,[7]
      Or glorious died.

Oh, sweet are Coila's haughs[8] an' woods,
When lintwhites[9] chant amang the buds,
And jinking hares, in amorous whids,[10]
      Their loves enjoy,
While thro' the braes the cushat croods[11]
      Wi' wailfu' cry!

Even winter bleak has charms to me,
When winds rave thro' the naked tree;
Or frosts on hills of Ochiltree
      Are hoary gray;
Or blinding drifts wild furious flee,
      Darkening the day!

---

[1] Foot.—[2] Make.—[3] Rivers and brooks.—[4] Fields.—[5] Obtained the victory.
—[6] Englishmen.—[7] To walk in blood over the shoe-tops.—[8] Valleys.—[9] Linnets.—[10] The motion of a hare in running, when not frightened.—[11] The dove coos.

O Nature! a' thy shows an' forms
To feeling, pensive hearts hae charms;
Whether the summer kindly warms
                Wi' life an' light,
Or winter howls, in gusty storms,
                The lang, dark night!

The Muse, nae Poet ever fand[1] her,
Till by himsel' he learn'd to wander,
Adown some trotting burn's meander,
                And no think lang;[2]
Oh, sweet to stray and pensive ponder
                A heart-felt sang!

The warly race may drudge an' drive,
Hog-shouther,[3] jundie,[4] stretch an' strive,
Let me fair Nature's face descrive,[5]
                And I, wi' pleasure,
Shall let the busy, grumbling hive
                Bum[6] owre their treasure.

Fareweel, "my rhyme-composing brither"
We 've been owre lang unkenn'd[7] to ither,
Now let us lay our heads thegither,
                In love fraternal:
May Envy wallop in a tether,[8]
                Black fiend infernal!

While Highlandmen hate tolls an' taxes;
While moorlan' herds like guid fat braxies;[9]
While *terra firma* on her axis
                Diurnal turns,
Count on a friend, in faith an' practice,
                In ROBERT BURNS.

POSTSCRIPT.

My memory 's no worth a preen;[10]
I had amaist forgotten clean,
You bade me write you what they mean
                By this new-light,[11]

---

[1] Found.—[2] And not think the time long, or be weary.—[3] Justle with the shoulder.—[4] Justle.—[5] Describe.—[6] To hum.—[7] Unknown to each other.—[8] Struggle as an animal whose tether gets entangled.—[9] Morbid sheep.—[10] A pin.

[11] New-light, a cant phrase in the west of Scotland for those religious opinions which Dr. Taylor, of Norwich, defended so strenuously.

'Bout which our herds sae aft hae been
　　　Maist like to fight.

In days when mankind were but callans[1]
At grammar, logic, and sic talents,
They took nae pains their speech to balance,
　　　Or rules to gie,
But spak their thoughts in plain, braid Lallans,[2]
　　　Like you or me.

In thae[3] auld times they thought the moon
Just like a sark,[4] or pair o' shoon,
Wore by degrees, till her last roon,[5]
　　　Gaed past their viewin',
An' shortly after she was done,
　　　They gat a new one.

This past for certain, undisputed,
It ne'er came i' their heads to doubt it,
Till chiels gat up an' wad confute it,
　　　An' ca'd it wrang;
An' muckle din there was about it,
　　　Bath loud an' lang.

Some herds, weel learn'd upo' the beuk,[6]
Wad threap[7] auld folk the thing misteuk;
For 'twas the auld moon turn'd a neuk,[8]
　　　An' out o' sight,
An' backlins-comin'[9] to the leuk,
　　　She grew mair bright.

This was denied—it was affirm'd:
The herds and hissels[10] were alarm'd;
The reverend gray-beards raved an' storm'd,
　　　That beardless laddies
Should think they better were inform'd
　　　Than their auld daddies.

Frae less to mair it gaed to sticks;
Frae words an' aiths to clours[11] an' nicks;

---

[1] Boys.—[2] The Scottish dialect.—[3] These.—[4] A shirt.—[5] A shred.—[6] Book.
—[7] Maintain by dint of assertion.—[8] Corner.—[9] Returning.—[10] So many cattle
as one person can attend.—[11] A wound occasioned by a blow.

And monie a fallow gat his licks,
        Wi' hearty crunt;[1]
An' some, to learn them for their tricks,
        Were hang'd an' brunt.[2]

This game was play'd in monie lands,
An' auld-light caddies' bure[4] sic hands,
That, faith, the youngsters took the sands
        Wi' nimble shanks,
The lairds forbade, by strict command,
        Sic bluidy pranks.

But new-light herds gat sic a cowe,[5]
Folk thought them ruin'd stick-an'-stowe,[6]
Till now amaist on every knowe,[7]
        Ye'll find ane placed;
An' some their new-light fair avow,
        Just quite barefaced.

Nae doubt the auld-light flocks are bleatin';
Their zealous herds are vex'd an' sweatin';
Mysel, I've even seen them greetin'[8]
        Wi' girnin'[9] spite,
To hear the moon sae sadly lied on
        By word an' write.[10]

But shortly they will cowe the louns!
Some auld-light herds in neebor towns
Are mind 't, in things they ca' balloons,
        To tak a flight,
And stay ae month amang the moons
        An' see them right.

Guid observation they will gie them;
An' when the auld-moon 's gaen to lea'e them,
The hindmost shaird,[11] they'll fetch it wi' them,
        Just i' their pouch,
An' when the new-light billies[12] see them,
        I think they'll crouch!

[1] A blow on the head with a cudgel.—[2] Burnt.
[3] Literally ticket-porters, or trusty persons who are employed on errands; but the appellation is frequently used in a more general way, and applied to other persons.
[4] Did bear.—[5] A fright or beating.—[6] Altogether.—[7] Hillock.—[8] Weeping. —[9] With rage, or agony of spirit.—[10] Both in conversation and books.—[11] A shred.—[12] Brethren.

Sae, ye observe that a' this clatter
Is naething but a moonshine matter;
But tho' dull prose-folk Latin splatter
    In logic tulzie,[1]
I hope we bardies ken some better,
        Than mind sic brulzie.[2]

TO JOHN GOUDIE, KILMARNOCK,

On the publication of his Essays.

O GOUDIE! terror o' the Whigs,
Dread o' black coats an' reverend wigs,
Sour Bigotry, on her last legs,
    Girnin[3] looks back,
Wishin' the ten Egyptian plagues
        Wad seize you quick.

Poor gapin', glowrin'[4] Superstition,
Waes me! she's in a sad condition;
Fie! bring Black Jock her state physician
    To see her water!
Alas! there's ground o' great suspicion
        She'll ne'er get better.

Auld Orthodoxy lang did grapple,
But now she's got an unco ripple,[5]
Haste, gie her name up i' the chapel,[6]
    Nigh unto death;
See how she fetches at the thrapple,
        An' gasps for breath.

Enthusiasm's past redemption,
Gaen[7] in a gallopping consumption,
Not a' the quacks wi' a' their gumption[8]
    Will ever mend her,
Her feeble pulse gies strong presumption
        Death soon will end her.

To quarrel.—[2] A broil.—[3] Twisting the features in agony.—[4] Staring.—
Great weakness in the back, or loins.—[6] That the prayers of the congrega-
tion may be offered up in her behalf.—[7] Going.—[8] Skill

'Tis you and Taylor[1] are the chief
Wha are to blame for this mischief;
But gin[2] the Lord's ain focks[3] gat leave,
    A toom[4] tar-barrel
And twa red peats[5] wad send relief,
    An' end the quarrel.

———

TO J. RANKINE,

Inclosing some poems.

O ROUGH, rude, ready-witted Rankine,
The wale[6] o' cocks for fun and drinkin'!
There's monie godly folks are thinkin',
    Your dreams' an' tricks
Will send you, Korah-like, a-sinkin',
    Straught to auld Nick's.

Ye hae sae monie cracks[8] an' cants,
And in your wicked, drucken rants,
Ye mak a devil o' the saunts,
    An' fill them fou;[9]
And then their failings, flaws, an' wants,
    Are a' seen thro'.

Hypocrisy, in mercy spare it!
That holy robe, oh dinna tear it,
Spare 't for their sakes wha aften wear it,
    The lads in black;
But your curst wit, when it comes near it,
    Rives 't[10] aff their back.

Think, wicked sinner, wha ye're skaithing,[11]
It 's just the blue-gown badge an' claithing
O' saunts;[12] tak that, ye la'e[13] them naething
    To ken them by,
Frae onie unregenerate heathen
    Like you or I.

---

[1] Dr. Taylor of Norwich.—[2] If, against.—[3] Folk, people.—[4] Empty.—[5] Two red-hot turfs, such as are used for fuel.—[6] Choice.

[7] A certain humorous dream of his was then making a noise in the country-side.

[8] Conversation. —[9] Make them drunk.—[10] Rends.—[11] Injuring.—[12] Saints. —[13] Leave.

I 've sent you here some rhyming ware,
A' that I bargain'd for, an' mair:
Sae, when you hae an hour to spare.
   I will expect
Yon sang,[1] ye 'll sen 't wi' cannie[2] care,
   And no neglect.

Tho' faith, sma' heart hae I to sing!
My Muse dow[3] scarcely spread her wing!
I 've play'd mysel a bonnie spring,[4]
   An' danced my fill;
I 'd better gaen an' sair'd[5] the king
   At Bunker's Hill.

'Twas ae night, lately, in my fun,
I gaed a-roving wi' the gun,
An' brought a paitrick[6] to the grun',[7]
   A bonnie hen,
An' as the twilight was begun,
   Thought nane wad ken.

The poor wee thing was little hurt;
I straiket[8] it a wee for sport,
Ne'er thinkin' they wad fash[9] me for 't;
   But deil-ma-care!
Somebody tells the poacher-court
   The hale[10] affair.

Some auld-used hands had taen a note,
That sic a hen had got a shot;
I was suspected for the plot:
   I scorn'd to lie.
So gat the whissle o' my groat,[11]
   An' pay't the fee.

But, by my gun, o' guns the wale,[12]
An' by my pouther an' my hail,[13]
An' by my hen, an' by her tail,
   I vow an' swear!
The game shall pay o'er moor an' dale,
   For this, neist year.

[1] A song he had promised the Author.—[2] Dexterous.—[3] Can, or dare.—
[4] A Scottish reel.—[5] Served.—[6] A partridge.—[7] Ground.—[8] Stroked.—
[9] Trouble.—[10] Whole.—[11] I played a losing game.—[12] The choice.—[13] Shot.

As soon 's the clocking-time[1] is by,
An' the wee pouts begun to cry,
Lord, I 'se hae sporting by an' by,
      For my gowd guinea,
Tho' I should herd the buckskin kye[2]
      For 't in Virginia.

Trowth, they had muckle for to blame!
'Twas neither broken wing nor limb,
But twa-three draps about the wame[3]
      Scarce thro' the feathers;
And baith a yellow George to claim,
      An' thole their blethers![4]

It pits me ay as mad 's a hare;
So I can rhyme nor write nae mair;
But pennyworths again is fair,
      When time 's expedient;
Meanwhile I am, respected sir,
      Your most obedient.

TO THE SAME,

On his writing to the Author that a girl was with child by him.

I AM a keeper of the law
In some sma' points, altho' not a';
Some people tell me gin[5] I fa'
      Ae way or ither,
The breaking of ae point, tho' sma',
      Breaks a' thegither.

I hae been in for 't ance or twice,
And winna say o'er far for thrice,
Yet never met with that surprise
      That broke my rest,
But now a rumor 's like to rise,
      A whaup[6] 's i' the nest.

---

[1] Hatching time.—[2] Be transported to America, and made a cow-herd.—[3] Belly.—[4] Endure their abuse.—[5] If.—[6] Curlew.

TO DR. BLACKLOCK.

ELLISLAND, Oct. 21, 1789.

Wow, but your letter made me vauntie![1]
And are ye hale, and weel, and cantie?[2]
I kenn'd it still your wee bit jauntie[3]
    Wad bring ye to:
Lord send you ay as weel 's I want ye,
    And then ye 'll do.

The ill-thief blaw the Heron[4] south!
And never drink be near his drouth!
He tald mysel', by word o' mouth,
    He 'd tak my letter!
I lippen'd[5] to the chiel[6] in trouth,
    And bade nae better.

But aiblins[7] honest Master Heron
Had at the time some dainty fair one,
To wear his theologic care on,
    And holy study;
An' tired o' sauls to waste his lear[8] on,
    E'en tried the body.

But what d' ye think, my trusty fier?[9]
I 'm turn'd a gauger—peace be here!
Parnassian queens, I fear, I fear,
    Ye 'll now disdain me,
And then my fifty pounds a year
    Will little gain me.

Ye glaiket,[10] gleesome, dainty damies,
Wha by Castalia's wimplin[11] streamies,
Loup, sing, and lave your pretty limbies,
    Ye ken, ye ken,
That strang necessity supreme is
    'Mang sons o' men.

I hae a wife and twa wee[12] laddies,
They maun hae brose and brats o' duddies;[13]

---

[1] Proud.—[2] Cheerful.—[3] Short journey.—[4] Mr. Heron, author of a History of Scotland, and of various other works.—[5] Depended.—[6] Fellow.—[7] Perhaps.
—[8] Learning.—[9] Friend.—[10] Inattentive.—[11] Meandering.—[12] Little—
[13] Food and raiment.

Ye ken yoursel my heart right proud is,
  I needna vaunt,
But I 'll sned[1] besoms—thraw saugh woodies,[2]
  Before they want.

Lord help me thro' this warld o' care!
I 'm weary sick o 't late and air![3]
Not but I hae a richer share
  Than monie ithers;
But why should ae man better fare,
  And a' men brithers?

Come, Firm Resolve, take thou the van,
Thou stalk o' carl-hemp in man!
And let us mind faint heart ne'er wan
  A lady fair:
Wha does the utmost that he can,
  Will whyles[4] do mair.

But to conclude my silly rhyme,
(I 'm scant o' verse, and scant o' time,)
To make a happy fireside clime
  To weans and wife,
That 's the true pathos and sublime
  Of human life.

My compliments to sister Beckie;
And eke the same to honest Luckie;
I wat[5] she is a daintie chuckie,
  As e'er tread clay!
An' gratefully, my guid auld cockie,
  I 'm yours for ay.
      ROBERT BURNS.

TO COLONEL DE PEYSTER.

DUMFRIES, 1796.

My honor'd Colonel, deep I feel
Your interest in the Poet's weal;
Ah! now sma' heart hae I to speel[6]
  The steep Parnassus,

---

[1] Lop, or cut.—[2] Twist willow ropes.—[3] Late and early.—[4] Sometimes.—
[5] Know.—[6] To climb.

Surrounded thus by bolus pill
   And potion glasses.

Oh what a cantie[1] warl were it,
Would pain, and care, and sickness spare it;
And Fortune favor worth and merit,
   As they deserve;
(And ay a rowth[2] roast-beef and claret,
   Syne[3] wha wad starve?)

Dame Life, tho' fiction out may trick her,
And in paste gems and frippery deck her;
Oh! flickering, feeble, and unsicker[4]
   I 've found her still,
Ay wavering like the willow-wicker,
   'Tween good and ill.

Then that curst carmagnole, auld Satan,
Watches, like baudrans[5] by a rattan,[6]
Our sinfu' saul to get a claut[7] on
   Wi' felon ire;
Syne, whip! his tail ye 'll ne'er cast saut on,
   He 's aff like fire.

Ah Nick! ah Nick! it is na fair,
First showing us the tempting ware,
Bright wines and bonnie lasses rare,
   To put us daft;[8]
Syne weave, unseen, thy spider snare,
   O' hell's damn'd waft.

Poor man, the fly, aft bizzes[9] by,
And aft as chance he comes thee nigh,
Thy auld damn'd elbow yeuks[10] wi' joy,
   And hellish pleasure;
Already in thy fancy's eye,
   Thy sicker[11] treasure.

Soon heels-o'er-gowdie![12] in he gangs,
And like a sheep-head on a tangs,

---

[1] Cheerful.—[2] Plenty.—[3] Then.—[4] Unsteady.—[5] The cat.—[6] A rat.—[7] To get hold of.—[8] Mad, or off our guard.—[9] To buzz.

[10] Literally, itches. Some persons manifest a high degree of pleasure by a quick motion of the elbow.

[11] Sure.—[12] Topsy-turvy.

Thy girning[1] laugh enjoys his pangs
          And murdering wrestle,
As dangling in the wind he hangs
          A gibbet's tassel.

But lest you think I am uncivil,
To plague you with this draunting[2] drivil,
Abjuring a' intentions evil,
          I quit my pen:
The Lord preserve us frae the Devil!
          Amen! Amen!

TO A TAILOR,

In answer to an epistle which he had sent to the Author.

WHAT ails ye now, ye lousie b—ch,
To thresh my back at sic a pitch?
Losh man! hae mercy wi' your natch,
          Your bodkin 's bauld,
I did na suffer half sae much
          Frae daddie Auld.

What tho' at times, when I grow crouse,
I gie their wames a random pouse,
Is that enough for you to souse
          Your servant sae?
Gae mind your seam, ye prick the louse,
          An' jag the flae.

King David, o' poetic brief,
Wrought 'mang the lasses sic mischief
As fill'd his after life with grief
          An' bluidy rants,
An' yet he 's rank'd amang the chief
          O' lang-syne saunts.

---

[1] Grinning hideously.—[2] Drawling.
[3] This answer to a trimming letter, is omitted in Dr. Currie's edition o
the Poems, published for the benefit of the Author's family; not because he
had any doubt that the verses were written by Burns, but because he was of
opinion that they were discreditable to his memory—and for the same rea-
son, the editor and commentator, in this edition, has forborne to elucidate
what he deems already sufficiently indelicate.

And maybe, Tam, for a' my cants,
My wicked rhymes, an' drucken rants,
I 'll gie auld cloven Clooty's haunts
    An unco slip yet,
An' snugly sit amang the saunts,
    At Davie 's hip yet.

But fegs, the Session says I maun
Gae fa' upo' anither plan,
Than garrin lasses cowp the cran
    Clean heels owre body,
And sairly thole their mither's ban,
    Afore the howdy.

This leads me on to tell for sport,
How I did wi' the Session sort—
Auld Clinkum, at the inner po.t,
    Cried three times, "Robin!
Come hither lad, an' answer for 't,
    Ye 're blamed for jobbin'!"

Wi' pinch I put a Sunday face on,
An' snoov'd awa before the Session—
I made an open, fair confession,
    I scorn to lie;
And syne Mess John, beyond expression,
    Fell foul o' me.

A fornicator loun he call'd me,
An' said my faut frae bliss expell'd me;
I own'd the tale was true he tell'd me;
    "But what the matter,"
Quo' I, "I fear, unless ye geld me,
    I 'll ne'er be better."

"Geld you!" quo' he, "and whatfore no!
If that your right hand, leg, or toe,
Should ever prove your spiritual foe,
    You should remember
To cut it aff, an' whatfore no
    Your dearest member?"

"Na, na," quo' I, "I 'm no for that,
Gelding 's nae better than 'tis ca't,
I 'd rather suffer for my faut
    A hearty flewit,
22

As sair owre hip as ye can draw 't!
       Tho' I should rue it.

" Or gin ye like to end the bother,
To please us a', I 've just ae ither,
When next wi' yon lass I forgather,
       Whate'er betide it,
I 'll frankly gie her 't a' thegither,
       An' let her guide it !"

But, Sir, this pleased them warst ava,
And, therefore, Tam, when that I saw,
I said, " Gude night," and cam awa',
       An' left the Session ;
I saw they were resolvéd a'
       On my oppression.

THE INVENTORY,

In answer to a mandate by Mr. Aikin, Surveyor of the Taxes.

SIR, as your mandate did request,
I send you here a faithfu' list
O' gudes an' gear, an' a' my graith,[1]
To which I'm clear to gie my aith.[2]

   Imprimis then, for carriage cattle,
I have four brutes o' gallant mettle,
As ever drew afore a pettle.[3]
My han'-afore,[4] a guide auld has been,
An' wight an' wilfu' a' his days been.
My han'-ahin[5] 's a weel gaun[6] fillie,
That att has borne me hame frae Killie,[7]
An' your auld burro', monie a time,
In days when riding was nae crime.
But ance when in my wooing pride,
I, like a blockhead boost[8] to ride,
The wilfu' creature sae I pat[9] to,
(L—d pardon a' my sins and that too !)
I play'd my fillie sic a shavie,[10]

---

[1] Tackle.—[2] Oath.—[3] A plough-staff.—[4] The fore-horse on the left hand in the plough.—[5] The hindmost horse on the same side.—[6] Going.—[7] Kilmarnock.—[8] Must needs.—[9] Put.—[10] Trick, frolic.

She 's a' be-devil'd wi' the spavie.[1]
My fur-ahin 's[2] a wordy[3] beast,
As e'er in tug or tow[4] was traced.
The fourth 's a Highland Donald hastie,
A damn'd red-wud[5] Kilburnie blastie ;[6]
Forbye[7] a cowte[8] o' cowtes the wale,[9]
As ever ran afore a tail.
An' he be spared to be a beast,
He 'll draw me fifteen pun'[10] at least.

Wheel-carriages I hae but few,
Three carts, an' twa are feckly[11] new ;
Ae auld wheel-barrow, mair for token,
Ae leg and baith the trams[12] are broken ;
I made a poker o' the spin'le,
And my auld mither brunt the trin'le.[13]

For men, I 've three mischievous boys,
Run[14] deils for rantin' an' for noise ;
A gaudsman[15] ane, a thrasher t' other ;
Wee Davock hauds the nowte in fother.[16]
I rule them as I ought, discreetly,
And aften labor them completely ;
An' ay on Sundays duly nightly,
I on the Questions tairge[17] them tightly,
Till, faith, wee Davock 's turn'd sae gleg,[18]
Tho' scarcely langer than your leg,
He 'll screed[19] you aff *Effectual Calling*,
As fast as onie in the dwalling.

I 've nane in female servan' station,
(Lord keep me ay frae a' temptation !)
I hae nae wife—and that my bliss is,
An' ye have laid nae tax on misses ;
An' then if Kirk folks dinna clutch me,
I ken the devils daur na touch me.

Wi' weans[20] I 'm mair than weel contented,
Heaven sent me ane mae[21] than I wanted.

---

[1] Spavin.—[2] The hindmost horse on the right hand in the plough.—
[3] Worthy.—[4] Rope. —[5] Stark mad.—[6] A term of contempt.—[7] Besides.—
[8] A colt.—[9] Choice.—[10] Pounds.—[11] Partly, nearly.—[12] Handles.—[13] Burnt
the wheel.—[14] Right down.—[15] The boy who drives the horses in the plough.
—[16] Little David fothers the black cattle.—[17] Examine.—[18] Sharp, ready.—
To repeat any thing fluently.—[20] Children.—[21] One more.

My sonsie, smirking, dear-bought Bess,
She stares the daddy in her face,
Enough of aught ye like but grace;
But her my bonnie, sweet wee lady,
I 've paid enough for her already,
An' gin[2] ye tax her or her mither,
B' the Lord! ye 'se get them a' thegither.

And now remember, Mr. Aikin,
Nae kind of license out I 'm takin';
Frae this time forth, I do declare,
I 'se ne'er ride horse nor hizzie[3] mair;
Thro' dirt and dub for life I 'll paidle,
Ere I sae dear pay for a saddle;
My travel, a' on foot I 'll shank it,
I 've sturdy bearers, Gude be thankit.

The Kirk an' you may tak you that,
It puts but little in your pat;[4]
Sae dinna put me in your buke
Nor for my ten white shillings luke.

This list, wi' my ain hand I wrote it,
Day and date as under notit,
Then know all ye whom it concerns,
Subscripsi huic　　　　　　ROBERT BURNS.
MOSSGIEL, Feb. 22, 1786.

———

TO J—S T—T, GL—NC—R.

AULD comrade dear and brither sinner,
How 's a' the folk about Gl—nc—r?
How do you this blae eastlin' wind,
That 's like to blaw a body blind!
For me my faculties are frozen,
My dearest member nearly dozen'd.[5]
I 've sent you here, by Johnie Simson,
Twa sage philosophers to glimpse on;
Smith, wi' his sympathetic feeling,
An' Reid, to common sense appealing.

———

• Having a sweet engaging countenance.—[2] If.—[3] Filly, or mare.—[4] Pot.
—[5] Impotent.

Philosophers have fought and wrangled,
An' meikle[1] Greek an' Latin mangled,
Till wi' their logic jargon tired,
An' in the depth of science mired,
To common sense they now appeal,
What wives and wabsters[2] see an' feel.
But hark ye, friend, I charge you strictly
Peruse them an' return them quickly;
For now I 'm grown sae cursèd douce,[3]
I pray an' ponder butt[4] the house;
My shins, my lane,[5] I there sit roasting,
Perusing Bunyan, Brown, and Boston;
Till by an' by, if I haud[6] on,
I 'll grunt a real gospel groan:
Already I begin to try it,
To cast my een up like a pyet,[7]
When, by the gun, she tumbles o'er,
Fluttering an' gasping in her gore:
Sae shortly you shall see me bright,
A burning an' a shining light.
    My heart-warm love to guid auld Glen,
The ace an' wale[8] of honest men;
When bending down with auld gray hairs,
Beneath the load of years and cares,
May He who made him still support him,
An' views beyond the grave comfort him:
His worthy family far and near,
God bless them a' wi' grace and gear.[9]
    My auld school-fellow, preacher Willie,
The manly tar, my mason Billie,
An' Auchenbay, I wish him joy;
If he 's a parent, lass or boy,
May he be dad, and Meg the mither,
Just five-an'-forty years thegither!
An' no forgetting wabster Charlie,
I 'm tauld he offers very fairly.
And Lord remember singing Sannock,
Wi' hale breeks, saxpence, an' a bannock.
An' next my auld acquaintance Nancy,
Since she is fitted to her fancy;

· Much.—[2] Weavers.—[3] Sober.—[4] The country kitchen.—[5] Myself alone.
—[6] Hold.—[7] Magpie.—[8] Choice.—[9] Riches.

An' her kind stars hae airted[1] till her
A guid chiel[2] wi' a pickle siller.[3]
My kindest, best respects I sen' it,
To cousin Kate and sister Janet;
Tell them frae me, wi' chiels be cautious,
For, faith, they 'll aiblins[4] find them fashious;[5]
To grant a heart is fairly civil,
But to grant a maidenhead 's the devil!
An' lastly, Jamie, for yoursel,
May guardian angels tak a spell,
An' steer you seven miles south o' hell:
But first, before you see heaven's glory,
May ye get monie a merry story,
Monie a laugh, and monie a drink,
An' ay eneugh o' needfu' clink.

   Now fare you weel, an' joy be wi' you:
For my sake this I beg it o' you,
Assist poor Simson a' ye can,
Ye 'll find him just an honest man;
Sae I conclude and quit my chanter,
  Yours, saint or sinner,
                Rob the Ranter.

TO A GENTLEMAN,

Who had sent him a newspaper, and offered to continue it free of expense.

ELLISLAND, 1790.

Kind Sir, I 've read your paper through,
And faith, to me, 'twas really new!
How guess'd ye, Sir, what maist I wanted?
This monie a day I 've grain'd[6] and gaunted,
To ken what French mischief was brewin';
Or what the drumlie[7] Dutch were doin';
That vile doup-skelper,[8] Emperor Joseph,
If Venus yet had got his nose off;
Or how the collieshangie[9] works
Atween the Russians and the Turks;

---

[1] Moved to her; an allusion to the wind shifting to a particular quarter.—
[2] Good fellow.—[3] A quantity of silver.—[4] Perhaps.—[5] Troublesome.—
[6] Groaned. —[7] Muddy.—[8] One who strikes the tail. —[9] Quarrelling.

Or if the Swede, before he halt,
Would play anither Charles the Twalt;[1]
If Denmark, any body spak o't!
Or Poland, wha had now the tack[2] o't;
How cut-throat Prussian blades were hingin',[3]
How libbet[4] Italy was singin';
If Spaniard, Portuguese, or Swiss
Were sayin' or takin' aught amiss:
Or how our merry lads at hame,
In Britain's court keep up the game;
How Royal George, the Lord leuk o'er him!
Was managing St. Stephen's quorum;
If sleekit[5] Chatham Will[6] was livin',
Or glaiket[7] Charlie[8] gat his nieve[9] in:
How daddie Burke the plea was cookin',
If Warren Hastings' neck was yeukin';[10]
How cesses, stents,[11] and fees were rax'd,[12]
Or if bare a—s yet were tax'd;
The news o' princes, dukes, and earls,
Pimps, sharpers, bawds, and opera-girls;
If that daft buckie, Geordie Wales,
Was threshin' still at hizzies' tails,
Or if he was grown oughtlins doucer,[13]
And no a perfect kintra cooser:[14]
A' this and mair I never heard of;
And but for you I might despair'd of;
So, gratefu', back your news I send' you,
And pray, a' guid things may attend you!

TO GAVIN HAMILTON, ESQ.

[A Dedication.]

Expect na, Sir, in this narration,
A fleechin',[15] fletherin',[16] dedication,
To roose[17] you up, an' ca' you guid,
An' sprung o' great an' noble biuid,

---

[1] Twelfth.—[2] The guiding, or governing of it.—[3] Hanging.—[4] Castrated.—
[5] Slender.—[6] William Pitt, son of the Earl of Chatham.—[7] Thoughtless,
giddy.—[8] The celebrated Charles James Fox.—[9] The fist.—[10] Yoked.—
[11] Tribute, dues.—[12] Stretched, increased.—[13] Wiser.—[14] Country stallion.—
[15] Supplicating.—[16] Flattering.—[17] To praise.

Because ye 're surnamed like His Grace,
Perhaps related to the race;
Then when I 'm tired—and sae are ye,
Wi' monie a fulsome, sinfu' lie,
Set up a face, how I stopt short,
For fear your modesty be hurt.

   This may do—maun[1] do, Sir, wi' them wha
Maun please the great folk for a wamefou';[2]
For me! sae laigh[3] I needna bow,
For, Lord be thankit, I can plough;
And when I downa[4] yoke a naig,
Then, Lord be thankit, I can beg;
Sae I shall say, an' that 's nae flatt'rin',
It 's just sic Poet an' sic Patron.

   The Poet, some guid angel help him,
Or else, I fear some ill ane skelp[5] him,
He may do weel for a' he 's done yet,
But only he 's no just begun yet.

   The Patron, (Sir, ye maun forgie me,
I winna lie, come what will o' me,)
On every hand it will allow'd be,
He 's just nae better than he should be.

   I readily and freely grant,
He downa see a poor man want;
What 's no his ain he winna tak it,
What ance he says he winna break it;
Aught he can lend he 'll no refuse 't,
Till aft his goodness is abused:
And rascals whyles that him do wrang,
E'en that he does not mind it lang;
As master, landlord, husband, father,
He does na fail his part in either.

   But then, nae thanks to him for a' that;
Nae godly symptom ye can ca' that;
It 's naething but a milder feature,
Of our poor, sinfu' corrupt nature:
Ye 'll get the best o' moral works,
'Mang black Gentoos and pagan Turks,
Or hunters wild of Ponotaxi,
Wha never heard of orthodoxy.
That he 's the poor man's friend in need,

---

[1] Must.—[2] Bellyful.—[3] Low.—[4] Cannot.—[5] To strike

The gentleman in word and deed,
It 's no thro' terror of damnation :
It 's just a carnal inclination.
  Morality! thou deadly bane,
Thy tens o' thousands thou hast slain!
Vain is his hope, whose stay and trust is
In moral mercy, truth, and justice!
  No—stretch a point to catch a plack ;
Abuse a brother to his back ;
Steal thro' a winnock¹ frae a whore,
But point the rake that takes the door ;
Be to the poor like onie whunstane,²
And haud their noses to the grunstane ;³
Ply every art o' legal thieving ;
No matter—stick to sound believing.
  Learn three-mile prayers, and half-mile graces,
Wi' weel-spread looves,⁴ an' lang wry faces,
Grunt up a solemn, lengthen'd groan,
And damn a' parties but your own ;
I 'll warrant then, ye 're nae deceiver,
A steady, sturdy, stanch believer.
  O ye wha leave the springs of Calvin,
For gumlie⁵ dubs⁶ of your ain delvin' !
Ye sons of heresy and error,
Ye 'll some day squeel⁷ in quakin' terror !
When Vengeance draws the sword in wrath,
And in the fire throws the sheath ;
When Ruin with his sweeping besom,
Just frets till Heaven commission gies him :
While o'er the harp pale Misery moans,
And strikes the ever-deepening tones,
Still louder shrieks, and heavier groans !
  Your pardon, Sir, for this digression.
I maist⁸ forgat my dedication !
But when divinity comes 'cross me,
My readers still are sure to lose me.
  So, Sir, ye see 'twas nae daft⁹ vapor,
But I maturely thought it proper,
When a' my works I did review,
To dedicate them, Sir, to You ;

Because (ye needna tak it ill)
I thought them something like yoursel.
   Then patronize them wi' your favor,
And your petitioner shall ever—
I had amaist said, *ever pray*,
But that's a word I needna say:
For prayin' I hae little skill o't;
I 'm baith dead-sweer[1] an' wretched ill o't;
But I 'se repeat each poor man's prayer,
That kens or hears about you, Sir:—
   "May ne'er misfortune's growling bark
Howl thro' the dwelling o' the Clerk!·
May ne'er his generous, honest heart,
For that same generous spirit smart:
May Kennedy's far-honor'd fame,
Lang beet[2] his hymeneal flame,
Till Hamiltons, at least a dizen,
Are frae their nuptial labors risen:
Five bonnie lasses round their table,
And seven braw fellows, stout an' able
To serve their king and country weel,
By word, or pen, or pointed steel!
May health and peace, with mutual rays,
Shine on the evening o' his days;
Till his wee curlie John's ier-oe,[3]
When ebbing life nae mair shall flow,
The last, sad mournful rites bestow!"
   I will not wind a lang conclusion,
Wi' complimentary effusion:
But whilst your wishes and endeavors
Are blest wi' Fortune's smiles and favors,
I am, dear Sir, with zeal most fervent,
Your much indebted, humble servant.
   But if (which Powers above prevent!)
That iron-hearted carl, Want,
Attended in his grim advances,
By sad mistakes and black mischances,
While hopes, and joys, and pleasures fly him,
Make you as poor a dog as I am,
Your humble servant then no more;
For who would humbly serve the poor?

---

[1] Averse.—[2] Add fuel to.—[3] Great-grandchild

But, by a poor man's hopes in Heaven!
While recollection's power is given,
If, in the vale of humble life,
The victim sad of Fortune's strife,
I, thro' the tender gushing tear,
Should recognize my master dear,
If, friendless, low, we meet together,
Then, Sir, your hand—my friend and brother!

TO THE SAME,

(Recommending a boy.)

MOSGAVILLE, May 3, 1796

I HOLD it, Sir, my bounden duty
To warn you how that Master Tootie,
Alias, Laird M'Gaun,[1]
Was here to hire yon lad away
'Bout whom ye spak the tither day,
    An' wad hae done 't aff han':[2]
But lest he learn the callan[3] tricks,
    As faith I muckle doubt him,
Like scrapin' out auld crummie's[4] nicks,
    An' tellin' lies about them;
    As lieve[5] then I 'd have then,
        Your clerkship he should sair,[6]
    If sae be, ye may be
        Not fitted otherwhere.

Altho' I say 't, he 's gleg[7] enough,
An' bout a house that 's rude an' rough,
    The boy might learn to swear;
But then wi' you, he 'll be sae taught,
An' get sic fair example straught,
    I hae na ony fear.
Ye 'll catechise him every quirk,
    An' shore[8] him weel wi' hell;

---

[1] Master Tootie then lived in Mauchline; a dealer in cows. It was his common practice to cut the nicks or markings from the horns of cattle, to disguise their age. He was an artful, trick-contriving character; hence he is called a *snick-drawer*. In the Poet's "Address to the Deil," he styles that august personage an *auld, snick-drawing* dog!—*Reliques*, p. 897.

[2] Off hand.—[3] Boy.—[4] Old cow.—[5] Rather.—[6] Serve.—[7] Sharp.—[8] Threaten

An' gar him follow to the kirk ——
    —Ay when ye gang yoursel.
If ye then, maun be then
    Frae hame this comin' Friday,
Then please, Sir, to lea'e, Sir,
    The orders wi' your lady.

My word of honor I hae gien,
In Paisley John's, that night at e'en,
    To meet the Warld's worm;
To try to get the twa to gree,[1]
An' name the airles[2] an' the fee,
    In legal mode an' form:
I ken he weel a snick can draw,
    When simple bodies let him;
An' if a Devil be at a',
    In faith he's sure to get him.
    To phrase you an' praise you,
      Ye ken your Laureat scorns:
    The prayer still, you share still,
      Of grateful Minstrel Burns.

TO ROBERT GRAHAM, ESQ, OF FINTRA.

WHEN Nature her great master-piece design'd,
And framed her last, best work, the human mind,
Her eye intent on all the mazy plan,
She form'd of various parts the various man.
    Then first she calls the useful many forth:
Plain, plodding industry, and sober worth:
Thence peasants, farmers, native sons of earth,
And merchandise' whole genus take their birth.
Each prudent cit a warm existence finds,
And all mechanics' many-apron'd kinds.
Some other rarer sorts are wanted yet,
The lead and buoy are needful to the net:
The *caput mortuum* of gross desires
Makes a material for mere knights and squires;
The martial phosphorus is taught to flow,
She kneads the lumpish, philosophic dough,

----

[1] Agree.—[2] Earnest money.

Then marks the unyielding mass with grave designs,
Law, physic, politics, and deep divines:
Last, she sublimes the Aurora of the poles,
The flashing elements of female souls.
  The order'd system fair before her stood,
Nature, well-pleased, pronounced it very good;
But here she gave creating labor o'er,
Half-jest, she tried one curious labor more.
Some spumy, fiery *ignis fatuus* matter;
Such as the slightest breath of air might scatter;
With arch-alacrity and conscious glee
(Nature may have her whim as well as we,
Her Hogarth-art perhaps she meant to show it)
She forms the thing, and christens it—a Poet.
Creature, tho' oft the prey of care and sorrow,
When blest to-day unmindful of to-morrow.
A being form'd to amuse his graver friends,
Admired and praised—and there the homage ends;
A mortal quite unfit for Fortune's strife,
Yet oft the sport of all the ills of life;
Prone to enjoy each pleasure riches give,
Yet haply wanting wherewithal to live;
Longing to wipe each tear, to heal each groan,
Yet freqent all unheeded in his own.
  But honest Nature is not quite a Turk;
She laugh'd at first, then felt for her poor work:
Pitying the propless climber of mankind,
She cast about a standard-tree to find;
And, to support his helpless woodbine state,
Attach'd him to the generous truly great—
A title, and the only one I claim,
To lay strong hold for help on bounteous Graham.
  Pity the tuneful Muses' hapless train,
Weak, timid landsmen on life's stormy main!
Their hearts no selfish, stern, absorbent stuff,
That never gives—though humbly takes enough;
The little fate allows, they share as soon,
Unlike sage, proverb'd Wisdom's hard-wrung boon.
The world were blest did bliss on them depend:
Ah! that the friendly e'er should want a friend!
Let prudence number o'er each sturdy son,
Who life and wisdom at one race begun,
Who feel by reason, and who give by rule,

(Instinct's a brute, and sentiment a fool!)
Who make poor *will do* wait upon *I should*—
We own they're prudent; but who feels they're good
   Ye wise ones, hence! ye hurt the social eye!
God's image rudely etch'd on base alloy!
But come, ye who the godlike pleasure know—
Heaven's attribute distinguish'd—to bestow!
Whose arms of love would grasp the human race:
Come, thou who giv'st with all the courtier's grace,
Friend of my life, true patron of my rhymes!
Prop of my dearest hopes for future times.
Why shrinks my soul half-blushing, half-afraid,
Backward, abash'd to ask thy friendly aid?
I know my need, I know thy giving hand,
I crave thy friendship at thy kind command;
But there are such who court the tuneful nine—
Heavens! should the branded character be mine!
Whose verse in manhood's pride sublimely flows,
Yet vilest reptiles in their begging prose.
Mark, how their lofty, independent spirit
Soars on the spurning wing of injured merit!
Seek not the proofs in private life to find;
Pity the best of words should be but wind!
So to heaven's gates the lark's shrill song ascends,
But grovelling on the earth the carol ends.
In all the clamorous cry of starving want,
They dun benevolence with shameless front:
Oblige them, patronize their tinsel lays,
They persecute you all your future days!
Ere my poor soul such deep damnation stain,
My horny fist assume the plough again;
The piebald jacket let me patch once more:
On eighteen-pence a-week I've lived before.
Though, thanks to Heaven, I dare even that last shift.
I trust, meantime, my boon is in thy gift:
That placed by thee upon the wish'd-for height,
Where, Man and Nature fairer in her sight,
My Muse may imp her wing for some sublimer flight.

TO THE SAME.

LATE crippled of an arm, and now a leg,
About to beg a pass for leave to beg;
Dull, listless, teased, dejected, and deprest,
(Nature is adverse to a cripple's rest;)
Will generous Graham list to his Poet's wail?
(It soothes poor Misery hearkening to her tale)
And hear him curse the light he first survey'd,
And doubly curse the luckless rhyming trade?
  Thou, Nature, partial Nature, I arraign;
Of thy caprice maternal I complain.
The lion and the bull thy care have found,
One shakes the forest, and one spurns the ground:
Thou giv'st the ass his hide, the snail his shell,
The envenom'd wasp, victorious, guards his cell.
Thy minions, kings, defend, control, devour,
In all the omnipotence of rule and power.
Foxes and statesmen, subtle wiles insure;
The cit and polecat stink, and are secure.
Toads with their poison, doctors with their drug,
The priest and hedgehog in their robes are snug.
Even silly woman has her warlike arts,
Her tongue and eyes, her dreaded spear and darts.
  But oh! thou bitter step-mother and hard,
To thy poor, fenceless, naked child—the Bard!
A thing unteachable in world's skill,
And half an idiot too, more helpless still.
No heels to bear him from the opening dun;
No claws to dig, his hated sight to shun;
No horns, but those by luckless Hymen worn,
And those, alas! not Amalthea's horn:
No nerves olfact'ry, Mammon's trusty cur,
Clad in rich Dulness' comfortable fur,
In naked feeling, and in aching pride,
He bears the unbroken blast from every side:
Vampyre booksellers drain him to the heart,
And scorpion critics cureless venom dart.
  Critics! appall'd, I venture on the name,
Those cut-throat bandits in the paths of fame,
Bloody dissectors, worse than ten Monroes;
He hacks to teach, they mangle to expose.

His heart by causeless, wanton malice wrung,
By blockheads' daring into madness stung;
His well-won bays, than life itself more dear,
By miscreants torn, who ne'er one sprig must wear.
Foil'd, bleeding, tortured, in the unequal strife,
The hapless Poet flounders on through life.
Till fled each hope that once his bosom fired,
And fled each Muse that glorious once inspired,
Low sunk in squalid, unprotected age,
Dead, even resentment, for his injured page,
He heeds or feels no more the ruthless critic's rage!
    So, by some hedge, the generous steed deceased,
For half-starved, snarling curs a dainty feast;
By toil and famine wore to skin and bone,
Lies senseless of each tugging bitch's son.
    O Dulness! portion of the truly blest!
Calm shelter'd haven of eternal rest!
Thy sons ne'er madden in the fierce extremes
Of Fortune's polar frost, or torrid beams.
If mantling high she fills the golden cup,
With sober, selfish ease they sip it up:
Conscious the bounteous meed they well deserve,
They only wonder some folks do not starve.
The grave, sage hern thus easy picks his frog,
And thinks the mallard a sad worthless dog.
When Disappointment snaps the clue of hope,
And through disastrous night they darkling grope,
With deaf endurance sluggishly they bear,
And just conclude that fools are Fortune's care.
So, heavy, passive to the tempest's shocks,
Strong on the sign-post stands the stupid ox.
    Not so the idle Muses' mad-cap train,
Not such the workings of their moon-struck brain;
In equanimity they never dwell,
By turns in soaring heaven or vaulted hell.
    I dread thee, Fate, relentless and severe,
With all a poet's, husband's, father's fear!
Already one strong hold of hope is lost,
Glencairn, the truly noble, lies in dust;
(Fled, like the sun eclipsed at noon appears,
And left us darkling in a world of tears:)
Oh! hear my ardent, grateful, selfish prayer!
Fintra, my other stay, long bless and spare!

Thro' a long life his hopes and wishes crown;
And bright in cloudless skies his sun go down:
May bliss domestic smooth his private path;
Give energy to life; and soothe his latest breath,
With many a filial tear circling the bed of death!

TO THE SAME,

ON RECEIVING A FAVOR.

I CALL no goddess to inspire my strains,
A fabled muse may suit a bard that feigns;
Friend of my life! my ardent spirit burns,
And all the tribute of my heart returns,
For boons accorded, goodness ever new,
The gift still dearer, as the giver you.
    Thou orb of day! thou other paler light!
And all ye many sparkling stars of night!
If aught that giver from my mind efface;
If I that giver's bounty e'er disgrace;
Then roll to me, along your wandering spheres,
Only to number out a villain's years!

TO MRS. DUNLOP,

ON NEW-YEAR'S DAY.

THIS day, Time winds the exhausted chain,
To run the twelvemonth's length again:
I see the old bald-pated fellow,
With ardent eyes, complexion sallow,
Adjust the unimpair'd machine,
To wheel the equal, dull routine.
    The absent lover, minor heir,   ·
· In vain assail him with their prayer;
Deaf as my friend, he sees them press,
Nor makes the hour one moment less.
    Will you (the Major's with the hounds,
The happy tenants share his rounds;
Coila's fair Rachel's care to-day,[1]

[1] This young lady was drawing a picture of Coila, from the "Vision."

And blooming Keith's engaged with Gray)
From housewife cares a minute borrow,
(That grandchild's cap will do to-morrow)
And join with me a-moralizing?
This day's propitious to be wise in.
　First, what did yesternight deliver?
"Another year is gone forever."
And what is this day's strong suggestion?
"The passing moment's all we rest on!"
Rest on—for what? what do we here?
Or why regard the passing year?
Will Time, amused with proverb'd lore,
Add to our date one minute more?
A few days may—a few years must—
Repose us in the silent dust.
Then is it wise to damp our bliss?
Yes—all such reasonings are amiss!
The voice of nature loudly cries,
And many a message from the skies,
That something in us never dies;
That on this frail uncertain state,
Hang matters of eternal weight;
That future life, in worlds unknown,
Must take its hue from this alone;
Whether as heavenly glory bright,
Or dark as misery's woeful night.
　Since, then, my honor'd first of friends,
On this poor being all depends;
Let us the important *now* employ,
And live as those that never die.
　Tho' you, with days and honors crown d,
Witness that filial circle round,
(A sight life's sorrows to repulse,
A sight pale envy to convulse,)
Others now claim your chief regard;
Yourself, you wait your bright reward.

TO THE SAME,

ON SENSIBILITY.

Sensibility, how charming,
  Thou, my friend, canst truly tell;
But distress with horrors arming,
  Thou hast also known too well;

Fairest flower, behold the lily,
  Blooming in the sunny ray:
Let the blast sweep o'er the valley;
  See it prostrate on the clay.

Hear the wood-lark charm the forest,
  Telling o'er his little joys:
Hapless bird! a prey the surest,
  To each pirate of the skies.

Dearly bought the hidden treasure
  Finer feelings can bestow;
Chords that vibrate sweetest pleasure,
  Thrill the deepest notes of woe!

TO A YOUNG FRIEND.[1]

MAY, 1786.

I lang hae thought, my youthfu' friend,
  A something to have sent you,
Tho' it should serve nae other end
  Than just a kind memento.
But how the subject-theme may gang,
  Let time and chance determine;
Perhaps it may turn out a sang,
  Perhaps turn out a sermon.

Ye'll try the world soon, my lad,
  And, Andrew dear, believe me,
Ye'll find mankind an unco[2] squad,
  And muckle they may grieve ye:

[1] Mr. A. A. Aikin, now of Liverpool, the son of Robert Aikin, Esq. — [2] Uncouth, untoward.

For care and trouble set your thought,
   E'en when your end's attain'd;
And a' your views may come to naught,
   When every nerve is strain'd.

I'll no say, men are villains a';
   The real, harden'd wicked,
Wha hae nae check but human law,
   Are to a few restricked:[1]
But, och! mankind are unco[2] weak,
   An' little to be trusted;
If self the wavering balance shake,
   It's rarely right adjusted!

Yet they wha fa' in Fortune's strife,
   Their fate we should na censure,
For still the important end of life,
   They equally may answer:
A man may hae an honest heart,
   Tho' poortith[3] hourly stare him;
A man may tak a neebor's part,
   Yet hae nae cash to spare him.

Ay free aff han' your story tell,
   When wi' a bosom cronie:
But still keep something to yoursel
   Ye scarcely tell to onie.
Conceal yoursel as weel's ye can,
   Frae critical dissection;
But keek[4] thro' every other man,
   Wi' sharpen'd sly inspection.

The sacred lowe[5] o' weel-placed love,
   Luxuriantly indulge it:
But never tempt the illicit rove,
   Tho' naething should divulge it:
I wave the quantum o' the sin,
   The hazard of concealing;
But, och! it hardens a' within,
   And petrifies the feeling!

---

[1] Restricted. In the use of this word, in common with many other English words, Burns has perhaps taken more than a poet's liberty with the orthography, in order to accommodate his rhyme.
[2] Very.—[3] Poverty.—[4] Peep into, or scrutinize.—[5] Flame.

To catch dame Fortune's golden smile,
    Assiduous wait upon her;
And gather gear by every wile
    That's justified by honor:
Not for to hide it in a hedge,
    Nor for a train-attendant;
But for the glorious privilege
    Of being independent.

The fear o' hell's a hangman's whip
    To haud the wretch in order;
But where ye feel your honor grip,[1]
    Let ay that be your border:
Its slightest touches, instant pause—
    Debar a' side pretences;
And resolutely keep its laws,
    Uncaring consequences.

The great Creator to revere,
    Must sure become the creature;
But still the preaching cant forbear,
    And even the rigid feature:
Yet ne'er with wits profane to range,
    Be complaisance extended;
An atheist's laugh's a poor exchange
    For Deity offended!

When ranting round in pleasure's ring,
    Religion may be blinded;
Or if she gie a random sting,
    It may be little minded:
But when on life we're tempest driven,
    A conscience but a canker—
A correspondence fix'd wi' Heaven,
    Is sure a noble anchor.

Adieu, dear, amiable youth!
    Your heart can ne'er be wanting;
May prudence, fortitude, and truth
    Erect your brow undaunting!
In ploughman phrase, "God send you speed,"
    Still daily to grow wiser!
And may you better reck the rede,[2]
    Than ever did the adviser.

[1] Pinch.—[2] Take heed, or pay due attention to good advice.

TO THE REV. JOHN M'MATH.

Inclosing a copy of Holy Willie's Prayer, which he had requested.

Sept. 17th, 1785.

WHILE at the stook[1] tho shearers cower
To shun the bitter blaudin'[2] shower,
Or in gulravage[3] rinnin' scower,
       To pass the time,
To you I dedicate the hour
       In idle rhyme.

My musie, tired wi' mony a sonnet
On gown, an' ban', an' douse black bonnet,
Is grown right eerie[4] now she's done it,
       Lest they should blame her,
An' rouse their holy thunder on it
       And anathem her.

I own 't was rash, an' rather hardy,
That I, a simple, kintra[5] bardie,
Should meddle wi' a pack sae sturdy,
       Wha, if they ken me,
Can easy, wi' a single wordie,
       Lowse h—ll upon me.

But I gae mad at their grimaces,
Their sighin', cantin', grace-prood faces,
Their three-mile prayers, an' half-mile graces,
       Their raxin'[6] conscience,
Whase greed, revenge, an' pride disgraces
       Waur nor[7] their nonsense.

There's Gaun,[8] miska't[9] waur than a beast,
Wha has mair honor in his breast
Than mony scores as guid's the priest
       Wha sae abus't him;
An' may a bard no crack his jest
       What way they've use't him?

See him,[10] the poor man's friend in need,
The gentleman in word an' deed;

[1] Shock of corn.—[2] Pelting.—[3] Riotous merriment.—[4] Frighted.—[5] Country.—[6] Stretching.—[7] Worse than.—[8] Gavin Hamilton, Esq.—[9] Miscalled.
[10] The poet has introduced the first two lines of this stanza into the dedication of his works to Mr. Hamilton.

An' shall his fame an' honor bleed
   By worthless skellums,[1]
An' not a muse erect her head
   To cowe the blellums?[2]

O Pope, had I thy satire's darts
To gie the rascals their deserts,
I'd rip their rotten, hollow hearts,
   An' tell aloud
Their jugglin' hocus-pocus arts,
   To cheat the crowd.

God knows, I'm no the thing I should be,
Nor am I even the thing I could be,
But twenty times I rather would be,
   An atheist clean,
Than under gospel colors hid be
   Just for a screen.

An honest man may like a glass,
An honest man may like a lass,
But mean revenge, an' malice fause,[3]
   He'll still disdain,
An' then cry zeal for gospel laws,
   Like some we ken.

They take religion in their mouth;
They talk o' mercy, grace, an' truth,
For what? to gie their malice skouth[4]
   On some puir wight,
An' hunt him down, o'er right an' ruth,
   To ruin streight.

All hail, Religion! maid divine!
Pardon a muse sae mean as mine,
Who in her rough imperfect line
   Thus daurs to name thee;
To stigmatize false friends of thine
   Can ne'er defame thee.

Tho' blotcht an' foul wi' mony a stain,
An' far unworthy of thy train,
With trembling voice I tune my strain
   To join with those,

---

[1] Fellows.—[2] Idle talkers.—[3] False.—[4] Scope.

Who boldly dare thy cause maintain
　　In spite of foes:

In spite o' crowds, in spite o' mobs,
In spite of undermining jobs,
In spite o' dark banditti stabs
　　At worth an' merit,
By scoundrels, even wi' holy robes,
　　But hellish spirit.

O Ayr, my dear, my native ground,
Within thy presbytereal bound
A candid, liberal band is found
　　Of public teachers,
As men, as Christians too, renown'd,
　　An' manly preachers.

Sir, in that circle you are named;
Sir, in that circle you are famed;
An' some by whom your doctrine 's blamed,
　　(Which gies you honor,)
Even, Sir, by them your heart 's esteem'd,
　　An' winning manner.

Pardon this freedom I have ta'en,
An' if impertinent I've been,
Impute it not, good Sir, in ane
　　Whase heart ne'er wrang'd ye,
But to his utmost would befriend
　　Aught that belang'd ye.

TO MR. M'ADAM, OF CRAIGEN-GILLAN,

In answer to an obliging letter he sent in the commencement of my poetic career.

Sir, o'er a gill I gat your card,
　　I trow it made me proud:
See wha takes notice o' the bard,
　　I lap[1] and cried fu' loud.

Now deil-ma-care about their jaw,
　　The senseless, gawky million;

[1] Did leap.

I 'll cock my nose aboon them a',
    I 'm roosed by Craigen-Gillan!

'Twas noble, Sir; 'twas like yoursel,
    To grant your high protection;
A great man's smile ye ken fu' well,
    Is ay a blest infection.

Though, by his banes wha in a tub
    Match'd Macedonian Sandy!
On my ain legs thro' dirt an' dub,
    I independent stand ay.—

And when those legs to guid, warm kail,
    Wi' welcome canna bear me;
A lee[1] dyke[2]-side, a sybow[3]-tail,
    And barley-scone[4] shall cheer me.

Heaven spare you lang to kiss the breath
    O' mony flowery simmers![5]
And bless your bonnie lasses baith,[6]
    I 'm tald they 're loosome kimmers![7]

And God bless young Dunaskin's laird,
    The blossom of our gentry!
And may he wear an auld man's beard,
    A credit to his country!

TO TERRAUGHTY[8] ON HIS BIRTH-DAY.

HEALTH to the Maxwells' veteran chief;
Health, ay unsour'd by care or grief:
Inspired, I turn'd Fate's sibyl leaf,
        This natal morn,
I see thy life is stuff o' prief,[9]
        Scarce quite half-worn.—

This day thou metes three-score eleven,
And I can tell that bounteous Heaven,

---

[1] Shaded, or grassy.—[2] Wall.—[3] A sort of leek.—[4] Cake.—[5] Summers.—
[6] Both.—[7] Lovely girls.—[8] Mr. Maxwell, of Terraughty, near Dumfries.—
[9] Proof.

(The second sight, ye ken, is given
                To ilka poet,)
On thee a tack o' seven times seven
                Will yet bestow it.

If envious buckies view wi' sorrow,
Thy lengthen'd days on this blest morrow,
May desolation's lang-teeth'd harrow,
                Nine miles an hour,
Rake them like Sodom and Gomorrah,
                In brunstane stoure.[1]

But for thy friends, and they are monie,
Baith honest men and lasses bonnie,
May couthie[2] fortune, kind and cannie,
                In social glee,
Wi' mornings blythe and e'enings funny,
                Bless them and thee!

Fareweel, auld birkie![3] Lord be near ye,
And then the Deil he daur na steer[4] ye:
Your friends ay love, your faes ay fear ye;
                For me, shame fa' me,
If neist[5] my heart I dinna wear ye,
                While BURNS they ca' me.

TO CAPTAIN RIDDEL, GLENRIDDEL.

(Extempore lines on returning a newspaper.)

ELLISLAND, *Monday Evening.*

YOUR news and review, Sir, I've read through and
                through, Sir,
With little admiring or blaming;
The papers are barren of home news or foreign,
No murders or rapes worth the naming.

Our friends the reviewers, those chippers and hewers,
Are judges of mortar and stone, Sir;
But of meet, or unmeet, in a fabric complete,
I'll boldly pronounce they are none, Sir.

[1] Brimstone dust.—[2] Loving.—[3] Clever fellow.—[4] Dare not molest.—[5] Next

My goose-quill too rude is, to tell all your goodness
Bestow'd on your servant, the Poet;
Would to God I had one like a beam of the sun,
And then all the world, Sir, should know it!

TO MR. MITCHELL,

Collector of Excise, Dumfries, 1796.

FRIEND of the poet, tried and leal,[1]
Wha wanting thee, might beg or steal;
Alake, alake, the meikle deil
   Wi' a' his witches
Are at it, skelpin'l[2] jig and reel,
   In my poor pouches.

I modestly fu' fain[3] wad hint it,
That one pound one, I sairly want it:
If wi' the hizzie[4] down ye sent it,
   It would be kind;
And while my heart wi' life-blood dunted.[5]
   I 'd bear 't in mind.

So may the auld year gang out moaning
To see the new come laden, groaning,
Wi' double plenty o'er the loanin',[6]
   To thee and thine;
Domestic peace and comforts crowning
   The hale[7] design.

POSTSCRIPT.

Ye 've heard this while how I 've been licket,
And by fell death was nearly nicket:
Grim loun! he gat me by the fecket,[8]
   And sair me sheuk;
But by guid luck I lap[9] a wicket,
   And turn'd a neuk.[10]

---

[1] Stanch, faithful.—[2] Tripping.—[3] Very desirous.—[4] The girl.—[5] Beats.—
The place of milking.—[7] Whole.—[8] A jacket.—[9] Leaped.—[10] Corner.

But by that health, I've got a share o't,
And by that life, I'm promised mair o't,
My hale and weel,[1] I 'll take a care o't
         A tentier[2] way;
Then farewell folly, hide and hair o't,
          For ance and ay.

TO A GENTLEMAN WHOM HE HAD OFFENDED

THE friend whom wild from wisdom's way
   The fumes of wine infuriate send
(Not moony madness more astray;)
   Who but deplores that hapless friend?

Mine was the insensate frenzied part,
   Ah why should I such scenes outlive!
Scenes so abhorrent to my heart!
   'Tis thine to pity and forgive.

TO AN OLD SWEETHEART,
After her marriage, with a present of a copy of his Poems.

ONCE fondly loved, and still remember'd dear,
   Sweet early object of my youthful vows,
Accept this mark of friendship, warm, sincere,
   Friendship!—'tis all cold duty now allows:—

And when you read the simple, artless rhymes,
   One friendly sigh for him, (he asks no more,)
Who distant burns in flaming, torrid climes,
   Or haply lies beneath the Atlantic roar.

TO MISS LOGAN,
With Beattie's Poems, as a New-Year's gift.
JAN. 1, 1787.

AGAIN the silent wheels of time
   Their annual round have driven,

---

[1] Health and welfare.—[2] More cautious.

And you tho' scarce in maiden prime,
    Are so much nearer heaven.

No gifts have I from Indian coasts
    The infant year to hail;
I send you more than India boasts,
    In Edwin's simple tale.

Our sex with guile and faithless love
    Is charged, perhaps, too true;
But may, dear maid, each lover prove
    An Edwin still to you.

TO A YOUNG LADY,

Miss Jessy Lewars, Dumfries; with a present of books.

THINE be the volumes, Jessy fair,
And with them take the Poet's prayer—
That Fate may in her fairest page,
With every kindliest, best presage
Of future bliss enrol thy name:
With native worth, and spotless fame,
And wakeful caution still aware
Of ill—but chief, man's felon snare;
All blameless joys on earth we find,
And all the treasures of the mind—
These be thy guardian and reward;
So prays thy faithful friend, the Bard.

TO A YOUNG LADY,

With a present of songs.

HERE, where the Scottish Muse immortal lives,
    In sacred strains and tuneful numbers join'd,
Accept the gift; tho' humble he who gives,
    Rich is the tribute of the grateful mind.

So may no ruffian-feeling in thy breast,
    Discordant, jar thy bosom chords among;
But peace attune thy gentle soul to rest,
    Or love ecstatic wake his seraph song:

Or pity's notes, in luxury of tears,
  As modest want the tale of woe reveals;
While conscious virtue all the strain endears,
  And heaven-born piety her sanction seals.

TO A LADY,

With a present of a pair of drinking-glasses.

FAIR empress of the Poet's soul,
  And queen of Poetesses—
Clarinda, take this little boon,
  This humble pair of glasses.

And fill them high with generous juice,
  As generous as your mind;
And pledge me in the generous toast—
  "The whole of human kind!"

"To those who love us!"—second fill!
  But not to those whom we love;
Lest we love those who love not us!
  A third—"To thee and me, love!"

TO MISS CRUICKSHANKS,

A very young lady, with a present of a book.

BEAUTEOUS rose-bud, young and gay,
Blooming on thy early May,
Never may'st thou, lovely flower
Chilly shrink in sleety shower!
Never Boreas' hoary path,
Never Eurus' pois'nous breath,
Never baleful stellar lights,
Taint thee with untimely blights!
Never, never reptile thief
Riot on thy virgin leaf!
Nor even Sol too fiercely view
Thy bosom blushing still with dew!
  May'st thou long, sweet crimson gem,
Richly deck thy native stem;

Till some evening, sober, calm,
Dropping dews, and breathing balm,
While all around the woodland rings,
And every bird thy requiem sings:
Thou amid the dirgeful sound,
Shed thy dying honors round,
And resign to parent earth
The loveliest form she e'er gave birth!

TO A LADY,

Whom the Author had often celebrated under the name of Chloris, with a
present of a copy of his Poems.

'Tis Friendship's pledge, my young fair friend,
    Nor thou the gift refuse,
Nor with unwilling ear attend
    The moralizing muse.

Since thou, in all thy youth and charms,
    Must bid the world adieu,
(A world 'gainst peace in constant arms)
    To join the friendly few:

Since, thy gay morn of life o'ercast,
    Chill came the tempest's lower,   ·
(And ne'er misfortune's eastern blast
    Did nip a fairer flower:)

Since life's gay scenes must charm no more,
    Still much is left behind;
Still nobler wealth hast thou in store,
    The comforts of the mind!

Thine is the self-approving glow,
    On conscious honor's part;
And, dearest gift of Heaven below,
    Thine friendship's truest heart.

The joys refined of sense and taste,
    With every Muse to rove:
And doubly were the Poet blest
    Those joys could he improve.

TO MRS. SCOTT, OF WAUCHOPE-HOUSE,

In answer to an epistle which she had sent the Author.

MARCH, 1787.

I MIND it weel, in early date,
When I was beardless, young, and blate,[1]
  And first could thresh the barn;
Or haud[2] a yokin' at the pleugh;
An' though forfoughten[3] sair eneugh,
  Yet unco proud to learn!
When first amang the yellow corn
  A man I reckon'd was,
And wi' the lave[4] ilk merry morn
  Could rank my rig and lass;
    Still shearing and clearing,
      The tither stooked raw,[5]
    Wi' clavers[6] an' haivers,[7]
      Wearing the day awa.

Even then, a wish, (I mind its power),
A wish that to my latest hour
  Shall strongly heave my breast—
That I for poor auld Scotland's sake
Some usefu' plan or book could make,
  Or sing a sang at least.
The rough burr-thistle, spreading wide
  Amang the bearded bear,[8]
I turn'd the weedin'-heuk[9] aside,
  An' spared the symbol dear;
    No nation, no station,
      My envy e'er could raise,
    A Scot still, but[10] blot still,
      I knew nae higher praise.

But still the elements o' sang
In formless jumble, right au' wrang,
  Wild floated in my brain;
Till on that har'st[11] I said before,
My partner in the merry core,
  She roused the forming strain:

---

[1] Bashful.—[2] Hold.—[3] Fatigued.—[4] Others.—[5] Sheaves of corn in rows.—
[6] Idle stories.—[7] Nonsense.—[8] Barley.—[9] Hook.—[10] Without.—[11] Harvest.

I see her yet, the sonsie[1] quean,
  That lighted up her jingle,
Her witching smile, her pawky[2] een,
  That gart[3] my heart-strings tingle.
    I fired, inspired,
      At every kindling keek,[4]
    But bashing, and dashing,
      I feared ay to speak.

Hale[5] to the set, ilk guid chiel[6] says,
Wi' merry dance in winter days,
  An' we to share in common;
The gust o' joy, the balm of woe,
The saul[7] o' life, the heaven below,
  Is rapture-giving woman.
Ye surly sumphs,[8] who hate the name,
  Be mindfu' o' your mither;
She, honest woman, may think shame
  That ye 're connected with her.
    Ye 're wae men, ye 're nae men,
      That slight the lovely dears;
    To shame ye, disclaim ye,
      Ilk honest birkie swears.

For you, no bred to barn or byre,[9]
Wha sweetly tune the Scottish lyre,
  Thanks to you for your line,
The marléd[10] plaid ye kindly spare,
By me should gratefully be ware;
  'Twad please me to the nine.
I 'd be mair vauntie o' my hap,[11]
  Douse hinging o'er my curple,[12]
Than onie ermine ever lap,
  Or proud imperial purple.
    Fareweel then, lang hale then,
      An' plenty be your fa':
    May losses and crosses
      Ne'er at your hallan[13] ca'.
              R. BURNS.

---

[1] Having sweet engaging looks.—[2] Sly.—[3] Made, or forced.—[4] Peep.—[5] Health.—[6] Good fellow.—[7] Soul.—[8] Stupid, sullen fellow.—[9] Cow-stable.—[10] Variegated.—[11] Mantle.—[12] Decently hanging over my loins.—[13] A seat of turf outside a cottage door.

SATIRES.

THE HOLY FAIR.[1]

A robe of seeming truth and trust
Hid crafty Observation ;
And secret hung, with poison'd crust.
The dirk of Defamation :
A mask that like the gorget show'd,
Dye-varying, on the pigeon;
And for a mantle large and broad,
He wrapt him in Religion.

Hypocrisy a-la-Mode

Upon a simmer Sunday morn,
　When Nature's face is fair,
I walkéd forth to view the corn,
　An' snuff the caller[2] air.
The rising sun owre Galston[3] muirs,
　Wi' glorious light was glintin';[4]
The hares were hirplin'[5] down the furs,[6]
　The lav'rocks they were chantin'
　　　Fu' sweet that day.

As lightsomely I glower'd[7] abroad,
　To see a scene sae gay,
Three hizzies, early at the road,
　Cam skelpin'[8] up the way;
Twa had manteeles o' dolefu' black,
　But ane wi' lyart[9] lining;
The third, that gaed a wee aback,[10]
　Was in the fashion shining,
　　　Fu' gay that day.

The twa appear'd like sisters twin,
　In feature, form, an' claes;[11]

---

[1] Holy Fair is a common phrase in the west of Scotland for a sacramental occasion.

[2] Fresh.—[3] The name of a parish adjoining Mauchline.—[4] Peeping.—[5] Creeping.—[6] Furrows.—[7] Looked,—[8] Walking.—[9] Gray.—[10] Went a little aloof.—[11] Clothes.

SATIRES.

287

Their visage, wither'd, lang, an' thin,
An' sour as onie slaes;[1]
The third cam up, hap-step-an'-loup,[2]
As light as onie lammie,
An' wi' a curchie low did stoop,
As soon as e'er she saw me,
Fu' kind that day.

Wi' bonnet aff, quoth I, "Sweet lass,
I think ye seem to ken me;
I'm sure I've seen that bonnie face,
But yet I canna name ye."
Quo' she, and laughin' as she spak,
An' taks me by the hands,
"Ye, for my sake, hae gien the feck[3]
Of a' the ten commands
A screed[4] some day.

"My name is Fun—your cronie dear,
The nearest friend ye hae;
An' this is Superstition here,
An' that's Hypocrisy.
I'm gaun to Mauchline Holy Fair,
To spend an hour in daffin':[5]
Gin ye'll go there, yon runkled[6] pair,
We will get famous laughin'
At them this day."

Quoth I, "With a' my heart, I'll do't;
I'll get my Sunday's sark[7] on,
An' meet you on the holy spot;
Faith we's hae fine remarkin'"!
Then I gaed[8] hame at crowdie-time,[9]
An' soon I made me ready;
For roads were clad, frae side to side,
Wi' monie a weary body,
In droves that day.

Here farmers gash,[10] in riding graith,[11]
Gaed hoddin[12] by their cotters;

---

[1] Sloes.—[2] Hop, step, and jump.—[3] The greater part.—[4] A rent, or tear.—
[5] Merriment.—[6] Wrinkled.—[7] Shirt.—[8] Went.—[9] Breakfast-time.—[10] Talkative.—[11] Accoutrements.—[12] The motion of a sage countryman riding a cart-horse.

There, swankies[1] young, in braw braid claith,
  Are springing o'er the gutters.
The lasses, skelpin[2] bare-fit, thrang,
  In silks an' scarlets glitter;
Wi' sweet-milk-cheese, in monie a whang,[3]
  An' farls[4] baked wi' butter
      Fu' crump that day.

When by the plate we set our nose,
  Weel heapéd up wi' ha'pence,
A greedy glow'r[5] Black Bonnet throws,
  An' we maun[6] draw our tippence.
Then in we go to see the show,
  On every side they 're gath'rin',
Some carrying deals, some chairs an' stools,
  An' some are busy bleth'rin'[7]
      Right loud that day.

Here stands a shed to fend the showers,
  An' screen our countra gentry,
There, racer Jess, an' twa-three[8] w—s,
  Are blinkin' at the entry.
Here sits a raw of tittlin[9] jads,
  Wi' heavin' breast and bare neck,
An' there a batch of wabster[10] lads,
  Blackguarding frae Kilmarnock,
      For fun this day.

Here some are thinkin' on their sins,
  An' some upo' their claes;
Ane curses feet that fyl'd[11] his shins,
  Anither sighs an' prays:
On this hand sits a chosen swatch,[12]
  Wi' screw'd-up grace-proud faces;
On that a set o' chaps at watch,
  Thrang[13] winkin' on the lasses
      To chairs that day.

Oh happy is that man and blest!
  (Nae wonder that it pride him!)
Whase ain dear lass, that he likes best,
  Comes clinkin' down beside him!

---

[1] A tight, strapping young fellow.—[2] Walking barefoot.—[3] A large, thick
slice.—[4] A cake of bread.—[5] Look.—[6] Must.—[7] Talking idly.—[8] A few.—
[9] Whispering.—[10] A weaver.—[11] Defiled.—[12] A sample.—[13] Busy.

Wi' arm reposed on the chair back,
  He sweetly does compose him!
Which, by degrees, slips round her neck,
  An' 's loof[1] upon her bosom,
                Unkenn'd that day.

Now a' the congregation o'er
  Is silent expectation;
For ***** speels[2] the holy door,
  Wi' tidings o' *damnation*.[3]
Should Hornie, as in ancient days,
  'Mang sons o' God present him,
The very sight o' *****'s face,
  To 's ain het[4] hame had sent him
                Wi' fright that day.

Hear how he clears the points o' faith
  Wi' rattlin' an' wi' thumpin'!
Now meekly calm, now wild in wrath,
  He 's stampin' an' he 's jumpin'!
His lengthen'd chin, his turn'd-up 'snout,
  His eldritch squeel[5] and gestures,
Oh how they fire the heart devout,
  Like cantharidian plasters,
                On sic a day!

But, hark! the tent[6] has changed its voice;
  There 's peace an' rest nae langer;
For a' the real judges rise,
  They canna sit for anger!
***** opens out his cauld harangues,
  On practice and on morals;
An' aff the godly pour in thrangs,
  To gie the jars an' barrels
                A lift that day.

What signifies his barren shine
  Of moral powers and reason?
His English style an' gestures fine
  Are a' clean out o' season.

[1] Palm of the hand.—[2] To climb.
[3] This word was originally printed *salvation*. The present reading was
adopted in the Edinburgh edition, at the suggestion of Dr. Blair, by which
the wit of the verse is undoubtedly improved.
[4] Hot home.—[6] Frightful scream.—[6] A field pulpit.

Like Socrates or Antonine,
　　Or some auld pagan heathen,
The moral man he does define,
　　But ne'er a word o' faith in
　　　　　　That 's right that day.

In guid time comes an antidote
　　Against sic poison'd nostrum;
For ******, frae the water-fit,[1]
　　Ascends the holy rostrum:
See, up he 's got the word o' God,
　　An' meek an' mim[2] has view'd it,
While *Common Sense* has taen the road,
　　An' aff an' up the Cowgate,[3]
　　　　　　Fast, fast, that day.

Wee ****** niest[4] the guard relieves,
　　An' Orthodoxy raibles,[5]
Tho' in his heart he weel believes,
　　An' thinks it auld wives' fables:
But, faith! the birkie[6] wants a manse,[7]
　　So, cannily he hums them;
Altho' his carnal wit and sense
　　Like hafflins-ways[8] o'ercomes him
　　　　　　At times that day.

Now, butt an' ben[9] the change-house[10] fills,
　　Wi' yill-caup[11] commentators:
Here 's crying out for bakes and gills,
　　An' there the pint stowp[12] clatters;
While thick an' thrang, an' loud an' lang,
　　Wi' logic and wi' Scripture,
They raise a din, that in the end,
　　Is like to breed a rupture
　　　　　　O' wrath that day.

Leeze me[13] on drink! it gies us mair
　　Than either school or college:
It kindles wit, it waukens lear,[14]
　　It pangs us fou[15] o' knowledge.

---

[1] Water-foot.—[2] Prim.—[3] A street so called.—[4] Next.—[5] To rattle nonsense.—[6] A clever fellow.—[7] The parsonage-house where the minister lives.—[8] Partly, nearly half.—[9] Kitchen and parlor.—[10] Country inn, or ale-house.—[11] Ale-cup.—[12] Pint-pot.—[13] A phrase of endearment.—[14] Learning.
　[15] Crams us full.

Be 't whisky gill[1] or penny wheep,[2]
  Or onie stronger potion,
It never fails, on drinking deep,
  To kittle[3] up our notion
          By night or day.

The lads an' lasses blythely bent
  To mind baith saul an' body,
Sit round the table weel content,
  An' steer about the toddy.
On this ane's dress, an' that ane's leuk,[4]
  They 're making observations;
While some are cozie i' the neuk,[5]
  An' forming assignations,
          To meet some day.

But now the Lord's ain trumpet touts,[6]
  Till a' the hills are rairin',[7]
An' echoes back return the shouts:
  Black ****** is nae spearin':
His piercing words, like Highland swords,
  Divide the joints an' marrow;
His talk o' hell, where devils dwell,
  Our vera sauls does harrow[8]
          Wi' fright that day.

A vast, unbottom'd, boundless pit,
  Fill'd fou o' lowin' brunstane,[9]
Whase raging flame an' scorchin' heat,
  Wad melt the hardest whunstane![10]
The half-asleep start up wi' fear,
  An' think they hear it roarin',
When presently it does appear
  'T was but some neebor snorin'
          Asleep that day.

'T wad be owre lang a tale to tell
  How monie stories past,
An' how they crowded to the yill,[11]
  When they were a' dismist:

---

[1] A gill of whisky.—[2] Small beer.—[3] Tickle.—[4] Look, appearance.—[5] Snug in the corner.—[6] The blast of a trumpet.—[7] Roaring.—[8] Shakspeare's Hamlet.—[9] Flaming brimstone.—[10] The hard rock found in the Ayrshire quarries.—• Ale.

How drink gaed round in cogs an' caups,
    Amang the furms an' benches;
An' cheese an' bread, frae women's laps,
    Were dealt about in lunches
           An' dawds[1] that day.

In comes a gaucie,[2] gash[3] guidwife,
    An' sits down by the fire,
Syne[4] draws her kebbuck[5] an' her knife:
    The lasses they are shyer.
The auld guidmen, about the *grace*,
    Frae side to side they bother,
Till some ane by his bonnet lays,
    An' gies them 't like a tether,
           Fu' lang that day.

Waesucks[6] for him that gets nae lass,
    Or lasses that hae naething!
Sma' need has he to say a grace,
    Or melvie[7] his braw claithing!
O wives, be mindfu' ance yoursel
    How bonnie lads ye wanted,
An' dinna, for a kebbuck-heel,[8]
    Let lasses be affronted
           On sic a day!

Now Clinkumbell,[9] wi' rattlin' tow,[10]
    Begins to jow an' croon;[11]
Some swagger hame the best they dow,[12]
    Some wait the afternoon.
At slaps[13] the billies[14] halt a blink,[15]
    Till lasses slip their shoon:
Wi' faith and hope, an' love an' drink,
    They 're a' in famous tune
           For crack[16] that day.

How monie hearts this day converts
    O' sinners and o' lasses!
Their hearts o' stane, gin night, are gane
    As saft as onie flesh is.

---

[1] Large pieces.—[2] Jolly.—[3] Sagacious.—[4] Then.—[5] Cheese.—[6] Alas!—[7] To soil with meal.—[8] The heel of cheese.—[9] Who rings the church bell.—[10] Rope. —[11] The motion of ringing, and sound of the bell.—[12] As well as they can.— [13] Gates.—[14] Young men.—[15] A little time.—[16] Talk.

There 's some are fou[1] o' love divine;
There 's some are fou o' brandy;
An' monie jobs that day begin,
May end in houghmagandie[2]
Some ither day.

THE ORDINATION.

For sense they little owe to frugal Heaven—
To please the mob, they hide the little given.

KILMARNOCK wabsters,[3] fidge an' claw,[4]
An' pour your creshie[5] nations;
An' ye wha leather rax[6] an' draw,
Of a' denominations—
Swith to the Laigh Kirk, ane an' a',
An' there tak up your stations;
Then aff to Begbie's in a raw,[7]
An' pour divine libations
For joy this day.

Curst Common Sense, that imp o' hell,
Cam in wi' Maggie Lauder,[8]
But O ****** aft made her yell,
An' Russel sair misca'd her;
This day M'Kinlay taks the flail,
An' he 's the boy will blaud[9] her;
He 'll clap a shangan[10] on her tail,
An' set the bairns[11] to daub her
Wi' dirt this day.

Mak haste an' turn king David owre,
An' lilt[12] wi' holy clangor;
O' double verse come gie us four,
An' skirl[13] up the Bangor:

---

[1] Full.—[2] Fornication.—[3] Weavers.—[4] Scratch.—[5] Greasy.—[6] Stretch. An
allusion to shoemakers.—[7] Row.
[8] Alluding to a scoffing ballad which was made on the admission of the late
reverend and worthy Mr. L. to the Laigh Kirk.
[9] To slap or strike.—[10] A cleft stick, sometimes mischievously fastened to
the tail of a dog.—[11] Children.—[12] To sing.—[13] To shriek, or cry aloud.

This day the Kirk kicks up a stour,[1]
  Nae mair the knaves shall wrang her;
For Heresy is in her power,
  And gloriously she 'll whang[2] her
            Wi' pith this day.

Come, let a proper text be read,
  An' touch it aff wi' vigor,
How graceless Ham[3] leugh[4] at his dad,
  Which made Canaan a niger;[5]
Or Phineas[6] drove the murdering blade,
  Wi' w—e-abhorring rigor;
Or Zipporah,[7] the scauldin'[8] jade,
  Was like a bluidy[9] tiger
            I' th' inn that day.

There, try his mettle on the creed,
  And bind him down, wi' caution,
That stipend is a carnal weed
  He taks but for the fashion;
And gie him o'er the flock, to feed,
  And punish each transgression;
Especial rams, that cross the breed,
  Gie them sufficient threshin';
            Spare them nae day.

Now, auld Kilmarnock, cock thy tail,
  And toss thy horns fu' canty;[10]
Nae mair thou 'lt rowte[11] out-owre the dale,
  Because thy pasture 's scanty;
For lapfu's large o' gospel kail[12]
  Shall fill thy crib in plenty,
And runts[13] o' grace the pick and wale,[14]
  No gien by way o' dainty,
            But ilka[15] day.

Nae mair by Babel's streams we 'll weep,
  To think upon our Zion;
And hing[16] our fiddles up to sleep,
  Like baby-clouts a-dryin':

---

[1] Dust.—[2] To give the strappado.—[3] Gen. ix. 22.—[3] Did laugh.—[5] A negro.
—[6] Numb. xxv. 8.—[7] Exod. iv. 25.—[8] Scolding.—[9] Bloody.—[10] Merrily.—
[11] Roar, bellow.—[12] Colewort.—[13] The stems of colewort, or cabbage.—
[4] Choice.—[15] Every.—[14] Hang.

Come, screw the pegs wi' tunefu' cheep,[1]
And o'er the thairms[2] be tryin';
O rare! to see our elbucks[3] wheep,[4]
An' a' like lamb-tails flyin'
    Fu' fast this day!

Lang Patronage, wi' rod o' airn,[5]
Has shored[6] the Kirk's undoin',
As lately Fenwick, sair forfairn,[7]
Has proven to its ruin:
Our Patron, honest man! Glencairn,
He saw mischief was brewin';
And, like a godly elect bairn,
He 's waled[8] us out a true ane,
    And sound this day.

Now R******* harangue nae mair,
But steek your gab[9] forever:
Or try the wicked town of Ayr,
For there they 'll think you clever:
Or, nae reflection on your lear,[10]
Ye may commence a shaver;
Or to the Netherton repair,
And turn a carpet-weaver
    Aff-hand this day.

M***** and you were just a match,
We never had sic twa drones:
Auld Hornie did the Laigh Kirk watch,
Just like a winkin' baudrons;[11]
And ay he catch'd the tither wretch,
To fry them in his caudrons;
But now his honor maun detach,
Wi' a' his brimstone squadrons,
    Fast, fast this day.

See, see auld Orthodoxy's faes[12]
She 's swingin'[13] thro' the city:
Hark! how the nine-tail'd cat she plays!
I vow it 's unco[14] pretty:
There, Learning, wi' his Greekish face,
Grunts out some Latin ditty;

[1] (*) p.—[2] Fiddle-strings.—[3] Elbows.—[4] Move nimbly.—[5] Iron.—[6] Offered, or attempted.—[7] Distressed.—[8] Picked.—[9] Shut your mouth.—[10] Learning.—[11] A cat.—[12] Foes.—[13] Whipping.—[14] Very.

An' Common Sense is gaun, she says,
    To mak to Jamie Beattie[1]
                Her plaint this day.

But there 's Morality himsel,
    Embracing all opinions;
Hear, how he gies the tither yell
    Between his twa companions!
See, how she peels the skin an' fell,[2]
    As ane were peeling onions!
Now there—they 're packèd aff to hell,
    And banish'd our dominions,
                Henceforth this day.

O happy day! rejoice, rejoice!
    Come, bouse about the porter!
Morality's demure decoys
    Shall here nae mair find quarter:
M'Kinlay, Russel, are the boys,
    That Heresy can torture;
They 'll gie her on a rape[3] a hoyse,[4]
    And cowe[5] her measure shorter
                By th' head some day.

Come, bring the tither mutchkin[6] in;
    And here 's, for a conclusion,
To every *new-light*[7] mother's son,
    From this time forth, confusion;
If mair they deave[8] us wi' their din,
    Or patronage intrusion,
We 'll light a spunk,[9] and every skin,
    We 'll rin[10] them aff in fusion
                Like oil some day.

[1] James Beattie, LL.D., author of "The Minstrel," 'Evidences of the Christian Religion," &c.
[2] The flesh immediately under the skin.—[3] Rope.—[4] Hoist.—[5] To lop, or cut off.—[6] An English pint.—[7] See note 11, p. 242.—[8] To deafen.—[9] A fire. —[10] Run.

ADDRESS TO THE UNCO GUID,

OR THE RIGIDLY RIGHTEOUS.

My son, these maxims make a rule,
  And lump them ay thegither;[1]
The rigid Righteous is a fool,
  The rigid Wise anither:
The cleanest corn that e'er was dight[2]
  May hae some pyles o' caff[3] in;
So ne'er a fellow-creature slight
  For random fits o' daffin'.[4]
                      Solomon.—Eccles. vii. 17.

O YE wha are sae guid yoursel,
  Sae pious and sae holy,
Ye 've naught to do but mark and tell
  Your neebor's faults and folly!
Whase life is like a weel-gaun[5] mill,
  Supplied wi' store o' water,
The heapet happer[6]'s ebbing still,
  And still the clap[7] plays clatter.

Hear me, ye venerable core,
  As counsel for poor mortals,
That frequent pass douce[8] Wisdom's door
  For glaikit[9] Folly's portals;
I, for their thoughtless, careless sakes,
  Would here propone defences,
Their donsie[10] tricks, their black mistakes,
  Their failings and mischances.

Ye see your state wi' theirs compared,
  And shudder at the niffer;[11]
But cast a moment's fair regard,
  What maks the mighty differ?
Discount what scant occasion gave
  That purity ye pride in,
And (what's aft mair than a' the lave[12])
  Your better art o' hiding.

Think, when your castigated pulse
  Gies now and then a wallop,

---

[1] Always together.—[2] Cleaned from chaff.—[3] Grains of chaff.—[4] Merriment.—[5] Well-going.—[6] Heaped hopper.—[7] Clapper of a mill.—[8] Sober.—[9] Thoughtless.—[10] Unlucky.—[11] Exchange.—[12] All the rest.

What ragings must his veins convulse,
  That still eternal gallop:
Wi' wind and tide fair i' your tail,
  Right on ye scud your sea-way;
But in the teeth o' baith[1] to sail,
  It makes an unco[2] lee-way.

See social life and glee sit down,
  All joyous and unthinking,
Till, quite transmugrified, they 're grown
  Debauchery and drinking:
Oh, would they stay to calculate
  Th' eternal consequences;
Or, your more dreaded hell to state,
  Damnation of expenses!

Ye high, exalted, virtuous dames,
  Tied up in godly laces,
Before ye gie poor Frailty names,
  Suppose a change o' cases;
A dear loved lad, convenience snug,
  A treacherous inclination—
But, let me whisper i' your lug,
  Ye 're aiblins[3] nae temptation.

Then gently scan your brother man,
  Still gentler sister woman;
Tho' they may gang a kennin'[4] wrang;
  To step aside is human:
One point must still be greatly dark,
  The moving *why* they do it:
And just as lamely can ye mark,
  How far perhaps they rue it.

Who made the heart, 'tis He alone
  Decidedly can try us:
He knows each chord—its various tone;
  Each spring—its various bias:
Then at the balance let 's be mute,
  We never can adjust it:
What 's *done* we partly may compute,
  But know not what 's *resisted*.

[1] Both.—[2] Awkward.—[3] Perhaps.—[4] A little, a small matter.

THE TWA HERDS.[1]

The "Twa Herds" were Mr. Moodie, minister of Riccarton, and Mr. John Russel, then minister of Kilmarnock, and afterwards of Stirling.

O A' ye pious godly flocks,
Weel fed on pastures orthodox,
Wha now will keep ye frae the fox,
    Or worrying tykes,[2]
Or wha will tent the waifs[3] and crocks,[4]
    About the dykes?

The twa best Herds in a' the wast,
That e'er gae gospel horn a blast,
These five-and-twenty simmers past,
    Oh, dool[5] to tell!
Hae had a bitter, black outcast[6]
    Atween themsel.

O M'Kinlay, man, and wordy[7] Russel,
How could you raise so vile a bustle?
Ye 'll see how *new-light* herds will whistle,
    And think it fine!
The Lord's cause ne'er gat sic a twistle,[8]
    Sin' I hae mine.

O, Sirs! whae'er wad hae expeckit,
Your duty ye wad sae negleckit,
Ye wha were ne'er by lairds respeckit,
    To wear the plaid,
But by the brutes themselves eleckit,[9]
    To be their guide.

What flock wi' M'Kinlay's flock could rank,
Sae hale and hearty every shank!
Nae poison'd sour Arminian stank,[10]
    He let them taste;
Frae Calvin's well, ay clear they drank—
    O sic a feast!

---

[1] "This is the first of my poetic offspring that saw the light."—*Burns's Letters.*
[2] Dogs.—[3] Strayed, and not yet claimed.—[4] Ewes too old for breeding.—[5] Sorrowful.—[6] Quarrel.—[7] Worthy.—[8] To twist, to twine.—[9] Elected.—[10] Pool of standing water.

The thummart,[1] wil'-cat, brock,[2] and tod,[3]
Weel kenn'd his voice thro' a' the wood,
He smell'd their ilka hole and road,
      Baith out and in,
And weel he lik'd to shed their bluid,
      And sell their skin.

What herd like Russel tell'd his tale?
His voice was heard thro' muir and dale;
He kenn'd the Lord's sheep, ilka tail,
      O'er a' the height,
And saw gin[4] they were sick or hale,[5]
      At the first sight.

He fine a mangy sheep could scrub,
Or nobly fling the gospel club,
And *new-light* herds could nicely drub,
      Or pay their skin;
Could shake them o'er the burnin' dub,[6]
      Or heave them in.

Sic twa!—oh, do I live to see't!—
Sic famous twa should disagreet,
An' names, like villain, hypocrite,
      Ilk ither gien,[7]
While *new-light* herds, wi' laughin' spite,
      Say neither's liein'!

A' ye wha tent the gospel fauld,
There's D——n deep, and P——s shaul;[8]
But chiefly thou, apostle Auld,
      We trust in thee,
That thou wilt work them, hot and cauld,
      Till they agree.

Consider, Sirs, how we're beset,
There's scarce a new herd that we get,
But comes frae 'mang that cursed set,
      I winna name,
I hope frae heaven to see them yet
      In fiery flame.

Dalrymple has been lang our fae,
M'Gill has wrought us meikle wae,[9]

---

[1] Pole-cat.—[2] Badger.—[3] Fox.—[4] If.—[5] Healthy.—[6] Pond.—[7] Each other give.—[8] Shallow.—[9] Much woe.

And that cursed rascal ca'd M——e,
  And baith the Shaws,
That aft hae made us black and blae,
  Wi' vengefu' paws.

Auld W——w lang has hatch'd mischief,
We thought ay death wad bring relief,
But he has gotten, to our grief,
  Ane to succeed him,
A chiel wha 'll soundly buff our beef;
  I meikle dread him.

And monie a ane that I could tell,
Wha fain would openly rebel,
Forbye turn-coats amang oursel,
  There 's S——h for ane,
I doubt he 's but a gray-nick quill,
  An' that ye 'll fin'.

Oh! a' ye flocks, o'er a' the hills,
By mosses, meadows, moors, and fells,
Come join your counsel and your skills,
  To cowe[1] the lairds,
And get the brutes the power themsels,
  To choose their herds.

Then Orthodoxy yet may prance,
And Learning in a woodie dance,[2]
And that fell cur ca'd Common Sense,
  That bites sae sair,
Be banish'd o'er the sea to France ;
  Let him bark there.

Then Shaw's and D'rymple's eloquence,
M'Gill's close nervous excellence,
M'Q——'s pathetic manly sense,
  And guid M'Math,[3]
Wi' Smith, wha thro' the heart can glance,
  May a' pack aff.

[1] Frighten.— [2] Dance in a rope, i. e. be hanged.—[3] See page 274.
26

THE KIRK'S ALARM.[1]

ORTHODOX, Orthodox,
  Wha believe in John Knox,
Let me sound an alarm to your conscience;
    There 's a heretic blast,
    Has been blawn in the wast,
That what is no sense must be nonsense.

    Dr. Mac,[2] Dr. Mac,
    You should stretch on a rack,
To strike evil-doers wi' terror;
    To join faith and sense
    Upon onie pretence,
Is heretic, damnable error.

    Town of Ayr, town of Ayr,
    It was mad, I declare,
To meddle wi' mischief a-brewin';
    Provost John is still deaf
    To the church's relief,
And orator Bob[3] is its ruin.

    D'rymple mild, D'rymple mild,
    Though your heart 's like a child,
And your life like the new driven snaw,
    Yet that winna save ye,
    Auld Satan must have ye,
For preaching that three 's ane and twa.

    Rumble John,[4] Rumble John,
    Mount the steps wi' a groan,
Cry the book is wi' heresy cramm'd;
    Then lug out your ladle,
    Deal brimstone like adle,[5]
And roar every note of the damn'd.

    Simper James,[6] Simper James,
    Leave the fair Killie dames

[1] This poem was written a short time after the publication of Dr. M'Gill's Essay.
[2] Dr. M'Gill.—[3] Robert Aiken.—[4] Mr. Russell.—[5] Putrid water.—[6] Mr. M'Kinlay.

There 's a holier chase in your view ;
   I 'll lay on your head,
   That the pack ye 'll soon lead,
For puppies like you there 's but few.

   Signet Sawney,[1] Signet Sawney,
   Are ye herding the penny,
Unconscious what evils await?
   Wi' a jump, yell, and howl,
   Alarm every soul,
For the foul thief is just at your gate.

   Daddy Auld,[2] Daddy Auld,
   There 's a tod[3] in your fauld,
A tod meikle waur than the clerk ;
   Though ye can do little skaith,[4]
   Ye 'll be in at the death,
And gif ye canna bite ye may bark.

   Davie Bluster,[5] Davie Bluster,
   If for a saint ye do muster,
The corps is no nice of recruits ;
   Yet to worth let 's be just,
   Royal blood ye might boast,
If the ass was the king of the brutes.

   Jamie Goose,[6] Jamie Goose,
   Ye hae made but toom roose,[7]
In hunting the wicked lieutenant ;
   But the doctor 's your mark,
   For the Lord's holy ark,
He has cooper'd and caw'd[8] a wrang pin in 't.

   Poet Willie,[9] Poet Willie,
   Gie the doctor a volley,
Wi' your liberty's chain and your wit ;
   O'er Pegasus' side
   Ye ne'er laid astride,
Ye but smelt, man, the place where he s—t.

   Andro Gouk,[10] Andro Gouk,
   Ye may slander the book,

---

[1] Mr. M....y.—[2] Mr. A....d.—[3] Fox.—[4] Harm.— Mr. G....t of O. l..e.
—[6] Mr. Y....g of C..n..k.—[7] Empty praise.—[8] Driven.—[9] Mr. P..b..s of
Ayr.—[10] Dr. A. M....ll.

And the book nane the waur,[1] let me tell ye!
　　Ye are rich, and look big,
　　But lay by hat and wig,
And ye 'll hae a calf's head o' sma' value.

　　Barr Steenie,[2] Barr Steenie,
　　What mean ye? what mean ye?
If ye 'll meddle nae mair wi' the matter,
　　Ye may hae some pretence
　　To havins[3] and sense,
Wi' people wha ken ye nae better.

　　Irvine Side,[4] Irvine Side,
Wi' your turkey-cock pride,
Of manhood but sma' is your share:
　　Ye 've the figure, 'tis true,
　　E'en your foes will allow,
And your friends, they dare grant you nae mair.

　　Muirland Jock,[5] Muirland Jock,
　　When the Lord makes a rock
To crush Common Sense for her sins,
　　If ill manners were wit,
　　There 's no mortal so fit
To confound the poor doctor at once.

　　Holy Will,[6] Holy Will,
　　There was wit i' your skull,
When ye pilfer'd the alms o' the poor;
　　The timmer[7] is scant
　　When ye 're taen for a saunt,
Wha should swing in a rape[8] for an hour.

　　Calvin's sons, Calvin's sons,
　　Seize your spiritual guns,
Ammunition you never can need;
　　Your hearts are the stuff,
　　Will be pouther[9] enough,
And your skulls are storehouses o' lead.

　　Poet Burns, Poet Burns,
　　Wi' your priest-skelping turns,

---

[1] None the worse.—[2] S....n Y....g of B....r.—[3] Good manners.—[4] Mr.
B ...h of G....n.—[5] Mr. S....d.—[6] An Elder in M....e.—[7] Timber.—
Rope.—[9] Powder.

Why desert ye your auld native shire?
Your Muse is a gypsie,
E'en though she were tipsie,
She could ca' us nae waur' than we are.

HOLY WILLIE'S PRAYER.[2]

O Thou, wha in the heavens dost dwell,
Wha, as it pleases best thysel',
Sends ane to heaven and ten to hell,
   A' for thy glory,
And no for onie guid or ill
    They 've done afore thee :

I bless and praise thy matchless might,
Whan thousands thou hast left in night,
That I am here afore thy sight,
   For gifts an' grace,
A burnin' an' a shinin' light,
    To a' this place.

What was I, or my generation,
That I should get such exaltation?
I, wha deserve such just damnation,
   For broken laws,
Five thousand years 'fore my creation,
    Through Adam's cause.

When frae my mither's womb I fell,
Thou might hae plunged me into hell,
To gnash my gums, to weep and wail,
   In burnin' lake,
Where damnéd devils roar and yell,
    Chain'd to a stake.

Yet I am here a chosen sample,
To show thy grace is great and ample;

Worse.

 [2] "Holy Willie's Prayer is a piece of satire more exquisitely severe than any which Burns ever afterwards wrote; but, unfortunately, cast in a form most daringly profane."—*Sir Walter Scott, Quarterly Review*, vol. i. p. 22

I 'm here a pillar in thy temple,
          Strong as a rock,
A guide, a buckler, an' example
          To a' thy flock.

O Lord, thou kens what zeal I bear,
When drinkers drink, and swearers swear,
And singin' there and dancin' here,
          Wi' great and sma':
For I am keepit by thy fear,
          Free frae them a'.

But yet, O Lord! confess I must,
At times I 'm fash'd wi' fleshly lust,
An' sometimes too, wi' warldly trust,
          Vile self gets in;
But thou remembers we are dust,
          Defiled in sin.

O Lord! yestreen, thou kens, wi' Meg—
Thy pardon I sincerely beg,
Oh! may 't ne'er be a livin' plague
          To my dishonor,
An' I 'll ne'er lift a lawless leg
          Again upon her.

Besides, I farther maun allow,
Wi' Lizzie's lass, three times I trow;
But, Lord, that Friday I was fou,
          When I came near her,
Or else thou kens thy servant true
          Wad ne'er hae steer'd her.

Maybe thou lets this fleshly thorn
Beset thy servant e'en and morn,
Lest he owre high and proud should turn,
          'Cause he 's sae gifted;
If sae, thy hand maun e'en be borne,
          Until thou lift it.

Lord, bless thy chosen in this place,
For here thou hast a chosen race;
But God confound their stubborn face,
          And blast their name,
Wha bring thy elders to disgrace,
          An' public shame.

Lord, mind Gavin Hamilton's deserts,
He drinks, an' swears, an' plays at cartes,
Yet has sae monie takin' arts,
    Wi' grit an' sma',
Frae God's ain priest the people's hearts
    He steals awa'.

An' whan we chasten'd him therefor,
Thou kens how he bred sic a splore,
As set the warld in a roar
    O' laughin' at us;
Curse thou his basket and his store,
    Kail and potatoes!

Lord, here my earnest cry an' prayer,
Against that presbyt'ry o' Ayr;
Thy strong right hand, Lord, make it bare
    Upo' their heads;
Lord weigh it down, and dinna spare,
    For their misdeeds.

O Lord my God, that glib-tongued[1] Aiken,
My very heart and saul are quakin',
To think how we stood sweatin', shakin',
    An' p—d wi' dread,
While he, wi' hingin' lips an' snakin',
    Held up his head.

Lord, in the day of vengeance try him ·
Lord, visit them wha did employ him,
And pass not in thy mercy by 'em,
    Nor hear their prayer;
But, for thy people's sake, destroy 'em,
    And dinna spare.

But, Lord, remember me and mine,
Wi' mercies temporal and divine,
That I for gear and grace may shine,
    Excell'd by nane,
An' a' the glory shall be thine,
    Amen, Amen.

---

[1] Having readiness of speech.

EPITAPH ON HOLY WILLIE.

HERE Holy Willie's sair worn clay,
    Taks up its last abode;
His saul has taen some other way,
    I fear the left-hand road.

Stop! there he is, as sure's a gun!
    Poor silly body, see him;
Nae wonder he's as black's the grun,
    Observe wha's standing wi' him.

Your brunstane devilship, I see,
    Has got him there before ye;
But haud your nine-tail cat a-wee,
    Till ance you've heard my story.

Your pity I will not implore,
    For pity ye have nane;
Justice, alas! has gien him o'er,
    And mercy's day is gane.

But hear me, Sir: deil as ye are,
    Look something to your credit;
A coof like him wad stain your name,
    If it were kent ye did it.

THE CALF.

TO THE REVEREND MR. ———,

On his text, Malachi iv. 2—"And they shall go forth, and grow up, like
calves of the stall."

RIGHT, Sir! your text, I'll prove it true,
    Tho' heretics may laugh;
For instance, there's yoursel just now,
    God knows, an unco[1] calf!

And should some patron be so kind,
    As bless you wi' a kirk,
I doubt na, Sir, but then we'll find
    Ye're still as great a stirk![2]

[1] A very calf.—[2] A yearling bullock.

But, if the lover's raptured hour
Shall ever be your lot,
Forbid it, every heavenly power,
You e'er should be a stot![1]

Tho', when some kind, connubial dear,
Your butt-and-ben[2] adorns,
The like has been, that you may wear
A noble head of horns!

And in your lug, most reverend James,
To hear you roar and rowte,[3]
Few men o' sense will doubt your claims
To rank amang the nowte![4]

And when ye're number'd wi' the dead,
Below a grassy hillock,
Wi' justice they may mark your head—
"Here lies a famous bullock!"

TO A LOUSE,

On seeing one on a lady's bonnet at church.

Ha! whare ye gaun, ye crowlin[5] ferlie?[6]
Your impudence protects you sairly;
I canna say but ye strunt[7] rarely
        Owre gauze and lace;
Tho', faith, I fear ye dine but sparely
        On sic a place.

Ye ugly, creepin', blastit wonner,[8]
Detested, shunn'd, by saunt an' sinner,
How dare you set your fit[9] upon her,
        Sae fine a lady!
Gae somewhere else and seek your dinner,
        On some poor body.

Swith,[10] in some beggar's haffet[11] squattle;[12]
There ye may creep, and sprawl, and sprattle

- An ox.—[2] The country kitchen and parlor.—[3] To bellow.—[4] Black cattle. —[5] Crawling.—[6] A term of contempt.—[7] To walk sturdily.—[8] A contemptuous appellation.—[9] Feet.—[10] Get away.—[11] The side of the head.—[12] To sprawl.

Wi ither kindred, jumpin' cattle,
       In shoals and nations;
Whare horn nor bane ne'er dare unsettle
       Your thick plantations.

Now haud ye there, ye 're out o' sight,
Below the fatt'rils,[1] snug and tight;
Na, faith ye yet! ye 'll no be right
       Till ye 've get on it,
The vera tapmost, towering height
          O' Miss's bonnet.

My sooth! right bauld ye set your nose out,
As plump and gray as onie grozet;[2]
O for some rank, mercurial rozet,[3]
       Or fell, red smeddum,[4]
I'd gie you sic a hearty dose o 't,
       Wad dress your droddum![5]

I wad na be surprised to spy
You on an auld wife's flainen toy;[6]
Or aiblins[7] some bit duddie[8] boy,
       On 's wyliecoat;[9]
But Miss's fine Lunardi! fie,
       How dare ye do 't?

O Jenny, dinna toss your head,
An' set your beauties a' abread![10]
Ye little ken what cursèd speed
       The blastie 's makin'!
Thae[11] winks and finger-ends I dread,
       Are notice takin'!

O wad some power the giftie gie us
To see oursels as others see us!
It wad frae monie a blunder free us
       And foolish notion:
What airs in dress an' gait wad lea'e us,
       And e'en devotion!

---

[1] Trimmings.—[2] Gooseberry.—[3] Rosin.—[4] Powder.—[5] Breech.—[6] An ancient head-dress.—[7] Perhaps.—[8] Ragged.—[9] A flannel vest.—[10] Abroad.—[11] Those.

ODE,

DWELLER in yon dungeon dark,
Hangman of creation! mark
Who in widow-weeds appears,
Laden with unhonor'd years,
Noosing with care a bursting purse,
Baited with many a deadly curse!

STROPHE.

View the wither'd beldam's face—
Can thy keen inspection trace
Aught of humanity's sweet melting grace?
Note that eye, 'tis rheum o'erflows,
Pity's flood there never rose.
See those hands, ne'er stretch'd to save,
Hands that took—but never gave.
Keeper of Mammon's iron chest,
Lo! there she goes—unpitied and unblest!
She goes—but not to realms of everlasting rest!

ANTISTROPHE.

Plunderer of armies, lift thine eyes,
(Awhile forbear, ye torturing fiends,)
Seest thou whose step unwilling hither bends?
No fallen angel, hurl'd from upper skies;
'Tis thy trusty *quondam mate*,
Doom'd to share thy fiery fate,
    She, tardy, hell-ward plies.

EPODE.

And are they of no more avail,
Ten thousand glittering pounds a-year?
    In other worlds can Mammon fail,
Omnipotent as he is here?
Oh, bitter mockery of the pompous bier,
While down the wretched vital part is driven!
The cave-lodged beggar, with a conscience clear,
Expires in rags, unknown, and goes to heaven.

MONODY

How cold is that bosom which folly once fired!
   How pale is that cheek where the rouge lately
      glisten'd!
How silent that tongue which the echoes oft tired!
   How dull is that ear which to flattery so listen'd!

If sorrow and anguish their exit await,
   From friendship and dearest affection removed,
How doubly severer, Eliza, thy fate—
   Thou diedst unwept as thou livedst unloved!

Loves, Graces, and Virtue, I call not on you;
   So shy, grave, and distant, ye shed not a tear:
But come all ye offspring of Folly so true,
   And flowers let us cull for Eliza's cold bier.

We'll search thro' the garden for each silly flower,
   We'll roam thro' the forest for each idle weed;
But chiefly the nettle, so typical, shower,
   For none e'er approach'd her but rued the rash
      deed.

We'll sculpture the marble, we'll measure the lay:
   Here Vanity strums on her idiot lyre;
There keen Indignation shall dart on her prey,
   Which spurning Contempt shall redeem from
      her ire.

THE EPITAPH.

Here lies, now a prey to insulting neglect,
   What once was a butterfly, gay in life's beam;
Want only of wisdom denied her respect,
   Want only of goodness denied her esteem.

ELEGIES.

ELEGY ON MISS BURNET, OF MONBODDO.

Life ne'er exulted in so rich a prize,
As Burnet, lovely, from her native skies;
Nor envious Death so triumph'd in a blow,
As that which laid the accomplish'd Burnet low.

Thy form and mind, sweet maid, can I forget?
In richest ore the brightest jewel set!
In thee, high Heaven above was truest shown,
As by his noblest work the Godhead best is known.

In vain ye flaunt in summer's pride, ye groves;
   Thou crystal streamlet with thy flowery shore,
Ye woodland choir that chant your idle loves,
   Ye cease to charm—Eliza is no more!

Ye heathy wastes, immix'd with reedy fens;
   Ye mossy streams, with sedge and rushes stored ·
Ye rugged cliffs, o'erhanging dreary glens,
   To you I fly—ye with my soul accord.

Princes, whose cumbrous pride was all their worth,
   Shall venal lays their pompous exit hail?
And thou, sweet excellence! forsake our earth,
   And not a Muse in honest grief bewail?

We saw thee shine in youth and beauty's pride,
   And virtue's light, that beams beyond the spheres;
But like the sun eclipsed at morning tide,
   Thou left'st us darkling in a world of tears.

The parent's heart that nestled fond in thee,
   That heart now sunk, a prey to grief and care;
So deck'd the woodbine sweet yon agéd tree,
   So from it ravish'd, leaves it bleak and bare.

ON THE DEATH OF ROBERT RIDDEL, ESQ,

OF GLEN-RIDDEL, APRIL, 1794.

No more, ye warblers of the wood, no more,
  Nor pour your descant, grating, on my soul:
  Thou young-eyed Spring, gay in thy verdant stole,
More welcome were to me grim Winter's wildest roar.

How can ye charm, ye flowers, with all your dyes?
  Ye blow upon the sod that wraps my friend:
  How can I to the tuneful strain attend?
That strain flows round the untimely tomb where
    Riddel lies.

Yes, pour, ye warblers, pour the notes of woe,
  And soothe the Virtues weeping on this bier:
  The Man of Worth, who has not left his peer,
Is in his narrow house forever darkly low.

Thee, Spring, again with joy shall others greet;
Me, memory of my loss will only meet.

ON THE DEATH OF SIR JAMES HUNTER BLAIR.

THE lamp of day, with ill-presaging glare,
  Dim, cloudy, sunk beneath the western wave;
The inconstant blast howl'd though the darkening air,
  And hollow whistled in the rocky cave.

Lone, as I wander'd by each cliff and dell,
  Once the loved haunts of Scotia's royal train;[1]
Or mused where limpid streams, once hallow'd well,[2]
  Or mouldering ruins mark'd the sacred fane;[3]

The increasing blast roared round the beetling rocks,
  The clouds, swift-wing'd, flew o'er the starry sky,
The groaning trees untimely shed their locks,
  And shooting meteors caught the startled eye;

The paly moon rose in the livid east,
  And 'mong the cliffs disclosed a stately form,

[1] The King's Park, at Holyrood-house.—[2] St. Anthony's Well.—[3] St. Anthony's Chapel.

In weeds of woe that frantic beat her breast,
    And mix'd her wailings with the raving storm.

Wild to my heart the filial pulses glow,
    'Twas Caledonia's trophied shield I view'd;
Her form majestic droop'd in pensive woe,
    The lightning of her eye in tears imbued.

Reversed that spear, redoubtable in war,
    Reclined that banner, erst in fields unfurl'd,
That like a deathful meteor gleam'd afar,
    And braved the mighty monarchs of the world:

"My patriot Son fills an untimely grave!"
    With accents wild, and lifted arms, she cried—
"Low lies the hand that oft was stretch'd to save,
    Low lies the heart that swell'd with honest pride!

"A weeping country joins a widow's tear,
    The helpless poor mix with the orphan's cry;
The drooping Arts surround their Patron's bier,
    And grateful Science heaves the heartfelt sigh.

"I saw my sons resume their ancient fire;
    I saw fair Freedom's blossoms richly blow;
But, ah! how hope is born but to expire!
    Relentless Fate has laid this Guardian low.

"My patriot falls—and shall he lie unsung,
    While empty greatness saves a worthless name?
No; every Muse shall join her tuneful tongue,
    And future ages hear his growing fame.

"And I will join a mother's tender cares,
    Thro' future times to make his virtues last,
That distant years may boast of other Blairs."—
    She said, and vanish'd with the sweeping blast.

ON READING, IN A NEWSPAPER, THE DEATH OF JOHN M'LEOD, ESQ.,

BROTHER TO A YOUNG LADY, A PARTICULAR FRIEND OF THE AUTHOR'S.

SAD thy tale, thou idle page,
    And rueful thy alarms:

Death tears the brother of her love
  From Isabella's arms.

Sweetly deck'd with pearly dew
  The morning rose may blow;
But cold successive noontide blasts
  May lay its beauties low.

Fair on Isabella's morn
  The sun propitious smiled;
But, long ere noon, succeeding clouds
  Succeeding hopes beguiled.

Fate oft tears the bosom chords
  That Nature finest strung:
So Isabella's heart was form'd,
  And so that heart was wrung.

Dread Omnipotence alone
  Can heal the wound he gave;
Can point the brimful grief-worn eyes
  To scenes beyond the grave.

Virtue's blossoms there shall blow,
  And fear no withering blast,
There Isabella's spotless worth
  Shall happy be at last.

ELEGY ON CAPTAIN MATTHEW HENDERSON,

A GENTLEMAN WHO HELD THE PATENT FOR HIS HONORS IMMEDIATZLY
FROM ALMIGHTY GOD.

> But now his radiant course is run,
>   For Matthew's course was bright:
> His soul was like the glorious sun,
>   A matchless, heavenly light!

O DEATH! thou tyrant fell and bloody!
The muckle Devil wi' a woodie[1]
Haurl thee hame to his black smiddie,[2]
  O'er hurcheon[3] hides,
And like stock-fish come o'er his studdie[4]
  Wi' thy auld sides!

------

[1] A halter.—[2] Smithy.—[3] Hedgehog.—[4] An anvil. An allusion is here had
to the beating of dried stock-fish, to make them tender.

He's gane! he's gane! he's frae us torn,
The ae best fellow e'er was born!
Thee, Matthew, Nature's sel' shall mourn
    By wood and wild,
Where, haply, Pity strays forlorn,
    Frae man exiled.

Ye hills, near neebors o' the starns,[1]
That proudly cock your cresting cairns [2]
Ye cliffs, the haunts of sailing yearns,[3]
    Where Echo slumbers!
Come join, ye Nature's sturdiest bairns,[4]
    My wailing numbers!

Mourn ilka grove the cushat[5] kens!
Ye hazelly shaws and briery dens!
Ye burnies,[6] wimplin[7] down your glens,
    Wi' todlin[8] din,
Or foaming strang, wi' hasty stens,[9]
    Frae linn to linn![10]

Mourn, little harebells owre the lee;
Ye stately foxgloves fair to see;
Ye woodbines hanging bonnilie,
    In scented bowers;
Ye roses on your thorny tree,
    The first o' flowers!

At dawn, when every grassy blade
Droops with a diamond at his head,
At even, when beans their fragrance shed
    I' th' rustling gale,
Ye maukins,[11] whiddin[12] thro' the glade,
    Come, join my wail!

Mourn, ye wee songsters o' the wood;
Ye grouse that crap the heather bud;
Ye curlews calling through a clud;[13]
    Ye whistling plover;

---

[1] Stars.—[2] A heap of stones piled up in the form of a cone.
[3] Eagles: they are here called "sailing yearns," in allusion to their flying without that motion of the wings which is common to most other birds.
[4] Children.—[5] The dove, or wood-pigeon.—[6] Rivulets.—[7] Meandering.—
[8] Wimpling.—[9] To rear as a horse.—[10] A water-fall.—[11] Hares.—[12] Running as a hare.—[13] Cloud.

And mourn, ye whirring[1] paitrick brood·
        He's gane forever!

Mourn, sooty coots, and speckled teals,
Ye fisher herons, watching eels;
Ye duck and drake, wi' airy wheels
        Circling the lake;
Ye bitterns, till the quagmire reels,
        Rair[2] for his sake!

Mourn, clamoring craiks,[3] at close o' day,
'Mang fields o' flowering clover gay!
And when ye wing your annual way
        Frae our cauld shore,
Tell thae[4] far warlds, wha lies in clay,
        Wham we deplore.

Ye howlets,[5] frae your ivy bower,
In some auld tree, or eldritch[6] tower,
What time the moon, wi' silent glower,
        Sets up her horn,
Wail through the weary midnight hour
        Till waukrife[7] morn!

O rivers, forests, hills, and plains!
Oft have ye heard my cantie[8] strains:
But now, what else for me remains
        But tales of woe;
And frae my een the drapping rains
        Maun ever flow!

Mourn, Spring, thou darling of the year!
Ilk[9] cowslip cup shall kep[10] a tear:
Thou, Simmer, while each corny spear
        Shoots up his head,
Thy gay, green, flowery tresses shear,
        For him that's dead!

Thou, Autumn, wi' thy yellow hair,
In grief thy sallow mantle tear!
Thou, Winter, hurling through the air
        The roaring blast,

---

[1] The noise made by the wings of a covey of partridges.—[2] To roar.—
Birds called in England landrails, in Scotland, corn-craiks.—[4] Those.—
Owls.—[6] Ghastly.—[7] The waking hour.—[8] Cheerful.—[9] Each.—[10] Catch.

Wide o'er the naked world declare
    The worth we 've lost!

Mourn him, thou Sun, great source of light!
Mourn, empress of the silent night!
And you, ye twinkling starnies bright,
    My Matthew mourn!
For through your orbs he 's taen[1] his flight,
    Ne'er to return.

O Henderson! the man! the brother!
And art thou gone, and gone forever?
And hast thou cross'd that unknown river,
    Life's dreary bound?
Like thee, where shall I find another,
    The world around?

Go to your sculptured tombs, ye great,
In a' the tinsel trash o' state!
But by thy honest turf I 'll wait,
    Thou man of worth!
And weep the ae best fellow's fate
    E'er lay in earth.

EPITAPH.

Stop, passenger! my story 's brief;
    And truth I shall relate, man;
I tell nae common tale o' grief,
    For Matthew was a great man.

If thou uncommon merit hast,
    Yet spurn'd at Fortune's door, man;
A look of pity hither cast,
    For Matthew was a poor man

If thou a noble sodger art,
    That passest by this grave, man,
There moulders here a gallant heart,
    For Matthew was a brave man.

If thou on men, their works and ways,
    Canst throw uncommon light, man;
Here lies wha weel had won thy praise,
    For Matthew was a bright man.

[1] Taken.

If thou at friendship's sacred ca⁷¹
   Wad² life itself resign, man;
Thy sympathetic tear maun fa',¹
   For Matthew was a kind man.

If thou art stanch without a stain,
   Like the unchanging blue, man;
This was a kinsman o' thy ain,
   For Matthew was a true man.

If thou hast wit, and fun, and fire,
   And ne'er guid wine did fear, man;
This was thy billie,⁴ dam, and sire,
   For Matthew was a queer man.

If onie whiggish, whingin'⁵ sot,
   To blame poor Matthew dare, man;
May dool⁶ and sorrow be his lot,
   For Matthew was a rare man.

— — —

TAM SAMSON'S⁷ ELEGY.

An honest man 's the noblest work of God.—*Pope.*

Has auld K********* seen the Deil?
Or great M'******** thrawn⁹ his heel?
Or R********¹⁰ again grown weel,
       To preach an' read?
"Na, waur¹¹ than a'!" cries ilka¹² chiel,
       "Tam Samson's dead!"

K********* lang may grunt and grane,
An' sigh, an' sab, an' greet her lane,¹³

¹ Call.—² Would.—³ Fall.—⁴ Brother.—⁵ Fretful.—⁶ Lamentation.

⁷ When this worthy old sportsman went out last muirfowl season, he supposed it to be, in Ossian's phrase, "the last of his fields;" and expressed an ardent wish to die and be buried in the muirs. On this hint the Author composed his Elegy and Epitaph.

⁸ A certain preacher, a great favorite with the million. Vide the Ordination, stanza ii.—⁹ Sprained.

¹⁰ Another preacher, an equal favorite with the few, who was at that time ailing. For him, see also the Ordination, stanza ix.

¹¹ Worse.—¹² Every.—¹³ Weep alone.

An' cleed her bairns,[1] man, wife, an' wean,[2]
In mourning weed;
To death she's dearly paid the kane,[3]
Tam Samson's dead!

The brethren of the mystic level,
May hing[4] their head in wofu' bevel,[5]
While by their nose the tears will revel,
Like onie bead;
Death's gien the lodge an unco devel;[6]
Tam Samson's dead!

When Winter muffles up his cloak,
And binds the mire up like a rock;
When to the lochs[7] the curlers[8] flock,
Wi' gleesome speed,
Wha will they station at the cock?[9]
Tam Samson's dead!

He was the king o' a' the core,
To guard, or draw, or wick[10] a bore,
Or up the rink[11] like Jehu roar
In time o' need;
But now he lags on death's hog-score,[12]
Tam Samson's dead!

Now safe the stately sawmont[13] sail,
And trouts bedropp'd wi' crimson hail,
And eels weel kenn'd for souple tail,
And geds[14] for greed,[15]
Since dark in death's fish-creel[16] we wail
Tam Samson dead!

Clothe her children.—[2] A young child.—[3] Rent, paid in fowls.—[4] Hang.
—[5] In sorrowful posture.—[6] An awkward blow.—[7] A large pond, or sheet of water.
[8] Those who play at the game of curling. Curling is a game of high celebrity in Scotland, and in some degree resembles the game of coits, or bowls.—An iron pin, called a cock, is driven into the ice as a mark, at which heavy pieces of stone (with an iron handle fixed in the upper part, and having a flat and smooth surface at the bottom, so as to glide on the ice) are hurled.—The party who lodge their stones nearest to the cock are the victors.
[9] The winning place in curling.—[10] To strike a stone in an oblique direction.—[11] The course of the stones at the game of curling.—[12] A kind of distance line, in curling, drawn across the rink.—[13] Salmon.—[14] Pike.—[15] Greediness.—[16] Fish-basket.

Rejoice, ye birring paitricks[1] a';
Ye cootie[2] muircocks crousely craw;[3]
Ye maukins,[4] cock your fud fu' braw,[5]
    Withouten dread;
Your mortal fae is now awa',
    Tam Samson's dead!

That waefu' morn be ever mourn'd,
Saw him in shootin' graith[6] adorn'd,
While pointers round impatient burn'd,
    Frae couples freed;
But, och! he gaed and ne'er return'd,
    Tam Samson's dead!

In vain auld age his body batters;
In vain the gout his ankles fetters;
In vain the burns[7] came down like waters
    An acre braid![8]
Now every auld wife, greetin[9] clatters,
    "Tam Samson's dead!"

Owre many a weary hag[10] he limpit,[11]
An' ay the tither shot he thumpit,
Till coward Death behind him jumpit,
    Wi' deadly feide;[12]
Now he proclaims, wi' tout[13] o' trumpet,
    "Tam Samson's dead!"

When at his heart he felt the dagger,
He reel'd his wonted bottle-swagger,
But yet he drew the mortal trigger,
    Wi' weel-aim'd heed;
"Lord, five!"[14] he cried, and owre did stagger;
    Tam Samson's dead!

Ilk hoary hunter mourn'd a brither;
Ilk sportsman youth bemoan'd a father;
Yon auld gray stane, amang the heather,
    Marks out his head,
Whare Burns has wrote, in rhyming blether,
    "Tam Samson's dead!"

[1] Partridges.—[2] Birds which have feathers on the legs are said to be cootie.—[3] Crow courageously.—[4] Hares.—[5] Cock your tail handsomely.—[6] Accoutrements.—[7] Rivulets.—[8] Broad.—[9] Crying.—[10] A scar or gulf in mosses or moors.—[11] Limped, or hobbled.—[12] Feud, enmity.—[13] Blast.—[14] An exclamation at finding he had killed five birds.

There low he lies, in lasting rest;
Perhaps upon his mouldering breast
Some spitefu' muirfowl bigs[1] her nest,
          To hatch an' breed ;
Alas! nae mair he 'll them molest!
          Tam Samson 's dead!

When August winds the heather wave,
And sportsmen wander by yon grave,
Three volleys let his memory crave
          O' pouther an' lead,
Till Echo answer frae her cave,
          "Tam Samson 's dead!"

Heaven rest his saul, where'er it be!
Is the wish o' monie mae[2] than me;
He had twa faults, or maybe three,
          Yet what remead?[3]
Ae social, honest man want we:
          Tam Samson 's dead!

THE EPITAPH.

Tam Samson's weel-worn clay here lies ;
    Ye canting zealots, spare him!
If honest worth in heaven rise,
    Ye 'll mend or ye win[4] near him.

PER CONTRA.

Go, Fame, and canter like a filly
Thro' a' the streets an' neuks o' Killie,[5]
Tell every social, honest billie[6]
          To cease his grievin',
For yet, unskaith'd[7] by Death's gleg gullie,[8]
          Tam Samson 's livin'.

ON A SCOTTISH BARD,
Gone to the West Indies.

A' ye wha live by soups o' drink,
A' ye wha live by crambo-clink,[9]
A' ye wha live and never think,

- Builds.—[2] Many more.—[3] Remedy.—[4] Get.—[5] Kilmarnock.—[6] Honest
fellow.—[7] Unhurt.—[8] Sharp knife.—[9] Rhymes; doggerel verses.

Come, mourn wi' me!
Our billie 's gien[1] us a' the jink,[2]
　　　An' owre the sea.

Lament him, a' ye rantin' core,
Wha dearly like a random splore,[3]
Nae mair he 'll join the merry roar,
　　　In social key;
For now he 's taen anither shore,
　　　An' owre the sea.

The bonnie lasses weel may wiss[4] him,
And in their dear petitions place him;
The widows, wives, an' a' may bless him,
　　　Wi' tearfu' e'e;
For weel I wat they 'll sairly miss him,
　　　That 's owre the sea.

O Fortune! they hae room to grumble
Hadst thou taen aff some drowsy bummle,[5]
Wha can do naught but fyke[6] an' fumble,
　　　'Twad been nae plea;
But he was gleg[7] as onie wumble,[8]
　　　That 's owre the sea.

Auld cantie Kyle[9] may weepers wear,
And stain them wi' the saut,[10] saut tear,
'Twill mak her poor auld heart, I fear,
　　　In flinders[11] flee;
He was her *laureate* monie a year,
　　　That 's owre the sea.

He saw misfortune's cauld nor'west
Lang mustering up a bitter blast;
A jillet[12] brak his heart at last,
　　　Ill may she be!
So, took a berth afore the mast,
　　　An' owre the sea.

To tremble under Fortune's cummock,[13]
On scarce a bellyfu' o' drummock,[14]
Wi' his proud, independent stomach,
　　　Could ill agree;

---

[1] Given.—[2] A dodge.—[3] A frolic.—[4] Wish.—[5] A blunderer.—[6] Trifle.—
[7] Sharp, ready.—[8] Wimble.—[9] A district in Ayrshire.—[10] Salt.—[11] Broken
pieces.—[12] Jilt.—[13] Rod, or staff.—[14] Raw meal and water.

So, row'd[1] his hurdies[2] in a hammock,
    An' owre the sea.

He ne'er was gien to great misguidin',
Yet coin his pouches[3] wad na bide in;
Wi' him it ne'er was under hiding;
    He dealt it free;
The Muse was a' that he took pride in,
    That 's owre the sea.

Jamaica bodies, use him weel,
An' hap[4] him in a cozie biel:[5]
Ye 'll find him ay a dainty chiel,
    And fou o' glee;
He wad na wrang'd the vera Deil,
    That 's owre the sea.

Fareweel, my rhyme-composing billie!
Your native soil was right ill-willie;[6]
But may ye flourish like a lily,
    Now bonniely!
I 'll toast ye in my hindmost gillie,[7]
    Though owre the sea.

ELEGY ON THE YEAR 1788.

JANUARY 1, 1789.

For lords or kings I dinna mourn,
E'en let them die—for that they 're born!
But oh! prodigious to reflect,
A towmont,[8] sirs, is gane to wreck!
O Eighty-eight, in thy sma' space
What dire events hae taken place!
Of what enjoyments thou hast reft us!
In what a pickle thou hast left us!

The Spanish empire 's tint[9] a head,
And my auld teethless Bawtie 's[10] dead;
The toolzie 's[11] teugh[12] 'tween Pitt and Fox,
An' our gudewife's wee birdie cocks;

---

[1] Rolled, wrapped.—[2] Loins, or backside.—[3] Pockets.—[4] To wrap, to cover.
—[5] Snug shelter.—[6] Ill-natured, malicious.—[7] Diminutive of Gill.—
[8] Twelvemonth.—[9] Lost.—[10] Name for a dog.—[11] Quarrel.—[12] Obstinate.

The tane is game, a bluidy devil,
But to the hen-birds unco civil;
The tither 's dour,[1] has nae sic breedin',
But better stuff ne'er claw'd a midden.[2]

Ye ministers, come mount the pulpit,
An' cry till ye be hearse an' rupit;[3]
For Eighty-eight he wish'd you weel,
And gied[4] ye a' baith gear[5] an' meal;
E'en monie a plack,[6] an' monie a peck,
Ye ken yoursels, for little feck![7]

Ye bonnie lasses, dight[8] your een,
For some o' you hae tint a frien':
In Eighty-eight, ye ken, was taen
What ye 'll ne'er hae to gie again.

Observe the very nowt[9] an' sheep,
How dowff[10] an' dowie[11] now they creep;
Nay, e'en the yirth[12] itself does cry,
For E'nbrugh wells are grutten[13] dry.

O Eighty-nine, thou 's but a bairn,
An' no owre auld, I hope, to learn!
Thou beardless boy, I pray tak care!
Thou now hast got thy daddie's chair;
Nae hand-cuff'd, muzzled, half-shackled regent,
But, like himsel', a full, free agent.
Be sure to follow out the plan
Nae waur[14] than he did, honest man.
As muckle better as you can.

ELEGY ON THE DEATH OF ROBERT RUISSEAUX.[15]

Now Robin lies in his last lair,[16]
He 'll gabble rhyme, nor sing nae mair,
Cauld poverty, wi' hungry stare,
   Nae mair shall fear him;

---

[1] Inflexible, unbending.—[2] Dunghill.—[3] Hoarse.—[4] Gave.—[5] Goods, effects.
—[6] An old coin, the third part of a Scotch penny.—[7] Value, or consideration.
—[8] Wipe.—[9] Black cattle.—[10] Pithless.—[11] Worn with grief.—[12] Earth.—
[13] Wept.—[14] Worse.—[15] Ruisseaux, a play on his own name.—[16] A place
for lying down.

Nor anxious fear, nor cankert[1] care,
    E'er mair come near him.

To tell the truth, they seldom fasht[2] him;
Except the moment that they crusht him;
For sune as chance or fate had husht 'em,
    Though e'er sae short,
Then wi' a rhyme or song he lasht 'em,
    An' thought it sport.——

Though he was bred to kintra[3] wark,
And counted was baith wight and stark,[4]
Yet that was never Robin's mark
    To mak a man;
But tell him he was learn'd and clark,[5]
    Ye roos'd him then!

ELEGY ON THE DEATH OF PEG NICHOLSON,

A favorite mare belonging to Mr. W. Nicol, of the High School, Edinburgh—
the "Willie that brew'd a peck o' maut."

Peg Nicholson was a gude bay mare,
    As ever trode on airn;[6]
But now she's floating down the Nith,
    An' past the Mouth o' Cairn.[7]

Peg Nicholson was a gude bay mare,
    An' rode through thick an' thin;
But now she 's floating down the Nith,
    An' wanting even the skin.

Peg Nicholson was a gude bay mare,
    An' ance she bare[8] a priest;
But now she 's floating down the Nith,
    For Solway fish a feast.

Peg Nicholson was a gude bay mare,
    An' the priest he rode her sair;
An' meikle[9] oppress'd an' bruised she was,
    As priest-rid cattle are.

---

[1] Cross, ill-conditioned.—[2] Troubled.—[3] Country.—[4] Strong, powerful.—
[5] Learned and clever.—[6] Iron.—[7] A tributary stream of the Nith.—[8] Did
bear.—[9] Much.

EPIGRAMS, ETC.

EPIGRAM
On Elphinstone's translation of Martial's Epigrams.

O THOU whom Poetry abhors,
Whom Prose has turnéd out of doors,
Heard'st thou that groan?—proceed no further,
'Twas laurell'd Martial roaring murder.

WRITTEN IN A LADY'S POCKET-BOOK.

GRANT me, indulgent Heaven, that I may live
To see the miscreants feel the pains they give:
Deal Freedom's sacred treasures free as air,
Till slave and despot be but things which were.

VERSES
Written on the windows of the Globe Tavern, Dumfries.

THE gray-beard, old Wisdom, may boast of his treasures,
    Give me with gay Folly to live;
I grant him his calm-blooded, time-settled pleasures,
    But Folly has raptures to give.

      *   *   *   *   *

I MURDER hate by field or flood,
    Tho' glory's name may screen us;
In wars at hame I'll spend my blood,
    Life-giving wars of Venus.

The deities that I adore,
    Are social Peace and Plenty;
I'm better pleased to make one more,
    Than be the death of twenty.

*   *   *   *   *

In politics if thou would'st mix,
And mean thy fortunes be;
Bear this in mind, "Be deaf and blind;
Let great folks hear and see."

EPIGRAM ON CAPTAIN GROSE.

The Devil got notice that Grose was a-dying,
So whip! at the summons, old Satan came flying;
But when he approach'd where poor Francis lay
    moaning,
And saw each bed-post with its burden a-groaning,
Astonish'd, confounded, cried Satan, "By G—d,
I'll want 'im ere I take such a damnable load!"[1]

EXTEMPORE,

In answer to an invitation to spend an hour at a tavern.

The King's most humble servant, I
Can scarcely spare a minute;
But I'll be wi' you by and by;
Or else the Deil's be in it.

EPIGRAM.

[Burns, accompanied by a friend, having gone to Inverary at a time when
some company were there on a visit to the Duke of Argyll, finding himself
entirely neglected by the innkeeper, whose attention was occupied by the
visitors of his Grace, expressed his disapprobation of the incivility with
which they were treated in the following lines.]

Whoe'er he be that sojourns here,
I pity much his case,
Unless he comes to wait upon
The Lord, their God, his Grace.

[1] Mr. Grose was exceedingly corpulent, and used to rally himself, with the
greatest good humor, on the singular rotundity of his figure. This Epigram,
written by Burns in a moment of festivity, was so much relished by the an-
tiquarian, that he made it serve as an excuse for prolonging the convivial oc-
casion that gave it birth to a very late hour.

There's naething here but Highland pride,
  And Highland scab and hunger;
If Providence has sent me here,
  'Twas surely in an anger.

A VERSE,

Presented, by the Author, on taking leave, to the master of a house in the
Highlands, by whom he had been hospitably entertained.

When Death's dark stream I ferry o'er,
  A time that surely shall come;
In heaven itself, I'll ask no more,
  Than just a Highland welcome.

THE TOAST.

[Written with a diamond pencil on a glass tumbler, and presented to Miss
Jessy Lewars, now Mrs. Thomson, Dumfries; a deservedly great favorite
of the Poet's, and a kind and soothing friend to Mrs. Burns at the time of
his death.]

Fill me with the rosy wine,
Call a toast, a toast divine;
Give the Poet's darling flame,
Lovely Jessy be the name;
Then thou mayest freely boast,
Thou hast given a peerless toast.

EPITAPH ON MISS JESSY LEWARS.

[The same lady complaining of some slight indisposition, Burns told her
he should take care to have an epitaph ready for her in case of the worst,
which he likewise wrote on a glass tumbler, to make a pair with the other
as follows:]

Say, sages, what's the charm on earth,
  Can turn Death's dart aside?
It is not purity and worth,
  Else Jessy had not died.

ON HER RECOVERY.

But rarely seen since Nature's birth,
    The natives of the sky;
Yet still one Seraph 's left on earth,
    For Jessy did not die.

TO THE SAME.

[About the end of May, 1796, the surgeon who attended Burns in his last
illness, happened to call on him at the same time with Miss Jessy Lewars.
In the course of conversation Mr. Brown mentioned that he had been to
see a collection of wild beasts just arrived in Dumfries. By way of aid-
ing his description, he took the advertisement (containing a list of the
animals to be exhibited) from his pocket. As he was about to hand it
to Miss Lewars, the Poet took it out of his hand, and with some red ink
standing beside him, wrote on the back of the advertisement the following
lines.]

Talk not to me of savages
    From Afric's burning sun,
No savage e'er could rend my heart,
    As, Jessy, thou hast done.

But Jessy's lovely hand in mine,
    A mutual faith to plight,
Not even to view the heavenly choir
    Would be so blest a sight.

LINES

WRITTEN ON THE BACK OF A BANK NOTE.

Wae worth thy power, thou cursèd leaf,
Fell source o' a' my woe and grief;
For lack o' thee I 've lost my lass,
For lack o' thee I scrimp my glass.
I see the children of affliction
Unaided, through thy cursed restriction.
I 've seen the oppressor's cruel smile
Amid his hapless victim's spoil:

And for thy potence vainly wish'd,
To crush the villain in the dust.
For lack o' thee I leave this much-loved shore,
Never, perhaps, to greet old Scotland more.

KYLE.   R. B

LINES ON MISS J. SCOTT, OF AYR.

OH! had each Scot of ancient times,
    Been, Jeany Scott, as thou art,
The bravest heart on English ground
    Had yielded like a coward.

LINES

On being asked, why God had made Miss Davies so little, and
Mrs. * * * so large.

WRITTEN ON A PANE OF GLASS IN THE INN AT MOFFAT.

ASK why God made the gem so small,
    And why so huge the granite?
Because God meant mankind should set
    The higher value on it.

LINES

Written under the picture of the celebrated Miss Burns.

CEASE, ye prudes, your envious railing,
    Lovely Burns has charms—*confess;*
True it is, she had one failing—
    Had a woman ever less.

LINES

Written and presented to Mrs. Kemble, on seeing her in the character
of Yarico.

KEMBLE, thou cur'st my unbelief
    Of Moses and his rod;
At Yarico's sweet notes of grief
    The rock with tears had flow'd.

Dumfries Theatre, 1794.

LINES

Written on a window at the King's Arms Tavern, Dumfries.

YE men of wit and wealth, why all this sneering
'Gainst poor Excisemen? give the cause a hearing:
What are your landlords' rent-rolls? taxing ledgers;
What premiers, what? even Monarchs' mighty guagers:
Nay, what are priests? those seeming godly wisemen;
What are they, pray? but spiritual Excisemen.

VERSES

Written on a window of the inn at Carron.

WE cam na here to view your warks
    In hopes to be mair wise,
But only, lest we gang[1] to hell,
    It may be nae surprise:

But when we tirl'd[2] at your door,
    Your porter dought na[3] hear us;
Sae may, should we to hell's yetts[4] come,
    Your billy[5] Satan sair[6] us!

TO DR. MAXWELL.

On Miss Jessy Staig's recovery.

MAXWELL, if merit here you crave,
    That merit I deny—
You save fair Jessy from the grave!
    An angel could not die.

. Go.—[2] Knocked.—[3] Was unable to.—[4] Gates.—[5] Brother.— Serve

EPIGRAM ON A HENPECKED COUNTRY SQUIRE.

O DEATH! hadst thou but spared his life,
  Whom we this day lament;
We freely wad exchanged the wife,
  And a' been weel content.

E'en as he is, cauld in his graff,[1]
  The swap[2] we yet will do 't;
Tak you the carlin's[3] carcase aff,
  Thou 'se get the saul to boot.

ANOTHER.

ONE Queen Artemisia, as old stories tell,
When deprived of her husband she loved so well,
In respect for the love and affection he 'd shown her,
She reduced him to dust, and she drank up the powder.
But Queen N*******, of a different complexion,
When call'd on to order the funeral direction,
Would have eat her dead lord on a slender pretence,
Not to show her respect, but—to save the expense.

A TOAST

[At a meeting of the Dumfries-shire Volunteers, held to commemorate the anniversary of Rodney's victory, April 12, 1782, Burns was called upon for a song, instead of which he delivered the following lines *extempore*.]

INSTEAD of a song, boys, I 'll give you a toast—
Here 's the memory of those on the twelfth that we lost;
That we lost, did I say? nay, by Heaven, that we found,
For their fame it shall last while the world goes round.
The next in succession, I 'll give you the King,
Whoe'er would betray him, on high may he swing;
And here 's the grand fabric, our free Constitution,
As built on the base of the great Revolution;
And longer with politics, not to be cramm'd,
Be anarchy cursed, and be tyranny d—d!
And who would to Liberty e'er prove disloyal,
May his son be a hangman, and he his first trial.

[1] Grave.—[2] Exchange.—[3] Stout old woman.

IMPROMPTU

On Mrs. R——'s birthday, 4th Nov. 1793.

OLD Winter with his frosty beard,
Thus once to Jove his prayer preferr'd:
"What have I done, of all the year,
To bear this hated doom severe?
My cheerless sons no pleasure know;
Night's horrid car drags dreary, slow:
My dismal months no joys are crowning,
But spleeny English hanging, drowning.
  "Now, Jove, for once, be mighty civil,
To counterbalance all this evil;
Give me, and I 've no more to say,
Give me Maria's natal day!
That brilliant gift will so enrich me,
Spring, summer, autumn, cannot match me."
"'T is done!" says Jove;—so ends my story,
And Winter once rejoiced in glory.

THE LOYAL NATIVES' VERSES.[1]

YE sons of sedition, give ear to my song,
Let Syme, Burns, and Maxwell, pervade every throng,
With Cracken, the attorney, and Mundell, the quack,
Send Willie the monger to hell with a smack.

BURNS—EXTEMPORE.

YE true "Loyal Natives," attend to my song,
In uproar and riot rejoice the night long;
From envy and hatred your corps is exempt;
But where is your shield from the darts of contempt?

[1] At this period of our Poet's life, when political animosity was made the
ground of private quarrel, the above foolish verses were sent as an attack on
Burns and his friends for their political opinions. They were written by
some member of a club styling themselves the "Loyal Natives" of Dumfries,
or rather by the united genius of that club, which was more distinguished for
drunken loyalty, than either for respectability or poetical talent. The verses
were handed over the table to Burns at a convivial meeting, and he instantly
endorsed the subjoined reply.—*Reliques*, p. 108.

EXTEMPORANEOUS EFFUSION

On being appointed to the Excise.

SEARCHING auld wives' barrels,
    Och, ho! the day!
That clarty barm[1] should stain my laurels,
    But—what 'll ye say?
These muvin'[2] things ca'd wives and weans
Wad muve the very hearts o' stanes!

ON SEEING THE BEAUTIFUL SEAT OF LORD G.

WHAT dost thou in that mansion fair?
    Flit, G——, and find
Some narrow, dirty, dungeon cave,
    The picture of thy mind!

ON THE SAME.

No Stewart art thou, G——,
    The Stewarts all were brave;
Besides, the Stewarts were but fools—
    Not one of them a knave.

ON THE SAME.

BRIGHT ran thy line, O G——,
    Thro' many a far-famed sire!
So ran the far-famed Roman way—
    So ended in a mire.

[1] Dirty yeast.—[2] Moving.

TO THE SAME,

On the Author being threatened with his resentment.

SPARE me thy vengeance, G——,
  In quiet let me live:
I ask no kindness at thy hand,
  For thou hast none to give.

EXTEMPORE IN THE COURT OF SESSION.

TUNE.—*Gillicrankie.*

LORD A——TE.

HE clench'd his pamphlets in his fist,
  He quoted and he hinted,
Till in a declamation mist,
  His argument he tint' it:
He gap'd for 't, he grap'd for 't,
  He fand it was awa, man;
But what his common sense came short,
  He eked it out wi' law, man.

MR. ER——NE.

COLLECTED Harry stood awee,
  Then open'd out his arm, man;
His lordship sat wi' ruefu' e'e,
  And eyed the gathering storm, man:
Like wind-driven hail it did assail,
  Like torrents owre a linn,[2] man;
The Bench sae wise, lift up their eyes,
  Half-wauken'd wi' the din, man.

ON HEARING THAT THERE WAS FALSEHOOD IN THE REV. DR. B——'S
VERY LOOKS.

THAT there is falsehood in his looks
  I must and will deny:
They say their master is a knave—
  And sure they do not lie.

[1] Lost.—[2] Waterfall.
29

EXTEMPORE,

On the late Mr. William Smellie, Author of the Philosophy of Natural History,
and Member of the Antiquarian and Royal Societies of Edinburgh.

To Crochallan came
The old cock'd hat, the gray surtout, the same;
His bristling beard just rising in its might,
'Twas four long nights and days till shaving night;
His uncomb'd grizzly locks wild staring, thatch'd
A head for thought profound and clear, unmatch'd;
Yet tho' his caustic wit was biting, rude,
His heart was warm, benevolent, and good.

EXTEMPORE, TO MR. SYME,[1]

On refusing to dine with him, after having been promised the first of company,
and the first of cookery; 17th Dec., 1795.

No more of your guests, be they titled or not,
   And cookery the first of the nation;
Who is proof to thy personal converse and wit,
   Is proof to all other temptation.

TO MR. S**E,

With a present of a dozen of porter.

Oh, had the malt thy strength of mind,
   Or hops the flavor of thy wit,
'Twere drink for first of human kind,
   A gift that e'en for S**e were fit.

JERUSALEM TAVERN, Dumfries.

LINES ADDRESSED TO MR. J. RANKINE,

While he occupied the farm of Adamhill, in Ayrshire.

AE day, as Death, that grusome carl,[2]
Was driving to the tither warl',[3]

---

[1] An intimate friend of the Poet's, with whom he made a very pleasant tour
over the counties of Kirkcudbright and Galloway, in July and August, 1793.
[2] Grim old man,—[3] Other world.

A mixtie-maxtie[1] motley squad,
And monie a guilt-bespotted lad;
Black gowns of each denomination,
And thieves of every rank and station,
From him that wears the star and garter,
To him that wintles[2] in a halter;
Ashamed himself to see the wretches,
He mutters, glowering at the bitches:
  "By God, I'll not be seen behint them,
Nor 'mang the spiritual corps present them,
Without at least ae honest man,
To grace this damn'd infernal clan."
  By Adamhill a glance he threw,
"Lord God!" quoth he, "I have it now;
There's just the man I want, i' faith;"
And quickly stoppéd Rankine's breath.

LINES WRITTEN BY BURNS,

While on his death-bed, to John Rankine, and forwarded to him immediately after the Poet's death.

HE who of Rankine sang, lies stiff and dead,
And a green grassy hillock hides his head;
Alas! alas! a devilish change indeed!

[1] Confusedly mixed.—[2] Swings.

EPITAPHS.

EPITAPH FOR THE AUTHOR'S FATHER.

O YE, whose cheek the tear of pity stains,
    Draw near with pious reverence and attend!
Here lie the loving husband's dear remains,
    The tender father, and the generous friend.

The pitying heart that felt for human woe;
    The dauntless heart that fear'd no human pride;
The friend of man, to vice alone a foe;
    "For even his failings lean'd to virtue's side."[1]

INSCRIPTION TO THE MEMORY OF FERGUSSON.

HERE LIES ROBERT FERGUSSON, POET.

Born September 5th, 1750.—Died 16th October, 1774.

No sculptured marble here, nor pompous lay,
    "No storied urn nor animated bust,"
This simple stone directs pale Scotia's way
    To pour her sorrows o'er her Poet's dust.

FOR ROBERT AIKEN, ESQ.

KNOW thou, O stranger to the fame
Of this much loved, much honor'd name!
(For none that knew him need be told)
A warmer heart Death ne'er made cold.

---

[1] Goldsmith.

A BARD'S EPITAPH.

Is there a whim-inspiréd fool,
Owre[1] fast for thought, owre hot for rule,
Owre blate[2] to seek, owre proud to snool,[3]
    Let him draw near;
And owre[4] this grassy heap sing dool,[5]
    And drap a tear.

Is there a Bard of rustic song,
Who, noteless, steals the crowds among
That weekly this area throng,
    Oh pass not by!
But with a frater-feeling strong,
    Here heave a sigh.

Is there a man, whose judgment clear
Can others teach the course to steer,
Yet runs himself life's mad career,
    Wild as the wave;
Here pause—and, thro' the starting tear,
    Survey this grave.

The poor inhabitant below,
Was quick to learn and wise to know,
And keenly felt the friendly glow,
    And softer flame,
But thoughtless follies laid him low,
    And stain'd his name.

Reader, attend—whether thy soul
Soars fancy's flights beyond the pole,
Or darkling grubs this earthy hole,
    In low pursuit;
Know, prudent, cautious, self-control,
    Is wisdom's root.

ON A FRIEND.

An honest man here lies at rest,
As e'er God with his image blest;

---

[1] Too.—[2] Bashful.—[3] To submit tamely, to sneak.—[4] Over.—[5] To lament, to mourn

The friend of man, the friend of truth;
The friend of age, and guide of youth;
Few hearts like his, with virtue warm'd,
Few heads with knowledge so inform'd:
If there's another world, he lives in bliss;
If there is none, he made the best of this.

FOR GAVIN HAMILTON, ESQ.

THE poor man weeps—here Gavin sleeps,
  Whom canting wretches blamed:
But with such as he, where'er he be,
  May I be saved or d——d!

ON W. NICHOL.

YE maggots, feed on Nichol's brain,
  For few sic feasts you've gotten;
And fix your claws in Nichol's heart,
  For deil a bit o't's rotten.

ON A WAG IN MAUCHLINE.

LAMENT him, Mauchline husbands a',
  He aften did assist ye:
For had ye staid whole weeks awa',
  Your wives they ne'er had miss'd ye.

Ye Mauchline bairns, as on ye pass
  To school in bands thegither,
O tread you lightly on his grass,
  Perhaps he was your father!

ON A HENPECKED COUNTRY SQUIRE.

As father Adam first was fool'd,
    (A case that's still too common,)
Here lies a man a woman ruled,
    The Devil ruled the woman.

———

ON A NOISY POLEMIC.

Below thir stanes lie Jamie's banes;
    O Death! it's my opinion,
Thou ne'er took such a bleth'rin' bitch,
    Into thy dark dominion!

———

ON A CELEBRATED RULING ELDER.

Here souter Will in death does sleep;
    To hell, if he's gane thither,
Satan, gie him thy gear to keep,
    He'll haud it weel thegither.

———

ON JOHN DOVE, INN-KEEPER, MAUCHLINE.

Here lies Johnie Pidgeon—
What was his religion,
Whae'er desires to ken,
To some other warl'
Maun follow the carl,
For here Johnie Pidgeon had nane.
    Strong ale was ablution,
Small beer persecution,
A dram was *memento mori;*
But a full-flowing bowl
Was the saving his soul,
And port was celestial glory.

ON WEE JOHNIE.

Hic jacet wee Johnie.

WHOE'ER thou art, O reader, know,
　That death has murder'd Johnie!
And here his *body* lies fu' low—
　For *saul* he ne'er had onie!

ON J——Y B——Y, WRITER IN DUMFRIES.

HERE lies J——y B——y, *honest man !*
Cheat him, Devil, if *you can.*

ON A PERSON NICKNAMED THE MARQUIS,

Who desired Burns to write one on him.

HERE lies a mock Marquis, whose titles were shamm'd,
If ever he rises it will be to be *d—d.*

ON A SCHOOLMASTER IN CLEISH PARISH, FIFESHIRE.

HERE lie Willie M—hie's banes:
　O Satan, when ye tak him,
Gie him the schulin'[1] of your weans ;[2]
　For clever Deils he 'll mak 'em!

FOR MR. GABRIEL RICHARDSON,

Brewer, Dumfries; (but who, much to the satisfaction of his friends, has not yet needed one, 1819.

HERE Brewer Gabriel's fire 's extinct,
　And empty all his barrels:
He 's blest—if, as he brew'd, he drink
　In upright honest morals.

Educating.—[2] Children.

ON WALTER S——

Sic a reptile was Wat,
  Sic a miscreant slave,
That the worms e'en d——d him
  When laid in his grave.

In his flesh there's a famine,
  A starved reptile cries;
And his heart is rank poison,
  Another replies.

ON A LAP-DOG NAMED ECHO.

In wood and wild, ye warbling throng,
  Your heavy loss deplore;
Now half-extinct your powers of song,
  Sweet Echo is no more.

Ye jarring, screeching things around,
  Scream your discordant joys;
Now half your din of tuneless sound
  With Echo silent lies.

SONGS AND BALLADS.

BANNOCKBURN.

ROBERT BRUCE'S ADDRESS TO HIS ARMY.

'I am delighted," says Burns to Mr. Thomson, "with many little melodies which
the learned musician despises as silly and insipid. I do not know whether the old
air "Hev tuttie tattie," may rank among this number; but well I know that,
with Frazer's hautboy, it has filled my eyes with tears. There is a tradition,
which I have met with in many places of Scotland, that it was Robert Bruce's
march at the battle of Bannockburn. This thought, in my solitary wanderings,
warmed me to a pitch of enthusiasm on the theme of liberty and independence,
which I threw into a kind of Scottish ode, fitted to the air, that one might sup-
pose to be the gallant royal Scot's address to his heroic followers on that eventful
morning."

TUNE—*Hey tuttie tattie*

Scots, wha hae wi' Wallace bled;
Scots, wham Bruce has aften led;
Welcome to your gory bed,
  Or to victorie.

Now's the day, and now's the hour;
See the front o' battle lower;
See approach proud Edward's power—
  Chains and slaverie!

Wha will be a traitor knave?
Wha can fill a coward's grave?
Wha sae base as be a slave?
  Let him turn and flee!

Wha for Scotland's king and law
Freedom's sword will strongly draw,
Free-man stand, or free-man fa'?
  Let him follow me!

By oppression's woes and pains!
By your sons in servile chains!
We will drain our dearest veins,
  But they shall be free!

Lay the proud usurpers low!
Tyrants fall in every foe!
Liberty 's in every blow!
    Let us do, or die![1]

THE SAME.

As altered, at the suggestion of Mr. Thomson, to suit the air of
"Lewie Gordon."

Scots, wha hae wi' Wallace bled;
Scots, wham Bruce has aften led!
Welcome to your gory bed,
    Or to glorious victorie.

Now 's the day, and now 's the hour;
See the front o' battle lower;
See approach proud Edward's power—
    Edward! chains and slaverie!

Wha will be a traitor knave?
Wha can fill a coward's grave?
Wha sae base as be a slave?
    Traitor! coward! turn and flee!

Wha for Scotland's king and law
Freedom's sword will strongly draw,
Free-man stand, or free-man fa'?
    Caledonian! on wi' me!

By oppression's woes and pains!
By your sons in servile chains!
We will drain our dearest veins,
    But they shall be—shall be free!

Lay the proud usurpers low!
Tyrants fall in every foe!
Liberty 's in every blow!
    Forward! let us do, or die!

· This verse is chiefly borrowed from Blind Harry's Wallace:
    "A false usurper sinks in every foe,
    And Liberty returns with every blow."

AULD LANG SYNE.

Burns gave this song to the public as a production of the "olden time;" but it was afterwards discovered to be his own.

"Auld Lang Syne" owes all its attractions, if it owes not its origin, to the muse of Burns. So exquisitely has the poet eked out the old with the new, that it would puzzle a very profound antiquary to separate the ancient from the modern.

SHOULD auld acquaintance be forgot,
  And never brought to min'!
Should auld acquaintance be forgot,
  And days o' lang syne?

    For auld lang syne, my dear,
    For auld lang syne,
    We'll tak a cup o' kindness yet,
    For auld lang syne.

We twa hae run about the braes,
  And pu'd the gowans[1] fine;
But we've wander'd mony a weary foot,
  Sin' auld lang syne.
    For auld lang syne, &c.

We twa hae paidl't[2] i' the burn,[3]
  Frae mornin' sun till dine;
But seas between us braid hae roar'd,
  Sin' auld lang syne.
    For auld lang syne, &c.

And here's a hand, my trusty fier,[4]
  And gie's a haud o' thine;
And we'll tak a right guid-willie waught,[5]
  For auld lang syne.
    For auld lang syne, &c.

And surely ye'll be your pint-stowp,
  As sure as I'll be mine;
And we'll tak a cup o' kindness yet,
  For auld lang syne.
    For auld lang syne, &c.

[1] Wild daisies.—[2] To wade or walk in the water.—[3] Rivulet.—[4] Friend.—
[5] Liberal draught.

DAINTY DAVIE.

'Dainty Davie" is the title of an old song from which Burns has taken
nothing but the name and the measure.

Now rosy May comes in wi' flowers,
To deck her gay, green-spreading bowers;
And now comes in my happy hours,
    To wander wi' my Davie.

Meet me on the warlock knowe,
    Dainty Davy, dainty Davie,
There I'll spend the day wi' you,
    My ain dear dainty Davie.

The crystal waters round us fa',
The merry birds are lovers a',
The scented breezes round us blaw,
    A wandering wi' my Davie.
        Meet me, &c.

When purple morning starts the hare
To steal upon her early fare,
Then thro' the dews I will repair,
    To meet my faithfu' Davie.
        Meet me, &c.

When day, expiring in the west,
The curtain draws o' nature's rest,
I'll flee to his arms I lo'e best,
    And that's my ain dear Davie.

Meet me on the warlock knowe,
    Bonnie Davy, daintie Davie,
There I'll spend the day wi' you,
    My ain dear dainty Davie.

BEHOLD THE HOUR, THE BOAT ARRIVE.

"September, 1793. I have this moment finished the song for Oran Gaoil, so you
have it glowing from the mint. If it suit you, well!—if not, 'tis also well."—*Burns
to Thomson.*

TUNE—*Oran Gaoil.*

BEHOLD the hour, the boat arrive;
    Thou goest, thou darling of my heart!
Sever'd from thee, can I survive?
    But fate has will'd, and we must part
30

I'll often greet this surging swe.l,
    Yon distant isle will often hail;
"E'en here I took the last farewell;
    There latest mark'd her vanish'd sail."

Along the solitary shore,
    While flitting sea-fowl round me cry,
Across the rolling, dashing roar
    I'll westward turn my wistful eye:
Happy, thou Indian grove, I'll say,
    Where now my Nancy's path may be;
While through thy sweets she loves to stray,
    O tell me, does she muse on me?

THOU HAST LEFT ME EVER, JAMIE.

I inclose you the music of 'Fee him, Father,' with two verses, which I composed at the time in which Patie Allan's mither died, that was about the back o' midnight, and by the lee-side of a bowl of punch, which had overset every mortal in company except the hautboys and the music."—Burns to Thomson.

TUNE—*Fee him, Father.*

THOU hast left me ever, Jamie,
    Thou hast left me ever,
Thou hast left me ever, Jamie,
    Thou hast left me ever.
Aften hast thou vow'd that death
    Only should us sever,
Now thou'st left thy lass for ay—
    I maun see thee never, Jamie,
        I'll see thee never.

Thou hast me forsaken, Jamie,
    Thou hast me forsaken,
Thou hast me forsaken, Jamie,
    Thou hast me forsaken.
Thou canst love anither jo,
    While my heart is breaking,
Soon my weary een I'll close—
    Never mair to waken, Jamie,
        Never mair to waken.

FAIR JENNY.[1]

Tune—Saw ye my Father?

WHERE are the joys I have met in the morning,
  That danced to the lark's early song?
Where is the peace that awaited my wandering,
  At evening the wild woods among?

No more a-winding the course of yon river,
  And marking sweet flowerets so fair;
No more I trace the light footsteps of pleasure,
  But sorrow and sad sighing care.

Is it that summer 's forsaken our valleys,
  And grim, surly winter is near?
No, no, the bees humming round the gay roses,
  Proclaim it the pride o' the year.

Fain would I hide what I fear to discover,
  Yet long, long too well have I known,
All that has caused this wreck in my bosom,
  Is Jenny, fair Jenny alone.

Time cannot aid me, my griefs are immortal,
  Nor hope dare a comfort bestow;
Come then, enamor'd and fond of my anguish,
  Enjoyment I 'll seek in my woe.

DELUDED SWAIN, ETC.

In a letter to Mr. Thomson, inclosing this song, Burns quaintly calls it "an old Bacchanal." It is, however, well known to be one of his own.

Tune—The Collier's Dochter.

DELUDED swain, the pleasure
  The fickle Fair can give thee,
Is but a fairy treasure;
  Thy hopes will soon deceive thee.

[1] Written for Mr. Thomson's Collection, to whom the Poet thus speaks concerning it: "I have finished my song to 'Saw ye my Father?' and in English, as you will see. There is a syllable too much for the expression of the air, but the mere dividing of a dotted crotchet into a crotchet and a quaver is no great matter. Of the poetry, I speak with confidence; but the music is a business where I hint my ideas with the utmost diffidence."

The billows on the ocean,
  The breezes idly roaming,
The clouds' uncertain motion,
  They are but types of woman.

Oh, art thou not ashaméd,
  To doat upon a feature?
If man thou wouldst be naméd
  Despise the silly creature.

Go, find an honest fellow;
  Good claret set before thee;
Hold on till thou art mellow,
  And then to bed in glory.

TO ANNA.

Written on the "Anna" of the song beginning—"Yestreen I had
a pint o' wine."

ANNA, thy charms my bosom fire,
  And waste my soul with care;
But, ah! how bootless to admire,
  When fated to despair!

Yet in thy presence, lovely Fair,
  To hope may be forgiven;
For sure 'twere impious to despair,
  So much in sight of Heaven.

ANNA.

Burns considered this to be the best love song he ever composed. The
Postscript, which former editors have suppressed, is here restored.

TUNE—*Banks of Banna.*

YESTREEN I had a pint o' wine,
  A place where body saw na;
Yestreen lay on this breast o' mine
  The raven locks of Anna:
The hungry Jew, in wilderness,
  Rejoicing o'er his manna,
Was naething to my honey bliss
  Upon the lips of Anna.

Ye monarchs, take the east and west,
    Frae Indus to Savannah;
Gie me within my straining grasp
    The melting form of Anna.
Then I'll despise imperial charms,
    An empress or sultana;
While dying raptures in her arms,
    I give and take wi' Anna.

Awa, thou flaunting god o' day!
    Awa, thou pale Diana!
Ilk star gae hide thy twinkling ray,
    When I'm to meet my Anna!
Come in thy raven plumage, night;
    Sun, moon, and stars, withdraw a';
And bring an angel pen to write
    My transports wi' my Anna.

POSTSCRIPT.

The kirk and state may join, and tell
    To do such things I mauna:
The kirk and state may gae to h–ll,
    And I'll gae to my Anna.
She is the sunshine o' my e'e,
    To live but her[1] I canna;
Had I on earth but wishes three,
    The first should be my Anna.

THE RIGS O' BARLEY.

One of our Poet's earliest productions.—*J. G. Lockhart's Life of Burns.*

TUNE—Corn rigs are bonnie.

It was upon a Lammas night,
    When corn rigs are bonnie,
Beneath the moon's unclouded light,
    I held awa' to Annie:
The time flew by wi' tentless heed,
    Till 'tween the late and early,
Wi' sma' persuasion she agreed,
    To see me thro' the barley.

[1] Without her.

The sky was blue, the wind was still,
　　The moon was shining clearly;
I set her down wi' right good will
　　Amang the rigs o' barley.
I kent her heart was a' my ain;
　　I loved her most sincerely;
I kiss'd her owre and owre again
　　Amang the rigs o' barley.

I lock'd her in my fond embrace;
　　Her heart was beating rarely!
My blessings on that happy place
　　Amang the rigs o' barley.
But by the moon and stars sae bright,
　　That shone that hour sae clearly!
She ay shall bless that happy night,
　　Amang the rigs o' barley.

I hae been blithe wi' comrades dear;
　　I hae been merry drinking;
I hae been joyfu' gathering gear;
　　I hae been happy thinking;
But a' the pleasures e'er I saw,
　　Though three times doubled fairly,
That happy night was worth them a'
　　Amang the rigs o' barley.

　　　Corn rigs an' barley rigs,
　　　　And corn rigs are bonnie;
　　　I'll ne'er forget that happy night
　　　　Amang the rigs wi' Annie.

THE BLUE-EYED LASSIE.

The lady, in honor of whose blue eyes this fine song was written, was Miss Jeffrey
of Lochmaben, now (1825) residing at New York, in America—a wife and a mother
—*Allan Cunningham.*

Tune—*The b'a'h. i. o 't.*

I GAED[1] a waefu' gate[2] yestreen,
　　A gate, I fear, I'll dearly rue;
I gat my death frae twa sweet een,
　　Twa lovely een o' bonnie blue.

[1] Went.—[2] Way, manner, road

'Twas not her golden ringlets bright;
  Her lips like roses wat wi' dew—
Her heaving bosom, lily-white—
  It was her een sae bonnie blue.

She talk'd, she smiled, my heart she wyled,
  She charm'd my soul, I wist na how;
And aye the stound,[2] the deadly wound,
  Cam frae her een sae bonnie blue.
But spare to speak, and spare to speed;
  She 'll aiblins listen to my vow:
Should she refuse, I 'll lay my dead
  To her twa een sae bonnie blue.

BLYTHE WAS SHE.

This song was written during a visit of the Poet at Ochtertyre with Sir William Murray. The lady, whom it celebrates, and who was there at the time, was Miss Euphemia Murray, of Lentrose. She was called, by way of eminence, the Flower of Strathmore. The chorus is from an old song of the same measure.

TUNE—Andro and his cutty gun.

Blythe, blythe, and merry was she,
  Blythe was she but and ben ;[3]
Blythe by the banks of Ern,
  And blythe in Glenturit glen.

By Ochtertyre grows the aik,[4]
  On Yarrow banks the birken shaw ;[5]
But Phemie was a bonnier lass
  Than braes o' Yarrow ever saw.
        Blythe, &c.

Her looks were like a flower in May,
  Her smile was like a simmer morn;
She trippéd by the banks of Ern,
  As light 's a bird upon a thorn.
        Blythe, &c.

Her bonnie face it was as meek
  As onie lamb upon a lee;

---

[1] Beguiled.—[2] A shooting pain.—[3] The country kitchen and parlor.—[4] Oak.—[5] A small wood.

The evening sun was ne'er sae sweet
    As was the blink o' Phemie's e'e.
                Blythe, &c.

The Highland hills I 've wander'd wide,
    And o'er the Lowlands I hae been;
But Phemie was the blythest lass
    That ever trod the dewy green.
                Blythe, &c.

DECEMBER NIGHT.

This song was first printed in Johnson's "Musical Museum." "The contrast of the first and last verses," says an eminent critic and poet, "is very great, yet very natural. The Poet imagines himself warmed with wine, and seated among his companions, to whom he announces, as the glass goes round, the attractions of his mistress, and his good fortune in her affections. His confidence goes no farther;—the name of his love is not to be told; and for this poetical tyranny there is no remedy."

O MAY, thy morn was ne'er sae sweet,
    As the mirk night o' December;
For sparkling was the rosy wine,
    And private was the chamber:
And dear was she I dare na name,
    But I will ay remember.
                And dear was she, &c.

And here 's to them, that like oursel,
    Can push about the jorum;
And here 's to them that wish us weel,
    May a' that 's good watch o'er them;
And here 's to them we dare na tell,
    The dearest o' the quorum.
                And here 's to them, &c.

PEGGY'S CHARMS.

"This song I composed on one of the most accomplished of women, Miss Peggy Chalmers that was, now Mrs. Lewis Hay, of Forbes & Co.'s Bank, Edinburgh."— *Burns's Reliques.*

TUNE—*Neil Gow's Lament for Abercairny.*

WHERE braving angry winter's storms,
    The lofty Ochils rise,
Far in the shade my Peggy's charms
    First blest my wondering eyes:

As one who by some savage stream
A lonely gem surveys,
Astonish'd, doubly marks its beam,
With art's most polish'd blaze.

Blest be the wild, sequester'd shade,
And blest the day and hour,
Where Peggy's charms I first survey'd.--
When first I felt their power!
The tyrant Death, with grim control,
May seize my fleeting breath;
But tearing Peggy from my soul
Must be a stronger death.

TAM GLEN.

Burns submitted this song to several of his friends as a lyric of the olden time,
and heard it praised before he acknowledged it his own. The old "Tam Glen"
however, has assisted both in the conception and expression of the *new*.

TUNE—*The mucking o' Geordie's byre.*

My heart is a breaking, dear Tittie,[1]
Some counsel unto me come len';[2]
To anger them a' is a pity,
But what will I do wi' Tam Glen?

I'm thinking, wi' sic a braw fellow,
In poortith[3] I might mak a fen':[4]
What care I in riches to wallow,
If I mauna[5] marry Tam Glen?

There's Lowrie, the laird o' Drumeller,
"Gude day to you, brute," he comes ben:[6]
He brags and he blaws o' his siller,
But when will he dance like Tam Glen?

My minnie[7] does constantly deave[8] me,
And bids me beware o' young men:
They flatter, she says, to deceive me,
But wha can think sae o' Tam Glen?

[1] A female confidante —[2] Lend.—[3] Poverty.—[4] Fend; to live comfortably
—[5] Must not.—[6] Into the parlor.—[7] Mother.—[8] To deafen.

My daddie says, gin[1] I 'll forsake him,
   He 'll gie me gude hunder[2] marks ten;
But, if it 's ordain'd I maun[3] take him,
   Oh wha will I get but Tam Glen?

Yestreen,[4] at the valentines' dealing,
   My heart to my mou gied a sten;[5]
For thrice I drew ane without failing,
   And thrice it was written, " Tam Glen!"

The last Halloween I was waukin'[6]
   My droukit[7] sark[8]-sleeve, as ye ken,
His likeness cam up the house staukin',
   And the very gray breeks o' Tam Glen!

Some counsel, dear Tittie, don't tarry;
   I 'll gie you my bonnie black hen,
Gif[9] ye will advise me to marry
   The lad I lo'e dearly, Tam Glen.

YOUNG JOCKEY.

First published in the Reliques, from a copy communicated to the editor,
by R. Riddel, Esq., of Glenriddel.

YOUNG Jockey was the blythest lad
   In a' our town or here awa;
Fu' blythe he whistled at the gaud,[10]
   Fu' lightly danced he in the ha'!
He roos'd[11] my een sae bonnie blue,
   He roos'd my waist sae genty[12] sma';
And ay my heart came to my mou,[13]
   When ne'er a body heard or saw.

My Jockey toils upon the plain,
   Thro' wind and sleet, thro' frost and snaw;
And o'er the lee[14] I look fu' fain
   When Jockey's owsen[15] hameward ca'.[16]

[1] If.—[2] An hundred.—[3] Must.—[4] Yesternight. [5] To rise or rear like a
horse.—[6] Stiffening, or thickening. [7] Wet. [8] Shirt. [9] If. [10] Plough.—
[11] Praised. [12] Elegantly formed.—[13] Mouth. [14] Grass fields.—[15] Oxen.—
[16] Drive.

And ay the night comes round again,
    When in his arms he taks me a';
And ay he vows he'll bo my ain
    As lang's he has a breath to draw.

BLYTHE HAE I BEEN ON YON HILL.

'Liggeram cosh" is a delightful air. I have become such an enthusiast about it, that I have made a song for it, which I think is not in my worst manner.—*Letter to Mr. Thomson.*

TUNE—*Liggeram cosh.*

BLYTHE hae I been on yon hill,
    As the lambs before me;
Careless ilka thought and free,
    As the breeze flew o'er me:
Now nae langer sport and play,
    Mirth or sang can please me;
Leslie is sae fair and coy,
    Care and anguish seize me.

Heavy, heavy is the task,
    Hopeless love declaring:
Trembling, I do nocht but glower,
    Sighing, dumb, despairing!
If she winna ease the thraws
    In my bosom swelling,
Underneath the grass-green sod
    Soon maun be my dwelling.

JOHN ANDERSON, MY JO.

In the first volume of a collection, entitled "Poetry, Original and Selected," published by Brash and Reid, of Glasgow, in 1801, this song is inserted, with four additional stanzas, said to be by Robert Burns. Of these *additional stanzas,* Dr. Currie says, "Every reader of discernment will see they are by an inferior hand."

JOHN ANDERSON, my jo,[1] John,
    When we were first acquent,
Your locks were like the raven,
    Your bonnie brow was brent;[2]

[1] Sweetheart.—[2] Smooth.

But now your brow is bald, John,
  Your locks are like the snow;
But blessings on your frosty pow,
  John Anderson, my jo.

John Anderson, my jo, John,
  We clamb the hill thegither,
And monie a cantie[2] day, John,
  We've had wi' ane anither.
Now we maun totter down, John,
  But hand in hand we'll go;
And sleep thegither at the foot,
  John Anderson, my jo.

OLD AGE.

"This song," says Allan Cunningham, "has never been a favorite. Youth wishes to enjoy the golden time upon its hand, and age is far from fond of chanting of declining strength, white pows, and general listlessness."

TUNE—*The death of the Linnet.*

BUT lately seen in gladsome green
  The woods rejoiced the day,
Thro' gentle showers the laughing flowers
  In double pride were gay:
But now our joys are fled,
  On winter blasts awa;
Yet maiden May, in rich array,
  Again shall bring them a'.

But my white pow,[3] nae kindly thowe[4]
  Shall melt the snaws of age;
My trunk of eild,[5] but buss or bield,[6]
  Sinks in time's wintry rage.
Oh, age has weary days,
  And nights o' sleepless pain:
Thou golden time o' youthfu' prime,
  Why com'st thou not again?

---

[1] Gray hairs.—[2] Cheerful. — [3] Head.—[4] Thaw. —[5] Old age. —[6] Without shelter.

MARY MORRISON.

"Mary Morrison," says Burns in a letter to Thomson, "is one of my juvenile works. I do not think it very remarkable, either for its merits or demerits." All his critics and commentators, however, agree in thinking it one of the best songs he ever wrote.

TUNE—Bide ye yet.

O MARY, at thy window be,
    It is the wish'd, the trysted[1] hour;
Those smiles and glances let me see,
    That make the miser's treasure poor:
How blythely wad I bid the stoure,[2]
    A weary slave frae sun to sun,
Could I the rich reward secure,
    The lovely Mary Morrison.

Yestreen, when to the trembling string,
    The dance gaed round the lighted ha',[3]
To thee my fancy took its wing—
    I sat, but neither heard nor saw:
Though this was fair and that was braw,[4]
    And yon the toast of a' the town,
I sigh'd, and said, amang them a',
    "Ye are na Mary Morrison."

O Mary, canst thou wreck his peace,
    Wha for thy sake wad gladly die?
Or canst thou break that heart of his,
    Whase only fault is loving thee?
If love for love thou wilt na gie,[5]
    At least be pity to me shown;
A thought ungentle canna be
    The thought o' Mary Morrison.

SWEETEST MAY.

Altered from Allan Ramsay's song :—
    "There's my thumb, I 'll ne'er beguile thee."
                Tea Table Miscellany, vol. i. p. 70.

SWEETEST May, let love inspire thee;
Take a heart which he desires thee;

[1] Appointed.—[2] Dust in motion.—[3] Hall.—[4] Fine.—[5] Give.

As thy constant slave regard it;
For its faith and truth reward it.

Proof o' shot to birth or money,
Not the wealthy but the bonnie;
Not high-born, but noble-minded,
In love's silken band can bind it.

LOVELY NANCY.

Burns frequently went to the Bible for some of his finest sentiments.
The two lines

"Turn away these eyes of love,
Lest I die with pleasure,"

are almost the same as the following passage in the Song of Solomon, chap.
vi. ver. 5 : "Turn away thine eyes from me, for they have overcome me.".

TUNE—The Quaker's Wife.

THINE am I, my faithful fair,
Thine, my lovely Nancy;
Every pulse along my veins,
Every roving fancy.

To thy bosom lay my heart,
There to throb and languish:
Though despair had wrung its core,
That would heal its anguish.

Take away these rosy lips,
Rich with balmy treasure;
Turn away these eyes of love
Lest I die with pleasure.

What is life when wanting love?
Night without a morning:
Love 's the cloudless summer's sun,
Nature gay adorning.

HUSBAND AND WIFE.

TUNE—*My jo, Janet.*

This song was written for Mr. Thomson's collection. "Tell me," says Burns, in a letter to that gentleman, dated December, 1793, "how you like my song to 'Jo, Janet.'"

SHE.

HUSBAND, husband, cease your strife,
    Nor longer idly rave, sir,—
Though I am your wedded wife,
    Yet I am not your slave, sir.

HE.

One of two must still obey,
    Nancy, Nancy;
Is it man or woman, say,
    My spouse, Nancy?

SHE.

If 'tis still the lordly word,
    Service and obedience;
I 'll desert my sovereign lord,
    And so, good-by allegiance!

HE.

Sad will I be, so bereft,
    Nancy, Nancy;
Yet I 'll try to make a shift,
    My spouse, Nancy.

SHE.

My poor heart then break it must,
    My last hour I 'm near it:
When you lay me in the dust,
    Think, think how you will bear it.

HE.

I will hope and trust in Heaven,
    Nancy, Nancy;
Strength to bear it will be given,
    My spouse, Nancy.

SHE.

Well, sir, from the silent dead,
  Still I 'll try to daunt you;
Ever round your midnight bed,
  Horrid sprites shall haunt you.

HE.

I 'll wed another, like my dear
  Nancy, Nancy;
Then all hell will fly for fear,
  My spouse, Nancy.

POORTITH CAULD.

This excellent song has never become popular, owing, perhaps, to the want of unity between the music and the verses. The air is lively, the words plaintive.

Tune—I had a horse.

Oh poortith[1] cauld and restless love,
  Ye wreck my peace between ye;
Yet poortith a' I could forgive,
  An' 'twere na for my Jeanie.

  O why should Fate sic pleasure have,
    Life's dearest bands untwining?
  Or why sae sweet a flower as love,
    Depend on Fortune's shining?

This warld's wealth when I think on,
  It 's pride, and a' the lave[2] o 't,
Fie, fie on silly coward man,
  That he should be the slave o 't.
    O why should Fate, &c.

Her een, sae bonnie blue, betray
  How she repays my passion;
But prudence is her owre-word aye,
  She talks of rank and fashion.
    O why should Fate, &c.

[1] Poverty. — [2] Rest.

O wha can prudence think upon,
And sic a lassie by him?
O wha can prudence think upon,
And sae in love as I am?
O why should Fate, &c.

How blest the humble cotter's fate!
He woos his simple dearie;
The silly bogles,[1] wealth and state,
Can never make them eerie.[2]
O why should Fate, &c.

THE BANKS OF DOON.

On the "Banks of Doon," and near to each other, are the house in which
the Poet was born, and the ruins of "Alloway's auld haunted Kirk."

TUNE—*The Caledonian Hunt's Delight.*

YE banks and braes o' bonnie Doon,
How can ye bloom so fresh and fair,
How can ye chant, ye little birds,
And I sae weary, fu' o' care!
Thou 'lt break my heart, thou warbling bird,
That wantons thro' the flowering thorn:
Thou minds me o' departed joys,
Departed—never to return.

Oft hae I roved by bonnie Doon,
To see the rose and woodbine twine;
And ilka bird sang o' its love,
And fondly sae did I o' mine.
Wi' lightsome heart I pu'd a rose,
Fu' sweet upon its thorny tree;
And my fause lover stole my rose,
But, ah! he left the thorn wi' me.

[1] Hobgoblins.—[2] Afraid.

BANKS O' BONNIE DOON

The reader will perceive that the measure of this copy of the "Banks an' Braes o'
Bonnie Doon" differs considerably from the foregoing. The Poet was obliged to
adapt his words to a particular air, and in so doing, he lost much of the simplicity
and beauty which the original version of the song possesses.

YE flowery banks o' bonnie Doon,
How can ye blume[1] so fair;
How can ye chant, ye little birds,
And I sae fu' o' care?

Thou 'lt break my heart, thou bonnie bird,
That sings upon the bough;
Thou minds me o' the happy days
When my fause[2] luve[3] was true.

Thou 'lt break my heart, thou bonnie bird,
That sings beside thy mate;
For sae I sat, and sae I sang,
An' wist na o' my fate.

Aft hae I roved by bonnie Doon,
To see the woodbine twine;
An' ilka[4] bird sang o' its luve,
An' sae did I o' mine.

Wi' lightsome heart I pu'd[5] a rose
Frae aff its thorny tree,
And my fause luver staw[6] the rose,
And left the thorn wi' me.

DUNCAN GRAY.

This song has nothing in common with the old licentious ballad of the same name,
but the first line and part of the third. The rest is original.

DUNCAN GRAY came here to woo,
Ha, ha, the wooing o 't,
On blythe Yule night when we were fou,[7]
Ha, ha, the wooing o 't:

[1] Bloom.—[2] False.—[3] Love.—[4] Every.—[5] Did pull.—[6] Did steal.—[7] Drunk,
or had been drinking.

Maggie coost[1] her head fu' heigh,[2]
Look'd asklent[3] and unco skeigh,[4]
Gart[5] poor Duncan stand abeigh;[6]
    Ha, ha, the wooing o 't.

Duncan fleech'd,[7] and Duncan pray'd ;
    Ha, ha, the wooing o 't,
Meg was deaf as Ailsa Craig,[8]
    Ha, ha, the wooing o 't.
Duncan sigh'd baith out and in,
Grat his een baith bleer't and blin',[9]
Spak o' louping owre a linn;[10]
    Ha, ha, the wooing o 't.

Time and chance are but a tide,
    Ha, ha, the wooing o 't,
Slighted love is sair to bide!
    Ha, ha, the wooing o' t.
"Shall I, like a fool," quoth he,
" For a haughty hizzie die?
She may gae to—France for me!"
    Ha, ha, the wooing o 't.

How it comes—let doctors tell,
    Ha, ha, the wooing o 't,
Meg grew sick—as he grew well,
    Ha, ha, the wooing o 't.
Something in her bosom wrings,
· For relief a sigh she brings;
And oh, her een, they spak sic things!
    Ha, ha, the wooing o 't.

Duncan was a lad o' grace,
    Ha, ha, the wooing o 't,
Maggie's was a piteous case,
    Ha, ha, the wooing o 't.
Duncan could na be her death,
Swelling pity smoor'd[11] his wrath,
Now they 're crouse[12] and cantie[13] baith,
    Ha, ha, the wooing o 't.

---

[1] Cast, or carried.—[2] Full high.—[3] Asquint.—[4] Very proud.—[5] Made.—
[6] At a shy distance.—[7] Entreated.—[8] A well-known rock in the frith of
Clyde.—[9] Wept till his eyes were sore and dim.—[10] Talked of jumping over
a precipice, or waterfall.—[11] Smothered.—[12] Cheerful.—[13] Gentle.

THE COUNTRY LASSIE.

"I wish Burns had written more of his songs in this lively and dramatic way. The enthusiastic affection of the maiden, and the suspicious care and antique wisdom of the 'dame of wrinkled eild,' animate and lengthen the song without making it tedious. 'Robie' has indeed a faithful and eloquent mistress, who vindicates true love and poverty against all the insinuations of one whose speech is spiced with very pithy and biting proverbs."—*Allan Cunningham.*

TUNE—*John, come kiss me now.*

In simmer when the hay was mawn,
    And corn waved green in ilka field,
While clover blooms white o'er the lea,[1]
    And roses blaw in ilka bield;[2]
Blythe Bessy in the milking shiel,[3]
    Says, "I'll be wed, come o't what will;"
Out spak a dame in wrinkled eild,[4]
    "O' guid advisement comes nae ill.

"It's ye hae wooers monie ane,
    And, lassie, ye're but young, ye ken;
Then wait a wee,[5] and cannie wale[6]
    A routhie butt, a routhie ben:[7]
There's Johnie o' the Buskie-glen,
    Fu' is his barn, fu' is his byre;
Tak this frae me, my bonnie hen,
    It's plenty beets[8] the lover's fire."

"For Johnie o' the Buskie-glen,
    I dinna care a single flie;
He lo'es sae weel his craps[9] and kye,
    He has nae love to spare for me;
But blythe's the blink o' Robie's ee,
    And weel I wat he lo'es me dear:
Ae blink o' him I wad na gie
    For Buskie-glen and a' his gear."[10]

"O thoughtless lassie, life's a faught;[11]
    The canniest gate,[12] the strife is sair;[13]
But ay fu'-han't is fechtin' best,[14]
    A hungry care's an uncol[15] care;

[1] The green field.—[2] Every sheltered spot.—[3] Shed.—[4] Old age.—[5] Little.—[6] Choose.—[7] Plentiful or well-stocked house. [8] Adds fuel to.—[9] Crops.—[10] Wealth. [11] Fight.—[12] Gentlest manner.—[13] Sore.—[14] 'Tis always best to fight full-handed.—[15] Strange, or very great.

But some will spend, and some will spare,
    An' wilfu' folk maun hae their will;
Syne[1] as ye brew, my maiden fair,
    Keep mind that ye maun drink the yill."[2]

"Oh, gear will buy me rigs o' land,
    And gear will buy me sheep and kye;
But the tender heart o' leesome[3] love,
    The gowd and siller canna buy:
We may be poor—Robie and I,
    Light is the burden love lays on;
Content and love brings peace and joy,
    What mair hae queens upon a throne?"

BESSY AND HER SPINNING-WHEEL.

Written for Johnson's "Musical Museum." The old song of the "Lass and her Spinning-Wheel," though animated by love, must have suggested to Burns the idea of this eulogy to household thrift. It is a pity that there is now so little to do—in Scotland at least—for "spinning-wheels."

TUNE—Bottom of the Punch Bowl.

O LEEZE me[4] on my spinning-wheel,
O leeze me on my rock and reel;
Frae tap to tae that cleeds me bien,[5]
And haps me fiel[6] and warm at e'en!
I 'll set me down and sing and spin,
While laigh[7] descends the simmer sun,
Blest wi' content, and milk and meal—
O leeze me on my spinning-wheel.

On ilka[8] hand the burnies[9] trot,
And meet below my theekit[10] cot;
The scented birk[11] and hawthorn white
Across the pool their arms unite,
Alike to screen the birdie's nest,
And little fishes' caller rest;[12]
The sun blinks kindly in the biel,[13]
Where blythe I turn my spinning-wheel.

---

[1] Since.—[2] Ale.—[3] Pleasant.—[4] A phrase of attachment.—[5] Clothes me plentifully.—[6] Covers me soft.—[7] Low.—[8] Every.—[9] Rivulets.—[10] Thatched.—[11] Birch-tree.—[12] Cool.—[13] Shade.

On lofty aiks[1] the cushats[2] wail,
And echo cons the doolfu' tale;
The lintwhites[3] in the hazel braes,[4]
Delighted, rival ither's lays:
The craik[5] amang the claver[6] hay,
The paitrick whirrin' o'er the ley,[7]
The swallow jinkin' round my shiel,[8]
Amuse me at my spinning-wheel.

Wi' sma' to sell, and less to buy,
Aboon[9] distress, below envy,
Oh wha would leave this humble state
For a' the pride of a' the great?
Amid their flaring, idle toys,
Amid their cumbrous, dinsome joys,
Can they the peace and pleasure feel
Of Bessy at her spinning-wheel?

BONNIE JEAN.

The heroine of this ballad was Miss M. of Dumfries. She is not painted in the rank
which she held in life, but in the dress and character of a cottager.

THERE was a lass, and she was fair,
    At kirk and market to be seen;
When a' the fairest maids were met,
    The fairest maid was bonnie Jean.

And ay she wrought her mammie's wark,
    And ay she sang sae merrilie;
The blythest bird upon the bush
    Had ne'er a lighter heart than she.

But hawks will rob the tender joys
    That bless the little lintwhite's nest;
And frost will blight the fairest flowers,
    And love will break the soundest rest.

Young Robie was the brawest lad,
    The flower and pride of a' the glen;
And he had owsen, sheep, and kye,
    And wanton naigies[10] nine or ten.

----

[1] Oaks.—[2] Doves.—[3] Linnets.—[4] The slope of a hill.—[5] The landrail.—
[6] Clover.—[7] Pasture ground.—[8] Shed.—[9] Above.—[10] Horses.

He gaed wi' Jeanie to the tryst,[1]
   He danced wi' Jeanie on the down:
And lang ere witless Jeanie wist,
   Her heart was tint,[2] her peace was stown.

As in the bosom of the stream
   The moonbeam dwells at dewy e'en,
So, trembling, pure, was tender love,
   Within the breast o' bonnie Jean.

And now she works her mammie's wark,
   And ay she sighs wi' care and pain;
Yet wist na what her ail might be,
   Or what wad mak her weel again.

But did na Jeanie's heart loup[3] light,
   And did na joy blink in her ee,
As Robie tauld a tale o' love,
   Ae e'enin' on the lily lea?

The sun was sinking in the west,
   The birds sang sweet in ilka grove;
His cheek to hers he fondly prest,
   And whisper'd thus his tale of love.

"O Jeanie fair, I lo'e thee dear;
   Oh canst thou think to fancy me?
Or wilt thou leave thy mammie's cot,
   And learn to tent the farm wi' me?

"At barn or byre thou shalt na drudge,
   Or naething else to trouble thee;
But stray amang the heather-bells,
   And tent the waving corn wi' me."

Now what could artless Jeanie do?
   She had nae will to say him na:
At length she blush'd a sweet consent,
   And love was ay between them twa.

---

[1] Fair.—[2] Lost.—[3] Leap.

THE LASS THAT MADE THE BED TO ME.

This ballad is founded on an amour of Charles the Second, when skulking in the north, about Aberdeen, in the time of the usurpation. The lass that made the bed to him was a daughter of the house of Port Letham, where he was entertained The old verses are greatly inferior to this improved version of the story.

WHEN Januar' wind was blawing cauld,
   As to the north I took my way,
The mirksome[1] night did me enfauld,[2]
   I knew nae where to lodge till day.

By my good luck a maid I met,
   Just in the middle o' my care;
And kindly she did me invite
   To walk into a chamber fair.

I bow'd fu' low unto this maid,
   And thank'd her for her courtesie;
I bow'd fu' low unto this maid,
   And bade her mak a bed to me.

She made the bed baith large and wide,
   Wi' twa white hands she spread it down;
She put the cup to her rosy lips,
   And drank, "Young man, now sleep ye soun'."

She snatch'd the candle in her hand,
   And frae my chamber went wi' speed;
But I call'd her quickly back again
   To lay some mair[3] below my head.

A cod[4] she laid below my head,
   And served me wi' due respect;
And to salute her wi' a kiss,
   I put my arms about her neck.

"Haud aff your hands, young man," she says,
   "And dinna sae uncivil be:
If ye hae onie love for me,
   Oh wrang nae my virginitie!"

Her hair was like the links o' gowd,
   Her teeth were like the ivorie;
Her cheeks like lilies dipt in wine,
   The lass that made the bed to me.

[1] Darksome.—[2] Enfold.—[3] More.—[4] A sort of pillow.

Her bosom was the driven snaw,
  Twa drifted heaps sae fair to see;
Her limbs the polish'd marble stane,
  The lass that made the bed to me.

I kiss'd her owre and owre again,
  And aye she wist na what to say;
I laid her between me and the wa',
  The lassie thought nae lang till day.

Upon the morrow when we rose,
  I thank'd her for her courtesie;
But aye she blush'd, and aye she sigh'd,
  And said, "Alas! ye've ruin'd me."

I clasp'd her waist, and kiss'd her syne,[1]
  While the tear stood twinklin' in her ee;
I said, "My lassie, dinna cry,
  For ye aye shall mak the bed to me."

She took her mither's Holland sheets,
  And made them a' in sarks[2] to me:
Blythe and merry may she be,
  The lass that made the bed to me.

The bonnie lass made the bed to me,
  The braw lass made the bed to me:
I'll ne'er forget till the day I die,
  The lass that made the bed to me!

TO MR. CUNNINGHAM.

This gentleman was an intimate friend and correspondent of the Poet's. One of
the last letters he wrote, dated from Brow, Sea-bathing Quarters, July 7, 1796, four-
teen days before his death, was addressed to Mr. A. Cunningham.

TUNE—*The Hopeless Lover.*

Now spring has clad the groves in green,
  And strew'd the lea wi' flowers:
The furrow'd, waving corn is seen
  Rejoice in fostering showers:

---
[1] Then.—[2] Shirts.

While ilka thing in nature join
  Their sorrow to forego,
Oh why thus all alone are mine
  The weary steps of woe!

The trout within yon wimpling¹ burn
  Glides swift, a silver dart,
And safe beneath the shady thorn
  Defies the angler's art:
My life was ance that careless stream,
  That wanton trout was I;
But love, wi' unrelenting beam,
  Has scorch'd my fountain dry.

The little floweret's peaceful lot,
  In yonder cliff that grows,
(Which, save the linnet's flight, I·wot
  Nae ruder visit knows,)
Was mine; till love has o'er me past,
  And blighted a' my bloom,
And now beneath the withering blast
  My youth and joy consume.

The waken'd lav'rock² warbling springs,
  And climbs the early sky,
Winnowing blythe her dewy wings
  In morning's rosy eye;
As little reckt³ I sorrow's power,
  Until the flowery snare
O' witching love, in luckless hour,
  Made me the thrall o' care.

Oh had my fate been Greenland snows,
  Or Afric's burning zone,
Wi' man and nature leagued my foes,
  So Peggy ne'er I'd known!
The wretch whase doom is, "Hope nae mair!"
  What tongue his woes can tell?
Within whase bosom, save despair,
  Nae kinder spirits dwell.

¹ Meandering.—² Lark.—³ Heeded.

CA' THE YOWES TO THE KNOWES.

The chorus of this song is old. "The music," says Burns, in his Remarks on
Scottish Songs and Ballads (Reliques), "is in the true Scotch taste."

Ca' the yowes[1] to the knowes,[2]
Ca' them where the heather grows,
Ca' them where the burnie rows,
  My bonnie dearie.

HARK the mavis'[3] evening sang
Sounding Clouden's[4] woods amang;
Then a faulding[5] let us gang,[6]
  My bonnie dearie.
    Ca' the yowes, &c.

We'll gae down by Clouden side,
Thro' the hazels spreading wide,
O'er the waves that sweetly glide
  To the moon sae clearly.
    Ca' the yowes, &c.

Yonder Clouden's silent towers,
Where at moonshine, midnight hours,
O'er the dewy bending flowers,
  Fairies dance sae cheery.
    Ca' the yowes, &c.

Ghaist nor bogle shalt thou fear;
Thou 'rt to love and heaven sae dear,
Nocht[7] of ill may come thee near,
  My bonnie dearie.
    Ca' the yowes, &c.

Fair and lovely as thou art,
Thou hast stown my very heart;
I can die—but canna part,
  My bonnie dearie.
    Ca' the yowes, &c.

While waters wimple to the sea;
While day blinks in the lift[8] sae hie;
Till clay-cauld death shall blin' my ee,
  Ye shall be my dearie.
    Ca' the yowes, &c.

Ewes.—[2] Small hillocks.—[3] Thrush.—[4] The river Clouden, a tributary
stream to the Nith.—[5] Folding.—[6] Go.—[7] Naught.—[8] Sky.

BONNIE MARY.

In the notes to "Johnson's Museum," Burns claims all this song as his composi
tion, except the first four lines. It is written to the old melody, "The Silver Tas
sie." The air is Oswald's.

Go fetch to me a pint o' wine,
    And fill it in a silver tassie;[1]
That I may drink before I go,
    A service to my bonnie lassie.
The boat rocks at the pier of Leith;
    Fu' loud the wind blaws frae the ferry;
The ship rides by the Berwick-law—
    And I maun leave my bonnie Mary

The trumpets sound, the banners fly,
    The glittering spears are rankéd ready;
The shouts o' war are heard afar,
    The battle closes thick and bloody.
But it's not the roar o' sea or shore
    Wad make me langer wish to tarry;
Nor shout o' war that's heard afar,
    It's leaving thee, my bonnie Mary.

———

WILT THOU BE MY DEARIE?

"I like the music of the 'Sutor's Dochter'; your verses to it are
pretty."—*Thomson to Burns.*

TUNE—*The Sutor's Dochter.*

WILT thou be my dearie?
    When sorrow rings thy gentle heart,
Wilt thou let me cheer thee?
    By the treasure of my soul,
And that's the love I bear thee—
    I swear and vow that only thou
Shall ever be my dearie.
    Only thou, I swear and vow,
    Shall ever be my dearie.

Lassie, say thou lo'es me;
    Or, if thou wilt na be my ain,
Say na thou 'lt refuse me:
    If it winna, canna be,

[1] Cup.

Thou for thine may choose me—
Let me, lassie, quickly die,
Trusting that thou lo'es me.
Lassie, let me quickly die,
Trusting that thou lo'es me.

WHISTLE OWRE THE LAVE O 'T.

First published in the Reliques, from a copy communicated to the editor
by Mrs. Burns.

TUNE—*When more is meant than meets the ear.*

FIRST when Maggie was my care,
Heaven, I thought, was in her air:
Now we 're married—spier nae mair[1]—
Whistle owre the lave o 't.[2]
Meg was meek, and Meg was mild,
Bonnie Meg was nature's child—
Wiser men than me 's beguiled—
Whistle owre the lave o 't.

How we live, my Meg and me,
How we love and how we 'gree,
I care na by how few may see—
Whistle owre the lave o 't.
Wha I wish were maggots' meat,
Dish'd up in her winding-sheet,
I could write—but Meg maun see 't—
Whistle owre the lave o 't.

WHA IS THAT AT MY BOWER DOOR?

The idea of this song is taken from the "Auld Man's best Argument"
of Allan Ramsay, beginning—

"Oh wha 's that at my chamber door?
Fair widow, are ye waukin' ?"

WHA is that at my bower door?
Oh wha is it but Findlay?
Then gae your gate,[3] ye 'se nae be here:
Indeed maun I, quo' Findlay.

---

[1] Ask no more.—[2] Over the rest of it.—[3] Way.

What make ye sae like a thief?
  Oh come and see, quo' Findlay:
Before the morn ye 'll work mischief;
  Indeed will I, quo' Findlay.

If I rise and let you in—
  Let me in, quo' Findlay:
Ye 'll keep me waukin[1] wi' your din;[2]
  Indeed will I, quo' Findlay.
In my bower if ye should stay—
  Let me stay, quo' Findlay:
I fear ye 'll bide till break o' day;
  Indeed will I, quo' Findlay.

Here this night if ye remain—
  I 'll remain, quo' Findlay:
I dread ye 'll learn the gate[3] again—
  Indeed will I, quo' Findlay.
What may pass within this bower—
  Let it pass, quo' Findlay:
Ye maun conceal till your last hour;
  Indeed will I, quo' Findlay.

HONEST POVERTY.

"A great critic (Dr. Aiken) on song says, that love and wine are the exclusive themes for song writing. The following is on neither subject, and consequently is no song; but will be allowed to be, I think, two or three pretty good prose thoughts inverted into rhyme." In this manner Burns speaks of this witty, clever, masculine song.

Tune—*For a' that and a' that.*

Is there, for honest poverty,
  Wha hangs his head, and a' that?
The coward-slave, we pass him by,
  We dare be poor for a' that.
    For a' that, and a' that,
      Our toils obscure, and a' that,
    The rank is but the guinea stamp,
      The man 's the gowd[4] for a' that.

What tho' on hamely fare we dine,
  Wear hodden[5] gray, and a' that;
Gie fools their silks, and knaves their wine,
  A man 's a man for a' that.

----

[1] Awake.—[2] Noise.—[3] Road.—[4] Gold.—[5] Humble.

For a' that, and a' that,
    Their tinsel show, and a' that;
The honest man, though e'er sae poor,
    Is king o' men for a' that.

You see yon birkie[1] ca'd a lord,
    Wha struts, and stares, and a' that,
Tho' hundreds worship at his word,
    He 's but a coof[2] for a' that;
        For a' that, and a' that,
            His riband, star, and a' that;
        The man of independent mind,
            He looks and laughs at a' that.

A prince can mak a belted knight,
    A marquis, duke, and a' that;
But an honest man 's aboon[3] his might,
    Guid faith he mauna[4] fa' that!
        For a' that, and a' that,
            Their dignities, and a' that,
        The pith o' sense, and pride o' worth,
            Are higher ranks than a' that.

Then let us pray that come it may,
    As come it will for a' that,
That sense and worth, o'er a' the earth,
    May bear the gree,[5] and a' that.
        For a' that, and a' that,
            It 's coming yet, for a' that,
        When man to man, the warld o'er,
            Shall brothers be for a' that.

CAPTAIN GROSE.

The following verses were written in an envelope, inclosing a letter to
Captain Grose, to be left with Mr. Cardonnel, antiquarian.

TUNE—*Sir John Malcolm.*

KEN ye aught o' Captain Grose?
    Igo, & ago,
If he 's amang his friends or foes?
    Iram, coram, dago.

---

1 Fine fellow.—2 Blockhead.—3 Above.—4 He must not try, or attempt
that.—5 The laurel, the victory.

Is he south, or is he north?
      Igo, & ago,
Or drownéd in the river Forth?
      Iram, coram, dago.

Is he slain by Highland bodies?
      Igo, & ago,
And eaten like a wether-haggis?
      Iram, coram, dago.

Is he to Abraham's bosom gane?
      Igo, & ago,
Or haudin' Sarah by the wame?
      Iram, coram, dago.

Where'er he be, the Lord be near him,
      Igo, & ago,
As for the Deil, he daur na steer[1] him.
      Iram, coram, dago.

But please transmit th' incloséd letter,
      Igo, & ago,
Which will oblige your humble debtor.
      Iram, coram, dago.

So may ye hae auld stanes in store,
      Igo, & ago,
The very stanes that Adam bore.
      Iram, coram, dago.

So may ye get in glad possession,
      Igo, & ago,
The coins o' Satan's coronation!
      Iram, coram, dago.

[1] Dare not molest.

MY AIN KIND DEARIE O.

This is the first song which Burns wrote for Mr. Thomson's collection. Dr. Currie supposes it to have been suggested to the Poet's fancy by the old song of the "Ploughman," beginning—

> "My ploughman he comes hame at e'en,
> He's aften weet an' weary,
> Cast aff the weet, put on the dry,
> An' gae to bed, my dearie."

Tune—The Lea-rig.

When o'er the hill the eastern star
  Tells bughtin'-time[1] is near, my jo;
And owsen[2] frae the furrow'd field,
  Return sae dowf[3] and weary O;
Down by the burn, where scented birks
  Wi' dew are hanging clear, my jo,
I 'll meet thee on the lea-rig,[4]
  My ain kind dearie O.

In mirkest[5] glen, at midnight hour,
  I 'd rove, and ne'er be eerie[6] O,
If thro' that glen I gaed[7] to thee,
  My ain kind dearie O.
Altho' the night were ne'er sae wild,
  And I were ne'er sae wearie O,
I 'd meet thee on the lea-rig,
  My ain kind dearie O.

The hunter lo'es the morning sun,
  To rouse the mountain deer, my jo;
At noon the fisher seeks the glen,
  Along the burn to steer, my jo;
Gie me the hour o' gloamin'[8] gray,
  It maks my heart sae cheery O,
To meet thee on the lea-rig,
  My ain kind dearie O.

[1] The time of collecting the sheep in the pens to be milked.—[2] Oxen.—
[3] Pithless.—[4] Grassy ridge.—[5] Darkest.—[6] Frighted.—[7] Went.—[8] Twilight.

PEGGY'S CHARMS.

This is one of the many songs which Burns wrote for the Museum, and an excellent song it is. The second verse is admirable, both in sentiment and expression.

My Peggy's face, my Peggy's form,
The frost of hermit age might warm;
My Peggy's worth, my Peggy's mind,
Might charm the first of human kind.
I love my Peggy's angel air,
Her face so truly heavenly fair,
Her native grace so void of art;
But I adore my Peggy's heart.

The lily's hue, the rose's dye,
The kindling lustre of an eye;
Who but owns their magic sway?
Who but knows they all decay?
The tender thrill, the pitying tear,
The generous purpose, nobly dear,
The gentle look, that rage disarms—
These are all immortal charms.

LORD GREGORY.

This song appears to have been suggested to the Poet's fancy, by the " Lass of Lochroyan," a very old ballad, a fragment of which will be found in Herd's collection, 1774. A copy of it still more enlarged has since been published in the " Minstrelsy of the Scottish Border."

Oh mirk, mirk is this midnight hour,
  And loud the tempest's roar;
A waefu' wanderer seeks thy tower—
  Lord Gregory, ope thy door.

An exile frae her father's ha',
  And a' for loving thee;
At least some *pity* on me shaw,[1]
  If *love* it may na be.

Lord Gregory, mind'st thou not the grove,
  By bonnie Irwine side,
When first I own'd that virgin-love
  I lang, lang had denied?

[1] Show.

How aften didst thou pledge and vow,
    Thou wad for aye bo mine:
And my fond heart, itsel sae true,
    It ne'er mistrusted thine.

Hard is thy heart, Lord Gregory,
    And flinty is thy breast:
Thou dart of heaven, that flashest by,
    Oh! wilt thou give me rest?

Ye mustering thunders from above,
    Your willing victim see!
But spare and pardon my false love
    His wrangs to heaven and me.

FRAGMENT.

These are eight beautiful lines. They are too few to sing, too good to cast away, and too peculiar and happy ever to be eked out by a hand inferior to the hand of their Author. They will long continue a fragment.—*Cunningham's Scottish Songs.*

Her flowing locks, the raven's wing,
    Adown her neck and bosom hing;
How sweet unto that breast to cling,
    And round that neck entwine her!

Her lips are roses wat wi' dew,
    Oh what a feast her bonnie mou!
Her cheeks a mair celestial hue,
    A crimson still diviner!

THE BLISSFUL DAY.

"I composed this song," says Burns, "out of compliment to one of the happiest and worthiest married couples in the world—Robert Riddel, Esq., of Glenriddel, and his lady. At their fireside I have enjoyed more pleasant evenings than all the houses of fashionable people in this country put together; and to their kindness and hospitality I am indebted for many of the happiest hours of my life."

TUNE—*Seventh of November.*

The day returns, my bosom burns,
    The blissful day we twa did meet;
Tho' winter wild in tempest toil'd,
    Ne'er summer sun was half sae sweet:

Than a' the pride that loads the tide,
   And crosses o'er the sultry line;
Than kingly robes, and crowns and globes,
   Heaven gave me more, it made thee mine.

While day and night can bring delight,
   Or nature aught of pleasure give;
While joys above my mind can move,
   For thee, and thee alone, I live;
When that grim foe of life below
   Comes in between to make us part,
The iron hand that breaks our band,
   It breaks my bliss—it breaks my heart.

———

JEANIE'S BOSOM.

This is an early composition. It was the first of the Poet's songs composed
in praise of "Bonnie Jean," afterwards Mrs. Burns.

TUNE—*My mother's ay glowering owre me.*

Louis, what reck I by thee,
   Or Geordie on his ocean:
Dyvor,[1] beggar louns[2] to me,
   I reign in Jeanie's bosom.

Let her crown my love her law,
   And in her breast enthrone me
Kings and nations swith[3] awa,
   Rief randies,[4] I disown ye!

- - ———

WILLIE'S WIFE.

This song is founded on an old border ditty, beginning—

"Willie Wastle dwells in his castle,
An' nae a loun in a' the town
Can tak Willie Wastle doun."

TUNE—*Tibbie Fowler in the glen.*

WILLIE WASTLE dwalt on Tweed,
   The spot they ca'd it Linkumdoddie;
Willie was a wabster[5] guid

Bankrupt.—[2] Ragamuffins.—[3] Get away.—[4] Thievish queans.—[5] Weaver.

Cou'd stown[1] a clue wi' onie bodie;
He had a wife was dour and din,[2]
Oh, tinkler[3] Madgie was her mither:
   Sic a wife as Willie had,
   I wad na gie a button for her.

She has an ee, she has but ane,
   The cat has twa the very color;
Five rusty teeth, forbye[4] a stump,
   A clapper tongue wad deave[5] a miller;
A whiskin' beard about her mou,
   Her nose and chin they threaten ither:
   Sic a wife, &c.

She's bow-hough'd,[6] she's hein-shinn'd,[7]
   Ae limpin' leg a hand-breed[8] shorter;
She's twisted right, she's twisted left,
   To balance fair on ilka[9] quarter;
She has a hump upon her breast,
   The twin o' that upon her shouther:
   Sic a wife, &c.

Auld baudrans[10] by the ingle[11] sits,
   And wi' her loof[12] her face a-washin';
But Willie's wife is nae sae trig,
   She dights her grunzie wi' a hushion;[13]
Her walie nieves[14] like midden-creels,[15]
   Her face wad fyle[16] the Logan water:
   Sic a wife, &c.

---

[1] Stolen—supposed to allude to the dishonest practices of some weavers who purloin the yarn that is sent to the loom.
[2] Sullen and shallow.—[3] A gipsey woman.—[4] Besides.—[5] Deafen.—[6] Knock-kneed.—[7] Bony-shinned.—[8] Hand-breadth.—[9] Every.—[10] The cat.—[11] Fireplace.—[12] Hand.—[13] Cleans her mouth with a cushion.—[14] Large fists.—[15] Dung-baskets.—[16] Make dirty.

I HAE A WIFE O' MY AIN.

The Poet was accustomed to say that the most happy period of his life
was the first winter he spent at Elliesland,—for the first time under a roof of
his own—with his wife and children about him. It is known that he wel-
comed his wife to her roof-tree at Elliesland in this song.—*Lockhart.*

I HAE a wife o' my ain,
    I 'll partake wi' naebody;
I 'll tak cuckold frae nane,
    I 'll gie cuckold to naebody.

I hae a penny to spend,
    There—thanks to naebody;
I hae naething to lend,
    I 'll borrow frae naebody.

I am naebody's lord,
    I 'll be slave to naebody;
I hae a guid braid sword,
    I 'll tak dunts[1] frae naebody.

I 'll be merry and free,
    I 'll be sad for naebody;
If naebody care for me,
    I 'll care for naebody.

BONNIE WEE THING.

Composed," says Burns, "on my little idol, the charming, lovely Davies."

TUNE—*The Lads of Saltcoats.*

Bonnie wee thing, cannie wee thing,
    Lovely wee thing, wast thou mine,
I wad wear thee in my bosom,
    Lest my jewel I should tine.[2]

WISHFULLY I look and languish,
    In that bonnie face o' thine;
And my heart it stounds wi' anguish,
    Lest my wee thing be na mine.
    Bonnie wee thing, &c.

[1] Blows.—[2] Lose.

Wit and grace, and love and beauty,
    In ae constellation shine:
To adore thee is my duty,
    Goddess o' this soul o' mine.
        Bonnie wee thing, &c.

THE SOLDIER'S RETURN.

The " Poor and Honest Sodger" laid hold at once on public feeling, and it was
everywhere sung with enthusiasm, which only began to abate when Campbell's
Exile of Erin and Wounded Hussar were published.—*Lockhart's Life of Burns.*

TUNE—*The mill, mill, O.*

WHEN wild war's deadly blast was blawn,
    And gentle peace returning,
Wi' monie a sweet babe fatherless,
    And monie a widow mourning,
I left the lines and tented field,
    Where lang I 'd been a lodger,
My humble knapsack a' my wealth,
    A poor but honest sodger.

A leal, light heart was in my breast,
    My hand unstain'd wi' plunder,
And for fair Scotia hame again,
    I cheery on did wander.
I thought upon the banks o' Coil,
    I thought upon my Nancy,
I thought upon the witching smile
    That caught my youthful fancy.

At length I reach'd the bonny glen,
    Where early life I sported,
I pass'd the mill and trysting thorn,
    Where Nancy aft I courted;
Wha spied I but my ain dear maid,
    Down by her mother's dwelling!
And turn'd me round to hide the flood,
    That in my een was swelling.

Wi' alter'd voice, quoth I, " Sweet lass,
    Sweet as yon hawthorn's blossom,
Oh happy, happy may he be
    That 's dearest to thy bosom!

My purse is light, I 've far to gang,
  And fain would be thy lodger;
I 've served my king and country lang,
  Take pity on a sodger."

Sae wistfully she gazed on me,
  And lovelier was than ever;
Quo' she, " A sodger ance I lo'ed;
  Forget him shall I never:
Our humble cot, and hamely fare,
  Ye freely shall partake it;
That gallant badge, the dear cockade,
  Ye 're welcome for the sake o't."

She gazed—she redden'd like a rose—
  Syne pale like onie lily,
She sank within mine arms and cried,
  "Art thou my ain dear Willie?"
"By Him who made yon sun and sky,
  By whom true love 's regarded,
I am the man; and thus may still
  True lovers be rewarded!

"The wars are o'er, and I 'm come hame,
  And find thee still true-hearted;
Tho' poor in gear, we 're rich in love,
  And mair we 'se ne'er be parted."
Quo' she, " My grandsire left me gowd,
  A mailen[1] plenish'd fairly:
And come, my faithful sodger lad,
  Thou 'rt welcome to it dearly!"

For gold the merchant ploughs the main,
  The farmer ploughs the manor;
But glory is the sodger's prize,
  The sodger's wealth his honor:
The brave poor sodger ne'er despise,
  Nor count him as a stranger;
Remember he 's his country's stay,
  In day and hour of danger.

[1] Farm.

LOGAN BRAES.

The title of this song, but nothing more, is taken from the old verses on
Logan Water, beginning—

"Ae simmer night, on Logan braes,
I help'd a bonnie lass on wi' her claes,
First wi' her stockings, an' syne wi' her shoon—
But she gied me the glaiks[1] when a' was done!"

AIR—*Logan Water*.

O LOGAN, sweetly didst thou glide,
That day I was my Willie's bride;
And years sinsyne[2] hae o'er us run,
Like Logan to the simmer sun.
But now thy flowery banks appear
Like drumlie winter, dark and drear,
While my dear lad maun face his faes,
Far, far frae me and Logan braes.

Again the merry month o' May
Has made our hills and valleys gay;
The birds rejoice in leafy bowers,
The bees hum round the breathing flowers:
Blythe morning lifts his rosy eye,
And evening's tears are tears of joy;
My soul, delightless, a' surveys,
While Willie's far frae Logan braes.

Within yon milk-white hawthorn bush,
Amang her nestlings sits the thrush;
Her faithfu' mate will snare her toil,
Or wi' his song her cares beguile:
But I wi' my sweet nurslings here,
Nae mate to help, nae mate to cheer,
Pass widow'd nights and joyless days,
While Willie's far frae Logan braes.

Oh wae upon you, men o' state,
That brethren rouse to deadly hate!
As ye make monie a fond heart mourn,
Sae may it on your heads return!
How can your flinty hearts enjoy
The widow's tears, the orphan's cry?
But soon may peace bring happy days,
And Willie hame to Logan braes!

[1] Jilted me.---[2] Since then.

BY ALLAN STREAM, Etc.

Of this song Burns says, "I think it not in my worst style." It has nothing in common with the Allan Water of Ramsay, in the Tea Table Miscellany, vol. i. p. 86, out the title.

TUNE—*Allan Water.*

By Allan stream I chanced to rove,
　While Phœbus sank beyond Benleddi;[1]
The winds were whispering thro' the grove,
　The yellow corn was waving ready;
I listen'd to a lover's sang,
　And thought on youthfu' pleasures monie;
And ay the wild-wood echoes rang—
　"Oh, dearly do I love thee, Annie!"

Oh, happy be the woodbine bower,
　Nae nightly bogle make it eerie;
Nor ever sorrow stain the hour,
　The place and time I met my dearie!
Her head upon my throbbing breast,
　She, sinking, said, "I'm thine forever!"
While monie a kiss the seal imprest,
　The sacred vow, we ne'er should sever.

The haunt o' spring's the primrose brae,
　The simmer joys the flocks to follow;
How cheerly thro' her shortening day,
　Is autumn, in her weeds o' yellow!
But can they melt the glowing heart,
　Or chain the soul in speechless pleasure?
Or thro' each nerve the rapture dart,
　Like meeting her, our bosom's treasure?

SHE'S FAIR AND FAUSE.

The fickleness of a lady of the name of Stewart occasioned this vigorous and emphatic song. The four concluding lines are quoted and highly praised in the Edinburgh Review for January, 1809.

She's fair and fause[2] that causes my smart,
　I lo'ed her meikle and lang;[3]
She's broken her vow, she's broken my heart,
　And I may e'en gae hang.

[1] A mountain west of Strathallan, 3009 feet high.—[2] False.—[3] Much and long.

A coof[1] came in wi' routh o' gear,[2]
And I hae tint my dearest dear;
But woman is but warld's gear,
  Sae let the bonnie lass gang.

Whae'er ye be that woman love,
  To this be never blind,
Nae ferlie[3] 'tis though fickle she prove,
  A woman has 't by kind:
O woman lovely, woman fair!
An angel form 's faun[4] to thy share,
'Twad been owre meikle to gien thee mair,
  I mean an angel mind.

SHE SAYS SHE LO'ES ME BEST O' A'.

"She says she lo'es me best of a'," is one of the pleasantest table songs
I have seen, and henceforth shall be mine when the song is going round.
—*Thomson to Burns.*

TUNE—*Onagh's Waterfall.*

SAE flaxen were her ringlets,
  Her eyebrows of a darker hue,
Bewitchingly o'er-arching
  Twa laughing een o' bonnie blue.
Her smiling sae wyling,
  Wad make a wretch forget his woe
What pleasure, what treasure,
  Unto these rosy lips to grow!
Such was my Chloris' bonnie face,
  When first her bonnie face I saw,
And ay my Chloris' dearest charm,
  She says she lo'es me best of a'.

Like harmony her motion;
  Her pretty ankle is a spy
Betraying fair proportion,
  Wad make a saint forget the sky.
Sae warming, sae charming,
  Her faultless form and gracefu' air;
Ilk feature—auld Nature
  Declared that she could do nae mair:

---

[1] Blockhead.—[2] Plenty of wealth.—[3] Wonder.—[4] Fallen.

Hers are the willing chains o' love,
    By conquering beauty's sovereign law;
And ay my Chloris' dearest charm,
    She says she lo'es me best of a'.

Let others love the city,
    And gaudy show at sunny noon;
Gie me the lonely valley,
    The dewy eve and rising moon
Fair beaming, and streaming,
    Her silver light the boughs amang;
While falling, recalling,
    The amorous thrush concludes her sang:
There, dearest Chloris wilt thou rove
    By wimpling burn and leafy shaw,
And hear my vows o' truth and love,
    And say thou lo'es me best of a'?

LAMENT OF A MOTHER FOR THE DEATH OF HER SON.

Burns in this song personifies Mrs. Ferguson of Craigdarroch, who lost her son, a
promising youth of eighteen years of age. He composed it one morning, on horse-
back, after three o'clock, as he jogged on in the dark, from Nithsdale to Elliesland.

TUNE—*Finlayston House.*

FATE gave the word, the arrow sped,
    And pierced my darling's heart;
And with him all the joys are fled
    Life can to me impart.
By cruel hands the sapling drops,
    In dust dishonor'd laid;
So fell the pride of all my hopes,
    My age's future shade.

The mother-linnet in the brake
    Bewails her ravish'd young;
So I, for my lost darling's sake,
    Lament the live-day long.
Death, oft I've fear'd thy fatal blow,
    Now, fond I bare my breast,
Oh, do thou kindly lay me low
    With him I love at rest!

THE LOVELY LASS OF INVERNESS.

For an old and beautiful version of the "Lass of Inverness," see "Harp of Caledonia," vol. iii. p. 171.

THE lovely lass o' Inverness,
Nae joy nor pleasure can she see;
For e'en and morn she cries—"Alas!"
And ay the saut tear blin's her ee:
"Drumossie moor, Drumossie day,
A waefu' day it was to me;
For there I lost my father dear,
My father dear, and brethren three.

"Their winding-sheet the bluidy clay,
Their graves are growing green to see;
And by them lies the dearest lad
That ever blest a woman's ee.
Now wae to thee, thou cruel lord,
A bluidy man I trow thou be;
For monie a heart thou hast made sair,
That ne'er did wrong to thine or thee."

THE RAVING WINDS.

These verses were composed for Isabella M'Leod of Raza, as expressive of her feelings on the death of her sister, and the still more melancholy death of her sister's husband, the Earl of Loudon, who shot himself in consequence of some mortifications he suffered, owing to the deranged state of his finances.

TUNE—*M'Grigor of Roro's Lament.*

RAVING winds around her blowing,
Yellow leaves the woodlands strowing,
By a river hoarsely roaring
Isabella stray'd deploring:—
"Farewell, hours that late did measure
Sunshine days of joy and pleasure;
Hail, thou gloomy night of sorrow,
Cheerless night that knows no morrow.
O'er the past too fondly wandering,
On the hopeless future pondering;
Chilly grief my life-blood freezes,
Fell despair my fancy seizes.

Life, thou soul of every blessing,
Load to misery most distressing,
Oh how gladly I'd resign thee,
And to dark oblivion join thee!"

THE YOUNG HIGHLAND ROVER.

"The Young Highland Rover," is Prince Charles Stuart. Burns was
always a Jacobite, but more so after his tour to the Highlands, when this
song was composed.

TUNE—*Morag.*

LOUD blaw the frosty breezes,
  The snaws the mountains cover;
Like winter on me seizes,
  Since my young Highland Rover
  Far wanders nations over.
Where'er he go, where'er he stray,
  May Heaven be his warden:
Return him safe to fair Strathspey,
  And bonnie Castle-Gordon!

The trees now naked groaning,
  Shall soon wi' leaves be hinging,[1]
The birdies dowie[2] moaning,
  Shall a' be blythely singing,
  And every flower be springing.
Sae I'll rejoice the lee-lang[3] day,
  When by his mighty warden
My youth's return'd to fair Strathspey
  And bonnie Castle-Gordon.

STRATHALLAN'S LAMENT.

Strathallan, it is presumed, was one of the followers of the young Cheva-
lier, and is supposed, in the following verses, to be lying concealed in some
cave of the Highlands, after the battle of Culloden.

THICKEST night o'erhang my dwelling!
  Howling tempests o'er me rave!
Turbid torrents, wintry swelling,
  Still surround my lonely cave!

[1] Hanging.—[2] Worn with grief.—[3] Live-long.

Crystal streamlets gently flowing,
    Busy haunts of base mankind,
Western breezes softly blowing,
    Suit not my distracted mind.

In the cause of right engagéd,
    Wrongs injurious to redress,
Honor's war we strongly wagéd,
    But the Heavens denied success.

Ruin's wheel has driven o'er us,
    Not a hope that dare attend;
The wild world is all before us—
    But a world without a friend!

THE BANKS OF NITH.

A Fragment.

To thee, loved Nith, thy gladsome plains,
    Where late wi' careless thought I ranged,
Though prest wi' care and sunk in woe,
    To thee I bring a heart unchanged.

I love thee, Nith, thy banks and braes,
    Though memory there my bosom tear;
For there he roved that brak my heart—
    Yet to that heart, ah! still how dear!

FAREWELL TO NANCY.

The last four lines of the second verse of this song have furnished Byron
with a motto, and Scott has said that that motto is worth a thousand romances:

"Had we never loved sae kindly," &c.

Ae fond kiss, and then we sever!
Ae fareweel, alas, forever!
Deep in heart-wrung tears I 'll pledge thee,
Warring sighs and groans I 'll wage thee.
Who shall say that Fortune grieves him,
While the star of hope she leaves him?
Me, nae cheerfu' twinkle lights me;
Dark despair around benights me.

I 'll ne'er blame my partial fancy,
Naething could resist my Nancy:
But to see her, was to love her;
Love but her, and love forever.
Had we never loved sae kindly,
Had we never loved sae blindly,
Never met—or never parted,
We had ne'er been broken-hearted.

Fare thee weel, thou first and fairest!
Fare thee weel, thou best and dearest!
Thine be ilka joy and treasure,
Peace, enjoyment, love, and pleasure!
Ae fond kiss, and then we sever!
Ae fareweel, alas! forever!
Deep in heart-wrung tears I 'll pledge thee,
Warring sighs and groans I 'll wage thee.

FAREWELL TO ELIZA.

Written for Johnson's Museum. This song has latterly been rendered
popular by the musical talents of Miss Stephens.

TUNE—*Gilderoy.*

FROM thee, Eliza, I must go,
  And from my native shore;
The cruel fates between us throw
  A boundless ocean's roar:
But boundless oceans roaring wide
  Between my love and me,
They never, never can divide
  My heart and soul from thee.

Farewell, farewell, Eliza dear,
  The maid that I adore!
A boding voice is in my ear,
  We part to meet no more!
But the last throb that leaves my heart,
  While Death stands victor by,
That throb, Eliza, is thy part,
  And thine that latest sigh.

FAIR ELIZA.

"The bonnie brucket lassie," to the music of which this superior song is composed, was written by an eccentric character, who was well known in Edinburgh about forty years ago by the name of "Balloon Tytler." He also wrote the popular song, of "Loch Erroch Side."

TUNE—*The bonnie brucket lassie.*

Turn again, thou fair Eliza,
  Ae kind blink before we part,
Rue on thy despairing lover!
  Canst thou break his faithfu' heart?
Turn again, thou fair Eliza!
  If to love thy heart denies,
For pity hide the cruel sentence
  Under friendship's kind disguise!

Thee, dear maid, hae I offended?
  The offence is loving thee:
Canst thou wreck his peace forever
  Wha for thine wad gladly die?
While the life beats in my bosom,
  Thou shalt mix in ilka throe:
Turn again, thou lovely maiden,
  Ae sweet smile on me bestow!

Not the bee upon the blossom,
  In the pride o' sunny noon;
Not the little sporting fairy,
  All beneath the simmer moon;
Not the poet in the moment
  Fancy lightens in his ee,
Kens the pleasure, feels the rapture,
  That thy presence gies to me.

THOUGH CRUEL FATE, ETC.

This beautiful fragment is an early composition.

Though cruel Fate should bid us part,
  As far's the Pole and Line,
Her dear idea round my heart
  Should tenderly entwine.

34

Though mountains frown and deserts howl,
And oceans roar between;
Yet, dearer than my deathless soul,
I still would love my Jean.

THE HIGHLAND LASSIE.

Burns composed these verses in early life, before he was at all known in the
world. The object of his affection was Mary Campbell, a native of the Highlands.
The deep impression which she made on his mind can hardly be inferred from this
song. From those which follow, however, we can more readily imagine the intense
interest which she excited in his bosom.

TUNE—*The deuk's dang owre my daddy.*

NAE gentle dames, though e'er sae fair,
Shall ever be my Muse's care;
Their titles a' are empty show;
Gie me my Highland lassie, O.

Within the glen sae bushy, O,
Aboon the plain sae rushy, O,
I set me down wi' right good will
To sing my Highland lassie, O.

Oh, were yon hills and valleys mine,
Yon palace and yon gardens fine,
The world then the love should know
I bear my Highland lassie, O.
Within the glen, &c.

But fickle fortune frowns on me,
And I maun cross the raging sea;
But while my crimson currents flow
I'll love my Highland lassie, O.
Within the glen, &c.

Although thro' foreign climes I range,
I know her heart will never change,
For her bosom burns with honor's glow,
My faithful Highland lassie, O.
Within the glen, &c.

For her I'll dare the billow's roar,
For her I'll dare the distant shore,

That Indian wealth may lustre throw
Around my Highland lassie, O.
Within the glen, &c.

She has my heart, she has my hand,
By sacred truth and honor's band!
Till the mortal stroke shall lay me low,
I'm thine, my Highland lassie, O.

Farewell the glen sae bushy, O,
Farewell the plain sae rushy, O,
To other lands I now must go
To sing my Highland lassie, O.

TO MARY.

Another of the Poet's many songs in praise of " Highland Mary."

COULD aught of song declare my pains,
Could artful numbers move thee,
The Muse should tell in labor'd strains,
O Mary, how I love thee!

They who but feign a wounded heart,
May teach the lyre to languish;
But what avails the pride of art,
When wastes the soul with anguish?

Then let the sudden bursting sigh
The heart-felt pang discover;
And in the keen, yet tender eye,
Oh read the imploring lover.

For well I know thy gentle mind
Disdains art's gay disguising;
Beyond what fancy e'er refined,
The voice of nature prizing.

PRAYER FOR MARY.

Supposed to be written on the eve of the Poet's intended departure for the West Indies. First published in the *Reliques*, from a copy supplied by the Rev. James Gray, of Dumfries, the kind friend of the widow and family of the Poet.

Powers celestial, whose protection
　Ever guards the virtuous fair,
While in distant climes I wander,
　Let my Mary be your care:
Let her form, sae fair and faultless,
　Fair and faultless as your own—
Let my Mary's kindred spirit,
　Draw your choicest influence down.

Make the gales you waft around her,
　Soft and peaceful as her breast;
Breathing in the breeze that fans her,
　Soothe her bosom into rest:
Guardian angels, oh protect her,
　When in distant lands I roam!
To realms unknown while fate exiles me,
　Make her bosom still my home.

HIGHLAND MARY.

In this song, so exquisitely mournful, we see all the anticipations, all the hopes, of Burns laid low. His Prayer was not heard. His Mary was, as it were, struck dead at his feet. She met him, by appointment, in a sequestered spot by the banks of Ayr, where she spent the day with him in taking a farewell, before she should embark for the West Highlands, to arrange matters among her friends for her projected change in life. Shortly after she crossed the sea to meet him at Greenock, where she had scarcely landed when she was seized with a malignant fever, which hurried her to the grave in a few days, before he could even hear of her illness.

Tune—Katharine Ogie.

Ye banks, and braes, and streams around
　The castle o' Montgomery,
Green be your woods, and fair your flowers,
　Your waters never drumlie!
There simmer first unfald[1] her robes,
　And there the langest tarry!
For there I took the last farewel
　O' my sweet Highland Mary.

[1] Unfolds.

How sweetly bloom'd the gay green birk!
How rich the hawthorn's blossom!
As underneath their fragrant shade,
I clasp'd her to my bosom!
The golden hours, on angel wings,
Flew o'er me and my dearie;
For dear to me, as light and life,
Was my sweet Highland Mary.

Wi' monie a vow and lock'd embrace,
Our parting was fu' tender;
And pledging aft to meet again,
We tore oursels asunder:
But, oh! fell death's untimely frost,
That nipt my flower sae early!
Now green's the sod, and cauld's the clay,
That wraps my Highland Mary!

Oh pale, pale now, those rosy lips,
I aft hae kiss'd sae fondly!
And closed for ay the sparkling glance
That dwelt on me sae kindly!
And mouldering now in silent dust,
That heart that lo'ed me dearly!
But still within my bosom's core
Shall live my Highland Mary.

TO MARY IN HEAVEN.

We have seen Burns celebrate the youth and beauty of his Mary. We have seen him bewail her death in the most pathetic and agonizing strains. In this sublime and tender elegy, which he composed on the anniversary of her decease, his whole soul seems overwhelmed with sadness. Agitated by the tumult of his feelings, he retired from his family, then residing on the farm of Ellisland, and wandered on the banks of the Nith and about the farm-yard nearly the whole of the night. At length he threw himself on the side of a corn-stack, and gave utterance to his grief in this divine strain of sensibility—this heart-rending address "To Mary in Heaven."

Tune—Miss Forbes's Farewell to Banff.

Thou lingering star, with lessening ray,
That lov'st to greet the early morn,
Again thou usher'st in the day
My Mary from my soul was torn.

O Mary! dear departed shade!
  Where is thy place of blissful rest?
Seest thou thy lover lowly laid?
  Hear'st thou the groans that rend his breast?

That sacred hour can I forget,
  Can I forget the hallow'd grove,
Where by the winding Ayr we met,
  To live one day of parting love?
Eternity will not efface
  Those records dear of transports past—
Thy image at our last embrace!
  Ah! little thought we 'twas our last!

Ayr, gurgling, kiss'd his pebbled shore,
  O'erhung with wild-woods, thickening, green.
The fragrant birch, and hawthorn hoar,
  Twined amorous round the raptured scene.
The flowers sprang wanton to be prest,
  The birds sang love on every spray,
Till too, too soon, the glowing west
· Proclaim'd the speed of wingéd day.

Still o'er those scenes my memory wakes,
  And fondly broods with miser care;
Time but the impression deeper makes,
  As streams their channels deeper wear.
My Mary! dear departed shade!
  Where is thy place of blissful rest?
Seest thou thy lover lowly laid?
  Hear'st thou the groans that rend his breast?

- - -

THE AUTHOR'S FAREWELL

TO HIS NATIVE COUNTRY.

Burns intended this song as a farewell dirge to his native land, from which he
was to embark in a few days for Jamaica. "I had taken," says he, "the last fare-
well of my friends : my chest was on the road to Greenock : I composed the last
song I should ever measure in Caledonia—'The gloomy night is gathering fast.' "

TUNE—Rosslin Castle.

THE gloomy night is gathering fast,
Loud roars the wild inconstant blast,

Yon murky cloud is foul with rain,
I see it driving o'er the plain ;
The hunter now has left the moor,
The scatter'd coveys meet secure,
While here I wander, prest wi' care,
Along the bonnie banks of Ayr.

The Autumn mourns her ripening corn,
By early Winter's ravage torn ;
Across her placid azure sky,
She sees the scowling tempest fly :
Chill runs my blood to hear it rave,
I think upon the stormy wave,
Where many a danger I must dare,
Far from the bonnie banks of Ayr.

'Tis not the surging billow's roar,
'Tis not that fatal deadly shore :
Tho' death in every shape appear,
The wretched have no more to fear :
But round my heart the ties are bound,
That heart transpierced with many a wound :
These bleed afresh, those ties I tear,
To leave the bonnie banks of Ayr.

Farewell old Coila's hills and dales,
Her heathy moors and winding vales ;
The scenes where wretched fancy roves,
Pursuing past, unhappy loves !
Farewell, my friends ! farewell, my foes !
My peace with these, my love with those—
The bursting tears my heart declare,
Farewell the bonnie banks of Ayr !

THE FAREWELL

TO THE BRETHREN OF ST. JAMES'S LODGE, TARBOLTON.

Tune—Gude night and joy be wi' you a'.

ADIEU ! a heart-warm fond adieu,
　Dear brothers of the mystic tie !
Ye favor'd, ye enlighten'd few,
　Companions of my social joy !

Tho' I to foreign lands must hie,
   Pursuing fortune's slippery ba',[1]
With melting heart and brimful eye,
   I'll mind you still, tho' far awa.

Oft have I met your social band,
   And spent the cheerful, festive night;
Oft, honor'd with supreme command,
   Presided o'er the sons of light;
And by that hieroglyphic bright,
   Which none but craftsmen ever saw!
Strong memory on my heart shall write
   Those happy scenes when far awa.

May freedom, harmony, and love,
   Unite you in the grand design,
Beneath the omniscient Eye above,
   The glorious Architect divine!
That you may keep the unerring line,
   Still rising by the plummet's law,
Till order bright completely shine,
   Shall be my prayer, when far awa.

And you, farewell! whose merits claim,
   Justly, that highest badge to wear!
Heaven bless your honor'd, noble name,
   To Masonry and Scotia dear!
A last request, permit me here,—
   When yearly ye assemble a',
One ronnd, I ask it with a tear,
   To him—The Bard that's far awa!

THE RUINED MAID'S LAMENT.

On meikle do I rue, fause[2] love,
   Oh sairly do I rue,
That e'er I heard your flattering tongue,
   That e'er your face I knew.

[1] Ball.—[2] False.

Oh I hae tint my rosy cheeks,
  Likewise my waist sae sma';
And I hae lost my lightsome heart,
  That little wist a fa'.

Now I maun thole the scornfu' sneer
  O' monie a saucy quean;
When, gin the truth were a' but kent,
  Her life's been waur than mine.

Whene'er my father thinks on me,
  He stares into the wa';
My mither, she has taen the bed
  Wi' thinking on my fa'.

Whene'er I hear my father's foot,
  My heart wad burst wi' pain;
Whene'er I meet my mither's ee,
  My tears rin down like rain.

Alas! sae sweet a tree as love
  Sic bitter fruit should bear!
Alas! that e'er a bonnie face
  Should draw a saut y tear!

*   *   *   *   *   *

AND MAUN I STILL ON MENIE DOAT.

It was the opinion of Dr. Currie, that the chorus originally attached to the following beautiful stanzas, both interrupted the narrative, and marred the sentiment of each verse. We have therefore omitted it.

TUNE—*Johnny's gray breeks.*

AGAIN rejoicing Nature sees
  Her robe assume its vernal hues;
Her leafy locks wave in the breeze,
  All freshly steep'd in morning dews.

In vain to me these cowslips blaw,
  In vain to me these violets spring:
In vain to me, in glen or shaw,
  The mavis[1] and the lintwhite[2] sing.

[1] The thrush.—[2] The linnet.

The merry ploughboy cheers his team,
  Wi' joy the tentie[1] seedsman stalks,
But life 's to me a weary dream,
  A dream of ane that never wauks.

The wanton coot the water skims,
  Amang the reeds the ducklings cry,
The stately swan majestic swims,
  And every thing is blest but I.

The shepherd steeks his faulding slap,[2]
  And owre the moorlands whistles shrill;
Wi' wild, unequal, wandering step
  I meet him on the dewy hill.

And when the lark, 'tween light and dark,
  Blythe waukens by the daisie's side,
And mounts and sings on fluttering wings,
  A woe-worn ghaist I hameward glide.

Come, Winter, with thine angry howl,
  And raging bend the naked tree;
Thy gloom will soothe my cheerless soul
  When nature all is sad like me!

THE DEAN OF FACULTY.—A NEW BALLAD.

A fragment, first published in the "Reliques."

TUNE—*The Dragon of Wantley.*

DIRE was the hate at old Harlaw,
  That Scot to Scot did carry;
And dire the discord Langside saw,
  For beauteous, hapless Mary:
But Scot with Scot ne'er met so hot,
  Or were more in fury seen, Sir,
Than 'twixt Hal and Bob for the famous job—
  Who should be Faculty's Dean, Sir,

This Hal, for genius, wit, and lore,
  Among the first was number'd;

[1] Careful.—[2] Shuts the gate of his fold.

But pious Bob, 'mid learning's store,
    Commandment tenth remember'd.
Yet simple Bob the victory got,
    And wan his heart's desire;
Which shows that Heaven can boil the pot
    Though the Devil p ss in the fire.

Squire Hal besides had, in this case,
    Pretensions rather brassy,
For talents to deserve a place
    Are qualifications saucy;
So their worships of the Faculty,
    Quite sick of merit's rudeness,
Chose one who should owe it all, d' ye see,
    To their gratis grace and goodness.

As once on Pisgah purged was the sight
    Of a son of circumcision,
So may be, on this Pisgah height,
    Bob's purblind, mental vision:
Nay, Bobby's mouth may be open'd yet,
    Till for eloquence you hail him,
And swear he has the angel met
    That met the ass of Balaam.

JOHN BARLEYCORN.—A BALLAD.

This is partly composed on the plan of an old song known by the same name.

Therе were three kings into the east,
    Three kings both great and high,
An' they hae sworn a solemn oath
    John Barleycorn should die.

They took a plough and plough'd him down,
    Put clods upon his head,
And they hae sworn a solemn oath
    John Barleycorn was dead.

But the cheerful spring came kindly on,
    And showers began to fall;
John Barleycorn got up again,
    And sore surprised them all.

The sultry suns of summer came,
    And he grew thick and strong,
His head weel arm'd wi' pointed spears,
    That no one should him wrong.

The sober autumn enter'd mild,
    When he grew wan and pale;
His bending joints and drooping head
    Show'd he began to fail.

His color sicken'd more and more,
    He faded into age;
And then his enemies began
    To show their deadly rage.

They 've taen a weapon long and sharp,
    And cut him by the knee;
Then tied him fast upon a cart,
    Like a rogue for forgerie.

They laid him down upon his back,
    And cudgell'd him full sore:
They hung him up before the storm,
    And turn'd him o'er and o'er.

They fillèd up a darksome pit
    With water to the brim,
They heavèd in John Barleycorn,
    There let him sink or swim.

They laid him out upon the floor,
    To work him farther woe,
And still as signs of life appear'd,
    They toss'd him to and fro.

They wasted o'er a scorching flame
    The marrow of his bones;
But a miller used him worst of all,
    For he crush'd him between two stones.

And they hae taen his very heart's blood,
    And drank it round and round;
And still the more and more they drank,
    Their joy did more abound.

John Barleycorn was a hero bold
    Of noble enterprise,
For if you do but taste his blood,
    'Twill make your courage rise.

'Twill make a man forget his woe;
  'Twill heighten all his joy;
'Twill make the widow's heart to sing,
  Tho' the tear were in her eye.

Then let us toast John Barleycorn,
  Each man a glass in hand;
And may his great posterity
  Ne'er fail in old Scotland.

A BOTTLE AND A FRIEND.

First published in the "Reliques."

HERE's a bottle and an honest friend!
  What wad ye wish for mair, man?
Wha kens, before his life may end,
  What his share may be of care, man?

Then catch the moments as they fly,
  And use them as ye ought, man:
Believe me, happiness is shy,
  And comes not ay when sought, man.

WILLIE BREWED A PECK O' MAUT.

These verses were composed to celebrate a visit which the Poet and Allan
Masterton made to William Nichol, of the High-school, Edinburgh, who hap-
pened to be at Moffat during the autumn vacation. The air is by Masterton.

O WILLIE brew'd a peck o' maut,[1]
  And Rob and Allan cam to see;
Three blyther hearts that lee-lang[2] night,
  Ye wad na find in Christendie.[3]

We are na fou,[4] we're nae that fou,
  But just a drappie in our ee;
The cock may craw, the day may daw,[5]
  But ay we'll taste the barley-bree.[6]

Here are we met, three merry boys,
  Three merry boys I trow are we;
And monie a night we've merry been,
  And monie mae we hope to be!
    We are na fou, &c.

Malt.—[2] Live-long.—[3] Christendom.—[4] Drunk.—[5] Dawn.—[6] Juice.

It is the moon, I ken her horn,
  That's blinkin' in the lift[1] sae hie;
She shines sae bright to wyle[2] us hame;
  But by my sooth she'll wait a wee!
    We are na fou, &c.

Wha first shall rise to gang awa,
  A cuckold, coward loun is he!
Wha last beside his chair shall fa',
  He is the king amang us three!
    We are na fou, &c.

GUDEWIFE, COUNT THE LAWIN.

The following is one of the verses of the old Bacchanalian ditty which suggested this song to Burns:

"O, ilka day my wife tells me, that yill and brandy will ruin me,
But tho' gude drink should be my dead, I'se hae this written on my head—
'O gudewife, count the lawin, the lawin, the lawin,
O gudewife, count the lawin, an' bring a coggie mair.'"

GANE is the day, and mirk's[3] the night,
But we'll ne'er stray for faut o' light,
For ale and brandy's stars and moon,
And blude-red wine's the rising sun.

    Then, gudewife,[4] count the lawin,[5]
    The lawin, the lawin,
    Then, gudewife, count the lawin,
    And bring a coggie[6] mair.

There's wealth and ease for gentlemen,
And semple folk maun fecht[7] and fen';
But here we're a' in ae accord,
For ilka[8] man that's drunk's a lord.
    Then, gudewife, &c.

My coggie is a haly[9] pool,
That heals the wounds of care and dool;[10]
And pleasure is a wanton trout,
An' ye drink it a' ye'll find him out.
    Then, gudewife, &c.

[1] The sky.—[2] Beguile.—[3] Dark.—[4] The landlady, or mistress of the house.
—[5] The bill, or reckoning.—[6] A cup.—[7] Fight and struggle.—[8] Every.—
[9] Holy.—[10] Sorrow.

I'M OWRE YOUNG TO MARRY YET.

Of this song the chorus and second stanza are old.

I AM my mammie's ae bairn,[1]
  Wi' unco folk I weary, Sir;
And lying in a man's bed,
  I'm fley'd[2] wad mak me eerie, Sir.
    I'm owre young, I'm owre young,
      I'm owre young to marry yet;
    I'm owre young, 'twad be a sin
      To tak me frae my mammie yet.

My mammie coft[3] me a new gown,
  The kirk maun hae the gracing o't;
Were I to lie wi' you, kind Sir,
  I'm fear'd ye'd spoil the lacing o't.
    I'm owre young, &c.

Hallowmas is come and gane,
  The nights are lang in winter, Sir;
And you an' I in ae bed,
  In troth I dare na venture, Sir.
    I'm owre young, &c.

Fu' loud and shrill the frosty wind
  Blaws thro' the leafless timmer,[4] Sir;
But if ye come this gate[5] again,
  I'll aulder be gin simmer,[6] Sir.
    I'm owre young, &c.

THE LASS O' BALLOCHMYLE.

The scenery of this song was taken from real life. Burns had roved out as chance directed, in the favorite haunts of his Muse, on the banks of the Ayr, to view nature in all the gayety of the vernal year. In a corner of his prospect he spied one of the loveliest creatures that ever crowned a poetical landscape, or met a poet's eye. On his return home he composed the following verses in honor of her charms.

TUNE—*Miss Forbes's Farewell to Banff.*

'TWAS even—the dewy fields were green,
  On every blade the pearls hang;
The zephyr wanton'd round the bean
  And bore its fragrant sweets alang:

[1] Only child —[2] Afraid.—[3] Bought.—[4] Timber, trees.—[5] Way.—[6] I'll be older against summer.

In every glen the mavis sang,
  All nature listening seem'd the while,
Except where green-wood echoes rang,
  Amang the the bracs o' Ballochmyle.

With careless step I onward stray'd,
  My heart rejoiced in nature's joy,
When musing in a lonely glade,
  A maiden fair I chanced to spy;
Her look was like the morning's eye,
  Her air like nature's vernal smile;
Perfection whisper'd, passing by,
  Behold the lass o' Ballochmyle!

Fair is the morn in flowery May,
  And sweet is night in autumn mild,
When roving thro' the garden gay,
  Or wandering in a lonely wild:
But woman, nature's darling child!
  There all her charms she does compile;
Even there her other works are foil'd
  By the bonnie lass o' Ballochmyle.

Oh, had she been a country maid,
  And I the happy country swain,
Tho' shelter'd in the lowest shed
  That ever rose in Scotland's plain!
Thro' weary winter's wind and rain
  With joy, with rapture, I would toil;
And nightly to my bosom strain
  The bonnie lass o' Ballochmyle.

Then pride might climb the slippery steep,
  Where fame and honors lofty shine;
And thirst of gold might tempt the deep,
  Or downward seek the Indian mine:
Give me the cot below the pine,
  To tend the flocks or till the soil,
And every day have joys divine,
  With the bonnie lass o' Ballochmyle.

THE BRAES O' BALLOCHMYLE.

This song was written on the occasion of Sir John Whiteford leaving Ballochmyle. The Maria mentioned in the first stanza was the eldest daughter of that gentleman.

TUNE—*Miss Forbes's Farewell to Banff.*

THE Catrine woods were yellow seen,
    The flowers decay'd on Catrine lee;
Nae lav'rock sang on hillock green,
    But nature sicken'd on the ee.
Thro' faded groves Maria sang,
    Hersel in beauty's bloom the while,
And ay the wild-wood echoes rang,
    Fareweel the braes o' Ballochmyle!

Low in your wintry beds, ye flowers,
    Again ye'll flourish fresh and fair:
Ye birdies dumb, in withering bowers,
    Again ye'll charm the vocal air:
But here, alas! for me nae mair
    Shall birdie charm, or floweret smile;
Fareweel the bonnie banks of Ayr,
    Fareweel, fareweel, sweet Ballochmyle!

BONNIE LESLIE.

This song was composed on a charming Ayrshire girl, as she passed through Dumfries to England.

TUNE—*The collier's bonnie dochter.*

OH saw ye bonnie Leslie
    As she gaed o'er the border?
She's gane, like Alexander,
    To spread her conquests farther.

To see her is to love her,
    And love but her forever;
For Nature made her what she is,
    And ne'er made sic anither.

Thou art a queen, fair Leslie,
    Thy subjects we, before thee:
Thou art divine, fair Leslie,
    The hearts o' men adore thee.

The Deil he could na scaith[1] thee,
　Or aught that wad belang thee;
He 'd look into thy bonnie face,
　And say, "I canna wrang thee."

The Powers aboon[2] will tent[3] thee;
　Misfortune sha'na steer[4] thee;
Thou 'rt like themselves sae lovely,
　That ill they 'll ne'er let near thee.

Return again, fair Leslie!
　Return to Caledonia!
That we may brag, we hae a lass
　There 's nane again sae bonnie.

———— ——

ON A BANK OF FLOWERS, Etc.

Written for the "Museum" to the beautiful old melody "The lady of the
flowery field," included in Ritson's "Desiderata in Scottish Song," since
published in the Scots Magazine for Jan. 1802.

On a bank of flowers, in a summer day,
　For summer lightly drest,
The youthful, blooming Nelly lay,
　With love and sleep opprest:

When Willie, wandering through the wood,
Who for her favor oft had sued;
He gazed, he wish'd, he fear'd, he blush'd,
　And trembled where he stood.

Her closèd eyes, like weapons sheathed,
　Were seal'd in soft repose;
Her lips, still as she fragrant breathed,
　They richer dyed the rose.

The springing lilies sweetly prest,
Wild, wanton kiss'd her rival breast;
He gazed, he wish'd, he fear'd, he blush'd,
　His bosom ill at rest.

Her robes, light waving in the breeze,
　Her tender limbs embrace!
Her lovely form, her native ease,
　All harmony and grace!

[1] Injure.—[2] Above.—[3] Tend, guard.—[4] Molest.

Tumultuous tides his pulses roll,
A faltering, ardent kiss he stole;
He gazed, he wish'd, he fear'd, he blush'd,
And sigh'd his very soul!

As flies the partridge from the brake,
On fear-inspiréd wings;
So Nelly, starting, half awake,
Away affrighted springs:

But Willie follow'd—as he should,
He overtook her in the wood:
He vow'd, he pray'd, he found the maid
Forgiving all and good.

THE BANKS OF CREE.

The air of this song was composed by Lady Elizabeth Heron, of Heron.
The Cree is a beautiful romantic stream in Galloway.

HERE is the glen, and here the bower,
All underneath the birchen shade;
The village-bell has told the hour—
Oh what can stay my lovely maid?

'Tis not Maria's whispering call;
'Tis but the balmy-breathing gale,
Mixt with some warbler's dying fall,
The dewy star of eve to hail.

It is Maria's voice I hear!
So calls the wood-lark in the grove,
His little faithful mate to cheer;
At once 'tis music—and 'tis love!

And art thou come? and art thou true?
Oh welcome, dear, to love and me!
And let us all our vows renew,
Along the flowery banks of Cree.

YOUNG PEGGY.

This is one of the Poet's earliest compositions.   It is copied from a MS
book which he had before his first publication.—*Cromek*.

TUNE—*The last time I came owre the moor.*

YOUNG Peggy blooms our bonniest lass,
  Her blush is like the morning,
The rosy dawn, the springing grass,
  With pearly gems adorning.
Her eyes outshine the radiant beams
  That gild the passing shower,
And glitter o'er the crystal streams,
  And cheer each freshening flower.

Her lips more than the cherries bright,
  A richer dye has graced them;
They charm the admiring gazer's sight,
  And sweetly tempt to taste them.
Her smiles are like the evening mild,
  When feather'd pairs are courting,
And little lambkins wanton wild,
  In playful bands disporting.

Were fortune lovely Peggy's foe,
  Such sweetness would relent her;
As blooming spring unbends the brow
  Of savage, surly winter.
Detraction's eye no harm can join
  Her winning powers to lessen;
And spiteful envy grins in vain,
  The poison'd tooth to fasten.

Ye powers of honor, love, and truth,
  From every ill defend her;
Inspire the highly-favor'd youth
  The destinies intend her:
Still fan the sweet connubial flame,
  Responsive in each bosom;
And bless the dear parental name
  With many a filial blossom.

THENIEL MENZIE'S BONNIE MARY.

This song was communicated by Burns to the Musical Museum, with a mark, denoting it to be an old song with alterations or additions. As he published "Auld Lang Syne," and several of his songs, in a similar way, and as the *new* of "Bonnie Mary" cannot be known from the *old*, there is reason to believe it one of his own songs.

In coming by the brig of Dye,[1]
  At Dartlet we a blink did tarry;
As day was dying in the sky,
  We drank a health to bonnie Mary.
    Theniel Menzie's bonnie Mary,
    Theniel Menzie's bonnie Mary;
    Charlie Gregor tint his plaidie,
    In wooing Theniel's bonnie Mary.

Her een sae bright, her brow sae white,
  Her haffet locks as brown 's a berry,
An' ay they dimpled wi' a smile,
  The rosie cheeks o' bonnie Mary.
    Theniel Menzie's bonnie Mary,
    Theniel Menzie's bonnie Mary;
    She charm'd my heart an' my twa een,
    Theniel Menzie's bonnie Mary.

We lap an' danced the lee-lang night,
  Till piper lads were wan an' weary,
Yet rosie as the rising sun
  Was Theniel Menzie's bonnie Mary.
    Theniel Menzie's bonnie Mary,
    Theniel Menzie's bonnie Mary;
    Oh, sweet as light, and kind as night,
    Was Theniel Menzie's bonnie Mary.

LASSIE WI' THE LINT-WHITE LOCKS.

"This song," says Burns, has at least the merit of being a regular pastoral. The vernal morn, the summer noon, the autumnal evening, and the winter night, are all regularly rounded."

Tune—*Rothiemurchus' Rant.*

Lassie wi' the lint-white locks,
  Bonnie lassie, artless lassie,
Wilt thou wi' me tent the flocks?
  Wilt thou be my dearie O?

[1] A small river in Kincardineshire, near the birthplace of the Poet's father.

Now nature cleeds[1] the flowery lea,
And a' is young and sweet like thee;
Oh wilt thou share its joys wi' me,
    And say thou 'lt be my dearie O?
    Lassie, &c.

And when the welcome simmer-shower
Has cheer'd ilk[2] drooping little flower,
We 'll to the breathing woodbine bower,
    At sultry noon, my dearie O.
    Lassie, &c.

When Cynthia lights, wi' silver ray,
The weary shearer's hameward way,
Thro' yellow waving fields we 'll stray,
    And talk o' love, my dearie O.
    Lassie, &c.

And when the howling wintry blast
Disturbs my lassie's midnight rest;
Enclaspéd to my faithfu' breast,
    I 'll comfort thee, my dearie O.
    Lassie, &c.

O WAT YE WHA 'S IN YON TOWN.

The subject of this song was a lady, who afterwards died at Lisbon. Burns writes in the character of her husband. She was an accomplished and lovely woman, and worthy of this beautiful strain of sensibility.

Tune—I'll gang nae mair to yon town.

Oh wat[3] ye wha 's in yon town,
    Ye see the e'enin' sun upon?
The fairest dame 's in yon town,
    That e'enin' sun is shining on.

Now haply down yon gay green shaw,
    She wanders by yon spreading tree:
How blest ye flowers that round her blaw,
    Ye catch the glances o' her ee!

How blest ye birds that round her sing,
    And welcome in the blooming year;
And doubly welcome be the spring,
    The season to my Lucy dear.

Clothes.—[2] Every.—[3] To wot.

The sun blinks blythe on yon town,
   And on yon bonnie braes of Ayr;
But my delight in yon town,
   And dearest bliss, is Lucy fair.

Without my love, not a' the charms
   O' Paradise could yield me joy;
But gie me Lucy in my arms,
   And welcome Lapland's dreary sky.

My cave wad be a lover's bower,
   Tho' raging winter rent the air;
And she a lovely little flower,
   That I wad tent and shelter there.

Oh sweet is she in yon town,
   Yon sinking sun 's gaun down upon;
A fairer than 's in yon town,
   His setting beams ne'er shone upon.

If angry Fate is sworn my foe,
   And suffering I am doom'd to bear;
I careless quit aught else below,
   But spare me, spare me, Lucy dear.

For while life's dearest blood is warm,
   Ae thought frae her shall ne'er depart;
And she—as fairest is her form,
   She has the truest, kindest heart.

THE BIRKS OF ABERFELDY.

This is written in the measure of an old Scottish song of the same name,
from which Burns has borrowed nothing but the chorus. He composed it
while standing under the Falls of Aberfeldy, near Moness.

Bonnie lassie, will ye go,
Will ye go, will ye go--
Bonnie lassie, will ye go
   To the birks[1] of Aberfeldy?

Now simmer blinks on flowery braes,
And o'er the crystal streamlet plays,

[1] Birch-trees.

Come let us spend the lightsome days
 In the birks of Aberfeldy.
  Bonnie lassie, &c.

While o'er their heads the hazels hing,[1]
The little birdies blythely sing,
Or lightly flit on wanton wing,
 In the birks of Aberfeldy.
  Bonnie lassie, &c.

The braes[2] ascend like lofty wa's,
The foaming stream deep-roaring fa's,
O'erhung wi' fragrant spreading shaws,
 The birks of Aberfeldy.
  Bonnie lassie, &c.

The hoary cliffs are crown'd wi' flowers,
White o'er the linns[3] the burnie pours,
And, rising, weets[4] wi' misty showers
 The birks of Aberfeldy.
  Bonnie lassie, &c.

Let Fortune's gifts at random flee,
They ne'er shall draw a wish frae me,
Supremely blest wi' love and thee,
 In the birks of Aberfeldy,
  Bonnie lassie, &c.

O LET ME IN THIS AE[5] NIGHT.

You have displayed great address in your song, 'Let me in this ae night.' Her answer is excellent, and at the same time takes away the indelicacy that otherwise would have attached to his entreaties. I like the song as it now stands very much." *Thomson to Burns.*

O Lassie, art thou sleeping yet?
Or art thou waukin', I would wit?
For love has bound me hand and fit,[6]
 For I would fain be in, jo.[7]

  O let me in this ae night,
   This ae, ae, ae night,
  For pity's sake, this ae night,
   O rise and let me in, jo.

---

[1] Hang.—[2] Slope of a hill.—[3] A precipice.—[4] Wets.—[5] One.—[6] Foot.—[7] Sweetheart

Thou hear'st the winter wind and weet,[1]
Nae star blinks thro' the driving sleet;
Take pity on my weary feet,
    And shield me frae the rain, jo,
      O let me in, &c.

The bitter blast that round me blaws
Unheeded howls, unheeded fa's;
The cauldness o' thy heart 's the cause
    Of a' my grief and pain, jo.
      O let me in, &c.

HER ANSWER.

O TELL na me o' wind and rain,
Upbraid na me wi' cauld disdain!
Gae back the gate[2] ye cam again,
    I winna let you in, jo.

    I tell you now this ae night,
      This ae, ae, ae night;
    And, ance for a', this ae night,
      I winna let you in, jo.

The snellest[3] blast at mirkest[4] hours,
That round the pathless wanderer pours,
Is nocht[5] to what poor she endures,
    That 's trusted faithless man, jo.
      I tell you now, &c.

The sweetest flower that deck'd the mead,
Now trodden like the vilest weed;
Let simple maid the lesson read,
    The weird[6] may be her ain, jo.
      I tell you now, &c.

The bird that charm'd his summer-day,
Is now the cruel fowler's prey;
Let witless, trusting woman say
    How aft her fate's the same, jo.
      I tell you now, &c.

[1] Rain.—[2] Way.—[3] Bitterest.—[4] Darkest.—[5] Naught.—[6] Fate.

ADDRESS TO THE WOOD-LARK.

Written for Thomson's Collection in May, 1795. "Caledonia," "O whistle
an' I'll come to you, my lad," "This is no my ain house," &c., were also
productions of this period.

TUNE—*Where'll bonnie Annie lie, or Loch-Erroch side.*

O STAY, sweet warbling wood-lark, stay,
Nor quit for me the trembling spray,
A hapless lover courts thy lay,
    Thy soothing fond complaining.
Again, again that tender part,
That I may catch thy melting art;
For surely that wad touch her heart,
    Wha kills me wi' disdaining.

Say, was thy little mate unkind,
And heard thee as the careless wind?
Oh, nocht but love and sorrow join'd,
    Sic notes o' woe could wanken.
Thou tells o' never-ending care;
O' speechless grief, and dark despair;
For pity's sake, sweet bird, nae mair!
    Or my poor heart is broken!

THE ROSE-BUD.

This song was written on Miss Jenny Cruickshanks, only child of William
Cruickshanks, of the High-school, Edinburgh.

TUNE—*The Shepherd's Wife.*

A ROSE-BUD by my early walk,
A-down a corn-inclosèd bawk,[1]
Sae gently bent its thorny stalk,
    All on a dewy morning.

Ere twice the shades o' dawn are fled,
In a' its crimson glory spread,
And drooping rich the dewy head,
    It scents the early morning.

Within the bush, her covert nest,
A little linnet fondly prest,
The dew sat chilly on her breast
    Sae early in the morning.

[1] A narrow footpath across a field.

She soon shall see her tender brood,
The pride, the pleasure o' the wood,
Amang the fresh green leaves bedew'd,
    Awake the early morning.

So thou, dear bird, young Jenny fair,
On trembling string or vocal air,
Shall sweetly pay the tender care
    That tents thy early morning.

So thou, sweet rose-bud, young and gay,
Shall beauteous blaze upon the day,
And bless the parent's evening ray ,
    That watch'd thy early morning.

O TIBBIE, I HAE SEEN THE DAY.

Burns wrote this song when he was about seventeen years of age.

TUNE—*Invercauld's Reel.*

O Tibbie, I hae seen the day
Ye wad na been sae shy ;
For laik[1] o' gear ye lightly me,
But, troth, I care na by.

YESTREEN I met you on the moor,
Ye spak na, but gaed by like stoure ;[2]
Ye geck[3] at me because I 'm poor,
    But fient[4] a hair care I.
      O Tibbie, &c.

I doubt na, lass, but ye may think,
Because ye hae the name o' clink,[5]
That ye can please me at a wink,
    Whene'er ye like to try.
      O Tibbie, &c.

But sorrow tak him that 's sae mean,
Altho' his pouch[6] o' coin were clean,
Wha follows onie saucy quean
    That looks sae proud and high.
      O Tibbie, &c.

[1] Lack.—[2] Dust in motion.—[3] Toss the head in scorn.—[4] A petty oath of negation.—[5] Cash.—[6] Pocket.

Altho' a lad were e'er so smart,
If that he want the yellow dirt,
Ye 'll cast your head anither airt,[1]
  And answer him fu' dry.
    O Tibbie, &c.

But if he hae the name o' gear,
Ye 'll fasten to him like a brier,
Tho' hardly he, for sense or lear,[2]
  Be better than the kye.[3]
    O Tibbie, &c.

But Tibbie, lass, tak my advice,
Your daddie's gear maks you sae nice:
The deil a ane wad spier[4] your price,
  Were ye as poor as I.
    O Tibbie, &c.

There lives a lass in yonder park,
I wad na gie her in her sark,
For thee wi' a' thy thousand mark—
  Ye need na look sae high.
    O Tibbie, &c.

CASTLE GORDON.

This song was written by Burns when on his tour to the Highlands, and transmitted to Gordon Castle as an acknowledgment of the hospitality he had received from the noble family.

Tune—Morag.

Streams that glide in orient plains,
Never bound by winter's chains;
Glowing here on golden sands,
There commix'd with foulest stains
From tyranny's empurpled bands:
These, their richly-gleaming waves,
I leave to tyrants and their slaves;
Give me the stream that sweetly laves
  The banks by Castle-Gordon.

Spicy forests, ever gay,
Shading from the burning ray

---

[1] Quarter.—[2] Learning.—[3] Cows.—[4] Inquire.

Helpless wretches sold to toil,
Or the ruthless native's way,
Bent on slaughter, blood, and spoil:
Woods that ever verdant wave,
I leave the tyrant and the slave:
Give me the groves that lofty brave
    The storms, by Castle-Gordon.

Wildly here, without control,
Nature reigns and rules the whole;
· In that sober pensive mood,
Dearest to the feeling soul,
She plants the forest, pours the flood:
Life's poor day I 'll musing rave,
And find at night a sheltering cave,
    Where waters flow and wild-woods wave,
    By bonnie Castle-Gordon.

OH, FOR ANE-AND-TWENTY, TAM.

This excellent lyric was written for the "Museum." The air is from
an old and very indelicate song, which is now justly forgotten

Tune—*The Moudiewort.*

An' oh for ane-and-twenty, Tam !
    An' hey, sweet ane-and-twenty, Tam !
I 'll learn my kin[1] a rattlin' sang,
    Gin I saw ane-and-twenty, Tam !

THEY snool[2] me sair, and haud me down,
    An' gar me look like bluntie,[3] Tam !
But three short years will soon wheel roun',
    An' then comes ane-and-twenty, Tam !
        An' oh, &c.

A gleib o' land, a claut[4] o' gear,
    Was left me by my auntie, Tam ;
At kith[5] or kin I need na spier,[6]
    Gin I were ane-and-twenty, Tam !
        An' oh, &c.

[1] Kindred, relations.—[2] Oppress.—[3] A sniveller, a stupid person.—[4] Good
portion.—[5] Kindred.—[6] Ask.

They 'll hae me wed a wealthy coof,[1]
  Though I mysel hae plenty, Tam;
But, hear'st thou, laddie—there 's my loof,[2]
  I 'm thine at ane-and-twenty, Tam!
    An' oh, &c.

THE VISION.

This fragment is founded on a poem, bearing the same title, written by Allan Ramsay. The scenery, however, is taken from nature. The poet is supposed to be musing on the banks of the river Cluden, by the ruins of Lincluden Abbey, founded in the twelfth century, in the reign of Malcolm IV

TUNE—*Cumnock psalms.*

As I stood by yon roofless tower,
  Where the wa'-flower scents the dewy air,
Where the howlet mourns in her ivy bower,
  And tells the midnight moon her care:

The winds were laid, the air was still,
  The stars they shot alang the sky;
The fox was howling on the hill,
  And the distant-echoing glens reply.

The stream, adown its hazelly path,
  Was rushing by the ruin'd wa's,
Hasting to join the sweeping Nith,
  Whase distant roaring swells and fa's.

The cauld blue north was streaming forth
  Her lights wi' hissing eerie din;[3]
Athort[4] the lift[5] they start and shift,
  Like fortune's favors, tint as win.[6]

By heedless chance I turn'd mine eyes,
  And by the moonbeam shook to see
A stern and stalwart[7] ghaist arise,
  Attired as minstrels wont to be.

Had I a statue been o' stane,
  His daurin'[8] look had daunted me;
And on his bonnet graved was plain,
  The sacred posy—LIBERTIE!

- Blockhead.—[2] Palm of the hand.—[3] Frightful noise.—[4] Athwart.—[5] Sky
—[6] Lost as soon as won.—[7] Strong.—[8] Daring.

And frae[1] his harp sic[2] strains did flow,
    Might roused the slumbering dead to hear;
But oh, it was a tale of woe,
    As ever met a Briton's ear!

He sang wi' joy his former day,
    He weeping wail'd his latter times;
But what he said it was nae play,
    I winna venture 't in my rhymes.

O BONNIE WAS YON ROSY BRIER.

The fine old air to which this song is written, has also been supplied with
words by Mr. Jamison, the editor of "Old Scottish Ballads and Songs" in
2 vols. 8vo.—Edin. 1806.

TUNE—*I wish my love was in a mire.*

O BONNIE was yon rosy brier,
    That blooms sae far frae haunt o' man;
And bonnie she, and ah, how dear!
    It shaded frae the e'enin' sun.

Yon rose-buds in the morning dew,
    How pure amang the leaves sae green!
But purer was the lover's vow
    They witness'd in their shade yestreen.

All in its rude and prickly bower,
    That crimson rose, how sweet and fair!
But love is far a sweeter flower
    Amid life's thorny path o' care.

The pathless wild, and wimpling burn,
    Wi' Chloris in my arms, be mine;
And I, the world, nor wish, nor scorn,
    Its joys and griefs alike resign.

CAN I CEASE TO CARE?
TUNE—*Ay waukin' O.*

Long, long the night,
    Heavy comes the morrow,
While my soul's delight
    Is on her bed of sorrow.

[1] From.—[2] Such.

CAN I cease to care,
  Can I cease to languish,
While my darling fair
  Is on the couch of anguish?
    Long, &c.

Every hope is fled,
  Every fear is terror;
Slumber even I dread,
  Every dream is horror.
    Long, &c.

Hear me, Powers divine!
  Oh, in pity hear me!
Take aught else of mine,
  But my Chloris spare me!
    Long, &c.

CLARINDA.

The subject of this song was a young widow who encouraged a friendly
correspondence with Burns.

CLARINDA, mistress of my soul,
  The measured time is run!
The wretch beneath the dreary pole,
  So marks his latest sun.

To what dark cave of frozen night
  Shall poor Sylvander hie;
Deprived of thee, his life and light,
  The sun of all his joy?

We part—but by these precious drops
  That fill thy lovely eyes!
No other light shall guide my steps
  Till thy bright beams arise.

She, the fair sun of all her sex,
  Has blest my glorious day:
And shall a glimmering planet fix
  My worship to its ray?

JOCKEY'S TAEN THE PARTING KISS.

Written to the tune and in the manner of the old song, beginning—
"Come kiss wi' me, come clap wi' me,
An' sail nae mair the saut,[1] saut sea."

Jockey's taen the parting kiss,
  Owre the mountains he is gane,
And with him is a' my bliss,
  Naught but griefs with me remain.

Spare my love, ye winds that blaw,
  Plashy sleets and beating rain!
Spare my love, thou feathery snaw,
  Drifting owre the frozen plain!

When the shades of evening creep
  Owre the day's fair, gladsome ee,
Sound and safely may he sleep,
  Sweetly blythe his waukening be!

He will think on her he loves,
  Fondly he'll repeat her name;
For where'er he distant roves,
  Jockey's heart is still at hame.

THE BONNIE LAD THAT'S FAR AWA.

The original song to the tune of which the following is written, will be found in a volume of songs printed at Edinburgh, about 1670, black-letter, beginning—

'The Elphin Knight sits on yon hill,
  Ba, ba, ba, lilli ba,
He blew his horn baith loud an' shrill,
  The wind has blawn my plaid awa.'

TUNE—*Owre the hills and far awa.*

Oh how can I be blythe and glad,
  Or how can I gang brisk and braw,[2]
When the bonnie lad that I lo'e best
  Is owre the hills and far awa?

It's no the frosty winter wind,
  It's no the driving drift and snaw;
But ay the tear comes in my ee,
  To think o' him that's far awa.

[1] Salt.—[2] Fine.

My father pat[1] me frae[2] his door,
   My friends they hae disown'd me a ;
But I hae ane will tak my part,
   The bonnie lad that 's far awa.

A pair o' gloves he gave to me,
   And silken snoods[3] he gave me twa;
And I will wear them for his sake,
   The bonnie lad that 's far awa.

The weary winter soon will pass,
   And spring will cleed[4] the birken shaw ;[5]
And my sweet babie will be born,
   And he 'll come hame that 's far awa.

GREEN GROW THE RASHES.

This is the first song that Burns contributed to Johnson's Museum of Scottish Songs, a work of great merit, extending to five 8vo. volumes, commenced in 1787, and concluded in 1794. Besides many original contributions to that work, upwards of one hundred and fifty of the old songs and ballads inserted in it bear traces of his hand

Green grow the rashes, O !
Green grow the rashes, O !
The sweetest hours that e'er I spend
Are spent amang the lasses, O !

THERE 's naught but care on every han',
   In every hour that passes, O ;
What signifies the life o' man,
   An' 'twere na for the lasses, O !
     Green grow, &c.

The warly[6] race may riches chase,
   And riches still will fly them, O ;
And tho' at last they catch them fast,
   Their hearts can ne'er enjoy them, O !
     Green grow, &c.

But gie[7] me a cannie[8] hour at e'en,
   My arms about my dearie, O ;
An' warly cares, an' warly men,
   May a' gae tapsalteerie,[9] O !
     Green grow, &c.

---

[1] Put. [2] From.—[3] Ribbons for binding the hair.—[4] Clothe.—[5] Small wood —[6] Worldly.—[7] Give.—[8] Convenient.—[9] Topsy-turvy.

For you sae douce,[1] ye sneer at this,
  Ye 're naught but senseless asses, O;
The wisest man the warl' e'er saw,
  He dearly loved the lasses, O!
    Green grow, &c.

Auld Nature swears, the lovely dears,
  Her noblest work she classes, O;
Her 'prentice han' she tried on man,
  And then she made the lasses, O!
    Green grow, &c.

BONNIE ANN.

Burns composed this song out of compliment to Miss Ann Masterton, daughter of his friend Allan Masterton, author of the air of "Strathallan's Lament" "Willie brewed a peck o' maut," &c.

YE gallants bright I red[2] you right,
  Beware o' bonnie Ann;
Her comely face sae fu' o' grace,
  Your heart she will trepan.
Her een sae bright, like stars by night,
  Her skin is like the swan;
Sae gimply laced her genty[3] waist,
  That sweetly ye might span.

Youth, grace, and love, attendant move,
  And pleasure leads the van:
In a' their charms, and conquering arms,
  They wait on bonnie Ann.
The captive bands may chain the hands,
  But love enslaves the man;
Ye gallants braw, I red you a',
  Beware o' bonnie Ann.

UP IN THE MORNING EARLY.

The chorus of this song is old.

Up in the morning 's no for me,
  Up in the morning early;
When a' the hills are cover'd wi' snaw,
  I'm sure it 's winter fairly.

[1] Sober, prudent.—[2] Counsel.—[3] Elegantly formed.

CAULD blaws the wind frae east to west,
  The drift[1] is driving sairly;
Sae loud and shill 's[2] I hear the blast
  I 'm sure it 's winter fairly.
      Up in the morning, &c.

The birds sit chittering in the thorn,
  A' day they fare but sparely;
And lang 's the night frae e'en to morn,
  I 'm sure it 's winter fairly.
      Up in the morning, &c.

MY NANNIE, O.

In the earliest editions of this song the Stinchar was said to be Nannie's native stream; but afterwards the Poet replaced it with Lugar, for what reason he has not told us. Perhaps he had a similar one for changing his own name from Burness to Burns.

BEHIND yon hills where Lugar flows,
  'Mang moors and mosses many, O,
The wintry sun the day has closed,
  And I 'll awa to Nannie, O.
The westlin' wind blaws loud an' shill;
  The night 's baith mirk[3] and rainy, O;
But I 'll get my plaid, an' out I 'll steal,
  An' owre the hills to Nannie, O.

My Nannie 's charming, sweet, an' young;
  Nae artfu' wiles to win ye, O;
May ill befa' the flattering tongue
  That wad beguile my Nannie, O;
Her face is fair, her heart is true,
  As spotless as she 's bonnie, O;
The opening gowan[4] wet wi' dew,
  Nae purer is than Nannie, O.

A country lad is my degree,
  An' few there be that ken[5] me, O;
But what care I how few they be,
  I 'm welcome ay to Nannie, O.

[1] Drifted snow.—[2] Shrill.—[3] Dark.—[4] Wild daisy.—[5] Know

SONGS AND BALLADS.

432

My riches a' 's my penny-fee,[1]
  And I maun guide it cannie,[2] O;
But warl's gear[3] ne'er troubles me,
  My thoughts are a' my Nannie, O.

Our auld gudeman delights to view
  His sheep an' kye thrive bonnie, O;
But I'm as blythe that hauds his pleugh,
  An' has nae care but Nannie, O.
Come weal, come woe, I care na by,
  I'll tak what Heaven will sen' me, O;
Nae ither care in life hae I,
  But live, an' love my Nannie, O.

OH WHISTLE, AND I'LL COME TO YOU, MY LAD.

The humor and fancy of "Whistle, an' I'll come to you, my lad," will render it nearly as great a favorite as Duncan Gray. These songs of yours will descend with the music to the latest posterity.—*Thomson to Burns.*

Oh whistle, and I'll come to you, my lad,
Oh whistle, and I'll come to you, my lad,
Tho' father and mither and a' should gae mad,
Oh whistle, and I'll come to you, my lad.

But warily tent,[4] when ye come to court me,
And come na unless the back-yett[5] be a-jee;
Syne[6] up the back-style, and let naebody see,
And come as ye were na comin' to me:
And come as ye were na comin' to me.
    Oh whistle, &c.

At kirk, or at market, whene'er ye meet me,
Gang by me as though that ye cared na a flee:
But steal me a blink o' your bonnie black ee,
Yet look as ye were na looking at me:
Yet look as ye were na looking at me.
    Oh whistle, &c.

Ay vow and protest that ye care na for me,
And whiles ye may lightly[7] my beauty a wee;[8]

---

[1] The wages earned and paid half-yearly, or yearly, to servants.—[2] Dexterously.—[3] Worldly riches.—[4] Heed.—[5] Gate.—[6] Then.—[7] Sneer at.—[8] Little.

37

But court na anither, tho' jokin' ye be,
For fear that she wyle' your fancy frae me:
For fear that she wyle your fancy frae me.
    Oh whistle, &c.

OH WERE MY LOVE YON LILAC FAIR.

The two last stanzas of this song are old.   Burns prefixed the two first.

TUNE—*Hughie Graham.*

Oh were my love yon lilac fair,
  Wi' purple blossom to the spring;
And I a bird to shelter there,
  When wearied on my little wing:

How I wad mourn when it was torn,
  By autumn wild and winter rude!
But I wad sing, on wanton wing,
  When youthfu' May its bloom renew'd.

Oh gin² my love were yon red rose,
  That grows upon the castle wa',
And I mysel a drap o' dew,
  Into her bonnie breast to fa';

Oh there beyond expression blest,
  I 'd feast on beauty a' the night;
Seal'd on her silk-saft faulds to rest,
  Till fley'd³ awa by Phœbus' light.

THIS IS NO MY AIN LASSIE.

The chorus of the old song, to the air of which this beautiful lyric is
written is curious :

    " This is nae my ain house,
      I ken by the biggin o 't—
    Bread an' cheese are the door cheeks,
      An' pancakes the riggin' o 't.—"

TUNE—*This is no my ain house.*

Oh this is no my ain¹ lassie,
  Fair though the lassie be;
Oh weel I ken my ain lassie,
  Kind love is in her ee.

¹ Beguile.—² If.—³ Scared —⁴ Own.

I see a form, I see a face,
Ye weel may wi' the fairest place:
It wants, to me, the witching grace,
 The kind love that 's in her ee.
  Oh this is no, &c.

She 's bonnie, blooming, straight, and tall,
And lang has had my heart in thrall;
And ay it charms my very saul,
 The kind love that 's in her ee.
  Oh this is no, &c.

A thief sae pawkie[1] is my Jean,
To steal a blink by a' unseen;
But gleg[2] as light are lovers' een,
 When kind love is in the ee.
  Oh this is no, &c.

It may escape the courtly sparks,
It may escape the learnéd clerks;
But weel the watching lover marks
 The kind love that 's in her ee.
  Oh this is no, &c.

THE DUMFRIES VOLUNTEERS.

Burns was a member of this corps. He composed the following verses to stimulate their patriotism. For though he deplored the corruptions in the administration of government at home, he was unwilling to exchange even them for foreign domination.

Tune—Push about the jorum.

Does haughty Gaul invasion threat?
 Then let the louns[3] beware, Sir;
There 's wooden walls upon our seas,
 And volunteers on shore, Sir.
The Nith shall rin to Corsincon,[4]
 And Criffel[5] sink in Solway,
Ere we permit a foreign foe
 On British ground to rally!

---

[1] Cunning.—[2] Quick.—[3] Fellows, ragamuffins.—[4] A high hill at the source of the Nith.—[5] A high mountain at the mouth of the same river.

Oh, let us not, like snarling tykes,[1]
   In wrangling be divided;
Till slap come in an unco loon,[2]
   And wi' a rung[3] decide it.
Be Britain still to Britain true,
   Amang oursels united;
For never but by British hands
   Maun British wrangs be righted.

The kettle o' the kirk and state,
   Perhaps a claut may fail in 't;
But deil a foreign tinker loon
   Shall ever ca' a nail in 't;
Our fathers' blude the kettle bought,
   And wha would dare to spoil it,
By heaven, the sacrilegious dog
   Shall fuel be to boil it!

The wretch that wad a tyrant own,
   And the wretch (his true-born brother)
Who 'd set the mob aboon the throne,
   May they be d—d together!
Who will not sing "God save the king,"
   Shall hang as high 's the steeple;
But, while we sing "God save the king,"
   We 'll ne'er forget the people.

THE UNION.

At a meeting of a select party of gentlemen to celebrate the birth-day of the lineal descendant of the Scottish race of kings, the late unfortunate Prince Charles Stuart, Burns produced and sung the following song.

Tune—*Such a parcel of rogues in a nation.*

Fareweel to a' our Scottish fame,
   Fareweel our ancient glory!
Fareweel even to the Scottish name
   Sae fam'd in martial story!
Now Sark rins o'er the Solway sands,
   And Tweed rins to the ocean,
To mark where England's province stands;
   Such a parcel of rogues in a nation!

[1] Dogs.—[2] Strange fellow, a foreigner.—[3] Cudgel.

What force or guile could not subdue,
Through many warlike ages,
Is wrought now by a coward few,
For hireling traitors' wages.
The English steel we could disdain,
Secure in valor's station,
But English gold has been our bane:
Such a parcel of rogues in a nation.

Oh would or I had seen the day
That treason thus could sell us,
My auld gray head had lien in clay,
Wi' Bruce and loyal Wallace!
But pith and power, till my last hour,
I'll mak this declaration,
We're bought and sold for English gold:
Such a parcel of rogues in a nation!

THE WINDING NITH.

The Gaelic air to which this song is adapted is said to have been composed by Roderic Dall, an itinerant musician, formerly well known in the Highlands of Perthshire. He died about 1780, at a very advanced age.

TUNE—*Robie Donna Gorach.*

THE Thames flows proudly to the sea,
Where royal cities stately stand;
But sweeter flows the Nith to me,
Where Cummins ance had high command;
When shall I see that honor'd land,
That winding stream I love so dear?
Must wayward Fortune's adverse hand
Forever, ever keep me here?

How lovely, Nith, thy fruitful vales,
Where spreading hawthorns gayly bloom!
How sweetly wind thy sloping dales,
Where lambkins wanton thro' the broom!
Tho' wandering, now, must be my doom,
Far from thy bonnie banks and braes,
May there my latest hours consume,
Amang the friends of early days!

MY HEART IS SAIR.

Two additional verses were written for this song by the late Mr. R. A.
Smith, which are now printed along with it in most collections. The new
verses are not unworthy to accompany the old.

TUNE—*The Highland Watch's farewell.*

My heart is sair, I dare na tell,
    My heart is sair for somebody;
I could wake a winter night,
    For the sake o' somebody.
        Oh-hon! for somebody!
        Oh-hey! for somebody!
    I could range the world around,
    For the sake o' somebody.

Ye Powers that smile on virtuous love,
    Oh sweetly smile on somebody!
Frae ilka danger keep him free,
    And send me safe my somebody.
        Oh-hon! for somebody!
        Oh-hey! for somebody!
    I wad do—what wad I not?
    For the sake o' somebody!

DELIA.—AN ODE.

This ode was sent to the publisher of the London Star —in which paper it
first appeared, with the following letter:

"MR. PRINTER,—If the productions of a simple ploughman can merit a
place in the same paper with Sylvester Otway,1 and the other favorites of
the Muse, who illuminate the Star with the lustre of genius, your insertion
of the inclosed trifle will be succeeded by future communications from
                                "Yours, &c.,   R. BURNS.
    " ELLISLAND, near Dumfries, May 18, 1789."

FAIR the face of orient day,
    Fair the tints of opening rose;
But fairer still my Delia dawns,
    More lovely far her beauty blows.

The assumed name of a Mr. Oswald, an officer in the army, who fre
quently contributed verses to the Star newspaper.

Sweet the lark's wild-warbling lay,
   Sweet the tinkling rill to hear;
But, Delia, more delightful still
   Steal thine accents on mine ear.

The flower-enamor'd busy bee
   The rosy banquet loves to sip;
Sweet the streamlet's limpid lapse
   To the sun-brown'd Arab's lip;

But, Delia, on thy balmy lips
   Let me, no vagrant insect, rove;
Oh let me steal one liquid kiss;
   For, oh! my soul is parch'd by love!

COME, LET ME TAKE THEE TO MY BREAST.

This and the five following songs were addressed to Jean Armour, afterwards Mrs. Burns.

TUNE—*Kauld Kail.*

COME, let me take thee to my breast,
   And pledge we ne'er shall sunder;
And I shall spurn, as vilest dust,
   The warld's wealth and grandeur:

And do I hear my Jeanie own
   That equal transports move her?
I ask for dearest life alone,
   That I may live to love her.

Thus in my arms, wi' a' thy charms,
   I clasp my countless treasure;
I'll seek nae mair o' heaven to share,
   Than sic a moment's pleasure:

And by thy een, sae bonnie blue,
   I swear I'm thine forever!
And on thy lips I seal my vow,
   And break it shall I never!

I'LL AY CA' IN BY YON TOWN.

I'll ay ca'[1] in by yon town
   And by yon garden green again;
I'll ay ca' in by yon town,
   And see my bonnie Jean again.

There's nane sall ken,[2] there's nane sall guess,
   What brings me back the gate again,
But she, my fairest, faithfu' lass;
   And stowlins[3] we sall meet again.

She'll wander by the aiken[4]-tree,
   When trystin'-time draws near again;
And when her lovely form I see,
   Oh, haith, she's doubly dear again.

THE RANTING DOG THE DADDIE O 'T.

Burns says, "I composed this song pretty early in life, and sent it to a young girl, a very particular acquaintance of mine, who was at that time under a cloud."

Tune—East neuk o' Fife.

O wha my baby clouts[5] will buy?
Wha will tent[6] me when I cry?
Wha will kiss me whare I lie?
   The rantin' dog the daddie o 't.

Wha will own he did the faut?[7]
Wha will buy my groanin'-maut?[8]
Wha will tell me how to ca't?
   The rantin' dog the daddie o 't.

When I mount the creepie-chair,[9]
Wha will sit beside me there?
Gie me Rob, I seek nae mair,
   The rantin' dog the daddie o 't.

Wha will crack to me my lane?[10]
Wha will mak me fidgin' fain?
Wha will kiss me owre again?
   The rantin' dog the daddie o 't.

[1] Call.—[2] Shall know.—[3] In secret.—[4] Oak.—[5] Clothes.—[6] Heed.—[7] Fault.—[8] Malt.—[9] Stool of repentance.—[10] Talk to me in secret.

OF A' THE AIRTS THE WIND CAN BLAW.

This song was written in honor of Mrs. Burns, during the honey-moon.

TUNE—*Miss Admiral Gordon's Strathspey.*

OF a' the airts[1] the wind can blaw,
    I dearly like the west;
For there the bonnie lassie lives,
    The lassie I lo'e best:
There wild-woods grow, and rivers row,[2]
    And monie a hill between;
But day and night my fancy's flight
    Is ever wi' my Jean.

I see her in the dewy flowers,
    I see her sweet and fair:
I hear in the tunefu' birds,
    I hear her charm the air:
There's not a bonnie flower that springs
    By fountain, shaw, or green,
There's not a bonnie bird that sings,
    But minds me o' my Jean.

OH, WERE I ON PARNASSUS' HILL.

This song was also written in honor of Mrs. Burns, about the same time as the preceding.

TUNE—*My love is lost to me.*

OH, were I on Parnassus' hill!
Or had of Helicon my fill;
That I might catch poetic skill,
    To sing how dear I love thee.
But Nith maun be my Muse's well,
My Muse maun be thy bonnie sel';
On Corsincon I'll glower[3] and spell,
    And write how dear I love thee!

Then come, sweet Muse, inspire my lay
For a' the lee-lang[4] simmer's day,
I couldna sing, I couldna say,
    How much—how dear I love thee.

Quarters of the heavens, i. e. east, west, north, or south.—[2] Roll.—[3] To
look with earnest and fixed attention.—[4] Live-long.

I see thee dancing o'er the green,
Thy waist sae jimp,[1] thy limbs sae clean,
Thy tempting lips, thy roguish een—
    By heaven and earth, I love thee!

By night, by day, a-field, at hame,
The thoughts o' thee my breast inflame;
And ay I muse and sing thy name:
    I only live to love thee.
Tho' I were doom'd to wander on,
Beyond the sea, beyond the sun,
Till my last weary sand was run;
    'Till then—and then I love thee.

CRAIGIE-BURN WOOD.

Craigie-burn wood is situated on the banks of the river Moffat, about three miles distant from the village of that name, celebrated for its medicinal waters. This wood, and that of Duncrieff, were at one time favorite haunts of Burns. It was there he met the "Lassie wi' the lint-white locks," and composed several of his songs.

SWEET fa's the eve on Craigie-burn,
    And blythe awakes the morrow,
But a' the pride o' spring's return
    Can yield me nocht[2] but sorrow.

I see the flowers and spreading trees,
    I hear the wild-birds singing;
But what a weary wight can please,
    And care his bosom wringing?

Fain, fain would I my griefs impart,
    Yet dare na for your anger;
But secret love will break my heart,
    If I conceal it langer.

If thou refuse to pity me,
    If thou shalt love anither,
When yon green leaves fa' frae the tree,
    Around my grave they 'll wither!

* Slender.—² Naught.

MACPHERSON'S FAREWELL.

Burns composed this song to the beautiful air of "Macpherson's Farewell." Macpherson was a famous robber in the beginning of the last century, and was condemned to be hanged at the assizes at Inverness. His exploits, however, as a freebooter, were debased by no act of cruelty, no robbery of the widow, the fatherless, or the distressed; nor was any murder ever committed under his command. A dispute with one of his own troop, who wished to plunder a gentleman's house while his wife and two children lay on the bier for interment, was the cause of his being betrayed to the vengeance of the law. He was an admirable performer on the violin, and his talent for musical composition is evinced, not only in his "Rant" and "Pibroch," but also in his "Farewell," which he composed while he was in prison under sentence of death. He played his "Farewell" at the foot of the gallows; and then broke his violin over his knee. He died with the same fortitude as he had lived—a stranger to repentance, to remorse, and to fear. His sword is still preserved at Duff-house, a residence of the Earl of Fife.

TUNE—*Macpherson's Farewell.*

FAREWELL, ye dungeons dark and strong,
    The wretch's destinie!
Macpherson's time will not be long,
    On yonder gallows-tree.

Sae rantingly, sae wantonly,
    Sae dauntingly gaed he;
He play'd a spring[1] and danced it round,
    Below the gallows-tree.

Oh, what is death but parting breath?
    On monie a bludie plain
I 've dared his face, and in this place
    I scorn him yet again!
        Sae rantingly, &c.

Untie these bands from off my hands,
    And bring to me my sword;
And there 's not a man in all Scotland,
    But I 'll brave him at a word.
        Sae rantingly, &c.

I 've lived a life of sturt[2] and strife;
    I die by treacherie:
It burns my heart I must depart,
    And not avengéd be.
        Sae rantingly, &c.

[1] A quick air in music, a Scottish reel.—[2] Trouble.

Now farewell, light, thou sunshine bright,
  And all beneath the sky!
May coward shame distain his name,
  The wretch that dares not die!
    Sae rantingly, &c.

HOW LANG AND DREARY IS THE NIGHT.

"'How lang and dreary is the night.' I met with some such words," says Burns, "in a collection of songs somewhere, which I have altered and enlarged, and made to suit my favorite air, 'Cauld kail in Aberdeen.'"

    TUNE—*Cauld kail in Aberdeen.*

How lang and dreary is the night,
  When I am frae my dearie!
I restless lie frae e'en to morn,
  Tho' I were ne'er sae weary.

  For oh, her lanely nights are lang;
    And oh, her dreams are eerie,[1]
  And oh, her widow'd heart is sair,
    That's absent frae her dearie!

When I think on the lightsome days
  I spent wi' thee, my dearie;
And now what seas between us roar,
  How can I be but eerie?
    For oh, &c.

How slow ye move, ye heavy hours!
  The joyless day, how drearie!
It was na sae ye glinted[2] by,
  When I was wi' my dearie.
    For oh, &c.

BONNIE PEG.

First published in the Edinburgh Magazine for 1818.

As I came in by our gate end,
  As day was waxin' weary,
Oh wha came tripping down the street,
  But bonnie Peg, my dearie!

[1] Frightful.—[2] Peeped, passed quickly.

Her air sae sweet, and shape complete,
 Wi' nae proportion wanting,
The Queen of Love did never move
 Wi' motion mair enchanting.

Wi' linkéd hands, we took the sands
 A-down yon winding river;
And, oh! that hour and broomy bower,
 Can I forget it ever?

CONTENTED WI' LITTLE.

Burns has written nothing of the kind better than the following happy and most excellent song. "The old proverbial lore," says Allan Cunningham, "lends wisdom to the verse, the love of freedom is delicately expressed and vindicated, the sorrows of life are softened by song, and drink seems only to flow to set the tongue of the muse a-moving."

Tune—Lumps o' Pudding.

Contented wi' little, and cantie[1] wi' mair,
Whene'er I forgather wi' sorrow and care,
I gie them a skelp,[2] as they 're creepin' alang,
Wi' a cog[3] o' gude swats,[4] and an auld Scottish sang.

I whyles claw[5] the elbow o' troublesome thought;
But man is a sodger, and life is a faught:[6]
My mirth and gude humor are coin in my pouch,
And my freedom's my lairdship nae monarch dare
 touch.

A towmond[7] o' trouble, should that be my fa'.[8]
A night o' gude fellowship sowthers[9] it a':
When at the blythe end o' our journey at last,
Wha the Deil ever thinks o' the road he has past?

Blind Chance, let her snapper[10] and stoyte[11] on her
 way;
Be 't to me, be 't frae me, e'en let the jad gae:
Come ease, or come travail; come pleasure or pain,
My warst word is, "Welcome, and welcome again!"

------

[1] Cheerful.—[2] Slap, a smart stroke.—[3] Wooden dish.—[4] Ale.—[5] Scratch.—[6] Fight.—[7] Twelvemonth.—[8] Fate.—[9] Cements.—[10] Stumble.—[11] Stagger.

38

WANDERING WILLIE.

Perhaps in this song Burns has not much improved upon the old " Here
awa, there awa, wandering Willie."

HERE awa, there awa, wandering Willie,
  Here awa, there awa, haud awa hame;[1]
Come to my bosom, my ain only dearie,
  Tell me thou bring'st me my Willie the same.

Winter winds blew loud and cauld at our parting.
  Fears for my Willie brought tears in my ee;
Welcome now simmer, and welcome my Willie,
  The simmer to nature, my Willie to me.

Rest, ye wild storms, in the cave of your slumbers,
  How your dread howling a lover alarms!
Wauken, ye breezes, row[2] gently, ye billows,
  And waft my dear laddie ance mair to my arms.

But oh, if he's faithless, and minds na his Nannie,
  Flow still between us, thou wide-roaring main;
May I never see it, may I never trow it,
  But, dying, believe that my Willie's my ain!

OPEN THE DOOR TO ME, O!

Written to the old air of Lord Gregory; the second line was originally, "I
love it may na be, O!"

OH, open the door, some pity to show,
  Oh, open the door to me, O!
Tho' thou hast been false, I'll ever prove true,
  Oh, open the door to me, O!

Cauld is the blast upon my pale cheek,
  But caulder thy love for me, O!
The frost that freezes the life at my heart,
  Is naught to my pains frae thee, O!

The wan moon is setting behind the white wave,
  And time is setting with me, O!
False friends, false love, farewell! for mair
  I'll ne'er trouble them, nor thee, O!

_____
[1] Hold away home.—[2] Roll.

She has open'd the door, she has open'd it wide,
  She sees his pale corse on the plain, O!
"My true love!" she cried, and sank down by his side,
  Never to rise again, O!

MY NANNIE'S AWA.

TUNE—*There'll never be peace till Jamie comes hame.*

The air to which this pretty pastoral song is united, was a favorite of Burns's.
He wrote some excellent Jacobite verses to the same tune.

Now in her green mantle blythe nature arrays,
And listens the lambkins that bleat o'er the braes,
While birds warble welcome in ilka green shaw;[1]
But to me it's delightless—my Nannie's awa.

The snaw-drap and primrose our woodlands adorn,
And violets bathe in the weet o' the morn;
They pain my sad bosom, sae sweetly they blaw,
They mind me o' Nannie—and Nannie's awa.

Thou lav'rock[2] that springs frae the dews o' the lawn,
The shepherd to warn o' the gray-breaking dawn,
And thou mellow mavis,[3] that hails the night-fa',
Give over for pity—my Nannie's awa.

Come, autumn, sae pensive, in yellow and gray,
And soothe me wi' tidings o' nature's decay;
The dark, dreary winter, and wild-driving snaw,
Alane can delight me—now Nannie's awa.

MEG O' THE MILL.

TUNE—*O bonnie lass, will ye lie in a barrack?*

This song was originally written to a fine old air, called Jackie Hume's
Lament, but altered to suit the present tune. There is another and an older
Meg o' the Mill, which begins—

  "Oh ken ye what Meg o' the Mill has gotten?
  Oh ken ye what Meg o' the Mill has gotten?
  A braw new gown, an' the tail o' it rotten,
  An' that's what Meg o' the Mill has gotten."

Oh ken ye what Meg o' the Mill has gotten?
An' ken ye what Meg o' the Mill has gotten?
She has gotten a coof[4] wi' a claut[5] o' siller,
And broken the heart o' the barley Miller.

Every small wood.—[2] Lark.—[3] Thrush.—[4] Blockhead.—[5] Great quantity
of silver.

The miller was strappin', the miller was ruddy;
A heart like a lord, and a hue like a lady;
The laird was a widdiefu',[1] bleerit knurl;[2]
She 's left the gude fellow and taen the churl.

The miller he hecht[3] her a heart leal and loving;
The laird did address her wi' matter mair moving:
A fine pacing horse, wi' a clear-chainéd bridle,
A whip by her side, and a bonnie side-saddle.

Oh wae on the siller, it is sae prevailin'!
And wae on the love that 's fixed on a mailen![4]
A tocher 's[5] nae word in a true lover's parle,
But, gie me my love, and a fig for the warl'!

THE BANKS OF THE DEVON.

These verses were composed on Miss Hamilton,[6] sister to Gavin
Hamilton, of Mauchline.

How pleasant the banks of the clear-winding Devon,
  With green-spreading bushes, and flowers blooming
      fair;
But the bonniest flower on the banks of the Devon
  Was once a sweet bud on the braes of the Ayr

Mild be the sun on this sweet blushing flower,
  In the gay rosy morn as it bathes in the dew!
And gentle the fall of the soft vernal shower,
  That steals on the evening each leaf to renew!

Oh spare the dear blossom, ye orient breezes,
  With chill hoary wing, as ye usher the dawn!
And far be thou distant, thou reptile that seizes
  The verdure and pride of the garden and lawn.

Let Bourbon exult in his gay-gilded lilies,
  And England triumphant display her proud rose:
A fairer than either adorns the green valleys,
  Where Devon, sweet Devon, meandering flows.

---

[1] Deserving the gallows. -[2] Bleared dwarf. -[3] Offered.- [4] Farm.—[5] Marriage portion.

[6] To this lady Burns addressed several letters, which are, unfortunately
lost.

AULD ROB MORRIS.

The two first lines of this song are taken from an old ballad. The
rest are original.

THERE's auld Rob Morris who wons[1] in yon glen,
He's the king o' gude fellows and wale[2] of auld men;
He has gowd in his coffers, he has owsen and kine,
And ae bonnie lass, his darling and mine.

She's fresh as the morning, the fairest in May;
She's sweet as the ev'ning amang the new hay;
As blythe and as artless as the lamb on the lea,
And dear to my heart as the light to my ee.

But, oh! she's an heiress, auld Robin's a laird,
And my daddie has naught but a cot-house and yard
A wooer like me maunna hope to come speed,
The wounds I must hide that will soon be my dead.

The day comes to me, but delight brings me nane;
The night comes to me, but my rest it is gane;
I wander my lane, like a night-troubled ghaist,
And I sigh as my heart it wad burst in my breast.

Oh had she but been of a lower degree,
I then might hae hoped she wad smiled upon me;
Oh how past describing had then been my bliss,
As now my distraction no words can express!

THE BRAW WOOER.

The original of this song, the "Lothian Lassie," consisted of some nine or ten
very silly verses; one of them may be quoted:
"The mither cried butt the house, Jockie come here,
Ye've naething to do but the question to speir—
The question was speir'd, and the bargain was struck,
The neebors came in and wish'd them gude luck."

TUNE—*Lothian Lassie.*

LAST May a braw[3] wooer cam down the lang glen,
And sair wi' his love he did deave[4] me;
I said there was naething I hated like men!
The deuce gae wi' 'm to believe me, believe me,
The deuce gae wi' 'm to believe me.

1 Dwells.—2 Choice.—3 Handsome.—4 Deafen.

He spak o' the darts in my bonnie black een,
  And vow'd for my love he was dying:
I said he might die when he liked, for Jean,
  The Lord forgie me for lying, for lying,
  The Lord forgie me for lying.

A weel-stockéd mailen,¹ himsel for the laird,
  And marriage, aff-hand, were his proffers,
I never loot² on that I ken'd it, or cared,
  But thought I might hae waur³ offers, waur offers,
  But thought I might hae waur offers.

But what wad ye think? in a fortnight or less,
  (The deil tak his taste to gae near me!)
He up the lang loan to my black cousin Bess,
  Guess ye how, the jad! I could bear her, could bear her
  Guess ye how, the jad! I could bear her.

But a' the neist week as I fretted wi' care,
  I gaed to the tryste⁴ o' Dalgarnock,
And wha but my fine fickle wooer was there;
  I glowr'd⁵ as I'd seen a warlock,⁶ a warlock,
  I glowr'd as I'd seen a warlock.

But owre my left shouther I gae him a blink,
  Lest neebors might say I was saucy;
My wooer he caper'd as he'd been in drink,
  And vow'd I was his dear lassie, dear lassie,
  And vow'd I was his dear lassie.

I spier'd⁷ for my cousin, fu' couthy⁸ and sweet,
  Gin she had recover'd her hearin',
And how her new shoon⁹ fit her auld shackled feet;
  But, heavens! how he fell a-swearin', a-swearin',
  But, heavens! how he fell a-swearin'.

He beggéd, for gudesake! I wad be his wife,
  Or else I wad kill him wi' sorrow;
So, e'en to preserve the poor body in life,
  I think I maun wed him to-morrow, to-morrow,
  I think I maun wed him to-morrow.

¹ A well-stocked farm.—² Let.—³ Worse.—⁴ Fair.—⁵ Stared.—⁶ A wizard.
—⁷ Inquired.—⁸ Loving.—⁹ Shoes.

WHAT CAN A YOUNG LASSIE DO, Etc.

Burns is indebted to an old song for the following happy and very graphic
verses. They were written for Johnson's "Museum."

TUNE—What can a lassie do?

WHAT can a young lassie, what shall a young lassie,
   What can a young lassie do wi' an auld man?
Bad luck on the pennie that tempted my minnie[1]
   To sell her poor Jenny for siller an' lan'!
      Bad luck on the pennie, &c.

He's always compleenin' frae mornin' to e'enin',
   He hosts[2] and he hirples[3] the weary day lang;
He's doyl't[4] and he's dozin', his bluid it is frozen,
   Oh dreary's the night wi' a crazy auld man!
      He's doyl't and he's dozin', &c.

He hums and he hankers, he frets and he cankers,
   I never can please him, do a' that I can;
He's peevish and jealous of a' the young fellows,
   Oh dool[5] on the day I met wi' an auld man!
      He's peevish and jealous, &c.

My auld auntie Katie upon me taks pity,
   I'll do my endeavor to follow her plan:
I'll cross him, and wrack him, until I heart-break him,
   And then his auld brass will buy me a new pan.
      I'll cross him, and wrack him, &c.

HEY FOR A LASS WI' A TOCHER.

Your "Hey for a lass wi' a tocher" is excellent, and with you the subject is new
indeed. It is the first time I have seen you debasing the god of soft desire into an
amateur of acres and guineas.—*Thomson.*

TUNE—Balinamona ora.

AWA wi' your witchcraft o' beauty's alarms,
The slender bit beauty you grasp in your arms;
O gie me the lass that has acres o' charms,
O gie me the lass wi' the weel-stockit farms.

[1] Mother [2] Coughs.—[3] Creeps, or walks crazily.—[4] Stupid.—[5] Sorrow.

Then hey for a lass wi' a tocher,[1]
Then hey for a lass wi' a tocher,
Then hey for a lass wi' a tocher ;
The nice yellow guineas for me.

Your beauty 's a flower in the morning that blows,
And withers the faster, the faster it grows;
But the rapturous charm o' the bonnie green knowes,[2]
Iik spring they 're new deckit wi' bonnie white yowes.[3]
Then hey, &c.

And e'en when this beauty your bosom has blest,
The brightest o' beauty may cloy when possest;
But the sweet yellow darlings wi' Geordie imprest,
The langer ye hae them the mair they 're carest.
Then hey, &c.

THE BIG-BELLIED BOTTLE.

To two old "bottle" songs we are partly indebted for the following verses. From
the one the Poet has borrowed the title ; from the other the tune.

TUNE—Prepare, my dear brethren, to the tavern let's fly.

No churchman am I for to rail and to write,
No statesman or soldier to plot or to fight,
No sly man of business contriving some snare,
For a big-bellied bottle 's the whole of my care.

The peer I don't envy, I give him his bow;
I scorn not the peasant, though ever so low;
But a club of good fellows, like those that are here,
And a bottle like this, are my glory and care.

Here passes the squire on his brother—his horse;
There centum per centum. the cit with his purse;
But see you the Crown, how it waves in the air,
There a big-bellied bottle still eases my care.

The wife of my bosom, alas! she did die;
For sweet consolation to church I did fly;
I found that old Solomon provéd it fair,
That a big-bellied bottle 's a cure for all care.

[1] A marriage portion.—[2] Hillocks.—[3] Ewes.

I once was persuaded a venture to make;
A letter inform'd me that all was to wreck;
But the pursy old landlord just waddled up stairs,
With a glorious bottle that ended my cares.

"Life's cares they are comforts"[1]—a maxim laid down
By the bard, what d'ye call him, that wore the black gown;
And faith, I agree with the old prig to a hair;
For a big-bellied bottle's a heaven of care.

A STANZA ADDED IN A MASON LODGE.

Then fill up a bumper and make it o'erflow,
And honors masonic prepare for to throw;
May every true brother of the compass and square
Have a big-bellied bottle when harass'd with care.

SONG OF DEATH.

"The circumstance," says Burns, "that gave rise to the following verses, was looking over, with a musical friend, M'Donald's Collection of Highland airs. I was struck with one, entitled 'Oran an Aoig,' or 'The song of Death,' to the measure of which I have adapted my stanzas."

Scene—A field of battle. Time of the day—Evening. The wounded and dying of the victorious army are supposed to join in the song.

FAREWELL, thou fair day, thou green earth, and ye skies,
    Now gay with the bright setting sun!
Farewell, loves and friendships, ye dear, tender ties,
    Our race of existence is run!

Thou grim king of terrors, thou life's gloomy foe,
    Go, frighten the coward and slave!
Go, teach them to tremble, fell tyrant! but know,
    No terrors hast thou for the brave!

Thou strik'st the poor peasant—he sinks in the dark,
    Nor saves e'en the wreck of a name:
Thou strik'st the young hero—a glorious mark!
    He falls in the blaze of his fame!

In the field of proud honor—our swords in our hands,
    Our king and our country to save—
While victory shines on life's last ebbing sands—
    Oh! who would not die with the brave?

[1] Young's Night Thoughts.

OUT-OVER THE FORTH, Etc.

The second of the following verses was first published by Currie, the first by Cromek. United, they make an exquisite little song.

Out-over the Forth I look to the north,
  But what is the north and its Highlands to me?
The south nor the east give ease to my breast,
  The far foreign land nor the wild rolling sea.

But I look to the west, when I gae to rest,
  That happy my dreams and my slumbers may be,
For far in the west lives he I lo'e best,
  The lad that is dear to my babie and me.

BY YON CASTLE WA', Etc.

Written in imitation of an old Jacobite song, of which the following are two lines—

> "My lord 's lost his land, and my lady her name,
> There 'll never be right till Jamie comes hame."

By yon castle wa', at the close o' the day,
I heard a man sing, though his head it was gray;
And as he was singing, the tears fast down came—
There 'll never be peace till Jamie comes hame.

The church is in ruins, the state is in jars,
Delusions, oppressions, and murderous wars;
We dare na weel say 't, but we ken wha 's to blame—
There 'll never be peace till Jamie comes hame.

My seven braw sons for Jamie drew sword,
And now I greet round their green beds in the yird;[1]
It brak the sweet heart o' my faithfu' auld dame—
There 'll never be peace till Jamie comes hame.

Now life is a burden that sair bows me down,
Sin' I tint[2] my bairns,[3] and he tint his crown:
But till my last moment my words are the same—
There 'll never be peace till Jamie comes hame.

[1] Earth.—[2] Lost.—[3] Children.

THE CHEVALIER'S LAMENT.

"When Prince Charles Stuart saw that utter ruin had fallen on a l those who loved him and fought for him—that the axe and the cord were busy with their persons, and that their wives and children were driven desolate, he is supposed by Burns to have given utterance to his feelings in this Lament."—*Allan Cunningham.*

TUNE—*Captain O'Kaine.*

The small birds rejoice in the green leaves returning;
 The murmuring streamlet winds clear thro' the vale;
The hawthorn trees blow in the dews of the morning,
 And wild scatter'd cowslips bedeck the green dale:

But what can give pleasure, or what can seem fair,
 While the lingering moments are number'd by care?
No flowers gayly springing, nor birds sweetly singing,
 Can soothe the sad bosom of joyless despair.

The deed that I dared, could it merit their malice,
 A king and a father to place on his throne?
His right are these hills, and his right are these valleys,
 Where the wild beasts find shelter, but I can find none.

But 'tis not my sufferings, thus wretched, forlorn,
 My brave gallant friends, 'tis your ruin I mourn;
Your deeds proved so loyal in hot bloody trial, .
 Alas! can I make you no sweeter return?

THEIR GROVES O' SWEET MYRTLE, ETC.

"Love of country and domestic affection have combined to endear this song to every bosom. It was written in honor of Mrs. Burns."—*Allan Cunningham.*

TUNE—*Humors of Glen.*

Their groves o' sweet myrtle let foreign lands reckon,
 Where bright-beaming summers exalt the perfume,
Far dearer to me yon lone glen o' green breckan,[1]
 Wi' the burn stealing under the lang yellow broom:
Far dearer to me are yon humble broom bowers,
 Where the blue-bell and gowan[2] lurk lowly unseen:
For there, lightly tripping amang the wild flowers,
 A-listening the linnet, aft wanders my Jean.

[1] Fern.—[2] The wild daisy

Tho' rich is the breeze in their gay sunny valleys,
   And cauld Caledonia's blast on the wave;
Their sweet-scented woodlands that skirt the proud
      palace,
   What are they? the haunt o' the tyrant and slave!
The slave's spicy forests, and gold-bubbling fountains,
   The brave Caledonian views wi' disdain;
He wanders as free as the winds of his mountains,
   Save love's willing fetters, the chains o' his Jean.

CALEDONIA.

This excellent national song was first published by Dr. Currie. It has never become, popular, however. The words and the tune are by no means a very suitable pair.

TUNE—*The Caledonian Hunt's Delight.*

THERE was once a day, but old Time then was young,
   That brave Caledonia, the chief of her line,
From some of your northern deities sprung,
   (Who knows not that brave Caledonia's divine?)
From Tweed to the Orcades was her domain,
   To·hunt, or to pasture, or do what she would:
Her heavenly relations there fixèd her reign,
   And pledged her their godheads to warrant it good.

A lambkin in peace, but a lion in war,
   The pride of her kindred, the heroine grew:
Her grandsire, old Odin, triumphantly swore—
   " Whoe'er shall provoke thee, the encounter shall
      rue !"
With tillage or pasture at times she would sport,
   To feed her fair flocks by her green rustling corn;
But chiefly the woods were her favorite resort;
   Her darling amusement, the hounds and the horn.

Long quiet she reign'd; till thitherward steers
   A flight of bold eagles from Adria's strand :[1]
Repeated, successive, for many long years,
   They darken'd the air, and they plunder'd the land;

[1] The Romans

Thus Robert, victorious, the triumph has gain'd;
Which now in his house has for ages remain'd;
Till three noble chieftains, and all of his blood,
The jovial contest again have renew'd.

Three joyous good fellows, with hearts clear of flaw;
Craigdarroch, so famous for wit, worth, and law;
And trusty Glenriddel, so skill'd in old coins;
And gallant Sir Robert, deep read in old wines.

Craigdarroch began, with a tongue smooth as oil,
Desiring Glenriddel to yield up the spoil;
Or else he would muster the heads of the clan,
And once more, in claret, try which was the man.

"By the gods of the ancients!" Glenriddel replies,
"Before I surrender so glorious a prize,
I'll conjure the ghost of the great Rorie More,[1]
And bumper his horn with him twenty times o'er."

Sir Robert, a soldier, no speech could pretend,
But he ne'er turn'd his back on his foe or his friend,
Said, "Toss down the whistle, the prize of the field,
And knee-deep in claret, he'd die, or he'd yield."

To the board of Glenriddel our heroes repair,
So noted for drowning of sorrow and care;
But for wine and for welcome not more known to fame,
Than the sense, wit, and taste of a sweet lovely dame.

A bard was selected to witness the fray,
And tell future ages the feats of the day;
A bard who detested all sadness and spleen,
And wish'd that Parnassus a vineyard had been.

The dinner being over, the claret they ply,
And every new cork is a new spring of joy;
In the bands of old friendship and kindred so set,
And the bands grew the tighter the more they were wet.

Gay pleasure ran riot as bumpers ran o'er:
Bright Phœbus ne'er witness'd so joyous a core,
And vow'd that to leave them he was quite forlorn,
Till Cynthia hinted he'd see them next morn.

[1] See Johnson's Tour to the Hebrides.

Six bottles a-piece had well wore out the night,
When gallant Sir Robert, to finish the fight,
Turn'd o'er in one bumper a bottle of red,
And swore 'twas the way that their ancestors did.

Then worthy Glenriddel, so cautious and sage,
No longer the warfare, ungodly, would wage:
A high-ruling elder to wallow in wine!
He left the foul business to folks less divine.

The gallant Sir Robert fought hard to the end;
But who can with fate and quart bumpers contend?
Tho' fate said—a hero should perish in light;
So up rose bright Phœbus—and down fell the knight

Next up rose our Bard, like a prophet in drink:
"Craigdarroch, thou 'lt soar when creation shall sink.
But if thou would flourish immortal in rhyme,
Come—one bottle more—and have at the sublime!

"Thy line, that has struggled for freedom with Bruce,
Shall heroes and patriots ever produce;
So thine be the laurel, and mine be the bay;
The field thou hast won, by yon bright god of day!"

AFTON WATER.

Afton Water is one of the tributary streams of the Nith. The song was written in
honor of Mrs. Dugald Stewart, of Afton Lodge, a lady of considerable literary abili-
ties. She wrote the beautiful and well-known song—"The tears I shed must ever
fall."

Flow gently, sweet Afton, among the green braes,
Flow gently, I 'll sing thee a song in thy praise;
My Mary's asleep by thy murmuring stream,
Flow gently, sweet Afton, disturb not her dream.

Thou stock-dove whose echo resounds thro' the glen,
Ye wild whistling blackbirds in yon thorny den,
Thou green-crested lapwing, thy screaming forbear,
I charge you disturb not my slumbering fair.

How lofty, sweet Afton, thy neighboring hills,
Far mark'd with the courses of clear winding rills!
There daily I wander as noon rises high,
My flocks and my Mary's sweet cot in my eye.

How pleasant thy banks and green valleys below,
Where wild in the woodlands the primroses blow !
There oft as mild evening weeps over the lea,
The sweet-scented birk[1] shades my Mary and me.

Thy crystal stream, Afton, how lovely it glides,
And winds by the cot where my Mary resides;
How wanton thy waters her snowy feet lave,
As gathering sweet flow'rets she stems thy clear wave.

Flow gently, sweet Afton, among thy green braes,[2]
Flow gently, sweet river, the theme of my lays ;
My Mary's asleep by thy murmuring stream,
Flow gently, sweet Afton, disturb not her dream.

THE BELLES OF MAUCHLINE.

This is one of our Bard's early productions.—Miss Armour was afterwards Mrs. Burns.

TUNE—*Bonnie Dundee.*

In Mauchline there dwells six proper young Belles,
    The pride of the place and its neighborhood a',
Their carriage and dress, a stranger would guess,
    In Lon'on or Paris they'd gotten it a':

Miss Miller is fine, Miss Markland's divine,
    Miss Smith she has wit, and Miss Betty is braw ;
There's beauty and fortune to get wi' Miss Morton,
    But Armour's the jewel for me o' them a'.

MY HARRY WAS A GALLANT GAY.

" The oldest title," says Burns, " I ever heard to this air was 'The Highland Watch's Farewell to Ireland.' The chorus I picked up from an old woman in Dunblane ; the rest of the song is mine."

TUNE—*Highlander's Lament.*

My Harry was a gallant gay,
    Fu' stately strade he on the plain !
But now he's banish'd far away,
    I'll never see him back again.

[1] Birch-tree.—[2] The slope of a hill.

Oh for him back again,
Oh for him back again,
I wad gie a' Knockhaspie's land
For Highland Harry back again

When a' the lave[1] gae to their bed,
 I wander dowie[2] up the glen;
I sit me down and greet[3] my fill,
 And ay I wish him back again.
     Oh for him, &c.

Oh were some villains hangit high,
 And ilka body had their ain,
Then I might see the joyfu' sight,
 My Highland Harry back again!
     Oh for him, &c.

WHEN GUILFORD GOOD OUR PILOT STOOD.

A FRAGMENT.

This ballad made its first appearance in the Edinburgh edition of the Poet's
works. When Dr. Blair read it, he uttered this pithy criticism—"Burns's
politics always smell of the smithy."

TUNE—Gillicrankie.

WHEN Guilford good our pilot stood,
 And did our hellim thraw, man,
Ae night, at tea, began a plea,
 Within America, man:
Then up they gat the maskin-pat,[4]
 And in the sea did jaw,[5] man;
An' did nae less, in full congress,
 Than quite refuse our law, man.

Then through the lakes Montgomery takes,
 I wat he was na slaw, man!
Down Lowrie's burn he took a turn,
 And Carleton did ca', man:

----

[1] Rest.—[2] Worn with grief.—[3] Cry.—[4] Teapot.
[5] To pour out—to jerk, or cast away. It will be recollected that when the
English parliament imposed an excise duty upon tea imported into North
America, the East India Company sent several ships laden with that article
to Boston, and the natives went on board these ships by force of arms, and
emptied all the chests of tea into the sea.

But yet, what-reck, he, at Quebec,
    Montgomery-like did fa', man,
Wi' sword in hand, before his band,
    Amang his enemies a', man.

Poor Tammy Gage, within a cage,
    Was kept at Boston ha', man;
Till Willie Howe took o'er the knowe[1]
    For Philadelphia, man:
Wi' sword an' gun he thought a sin
    Guid Christian blood to draw, man;
But at New York, wi' knife an' fork,
    Sirloin he hacked sma', man.

Burgoyne gaed up, like spur an' whip,
    Till Fraser brave did fa', man;
Then lost his way, ae misty day,
    In Saratoga shaw, man.
Cornwallis fought as lang 's he dought,[2]
    An' did the buckskins[3] claw, man;
But Clinton's glaive[4] frae rust to save,
    He hung it to the wa', man.

Then Montague, and Guilford too,
    Began to fear a fa', man;
And Sackville doure,[5] wha stood the stoure,[6]
    The German chief to thraw, man:
For Paddy Burke, like ony Turk,
    Nae mercy had at a', man;
And Charlie Fox threw by the box,
    And lows'd his tinkler[7] jaw, man.

Then Rockingham took up the game,
    Till death did on him ca', man;
When Shelburne meek held up his cheek,
    Conform to gospel law, man;
Saint Stephen's boys, wi' jarring noise,
    They did his measures thraw, man,
For North an' Fox united stocks,
    An' bore him to the wa', man.

---

[1] A hillock.—[2] Was able.—[3] Natives of Virginia.—[4] A sword.—[5] Stout, stubborn.—[6] Dust.—[7] Let loose in a strain of coarse raillery against the Ministry.

Then clubs an' hearts were Charlie's cartes,
  He swept the stakes awa', man,
Till the diamond's ace, of Indian race,
  Led him a sair *faux pas*, man:
The Saxon lads, wi' loud placads,[1]
  On Chatham's boy did ca', man:
An' Scotland drew her pipe, an' blew,
  "Up, Willie, waur[2] them a', man!"

Behind the throne then Grenville's gone,
  A secret word or twa, man;
While slee Dundas aroused the class
  Be-north the Roman wa', man:
An' Chatham's wraith, in heavenly graith,[3]
  (Inspired bardies saw, man,)
Wi' kindling eyes cried, "Willie, rise!
  Would I hae fear'd them a', man?"

But, word an' blow, North, Fox, and Co.
  Gowff'd[4] Willie like a ba', man,
Till Suthron[5] raise, and coost their claise[6]
  Behind him in a raw, man;
An' Caledon threw by the drone,
  And did her whittle[7] draw, man;
And swoor[8] fu' rude, thro' dirt an' blood,
  To mak it guid in law, man.

    *   *   *   *   *

NOW WESTLIN' WINDS, Etc.

This is an early production. It was published in the Kilmarnock edition.

Tune—*I had a horse, I had nae mair.*

Now westlin' winds, and slaughtering guns
  Bring Autumn's pleasant weather;
The moorcock springs, on whirring wings,
  Amang the blooming heather:
Now waving grain, wide o'er the plain,
  Delights the weary farmer;
And the moon shines bright, when I rove at night,
  To muse upon my charmer.

[1] Proclamation. — [2] To worst; to defeat. — [3] Dress, accoutrements.
[4] Struck. — [5] An old name for the English nation. — [6] Cast their clothes. — [7] Knife, or sword. — [8] Swore.

Tho partridge loves the fruitful fells;[1]
    The plover loves the mountains;
The woodcock haunts the lonely dells;
    The soaring hern the fountains:
Thro' lofty groves the cushat[2] roves,
    The path of man to shun it;
The hazel bush o'erhangs the thrush,
    The spreading thorn the linnet.

Thus every kind their pleasure find,
    The savage and the tender;
Some social join, and leagues combine;
    Some solitary wander:
Avaunt, away! the cruel sway,
    Tyrannic man's dominion;
The sportsman's joy, the murdering cry,
    The fluttering, gory pinion!

But Peggy dear, tho evening's clear,
    Thick flies the skimming swallow:
The sky is blue, the fields in view,
    All fading green and yellow:
Come let us stray our gladsome way,
    And view the charms of nature!
Tho rustling corn, the fruited thorn,
    And every happy creature.

We'll gently walk, and sweetly talk,
    Till the silent moon shine clearly;
I'll grasp thy waist, and, fondly prest,
    Swear how I love thee dearly:
Not vernal showers to budding flowers,
    Not autumn to the farmer,
So dear can be as thou to me,
    My fair, my lovely charmer!

TO MARY.

"In my early years, when I was thinking of going to the West Indies, I took this fareweel of a dear girl."—*Burns to Thomson.*

TUNE—*Ewe-bughts, Marion.*

WILL ye go to the Indies, my Mary,
    And leave auld Scotia's shore?

[1] A field pretty level on the side or top of a hill.—[2] The dove, or wood-pigeon.

Will ye go to the Indies, my Mary,
　　Across th' Atlantic's roar?

Oh sweet grows the lime and the orange,
　　And the apple on the pine;
But a' the charms o' the Indies,
　　Can never equal thine.

I hae sworn by the heavens to my Mary,
　　I hae sworn by the heavens to be true;
And sae may the heavens forget me,
　　When I forget my vow!

Oh plight me your faith, my Mary,
　　And plight me your lily-white hand;
Oh plight me your faith, my Mary,
　　Before I leave Scotia's strand.

We hae plighted our troth, my Mary,
　　In mutual affection to join,
And curst be the cause that shall part us!
　　The hour and the moment o' time!

MY WIFE 'S A WINSOME WEE THING.

"These lines," says Burns, "are extempore. I might have tried
something more profound, yet it might not have suited the light-horse
gallop of the air so well as this random clink."

Sне is a winsome[1] wee[2] thing,
She is a handsome wee thing,
She is a bonnie wee thing,
This sweet wee wife o' mine.

I never saw a fairer,
I never lo'ed a dearer,
And neist[3] my heart I 'll wear her,
For fear my jewel tine.[4]

She is a winsome wee thing,
She is a handsome wee thing,
She is a bonnie wee thing,
This sweet wee wife of mine.

[1] Gay.—[2] Little.—[3] Nearest.—[4] Be lost.

Their pounces were murder, and terror their cry,
 They'd conquer'd and ruin'd a world beside:
She took to her hills, and her arrows let fly,
 The daring invaders they fled or they died.

The fell harpy-raven took wing from the north,
 The scourge of the seas and the dread of the shore;[1]
The wild Scandinavian boar issued forth
 To wanton in carnage, and wallow in gore;[2]
O'er countries and kingdoms their fury prevail'd,
 No arts could appease them, no arms could repel;
But brave Caledonia in vain they assail'd,
 As Largs well can witness, and Loncartie tell.[3]

The Cameleon-savage disturb'd her repose,
 With tumult, disquiet, rebellion, and strife;
Provoked beyond bearing, at last she arose,
 And robb'd him at once of his hopes and his life:[4]
The Anglian lion, the terror of France,
 Oft prowling, ensanguined the Tweed's silver flood;
But taught by the bright Caledonian lance,
 He learnéd to fear his own native wood.

Thus bold, independent, unconquer'd and free,
 Her bright course of glory forever shall run:
For brave Caledonia immortal must be;
 I'll prove it from Euclid as clear as the sun:
Rectangle-triangle, the figure we'll choose,
 The upright is Chance, and old Time is the base
But brave Caledonia's the hypothenuse;
 Then ergo she'll match them, and match them
  always.[5]

---

[1] The Saxons.—[2] The Danes.—[3] The two famous battles in which the Danes or Norwegians were defeated.—[4] The Highlanders of the Isles.
[5] This singular figure of poetry refers to the famous proposition of Pythagoras, the 47th of Euclid. In a right-angled triangle, the square of the hypothenuse is always equal to the squares of the two other sides.

To equal young Jessie seek Scotland all over;
   To equal young Jessie, you seek it in vain;
Grace, beauty, and elegance, fetter her lover,
   And maidenly modesty fixes the chain.

Oh fresh is the rose in the gay, dewy morning,
   And sweet is the lily at evening close;
But in the fair presence o' lovely young Jessie,
   Unseen is the lily, unheeded the rose.
Love sits in her smile, a wizard ensnaring;
   Enthroned in her een he delivers his law;
And still to her charms she alone is a stranger!
   Her modest demeanor 's the jewel of a'.

PHILLIS THE FAIR.

Speaking of this song to Thomson, Burns says, " I have tried my hand
on ' Robin Adair,' and you will probably think with little success; but
it is such a cursed, cramp, out-of-the-way measure, that I despair of doing
any thing better to it."

TUNE—Robin Adair.

WHILE larks with little wing
   Fann'd the pure air,
Tasting the breathing spring,
   Forth I did fare:
Gay the sun's golden eye
Peep'd o'er the mountains high!
Such thy morn! did I cry,
   Phillis the fair.

In each bird's careless song,
   Glad did I share;
While yon wild-flowers among,
   Chance led me there:
Sweet to the opening day,
Rosebuds bent the dewy spray;
Such thy bloom! did I say,
   Phillis the fair.

Down in a shady walk,
   Doves cooing were,
I mark'd the cruel hawk
   Caught in a snare:

So kind may Fortune be,
Such make his destiny,
He who would injure thee,
Phillis the fair.

HAD I A CAVE, Etc.

An unfortunate circumstance which happened to his friend Cunningham, sug
gested this fine pathetic song to the Poet's fancy.

TO THE SAME TUNE.

Had I a cave on some wild, distant shore,
Where the winds howl to the waves' dashing roar,
There would I weep my woes,
There seek my lost repose,
Till grief my eyes should close,
Ne'er to wake more.

Falsest of womankind, canst thou declare,
All thy fond plighted vows—fleeting as air?
To thy new lover hie,
Laugh o'er thy perjury,
Then in thy bosom try,
What peace is there!

ADOWN WINDING NITH.

"A favorite air of mine," says Burns, "is 'The muckin' o' Geordie's Byre,'
when sung slow, with expression. I have often wished that it had had better
poetry: that I have endeavored to supply as follows."

TUNE—*The muckin' o' Geordie's Byre.*

Adown winding Nith I did wander,
To mark the sweet flowers as they spring;
Adown winding Nith I did wander,
Of Phillis to muse and to sing.

Awa wi' your belles and your beauties,
They never wi' her can compare:
Whaever has met wi' my Phillis,
Has met wi' the queen o' the fair.

The daisy amused my fond fancy,
  So artless, so simple, so wild;
Thou emblem, said I, o' my Phillis,
  For she is simplicity's child.
      Awa, &c.

The rose-bud 's the blush o' my charmer,
  Her sweet balmy lip when 'tis prest:
How fair and how pure is the lily!
  But fairer and purer her breast.
      Awa, &c.

Yon knot of gay flowers in the arbor,
  They ne'er with my Phillis can vie:
Her breath is the breath o' the woodbine,
  Its dew-drop o' diamond her eye.
      Awa, &c.

Her voice is the song o' the morning,
  That wakes thro' the green-spreading grove,
When Phœbus peeps over the mountains
  On music, and pleasure, and love.
      Awa, &c.

But beauty how frail and how fleeting,
  The bloom of a fine summer's day!
While worth in the mind o' my Phillis
  Will flourish without a decay.
      Awa, &c.

ON THE SEAS AND FAR AWAY.

"I do not think 'On the Seas and far away' one of your very happy produc-
tions, though it certainly contains stanzas that are worthy of all acceptation."—
Thomson to Burns.

TUNE—*O'er the hills, &c.*

How can my poor heart be glad,
When absent from my sailor lad?
How can I the thought forego,
He 's on the seas to meet the foe?
Let me wander, let me rove,
Still my heart is with my love;
Nightly dreams and thoughts by day
Are with him that 's far away.

On the seas and far away,
On stormy seas and far away ;
Nightly dreams and thoughts by day,
Are ay with him that's far away.

When in summer's noon I faint,
As weary flocks around me pant,
Haply in this scorching sun
My sailor's thundering at his gun:
Bullets, spare my only joy !
Bullets, spare my darling boy !
Fate, do with me what you may,
Spare but him that's far away!
    On the seas, &c.

At the starless midnight hour,
When winter rules with boundless power;
As the storms the forest tear,
And thunders rend the howling air,
Listening to the doubling roar,
Surging on the rocky shore,
All I can—I weep and pray,
For his weal that's far away.
    On the seas, &c.

Peace, thy olive wand extend,
And bid wild war his ravage end,
Man with brother man to meet,
And as a brother kindly greet:
Then may heaven with prosperous gales,
Fill my sailor's welcome sails,
To my arms their charge convey,
My dear lad that's far away.
    On the seas, &c.

SAW YE MY PHELY!

Written for the Museum. The air must have been altered to suit the present verses, as the measure of the old song is very different—"When she cam ben she bobbit *fu' low*."

   Tune—*When she cam ben she bobbit.*

Oh saw ye my dear, my Phely?
Oh saw ye my dear, my Phely?
She's down i' the grove, she's wi' a new love,
 She winna come hame to her Willy.

What says she, my dearest, my Phely?
What says she, my dearest, my Phely?
She lets thee to wit that she has thee forgot,
    And forever disowns thee her Willy.

Oh had I ne'er seen thee, my Phely!
Oh had I ne'er seen thee, my Phely!
As light as the air, and fause as thou 's fair,
    Thou 's broken the heart o' thy Willy.

LET NOT WOMAN E'ER COMPLAIN.

Duncan Gray was a favorite air of the Poet's. He had already written to
it his admirable Scottish song "Duncan Gray cam here to woo." The fol-
lowing is an attempt to dress it in English.

TUNE—*Duncan Gray.*

LET not woman e'er complain,
    Of inconstancy in love;
Let not woman e'er complain,
    Fickle man is apt to rove:

Look abroad through Nature's range,
Nature's mighty law is change;
Ladies, would it not be strange,
    Man should then a monster prove?

Mark the winds, and mark the skies:
    Ocean's ebb, and ocean's flow:
Sun and moon but set to rise,
    Round and round the seasons go.

Why then ask of silly man,
To oppose great Nature's plan?
We 'll be constant while we can—
    You can be no more, you know.

SLEEP'ST THOU, OR WAK'ST THOU, Etc.

Written for Thomson's collection. For some curious alterations of this song
see Currie's edition, vol. iv. page 137.

TUNE—*Deil tak the Wars.*

SLEEP'ST thou, or wak'st thou, fairest creature?
    Rosy morn now lifts his eye,
Numbering ilka bud which Nature

Waters wi' the tears o' joy:
Now to the streaming fountain,
Or up the heathy mountain,
Wild Nature's tenants freely, gladly stray;
The lintwhite[1] in his bower
Chants o'er the breathing flower;
The lav'rock to the sky
Ascends wi' sangs o' joy,
While the sun and thou arise to bless the day.

Phœbus gilding the brow o' morning,
Banishes ilk darksome shade,
Nature gladdening and adorning;
Such to me, my lovely maid,
When frae my Chloris parted,
Sad, cheerless, broken-hearted,
Night's gloomy shades, cloudy, dark, o'ercast my sky:
But when, in beauty's light,
She meets my ravish'd sight,
When through my very heart
Her beaming glories dart;
'Tis then I wake to life, to light, and joy.

MY CHLORIS, MARK HOW GREEN THE GROVES.

"How do you like," says Burns to Thomson, 'the simplicity and tenderness of this pastoral? I think it pretty well."

Tune—My lodging is on the cold ground.

My Chloris, mark how green the groves,
The primrose banks how fair:
The balmy gales awake the flowers,
And wave thy flaxen hair.

The lav'rock shuns the palace gay,
And o'er the cottage sings:
For nature smiles as sweet, I ween,
To shepherds as to kings.

Let minstrels sweep the skilfu' string
In lordly lighted ha':[2]
The shepherd stops his simple reed,
Blythe, in the birken shaw.[3]

[1] Linnet.—[2] Hall.—[3] Small wood in a hollow.

The princely revel may survey
    Our rustic dance wi' scorn;
But are their hearts as light as ours
    Beneath the milk-white thorn?

The shepherd, in the flowery glen,
    In shepherd's phrase will woo;
The courtier tells a finer tale,
    But is his heart as true?

These wild-wood flowers I 've pu'd,[1] to deck
    That spotless breast o' thine:
The courtiers' gems may witness love—
    But 'tis na love like mine.

IT WAS THE CHARMING MONTH OF MAY.

Altered from an old English song.

TUNE—*Dainty Davie.*

It was the charming month of May,
When all the flowers were fresh and gay,
One morning by the break of day,
    The youthful, charming Chloe;

From peaceful slumber she arose,
Girt on her mantle and her hose,
And o'er the flowery mead she goes,
    The youthful, charming Chloe.

    Lovely was she by the dawn,
      Youthful Chloe, charming Chloe,
    Tripping o'er the pearly lawn,
      The youthful, charming Chloe.

The feather'd people you might see,
Perch'd all around on every tree,
In notes of sweetest melody,
    They hail the charming Chloe;

Till, painting gay the eastern skies,
The glorious sun began to rise,
Out-rivall'd by the radiant eyes
    Of youthful, charming Chloe.
      Lovely was she, &c.

----

[1] Pulled, gathered.

FAREWELL, THOU STREAM, Etc.

This song has nothing in common with the old verses—
"Nancy 's to the greenwood gane,
To gain her love by flattering."

TUNE—*Nancy 's to the greenwood gane.*

FAREWELL, thou stream that winding flows
  Around Eliza's dwelling!
O memory spare the cruel throes
  Within my bosom swelling:
Condemn'd to drag a hopeless chain,
  And yet in secret languish,
To feel a fire in every vein,
  Nor dare disclose my anguish.

Love's veriest wretch, unseen, unknown,
  I fain my griefs would cover;
The bursting sigh, the unweeting groan,
  Betray the hapless lover.
I know thou doom'st me to despair,
  Nor wilt, nor canst relieve me;
But oh, Eliza, hear one prayer,
  For pity's sake forgive me.

The music of thy voice I heard,
  Nor wist while it enslaved me;
I saw thine eyes, yet nothing fear'd,
  Till fears no more had saved me:
The unwary sailor thus aghast,
  The wheeling torrent viewing,
'Mid circling horrors sinks at last
  In overwhelming ruin.

PHILLY[1] AND WILLY.—A DUET.

"I am much pleased," says the Poet, in a letter to George Thomson,
"with your idea of singing our songs in alternate stanzas. I regret that you
did not hint it to me sooner."

TUNE—*The Sow's Tail.*

HE.

O PHILLY, happy be the day
When roving through the gather'd hay,

[1] The common abbreviation of Phillis.

My youthfu' heart was stown away,
  And by thy charms, my Philly.

SHE.

O Willy, ay I bless the grove
Where first I own'd my maiden love,
Whilst thou didst pledge the Powers above
  To be my ain dear Willy.

HE.

As songsters of the early year
Are ilka day mair sweet to hear,
So ilka day to me mair dear
  And charming is my Philly.

SHE.

As on the brier the budding rose
Still richer breathes and fairer blows,
So in my tender bosom grows
  The love I bear my Willy.

HE.

The milder sun and bluer sky,
That crown my harvest cares wi' joy,
Were ne'er sae welcome to my eye
  As is a sight o' Philly.

SHE.

The little swallow's wanton wing,
Tho' wafting o'er the flowery spring,
Did ne'er to me sic tidings bring
  As meeting o' my Willy.

HE.

The bee that thro' the sunny hour
Sips nectar in the opening flower,
Compared wi' my delight is poor,
  Upon the lips o' Philly.

SHE.

The woodbine in the dewy weet
When evening shades in silence meet,
Is nocht sae fragrant or sae sweet
  As is a kiss o' Willy.

HE.

Let fortune's wheel at random rin,
And fools may tyne,[1] and knaves may win;
My thoughts are a' bound up in ane,
    And that's my ain dear Philly.

SHE.

What's a' the joys that gowd[2] can gie!
I care na wealth a single flie;
The lad I love's the lad for me,
    And that's my ain dear Willy.

CANST THOU LEAVE ME THUS, MY KATY?

Of this song, Burns says, "Well! I think, to be done in two or three turns across my room, and with two or three pinches of Irish blackguard,[3] it is not so far amiss."

TUNE—*Roy's Wife.*

Canst thou leave me thus, my Katy?
Canst thou leave me thus, my Katy?
Well thou know'st my aching heart,
And canst thou leave me thus for pity?

Is this thy plighted, fond regard,
    Thus cruelly to part, my Katy?
Is this thy faithful swain's reward—
    An aching, broken heart, my Katy?
    Canst thou, &c.

Farewell! and ne'er such sorrows tear
    That fickle heart of thine, my Katy!
Thou mayst find those will love thee dear—
    But not a love like mine, my Katy.
    Canst thou, &c.

'TWAS NA HER BONNIE BLUE EE WAS MY RUIN.

The following is a verse of the old song:

  "Lang hae we parted been, lassie my dearie,
  Now we are met again, lassie, lie near me;
  Near me, near me, lassie, lie near me,
  Lang hast thou lien thy lane, lassie, lie near me."

TUNE—*Lassie, lie near me.*

'Twas na her bonnie blue ee was my ruin;
Fair tho' she be, that was ne'er my undoing:

[1] Lose.—[2] Gold —[3] Snuff.

'Twas the dear smile when naebody did mind us,
'Twas the bewitching, sweet, stown[1] glance o' kindness.

Sair do I fear that to hope is denied me,
Sair do I fear that despair maun abide me;
But tho' fell fortune should fate us to sever,
Queen shall she be in my bosom forever.

Mary, I'm thine wi' a passion sincerest,
And thou hast plighted me love o' the dearest!
And thou 'rt the angel that never can alter,
Sooner the sun in his motion would falter.

HOW CRUEL ARE THE PARENTS.

Altered from an old English song.

TUNE—*John Anderson, my jo.*

How cruel are the parents
    Who riches only prize:
And to the wealthy booby,
    Poor woman sacrifice!
Meanwhile the hapless daughter
    Has but a choice of strife;
To shun a tyrant father's hate,
    Become a wretched wife.

The ravening hawk pursuing,
    The trembling dove thus flies,
To shun impending ruin
    Awhile her pinions tries;
Till of escape despairing,
    No shelter or retreat,
She trusts the ruthless falconer,
    And drops beneath his feet.

MARK YONDER POMP OF COSTLY FASHION.

The Chloris of this song has inspired some of the Poet's sweetest strains.
She is said to have died lately in great poverty.

TUNE—*Deil take the wars.*

MARK yonder pomp of costly fashion,
    Round the wealthy, titled bride:
But when compared with real passion,
    Poor is all that princely pride.

[1] Stolen.

What are the showy treasures?
What are the noisy pleasures?
The gay, gaudy glare of vanity and art;
  The polish'd jewel's blaze
  May draw the wondering gaze,
  And courtly grandeur bright
  The fancy may delight,
But never, never can come near the heart.

  But did you see my dearest Chloris,
    In simplicity's array,
  Lovely as yonder sweet opening flower is,
    Shrinking from the gaze of day;
  Oh then, the heart alarming,
  And all resistless charming,
In Love's delightful fetters she chains the willing
        soul!
    Ambition would disown
    The world's imperial crown,
    Ev'n Avarice would deny
    His worshipp'd deity,
And feel thro' every vein Love's raptures roll.

FORLORN, MY LOVE, NO COMFORT NEAR.

"I have written this song," says Burns in one of his letters, "in the
course of an hour; so much for the *speed* of my Pegasus, but what say
you to his *bottom* ?"

TUNE—*Let me in this ae night.*

FORLORN, my love, no comfort near,
Far, far from thee, I wander here:
Far, far from thee, the fate severe
  At which I most repine, love.

  Oh wert thou, love, but near me,
  But near, near, near me:
  How kindly thou wouldst cheer me,
    And mingle sighs with mine, love!

Around me scowls a wintry sky,
That blasts each bud of hope and joy,
And shelter, shade, nor home, have I,
  Save in those arms of thine, love.
        Oh wert, &c.

Cold, alter'd friendship's cruel part,
To poison fortune's ruthless dart—
Let me not break thy faithful heart,
   And say that fate is mine, love.
     Oh wert, &c.

But dreary tho' the moments fleet,
Oh let me think we yet shall meet!
That only ray of solace sweet
   Can on thy Chloris shine, love.
     Oh wert, &c.

WHY, WHY TELL THY LOVER.

A FRAGMENT.

TUNE—*The Caledonian Hunt's Delight.*

WHY, why tell thy lover,
   Bliss he never must enjoy?
Why, why undeceive him,
   And give all his hopes the lie?

Oh why, while fancy, raptured, slumbers,
   Chloris, Chloris all the theme;
Why, why wouldst thou, cruel,
   Wake thy lover from his dream?

HERE'S A HEALTH TO ANE I LO'E DEAR.

This song was written for Mr. Thomson's Collection. The three first verses were sent in a letter to that gentleman, a few days before the Poet's death, which took place on the 21st July, 1796; the fourth verse was afterwards found among his manuscripts; so that this beautiful song, written under much distress of body and trouble of mind, was, in all probability, the last finished offspring of his muse.

TUNE—*Here's a health to them that's awa, hiney.*

Here's a health to ane I lo'e dear,
Here's a health to ane I lo'e dear;
Thou art sweet as the smile when fond lovers meet,
And soft as the parting tear—Jessy!

ALTHO' thou maun never be mine,
   Altho' even hope is denied:

'Tis sweeter for thee despairing,
  Than aught in the world beside—Jessy!
    Here's a health, &c.

I mourn thro' the gay, gaudy day,
  As, hopeless, I muse on thy charms;
But welcome the dream o' sweet slumber,
  For then I am lock'd in thy arms—Jessy!
    Here's a health, &c.

I guess by the dear angel smile,
  I guess by the love-rolling ee;
But why urge the tender confession
  'Gainst fortune's fell cruel decree—Jessy!
    Here's a health, &c.

FAIREST MAID ON DEVON BANKS.

This song was written at Brow, on the Solway Firth, a few days before
the Poet's death.

Tune—*Rothermurchie's Rant.*

Fairest maid on Devon banks,
  Crystal Devon, winding Devon,
Wilt thou lay that frown aside,
  And smile as thou wert wont to do?

Full well thou know'st I love thee dear,
Couldst thou to malice lend an ear?
Oh, did not Love exclaim, "Forbear,
  Nor use a faithful lover so?"
    Fairest maid, &c.

Then come, thou fairest of the fair,
Those wonted smiles, oh, let me share!
And by thy beauteous self I swear,
  No love but thine my heart shall know!
    Fairest maid, &c.

41

STAY, MY CHARMER, CAN YOU LEAVE ME.

"The peculiar rhythm of this fine Gaelic air, and the consequent difficulty of making verses to suit it, must excuse the shortness of this song."—*Morrison.*

TUNE—*An Gille dubh ciar dhubh.*

STAY, my charmer, can you leave me?
Cruel, cruel to deceive me;
Well you know how much you grieve me;
 Cruel charmer, can you go?
 Cruel charmer, can you go?

By my love so ill requited;
By the faith you fondly plighted;
By the pangs of lovers slighted;
 Do not, do not leave me so!
 Do not, do not leave me so!

MUSING ON THE ROARING OCEAN.

Written in compliment to Miss Hamilton, the sister of the Poet's early friend and patron, G. Hamilton, Esq.

TUNE—*Druimion dubh.*

MUSING on the roaring ocean,
 Which divides my love and me,
Wearying Heaven in warm devotion,
 For his weal, where'er he be.

Hope and fear's alternate billow,
 Yielding late to nature's law;
Whispering spirits round my pillow
 Talk of him that's far awa!

Ye whom sorrow never wounded,
 Ye who never shed a tear,
Care-untroubled, joy-surrounded,
 Gaudy day to you is dear.

Gentle night, do thou befriend me:
 Downy sleep, the curtain draw;
Spirits kind, again attend me,
 Talk of him that's far awa!

THE LAZY MIST, Etc.

This is an early production. It was originally written for the Museum, but since considerably altered.

IRISH AIR—*Coolun.*

THE lazy mist hangs from the brow of the hill,
Concealing the course of the dark-winding rill;
How languid the scenes, late so sprightly, appear,
As autumn to winter resigns the pale year!
The forests are leafless, the meadows are brown,
And all the gay foppery of summer is flown:
Apart let me wander, apart let me muse,
How quick time is flying, how keen fate pursues!
How long I have lived—but how much lived in vain!
How little of life's scanty span may remain!
What aspects, old Time in his progress has worn!
What ties, cruel fate in my bosom has torn!
How foolish, or worse, till our summit is gain'd!
And downward, how weaken'd, how darken'd, how
    pain'd!
This life's not worth having with all it can give,
For something beyond it poor man sure must live.

MY TOCHER'S THE JEWEL.

This clever, sensible song is also an early production, and was likewise written for the Museum.

On meikle[1] thinks my luve o' my beauty,
    And meikle thinks my luve o' my kin;
But little thinks my luve I ken brawlie,[2]
    My tocher's[3] the jewel has charms for him.
It's a' for the apple he'll nourish the tree;
    It's a' for the hiney[4] he'll cherish the bee;
My laddie's sae meikle in luve wi' the siller,
    He can na hae luve to spare for me.

Your proffer o' luve's an airl-penny,[5]
    My tocher's the bargain ye wad buy;
But an ye be crafty, I am cunnin',[6]
    Sae ye wi' anither your fortune maun try.

[1] Much.—[2] Know very well.—[3] Money.—[4] Honey.—[5] Earnest-money.—
[6] Cunning.

Ye 're like to the timmer[1] o' yon rotten wood,
Ye 're like to the bark o' yon rotten tree,
Ye 'll slip frae me like a knotless thread,
Ye 'll crack your credit wi' mae[2] nor me.

THE POSIE.

The air of this song was taken down from the singing of Mrs. Burns. The fol
lowing is the first verse of the old song to the same tune :

"There was a pretty May, and a milking she went,
Wi' her red rosie cheeks, an' her coal black hair."

Oh luve will venture in where it daur na weel[3] be seen,
Oh luve will venture in where wisdom ance has been;
But I will down yon river rove, among the wood sae green,
  And a' to pu'[4] a posie to my ain dear May.

The primrose I will pu', the firstlin' o' the year,
And I will pu' the pink, the emblem o' my dear,
For she 's the pink o' womankind, and blooms without a peer;
  And a' to be a posie to my ain dear May.

I 'll pu' the budding rose, when Phœbus peeps in view,
For it 's like a baumy kiss o' her bonnie sweet mou;
The hyacinth 's for constancy, wi' its unchanging blue,
  And a' to be a posie to my ain dear May.

The lily it is pure, and the lily it is fair,
In her lovely bosom I 'll place the lily there;
The daisy 's for simplicity and unaffected air,
  And a' to be a posie to my ain dear May.

The hawthorn I will pu', wi' its locks o' siller gray,
Where, like an agéd man, it stands at break o' day,
But the songster's nest within the bush I winna tak away;
  And a' to be a posie to my ain dear May.

The woodbine I will pu' when the e'ening star is near,
And the diamond-draps o' dew shall be her een sae clear;
The violet 's for modesty, which weel she fa's to wear,
  And a' to be a posie to my ain dear May.

I 'll tie the posie round wi' the silken band o' luve,
And I 'll place it in her breast, and I 'll swear by a' above,
That to my latest draught o' life the band shall ne'er remuve,
  And this will be a posie to my ain dear May.

Timber.—[2] More.—[3] Dare not well.—[4] Pull.

GLOOMY DECEMBER.

The old air, "Wat ye how the play began," to which this song was written, is lively—the words plaintive. Burns frequently united music and poetry together, without considering much the natural dispositions of the parties.

Ance mair[1] I hail thee, thou gloomy December!
  Ance mair I hail thee, wi' sorrow and care;
Sad was the parting thou makes me remember,
  Parting wi' Nancy—oh, ne'er to meet mair!
Fond lovers' parting is sweet painful pleasure;
  Hope beaming mild on the soft parting hour;
But the dire feeling, *Oh farewell forever*,
  Is anguish unmingled and agony pure.

Wild as the winter now tearing the forest,
  Till the last leaf of the summer is flown,
Such is the tempest has shaken my bosom,
  Since my last hope and last comfort is gone;
Still as I hail thee, thou gloomy December,
  Still shall I hail thee wi' sorrow and care;
For sad was the parting thou makes me remember
  Parting wi' Nancy—oh, ne'er to meet mair!

BONNIE BELL.

In the "Edinburgh Miscellany," 1809, a copy of this song is printed with two additional verses; but they do not appear to be the work of Burns.

The smiling Spring comes in rejoicing,
  And surly Winter grimly flies:
Now crystal clear are the falling waters,
  And bonnie blue are the sunny skies;
Fresh o'er the mountains breaks forth the morning,
  The evening gilds the ocean's swell,
All creatures joy in the sun's returning,
  And I rejoice in my bonnie Bell.

The flowery Spring leads sunny Summer,
  And yellow Autumn presses near,

[1] Once more.

Then in his turn comes gloomy Winter,
   Till smiling Spring again appear.
Thus seasons dancing, life advancing,
   Old Time and Nature their changes tell,
But never ranging, still unchanging,
   I adore my bonnie Bell.

THE GALLANT WEAVER.

In some of the earlier editions of this song, "sailor" is substituted for
"weaver."

Tune—The auld wife ayont the fire.

WHERE Cart[1] rins rowin'[2] to the sea,
By mony a flower and spreading tree,
There lives a lad, the lad for me,
   He is a gallant weaver.

Oh I had wooers aught[3] or nine,
They gied me rings and ribbons fine;
And I was fear'd my heart would tine,[4]
   And I gied it to the weaver.

My daddie sign'd my tocher-band,[5]
To gie the lad that has the land,
But to my heart I'll add my hand,
   And gie it to the weaver.

While birds rejoice in leafy bowers;
While bees rejoice in opening flowers;
While corn grows green in simmer showers,
   I'll love my gallant weaver.

---

[1] The name of a river.—[2] Runs rolling.—[3] Eight.—[4] Would be lost.—[5] Marriage-bond.

A RED, RED ROSE.

The air and the first verse of this song are taken from an old Ayrshire ballad.

Oh, my luve's like a red, red rose,
    That's newly sprung in June:
Oh, my luve's like the melodie
    That's sweetly play'd in tune.

As fair art thou, my bonnie lass,
    So deep in luve am I;
And I will luve thee still, my dear,
    Till a' the seas gang[1] dry.

Till a' the seas gang dry, my dear,
    And the rocks melt wi' the sun:
I will luve thee still, my dear,
    While the sands of life shall run.

And fare thee weel, my only luve!
    And fare thee weel a while!
And I will come again, my luve,
    Tho' it were ten thousand mile.

ON THE BATTLE OF SHERIFF-MUIR,

BETWEEN THE DUKE OF ARGYLE AND THE EARL OF MAR, FOUGHT NOV. 13, 1715.

TUNE—*The Cameronian Rant.*

"Oh cam ye here the fight to shun,
    Or herd the sheep wi' me, man?
Or were you at the Sherra-muir,
    And did the battle see, man?"
I saw the battle, sair[2] and tough,
And reekin'-red ran mony a sheugh,[3]
My heart, for fear, gae sough[4] for sough,
To hear the thuds,[5] and see the cluds,[6]
O' clans frae woods, in tartan duds,[7]
    Wha glaum'd[8] at kingdoms three, man.

Go.—[2] Sore.—[3] Ditch.—[4] Sign.—[5] A loud intermitting noise.—[6] Clouds
—[7] In clothing made of the tartan check.—[8] Aimed at.

The red-coat lads wi' black cockades
   To meet them were na slaw, man;
They rush'd and push'd, and blude outgush'd,
   And mony a bonk[1] did fa', man:
The great Argyle led on his files,
I wat they glancéd twenty miles:
They hack'd and hash'd, while broadswords clash'd,
And thro' they dash'd, and hew'd and smash'd,
   Till fey[2] men died awa, man.

But had you seen the philibegs,[3]
   And skyrin' tartan trews,[4] man,
When in the teeth they dared our whigs
   And covenant true blues, man;
In lines extended lang and large,
When bayonets opposed the targe,[5]
And thousands hasten'd to the charge,
Wi' Highland wrath they frae the sheath
Drew blades o' death, till, out o' breath,
   They fled like frighted doos,[6] man.

"Oh how deil Tam can that be true?
   The chase gaed frae the north, man:
I saw myself, they did pursue
   The horsemen back to Forth, man;
And at Dumblane, in my ain sight,
They took the brig[7] wi' a' their might,
And straught to Stirling wing'd their flight;
But, cursèd lot! the gates were shut,
And mony a huntit, poor red-coat,
   For fear amaist did swarf,[8] man."

My sister Kate cam up the gate
   Wi' crowdie unto me, man;
She swore she saw some rebels run
   Frae Perth unto Dundee, man;
Their left-hand general had nae skill,
The Angus lads had nae good will
That day their neebors' blood to spill;
For fear, by foes, that they should lose
Their cogs o' brose;[9] all crying woes,
   And so it goes, you see, man.

[1] Vomiting.—[2] Foe.—[3] A short petticoat worn by the Highlanders.—
[4] Shining checkered trowsers.—[5] Target.—[6] Doves.—[7] Bridge.—[8] Swoon.—
[9] Cups of broth.

They 've lost some gallant gentlemen,
    Amang the Highland clans, man;
I fear my lord Panmure is slain,
    Or fallen in whiggish hands, man:
Now wad ye sing this double fight,
Some fell for wrang and some for right;
But mony bade the world guid-night;
Then ye may tell, how pell and mell,
By red claymores,[1] and muskets' knell,
Wi' dying yell, the tories fell,
    And whigs to hell did flee, man.

OH WERT THOU IN THE CAULD BLAST.

This song was found among the manuscripts of Burns, after his
death, entitled " An Address to a Lady."

TUNE—*The lass of Livingstone.*

Oh wert thou in the cauld blast,
    On yonder lea, on yonder lea;
My plaidie[2] to the angry airt,[3]
    I 'd shelter thee, I 'd shelter thee:
Or did misfortune's bitter storms
    Around thee blaw, around thee blaw,
Thy bield[4] should be my bosom,
    To share it a', to share it a'.

Or were I in the wildest waste,
    Sae black and bare, sae black and bare,
The desert were a paradise,
    If thou wert there, if thou wert there.
Or were I monarch o' the globe,
    Wi' thee to reign, wi' thee to reign;
The brightest jewel in my crown,
    Wad be my queen, wad be my queen.

[1] A broadsword.—[2] Cloak.—[3] The quarter from which the wind or weather comes.—[4] Shelter.

OH WHA IS SHE THAT LO'ES ME.

This song was also found among the manuscripts of the Poet, after his death. He was very fond of the air "Morag," and wrote other songs to it.

TUNE—*Morag.*

OH wha is she that lo'es me,
  And has my heart a keeping?
Oh sweet is she that lo'es me,
  As dews o' simmer weeping,
  In tears the rose-buds steeping.

    Oh that's the lassie o' my heart,
     My lassie ever dearer ;
    Oh that's the queen o' woman-kind,
     And ne'er a ane to peer her.

If thou shalt meet a lassie
  In grace and beauty charming,
That e'en thy chosen lassie,
  Erewhile thy breast sae warming,
  Had ne'er sic powers alarming;
    Oh that's, &c.

If thou hadst heard her talking,
  And thy attentions plighted,
That ilka body talking
  But her by thee is slighted;
  And thou art all delighted;
    Oh that's, &c.

If thou hast met this fair one;
  When frae her thou hast parted,
If every other fair one
  But her thou hast deserted,
  And thou art broken-hearted;
    Oh that's, &c.

ADDRESS TO GENERAL DUMOURIER.

First published in the " Reliques."

(A PARODY ON " ROBIN ADAIR.")

YOU'RE welcome to despots, Dumourier;
You're welcome to despots, Dumourier.—

How does Dampiere do?
Aye, and Bournonville too?
Why did they not come along with you, Dumourier?

I will fight France with you, Dumourier,—
I will fight France with you, Dumourier:—
I will fight France with you,
I will take my chance with you;
By my soul I'll dance a dance with you, Dumourier.

Then let us fight about, Dumourier;
Then let us fight about, Dumourier;
Then let us fight about,
Till freedom's spark is out,
Then we'll be d—mn'd no doubt—Dumourier.

OH ONCE I LOVED A BONNIE LASS.

This was our Poet's first attempt.

TUNE—*I am a man unmarried.*

Oh once I loved a bonnie lass,
    Ay, and I love her still,
And whilst that honor warms my breast,
    I'll love my handsome Nell.
            Fal lal de ral, &c.

As bonnie lasses I hae seen,
    And mony[1] full as braw,[2]
But for a modest gracefu' mien,
    The like I never saw.

A bonnie lass, I will confess,
    Is pleasant to the ee,
But without some better qualities
    She's no a lass for me.

But Nelly's looks are blythe and sweet,
    And what is best of a',
Her reputation is complete,
    And fair without a flaw.

[1] Many.—[2] Fine.

She dresses ay sae clean and neat,
  Both decent and genteel:
And then there's something in her gait
  Gars[1] ony dress look weel.

A gaudy dress and gentle air
  May slightly touch the heart,
But it's innocence and modesty
  That polishes the dart:

'Tis this in Nelly pleases me,
  'Tis this enchants my soul;
For absolutely in my breast
  She reigns without control.
          Fal lal de ral, &c.

I DREAM'D I LAY WHERE FLOWERS WERE SPRINGING.

"These two stanzas I composed when I was seventeen,[2] and are among the oldest of my printed pieces."—*Burns's Reliques.*

I DREAM'D I lay where flowers were springing,
  Gayly in the sunny beam;
Listening to the wild birds singing,
  By a falling, crystal stream:
Straight the sky grew black and daring;
  Thro' the woods the whirlwinds rave;
Trees with agéd arms were warring,
  O'er the swelling, drumlie[3] wave.

Such was my life's deceitful morning,
  Such the pleasures I enjoy'd;
But lang or noon,[4] loud tempest storming,
  A' my flowery bliss destroy'd.
Tho' fickle fortune has deceived me,
  (She promised fair, and perform'd but ill;)
Of mony a joy and hope bereaved me,
  I bear a heart shall support me still.

[1] Makes.
[2] It is perhaps worthy of remark, that in this song of *seventeen*, there is, strictly speaking, only one Scotch word - the word *drumlie*—a circumstance that promised little for our author's future eminence as a Scottish Poet.
[3] Muddy.—[4] Long before noon.

THERE'S A YOUTH IN THIS CITY.

This air is claimed by Neil Gow, who calls it his lament for his brother,
The first half-stanza of the song is old.

THERE's a youth in this city, it were a great pity,
   That he from our lasses should wander awa;
For he's bonnie and braw, weel-favor'd with a',
   And his hair has a natural buckle and a'.
His coat is the hue of his bonnet sae blue;
   His fecket[1] is white as the new-driven sraw;
His hose they are blae, and his shoon[2] like the slae,
   And his clear siller buckles they dazzle us a'.
      His coat is the hue, &c.

For beauty and fortune the laddie's been courtin';
   Weel featur'd, weel tocher'd, weel mounted and braw
But chiefly the siller, that gars him gang till her;[3]
   The pennie's the jewel that beautifies a'.—
There's Meg wi' the mailen,[4] that fain wad a haen him,[5]
   And Susy, whase daddy was Laird o' the ha';
There's lang-tocher'd Nancy[6] maist fetters his fancy,
   —But the laddie's dear sel he lo'es dearest of a'.

MY HEART'S IN THE HIGHLANDS.

The first half-stanza of this song is old.

My heart's in the Highlands, my heart is not here;
My heart's in the Highlands a chasing the deer;
Chasing the wild deer, and following the roe,
My heart's in the Highlands wherever I go.
Farewell to the Highlands, farewell to the North,
The birthplace of valor, the country of worth;
Wherever I wander, wherever I rove,
The hills of the Highlands forever I love.

Farewell to the mountains high cover'd with snow;
Farewell to the straths and green valleys below;

---

[1] An under-waistcoat with sleeves.—[2] Shoes.—[3] Causes him to go to her
—[4] Farm.—[5] Would have had him.—[6] Nancy with a great marriage portion

Farewell to the forests and wild-hanging woods;
Farewell to the torrents and loud-pouring floods.
My heart's in the Highlands, my heart is not here,
My heart's in the Highlands a chasing the deer:
Chasing the wild deer, and following the roe,
My heart's in the Highlands, wherever I go.

CRAIGIE-BURN WOOD.

This song, says Burns, was composed on a passion which a Mr. Gillespie, a particular friend of mine, had for a Miss Lorimer, afterwards a Mrs. Whelpdale. The young lady was born at Craigie-burn wood. The chorus is part of an old foolish ballad. Another copy of this will be found, ante, p. 442.

Beyond thee, dearie, beyond thee, dearie,
And oh to be lying beyond thee,
Oh sweetly, soundly, weel may he sleep,
That's laid in the bed beyond thee.

SWEET closes the evening on Craigie-burn wood,
  And blythely awakens the morrow;
But the pride of the spring in the Craigie-burn wood,
  Can yield to me nothing but sorrow.
    Beyond thee, &c.

I see the spreading leaves and flowers,
  I hear the wild-birds singing;
But pleasure they hae nane for me,
  While care my heart is wringing.
    Beyond thee, &c.

I canna tell, I maunna tell,
  I dare na for your anger;
But secret love will break my heart
  If I conceal it langer.
    Beyond thee, &c.

I see thee gracefu', straight, and tall,
  I see thee sweet and bonnie,
But oh, what will my torments be,
  If thou refuse thy Johnie!
    Beyond thee, &c.

To see thee in anither's arms,
In love to lie and languish,
'Twad be my dead, that will be seen,
My heart wad burst wi' anguish.
Beyond thee, &c.

But Jeanie, say thou wilt be mine,
Say, thou lo'es nane before me;
An' a' my days o' life to come
I'll gratefully adore thee.
Beyond thee, &c.

I DO CONFESS THOU ART SAE FAIR.

This song is altered from a poem by Sir Robert Ayton, private secretary
to Mary and Anne, queens of Scotland.

I DO confess thou art sae fair,
I wad been o'er the lugs[1] in luve,
Had I na[2] found the slightest prayer
That lips could speak, thy heart could muve.

I do confess thee sweet, but find
Thou art sae thriftless o' thy sweets,
Thy favors are the silly wind
That kisses ilka[3] thing it meets.

See yonder rose-bud, rich in dew,
Amang its native briers sae coy,
How sune it tines[4] its scent and hue,
When pu'd and worn a common toy!

Sic fate ere lang shall thee betide,
Tho' thou may gayly bloom a while;
Yet sune thou shalt be thrown aside,
Like ony common weed and vile.

YON WILD MOSSY MOUNTAINS.

Written for the "Caledonian Musical Repository," a collection of Scottish songs and
airs, published at Edinburgh in 1789; and set to the old tune of "Falkland Fair."

Yon wild mossy mountains, sae lofty and wide,
That nurse in their bosom the youth o' the Clyde.

[1] Ears.—[2] Not.—[3] Every.—[4] Soon it loses.

Where the grouse lead their coveys thro' the heather to
    feed,
And the shepherd tents his flock as he pipes on his reed.
            Where the grouse, &c.

Not Gowrie's rich valley, nor Forth's sunny shores,
To me hae the charms o' yon wild, mossy moors;
For there, by a lanely, sequester'd, clear stream,
Beside a sweet lassie, my thought and my dream.

Amang thae wild mountains shall still be my path,
Ilk stream foaming down its ain green narrow strath;
For there, wi' my lassie, the day lang I rove,
While o'er us, unheeded, flie the swift hours o' love.

She is not the fairest, altho' she is fair;
O' nice education but sma' is her share;
Her parentage humble as humble can be,
But I lo'e the dear lassie because she lo'es me.

To beauty what man but maun yield him a prize,
In her armor of glances, and blushes, and sighs;
And when wit and refinement hae polish'd her darts,
They dazzle our een, as they flie to our hearts.

But kindness, sweet kindness, in the fond sparkling ee,
Has lustre outshining the diamond to me;
And the heart-beating love, as I 'm clasp'd in her arms,
Oh these are my lassie's all-conquering charms!

MY FATHER WAS A FARMER.

"This song is a wild rhapsody, miserably deficient in versification, but as the
sentiments are the genuine feelings of my heart, for that reason I have a particular
pleasure in conning it over."—*Burns's Reliques*, p. 329.

Tune—The Weaver and his Shuttle, O.

My father was a farmer
    Upon the Carrick border, O,
And carefully he bred me
    In decency and order, O;
He bade me act a manly part,
    Though I had ne'er a farthing, O;
For without an honest manly heart,
    No man was worth regarding, O.

Then out into the world
  My course I did determine, O ;
Tho' to be rich was not my wish,
  Yet to be great was charming, O ;
My talents they were not the worst,
  Nor yet my education, O :
Resolved was I, at least to try,
  To mend my situation, O.

In many a way, and vain essay,
  I courted fortune's favor, O ;
Some cause unseen, still stept between,
  To frustrate each endeavor, O :
Sometimes by foes I was o'erpower'd ;
  Sometimes by friends forsaken, O ;
And when my hope was at the top,
  I still was worst mistaken, O.

Then sore harass'd, and tired at last,
  With fortune's vain delusion, O,
I dropt my schemes, like idle dreams,
  And came to this conclusion, O :
The past was bad, and the future hid ;
  Its good or ill untriéd, O ;
But the present hour was in my power ;
  And so I would enjoy it, O.

No help, nor hope, nor view had I ;
  Nor person to befriend me, O ;
So I must toil, and sweat and broil,
  And labor to sustain me, O,
To plough and sow, to reap and mow,
  My father bred me early, O ;
For one, he said, to labor bred,
  Was a match for fortune fairly, O.

Thus all obscure, unknown and poor,
  Thro' life I 'm doom'd to wander, O,
Till down my weary bones I lay,
  In everlasting slumber, O ;
No view nor care, but shun whate'er
  Might breed me pain or sorrow, O ;
I live to-day, as well 's I may,
  Regardless of to-morrow, O.

But cheerful still, I am as well
  As a monarch in a palace, O,
Tho' fortune's frown still hunts me down,
  With all her wonted malice, O;
I make, indeed, my daily bread,
  But ne'er can make it farther, O;
But as daily bread is all I need,
  I do not much regard her, O.

When sometimes by my labor
  I earn a little money, O,
Some unforeseen misfortune comes
  Generally upon me, O;
Mischance, mistake, or by neglect,
  Or my good-natured folly, O:
But come what will, I 've sworn it still,
  I 'll ne'er be melancholy, O.

All you who follow wealth and power
  With unremitting ardor, O.
The more in this you look for bliss,
  You leave your view the farther, O;
Had you the wealth Potosi boasts,
  Or nations to adore you, O,
A cheerful honest-hearted clown
  I will prefer before you, O.

I 'LL KISS THEE YET.

"The name of Peggy Allison gives an air of truth and reality to this little warm affectionate song."—*See Scottish Songs.*

Our Poet was sometimes not very happy in naming his heroines: the names of Chloris, Phillis, &c., look strangely in a Scottish song.

TUNE—*Braes o' Balquhidder.*

I 'll kiss thee yet, yet,
  An' I 'll kiss thee o'er again,
An' I 'll kiss thee yet, yet,
  My bonnie Peggy Allison !

ILK[1] care and fear, when thou art near,
  I ever mair defy them, O;
Young kings upon their hansel[2] throne
  Are no sae blest as I am, O !
    I 'll kiss thee, &c.

[1] Each.—[2] When they first mount the throne

When in my arms, wi' a' thy charms,
    I clasp my countless treasure, O ;
I seek nae mair o' Heaven to share,
    Than sic' a moment's pleasure, O !
        I'll kiss thee, &c.

And by thy een, sae bonnie blue,
    I swear I'm thine forever, O ;—
And on thy lips I seal my vow,
    And break it shall I never, O !
        I'll kiss thee, &c.

ON CESSNOCK BANKS THERE LIVES A LASS.

Recovered from the recitation of a lady in Glasgow, and first published
by Cromek.

Tune—*If he be a butcher neat and trim.*

On Cessnock banks there lives a lass—
    Could I describe her shape and mien ;
The graces of her weel-fared face,
    And the glancin' of her sparklin' een.[2]

She's fresher than the morning dawn
    When rising Phœbus first is seen,
When dew-drops twinkle o'er the lawn ;
    An' she's twa glancin' sparklin' een.

She's stately like yon youthful ash,
    That grows the cowslip braes between,
And shoots its head above each bush ;
    An' she's twa glancin' sparklin' een.

She's spotless as the flowering thorn,
    With flowers so white and leaves so green,
When purest in the dewy morn ;
    An' she's twa glancin' sparklin' een.

Her looks are like the sportive lamb,
    When flowery May adorns the scene,
That wantons round its bleating dam ;
    An' she's twa glancin' sparklin' een.

[1] Such.—[2] Eyes.

Her hair is like the curling mist
  That shades the mountain-side at e'en,
When flower-reviving rains are past;
  An' she 's twa glancin' sparklin' een.

Her forehead 's like the showery bow,
  When shining sunbeams intervene,
And gild the distant mountain's brow;
  An' she 's twa glancin' sparklin' een.

Her voice is like the evening thrush
  That sings in Cessnock banks unseen,
While his mate sits nestling in the bush;
  An' she 's twa glancin' sparklin' een.

Her lips are like the cherries ripe
  That sunny walls from Boreas screen,
They tempt the taste and charm the sight;
  An' she 's twa glancin' sparklin' een.

Her teeth are like a flock of sheep,
  With fleeces newly washen clean,
That slowly mount the rising steep;
  An' she 's twa glancin' sparklin' een.

Her breath is like the fragrant breeze
  That gently stirs the blossom'd bean,
When Phœbus sinks behind the seas;
  An' she 's twa glancin' sparklin' een.

But it 's not her air, her form, her face,
  Tho' matching Beauty's fabled Queen,
But the mind that shines in every grace,
  An' chiefly in her sparklin' een.

———

WAE IS MY HEART.

First published in the " Reliques."

Wae[1] is my heart, and the tear 's in my ee;[2]
Lang, lang joy 's been a stranger to me:
Forsaken and friendless my burden I bear,
And the sweet voice o' pity ne'er sounds in my ear.

---

[1] Woe.—[2] Eye.

Love, thou hast pleasures; and deep hae I loved;
Love, thou hast sorrows; and sair hae I proved:
But this bruised heart that now bleeds in my breast,
I can feel by its throbbings will soon be at rest.

Oh if I were, where happy I hae been,
Down by yon stream and yon bonnie castle green;
For there he is wandering and musing on me,
Wha wad soon dry the tear frae Phillis's ee.

THE DEIL'S AWA WI' THE EXCISEMAN.

At a meeting of his brother Excisemen in Dumfries, Burns being called upon
for a song, handed these verses extempore to the President, written on the back
of a letter.

THE Deil came fiddling thro' the town,
   And danced awa wi' the Exciseman;
And ilka wife cried, "Auld Mahoun,[1]
   We wish you luck o' the prize, man.

    "We'll mak our maut, and brew our drink,
      We'll dance, and sing, and rejoice, man;
    And monie thanks to the muckle black Deil,
      That danced awa wi' the Exciseman.

"There's threesome reels, and foursome reels,
   There's hornpipes and strathspeys, man;
But the ae best dance e'er cam to our lan',
   Was—the Deil's awa wi' the Exciseman.
       "*We'll mak our maut,*" &c.

I RED[2] YOU BEWARE AT THE HUNTING.

First published in the "Reliques," from a manuscript in the possession of the
Poet's intimate friend, Mr. Cunningham.

THE heather was blooming, the meadows were maun,[3]
Our lads gaed[4] a hunting, ae day at the dawn,
O'er moors and o'er mosses and mony a glen;
At length they discover'd a bonnie moor-hen.

---

[1] A name given to the Devil.—[2] Counsel, caution.—[3] Mown.—[4] Went.

I red you beware at the hunting, young men;
I red you beware at the hunting, young men;
Tak some on the wing, and some as they spring,
But cannily steal on a bonnie moor-hen.

Sweet brushing the dew from the brown heather bells,
Her colors betray'd her on yon mossy fells;
Her plumage out-lustred the pride o' the spring,
And oh! as she wantonéd gay on the wing,
      I red, &c.

Auld Phœbus himsel, as he peep'd o'er the hill,
In spite at her plumage he triéd his skill;
He levell'd his rays where she bask'd on the brae—
His rays were outshone, and but mark'd where she lay.
      I red, &c.

They hunted the valley, they hunted the hill;
The best of our lads wi' the best o' their skill;
But still as the fairest she sat in their sight,
Then, whirr! she was over, a mile at a flight.—
      I red, &c.

   *   *   *   *   *   *

AMANG THE TREES WHERE HUMMING BEES.

From the Poet's memorandum-book; first published in the "Reliques."

TUNE—*The King of France, he rade a race.*

AMANG the trees where humming bees
    At buds and flowers were hinging, O,
Auld Caledon drew out her drone,
    And to her pipe was singing, O.
'Twas pibroch,[1] sang, strathspey, or reels,
    She dirl'd[2] them aff, fu' clearly, O;
When there cam a yell o' foreign squeels,[3]
    That dang[4] her tapsalteerie,[5] O.

Their capon craws[6] and queer ha ha's,
    They made our lugs[7] grow eerie,[8] O;
The hungry bike[9] did scrape and pike
    Till we were wae and weary, O:

---

[1] A Highland war-song, adapted to the bagpipe.—[2] Struck slightly, yet quick.—[3] Screams.—[4] Drove.—[5] Topsy-turvy.—[6] Hen-crowing.—[7] Ears.—[8] Frightened.—[9] Bee-hive.

But a royal ghaist wha ance was cased
A prisoner aughteen years awa,
He fired a fiddler in the North
That dang them tapsalteerie, O.

*   *   *   *   *   *

ONE NIGHT AS I DID WANDER.

A FRAGMENT.

From the Poet's Common-place Book, published by Cromek.

TUNE—*John Anderson, my jo.*

ONE night as I did wander,
    When corn begins to shoot,
I sat me down to ponder
    Upon an auld tree root:

Auld Ayr ran by before me,
    And bicker'd to the seas;
A cushat[1] crooded o'er me,
    That echoed thro' the braes.

*   *   *   *   *   *

THERE WAS A LAD WAS BORN AT KYLE.

A FRAGMENT.

The following is also an extract from the same Common-place Book of
Observations, Hints, Songs, Scraps of Poetry, &c., by Robert Burness (for
so Burns in early life spelt his name), first published by Cromek.

TUNE—*Daintie Davie.*

THERE was a lad was born at Kyle,[2]
But what na day o' what na style—
I doubt it's hardly worth the while
    To be sae nice wi' Robin.

    Robin was a rovin' boy,
      Rantin' rovin', rantin' rovin':
    Robin was a rovin' boy,
      Rantin' rovin' Robin.

[1] The dove, or wild pigeon.—[2] A district of Ayrshire.

Our monarch's hindmost year but ane
Was five-and-twenty days begun,
'Twas then a blast o' Janwar' win
    Blew hansel in on Robin.

The gossip keekit[1] in his loof,[2]
Quo' scho, "Wha lives will see the proof,
This waly[3] boy will be nae coof,[4]
    I think we 'll ca' him Robin.

"He 'll hae misfortunes great and sma',
But ay a heart aboon them a';
He 'll be a credit till[5] us a',
    We 'll a' be proud o' Robin.

"But sure as three times three mak nine,
I see by ilka[6] score and line,
This chap will dearly like our kin',[7]
    So leeze[8] me on thee, Robin.

"Guid faith," quo' scho, "I doubt you, Sir,
Ye gar the lasses * * * *
But twenty fauts ye may hae waur[9]—
    So blessin's on thee, Robin!"

            Robin was a rovin' boy, &c.

WHEN FIRST I CAME TO STEWART KYLE.

A FRAGMENT.

TUNE—*I had a horse and I had nae mair.*

When first I came to Stewart Kyle,
    My mind it was na steady,
Where'er I gaed,[10] where'er I rade,
    A mistress still I had ay:

But when I came roun' by Mauchline town,
    Not dreadin' ony body,
My heart was caught before I thought,
    And by a Mauchline lady.[11]
        *   *   *   *   *   *   *

[1] Peeped.—[2] Palm of the hand.—[3] Jolly.—[4] Blockhead.—[5] To.—[6] Every.
—[7] Kind, sex.—[8] A phrase of congratulatory endearment.—[9] Worse.—
—[10] Went.—[11] Jean Armour, afterwards Mrs. Burns.

MONTGOMERIE'S PEGGY.

A FRAGMENT.

TUNE—*Galla Water.*

ALTHO' my bed were in yon muir,
  Amang the heather, in my pladdie,
Yet happy, happy would I be
  Had I my dear Montgomerie's Peggy.—

When o'er the hill beat surly storms,
  And winter nights were dark and rainy;
I'd seek some dell, and in my arms
  I'd shelter dear Montgomerie's Peggy.—

Were I a baron proud and high,
  And horse and servants waiting ready,
Then a' 'twad gie o' joy to me,
  The sharin' 't with Montgomerie's Peggy—
    *   *   *   *   *   *

OH, RAGING FORTUNE'S WITHERING BLAST

A FRAGMENT.

OH, raging fortune's withering blast
  Has laid my leaf full low, O!
Oh, raging fortune's withering blast
  Has laid my leaf full low, O!
My stem was fair, my bud was green,
  My blossom sweet did blow, O;
The dew fell fresh, the sun rose mild,
  And made my branches grow, O.
But luckless fortune's northern storms
  Laid a' my blossoms low, O;
But luckless fortune's northern storms
  Laid a' my blossoms low, O.

HERE'S A HEALTH TO TO THEM THAT'S AWA.

The first three verses of this excellent patriotic song were first published in the Edinburgh Magazine for 1818, from a manuscript in the handwriting of Burns. The remaining two verses appeared some time after in the same periodical, with a note by the editor, proving their authenticity. The first complete copy of the song was printed in a little volume entitled, "The Lyric Muse of Robert Burns," published in 1819, by the late John Smith, bookseller, Montrose.

HERE's a health to them that's awa,
   And here's to them that's awa;
And wha winna[1] wish guid luck to our cause,
   May never guid luck be their fa'![2]
It's guid to be merry and wise,
   It's guid to be honest and true,
It's guid to support Caledonia's cause,
   And bide by the buff and the blue.

Here's a health to them that's awa,
   And here's to them that's awa;
Here's a health to Charlie, the chief o' the clan,
   Altho' that his band be sma'.
May liberty meet wi' success!
   May prudence protect her frae evil!
May tyrants and tyranny tine[3] in the mist,
   And wander their way to the devil!

Here's a health to them that's awa,
   And here's to them that's awa;
Here's a health to Tammie, the Norland laddie,
   That lives at the lug[4] o' the law!
Here's freedom to him that wad read,
   Here's freedom to him that wad write!
There's nane ever fear'd that the truth should be heard,
   But they whom the truth wad indite.

Here's a health to them that's awa;
   And here's to them that's awa;
Here's Maitland and Wycombe, and wha does na
     like 'em
   We'll build in a hole o' the wa'.

[1] Will not.—[2] Fate, lot.—[3] Be lost.—[4] The ear; i. e. close to.

Here 's timmer[1] that 's red at the heart,
　Here 's fruit that 's sound at the core!
May he that would turn the buff and blue coat,
　Be turn'd to the back o' the door.

Here 's a health to them that 's awa,
　And here 's to them that 's awa;
Here 's Chieftain M'Leod, a chieftain worth gowd,
　Though bred amang mountains o' snaw!
Here 's friends on baith sides o' the Forth,
　And friends on baith sides o' the Tweed,
And wha would betray old Albion's rights,
　May they never eat of her bread.

THE PLOUGHMAN.

This and the two following Fragments are excellent; the second, "The Winter
it is past," &c., is particularly so. It is conceived in the spirit, and expressed in the
manner, of the old ballad.

As I was wandering ae morning in spring,
I heard a young Ploughman sae sweetly to sing,
And as he was singing thir[2] words he did say—
"There 's nae life like the Ploughman in the month o'
　sweet May.—

"The lav'rock in the morning she 'll rise frae her nest,
And mount to the air wi' the dew on her breast,
And wi' the merry Ploughman she 'll whistle and sing,
And at night she 'll return to her nest back again."

THE WINTER IT IS PAST, Etc.

A FRAGMENT.

The winter it is past, and the summer comes at last,
　And the small birds sing on every tree;
Now every thing is glad, while I am very sad,
　Since my true love is parted from me.

[1] Timber, wood.—[2] These.

The rose upon the brier by the waters running clear,
  May have charms for the linnet or the bee;
Their little loves are blest, and their little hearts at rest,
  But my true love is parted from me.

DAMON AND SYLVIA.

A FRAGMENT.

Yon wandering rill, that marks the hill,
  And glances o'er the brae, Sir,
Slides by a bower where mony a flower,
  Sheds fragrance on the day, Sir.

There Damon lay, with Sylvia gay:
  To love they thought nae crime, Sir;
The wild-birds sang, the echoes rang,
  While Damon's heart beat time, Sir.

POLLY STEWART.

This happy little song was written for the Museum. It is an early
production.

TUNE—*Ye're welcome, Charlie Stewart*

O lovely Polly Stewart,
  O charming Polly Stewart,
There's ne'er a flower that blooms in May
  That's half so fair as thou art.

The flower it blaws, it fades, it fa's,
  And art can ne'er renew it;
But worth and truth eternal youth
  Will gie to Polly Stewart.

May he whase arms shall fauld thy charms,
  Possess a leal and true heart;
To him be given to ken the heaven
  He grasps in Polly Stewart!
    O lovely, &c.

THERE WAS A BONNIE LASS.

A FRAGMENT.

THERE was a bonnie lass, and a bonnie, bonnie lass,
  And she lo'ed her bonnie laddie dear;
Till war's loud alarms tore her laddie frae her arms,
  Wi' monie a sigh and tear.

Over sea, over shore, where the cannons loudly roar,
  He still was a stranger to fear:
And nocht[1] could him quell, or his bosom assail,
  But the bonnie lass he lo'ed sae dear.

TIBBIE DUNBAR,

The person who composed the air of this song was a Girvan fiddler, a Johny
M'Gill—he named it after himself.

TUNE—*Johny M'Gill.*

OH wilt thou go wi' me, sweet Tibbie Dunbar?
Oh wilt thou go wi' me, sweet Tibbie Dunbar?
Wilt thou ride on a horse, or be drawn in a car,
Or walk by my side, O sweet Tibbie Dunbar?
I carena[2] thy daddie, his lands and his money,
I carena thy kin, sae high and sae lordly:
But say thou wilt hae me for better for waur,[3]
And come in thy coatie, sweet Tibbie Dunbar.

ROBIN SHURE IN HAIRST.

First published in the Poetry, "Original and Selected," by Brash and
Reid, of Glasgow.

Robin shure in hairst,[4]
  I shure wi' him,
Fient[5] a heuk[6] had I,
  Yet I stack[7] by him.

Nothing.—[2] Care not for.—[3] Worse.—[4] Did shear, or reap, in harvest.—
[5] A petty oath of negation.—[6] Reaping-hook.—[7] Stuck.

I GAED[1] up to Dunse,
  To warp a wab[2] o' plaiden,
At his daddie's yett,[3]
  Wha met me but Robin!

Was na Robin bauld,[4]
  Though I was a cotter,
Play'd me sic[5] a trick
  And me the eller's dochter?[6]
    Robin shure, &c.

Robin promised me
  A' my winter vittle,[7]
Fient haet he had but three
  Goose feathers and a whittle.
    Robin shure, &c.

MY LADY'S GOWN THERE'S GAIRS UPON 'T.

The original of this song will be found in Sibbald's "Chronicle of Scottish Poetry."

My lady's gown there's gairs upon 't,[8]
And gowden flowers sae rare upon 't;
But Jenny's jimps[9] and jirkinet,[10]
My lord thinks muckle mair[11] upon 't.

My lord a-hunting he is gane,
But hounds or hawks wi' him are nane,
By Colin's cottage lies his game,
If Colin's Jenny be at hame.
    My lady's gown, &c.,

My lady's white, my lady's red,
And kith[12] and kin o' Cassillis' blude,
But her ten-pund lands o' tocher[13] guid
Were a' the charms his lordship lo'ed.
    My lady's gown, &c.

Out o'er yon muir, out o'er yon moss,
Whare gor-cocks thro' the heather pass,

------

[1] Went. — [2] Web. — [3] Gate. — [4] Bold. — [5] Such. — [6] Elder's daughter. — [7] Victuals. — [8] Triangular pieces of cloth sewed on the bottom of it. — [9] Easy stays. — [10] Short gown. — [11] Much more. — [12] Kindred. — [13] Marriage portion.

There wons[1] auld Colin's bonnie lass,
A lily in a wilderness.
> *My lady's gown, &c.*

Sae sweetly move her genty[2] limbs,
Like music notes o' lover's hymns:
The diamond dew[3] in her een sae blue,
Where laughing love sae wanton swims.
> *My lady's gown, &c.*

My lady 's dink,[3] my lady 's drest,
The flower and fancy o' the west;
But the lassie that a man lo'es best,
Oh that 's the lass to make him blest.
> *My lady's gown, &c.*

WEE WILLIE GRAY.

This and the following two verses are imitations of old songs

Wee[4] Willie Gray, and his leather wallet;
Peel a willow-wand to be him boots and jacket:
The rose upon the brier will be him trouse and doublet,
The rose upon the brier will be him trouse and doublet.

Wee Willie Gray, and his leather wallet;
Twice a lily flower will be him sark and cravat:
Feathers of a flee[5] wad feather up his bonnet,
Feathers of a flee wad feather up his bonnet.

OH GUID ALE COMES.

> *Oh guid ale comes, and guid ale goes,*
> *Guid ale gars[6] me sell my hose,*
> *Sell my hose, and pawn my shoon,*
> *Guid ale keeps my heart aboon.*

I had sax owsen[7] in a pleugh,
They drew a' weel eneugh,
I sell'd them a' just ane by ane;
Guid ale keeps my heart aboon.

[1] Dwells.—[2] Elegantly formed.—[3] Neat, trim.—[4] Little.—[5] Fly.—[6] Makes.
—[7] Six oxen.

Guid ale hauds¹ me bare and busy,
Gars me moop wi' the servant lizzie,
Stand i' the stool² when I hae done,
Guid ale keeps my heart aboon.
Oh guid ale comes, &c.

OH LAY THY LOOF IN MINE, LASS.

Written for the Museum. The chorus is partly old

Oh lay thy loof³ in mine, lass,
In mine, lass, in mine, lass,
And swear in thy white hand, lass,
That thou wilt be my ain.

A SLAVE to love's unbounded sway,
He aft has wrought me meikle wae;⁴
But now he is my deadly fae,
Unless thou be my ain.
Oh lay thy loof, &c.

There's mony a lass has broke my rest,
That for a blink I hae lo'ed best;
But thou art queen within my breast,
Forever to remain.
Oh lay thy loof, &c.

EXTEMPORE.⁵

April, 1782.

Oh why the deuce should I repine,
And be an ill foreboder?
I'm twenty-three, and five feet nine—
I'll go and be a sodger.
I gat some gear wi' meikle care,
I held it weel thegither;
But now it's gane and something mair,
I'll go and be a sodger.

---

¹ Holds.—² Stool of repentance.—³ Palm of the hand.—⁴ Much woe.—
⁵ An early production.

OH LEAVE NOVELS.

Extracted from the Poet's memorandum-book, when farmer at Mossgiel.

Oh leave novels, ye Mauchline belles,
    Ye 're safer at your spinning-wheel;
Such witching books are baited hooks,
    For rakish rooks like Rob Mossgiel.
Your fine Tom Jones and Grandisons,
    They make your youthful fancies reel,
They heat your brains, and fire your veins,
    And then you 're prey for Rob Mossgiel.

Beware a tongue that 's smoothly hung;
    A heart that warmly seems to feel;
That feeling heart but acts a part,
    'Tis rakish art in Rob Mossgiel.
The frank address, the soft caress,
    Are worse than poison'd darts of steel;
The frank address, and politesse,
    Are all finesse in Rob Mossgiel.

OH AY MY WIFE SHE DANG ME.

The chorus and the two concluding lines of this song are from an old ballad
of considerable length, which tradition has still preserved in Kincardineshire.

Oh ay my wife she dang me,
*   An' aft my wife she bang'd me;*
If ye gie a woman a' her will,
*   Guid faith she 'll soon o'ergang ye.*

On peace and rest my mind was bent,
    And fool I was I married;
But never honest man's intent,
    As cursedly miscarried.

Some sairie[1] comfort still at last,
    When a' thir[2] days are done, man,
My pains o' hell on earth is past,
    I 'm sure o' bliss aboon, man.
    Oh ay my wife, &c.

[1] Sorry.—[2] These.

THE DEUK'S DANG O'ER MY DADDIE.

There is still much of the spirit of the old indelicate song of the same name, in the following verses.

THE bairns[1] gat out wi' an unco[2] shout,
  The deuk[3]'s dang[4] o'er my daddie, O!
The fient[5] ma care, quo' the feirie[6] auld wife,
  He was but a paidlin[7] body, O!
He paidles out, and he paidles in,
  An' he paidles late and early, O;
This seven lang years I hae lien by his side,
  An' he is but a fusionless[8] carlie, O.

Oh haud your tongue, my feirie auld wife,
  Oh haud your tongue now, Nansie, O:
I've seen the day, and sae hae ye,
  Ye wadna been sae donsie,[9] O:
I've seen the day ye butter'd my brose,
  And cuddled me late and earlie, O;
But downa[10] do 's come o'er me now,
  And, oh, I find it sairly, O!

THE FIVE CARLINS.—AN ELECTION BALLAD.

There is considerable humor in this ballad. It was written on a desperately contested election for the Dumfries district of boroughs, between Sir James Johnson of Wester-hall, and Mr. Miller of Dalswinton.

TUNE—*Chevy-chace.*

THERE were five Carlins[11] in the south,
  They fell upon a scheme,
To send a lad to Lon'on town
  To bring us tidings hame.

Not only bring us tidings hame,
  But do our errands there,
And aiblins[12] gowd and honor baith
  Might be that laddie's share.

[1] Children.—[2] Great.—[3] Duck.—[4] Driven or pushed.—[5] Fiend.—[6] Stout, vigorous.—[7] Infirm, walking with a feeble step.—[8] Dry, sapless.—[9] Unlucky.—[10] Unable, cannot.—[11] Stout old women.—[12] Perhaps.

There was Maggie by the banks o' Nith,[1]
  A dame wi' pride eneugh;
And Marjorie o' the monie Loch,[2]
  A Carlin auld an' teugh.[3]

And blinkin' Bess o' Annandale,[4]
  That dwells near Solway side,
And whisky Jean that took her gill[5]
  In Galloway so wide.

And auld black Joan frae Creighton peel,[6]
  O' gipsy kith an' kin,[7]
Five weightier Carlins were na found
  The south kintra[8] within.

To send a lad to Lon'on town
  They met upon a day,
And monie a Knight and monie a Laird,
  That errand fain would gae.

Oh! monie a Knight and monie a Laird,
  This errand fain would gae;
But nae ane could their fancy please,
  Oh! ne'er a ane but twae.

The first ane was a belted Knight,
  Bred o' a border band,
An' he wad gae to Lon'on town,
  Might nae man him withstand.

And he wad do their errands weel,
  And meikle he wad say,
And ilka ane at Lon'on court
  Wad bid to him guid day.

Then neist came in a sodger youth,
  And spak wi' modest grace,
An' he wad gae to Lon'on town,
  If sae their pleasure was.

He wad na hecht[9] them courtly gift,
  Nor meikle speech pretend;
But he wad hecht an honest heart—
  Wad ne'er desert his friend.

Dumfries.—[2] Lochmaben.—[3] Teugh.—[4] Annan.—[5] Kirkcudbright.—
[6] Sanquhar.—[7] Kindred.—[8] Country.—[9] Offer.

Now whom to choose and whom refuse:
　To strife thae Carlins fell;
For some had gentle-folk to please,
　And some wad please themsel.

Then out spak mim-mou'd Meg o' Nith,
　And she spak out wi' pride,
An' she wad send the sodger youth
　Whatever might betide.

For the auld guidman o' Lon'on court
　She did not care a pin,
But she wad send the sodger youth
　To greet his eldest son.

Then up sprang Bess o' Annandale:
　A deadly aith she 's ta'en,
That she wad vote the border Knight,
　Tho' she should vote her lane.

For far off fowls hae feathers fair,
　An' fools o' change are fain:
But I hae tried the border Knight,
　I 'll try him yet again.

Says auld black Joan frae Creighton peel,
　A Carlin stout and grim,
The auld guidman or young guidman,
　For me may sink or swim!

For fools may prate o' right and wrang,
　While knaves laugh them to scorn:
But the Sodger's friends hae blawn the best,
　Sae he shall bear the horn.

Then whisky Jean spak o'er her drink—
　Ye weel ken, kimmers¹ a',
The auld guidman o' Lon'on court,
　His back 's been at the wa':

And monie a friend that kiss'd his caup,²
　Is now a frammit³ wight;
But it 's ne'er sae wi' whisky Jean—
　We 'll send the border Knight.

---

¹ Gossips.—² Wooden drinking vessel.—³ Strange, or estranged.

Then slow raise Marjorie o' the Lochs,
    And wrinkled was her brow;
Her ancient weed was russet gray,
    Her auld Scots heart was true.

There 's some great folks set light by me,
    I set as light by them;
But I will send to Lon'on town,
    Wha I lo'e best at hame.

So how this weighty plea will end,
    Nae mortal wight can tell;
G—d grant the King and ilka man
    May look weel to himsel.

OH THAT I HAD NE'ER BEEN MARRIED.

Written for the Musical Museum—the chorus is old.

Oh that I had ne'er been married,
    I wad never had sic care—
Now I 've gotten wife an' bairns,
    An' they cry crowdie ever mair.

    Ance crowdie,[1] twice crowdie,
        Three times crowdie in a day;
    Gin ye crowdie ony mair,
        Ye 'll crowdie a' my meal away.

Waefu' want an' hunger fley[2] me,
    Glowrin[3] by the hallan[4] en'—
Sair I fecht[5] them at the door,
    But ay I 'm eerie[6] they come ben.[7]
        Ance crowdie, &c.

---

[1] A dish made by pouring boiling water on oatmeal, and stirring it.— [2] To make afraid.—[3] Staring.—[4] Partition wall.—[5] To fight.—[6] Frighted.—[7] Inwards.

THE JOLLY BEGGARS.

A CANTATA.

This spirited and humorous production was first introduced to the public
by Mr. T. Stewart of Greenock. It appeared in a thin octavo, published at
Glasgow in 1801, under the title of "Poems ascribed to Robert Burns, the
Ayrshire Bard." Dr. Currie refused to admit it into his collection, because
the Poet had trespassed slightly upon the limits of Presbyterian purity, and
spoken rather irreverently of courts and churches.

RECITATIVO.

WHEN lyart[1] leaves bestrow the yird,
Or wavering like the bauckie-bird,[2]
  Bedim cauld Boreas' blast;
When hail-stanes drive wi' bitter skyte,
And infant frosts begin to bite,
  In hoary cranreuch[4] drest;
Ae night at e'en a merry core
  O' randie,[8] gangrel[8] bodies,
In Posie-Nansie's[7] held the splore,[8]
  To drink their orra duddies:[9]
    Wi' quaffing and laughing,
      They ranted and they sang;
    Wi' jumping and thumping,
      The very girdle[10] rang.

First neist[11] the fire, in auld red rags,
Ane sat, weel braced wi' mealy bags,
  And knapsack a' in order;
His doxy lay within his arm,
Wi' usquebae an' blankets warm,
  She blinket on her sodger:
An' ay he gies the toozie[12] drab
  The tither skelpin[13] kiss,
While she held up her geedy gab[14]
  Just like an aumos[15] dish.

[1] Gray, or dead leaves.—[2] The razor-bill.—[8] To eject with great force.—
[4] Hoar-frost.—[5] Turbulent.—[6] Strolling.
[7] The landlady of a whisky-house, in the outskirts of Mauchline, in which
the beggars held their orgies, and where the present group actually met.
[8] A frolic.—[9] Superfluous rags, or pence: or whatever they could turn into
money.—[10] A round plate of iron for toasting cakes over the fire.—[11] Next.—
[12] Swarthy.—[13] Warm, eager.—[14] Mouth.—[15] An alms-dish.

Ilk smack still did crack still,
　Just like a cadger's[1] whip;
Then staggering and swaggering
　He roar'd this ditty up:

AIR.

TUNE—*Soldier's Joy.*

I AM a son of Mars,
Who have been in many wars,
And show my cuts and scars
　Wherever I come;
This here was for a wench,
And that other in a trench,
When welcoming the French
　At the sound of the drum.
　　Lal de daudle, &c.

My 'prenticeship I past
Where my leader breathed his last,
When the bloody die was cast
　On the heights of Abram;
I servéd out my trade
When the gallant game was play'd,
And the Moro low was laid
　At the sound of the drum.
　　Lal de daudle, &c.

I, lastly, was with Curtis,
Among the floating batt'ries,
And there I left for witness
　An arm and a limb;
Yet, let my country need me,
With Elliot to head me,
I 'd clatter on my stumps
　At the sound of the drum.
　　Lal de daudle, &c.

And now, tho' I must beg,
With a wooden arm and leg,
And many a tatter'd rag
　Hanging over my bum,

----

[1] A carrier.

I 'm as happy with my wallet,
My bottle and my callet,[1]
As when I used in scarlet
        To follow the drum.
            Lal de daudle, &c.

What tho', with hoary locks,
I must stand the winter shocks,
Beneath the woods and rocks
        Oftentimes for a home:
When the tother bag I sell,
And the tother bottle tell,
I could meet a troop of hell
        At the sound of the drum.
            Lal de daudle, &c.

RECITATIVO.

He ended; and the kebars[2] shook
    Aboon[3] the chorus roar;
While frighted rattons[4] backward look,
    And seek the benmost bore:[5]
A Merry-Andrew i' the nook,
    He skirl'd out, "Encore!"
But up arose the martial chuck,
    And laid the loud uproar:

AIR.

TUNE—*Soldier Laddie.*

I once was a maid, tho' I cannot tell when,
And still my delight is in proper young men:
Some one of a troop of dragoons was my daddie,
No wonder I 'm fond of a sodger laddie.
        Sing, Lal de lal, &c.

The first of my loves was a swaggering blade,
To rattle the thundering drum was his trade:
His leg was so tight, and his cheek was so ruddy,
Transported I was with my sodger laddie.
        Sing, Lal de lal, &c.

But the godly old chaplain left him in the lurch,
The sword I forsook for the sake of the church;

---

[1] A kind of cap. —[2] Rafters.—[3] Above.—[4] Rats.—[5] The innermost hole.

He ventured the soul, and I risk'd the body,
'Twas then I proved false to my sodger laddie.
Sing, Lal de lal, &c.

Full soon I grew sick of the sanctified sot,
The regiment at large for a husband I got;
From the gilded spontoon to the fife I was ready,
I asked no more but a sodger laddie.
Sing, Lal de lal, &c.

But the peace it reduced me to beg in despair.
Till I met my old boy at Cunningham fair;
His rags regimental they flutter'd so gaudy,
My heart it rejoiced at my sodger laddie.
Sing, Lal de lal, &c.

And now I have lived, I know not how long,
And still I can join in a cup and a song;
But whilst with both hands I can hold the glass steady
Here's to thee, my hero, my sodger laddie.
Sing, Lal de lal, &c,

RECITATIVO.

Poor Merry-Andrew, i' the neuk,[1]
Sat guzzling wi' a tinkler hizzie;[2]
They mind't na wha the chorus took,
Between themsels they were sae bizzy.
At length wi' drink and courting dizzy,
He stoiter'd[3] up and made a face;
Then turn'd and laid a smack on Grizzy,
Syne[4] tuned his pipes wi' grave grimace.

AIR.

TUNE—*Auld Sir Symon.*

Sir Wisdom's a fool when he's fou,[5]
Sir Knave is a fool in a session;
He's there but a 'prentice I trow,
But I am a fool by profession.

My grannie she bought me a book,
And I held awa to the school;
I fear I my talent mistook,
But what will ye hae of a fool?

---

[1] A nook, or corner.—[2] Tinker wench.—[3] Staggered.—[4] Then.—[5] Drunk.

For drink I would venture my neck;
    A hizzie's the half of my craft;
But what could ye other expect
    Of ane that's avowedly daft?[1]

I ance was tied up like a stirk,[2]
    For civilly swearing and quaffing;
I ance was abused i' the kirk,
    For touzling a lass i' my daffin.[3]

Poor Andrew that tumbles for sport,
    Let naebody name wi' a jeer;
There's even, I'm tauld, i' the court
    A tumbler ca'd the Premier.

Observed ye yon reverend lad
    Make faces to tickle the mob;
He rails at our mountebank squad,
    It's *rivalship* just i' the job.

And now my conclusion I'll tell,
    For faith I'm confoundedly dry,
The chield that's a fool for himsel',
    Gude L—d, he's far dafter[4] than I.

RECITATIVO.

Then neist[5] outspak a rancle carlin,[6]
Wha kent[7] fu' weel to cleek[8] the sterlin';
For monie a pursie she had hookit,
And had in monie a well been doukit;

Her dove had been a Highland laddie,
But weary fa' the waefu' woodie![9]
Wi' sighs and sobs she thus began
To wail her braw John Highlandman.

AIR.

Tune—*Oh an ye were dead, Gudeman.*

A HIGHLAND lad my love was born,
The Lowland laws he held in scorn;
But he still was faithfu' to his clan,
My gallant, braw[10] John Highlandman!

---

[1] Crazy, or foolish.—[2] A young bullock, or heifer.—[3] Pastime, gayety.—
[4] A greater fool.—[5] Next.—[6] Rash, contemptuous term for a woman.—
[7] Knew.—[8] To lay hold of as with a hook.—[9] The gallows, on which her husband had been hanged.—[10] Brave.

Sing, hey, my braw John Highlandman,
Sing, ho, my braw John Highlandman;
There's not a lad in a' the lan'
Was match for my John Highlandman.

With his philibeg[1] an' tartan[2] plaid,
An' guid claymore[3] down by his side,
The ladies' hearts he did trepan,
My gallant, braw John Highlandman!
   Sing, hey, &c.

We rangéd a' from Tweed to Spey,
And lived like lords and ladies gay;
For a Lowland face ha feared none,
My gallant, braw John Highlandman.
   Sing, hey, &c.

They banish'd him beyond the sea,
But ere the bud was on the tree,
Adown my cheeks the pearls ran,
Embracing my John Highlandman.
   Sing, hey, &c.

But, oh! they catch'd him at the last,
And bound him in a dungeon fast;
My curse upon them every one,
They've hang'd my braw John Highlandman.
   Sing, hey, &c.

And now, a widow, I must mourn
Departed joys that ne'er return;
No comfort but a hearty can,
When I think on John Highlandman.
   Sing, hey, &c.

RECITATIVO.

A pigmy scraper wi' his fiddle,
Wha used at trysts[4] and fairs to driddle,[5]
Her strappin[6] limb and gaucy[7] middle
   (He reach'd nae higher)
Had hol'd his heartie like a riddle,
   An' blawn 't on fire.

[1] A short petticoat worn by Highlandmen.—[2] Checkered cloak, or upper garment.—[3] A broadsword.—[4] Meetings appointed for dancing and frolic.—[5] To move slowly.—[6] Tall and handsome.—[7] Large, jolly.

Wi' hand on haunch, an' upward ee,
He croon'd[1] his gamut, one, two, three,
Then, in an *arioso* key,
          The wee Apollo
Set off, wi' *allegretto* glee,
          His *giga solo.*

AIR.

Tune—*Whistle owre the lave o't.*

Let me ryke[2] up to dight[3] that tear,
An' go wi' me an' be my dear;
An' then your every care and fear
    May whistle owre the lave o't.

I am a fiddler to my trade,
An' a' the tunes that e'er I play'd,
The sweetest still to wife or maid,
    Was " Whistle owre the lave o't."

At kirns[4] and weddings we 'se be there,
And oh sae nicely 's we will fare!
We 'll bouse about till daddie Care
    Sings " Whistle owre the lave o't."
          I am, &c.

Sae merrily 's the banes we 'll pyke,[5]
And sun oursels about the dyke,
And at our leisure, when ye like,
    We 'll whistle owre the lave o't.
          I am, &c.

But bless me wi' your heaven o' charms,
And while I kittle hair on thairms,[6]
Hunger, cauld, and a' sic harms,
    May whistle owre the lave o't.
          I am, &c.

RECITATIVO.

Her charms had struck a sturdy caird,[7]
    As weel as poor gut-scraper;
He taks the fiddler by the beard,
    And draws a rusty rapier :—

---

[1] Hummed.—[2] Use my power, or best endeavors.—[3] Wipe, or clean.—
[4] Harvest suppers.—[5] The bones we 'll pick.—[6] Tickle hair on guts; i. e.
play on the violin.—[7] Tinker.

He swore by a' was swearing worth,
    To spit him like a pliver,[1]
Unless he would from that time forth
    Relinquish her forever.

Wi' ghastly ee, poor tweedle-dee
    Upon his hunkers'[2] bended,
And pray'd for grace wi' ruefu' face,
    And sae the quarrel ended.
But though his little heart did grieve
    When round the tinker press'd her,
He feign'd to snirtle[3] in his sleeve,
    When thus the caird address'd her :

AIR.

Tune—*Clout the Cauldron.*

My bonnie lass, I work in brass,
    A tinkler is my station ;
I 've travell'd round all Christian ground,
    In this my occupation ;
I 've taen the gold, I 've been enroll'd
    In many a noble squadron ;
But vain they search'd, when off I march'd
    To go and clout[4] the cauldron.
        I 've taen the gold &c.

Despise that shrimp, that wither'd imp,
    Wi' a' his noise and cap'rin',
And take a share wi' those that bear
    The budget and the apron :
And by that stowp,[5] my faith and houp,
    And by that dear Kilbagie,[6]
If e'er ye want or meet wi' scant,
    May I ne'er weet my craigie ![7]
        And by that stowp, &c.

RECITATIVO.

The caird prevail'd—the unblushing fair
    In his embraces sunk,
Partly wi' love o'ercome sae sair,[8]
    And partly she was drunk.

---

[1] Spit him like a plover.—[2] The hams, or hinder part of the thighs.—[3] To laugh.—[4] To mend kettles or cauldrons.—[5] A jug.—[6] Whisky, so called from a celebrated distillery.—[7] Throat.—[8] Sore.

Sir Violino, with an air
  That show'd a man o' spunk,
Wish'd unison between the pair,
  And made the bottle clunk[1]
        To their health that night.

But urchin Cupid shot a shaft,
  That play'd a dame a shavie,[2]
The fiddler raked her fore and aft,
  Behind the chicken cavie.[3]
Her lord, a wight o' Homer's craft,[4]
  Though limping wi' the spavie,[5]
He hirpled[6] up, and lap like daft,[7]
  And shored[8] them Dainty Davie
        O' boot[9] that night.

He was a care-defying blade
  As ever Bacchus listed,
Though Fortune sair upon him laid,
  His heart she ever miss'd it.
He had no wish—but to be glad,
  Nor want—but when he thirsted;
He hated naught—but to be sad,
  And thus the Muse suggested
        His sang that night.

AIR.

Tune—For a' that, an' a' that.

I am a bard of no regard,
  Wi' gentle-folks, an a' that;
But Homer-like, the glowrin' byke,[10]
Frae town to town I draw that.

  For a' that, an' a' that,
    And twice as muckle's a' that,
  I've lost but ane, I've twa behin',
    I've wife enough for a' that.

I never drank the Muses' stank,[11]
  Castalia's burn,[12] and a' that;

---

[1] To gurgle in the manner of a bottle when emptying.—[2] A trick.—[3] A pen, or coop.—[4] Homer is allowed to be the oldest ballad-singer on record.—[5] Spavin.—[6] Limped.—[7] Leaped as if he was mad.—[8] Offered.—[9] To boot.—[10] Staring crowd.—[11] A standing pool of water.—[12] Rivulet.

But there it reams,[1] and richly streams,
   My Helicon I ca' that.
     For a' that, &c.

Great love I bear to a' the fair,
   Their humble slave, and a' that;
But lordly will I hold it still
   A mortal sin to thraw[2] that.
     For a' that, &c.

In raptures sweet, this hour we meet,
   Wi' mutual love, and a' that;
But for how lang the flie may stang,[3]
   Let inclination law[4] that.
     For a' that, &c.

Their tricks and craft hae put me daft,[5]
   They 've taen me in, and a' that;
But clear your decks, and—Here 's the sex!
   I like the jads for a' that.

   For a' that, an' a' that,
     And twice as muckle 's a' that,
   My dearest blude to do them gude,
     They 're welcome till 't[6] for a' that.

RECITATIVO.

So sung the bard—and Nansie's wa's
   Shook with a thunder of applause,
     Re-echo'd from each mouth:
They toom'd their pocks,[7] they pawn'd their duds,
   They scarcely left to co'er their fuds,[8]
     To quench their lowan[10] drouth.

Then owre again the jovial thrang
   The poet did request,
To lowse his pack, and wale a sang,
   A ballad o' the best;
     He, rising, rejoicing
       Between his twa Deborahs,
    Looks round him, and found them
     Impatient for the chorus.

---

[1] Froths, or foams.—[2] To contradict.—[3] Sting.—[4] Rule, or govern.—[5] Mad, vexed.—[6] To it.—[7] Emptied their bags.—[8] Rags.—[9] Cover their tails.—[10] Raging thirst.

AIR.

TUNE—*Jolly mortals, fill your glasses.*

SEE the smoking bowl before us!
Mark our jovial ragged ring!
Round and round take up the chorus,
And in raptures let us sing:

> *A fig for those by law protected,*
> *Liberty 's a glorious feast!*
> *Courts for cowards were erected,*
> *Churches built to please the priest.*

What is title? what is treasure?
What is reputation's care?
If we lead a life of pleasure,
'Tis no matter how or where.
   A fig, &c.

With the ready trick and fable,
Round we wander all the day;
And at night, in barn or stable,
Hug our doxies on the hay.
   A fig, &c.

Does the train-attended carriage
Through the country lighter rove?
Does the sober bed of marriage
Witness brighter scenes of love?
   A fig, &c.

Life is all a variorum,
We regard not how it goes;
Let them cant about decorum
Who have characters to lose.
   A fig, &c.

Here's to budgets, bags, and wallets!
Here's to all the wandering train!
Here's our ragged brats[1] and callets![2]
One and all cry out, Amen!
   A fig, &c.

[1] Clothing in general. —[2] A woman's cap made without a border,

MY HEART WAS ANCE.

The Poet in the Musical Museum has added a note, that "the chorus of
this song is old, the rest of it is mine."

TUNE—To the Weavers gin ye go.

My heart was ance as blythe and free
   As simmer days were lang,
But a bonnie, westlin weaver lad
   Has gart me change my sang.

    To the weavers gin ye go, fair maids,
      To the weavers gin ye go ;
    I rede[1] you right gang ne'er at night,
      To the weavers gin ye go.

My mither[2] sent me to the town,
   To warp a plaiden wab ;
But the weary, weary warpin o't
   Has gart me sigh and sab.

A bonnie westlin weaver lad
   Sat working at his loom ;
He took my heart as wi' a net,
   In every knot and thrum.

I sat beside my warpin-wheel,
   And ay I ca'd it roun' ;
But every shot and every knock,
   My heart it gae a stoun.

The moon was sinking in the west
   Wi' visage pale and wan,
As my bonnie westlin weaver lad
   Convoy'd me thro' the glen.

But what was said, or what was done,
   Shame fa' me gin I tell ;
But oh! I fear the kintra[3] soon
   Will ken[4] as weel 's mysel.

      To the weavers gin ye go, &c.

---

[1] To counsel.—[2] Mother.—[3] Country.—[4] Know.

THE PLOUGHMAN.

Tune—Up wi' the Ploughman.

The ploughman he's a bonnie lad,
  His mind is ever true, jo;
His garters knit below his knee,
  His bonnet it is blue, jo.

   Then up wi' my ploughman lad,
    And hey my merry ploughman!
   Of a' the trades that I do ken,
    Commend me to the ploughman.

My ploughman he comes hame at e'en,
  He's aften wat and weary;
Cast off the wat, put on the dry,
  And gae to bed, my dearie!

I will wash my ploughman's hose,
  And I will dress his o'erlay;
I will mak my ploughman's bed,
  And cheer him late and early.

I hae been east, I hae been west,
  I hae been at Saint Johnston;
The bonniest sight that e'er I saw
  Was the ploughman laddie dancin'.

Snaw-white stockins on his legs,
  And siller buckles glancin';
A guid blue bonnet on his head—
  And oh, but he was handsome!

Commend me to the barn-yard,
  And the corn-mou, man;
I never gat my coggie fou,
  Till I met wi' the ploughman.

THE SONS OF OLD KILLIE.

This song was sung by Burns in the Kilmarnock Kilwinning Lodge in 1786.

Tune—Shawnboy.

Ye sons of old Killie, assembled by Willie,
  To follow the noble vocation;

Your thrifty old mother has scarce such another
    To sit in that honoréd station.
I 've little to say, but only to pray,
    As praying 's the ton of your fashion ;
A prayer from the muse you well may excuse,
    'Tis seldom her favorite passion.

Ye powers who preside o'er the wind and the tide,
    Who markéd each element's border ;
Who forméd this frame with beneficent aim,
    Whose sovereign statute is order ;
Within this dear mansion may wayward contention
    Or witheréd envy ne'er enter ;
May secrecy round be the mystical bound,
    And brotherly love be the centre !

OH, WHAR DID YE GET.

Part of this song is old, but all that is natural and tender was added by Burns.

TUNE—*Bonnie Dundee.*

Oh, whar did ye get that hauver meal bannock ?
    Oh silly blind body, oh dinna ye see ?
I gat it frae a brisk young sodger laddie,
    Between Saint Johnston and bonnie Dundee.
Oh gin I saw the laddie that gae me 't !
    Aft has he doudled me up on his knee ;
May Heaven protect my bonnie Scots laddie,
    And send him safe hame to his babie and me !

My blessin 's upon thy sweet wee lippie,
    My blessin 's upon thy bonnie e'e brie !
Thy smiles are sae like my blythe sodger laddie,
    Thou 's ay the dearer and dearer to me !
But I 'll big a bower on yon bonnie banks,
    Where Tay rins wimplin' by sae clear ;
And I 'll cleed thee in the tartan sae fine,
    And mak thee a man like thy daddie dear.

THE JOYFUL WIDOWER.

Tune—Maggy Lauder.

I MARRIED with a scolding wife
    The fourteenth of November;
She made me weary of my life,
    By one unruly member.
Long did I bear the heavy yoke,
    And many griefs attended;
But, to my comfort be it spoke,
    Now, now her life is ended.

We lived full one-and-twenty years
    As man and wife together;
At length from me her course she steer'd,
    And gone I know not whither:
Would I could guess, I do profess,
    I speak, and do not flatter,
Of all the women in the world,
    I never could come at her.

Her body is bestowéd well,
    A handsome grave does hide her;
But sure her soul is not in hell,
    The deil would ne'er abide her.
I rather think she is aloft,
    And imitating thunder;
For why,—methinks I hear her voice
    Tearing the clouds asunder.

COME DOWN THE BACK STAIRS.

The air was composed by John Bruce, an excellent fiddler, who lived in
Dumfries. The sentiment is taken from an old song, but every line is very
much altered. It may be compared with the other version at page 433.

Tune—Whistle, and I'll come to you, my lad.

Oh whistle, and I'll come
    To you, my lad;
Oh whistle, and I'll come
    To you, my lad;
Though father and mither
    Should baith gae mad,
Oh whistle, and I'll come
    To you, my lad.

Come down the back stairs
  When ye come to court me;
Come down the back stairs
  When ye come to court me,
Come down the back stairs,
  And let naebody see,
And come as ye were na
  Coming to me.

BRAW LADS OF GALLA WATER.

Perhaps the air of this song is the sweetest of all the Scotch airs.
It was considered so by Haydn.

TUNE—*Galla Water.*

Braw, braw lads of Galla Water;
  Oh braw lads of Galla Water;
I'll kilt my coats aboon my knee,
  And follow my love through the water.

Sae fair her hair, sae brent her brow,
  Sae bonny blue her een, my dearie;
Sae white her teeth, sae sweet her mou',
  The mair I kiss she's ay my dearie.

O'er yon bank and o'er yon brae,
  O'er yon moss amang the heather;
I'll kilt my coats aboon my knee,
  And follow my love through the water.

Down amang the broom, the broom,
  Down amang the broom, my dearie,
The lassie lost a silken snood,
  That cost her mony a blirt and bleary.
    Braw, braw lads, &c.

MY HOGGIE.

TUNE—*What will I do gin my Hoggie die !*

What will I do gin my Hoggie die?
  My joy, my pride, my Hoggie!
My only beast, I had nae mae,
  And vow but I was vogie!

The lee-lang night we watch'd the fauld,
  Me and my faithfu' doggie;
We heard naught but the roaring linn,
  Amang the braes sae scroggie;
But the houlet cried frae the castle wa',
  The blitter frae the boggie,
The tod replied upon the hill,
  I trembled for my Hoggie.
When day did daw, and cocks did craw,
  The morning it was foggie;
An' unco tyke lap o'er the dyke,
  And maist has kill'd my Hoggie.

HER DADDIE FORBAD.

Some of these verses are by Burns, and part from a humorous old Ballad,
"Jumpin' John o' the green."

TUNE—*Jumpin' John.*

HER daddie[1] forbad, her minnie[2] forbad;
  Forbidden she wadna[3] be:
She wadna trow't, the browst she brew'd
  Wad taste sae bitterlie.
    The lang lad they ca' Jumpin' John,
      Beguiled the bonnie lassie,
    The long lad they ca' Jumpin' John,
      Beguiled the bonnie lassie.

A cow and a cauf, a yowe and a hauf,
  And thretty gude shillin's and three;
A vera gude tocher,[4] a cotter-man's dochter,
  The lass with the bonnie black e'e.
        The lang lad, &c.

— · —

HEY, THE DUSTY MILLER.

This is a cheerful air, and was formerly played as a single hornpipe in the
Scottish dancing-schools; the words are altered from an old song.

TUNE—*The Dusty Miller.*

HEY, the dusty miller,
  And his dusty coat;
He will win a shilling,
  Or he spend a groat.

[1] Father.—[2] Mother.—[3] Would not.—[4] Dowry.

Dusty was the coat,
Dusty was the color,
Dusty was the kiss
That I got frae the miller.

Hey, the dusty miller,
And his dusty sack;
Leeze me on the calling
Fills the dusty peck.
Fills the dusty peck,
Brings the dusty siller;
I wad gie my coatie
For the dusty miller.

THERE WAS A LASS.

The old song of this name, sung to the tune of "You'll ay be welcome
back again," is much inferior to the present in wit and delicacy.

TUNE—Duncan Davison.

THERE was a lass, they ca'd her Meg,
And she held o'er the moors to spin;
There was a lad that follow'd her,
They ca'd him Duncan Davison.
The moor was driegh,[1] and Meg was skiegh,[2]
Her favor Duncan could na win;
For wi' the roke she wad him knock,
And ay she shook the temper-pin.

As o'er the moor they lightly foor,
A burn was clear, a glen was green,
Upon the banks they eased their shanks,[3]
And ay she set the wheel between:
But Duncan swore a haly aith,[4]
That Meg should be a bride the morn;
Then Meg took up her spinnin' graith,
And flung them a' out o'er the burn.

We'll big a house—a wee, wee house,
And we will live like king and queen,
Sae blythe and merry we will be
When ye set by the wheel at e'en.

[1] Dreary.—[2] Proud.—[3] Legs.—[4] A holy oath.

A man may drink and no be drunk;
  A man may fight and no be slain;
A man may kiss a bonnie lass,
  And ay be welcome back again.

WEARY FA' YOU, DUNCAN GRAY.

Of this the Poet says, "It is that kind of light-horse gallop of an air which precludes sentiment. The ludicrous is its ruling feature." Another version will be found at page 366.

TUNE—*Duncan Gray.*

WEARY fa' you, Duncan Gray—
  Ha, ha, the girdin o't!
Wae gae by you, Duncan Gray—
  Ha, ha, the girdin o't!
When a' the lave gae to their play,
Then I maun sit the lee-lang day,
And jog the cradle wi' my tae,
  And a' for the girdin o't.

Bonnie was the Lammas moon—
  Ha, ha, the girdin o't!
Glowrin' a' the hills aboon—
  Ha, ha, the girdin o't!
The girdin brak, the beast cam down,
I tint my curch, and baith my shoon;
Ah! Duncan, ye're an unco loon—
  Wae on the bad girdin o't!

But, Duncan, gin ye'll keep your aith—
  Ha, ha, the girdin o't!
I'se bless you wi' my hindmost breath—
  Ha, ha, the girdin o't!
Duncan, gin ye'll keep your aith,
The beast again can bear us baith,
And auld Mess John will mend the skaith,
  And clout the bad girdin o't.

LANDLADY, COUNT THE LAWIN.

The two first verses are by Burns : the last is taken from an old song.

TUNE—*Hey tutti, taiti.*

LANDLADY, count the lawin,[1]
The day is near the dawin ;[2]
Ye 're a' blind drunk, boys,
And I 'm but jolly fou.[3]

> *Hey tutti, taiti,*
> *How tutti, taiti—*
> *Wha 's fou now ?*

Cog an' ye were ay fou,
Cog an' ye were ay fou,
I wad sit and sing to you
If ye were ay fou.

Weel may ye a' be!
Ill may we never see!
God bless the king, boys,
And the companie!
> *Hey tutti, &c.*

THE BLUDE RED ROSE AT YULE MAY BLAW.

The sentiment is taken from a Jacobite song of the same name.

TUNE—*To daunton me.*

THE blude[4] red rose at Yule may blaw,[5]
The simmer lilies bloom in snaw,[6]
The frost may freeze the deepest sea ;
But an auld man shall never daunton[7] me.

> *To daunton me, and me sae young,*
> *Wi' his fause heart and flattering tongue,*
> *That is the thing you ne'er shall see ;*
> *For an auld man shall never daunton me.*

---

[1] Reckoning. — [2] Dawn. — [3] Tipsy. — [4] Blood. — [5] Blow. — [6] Snow. —
[7] Fondle.

For a' his meal and a' his maut,
For a' his fresh beef and his saut,
For a' his gold and white monie,
An auld man shall never daunton me.

His gear may buy him kye and yowes,
His gear may buy him glens and knowes
But me he shall not buy nor fee,
For an auld man shall never daunton me.

He hirples twa fauld as he dow,
Wi' his teethless gab[1] and his auld beld pow,[2]
And the rain rains down frae his red bleer'd ee—
That auld man shall never daunton me.
To daunton me, &c.

COME BOAT ME O'ER TO CHARLIE.

Some of these lines are old; the second and most of the third stanza are original. 1

TUNE—*O'er the water to Charlie.*

Come boat me o'er, come row me o'er,
  Come boat me o'er to Charlie;
I'll gie John Ross another bawbee,
  To boat me o'er to Charlie.

    We'll o'er the water and o'er the sea,
      We'll o'er the water to Charlie;
    Come weal, come woe, we'll gather and go,
      And live or die wi' Charlie.

I lo'e weel my Charlie's name,
  Tho' some there be abhor him:
But oh, to see auld Nick gaun hame,
  And Charlie's faes before him!

I swear and vow by moon and stars,
  And sun that shines sae early,
If I had twenty thousand lives
  I'd die as aft for Charlie.
      We'll o'er the water, &c.

[1] Speech.—[2] Bald head.

RATTLIN', ROARIN' WILLIE.[1]

Tune—Rattlin', roarin' Willie.

O RATTLIN', roarin' Willie,
  Oh, he held to the fair,
An' for to sell his fiddle,
  An' buy some other ware;
But parting wi' his fiddle,
  The saut tear blin't his ee;
And rattlin', roarin' Willie,
  Ye 're welcome hame to me!

O Willie, come sell your fiddle,
  Oh sell your fiddle sae fine;
O Willie, come sell your fiddle,
  And buy a pint o' wine!
If I should sell my fiddle,
  The warl' would think I was mad;
For mony a rantin' day
  My fiddle and I hae had.

As I cam by Crochallan,
  I cannily keekit ben—
Rattlin', roarin' Willie
  Was sitting at yon board en';
Sitting at yon board en',
  And amang guid companie;
Rattlin', roarin' Willie,
  Ye 're welcome hame to me!

THE TAILOR.

The second and fourth verses are by Burns; the rest is very old. The air is beautiful, and is played by the Corporation of Tailors at their annual elections and processions.

Tune—The tailor fell thro' the bed, thimbles an' a'.

THE tailor fell thro' the bed, thimbles an' a',
The tailor fell thro' the bed, thimbles an' a';

[1] The hero of this song was William Dunbar, Esq., writer to the "Signet," Edinburgh, and colonel of the Crochallan corps, a club of wits, who took that title at the time of raising the Fencible regiments. Burns says, "he was one of the worthiest fellows in the world."

The blankets were thin, and the sheets they were sma'
The tailor fell thro' the bed, thimbles an' a'.

The sleepy bit lassie, she dreaded nae ill,
The sleepy bit lassie, she dreaded nae ill;
The weather was cauld, and the lassie lay still,
She thought that a tailor could do her nae ill.

Gie me the groat again, canny young man;
Gie me the groat again, canny young man;
The day it is short, and the night it is lang,
The dearest siller that ever I wan!

There's somebody weary wi' lying her lane;
There's somebody weary wi' lying her lane;
There's some that are dowie, I trow wad be fain
To see the bit tailor come skippin' again.

SIMMER'S A PLEASANT TIME.

The first verse is by Burns, the others are only revised by him.

TUNE—*Ay waukin O.*

SIMMER's a pleasant time,
   Flowers of every color;
The water rins o'er the heugh,[1]
   And I long for my true lover.

Ay waukin' O,
   Waukin still and wearie:
Sleep I can get nane[3]
   For thinking on my dearie.

When I sleep I dream,
   When I wauk I'm eerie;[4]
Sleep I can get nane
   For thinking on my dearie.

Lanely night comes on,
   A' the lave are sleeping;
I think on my bonnie lad,
   And I bleer my een with greetin'.
     Ay waukin, &c.

[1] Crag.—[2] Waking.—[3] None.—[4] Frightened.

WHEN ROSY MAY.

In other days every trade and vocation had a tune to dance or march to: the air of this song is the march of the gardeners; the title only is old; the rest is the work of Burns.—*Cunningham.*

TUNE—*The gardener wi' his paidle.*

WHEN rosy May comes in wi' flowers,
To deck her gay green-spreading bowers,
Then busy, busy are his hours—
    The gardener wi' his paidle.
The crystal waters gently fa';
The merry birds are lovers a';
The scented breezes round him blaw—
    The gardener wi' his paidle.

When purple morning starts the hare
To steal upon her early fare,
Then thro' the dews he maun repair—
    The gardener wi' his paidle.
When day, expiring in the west,
The curtain draws of nature's rest,
He flies to her arms he lo'es best—
    The gardener wi' his paidle.

MY LOVE SHE'S BUT A LASSIE YET.

The title and some lines are old; the rest of the song is by Burns.

TUNE—*Lady Badinscoth's Reel.*

MY love she's but a lassie yet;
    My love she's but a lassie yet;
We'll let her stand a year or twa,
    She'll no be half sae saucy yet.
I rue the day I sought her, O,
    I rue the day I sought her, O;
Wha gets her need na say she's woo'd,
    But he may say he's bought her, O!

Come, draw a drap o' the best o't yet,
    Come, draw a drap o' the best o't yet;
Gae seek for pleasure where ye will,
    But here I never miss'd it yet.

We're a' dry wi' drinking o't,
  We're a' dry wi' drinking o't;
The minister kiss'd the fiddler's wife,
  An' could na preach for thinking o't.

JAMIE, COME TRY ME.

Tune—*Jamie, come try me.*

Jamie, come try me,
Jamie, come try me;
If thou would win my love,
Jamie, come try me.

If thou should ask my love,
  Could I deny thee?
If thou would win my love,
  Jamie, come try me.

If thou should kiss me, love,
  Wha could espy thee?
If thou wad be my love,
  Jamie, come try me.
    Jamie, come, &c.

THE CAPTAIN'S LADY.

Part of this song is old, and part of it by Burns.

Tune—*Oh mount and go.*

Oh mount and go,
  Mount and make you ready;
Oh mount and go,
  And be the captain's lady.

When the drums do beat,
  And the cannons rattle,
Thou shalt sit in state,
  And see thy love in battle.

When the vanquish'd foe,
  Sues for peace and quiet,
To the shades we'll go,
  And in love enjoy it.
    Oh mount, &c.

OUR THRISSLES FLOURISHED, Etc.

The second and fourth stanzas are original; the others only revised
from a Jacobite song.

TUNE—*Awa Whigs, awa.*

Awa Whigs, awa!
  Awa Whigs, awa!
Ye 're but a pack o' traitor louns,
  Ye 'll do nae good at a'.

OUR thrissles flourish'd fresh and fair,
  And bonnie bloom'd our roses;
But Whigs came like a frost in June,
  And wither'd a' our posies.

Our ancient crown 's fa'n in the dust—
  Deil blin' them wi' the stoure o't;
And write their names in his black beuk,
  Wha gae the Whigs the power o't.

Our sad decay in Church and State
  Surpasses my descriving;
The Whigs came o'er us for a curse,
  And we hae done wi' thriving.

Grim vengeance lang has ta'n a nap,
  But we may see him wauken;
Gude help the day when royal heads
  Are hunted like a maukin.
         Awa, Whigs, &c.

———

MERRY HAE I BEEN TEETHIN' A HECKLE.

TUNE—*Lord Breadalbane's March.*

OH merry hae I been teethin' a heckle,
  And merry hae I been shapin' a spoon;
Oh merry hae I been cloutin a kettle,
  And kissin' my Katie when a' was done.
Oh a' the lang day I ca' at my hammer,
  An' a' the lang day I whistle and sing,
A' the lang night I cuddle my kimmer,
  An' a' the lang night as happy 's a king.

Bitter in dool I lickit my winnins,
  O' marrying Bess, to gie her a slave:
Bless'd be the hour she cool'd in her linens,
  An' blythe be the bird that sings on her grave.
Come to my arms, my Katie, my Katie,
  An' come to my arms, and kiss me again!
Drunken or sober, here's to thee, Katie!
  And bless'd be the day I did it again.

EPPIE ADAIR.

TUNE—*My Eppie.*

An' oh! my Eppie,
My jewel, my Eppie!
Wha wadna be happy
  Wi' Eppie Adair?
By love, and by beauty,
By law, and by duty,
I swear to be true to
  My Eppie Adair!

An' oh! my Eppie,
My jewel, my Eppie!
Wha wadna be happy
  Wi' Eppie Adair?
A' pleasure exile me,
Dishonor defile me,
If e'er I beguile thee,
  My Eppie Adair!

WHARE HAE YE BEEN.

Allusion is made in this song to the battle of Killiecrankie

TUNE—*Killiecrankie.*

WHARE hae ye been sae braw, lad?
  Whare hae ye been sae brankie, O?
Oh, whare hae ye been sae braw, lad?
  Cam ye by Killiecrankie, O?
An' ye had been whare I hae been,
  Ye wad na been so cantie, O;

An' ye had seen what I hae seen,
  On the braes of Killiecrankie, O.

I fought at land, I fought at sea;
  At hame I fought my auntie, O;
But I met the devil an' Dundee,
  On the braes o' Killiecrankie, O.
The bauld Pitcur fell in a furr,
  An' Clavers got a clankie, O;
Or I had fed an Athole gled,
  On the braes o' Killiecrankie, O.

FRAE THE FRIENDS AND LAND I LOVE.

Tune—*Carron Side.*

Frae the friends and land I love,
  Driven by fortune's felly spite,
Frae my best beloved I rove,
  Never mair to taste delight;
Never mair maun hope to find
  Ease frae toil, relief frae care:
When remembrance wracks the mind,
  Pleasures but unveil despair.

Brightest climes shall mirk appear,
  Desert ilka blooming shore,
Till the fates, nae mair severe,
  Friendship, love, and peace restore;
Till Revenge, wi' laurell'd head,
  Bring our banish'd hame again;
And ilk loyal bonnie lad
  Cross the seas and win his ain.

COCK UP YOUR BEAVER.[1]

Tune—*Cock up your beaver.*

When first my brave Johnie lad
Came to this town,

[1] On the accession of the house of Stuart, many sarcastic songs were directed by the English against the Scots: the latter took it all in very good humor, as they were generally benefited by the change, and even now do not object to exchange the bonnet for a good beaver. The poet produced the present from one of these

He had a blue bonnet
  That wanted the crown;
But now he has gotten
  A hat and a feather,—
Hey, brave Johnie lad,
  Cock up your beaver!

Cock up your beaver,
  And cock it fu' sprush,
We 'll over the border
  And gie them a brush;
There 's somebody there
  We 'll teach better behavior,—
Hey, brave Johnie lad,
  Cock up your beaver!

HOW CAN I BE BLYTHE AND GLAD?

This song is said to have been written in allusion to the treatment of Jean Armour by her father, when he learned that she still kept up a correspondence with the Poet.

TUNE—*The bonnie lad that 's far awa.*

OH how can I be blythe and glad,
  Or how can I gang brisk and braw,
When the bonnie lad that I lo'e best
  Is o'er the hills and far awa?
When the bonnie lad that I lo'e best
  Is o'er the hills and far awa?

It 's no the frosty winter wind,
  It 's no the driving drift and snaw;
But ay the tear comes in my e'e,
  To think on him that 's far awa.
But ay the tear comes in my e'e,
  To think on him that 's far awa.

My father pat me frae his door,
  My friends they hae disown'd me a',
But I hae ane will tak' my part,
  The bonnie lad that 's far awa.
But I hae ane will tak' my part,
  The bonnie lad that 's far awa.

A pair o' gloves he gae to me,
    And silken snoods he gae me twa;
And I will wear them for his sake,
    The bonnie lad that's far awa.
And I will wear them for his sake,
    The bonnie lad that's far awa.

SENSIBILITY HOW CHARMING.

The heroine of this song is said to be the fair Clarinda

Tune—Cornwallis's Lament for Colonel Muirhead.

SENSIBILITY how charming,
    Dearest Nancy! thou canst tell,
But distress with horrors arming,
    Thou hast also known too well.
Fairest flower, behold the lily,
    Blooming in the sunny ray—
Let the blast sweep o'er the valley,
    See it prostrate on the clay.

Hear the woodlark charm the forest,
    Telling o'er his little joys:
Hapless bird! a prey the surest
    To each pirate of the skies.
Dearly bought the hidden treasure,
    Finer feelings can bestow:
Chords that vibrate sweetest pleasure,
    Thrill the deepest notes of woe.

IT IS NA, JEAN, THY BONNIE FACE.

These verses were originally in English; Burns has bestowed on them a Scottish dress.

Tune—The Maid's Complaint.

IT is na, Jean, thy bonnie face,
    Nor shape, that I admire,
Although thy beauty and thy grace
    Might weel awake desire.

Something, in ilka part o' thee,
To praise, to love, I find;
But dear as is thy form to me,
Still dearer is thy mind.

Nae mair ungenerous wish I hae,
Nor stronger in my breast,
Than if I canna mak thee sae,
At least to see thee blest.
Content am I, if Heaven shall give
But happiness to thee:
And as wi' thee I 'd wish to live,
For thee I 'd bear to die.

OH SAW YE MY DEARIE.

Altered from the old song of Eppie Macnab, which has more wit than decency.

Tune—Eppie Macnab.

Oh saw ye my dearie, my Eppie M'Nab?
Oh saw ye my dearie, my Eppie M'Nab?
She 's down in the yard, she 's kissin' the laird,
She winna come hame to her ain Jock Rab.
Oh come thy ways to me, my Eppie M'Nab!
Oh come thy ways to me, my Eppie M'Nab!
Whate'er thou hast done, be it late, be it soon,
Thou 's welcome again to thy ain Jock Rab.

What says she, my dearie, my Eppie M'Nab?
What says she, my dearie, my Eppie M'Nab?
She lets thee to wit, that she has thee forgot,
And forever disowns thee, her ain Jock Rab.
Oh had I ne'er seen thee, my Eppie M'Nab!
Oh had I ne'er seen thee, my Eppie M'Nab!
As light as the air, and fause as thou 's fair,
Thou 's broken the heart o' thy ain Jock Rab.

THE TITHER MORN

TO A HIGHLAND AIR.

The tither morn
When I forlorn,
Aneath an aik sat moaning,
I did na trow,
I 'd see my Jo,
Beside me, gain the gloaming.
But he sae trig,
Lap o'er the rig,
And dawtingly did cheer me,
When I, what reck,
Did least expec',
To see my lad so near me.

His bonnet he,
A thought ajee,
Cock'd sprush when first he clasp'd me;
And I, I wat,
Wi' fainness grat,
While in his grips he press'd me.
Deil tak' the war!
I late and air,
Hae wish'd since Jock departed;
But now as glad
I 'm wi' my lad,
As short syne broken-hearted.

Fu' aft at e'en
Wi' dancing keen,
When a' were blythe and merry,
I cared na by,
Sae sad was I
In absence o' my dearie.
But, praise be blest,
My mind 's at rest,
I 'm happy wi' my Johnie:
At kirk and fair,
I 'se ay be there.
And be as canty 's onie.

LOVELY DAVIES.

Tune—*Miss Muir.*

Oh how shall I, unskilfu', try
    The poet's occupation,
The tunefu' powers, in happy hours,
    That whisper inspiration?
Even they maun dare an effort mair,
    Than aught they ever gave us,
Or they rehearse, in equal verse,
    The charms o' lovely Davies.
Each eye it cheers, when she appears,
    Like Phœbus in the morning,
When past the shower, and every flower
    The garden is adorning.
As the wretch looks o'er Siberia's shore,
    When winter-bound the wave is;
Sae droops our heart when we maun part
    Frae charming lovely Davies.

Her smile 's a gift, frae 'boon the lift,
    That maks us mair than princes;
A scepter'd hand, a king's command,
    Is in her darting glances;
The man in arms, 'gainst female charms,
    Even he her willing slave is;
He hugs his chain, and owns the reign
    Of conquering, lovely Davies.
My muse to dream of such a theme,
    Her feeble powers surrender;
The eagle's gaze alone surveys
    The sun's meridian splendor;
I wad in vain essay the strain,
    The deed too daring brave is;
I 'll drap the lyre, and mute admire
    The charms o' lovely Davies.

THE WEARY PUND O' TOW.

Tune—*The weary pund o' tow.*

The weary pund, the weary pund,
    The weary pund o' tow;

I think my wife will end her life
Before she spin her tow.

I BOUGHT my wife a stane o' lint[1]
  As gude as e'er did grow;
And a' that she has made o' that,
  Is ae poor pund[2] o' tow.

There sat a bottle in a bole,
  Beyont the ingle low,
And ay she took the tither souk[3]
  To drouk the stowrie tow.[4]

Quoth I, For shame, ye dirty dame,
  Gae spin your tap o' tow !
She took the rock, and wi' a knock
  She brak it o'er my pow.

At last her feet—I sang to see 't—
  Gaed foremost o'er the knowe;
And or I wad anither jad,
  I 'll wallop in a tow.
      The weary pund, &c.

KENMURE'S ON AND AWA.[5]

TUNE—*Oh, Kenmure's on and awa, Willie.*

OH, Kenmure 's on and awa, Willie !
  Oh, Kenmure 's on and awa !
And Kenmure's lord 's the bravest lord
  That ever Galloway saw.

Success to Kenmure's band, Willie !
  Success to Kenmure's band;
There 's no a heart that fears a Whig
  That rides by Kenmure's hand.

Here 's Kenmure's health in wine, Willie !
  Here 's Kenmure's health in wine;

---

1 Pound.—2 A stone-weight of flax.—3 Another drink.—4 To wash away
the dust of the tow.
  5 There is some doubt as to the portions of this song which belong to
Burns; it is presumed that the second and third stanzas are only original.
It alludes to the part taken by Viscount Kenmure in the rebellion of 1715.

There ne'er was a coward o' Kenmure's blude,
  Nor yet o' Gordon's line.

Oh, Kenmure's lads are men, Willie!
  Oh, Kenmure's lads are men;
Their hearts and swords are metal true—
  And that their faes shall ken.

They 'll live or die wi' fame, Willie!
  They 'll live or die wi' fame;
But soon, wi' sounding victorie,
  May Kenmure's lord come hame.

Here 's him that 's far awa, Willie!
  Here 's him that 's far awa;
And here 's the flower that I love best—
  The rose that 's like the snaw!

MY COLLIER LADDIE.

TUNE—*The Collier Laddie.*

WHERE live ye, my bonnie lass?
  An' tell me what they ca' ye;
My name, she says, is Mistress Jean,
  And I follow the Collier Laddie.
My name, she says, is Mistress Jean,
  And I follow the Collier Laddie.

See you not yon hills and dales,
  The sun shines on sae brawlie!
They a' are mine, and they shall be thine,
  Gin ye 'll leave your Collier Laddie.
They a' are mine, and they shall be thine,
  Gin ye 'll leave your Collier Laddie.

Ye shall gang in gay attire,
  Weel buskit up sae gaudy;
And ane to wait on every hand,
  Gin ye 'll leave your Collier Laddie.
And ane to wait on every hand,
  Gin ye 'll leave your Collier Laddie.

Tho' ye had a' the sun shines on,
  And the earth conceals sae lowly;

I wad turn my back on you and it a',
   And embrace my Collier Laddie.
I wad turn my back on you and it a',
   And embrace my Collier Laddie.

I can win my five pennies in a day,
   And spen 't at night fu' brawlie;
And make my bed in the Collier's neuk,
   And lie down wi' my Collier Laddie.
And make my bed in the Collier's neuk,
   And lie down wi' my Collier Laddie.

Luve for luve is the bargain for me,
   Tho' the wee cot-house should haud me;
And the world before me to win my bread,
   And fair fa' my Collier Laddie.
And the world before me to win my bread,
   And fair fa' my Collier Laddie.

NITHSDALE'S WELCOME HAME.

The Maxwells, after the fall of the house of Douglas, were the most powerful family in the south of Scotland; but the name is now no longer numbered with our nobility.

The noble Maxwells and their powers
   Are coming o'er the border,
And they 'll gae bigg Terreagle's towers,
   An' set them a' in order.
And they declare Terreagle 's fair,
   For their abode they choose it;
There 's no a heart in a' the land,
   But 's lighter at the news o't.

Tho' stars in skies may disappear,
   And angry tempests gather;
The happy hour may soon be near
   That brings us pleasant weather:
The weary night o' care and grief,
   May hae a joyful morrow;
So dawning day has brought relief—
   Fareweel our night o' sorrow!
        47

AS I WAS A-WANDERING.

This is an old Highland air, and the title means, "my love did deceive me."
There is much feeling expressed in this song.

TUNE—*Rinn Meudial mo Mhealladh.*

As I was a-wandering ae midsummer e'enin',
 The pipers and youngsters were making their game;
Amang them I spied my faithless fause lover,
 Which bled a' the wounds o' my dolour[1] again.

Weel, since he has left me, may pleasure gae wi' him;
 I may be distress'd, but I winna complain;
I flatter my fancy I may get anither,
 My heart it shall never be broken for ane.

I couldna get sleeping till dawin[2] for greetin',[3]
 The tears trickled down like the hail and the rain:
Had I na got greetin', my heart wad a broken,
 For, oh! love forsaken 's a tormenting pain.

Although he has left me for greed o' the siller,
 I dinna envy him the gains he can win;
I rather wad bear a' the lade o' my sorrow
 Than ever hae acted sae faithless to him.

Weel, since he has left me, may pleasure gae wi' him,
 I may be distress'd, but I winna complain;
I flatter my fancy I may get anither,
 My heart it shall never be broken for ane.

———— —

YE JACOBITES BY NAME.

This song was founded upon some old verses, in which it was intimated that
the extinction of the house of Stuart was sought for by other weapons than the
sword.

TUNE—*Ye Jacobites by name.*

Ye Jacobites by name, give an ear, give an ear,
 Ye Jacobites by name, give an ear;
 Ye Jacobites by name,
 Your fautes I will proclaim,
 Your doctrines I maun blame—
 You shall hear.

[1] Grief.—[2] Break of day.—[3] Crying.

What is right and what is wrang, by the law, by the law?
  What is right and what is wrang by the law?
    What is right and what is wrang?
      A short sword and a lang,
      A weak arm, and a strang
        For to draw.

What makes heroic strife, famed afar, famed afar?
  What makes heroic strife famed afar?
    What makes heroic strife?
      To whet the assassin's knife,
      Or hunt a parent's life
        Wi' bluidie war.

Then let your schemes alone, in the state, in the state;
  Then let your schemes alone in the state;
    Then let your schemes alone,
      Adore the rising sun,
      And leave a man undone
        To his fate.

LADY MARY ANN.

Tune—*Craigtown's growing.*

O LADY Mary Ann
  Looks o'er the castle wa',
She saw three bonnie boys
  Playing at the ba';
The youngest he was
  The flower amang them a';
My bonnie laddie's young,
  But he's growin' yet.

O father! O father!
  An' ye think it fit,
We'll send him a year
  To the college yet:
We'll sew a green ribbon
  Round about his hat,
And that will let them ken
  He's to marry yet.

Lady Mary Ann
　　Was a flower i' the dew,
Sweet was its smell,
　　And bonnie was its hue!
And the langer it blossom'd
　　The sweeter it grew;
For the lily in the bud
　　Will be bonnier yet.

Young Charlie Cochran·
　　Was the sprout of an aik!
Bonnie and bloomin'
　　And straught was its make:
The sun took delight
　　To shine for its sake,
And it will be the brag
　　O' the forest yet.

The simmer is gane
　　When the leaves they were green,
And the days are awa
　　That we hae seen;
But far better days
　　I trust will come again,
For my bonnie laddie 's young,
　　But he 's growin' yet.

THE CARLE OF KELLYBURN BRAES.[1]

TUNE—*Kellyburn Braes.*

THERE lived a carle on Kellyburn braes,
　　(Hey, and the rue grows bonnie wi' thyme,)
And he had a wife was the plague o' his days;
　　And the thyme it is wither'd, and rue is in prime.

Ae day as the carle gaed up the lang glen,
　　(Hey, and the rue grows bonnie wi' thyme,)
He met wi' the devil; says, "How do yow fen?"
　　And the thyme it is wither'd, and rue is in prime.

[1] The groundwork of this piece is old, but it underwent many alterations by Burns; the eleventh and twelfth verses are wholly his; and as for the other parts, Mrs. Burns told Mr. Cromek, "that he gae this ane a terrible brushing."

"I've got a bad wife, sir; that's a' my complaint,
   (Hey, and the rue grows bonnie wi' thyme,)
For, saving your presence, to her ye're a saint;
   And the thyme it is wither'd, and rue is in prime."

"It's neither your stot nor your staig I shall crave,
   (Hey, and the rue grows bonnie wi' thyme;)
But gie me your wife, man, for her I must have,
   And the thyme it is wither'd, and rue is in prime."

"Oh welcome, most kindly," the blythe carle said,
   (Hey, and the rue grows bonnie with thyme,)
"But if ye can match her ye're waur nor ye're ca'd,
   And the thyme it is wither'd, and rue is in prime."

The devil has got the auld wife on his back,
   (Hey, and the rue grows bonnie wi' thyme,)
And, like a poor peddler, he's carried his pack;
   And the thyme it is wither'd, and rue is in prime.

He's carried her hame to his ain hallan-door,
   (Hey, and the rue grows bonnie wi' thyme);
Syne bade her gae in, for a b—h and a w—e,
   And the thyme it is wither'd, and rue is in prime.

Then straight he makes fifty, the pick o' his band,
   (Hey, and the rue grows bonnie wi' thyme,)
Turn out on her guard in the clap of a hand;
   And the thyme it is wither'd, and rue is in prime.

The carlin gaed through them like ony wud bear,
   (Hey, and the rue grows bonnie wi' thyme,)
Whae'er she gat hands on came near her nae mair;
   And the thyme it is wither'd, and rue is in prime.

A reekit wee devil looks over the wa',
   (Hey, and the rue grows bonnie wi' thyme,)
"Oh, help, master, help, or she'll ruin us a',
   And the thyme it is wither'd, and rue is in prime."

The devil he swore by the edge o' his knife,
   (Hey, and the rue grows bonnie wi' thyme,)
He pitied the man that was tied to a wife;
   And the thyme it is wither'd, and rue is in prime.

The devil he swore by the kirk and the bell,
   (Hey, and the rue grows bonnie wi' thyme,)

He was not in wedlock, thank heaven, but in hell;
    And the thyme it is wither'd, and rue is in prime.

Then Satan has travelled again wi' his pack,
    (Hey, and the rue grows bonnie wi' thyme,)
An' to her auld husband he 's carried her back;
    And the thyme it is wither'd, and rue is in prime.

I hae been a devil the feck o' my life,
    (Hey, and the rue grows bonnie wi' thyme,)
But ne'er was in hell, till I met wi' a wife;
    And the thyme it is wither'd, and rue is in prime."

LADY ONLIE.

Tune—The Ruffian's Rant.

A' the lads o' Thornie-bank,
    When they gae to the shore o' Bucky,
They 'll step in an' tak' a pint
    Wi' Lady Onlie, honest Lucky!

Lady Onlie, honest Lucky,
    Brews gude ale at shore o' Bucky;
I wish her sale for her gude ale,
    The best on a' the shore o' Bucky.

Her house sae bien, her curch sae clean,
    I wat she is a dainty chucky;
And cheerlie blinks the ingle-gleed
    Of Lady Onlie, honest Lucky!
        Lady Onlie, &c.

THE CARLES OF DYSART.

It is presumed that this song is entirely original; the air is lively and old,
and the verses have an air of antiquity.

Tune—Hey, ca' thro'.

Up wi' the carles o' Dysart,
    And the lads o' Buckhaven,
An' the kimmers o' Largo,
    And the lasses o' Leven.

Hey, ca' thro', ca' thro',
    For we hae mickle ado:

Hey, ca' thro', ca' thro',
  For we hae mickle ado.

We hae tales to tell,
  And wo hae sangs to sing;
We hae pennies to spend,
  And we hae pints to bring.

We 'll live a' our days,
  And them that come behin',
Let them do the like,
  And spend the gear they win.
        Hey, ca' thro', &c.

HAD I THE WYTE.[1]

HAD I the wyte, had I the wyte,
  Had I the wyte she bade me;
She watch'd me by the hie-gate side,
  And up the loan she shawed me;
And when I wadna venture in,
  A coward loon she ca'd me;
Had kirk and state been in the gate,
  I lighted when she bade me.

Sae craftilie she took me ben,
  And bade me make nae clatter;
"For our ramgunshoch glum gudeman
  Is out and owre the water:"
Whae'er shall say I wanted grace
  When I did kiss and dawte her,
Let him be planted in my place,
  Syne say I was the fautor.

Could I for shame, could I for shame,
  Could I for shame refused her?
And wadna manhood been to blame,
  Had I unkindly used her?

The air to which Burns composed this song was called, "Come, kiss wi'
me, and clap wi' me," and some of the words may be found in an old lyric
called, "Had I the wyte she bade me."

He claw'd her wi' the ripplin-kame,
    And blue and bluidy bruised her;
When sic a husband was frae hame,
    What wife but had excused her?

I dighted ay her een sae blue,
    And bann'd the cruel randy;
And weel I wat her willing mou'
    Was e'en like sugar-candy.
A gloamin-shot it was I trow,
    I lighted on the Monday;
But I cam through the Tysday's dew,
    To wanton Willie's brandy.

COMING THROUGH THE RYE.

This is altered from an old favorite song of the same name.

TUNE—*Coming through the rye.*

COMING through the rye, poor body,
    Coming through the rye,
She draiglet a' her petticoatie,
    Coming through the rye.
Jenny 's a' wat, poor body,
    Jenny 's seldom dry;
She draiglet a' her petticoatie,
    Coming through the rye.

Gin a body meet a body—
    Coming through the rye;
Gin a body kiss a body—
    Need a body cry?

Gin a body meet a body
    Coming through the glen,
Gin a body kiss a body—
    Need the world ken?
Jenny 's a' wat, poor body,
    Jenny 's seldom dry;
She draiglet a' her petticoatie,
    Coming through the rye.

YOUNG JAMIE, PRIDE OF A' THE PLAIN.

Tune—The curlin o' the glen.

Young Jamie, pride of a' the plain,
Sae gallant and sae gay a swain;
Thro' a' our lasses he did rove,
And reign'd resistless king of love:
But now wi' sighs and starting tears,
He strays amang the woods and briers;
Or in the glens and rocky caves
His sad complaining dowie raves:

I wha sae late did range and rove,
And changed with every moon my love,
I little thought the time was near,
Repentance I should buy sae dear:
The slighted maids my torment see,
And laugh at a' the pangs I dree;
While she, my cruel, scornfu' fair,
Forbids me e'er to see her mair!

THE LASS OF ECCLEFECHAN.

This is altered from an old song; the language is rendered more delicate
and the sentiment less warm, than in the original.

Tune—Jacky Latin.

Gat ye me, oh gat ye me,
  Oh gat ye me wi' naething?
Rock and reel, and spinnin'-wheel,
  A mickle quarter basin.
Bye attour, my gutcher has
  A hich house and a laigh ane,
A' for bye, my bonnie sel',
  The toss of Ecclefechan.

Oh haud your tongue now, Luckie Laing,
  Oh haud your tongue and jauner;
I held the gate till you I met,
  Syne I began to wander:
I tint my whistle and my sang,
  I tint my peace and pleasure;
But your green graff, now, Luckie Laing,
  Wad airt me to my treasure.

THE COOPER O' CUDDIE.[1]

TUNE—Bab at the bowster.

THE cooper o' Cuddie cam' here awa,
And ca'd the girrs out owre us a'—
And our gude-wife has gotten a ca'
    That anger'd the silly gude-man, O.

We'll hide the cooper behind the door,
Behind the door, behind the door;
We'll hide the cooper behind the door,
    And cover him under a mawn, O.

He sought them out, he sought them in,
Wi', deil hae her! and, deil hae him!
But the body was sae doited and blin',
    He wist na where he was gaun, O.

They cooper'd at e'en, they cooper'd at morn,
'Till our gude-man has gotten the scorn;
On ilka brow she's planted a horn,
    And swears that they shall stan', O.

We'll hide the cooper behind the door,
Behind the door, behind the door;
We'll hide the cooper behind the door,
    And cover him under a mawn, O.

THE CARDIN' O'T.[2]

TUNE—Salt-fish and dumplings.

I COFT a stane o' haslock woo',
    To make a wat to Johnie o't;
For Johnie is my only jo,
    I lo'e him best of onie yet.

[1] The delicacy of this song cannot be compared to its wit. Burns was in all respects the poet of the people, and no man in wide Scotland had so many merry tales to tell, and so many joyous songs to sing.—*Cunningham.*
[2] The tenderness of Johnie's wife can only be fully felt by those who know that hanse-lock wool is the softest and finest of the fleece, and is shorn from the throats of sheep in the summer heat, to give them air and keep them cool.—*Cunningham.*

The cardin o't, the spinnin' o't,
The warpin' o't, the winnin' o't;
When ilka ell cost me a groat,
The tailor staw the lynin o't.

For though his locks be lyart gray,
  And tho' his brow be beld aboon,
Yet I hae seen him on a day,
  The pride of a' the parishen.
            The cardin o't, &c.

SAE FAR AWA.[1]

Tune—Dalkeith Maiden Bridge.

Oh sad and heavy should I part,
  But for her sake sae far awa;
Unknowing what my way may thwart,
  My native land sae far awa.
Thou that of a' things Maker art,
  That form'd this fair sae far awa,
Gie body strength, then I'll ne'er start
  At this my way sae far awa.

How true is love to pure desert,
  So love to her, sae far awa:
And nocht can heal my bosom's smart,
  While, oh! she is sae far awa.
Nane other love, nane other dart,
  I feel but hers, sae far awa;
But fairer never touch'd a heart
  Than hers, the fair sae far awa.

[1] The youth of Scotland for many years have been much influenced by the spirit of enterprise. With the exception of a few districts, in which manufactures have been introduced, the country is poor, and affords little encouragement to the hardy race to whom it gives birth. The present song is a beautiful expression of attachment to his fair one, who is "far awa."

O MAY, THY MORN.

The lady here celebrated is said to be the fair Clarinda.

Tune—May, thy morn.

O MAY, thy morn was ne'er sae sweet
  As the mirk night o' December;
For sparkling was the rosy wine,
  And private was the chamber:
And dear was she I dare na name,
  But I will ay remember.
But dear was she I dare na name,
  But I will ay remember.

And here's to them, that, like oursel,
  Can push about the jorum;
And here's to them that wish us weel,
  May a' that's guid watch o'er them!
And here's to them, we dare na tell,
  The dearest o' the quorum.
And here's to them we dare na tell,
  The dearest o' the quorum!

THE HIGHLAND LADDIE.[1]

Tune—If thou'll play me fair play.

THE bonniest lad that e'er I saw,
  Bonnie laddie, Highland laddie,
Wore a plaid, and was fu' braw,
  Bonnie Highland laddie.
On his head a bonnet blue,
  Bonnie laddie, Highland laddie;
His royal heart was firm and true,
  Bonnie Highland laddie.

Trumpets sound, and cannons roar,
  Bonnie lassie, Lowland lassie;
And a' the hills wi' echoes roar,
  Bonnie Lowland lassie.

[1] Burns compressed "The Highland lad and Lowland lassie" into these three stanzas. It has allusion to Prince Charles, and is expressive of the affection and constancy of the people to him and his family.

Glory, honor, now invite,
    Bonnie lassie, Lowland lassie,
For freedom and my king to fight,
    Bonnie Lowland lassie.

The sun a backward coorse shall take,
    Bonnie laddie, Highland laddie,
Ere aught thy manly courage shake,
    Bonnie Highland laddie.
Go, for yourself procure renown,
    Bonnie laddie, Highland laddie;
And for your lawful king his crown,
    Bonnie Highland laddie.

CASSILLIS' BANKS.

The stream of Girvan and the banks of Cassillis were ever present to the
feeling and fancy of Burns ; ne loved to return to the scenes of his youth.

Tune—Unknown.

Now bank an' brae are claith'd[1] in green,
    An' scatter'd cowslips sweetly spring;
By Girvan's fairy-haunted stream
    The birdies flit on wanton wing.
To Cassillis' banks when e'ening fa's,
    There wi' my Mary let me flee,
There catch her ilka glance of love,
    The bonnie blink o' Mary's e'e!

The child wha boasts o' warld's walth[2]
    Is aften laird o' meikle care;
But Mary she is a' my ain—
    Ah! fortune canna gie me mair.
Then let me range by Cassillis' banks,
    Wi' her, the lassie dear to me,
And catch her ilka glance o' love,
    The bonnie blink o' Mary's e'e!

[1] Clothed.—[2] World's wealth.

TO THEE, LOVED NITH.

TUNE—*Unknown.*

To thee, loved Nith, thy gladsome plains,
 Where late wi' careless thought I ranged,
Though prest wi' care and sunk in woe,
 To thee I bring a heart unchanged.

I love thee, Nith, thy banks and braes,
 Tho' memory there my bosom tear;
For there he roved that brake my heart,
 Yet to that heart, ah! still how dear!

BANNOCKS O' BARLEY.

The air to which these words were written gave the name to an old song.

TUNE—*The Killogie.*

BANNOCKS o' bear meal,
 Bannocks o' barley;
Here's to the Highlandman's
 Bannocks o' barley.
Wha in a brulzie
 Will first cry a parley?
Never the lads wi'
 The bannocks o' barley.

Bannocks o' bear meal,
 Bannocks o' barley;
Here's to the lads wi'
 The bannocks o' barley.
Wha in his wae-days
 Were loyal to Charlie?
Wha but the lads wi'
 The bannocks o' barley.

HEE BALOU.[1]

TUNE—*The Highland Balou.*

HEE balou! my sweet wee Donald,
Picture o' the great Clanronald;
Brawlie kens our wanton chief
Wha got my young Highland thief.

Leeze me on thy bonnie craigie,
An' thou live, thou 'll steal a naigie:
Travel the country thro' and thro',
And bring hame a Carlisle cow.

Thro' the Lawlands, o'er the border,
Weel, my babie, may thou furder:
Herry the louns o' the laigh countree,
Syne to the Highlands hame to me.

HERE'S HIS HEALTH IN WATER!

TUNE—*The Job of Journey-work.*

ALTHO' my back be at the wa',
  And tho' he be the fautor;
Altho' my back be at the wa',
  Yet, here 's his health in water!
Oh! wae gae by his wanton sides,
  Sae brawlie he could flatter;
Till for his sake I 'm slighted sair,
  And dree the kintra clatter.
But tho' my back be at the wa',
  And though he be the fautor;
But tho' my back be at the wa',
  Yet, here 's his health in water!

[1] The sentiment is that of an old Highland nursery song: the Highland chief and his clan were formerly little better than robbers; they taught it to their children from their cradle, that might was right, especially so far as the Lowland cattle were concerned. The origin of this song is said to be, that a Highland lady sung a song in Gaelic, and explained it in English to the poet, when he quickly rendered it as it now appears.

HERE'S TO THY HEALTH, MY BONNIE LASS.

This was a song of the Poet's youthful days.

TUNE—*Laggan Burn.*

HERE's to thy health, my bonnie lass,
　Gude night, and joy be wi' thee;
I 'll come nae mair to thy bower door,
　To tell thee that I lo'e thee.
Oh dinna think, my pretty pink,
　But I can live without thee;
I vow and swear I dinna care
　How lang ye look about ye.

Thou 'rt ay sae free informing me
　Thou hast nae mind to marry;
I 'll be as free informing thee
　Nae time hae I to tarry.
I ken thy friends try ilka means,
　Frae wedlock to delay thee;
Depending on some higher chance—
　But fortune may betray thee.

I ken they scorn my low estate,
　But that does never grieve me;
But I 'm as free as any he,
　Sma' siller will relieve me.
I count my health my greatest wealth,
　Sae long as I 'll enjoy it:
I 'll fear nae scant, I 'll bode nae want,
　As lang 's I get employment.

But far off fowls hae feathers fair,
　And ay until ye try them:
Tho' they seem fair, still have a care,
　They may prove waur than I am.
But at twal at night, when the moon shines bright,
　My dear, I 'll come and see thee;
For the man that lo'es his mistress weel
　Nae travel makes him weary.

THE FAREWELL.

Tune—It was a' for our rightfu' king.

There is some doubt as to the authorship of this song—Hogg attributes it to Captain Ogilvie, who was killed in 1695; but there is reason to believe that it was an old song revived by Burns for Johnson's Museum.

It was a' for our rightfu' king
   We left fair Scotland's strand;
It was a' for our rightfu' king
   We e'er saw Irish land,
          My dear;
   We e'er saw Irish land.

Now a' is done that men can do,
   And a' is done in vain;
My love and native land, farewell,
   For I maun cross the main,
          My dear;
   For I maun cross the main.

He turn'd him right, and round about,
   Upon the Irish shore;
And gae his bridle-reins a shake,
   With adieu for evermore,
          My dear;
   With adieu for evermore.

The sodger from the wars returns,
   The sailor frae the main;
But I hae parted frae my love,
   Never to meet again,
          My dear;
   Never to meet again.

When day is gane, and night is come,
   And a' folk bound to sleep;
I think on him that's far awa',
   The lee-lang night, and weep,
          My dear;
   The lee-lang night, and weep.

OH, STEER HER UP.

From an old song of the same name.

TUNE—*Oh, steer her up, and haud her gaun.*

OH, steer her up and haud her gaun,
　Her mother's at the mill, jo;
And gin she winna take a man,
　E'en let her take her will, jo;
First shore her wi' a kindly kiss,
　And ca' another gill, jo,
And gin she take the thing amiss,
　E'en let her flyte her fill, jo.

Oh, steer her up, and be na blate,
　An' gin she take it ill, jo,
Then lea'e the lassie till her fate,
　And time nae longer spill, jo:
Ne'er break your heart for ae rebute,
　But think upon it still, jo;
Then gin the lassie winna do 't,
　Ye'll fin' anither will, jo.

THE FÊTE CHAMPÊTRE.

On the occasion of a Fête Champêtre, given by Mr. Cunninghame, of Enterkin, on his coming to his estates—and from its novelty, it was supposed he had an intention of becoming a candidate for the representation of his county.

TUNE—*Killi crankie.*

OH, wha will to Saint Stephen's house,
　To do our errands there, man?
Oh, wha will to Saint Stephen's house,
　O' th' merry lads of Ayr, man?
Or will we send a man-o'-law?
　Or will we send a sodger?
Or him wha led o'er Scotland a'
　The meikle Ursa-Major?

Come, will ye court a noble lord,
　Or buy a score o' lairds, man?
For worth and honor pawn their word,
　Their vote shall be Glencaird's, man?

Ane gies them coin, ane gies them wine,
  Anither gies them clatter;
Anbank, wha guess'd the ladies' taste,
  He gies a Fête Champêtre.

When Love and Beauty heard the news,
  The gay green woods amang, man;
Where gathering flowers and busking bowers
  They heard the blackbird's sang, man,
A vow, they seal'd it with a kiss,
  Sir Politics to fetter,
As theirs alone, the patent-bliss,
  To hold a Fête Champêtre.

Then mounted Mirth, on gleesome wing,
  O'er hill and dale she flew, man:
Ilk wimpling burn, ilk crystal spring,
  Ilk glen and shaw she knew, man:
She summon'd every social sprite,
  That sports by wood or water,
On the bonny banks of Ayr to meet,
  And keep this Fête Champêtre.

Cauld Boreas, wi' his boisterous crew,
  Were bound to stakes like kye, man;
And Cynthia's car, o' silver fu',
  Clamb up the starry sky, man:
Reflected beams dwell in the streams,
  Or down the current shatter;
The western breeze steals through the trees
  To view this Fête Champêtre.

How many a robe sae gaily floats!
  What sparkling jewels glance, man!
To Harmony's enchanting notes,
  As moves the mazy dance, man.
The echoing wood, the winding flood,
  Like Paradise did glitter,
When angels met, at Adam's yett,
  To hold their Fête Champêtre.

When Politics came there, to mix
  And make his ether-stane, man!
He circled round the magic ground,
  But entrance found he nane, man:

He blush'd for shame, he quat his name,
　Forswore 't, every letter,
Wi' humble prayer to join and share
　The festive Fête Champêtre.

———

THE HIGHLAND WIDOW'S LAMENT.

This is no exaggerated picture of the desolation which was commanded
and sanctioned by the Duke of Cumberland in putting down the rebellion
in 1745.

Oh! I am come to the low countrie,
　Och-on, och-on, och-rie!
Without a penny in my purse,
　To buy a meal to me.

It was na sae in the Highland hills,
　Och-on, och-on, och-rie!
Nae woman in the country wide
　Sae happy was as me.

For then I had a score o' kye,
　Och-on, och-on, och-rie!
Feeding on yon hills so high,
　And giving milk to me.

And there I had threescore o' yowes,
　Och-on, och-on, och-rie!
Skipping on yon bonnie knowes,
　And casting woo' to me.

I was the happiest of a' the clan,
　Sair, sair may I repine;
For Donald was the brawest lad,
　And Donald he was mine.

Till Charlie Stuart cam' at last,
　Sae far to set us free;
My Donald's arm was wanted then,
　For Scotland and for me.

Their waefu' fate what need I tell,
　Right to the wrang did yield:
My Donald and his country fell
　Upon Culloden's field.

Oh! I am come to the low countrie,
   Och-on, och-on, och-rie!
Nae woman in the world wide
   Sae wretched now as me.

PEG-A-RAMSEY.

The old song of this name was a very famous amatory song.

TUNE—*Cauld is the e'ening blast.*

CAULD is the e'enin' blast
   O' Boreas o'er the pool,
And dawin' it is dreary
   When birks are bare at Yule.

Oh bitter blaws the e'enin' blast
   When bitter bites the frost,
And in the mirk and dreary drift
   The hills and glens are lost.

Ne'er sae murky blew the night
   That drifted o'er the hill,
But a bonnie Peg-a-Ramsey
   Gat grist to her mill.

THERE WAS A BONNIE LASS.

An unfinished sketch.

THERE was a bonnie lass,
   And a bonnie, bonnie lass,
And she lo'ed her bonnie laddie dear;
   Till war's loud alarms,
   Tore her laddie frae her arms,
Wi' mony a sigh and tear.

   Over sea, over shore,
   Where the cannons loudly roar,
He still was a stranger to fear:
   And nocht could him quell,
   Or his bosom assail,
But the bonnie lass he lo'ed sae dear.

OH, MALLY 'S MEEK, MALLY 'S SWEET.

This stands the last of the communications to the "Museum." It is said
to have been produced on seeing a young countrywoman with her shoes and
stockings packed carefully up, and her petticoats kilted, which showed

" Her straight bare legs, that whiter were than snaw."

Oh, Mally 's meek, Mally 's sweet,
    Mally 's modest and discreet,
Mally 's rare, Mally 's fair,
    Mally 's every way complete.
As I was walking up the street,
    A barefit maid I chanced to meet;
But oh, the road was very hard
    For that fair maiden's tender feet.

It were mair meet that those fine feet
    Were weel laced up in silken shoon;
And 'twere more fit that she should sit
    Within yon chariot gilt aboon.

Her yellow hair, beyond compare,
    Comes trinkling down her swan-white neck;
And her two eyes, like stars in skies,
    Would keep a sinking ship frae wreck.
Oh, Mally 's meek, Mally 's sweet,
    Mally 's modest and discreet,
Mally 's rare, Mally 's fair,
    Mally 's every way complete.

ADDITIONAL

MISCELLANEOUS PIECES.

THE FAREWELL.

These beautiful and affecting stanzas were composed under great distress
of mind, when his prospects in life were so gloomy, that his only hope for
success seemed to be directed to obtaining a situation in the West Indies.

FAREWELL, old Scotia's bleak domains,
Far dearer than the torrid plains.
　　Where rich ananas blow !
Farewell, a mother's blessing dear !
A brother's sigh ! a sister's tear !
　　My Jean's heart-rending throe !
Farewell, my Bess ! tho' thou 'rt bereft
　　Of my parental care ;
A faithful brother I have left,
　　My part in him thou 'lt share !
　　　　Adieu too, to you too,
　　　　　　My Smith, my bosom frien' ;
　　　　When kindly you mind me,
　　　　　　Oh then befriend my Jean !

What bursting anguish tears my heart !
From thee, my Jenny, must I part !
　　Thou weeping answerest no :
Alas ! misfortune stares my face,
And points to ruin and disgrace,
　　I for thy sake must go !
Thee, Hamilton, and Aiken dear,
　　A grateful, warm adieu !
I, with a much-indebted tear,
　　Shall still remember you !
　　　　All-hail then, the gale then,
　　　　　　Wafts me from thee, dear shore !
　　　　It rustles, and whistles,
　　　　　　I 'll never see thee more !

WILLIE CHALMERS.[1]

Wi' braw new branks in mickle pride,
    And eke a braw new brechan,
My Pegasus I 'm got astride,
    And up Parnassus pechin;
Whiles owre a bush wi' downward crush,
    The doited beastie stammers;
Then up he gets, and off he sets
    For sake o' Willie Chalmers.

I doubt na, lass, that weel-kenn'd name
    May cost a pair o' blushes;
I am nae stranger to your fame,
    Nor his warm-urgéd wishes.
Your bonnie face sae mild and sweet,
    His honest heart enamors,
And faith ye 'll no be lost a whit,
    Tho' waired on Willie Chalmers.

Auld Truth hersel' might swear ye 're fair,
    And Honor safely back her,
And Modesty assume your air,
    And ne'er a ane mistak her:
And sic twa love-inspiring e'en
    Might fire even holy Palmers;
Nae wonder then they 've fatal been
    To honest Willie Chalmers.

I doubt na fortune may you shore
    Some mim-mou'd pouther'd priestie,
Fu' lifted up wi' Hebrew lore,
    And band upon his breastie:
But oh! what signifies to you
    His lexicons and grammars;
The feeling heart 's the royal blue,
    An' that 's wi' Willie Chalmers.

[1] Mr. Lockhart has given the following account of this singular piece—he copied it from a small collection of MSS. sent by Burns to Lady Harriet Don, accompanied with the following explanation:—" W. Chalmers, a gentleman in Ayrshire, a particular friend of mine, asked me to write a poetical epistle to a young lady, his Dulcinea. I had seen her, but was scarcely acquainted with her, and wrote as above."

Some gapin', glowrin' countra laird,
    May warsle for your favor;
May claw his lug, and straik his beard,
    And host up some palaver.
My bonnie maid, before ye wed
    Sic clumsy-witted hammers,
Seek Heaven for help, and barefit skelp
    Awa' wi' Willie Chalmers.

Forgive the Bard! my fond regard
    For ane that shares my bosom,
Inspires my muse to gie 'm his dues.
    For deil a hair I roose him.
May powers aboon unite you soon,
    And fructify your amours,—
And every year come in mair dear
    To you and Willie Chalmers.

EPISTLE TO MAJOR LOGAN.[1]

Hail, thairm-inspirin', rattlin' Willie!
Though fortune's road be rough an' hilly
To every fiddling, rhyming billie,
            We never heed,
But take it like the unback'd filly,
            Proud o' her speed.

When idly goavan whyles we saunter
Yirr, fancy barks, awa' we canter
Uphill, down brae, till some mishanter,
            Some black bog-hole,
Arrests us, then the scathe an' banter
            We're forced to thole.

Hale be your heart! Hale be your fiddle!
Lang may your elbuck jink and diddle,
To cheer you through the weary widdle
            O' this wild warl',
Until you on a crummock driddle,
            A gray-hair'd carl.

This gentleman lived at Parkhouse, near Ayr, and was not only a first-rate performer on the violin, but a pleasant man, and not a little of a wit. The original of this piece is now in the possession of David Auld, Esq., Ayr.

Come wealth, come poortith, late or soon,
Heaven send your heart-strings ay in tune,
And screw your temper pins aboon
   A fifth or mair,
The melancholious, lazie croon
   O' cankrie care.

May still your life from day to day
Nae "lente largo" in the play,
But "allegretto forté" gay
   Harmonious flow
A sweeping, kindling, bauld strathspey—
   Encore! Bravo!

A blessing on the cheery gang
Wha dearly like a jig or sang,
An' never think o' right an' wrang
   By square an' rule,
But as the clegs o' feeling stang
   Are wise or fool.

My hand-waled curse keep hard in chase
The harpy, hoodock, purse-proud race,
Wha count on poortith as disgrace—
   Their tuneless hearts!
May fireside discords jar a base
   To a' their parts!

But come, your hand, my careless brither,
I' th' ither warl', if there's anither—
An' that there is I've little swither
   About the matter—
We cheek for chow shall jog thegither,
   I'se ne'er bid better.

We've faults and failings—granted clearly,
We're frail backsliding mortals merely,
Eve's bonnie squad priests wyte them sheerly
   For our grand fa';
But still, but still, I like them dearly—
   God bless them a'!

Ochon for poor Castalian drinkers,
When they fa' foul o' earthly jinkers,
The witching, cursed, delicious blinkers
   Hae put me hyte,

And gart me weet my waukrife winkers,
   Wi' girnan spite.

But by yon moon!—and that's high swearin'—
An' every star within my hearin'!
An' by her een wha was a dear ane!
   I 'll ne'er forget;
I hope to gie the jads a clearin'
   In fair play yet.

My loss I mourn, but not repent it,
I 'll seek my pursie whare I tint it;
Ance to the Indies I were wonted,
   Some cantraip hour,
By some sweet elf I 'll yet be dinted,
   Then, *vive l'amour !*

Faites mes baissemains respectueuse,
To sentimental sister Susie,
An' honest Lucky; no to roose you,
   Ye may be proud,
That sic a couple fate allows ye
   To grace your blood.

Nae mair at present can I measure,
An' trowth my rhymin' ware's nae treasure;
But when in Ayr, some half-hour's leisure,
   Be 't light, be 't dark,
Sir Bard will do himself the pleasure
   To call at Park.
        ROBERT BURNS.

MOSSGIEL, 30th October, 1786.

———

ON THE DEATH OF ROBERT DUNDAS, ESQ.[1]

OF ARNISTON, LATE LORD PRESIDENT OF THE COURT OF SESSION,

LONE on the bleaky hills the straying flocks
Shun the fierce storms among the sheltering rocks,

> [1] Burns has given the following account of these beautiful lines:—"The inclosed was written in consequence of your suggestion last time I had the pleasure of seeing you. It cost me an hour or two of next morning's sleep, but did not please me, so it laid by, an ill-digested effort, till the other day I gave it a critic-brush. These kinds of subjects are much hackneyed,

Down from the rivulets, red with dashing rains,
The gathering floods burst o'er the distant plains;
Beneath the blasts the leafless forests groan;
The hollow caves return a sullen moan.

Ye hills, ye plains, ye forests, and ye caves,
Ye howling winds, and wintry swelling waves!
Unheard, unseen, by human ear or eye,
Sad to your sympathetic scenes I fly;
Where to the whistling blast and waters' roar
Pale Scotia's recent wound I may deplore.

Oh, heavy loss, thy country ill could bear!
A loss these evil days can ne'er repair!
Justice, the high vicegerent of her God,
Her doubtful balance eyed, and sway'd her rod;
Hearing the tidings of the fatal blow
She sunk, abandon'd to the wildest woe.

Wrongs, injuries, from many a darksome den,
Now gay in hope explore the paths of men:
See from his cavern grim Oppression rise,
And throw on poverty his cruel eyes;
Keen on the helpless victim see him fly,
And stifle, dark, the feebly-bursting cry:

Mark ruffian Violence, distain'd with crimes,
Rousing elate in these degenerate times;
View unsuspecting Innocence a prey,
As guileful Fraud points out the erring way:
While subtile Litigation's pliant tongue
The life-blood equal sucks of Right and Wrong:
Hark, injured Want recounts the unlisten'd tale,
And much-wrong'd Misery pours the unpitied wail!

and, besides, the wailings of the rhyming tribe over the ashes of the great
are cursedly suspicious, and out of all character for sincerity. These ideas
damped my muse's fire: however I have done the best I could." And in
another letter to Dr. Geddes, he writes thus: "The foregoing poem has some
tolerable lines in it, but the incurable wound of my pride will not suffer me
to correct, or even peruse it. I sent a copy of it, with my best prose letter,
to the son of the great man, the theme of the piece, by the hands of one of
the noblest men in God's world, Alexander Wood, surgeon. When, behold!
his solicitorship took no more notice of my poem or me than I had been
a strolling fiddler, who had made free with his lady's name over a silly new
reel! Did the gentleman imagine that I looked for any dirty gratuity?"

Ye dark waste hills, and brown unsightly plains,
To you I sing my grief-inspired strains:
Ye tempests, rage! ye turbid torrents, roll!
Ye suit the joyless tenor of my soul.
Life's social haunts and pleasures I resign,
Be nameless wilds and lonely wanderings mine,
To mourn the woes my country must endure,
That wound degenerate ages cannot cure.

WRITTEN IN FRIARS-CARSE HERMITAGE,

ON THE BANKS OF NITH.

This is from the original rough draft of the poem, in the possession of Mrs. Hyslop.

Thou whom chance may hither lead,
Be thou clad in russet weed,
Be thou deckt in silken stole,
Grave these maxims on thy soul.

Life is but a day at most,
Sprung from night, in darkness lost;
Day, how rapid in its flight—
Day, how few must see the night;
Hope not sunshine every hour,
Fear not clouds will always lower.
Happiness is but a name,
Make content and ease thy aim.
Ambition is a meteor gleam;
Fame a restless idle dream:
Pleasures, insects on the wing,
Round Peace, the tenderest flower of Spring:
Those that sip the dew alone,
Make the butterflies thy own;
Those that would the bloom devour,
Crush the locusts—save the flower.
For the future be prepared,
Guard wherever thou canst guard;
But thy utmost duly done,
Welcome what thou canst not shun.
Follies past, give thou to air,
Make their consequence thy care:

Keep tho name of man in mind,
And dishonor not thy kind.
Reverence with lowly heart
Him whose wondrous work thou art;
Keep his goodness still in view,
Thy trust—and thy example, too.

Stranger, go! Heaven be thy guide!
Quod, the Beadsman on Nithside.

EPISTLE TO HUGH PARKER,

One of the Poet's earliest friends.

In this strange land, this uncouth clime,
A land unknown to prose or rhyme;
Where words ne'er crost the muse's heckles,
Nor limpet in poetic shackles;
A land that prose did never view it,
Except when drunk he stacher't through it,
Here, ambush'd by the chimla cheek,
Hid in an atmosphere of reek,
I hear a wheel thrum i' the neuk,
I hear it—for in vain I leuk.—
The red peat gleams, a fiery kernel,
Enhuskéd by a fog infernal:
Here, for my wonted rhyming raptures,
I sit and count my sins by chapters;
For life and spunk like ither Christians,
I'm dwindled down to mere existence,
Wi' nae converse but Gallowa' bodies,
Wi' nae kend face but Jenny Geddes.[1]
Jenny, my Pegasean pride!
Dowie she saunters down Nithside,
And ay a westlin leuk she throws,
While tears hap o'er her auld brown nose!
Was it for this, wi' canny care,
Thou bure the Bard through many a shire?
At howes or hillocks never stumbled,
And late or early never grumbled!—
Oh, had I power like inclination,
I'd heeze thee up a constellation,

[1] His mare.

To canter with the Sagitarre,
Or loup the ecliptic like a bar;
Or turn the pole like any arrow;
Or, when auld Phebus bids good-morrow,
Down the zodiac urge the race,
And cast dirt on his godship's face;
For I could lay my bread and kail
He 'd ne'er cast saut upo' thy tail.—
Wi' a' this care and a' this grief,
And sma', sma' prospect of relief,
And naught but peat reek i' my head,
How can I write what ye can read?—
Tarbolton, twenty-fourth o' June,
Ye 'll find me in a better tune;
But till we meet and weet our whistle,
Tak this excuse for nae epistle.

ROBERT BURNS.

TO JOHN M'MURDO, Esq.

He was steward to the Duke of Queensberry, and a warm friend of the Poet.

OH, could I give thee India's wealth,
  As I this trifle send!
Because thy joy in both would be
  To share them with a friend.

But golden sands did never grace
  The Heliconian stream;
Then take what gold could never buy—
  An honest Bard's esteem.

WRITTEN ON A PANE OF GLASS.

BLEST be M'Murdo to his latest day!
No envious cloud o'ercast his evening ray!
No wrinkle furrow'd by the hand of care,
Nor ever sorrow add one silver hair!
Oh, may no son the father's honor stain,
Nor ever daughter give the mother pain!

THE KIRK'S ALARM.[1]

A BALLAD.—(SECOND VERSION.)

ORTHODOX, orthodox,
  Who believe in John Knox,
Let me sound an alarm to your conscience—
    There's a heretic blast,
    Has been blawn i' the wast,
That what is not sense must be nonsense,
          Orthodox,
That what is not sense must be nonsense.

Doctor Mac, Doctor Mac,
  Ye should stretch on a rack,
To strike evil-doers wi' terror;
    To join faith and sense,
    Upon any pretence,
Was heretic, damnable error,
          Doctor Mac,
Was heretic, damnable error.

Town of Ayr, town of Ayr,
  It was rash, I declare,
To meddle wi' mischief a-brewin';
    Provost John is still deaf
    To the church's relief,
And orator Bob is its ruin,
          Town of Ayr,
And orator Bob is its ruin.

[1] Of this piece Burns has given the following account, in a letter to Graham of Fintray:—"Though I dare say you have none of the Solemn League and Covenant fire which shone so conspicuous in Lord George Gordon and the Kilmarnock weavers, yet I think you must have heard of Dr. M'Gill, one of the clergymen of Ayr, and his heretical book. God help him, poor man! Though he is one of the worthiest, as well as one of the ablest of the whole priesthood of the Kirk of Scotland, in every sense of that ambiguous term, yet the poor Doctor and his numerous family are in imminent danger of being thrown out (9th December, 1790) to the mercy of the winter winds. The inclosed ballad on that business is, I confess, too local, but I laughed myself at some conceits in it, though I am convinced in my conscience that there are a good many heavy stanzas in it, too."

To another correspondent the Poet says:—"Whether in the way of my trade I can be of any service to the Rev. Doctor, is, I fear, very doubtful. Ajax's shield consisted, I think, of seven bull-hides and a plate of brass,

D'rymple mild, D'rymple mild,
Tho' your heart's like a child,
And your life like the new-driven snaw,
Yet that winna save ye,
Old Satan must have ye
For preaching that three's ane an' twa,
D'rymple mild,
For preaching that three's ane an' twa.

Calvin's sons, Calvin's sons,
Seize your spiritual guns,
Ammunition ye never can need;
Your hearts are the stuff,
Will be powder enough,
And your skulls are a storehouse of lead,
Calvin's sons,
And your skulls are a storehouse of lead.

Rumble John, Rumble John,
Mount the steps with a groan,
Cry the book is with heresy cramm'd;
Then lug out your ladle,
Deal brimstone like aidle,
And roar every note o' the damn'd,
Rumble John,
And roar every note o' the damn'd.

Simper James, Simper James,
Leave the fair Killie dames,
There's a holier chase in your view;
I'll lay on your head,
That the pack ye'll soon lead,
For puppies like you there's but few,
Simper James,
For puppies like you there's but few.

Singet Sawnie, Singet Sawnie,
Are ye herding the penny,
Unconscious what danger awaits?

which altogether set Hector's utmost force at defiance. Alas! I am not a
Hector, and the worthy Doctor's foes are as securely armed as Ajax was
Ignorance, superstition, bigotry, stupidity, malevolence, self-conceit, envy,—
all strongly bound in a massy frame of brazen impudence."

With a jump, yell, and howl,
Alarm every soul,
For Hannibal 's just at your gates,
    Singet Sawnie,
For Hannibal 's just at your gates.

Andrew Gowk, Andrew Gowk,
Ye may slander the book,
And the book naught the waur—let me tell you;
Tho' ye 're rich and look big,
Yet lay by hat and wig,
And ye 'll hae a calf's-head o' sma' value,
    Andrew Gowk,
And ye 'll hae a calf's-head o' sma' value.

Poet Willie, Poet Willie,
Gie the doctor a volley,
Wi' your "liberty's chain" and your wit;
O'er Pegasus' side,
Ye ne'er laid astride,
Ye only stood by when he sh——,
    Poet Willie,
Ye only stood by when he sh——.

Barr Steenie, Barr Steenie,
What mean ye? what mean ye?
If ye 'll meddle nae mair wi' the matter,
Ye may hae some pretence man,
To havins and sense man,
Wi' people that ken you nae better,
    Barr Steenie,
Wi' people that ken you nae better.

Jamie Goose, Jamie Goose,
Ye hae made but toom roose,
O' hunting the wicked lieutenant;
But the doctor 's your mark,
For the L—d's holy ark,
He has cooper'd and ca'd a wrong pin in 't,
    Jamie Goose,
He has cooper'd and ca'd a wrong pin in 't.

Davie Bluster, Davie Bluster,
For a saunt if ye muster,
It 's a sign they 're no nice o' recruits;

Yet to worth let 's be just,
Royal blood ye might boast,
If the ass were the king o' the brutes,
      Davie Bluster,
If the ass were the king o' the brutes.

Muirland George, Muirland George,
  Whom the Lord made a scourge,
To claw common sense for her sins;
  If ill manners were wit,
  There 's no mortal so fit
To confound the poor doctor at ance,
      Muirland George,
To confound the poor doctor at ance.

Cessnockside, Cessnockside,
  Wi' your turkey-cock pride,
O' manhood but sma' is your share;
  Ye 've the figure, it 's true,
  Even our faes maun allow,
And your friends daurna say ye hae mair,
      Cessnockside,
And your friends daurna sae ye hae mair.

Daddie Auld, Daddie Auld,
  There 's a tod i' the fauld,
A tod meikle waur than the clerk;
  Tho' ye downa do skaith,
  Ye 'll be in at the death,
And if ye canna bite ye can bark,
      Daddie Auld,
And if ye canna bite ye can bark.

Poet Burns, Poet Burns,
  Wi' your priest-skelping turns,
Why desert ye your auld native shire?
  Tho' your Muse is a gipsy,
  Yet were she even tipsy,
She could ca' us nae waur than we are,
      Poet Burns,
She could ca' us nae waur than we are.

POSTSCRIPT.

Afton's Laird, Afton's Laird,
When your pen can be spared,

A copy o' this I bequeath,
  On the same sicker score
  I mention'd before,
To that trusty auld worthy Clackleith,
                Afton's Laird,
To that trusty auld worthy Clackieith.

TO ROBERT GRAHAM, ESQ., OF FINTRAY:

ON THE CLOSE OF THE DISPUTED ELECTION BETWEEN SIR JAMES JOHNSTON AND CAPTAIN MILLER, FOR THE DUMFRIES DISTRICT OF BOROUGHS.

FINTRAY, my stay in worldly strife,
Friend o' my muse, friend o' my life,
    Are ye as idle 's I am?
Come then, wi' uncouth, kintra fleg,
O'er Pegasus I 'll fling my leg,
    And ye shall see me try him.

I 'll sing the zeal Drumlanrig bears
Who left the all-important cares
    Of princes and their darlings ·
And, bent on winning borough towns,
Came shaking hands wi' wabster lowns,
    And kissing barefit carlins.

Combustion thro' our boroughs rode,
Whistling his roaring pack abroad
    Of mad unmuzzled lions;
As Queensberry buff and blue unfurl'd,
And Westerha' and Hopeton hurl'd
    To every Whig defiance.

But cautious Queensberry left the war,
The unmanner'd dust might soil his star;
    Besides, he hated bleeding;
But left behind him heroes bright,
Heroes in Cæsarean fight,
    Or Ciceronian pleading.

Oh! for a throat like huge Mons-meg,
To muster o'er each ardent Whig
    Beneath Drumlanrig's banner;

Heroes and heroines commix,
All in the field of politics,
   To win immortal honor.

M'Murdo and his lovely spouse,
(The enamor'd laurels kiss her brows!)
   Led on the loves and graces:
She won each gaping burgess' heart,
While he, all-conquering, play'd his part
   Among their wives and lasses.

Craigdarroch led a light-arm'd corps,
Tropes, metaphors, and figures pour,
   Like Hecla streaming thunder;
Glenriddel, skill'd in rusty coins,
Blew up each Tory's dark designs,
   And bared the treason under.

In either wing two champions fought,
Redoubted Staig,[1] who set at naught
   The wildest savage Tory:
And Welsh,[2] who ne'er yet flinch'd his ground,
High-waved his magnum-bonum round
   With Cyclopeian fury.

Miller brought up the artillery ranks,
The many-pounders of the Banks,
   Resistless desolation!
While Maxwelton, that baron bold,
'Mid Lawson's[3] port entrench'd his hold,
   And threaten'd worse damnation.

To these what Tory hosts opposed,
With these what Tory warriors closed,
   Surpasses my descriving:
Squadrons extended long and large,
With furious speed rush to the charge,
   Like raging devils driving.

What verse can sing, what prose narrate,
The butcher deeds of bloody fate
   Amid this mighty tulzie!
Grim Horror girn'd—pale Terror roar'd,
As Murther at his thrapple shored,
   And hell mix'd in the brulzie.

[1] Provost Staig of Dumfries.—[2] Sheriff Welsh.—[3] Lawson, a wine merchant
in Dumfries.

As Highland craigs by thunder cleft,
When lightnings fire the stormy lift,
                  Hurl down with crashing rattle:
As flames among a hundred woods;
As headlong foam a hundred floods,
                  Such is the rage of battle!

The stubborn Tories dare to die;
As soon the rooted oaks would fly
                  Before the approaching fellers:
The Whigs come on like Ocean's roar,
When all his wintry billows pour
                  Against the Buchan Bullers.

Lo, from the shades of Death's deep night,
Departed Whigs enjoy the fight,
                  And think on former daring:
The muffled murtherer[1] of Charles
The Magna Charta flag unfurls,
                  All deadly gules it's bearing.

Nor wanting ghosts of Tory fame,
Bold Scrimgeour[3] follows gallant Graham,[2]
                  Auld Covenanters shiver.
(Forgive, forgive, much-wrong'd Montrose!
Now death and hell engulf thy foes,
                  Thou liv'st on high forever!)

Still o'er the field the combat burns,
The Tories, Whigs, give way by turns;
                  But Fate the word has spoken:
For woman's wit and strength o' man,
Alas! can do but what they can!
                  The Tory ranks are broken.

Oh that my een were flowing burns,
My voice a lioness that mourns
                  Her darling cubs' undoing!
That I might greet, that I might cry,
While Tories fall, while Tories fly,
                  And furious Whigs pursuing!

---

[1] The executioner of Charles I. was masked.—[2] Scrimgeour, Lord Dundee.
—[3] Graham, Marquis of Montrose.

What Whig but melts for good Sir James?
Dear to his country by the names
   Friend, patron, benefactor!
Not Pulteney's wealth can Pulteney save!
And Hopeton falls, the generous brave!
   And Stewart,[1] bold as Hector.

Thou, Pitt, shalt rue this overthrow;
And Thurlow growl a curse of woe;
   And Melville melt in wailing!
How Fox and Sheridan rejoice!
And Burke shall sing, O Prince, arise,
   Thy power is all-prevailing!

For your poor friend, the Bard, afar,
He only hears and sees the war,
   A cool spectator purely!
So, when the storm the forest rends,
The robin in the hedge descends,
   And sober chirps securely.

ADDRESS OF BEELZEBUB

TO THE PRESIDENT OF THE HIGHLAND SOCIETY.

First published in the "Scots Magazine" for February, 1818.

Long life, my Lord, an' health be yours,
Unskaith'd by hunger'd Highland boors;
Lord grant nae duddie desperate beggar,
Wi' dirk, claymore, or rusty trigger,
May twin auld Scotland o' a life
She likes—as lambkins like a knife.
Faith, you and A——s were right
To keep the Highland hounds in sight,
I doubt na'! they wad bid nae better
Than let them ance out owre the water,
Then up amang thae lakes and seas
They'll mak what rules and laws they please;
Some daring Hancock, or a Franklin,
May set their Highland bluid a ranklin';
Some Washington again may head them,
Or some Montgomery fearless lead them,

1 Stewart of Hillside.

Till God knows what may be effected
When by such heads and hearts directed—
Poor dunghill sons of dirt and mire
May to patrician rights aspire!
Nae sage North, now, nor sager Sackville,
To watch and premier o'er the pack vile,
An' whare will ye get Howes and Clintons
To bring them to a right repentance,
To cowe the rebel generation,
An' save the honor o' the nation?
They an' be d——d! what right hae they
To meat or sleep, or light o' day?
Far less to riches, power, or freedom,
But what your lordship likes to gie them?

But hear, my lord! Glengarry, hear!
Your hand's owre light on them, I fear:
Your factors, grieves, trustees, and bailies,
I canna' say but they do gaylies;
They lay aside a' tender mercies,
An' tirl the hallions to the birses;
Yet while they're only poind't and herriet,
They'll keep their stubborn Highland spirit:
But smash them! crash them a' to spails!
An' rot the dyvors i' the jails!
The young dogs, swinge them to the labor;
Let wark an' hunger mak them sober!
The hizzies, if they're aughtlins fawsont,
Let them in Drury-lane be lesson'd!
An' if the wives an' dirty brats
E'en thigger at your doors an' yetts,
Flaffan wi' duds an' gray wi' beas',
Frightin' awa your deucks an' geese—
Get out a horsewhip or a jowler,
The langest thong, the fiercest growler,
An' gar the tatter'd gypsies pack
Wi' a' their bastarts on their back!
Go on, my lord! I lang to meet you,
An' in my house at hame to greet you;
Wi' common lords ye shanna mingle,
The benmost neuk beside the ingle,
At my right han' assign'd your seat
'Tween Herod's hip an' Polycrate,—

Or if you on your station tarrow,
Between Almagro and Pizarro,
A seat, I'm sure, ye're weel deservin't;
An' till ye come—Your humble servant,
BEELZEBUB.

TO JOHN TAYLOR.[1]

WITH Pegasus upon a day
  Apollo weary flying,
Through frosty hills the journey lay,
  On foot the way was plying.

Poor slip-shod giddy Pegasus
  Was but a sorry walker;
To Vulcan then Apollo goes,
  To get a frosty calker.

Obliging Vulcan fell to work,
  Threw by his coat and bonnet,
And did Sol's business in a crack;
  Sol paid him with a sonnet.

Ye Vulcan's sons of Wanlockhead,
  Pity my sad disaster;
My Pegasus is poorly shod—
  I'll pay you like my master.
           ROBERT BURNS.

EPISTLE FROM ESOPUS TO MARIA.

The Esopus of this epistle was Williamson, an actor, and the Maria to whom it is addressed was Mrs. Riddel.

FROM those drear solitudes and frowzy cells,
Where infamy with sad repentance dwells;
Where turnkeys make the jealous portal fast,
And deal from iron hands the spare repast;

[1] These verses were written, to induce a blacksmith to proceed at once "to sharpen his horse's shoes," as the roads had become slippery with ice. The blacksmith is said to have lived thirty years after to say that he had never been "weel paid but ance, and that was by a Poet, who paid him in money, paid him in drink, and paid him in verse."

Where truant 'prentices, yet young in sin,
Blush at the curious stranger peeping in;
Where strumpets, relics of the drunken roar,
Resolve to drink, nay half to whore, no more;
Where tiny thieves, not destined yet to swing,
Beat hemp for others, riper for the string:
From these dire scenes my wretched lines I date,
To tell Maria her Esopus' fate.

"Alas! I feel I am no actor here!"
'Tis real hangmen, real scourges bear!
Prepare, Maria, for a horrid tale
Will turn thy very rouge to deadly pale;
Will make thy hair, tho' erst from gipsy poll'd,
By barber woven, and by barber sold,
Though twisted smooth with Harry's nicest care,
Like hoary bristles to erect and stare.
The hero of the mimic scene, no more
I start in Hamlet, in Othello roar;
Or haughty Chieftain, 'mid the din of arms,
In Highland bonnet woo Malvina's charms;
While sans culottes stoop up the mountain high,
And steal from me Maria's prying eye.
Bless'd Highland bonnet! Once my proudest dress,
Now prouder still, Maria's temples press.
I see her wave thy towering plumes afar,
And call each coxcomb to the wordy war.
I see her face the first of Ireland's sons,[1]
And even out-Irish his Hibernian bronze;
The crafty colonel[2] leaves the tartan'd lines
For other wars, where he a hero shines:
The hopeful youth, in Scottish senate bred,
Who owns a Bushby's heart without the head;
Comes 'mid a string of coxcombs to display,
That *veni, vidi, vici*, is his way;
The shrinking bard adown an alley skulks,
And dreads a meeting worse than Woolwich hulks;
Though there his heresies in church and state
Might well award him Muir and Palmer's fate:
Still she undaunted reels and rattles on,
And dares the public like a noontide sun.

[1] Gillespie.—[2] Col. M'Dowal.

(What scandal call'd Maria's jaunty stagger
The ricket reeling of a crooked swagger?
Whose spleen e'en worse than Burns's venom when
He dips in gall unmix'd his eager pen,—
And pours his vengeance in the burning line,
Who christen'd thus Maria's lyre divine;
The idiot strum of vanity bemused,
And even the abuse of poesy abused!
Who call'd her verse a parish workhouse, made
For motley, foundling fancies, stolen or stray'd?)

A workhouse! ah, that sound awakes my woes,
And pillows on the thorn my rack'd repose!
In durance vile here must I wake and weep,
And all my frowzy couch in sorrow steep;
That straw where many a rogue has lain of yore,
And vermined gipsies litter'd heretofore.

Why, Lonsdale, thus thy wrath on vagrants pour,
Must earth no rascal save thyself endure?
Must thou alone in guilt immortal swell,
And make a vast monopoly of hell?
Thou know'st, the virtues cannot hate thee worse,
The vices also, must they club their curse?
Or must no tiny sin to others fall,
Because thy guilt's supreme enough for all?

Maria, send me too thy griefs and cares;
In all of thee sure thy Esopus shares.
As thou at all mankind the flag unfurls,
Who on my fair one satire's vengeance hurls?
Who calls thee, pert, affected, vain coquette,
A wit in folly, and a fool in wit?
Who says that fool alone is not thy due,
And quotes thy treacheries to prove it true?
Our force united on thy foes we'll turn,
And dare the war with all of woman born:
For who can write and speak as thou and I?
My periods that deciphering defy,
And thy still matchless tongue that conquers all reply.

ON SEEING MISS FONTENELLE

IN A FAVORITE CHARACTER.

SWEET naïveté of feature,
　　Simple, wild, enchanting elf,
Not to thee, but thanks to Nature,
　　Thou art acting but thyself.

Wert thou awkward, stiff, affected,
　　Spurning nature, torturing art;
Loves and graces all rejected,
　　Then indeed thou 'dst act a part.

R. B.

THE HERON BALLADS.

[BALLAD FIRST.]

These were written as election squibs to serve Patrick Heron, Esq, of
Kerroughtree, at two contested elections.

WHOM will you send to London town,
　　To Parliament and a' that?
Or wha in a' the country round
　　The best deserves to fa' that?
　　　　For a' that, and a' that,
　　　　Thro' Galloway and a' that;
　　　　Where is the laird or belted knight
　　　　The best deserves to fa' that?

Wha sees Kerroughtree's open yett,
　　And wha is 't never saw that
Wha ever wi' Kerroughtree met
　　And has a doubt of a' that?
　　　　For a' that, and a' that,
　　　　Here 's Heron yet for a' that;
　　　　The independent patriot,
　　　　The honest man, and a' that.
Tho' wit and worth in either sex,
　　St. Mary's Isle can shaw that;
Wi' dukes an' lords let Selkirk mix,
　　And weel does Selkirk fa' that.

For a' that, an' a' that,
Here 's Heron yet for a' that!
The independent commoner
Shall be the man for a' that.

But, why should we to nobles jouk,
  And it 's against the law that;
For why, a lord may be a gouk,
  Wi' ribbon, star, an' a' that,
    For a' that, an' a' that,
    Here 's Heron yet for a' that!
    A lord may be a lousy loun,
    Wi' ribbon, star, an' a' that.

A beardless boy comes o'er the hills,
  Wi' uncle's purse an' a' that;
But we 'll hae ane frae 'mang oursels,
  A man we ken, an' a' that.
    For a' that, an' a' that!
    Here 's Heron yet for a' that!
    For we 're not to be bought an' sold,
    Like naigs, an' nowt, an' a' that.

Then let us drink the Stewartry,
  Kerroughtree's laird, an' a' that,
Our representative to be,
  For weel he 's worthy a' that.
    For a' that, an' a' that,
    Here 's Heron yet for a' that!
    A House of Commons such as he,
    They would be blest that saw that.

THE ELECTION.

[BALLAD SECOND.]

Fy, let us a' to Kirkcudbright,
  For there will be bickerin' there;
For Murray's light-horse are to muster,
  And oh, how the heroes will swear!
An' there will be Murray commander,
  And Gordon the battle to win;
Like brothers they 'll stand by each other,
  Sae knit in alliance an' kin.

An' there will be black-lippit Johnie,
  The tongue o' the trump to them a';
An' he get nae hell for his haddin'
  The deil gets nae justice ava':
An' there will be Kempleton's birkie,
  A boy no sae black at the bane;
But as for his fine nabob fortune,
  We'el e'en let the subject alane.

An' there will be Wigton's new sheriff,
  Dame Justice fu' brawlie has sped,
She's gotten the heart of a Bushby,
  But, Lord, what's become o' the head?
An' there will be Cardoness' Esquire,
  Sae mighty in Cardoness' eyes;
A wight that will weather damnation,
  For the devil the prey will despise.

An' there will be Douglases doughty,
  New christening towns far and near,
Abjuring their democratic doings,
  By kissing the — o' a peer;
An' there will be Kenmure sae gen'rous,
  Whose honor is proof to the storm,
To save them from stark reprobation,
  He lent them his name to the firm.

But we winna mention Redcastle,
  The body e'en let him escape!
He'd venture the gallows for siller,
  An' 'twere na the cost o' the rape.
An' where is our king's lord lieutenant,
  Sae famed for his gratefu' return?
The billie is gettin' his questions,
  To say in St. Stephen's the morn.

An' there will be lads o' the gospel,
  Muirhead wha's gude as he's true;
An' there will be Buittle's apostle,
  Wha's more o' the black than the blue
An' there will be folk from St. Mary's,
  A house o' great merit and note,
The deil ane but honors them highly,—
  The deil ane will gie them his vote!

An' there will be wealthy young Richard,
    Dame Fortune should hing by the neck;
For prodigal, thriftless bestowing,
    His merit had won him respect:
An' there will be rich brother nabobs,
    Though nabobs, yet men of the first;
An' there will be Collieston's whiskers,
    An' Quintin, o' lads not the worst.

An' there will be stamp-office Johnie,
    Tak tent how ye purchase a dram;
An' there will be gay Cassencarrie,
    An' there will be gleg Colonel Tam;
An' there will be trusty Kerroughtree,
    Whose honor was ever his law,
If the virtues were pack'd in a parcel,
    His worth might be sample for a'.

An' can we forget the auld major,
    Wha 'll ne'er be forgot in the Greys?
Our flattery we 'll keep for some other,
    Him only 'tis justice to praise.
An' there will be maiden Kilkerran,
    And also Barskimming's gude knight;
An' there will be roarin' Birtwhistle,
    Wha luckily roars in the right.

An' there, frae the Niddisdale's borders,
    Will mingle the Maxwells in droves;
Teugh Johnie, stanch Geordie, an' Walie,
    That griens for the fishes an' loaves;
An' there will be Logan MacDouall,
    Sculdudd'ry an' he will be there,
An' also the wild Scot o' Galloway,
    Sodgerin', gunpowder Blair.

Then hey the chaste interest o' Broughton,
    An' hey for the blessings 'twill bring!
It may send Balmaghie to the Commons,
    In Sodom 'twould make him a king;
An' hey for the sanctified M——y,
    Our land who wi' chapels has stored;
He founder'd his horse among harlots,
    But gied the auld naig to the Lord.

AN EXCELLENT NEW SONG.

[BALLAD THIRD.]

Tune—*Buy broom besoms.*

WHA will buy my troggin,
  Fine election ware;
Broken trade o' Broughton.
  A' in high repair.

> *Buy braw troggin,*
>   *Frae the banks o' Dee ;*
> *Wha wants troggin*
>   *Let him come to me.*

There's a noble Earl's
  Fame and high renown,
For an auld song—
  It's thought the gudes were stown.
        Buy braw troggin, &c.

Here's the worth o' Broughton
  In a needle's ee;
Here's a reputation
  Tint by Balmaghie.
        Buy braw troggin, &c.

Here's an honest conscience
  Might a prince adorn;
Frae the downs o' Tinwald—
  So was never worn.
        Buy braw troggin, &c.

Here's its stuff and lining,
  Cardoness's head;
Fine for a sodger
  A' the wale o' lead.
        Buy braw troggin, &c.

Here's a little wadset
  Buittle's scrap o' truth,
Pawn'd in a gin shop
  Quenching holy drouth.
        Buy braw troggin, &c.

Here 's armorial bearings
  Frae the manse o' Urr;
The crest, an auld crab-apple
  Rotten at the core.
        Buy braw troggin, &c.

Here is Satan's picture,
  Like a bizzard gled,
Pouncing poor Redcastle
  Sprawlin' as a taed.
        Buy braw troggin, &c.

Here 's the worth and wisdom
  Collieston can boast;
By a thievish midge
  They had been nearly lost.
        Buy braw troggin, &c.

Here is Murray's fragments
  O' the ten commands;
Gifted by black Jock
  To get them aff his hands.
        Buy braw troggin, &c.

Saw ye e'er sic troggin?
  If to buy ye 're slack,
Hornie's turnin' chapman,—
  He 'll buy a' the pack.
        Buy braw troggin, &c.

TO A KISS.

HUMID seal of soft affections,
  Tenderest pledge of future bliss,
Dearest tie of young connections,
  Love's first snow-drop, virgin kiss!

Speaking silence, dumb confession,
  Passion's birth, and infant's play,
Dove-like fondness, chaste concession,
  Glowing dawn of brighter day.

Sorrowing joy, adieu's last action,
  When lingering lips no more must join,
What words can ever speak affection
  So thrilling and sincere as thine!

VERSES WRITTEN UNDER VIOLENT GRIEF.

These lines were written in 1786, when the Poet's circumstances were so embarrassed, that he had determined to emigrate to Jamaica as a means of improving them.

Accept the gift a friend sincere
    Wad on thy worth be pressin';
Remembrance oft may start a tear,
But oh! that tenderness forbear,
    Though 'twad my sorrows lessen.

My morning raise sae clear and fair,
    I thought sair storms wad never
Bedew the scene; but grief and care
In wildest fury hae made bare
    My peace, my hope, forever!

You think I'm glad; oh, I pay weel
    For a' the joy I borrow,
In solitude—then, then I feel
I canna to mysel' conceal
    My deeply ranklin' sorrow.

Farewell! within thy bosom free
    A sigh may whiles awaken;
A tear may wet thy laughin' ee,
For Scotia's son—ance gay like thee—
    Now hopeless, comfortless, forsaken!

THE HERMIT.

Written on a marble sideboard, in the hermitage belonging to the Duke of Athole, in the wood of Aberfeldy.

Whoe'er thou art, these lines now reading,
Think not, though from the world receding,
I joy my lonely days to lead in
            This desert drear;
That fell remorse a conscience bleeding
            Hath led me here.

No thought of guilt my bosom sours;
Free-will'd I fled from courtly bowers;

For well I saw in halls and towers
    That lust and pride,
The arch-fiend's dearest, darkest powers,
    In state preside.

I saw mankind with vice incrusted;
I saw that honor's sword was rusted;
That few for aught but folly lusted;
That he was still deceived who trusted
    To love or friend;
And hither came, with men disgusted,
    My life to end.

In this lone cave, in garments lowly,
Alike a foe to noisy folly,
And brow-bent gloomy melancholy,
    I wear away
My life, and in my office holy
    Consume the day.

This rock my shield, when storms are blowing,
The limpid streamlet yonder flowing
Supplying drink, the earth bestowing
    My simple food;
But few enjoy the calm I know in
    This desert wood.

Content and comfort bless me more in
This grot, than e'er I felt before in
A palace—and with thoughts still soaring
    To God on high,
Each night and morn, with voice imploring,
    This wish I sigh:—

"Let me, O Lord! from life retire,
Unknown each guilty worldly fire,
Remorse's throb, or loose desire;
    And when I die,
Let me in this belief expire—
    To God I fly."

Stranger, if full of youth and riot,
And yet no grief has marr'd thy quiet,
Thou haply throw'st a scornful eye at
    The hermit's prayer—
But if thou hast good cause to sigh at
    Thy fault or care:

If thou hast known false love's vexation,
Or hast been exiled from thy nation,
Or guilt affrights thy contemplation,
          And makes thee pine,
Oh, how must thou lament thy station,
          And envy mine!

TO MY BED.

Thou bed, in which I first began
To be that various creature—*Man!*
And when again the Fates decree,
The place where I must cease to be ;—
When sickness comes, to whom I fly,
To soothe my pain, or close mine eye ;—
When cares surround me, where I weep,
Or lose them all in balmy sleep ;—
When sore with labor, whom I court,
And to thy downy breast resort ;—
Where, too, ecstatic joys I find,
When deigns my Delia to be kind—
And full of love, in all her charms,
Thou giv'st the fair one to my arms.
The centre thou—where grief and pain,
Disease and rest, alternate reign.
Oh, since within thy little space
So many various scenes take place ;
Lessons as useful shalt thou teach,
As sages dictate—churchmen preach ;
And man, convinced by thee alone,
This great important truth shall own: --
"*That thin partitions do divide*
The bounds where good and ill reside ;
That naught is perfect here below ;
But BLISS *still bordering upon* WOE."

THE TREE OF LIBERTY.

HEARD ye o' the tree o' France,
    I watna what's the name o't;
Around it a' the patriots dance,
    Weel Europe kens the fame o't.

It stands where ance the Bastile stood,·
  A prison built by kings, man,
When Superstition's hellish brood
  Kept France in leading-strings, man.

Upo' this tree there grows sic fruit,
  Its virtues a' can tell, man;
It raises man aboon the brute,
  It maks him ken himsel', man.
Gif ance the peasant taste a bit,
  He's greater than a lord, man,
And wi' the beggar shares a mite
  O' a' he can afford, man.

This fruit is worth a' Afric's wealth,
  To comfort us 'twas sent, man;
To gie the sweetest blush o' health,
  And mak us a' content, man.
It clears the een, it cheers the heart,
  Maks high and low gude friends, man;
And he wha acts the traitor's part,
  It to perdition sends, man.

My blessings aye attend the chiel
  Wha pitied Gallia's slaves, man,
And staw'd a branch, spite o' the deil,
  Frae yont the western waves, man.
Fair Virtue water'd it wi' care,
  And now she sees wi' pride, man,
How weel it buds and blossoms there,
  Its branches spreading wide, man.

But vicious folk aye hate to see
  The works o' Virtue thrive, man;
The courtly vermin's bann'd the tree,
  And grat to see it thrive, man;
King Loui' thought to cut it down,
  When it was unco sma', man;
For this the watchman crack'd his crown,
  Cut aff his head and a', man.

A wicked crew syne, on a time,
  Did tak a solemn aith, man,
It ne'er should flourish to its prime,
  I wat they pledged their faith, man;

Awa they gaed wi' mock parade,
   Like beagles hunting game, man,
But soon grew weary o' the trade,
   And wish'd they 'd been at hame, man.

For Freedom, standing by the tree,
   Her sons did loudly ca', man;
She sang a sang o' liberty,
   Which pleased them ane and a', man.
By her inspired, the new-born race
   Soon drew the avenging, steel, man;
The hirelings ran—her foes gied chase,
   And bang'd the despot weel, man.

Let Britain boast her hardy oak,
   Her poplar and her pine, man,
Auld Britain ance could crack her joke,
   And o'er her neighbors shine, man:
But seek the forest round and round,
   And soon 'twill be agreed, man,
That sic a tree cannot be found
   'Twixt London and the Tweed, man.

Without this tree, alake! this life
   Is but a vale o' woe, man;
A scene o' sorrow mix'd wi' strife,
   Nae real joys we know, man.
We labor soon, we labor late,
   To feed the titled knave, man;
And a' the comfort we 're to get,
   Is that ayont the grave, man.

Wi' plenty o' sic trees, I trow,
   The warld would live in peace, man;
The sword would help to mak a plough,
   The din o' war wad cease, man.
Like brethren in a common cause,
   We 'd on each other smile, man;
And equal rights and equal laws
   Wad gladden every isle, man.

Wae worth the loon wha wadna eat
   Sic halesome dainty cheer, man;
I 'd gie my shoon frae aff my feet,
   To taste sic fruit, I swear, man.

Syne let us pray, auld England may
   Sure plant this far-famed tree, man;
And blythe we 'll sing, and hail the day
   That gave us liberty, man.

ON THE DEATH OF THE POET'S DAUGHTER.

These tender lines were written, it is said, on the death of his child, in 1795.

Oh sweet be thy sleep in the land of the grave,
   My dear little angel, forever;
Forever—oh no! let not man be a slave,
   His hopes from existence to sever.

Though cold be the clay where thou pillow'st thy head,
   In the dark silent mansions of sorrow,
The spring shall return to thy low narrow bed,
   Like the beam of the day-star to-morrow.

The flower-stem shall bloom like thy sweet seraph form,
   Ere the spoiler had nipt thee in blossom,
When thou shrunk frae the scowl of the loud winter storm,
   And nestled thee close to that bosom.

Oh still I behold thee, all lovely in death,
   Reclined on the lap of thy mother,
When the tear trickled bright, when the short stifled breath,
   Told how dear ye were aye to each other.

My child, thou art gone to the home of thy rest,
   Where suffering no longer can harm ye,
Where the songs of the good, where the hymns of the blest,
   Through an endless existence shall charm thee.

While he, thy fond parent, must sighing sojourn,
   Through the dire desert regions of sorrow,
O'er the hope and misfortune of being to mourn,
   And sigh for this life's latest morrow.

ON THE SAME.

Here lies a rose, a budding rose,
   Blasted before its bloom;
Whose innocence did sweets disclose
   Beyond that flower's perfume.

To those who for her loss are grieved,
  This consolation's given—
She's from a world of woe relieved,
  And blooms a rose in heaven.

VERSES ON THE DESTRUCTION OF THE WOODS NEAR DRUMLANRIG.

' The Duke of Queensberry stripped his domains of Drumlanrig in Dumfriesshire, and Neidpath in Peeblesshire, of all the wood fit for being cut, in order to enrich the Countess of Yarmouth, whom he supposed to be his daughter, and to whom, by a singular piece of good fortune on her part, Mr. George Selwyn, the celebrated wit, also left a fortune, under the same, and probably equally mistaken impression " *Chambers.*

As on the banks o' wandering Nith,
  Ae smiling simmer morn I stray'd,
And traced its bonnie howes and haughs,
  Where linties sang and lambkins play'd,
I sat me down upon a craig,
  And drank my fill o' fancy's dream,
When, from the eddying deep below,
  Uprose the Genius of the stream.

Dark, like the frowning rock, his brow,
  And troubled, like his wintry wave,
And deep, as sughs the boding wind
  Amang his caves, the sigh he gave—
"And came ye here, my son," he cried,
  "To wander in my birken shade?
To muse some favorite Scottish theme,
  Or sing some favorite Scottish maid?

"There was a time, it's nae lang syne,
  Ye might hae seen me in my pride,
When a' my banks sae bravely saw
  Their woody pictures in my tide;
When hanging beech and spreading elm
  Shaded my stream sae clear and cool;
And stately oaks their twisted arms
  Threw broad and dark across the pool:

"When, glinting through the trees, appear'd
  The wee white cot aboon the mill,
And peacefu' rose its ingle reek,
  That slowly curléd up the hill.

But now the cot is bare and cauld,
   Its branchy shelter 's lost and gane,
And scarce a stinted birk is left
   To shiver in the blast its lane."

" Alas!" said I, " what ruefu' chance
   Has twined ye o' your stately trees?
Has laid your rocky bosom bare?
   Has stripp'd the cleeding o' your braes?
Was it the bitter eastern blast,
   That scatters blight in early spring?
Or was 't the wil'fire scorch'd their boughs,
   Or canker-worm wi' secret sting?"

" Nae eastlin blast," the sprite replied;
   " It blew na here sae fierce and fell,
And on my dry and halesome banks
   Nae canker-worms get leave to dwell:
Man! cruel man!" the Genius sigh'd—
As through the cliffs he sank him down—
" The worm that gnaw'd my bonnie trees,
   That reptile wears a ducal crown."

THE BOOK-WORMS.

Written in a splendidly bound, but worm-eaten copy of Shakspeare, the property
of a nobleman.

Through and through the inspired leaves,
   Ye maggots, make your windings;
But, oh! respect his lordship's taste,
   And spare his golden bindings.

LINES ON STIRLING.

Written on a pane of glass, on visiting this ancient seat of Royalty, in 1787.

Here Stuarts once in glory reign'd,
And laws for Scotland's weal ordain'd;
But now unroof'd their palace stands,
Their sceptre 's sway'd by other hands;
The injured Stuart line is gone,
A race outlandish fills their throne.

THE REPROOF.

The lines on Stirling were considered imprudent by one of the Poet's friends, when he immediately wrote the "Reproof" underneath.

Rash mortal, and slanderous Poet, thy name
Shall no longer appear in the records of fame;
Dost not know that old Mansfield, who writes like the Bible,
Says the more 'tis a truth, sir, the more 'tis a libel?

THE KIRK OF LAMINGTON.

As cauld a wind as ever blew,
A caulder kirk, and in 't but few;
As cauld a minister's e'er spak,
Ye 'se a' be het ere I come back.

THE LEAGUE AND COVENANT.

This was spoken in reply to one who sneered at the sufferings of Scotland for conscience' sake.

The Solemn League and Covenant
    Cost Scotland blood—cost Scotland tears:
But it seal'd freedom's sacred cause—
    If thou 'rt a slave, indulge thy sneers.

INSCRIPTION ON A GOBLET.

There 's death in the cup—sae beware!
    Nay, more—there is danger in touching;
But wha can avoid the fell snare?
    The man and his wine 's sae bewitching!

THE TOAD-EATER.

Spoken in reply to one who was talking largely of his noble friends.

What of earls with whom you have supt,
    And of dukes that you dined with yestreen?
Lord! a louse, sir, is still but a louse,
    Though it crawl on the curls of a queen.

THE SELKIRK GRACE.

When on a visit to St. Mary's Isle, the Earl of Selkirk requested Burns to say grace at dinner ; he complied in these words.

SOME hae meat, and canna eat,
    And some wad eat that want it ;
But we hae meat and we can eat,
    And sae the Lord be thanket.

IMPROMPTU ON WILLIE STEWART.

These verses were written on a tumbler which was in the possession of the late Sir Walter Scott.

YOU 'RE welcome, Willie Stewart,
    You 're welcome, Willie Stewart ;
There 's ne'er a flower that blooms in May,
    That 's half sae welcome 's thou art.

Come, bumpers high, express your joy,
    The bowl we maun renew it ;
The tappit-hen gae bring her ben,
    To welcome Willie Stewart.

May foes be strang, and friends be slack,
    Ilk action may he rue it ;
May woman on him turn her back,
    That wrangs thee, Willie Stewart.

WRITTEN ON A PANE OF GLASS,

On the occasion of a national thanksgiving for a naval victory.

YE hypocrites ! are these your pranks ?—
To murder men, and gie God thanks !
For shame ! gie o'er, proceed no further—
God won't accept your thanks for murther !

A GRACE BEFORE MEAT.

O THOU, in whom we live and move,
    Who mad'st the sea and shore ;
Thy goodness constantly we prove,
    And grateful would adore.

And if it please thee, Power above,
  Still grant us, with such store,
The friend we trust, the fair we love,
  And we desire no more.

EPITAPH ON MR. W. CRUICKSHANKS.

HONEST Will 's to heaven gane,
  And mony shall lament him;
His faults they a' in Latin lay,
  In English nane e'er kent them.

EPITAPH ON W———.

STOP thief! dame Nature cried to Death,
As Willie drew his latest breath;
You have my choicest model taen,
How shall I make a fool again?

ON THE SAME.

REST gently, turf, upon his breast,
His chicken heart 's so tender;—
But rear huge castles on his head,
His skull will prop them under.

THE END.

Printed in the United States
150838LV00003B/138/P